The Religious Cultures of Dutch Jewry

Brill's Series in Jewish Studies

Founding Editor

David S. Katz (*Tel-Aviv University*)

Edited by

Joshua Holo (*Hebrew Union College – Jewish Institute of Religion*)

VOLUME 58

The titles published in this series are listed at *brill.com/bsjs*

The Religious Cultures of Dutch Jewry

Edited by

Yosef Kaplan
Dan Michman

BRILL

LEIDEN | BOSTON

Cover Illustration: Religious Ceremonies of Dutch Jews. Top – an Ashkenazi wedding ceremony. Bottom – a ceremony at the Feast of Tabernacles (Sukkot) in the Portuguese Synagogue (Amsterdam). Illustrations by Bernard Picart, from the early 18th century.

Library of Congress Cataloging-in-Publication Data

Names: Kaplan, Yosef, editor. | Michman, Dan, editor.
Title: The religious cultures of Dutch Jewry / edited by Yosef Kaplan, Dan
  Michman.
Description: Leiden ; Boston : Brill, [2017] | Series: Brill's series in
  Jewish studies, ISSN 0926-2261 ; volume 58 | Includes bibliographical
  references and index.
Identifiers: LCCN 2017008773 (print) | LCCN 2017010560 (ebook) | ISBN
  9789004343160 (E-book) | ISBN 9789004343153 (hardback : alk. paper)
Subjects: LCSH: Jews--Netherlands--History--To 1900. |
  Sephardim--Netherlands--History--To 1900. |
  Ashkenazim--Netherlands--History--To 1900. | Netherlands--History--To 1900.
Classification: LCC DS135.N4 (ebook) | LCC DS135.N4 R44 2017 (print) |
  DDC 296.09492--dc23
LC record available at https://lccn.loc.gov/2017008773

Typeface for the Latin, Greek, and Cyrillic scripts: "Brill". See and download: brill.com/brill-typeface.

ISSN 0926-2261
ISBN 978-90-04-34315-3 (hardback)
ISBN 978-90-04-34316-0 (e-book)

In Memoriam

Shlomo Berger
$(1953–2015)$

∴

Contents

Preface

In comparison to the history of other Jewish communities, the history of Dutch Jewry, which only began in the early modern age, is relatively short. However, as with other chapters in Jewish history, that of Dutch Jewry was molded by reciprocal relations between centripetal and centrifugal forces: the desire to retain the unity of Jewish existence versus inner trends of disintegration; the aspiration to remain separate from the non-Jewish society versus the longing to integrate into it; loyalty to the ancient religious tradition versus the drive to renew or even abandon it. These contradictory forces coexisted over the four hundred years of the history of Dutch Jewry and made their mark on the religious cultures that emerged within it, both in times of growth and flourishing and in times of crisis and decline.

From the time of the Dutch Republic (sixteenth to eighteenth centuries), the Netherlands have been a meeting place between Jews of various origins, who arrived with well-established religious traditions that took on a new character in the new location. The impressive economic growth of Amsterdam in the early modern period and the relative religious tolerance that prevailed there made it a lodestone for refugees and immigrants of many religions, from many countries. The flow of immigrants to the Dutch metropolis also included Marranos from Spain and Portugal, who returned to the Jewish religion, Ashkenazi refugees from throughout Germany, who fled the scourges of the Thirty Years War, and Jews from Poland and Lithuania, who fled the Swedish invasion and wars that struck Eastern Europe. The considerable numerical and visual presence of these Jewish immigrants made a unique mark on the social and cultural landscape of Amsterdam, especially after the inauguration of two large synagogues there, that of the Ashkenazim in 1670, and especially that of the Sephardim in 1675. These houses of worship attracted considerable attention not only within the local Christian population but also among tourists from other European countries. The splendid sanctuary of the Sephardi Jews, the Esnoga, was described with admiration in the diaries of Christian visitors, especially English tourists, who had never previously encountered either real live Jews, or, consequently, Jewish religious ceremonies. This house of worship became a display window for part of the Christian public in Western Europe, giving them their first glimpse of Jewish ceremonies and religious customs.

The Jews of these two communities, the Sephardi and Ashkenazi, belonged to separate ethnic Diasporas with different cultures, although consciously admitting their religious affinity. However, these cultures shared a common denominator: they were de-territorialized cultures, i.e., cultures that had lost a direct and binding link with a specific territory. The particular cultures of the Sephardi and of the Ashkenazi Jews who arrived in Amsterdam were cut off from any territorial connection, though the Land of Israel existed in their consciousness as an actual place, both in their faith and in their religious ceremonies.

In the seventeenth and eighteenth centuries, each of these communities played a central role in their Diasporas, a role that was more significant than their demographic presence in the Jewish world. From the 1640s on, the Sephardi community in Amsterdam became the major center of the Western Sephardi Diaspora, that is to say, of all the communities composed of former Marranos, which were founded in Western Europe and the New World. It provided economic support in times of crisis and distress and became the unchallenged center of their culture. Generations of rabbis in these communities were ordained in the Ets Haim Yeshiva in Amsterdam, and the cantors trained in the Dutch capital spread the rituals and melodies that were used in all the synagogues of the *Nação*. The architecture of the Amsterdam Esnoga was copied in several Sephardi synagogues elsewhere. Similarly, the rise of Jewish printing houses in Amsterdam in the early modern age gave Jewish books printed there an iconic position: "Printed in Amsterdam" became a valued trademark for Jewish books. The Jewish printers of Amsterdam produced a wide variety of books in Hebrew, comprising the main genres of Jewish religious literature, such as biblical and talmudical exegesis, halakhah, kabbalah, homiletics, and ethics, for Jewish communities throughout the Diaspora. They also printed books in Spanish and Portuguese for the Sephardi Diaspora, and they became the major suppliers of Yiddish literature for the Ashkenazi communities of Central and Eastern Europe.

By virtue of the high status of Jewish printing in the Dutch capital, Amsterdam Jewry became a central factor in distributing propaganda and polemical writing throughout the Jewish world in times of ferment and crisis. Thus, for example, in 1665–1666 when messianic expectations swept the Jewish world with the appearance of Shabbetai Tzvi, Amsterdam became the center for the circulation of letters and pamphlets on the messiah from Smyrna.

Toward the mid-eighteenth century, the Jewish presence spread to quite a few towns throughout the Netherlands, and along with the term "*Mokum*" (from the Hebrew word *makom*, meaning "place," in its Ashkenazi pronunciation), which the local Jews used for the city of Amsterdam, the Jewish settlements elsewhere in the country were called "*Mediene*" (the Ashkenazi pronunciation of the Hebrew word *medina*, originally meaning "state" but in Mishnaic and medieval Hebrew indicating the regions outside the capital; see Mishna, Ma'aser Sheni, 3:4). These two terms—*Mokum* and *Mediene*—took root in the consciousness of Dutch Jewry as unique expressions of Jewish life in the Netherlands during the whole modern age. The communities of the *Mediene* were almost all Ashkenazi, and a unique Jewish folklore emerged there, which was preserved in certain places until the Holocaust.

The exposure of the Sephardi social elite to the ideals of the early Enlightenment accelerated the processes of secularization of the Sephardi bourgeoisie in Amsterdam and The Hague. Spinoza's writings, which, despite censorship, were widely circulated in the Dutch Republic, made a deep impression on cultivated Sephardim. Some of them were sympathetic to the principles of biblical criticism, and a few of these were not reluctant to express harsh criticism of the Jewish religion. As early as the eighteenth century, especially in the second half of it, quite a few Sephardi Jews abandoned the community. Some of them assimilated into the majority society, sometimes by conversion and intermarriage. The Sephardi rabbinical leadership stood in firm opposition to these processes of disintegration, supported by a kernel of firm believers. In contrast to the many who had thrown off the yoke of the halakhah, a devout minority remained and entrenched itself within its confines.

The Ashkenazi community in Amsterdam was a separate, independent entity, and, in the eighteenth century, it became larger than the Sephardi community, but it still remained subordinate to Sephardi hegemony. However, in the 1730s the Ashkenazi community of Amsterdam had become a significant factor in the Ashkenazi world, and important rabbis were keen to go to Amsterdam and serve as chief rabbis. In contrast to the modest salary of former years, the chief rabbis were now paid more generously. Their presence ensured that Ashkenazi Amsterdam became an independent Torah center, exercising influence on Ashkenazi Jewry in Western Europe, and by means of its printing industry, even beyond.

The extensive educational and cultural activity of two Ashkenazi rabbinical scholars, Menahem Mann Amelander and Eleasar Soesman Rudelsum, commenced in the 1720s and laid the groundwork for the absorption of modern pedagogical systems in the Ashkenazi community as well. Amelander and Rudelsum sought to influence the manner of teaching and system of education in their community, taking a critical view of traditional education as it was practiced. In certain senses they can be seen as precursors of the pedagogy of the Jewish Enlightenment in Western Europe.

Despite the significant differences between the processes of modernization among the Sephardim and among the Ashkenazim, toward the end of the eighteenth century, a stratum of cultivated and open-minded Jews was active in both of the communities. They found a common language with the revolutionary authorities under the Batavian-French Republic, which granted emancipation to all the Jews in the country in 1796. Though the structure of the old communities did not change essentially (though a new Ashkenazi congregation, Adath Jeschurun, or the "*neie kille*" in common discourse, split off from the main congregation in Amsterdam in 1797), they were forced to adapt to the changes imposed upon all the Jews of the country. Upon order of King Louis Napoleon, in 1808 a Supreme Consistory was established, a central organization subject to the state, the vast majority of its members being sympathetic to revolutionary ideals. Thus the era of the traditional Orthodox hegemony over Jewish life in Holland came to an end, although most of the Jews in the country were still Orthodox.

The newly established (1815) centralized nation state, the Kingdom of the Netherlands, drew upon the major changes introduced in the "French period," the most important one being a state-supervised country-wide umbrella organization of the Jewish communities, yet also accepted the basic division between the *Hoogduitsche* ("High German," i.e., Ashkenazi) and *Portugeesche* (Portuguese, i.e., Sephardi) Jews, who, in the new emancipatory language, were called *Israeliten*. Consequently, two so-called *Kerkgenootschappen* (Church Organizations) were created. This structure has remained intact until today, although since the separation of state and church in the mid-nineteenth century, these umbrella organizations became voluntary. More importantly, in the new concept of the state, Jews were officially considered as belonging to a religion, not to an ethnic group, and their affairs were dealt with by the authorities as such.

The last decades of the nineteenth century and first decades of the twentieth were characterized by a gradual process of secularization as well as of accommodation to the Dutch society. This caused the replacement of Dutch Yiddish by Dutch in daily discourse, which caused rabbis, after some reluctance, to deliver their sermons in Dutch too. Following the spirit in the Dutch churches, the demand for *decorum* in services gained the upper hand. *Hazanut* also acquired an important place in these services. The independent Jewish daily schools, in which religion was taught, gradually vanished, while most Jewish children attended public schools. As a result, new paths for Jewish education had to be found; Sunday schools or additional lessons on other days were introduced, but the number of children attending them declined over time, and this impacted on the commitment to religious practices too.

In spite of these developments, the segmented composition of Dutch society, partially based on religious affiliation (to the Protestant or Catholic churches) caused Dutch Jewry to remain a sub-segment itself, with a relatively low percentage of intermarriage until WW II. Moreover, due to the policies of both *Kerkgenootschappen* to accept non-observing Jews as members as long as the Orthodox rules were officially kept, most Jews stayed within these organizations. In this context it is no surprise that only minor attempts to establish Reform Judaism in the Netherlands failed until 1929. And even though a trickle of Eastern European Jews (*Ostjuden*) came to the Netherlands within the great wave of immigration to Western Europe and overseas since the 1880s, the religious movements that had developed in Eastern Europe since the end of the eighteenth century—Hasidism and Mitnaggedism—did not have any real influence on the religious world of Dutch Jewry. The only movement of Orthodox revival with which there were certain intellectual contacts during the second half of the nineteenth century was German Neo-Orthodoxy.

Of considerable importance for the course of Dutch Orthodoxy in the last decades of the nineteenth century and the first decades of the twentieth, was the coming to Amsterdam of Rabbi Jozeph Zvi (Hirsch) Dünner. Born in Krakow and having studied first in a yeshiva in that city and afterward at Bonn University, he was called to Amsterdam in 1862 to serve as the rector of the Rabbinical Seminary (which also trained teachers of religion). He modernized the curriculum of the institution systematizing the curriculum and introducing modern scholarship. In 1874, he was nominated as chief rabbi of Amsterdam and North-Holland, a position he kept until his death in 1911. Under his influence, some new Jewish schools were established. Being a proto-Zionist from his early days (he corresponded with Moses Hess in the 1860s), he welcomed the establishment of the Zionist movement by Theodor Herzl in 1897, and was favorable of the religious Zionist *Mizrachi* afterward. This support was important for the status of the Zionist movement in the Netherlands, even though most of the rabbis whom he had raised at the seminary did not become Zionists, some even opposing the movement vehemently. Later on, also a branch of *Agudath Israel*, the anti-Zionist ultra-Orthodox political movement established in Kattowice in 1912, was established in the Netherlands.

The Zionist movement succeeded in its appeal to a considerable number of Jewish youth, especially religious ones who were looking also for religious revival. The coming of religious Zionist refugees of Eastern European origin from Belgium to the neutral Netherlands during WW I served as a trigger for the development of activities. The Zionist youth movement which would become the most important one in the Netherlands was religious: *Zichron Jaakov*; it was established in 1915 by the *Mizrachi* in Amsterdam. This vibrant movement became also the leading force in the umbrella organization of Zionist youth movements, the *Joodsche Jeugdfederatie*. In *Zichron* the pronunciation of Hebrew as it was spoken by the *yishuv* in Eretz Israel was adopted (vs. the Ashkenazi pronunciation), Hebrew was taught intensively, courses in Jewish history and religious sources became central. Consequently, some youngsters who had been in the movement made *aliya* in the 1920s and 1930s. Some of them trained themselves as *halutzim* when still in the Netherlands; next to general organizations for pioneers, separate ones for religious pioneers were set up: *Torah Vaarets* as a funding and supervising agency, and *Bahad* (*Brith Halutzim Datiyim*, Union of Religious Pioneers) as the organization of the pioneers themselves. In any case, the young religious Zionists were one of the most active groups in Dutch Jewry in the 1930s.

In the years after Hitler's ascendance to power (1933) and until the occupation of the country, thousands of refugees came to the Netherlands, the majority of them not affiliated to any religious stream. However, some of the Liberal-religious among them joined the tiny Liberal religious movement in Amsterdam and The Hague that had been initiated just shortly before 1933, thus strengthening it and giving Liberal Judaism for the first time a real stronghold in the Netherlands. In the Orthodox arena, the coming to the Rabbinical Seminary of the charismatic Rabbi Dr. Jakob Jekutiel Neubauer from Würzburg, was of importance. Yet, altogether, these years before the storm were too limited to allow for a lasting impact.

The occupation of the Netherlands by Nazi Germany in May 1940 changed the picture entirely. One can observe a series of efforts to intensify Jewish identity vis-à-vis the persecutions, both in the years before the beginning of the deportations (1940–1942), and afterward in the camps Westerbork and Vught, through educational activities emphasizing the historical past and religious origins and sources, carried out sometimes in settings such as synagogues; but this was short-lived and the arrests and deportations of 1942–1944 put an abrupt end to them. The hardships of this period challenged the faithful—rabbis as well as ordinary Jews—regarding the keeping to halakhic rules and raised theological questions. This would have an impact on the attitude and practices of the surviving remnant to the faith.

Post-war Dutch Jewry was a decimated remnant of the prewar considerable community: about 75% of the 140,000 Jews were murdered in the Shoah. As said above, already before 1940, religious life and culture had declined, and that had affected especially the little communities outside Amsterdam. Many communities did not have a *minyan* any more, and functionaries, including cantors, teachers and rabbis who had led religious life before the war, did not survive. Synagogues and ritual baths had been ruined or damaged.

Attempts at rehabilitation and revival were made though. The prewar community structure, anchored in law and tradition, was restored. The overall idea was to centralize activities and institutions; thus, in 1947, the official chief Orthodox rabbinate of the Netherlands was established, a novum. Religious and educational activities were undertaken in order to provide the remnant, and especially the children, with content to their Jewish identity, which had been under attack in the previous years. One result was that younger people, interested in belonging, moved to the big cities, mainly to Amsterdam. Consequently, most communities of the Ashkenazi umbrella organization declined in the ensuing decades, as did the overall membership. The Sephardi community continued its existence, but was extremely miniscule; new members, limited in number, would come from Sephardi Jews who immigrated since the 1960s from Middle Eastern and North African countries, as well as from Israel. The only Jewish religious community whose membership grew in the post-war period was the Liberal one, with its largest center in Amsterdam.

In the post-war years there was a relatively high number of proselytes. Trickles of a tendency among former secular Jews to embrace Orthodoxy evolved in the last quarter of the twentieth century. However, for many religious Jews, whether newcomers or from religious families, who wanted to live a fuller Jewish life, the Netherlands did not suffice any more, and many of them immigrated—to Israel (often due to the activities of the *Bnei Akiva* religious Zionist youth movement), the United States, the UK or other strong Jewish communities.

Dutch Jewry had never before had a *Haredi*-type of Jewry. This religious stream was introduced in Amsterdam in the 1970s with the establishment of a *Kolel* and shortly afterward a new school—the *Heder*. This group has remained limited in number, but has exerted a certain influence on several aspects of religious life in the city.

Altogether, in the beginning of the twenty-first century, the contents and varieties of religious culture within Dutch Jewry are very limited.

The Contributions in This Volume

The sixteen articles in this volume are based on the lectures given at the Twelfth International Symposium on the History of the Jews in the Netherlands on the topic of "Religious Cultures of Dutch Jewry," which took place in Jerusalem on 21–23 November 2011.

The first eight articles in this volume deal with various aspects of religious belief and practice of pre-emancipation Dutch Jewry. The two articles in the first section, **Messianic Hopes and Redemption**, treat the messianic consciousness common to both the first Sephardim to settle in Amsterdam and certain contemporaneous Calvinists in the Dutch Republic. Both of these groups attributed messianic significance to the historical events they experienced in opposition to Catholic Spain, their common enemy, discerning signs of the promised redemption, which was ostensibly commencing in their time.

Limor Mintz-Manor explores the religious and cultural context of the phoenix, which the Sephardi community in Amsterdam adopted as a symbol, along with the words "*Mi Kamokha*" [who is like unto Thee], from the Song of the Sea (Exodus 15:1–19). The association of the symbol of the phoenix with the Exodus from Egypt created a metaphor for them of the path of the Sephardi community from Christianity to Judaism and from exile in Spain and Portugal to redemption in Amsterdam. The first Sephardi Jews in Amsterdam were aware that in Catholic culture, the phoenix was a symbol of Jesus and the resurrection. By appropriating this decidedly Christian symbol, they emphasized their feelings about the deliverance they had won in their city of refuge—their departure from subjection in the lands of the Inquisition, which were comparable to ancient Egypt, and their arrival in a place of freedom and redemption. The article contains a detailed analysis of the symbolic meanings which Sephardi authors in Amsterdam gave to the redemptive function of the Dutch Republic and the special place of Amsterdam, "the Northern Jerusalem," as the "Promised Land," where they were able to adhere to their ancestral faith. The article by **Matt Goldish** is in direct dialogue with this one. **Goldish** points to a kind of pre-messianic redemption consciousness which was apparently shared by the Jews and certain Calvinists in the Dutch Republic. According to this consciousness, the messiah had yet to be revealed, but God's salvation was already palpable on earth. Goldish argues that signs of this kind of consciousness can be found in various works written by Sephardi Jews in Amsterdam in the seventeenth century, and that works by Dutch Calvinists of the same period show that the Dutch Republic often viewed itself as the New Jerusalem, a place in which God takes a unique interest and treats with special providence.

The second section, **Aspects of Daily Religious Life,** includes four articles on various subjects connected to the religious practice of both the Sephardim and the Ashkenazim in Amsterdam in the early modern period.

The comprehensive article by **Tirtsah Levie Bernfeld** discusses various aspects of the religiosity of Sephardi women in Amsterdam. Based on detailed examination of archival documents and works from that period, the author discusses the motivation of *conversas* to reach the Portuguese Jewish community in Amsterdam and their adjustment to the open profession of Judaism. Because of fear of the Inquisition and the need to keep the observance of Jewish customs in deep secrecy, the religious practices of the *conversos* became domestic and familial, in which women naturally played a dominant role. In many instances they bore the main burden of educating the younger generation in observance of the commandments. The transition to life in an

institutionalized Jewish community with a decidedly patriarchal ethos like
that of the Sephardi community of Amsterdam entailed a systemic overhaul
and radical change in the division of religious roles, both within the family
and in the public realm. The strong language used by Baruch Spinoza in the
eleventh chapter of *Tractatus Politicus* apparently reflects the rigid patriarchal
regime that prevailed in the Portuguese community in which the great philosopher was raised and the unflattering stereotypes of the character of women,
which he imbibed in his youth: "Wherever on the earth men are found, there
we see that men rule, and women are ruled." Levie Bernfeld indeed confirms
the subjection of women to male hegemony in the Amsterdam community.
However, at the same time, from the sensitive reading of hundreds of documents and printed texts, she shows that the Sephardi women in seventeenth-
century Amsterdam were involved in the religious activity of the community,
playing active roles in religious rituals and preserving customs in the family
framework.

The three other articles in this section relate to the religious practices of the
Ashkenazi Jews in the Dutch capital, touching upon different aspects of the
impact of the printed book. **Avriel Bar-Levav's** contribution relates to the way
in which the Ashkenazi Jews of Amsterdam rewrote their deathbed rituals and
made a significant contribution to a new genre of books and booklets, which
first appeared in Italy, referred to as "books for the sick and dying." The essay
analyzes one of the most important books of this genre, printed in Amsterdam
in 1703 in a bilingual Hebrew and Yiddish edition, written by Shimon Frankfurt, the rabbi of the Amsterdam Ashkenazi Burial Society. For the first time
in the history of the Jewish books for the sick and the dying, in addition to the
Hebrew text, the author added a separate volume in Yiddish, the spoken language of most of the Ashkenazi Jews of Europe during this period. This section
was intended for readers who were not well enough educated to understand
a text in Hebrew. Included in this category were women, the primary target
group of the old Yiddish literature, but not only them. The poorer members of
society and those living in remote rural areas also read Yiddish books, just as
their social counterparts among the peoples of Europe read books printed in
the vernacular. *Sefer ha-ḥayyim*, printed and summarized many times, reflects
both the proliferation of books for the sick and the dying and the widening of
the circle of readers to which they were directed.

The other two contributions in this section also treat the central role played
by Yiddish books in the culture of the Ashkenazi Jews. The article by **Shlomo
Berger** discusses at length the place that printing in the Yiddish language began to take in the religious life of the Ashkenazi Jews, seeing that few of them
had sufficient mastery of the Hebrew language. His article deals with the role

played by Yiddish books in Torah study in Ashkenazi society, with emphasis on the special value of the spread of ethical works in Yiddish. The reading of religious literature in Yiddish took on the significance of *"lernen"* (meaning "studying"), and this may be viewed as the beginning of a new diasporic and modern mode of Torah study. While this was less profound than the traditional method, at the same time it was more democratic. Yiddish had replaced Aramaic as the language of everyday speech, and for that reason it began to serve similar purposes to that of the ancient language of Torah study. Since Amsterdam had become a center of the Jewish book industry, the availability of books in Yiddish made the Ashkenazi community of the city the first European community that was exposed to this new type of *lernen*. Since until the nineteenth century, the Ashkenazi rabbis were brought from Central and Eastern Europe, and no Ashkenazi yeshiva was established until then, in the absence of an authentic Ashkenazi intellectual elite, these Yiddish books became significant messengers of Jewish tradition and custom.

The final article in this section, by **Marion Aptroot** discusses the appearance of *Yontev-bletlekh*, small broadsheets and brochures printed in Amsterdam in Yiddish and Dutch. They appeared around 1800 and were also known as *purim krantn* (Purim papers). These publications were a local expression of a general Ashkenazi tradition, a form of Purim entertainment of carnivalesque character. They showed sensitivity to social justice and often included subversive ideas. Neither the Yiddish language nor the traditional genre of the *yontev-bletlekh* were abandoned abruptly. Rather, the Yiddish, Dutch and bilingual *yontev-bletlekh* printed in Amsterdam indicate a transition period characterized by linguistic and literary code switching.

The third section in this volume, **Jewish Religion in Troubled Waters: The Dutch-Sephardi Diaspora Overseas,** focuses on the history of the Sephardi Jews in two of the Dutch colonies in the New World, Curaçao and Surinam. The Jewish communities in these colonies were often forced to cope with deviance and departure from the norms of rabbinical Judaism. Controversies that broke out following challenges to the leadership often made it difficult to maintain orderly communal life. The mother community of Amsterdam frequently had to intervene to calm turbulent spirits, to bolster the authority of the local Jewish leadership, and to protect the honor of the rabbis.

The article by **Evelyne Oliel-Grausz** presents a fascinating incident, which shocked the Jewish community in the Dutch colony of Curaçao in the 1740s. The central figure in this case was David Aboab, a colorful and enigmatic man who challenged the authority of the local rabbi. Aboab was a complex individual, undoubtedly a learned talmudist, who had received a rabbinical education in Italy, the land of his birth. He combined a measure of behavioral secularization and religious laxity. The description of the confrontation between him and the rabbi of the Curaçao community, Mendes de Solla, and the internecine controversies among the various factions of the Jews on the island sheds light on the differences between the religious culture of the Jews of the Caribbean islands and the religious norms prevalent in the leading community of Amsterdam. Years after leaving the island, Aboab converted to Christianity and became a Christian Hebraist, who was connected with the circle of Hutchinsonians in England.

Under the influence of the new winds blowing in France, which brought the ideas of the Enlightenment to the shores of the Caribbean and North America, the Jewish community of Surinam became a fertile soil for intellectual ferment and cultural experiments in the spirit of the ideas of the eighteenth-century *philosophes*. The article by **Jonathan Israel** analyzes the activity of a small group of Jewish youths in Surinam during the last thirty years of the eighteenth century. This group was headed by David Cohen Nassy, an enlightened Jewish intellectual who, years later, became a consistent fighter for Jewish emancipation. This group of young people established a Jewish literary and learned society, in which Christians also participated. It held discussions in French and Dutch and was exposed to the literature of the radical Enlightenment. One of the goals the circle proposed for itself was curtailment of the religious authority of the *Mahamad* in the name of equality and individual liberty. Nassy developed an educational curriculum intended for women as well, and central to it was to be the establishment of a Jewish school based on the principles of the Enlightenment.

The fourth section, **Ceremonial Dimensions** contains two articles about Dutch Jewry in the nineteenth century. Following the law of emancipation, trends of acculturation into the majority society grew stronger among the Jews of Holland. While most of the Jews remained Orthodox in their way of life, among the cultivated intelligentsia the influence of the Jewish Enlightenment, in its German version, was increasingly felt. The educated Jewish bourgeoisie sought to introduce certain changes in religious ceremonies, in order to endow them with decorum, in an effort to imitate the dignified atmosphere prevalent in the Calvinist churches. As early as the seventeenth century, the Sephardi community in Amsterdam passed ordinances calling for maintenance of order and discipline within the synagogue, stating that this was proper for *gente politica*, that is to say, civilized people, and it was expected that those committed to the values of *bom judesmo,* that is, proper Judaism, should behave in this manner. Among other things, the Sephardi worshipers were asked not to talk during prayers, not to rise and offer a seat to gentile visitors, and not to bang with hammers during the reading of the Scroll of Esther on Purim. However, under the influence of the reforms in the synagogue rite among German

Jewry, tendencies toward acculturation also began to emerge in the liturgy and ceremonies in the synagogues of the Jews of Holland.

Wout van Bekkum discusses developments in Jewish liturgy in the Netherlands, among both Ashkenazim and Sephardim. Van Bekkum states that there is almost no parallel to the situation of early nineteenth-century Dutch Jewry, which left its imprint on the content, appearance, and purpose of the Jewish prayer books, both Ashkenazi and Sephardi. Inspired by Moses Mendelssohn's ideas about *Bildung*, prayer books in which the prayers also appear in Dutch became the norm. The concept of *plegtig* (decorous) began to appear increasingly in the context of the way a service should be conducted in the synagogue, looking toward the Dutch Protestant example, and, to a lesser degree, under the influence of German Jewry.

It should be noted that among the Sephardi Jews in Western Europe, it was customary to print prayer books in Spanish for those who could not read Hebrew as early as the sixteenth century. This custom began among the *ponentini* Jews in Italy, that is to say, the Marranos who returned to Judaism, and it was transferred from them to the Sephardim in Amsterdam, and to the other communities of the Western Sephardi Diaspora. From 1721 on, among the Ashkenazim of Amsterdam as well, prayer books were printed in Yiddish, to enable worshipers who did not know Hebrew, to understand the content of the prayers that they murmured in the Holy Tongue. The main innovation in Dutch synagogues during the nineteenth century was that this change was motivated by a desire for acculturation in the majority society and the desire to resemble the Dutch Calvinists.

In the same context, out of the desire to give Jewish children an experience similar to that of Calvinist children, a consistent effort was made within nineteenth-century Dutch Jewry to introduce confirmation ceremonies in synagogues. This is the subject of the article by **Chaya Brasz**, who examines the way these ceremonies were actually introduced in Orthodox synagogues. However, the first Jewish children for whom these ceremonies were held were hearing- and speech-impaired children, "deaf and dumb," in the term of their time. The first ceremony took place in Groningen in 1829, with lip-reading and sign language. Afterward, under the influence of German Jewry, the ceremonies of this kind were held for all boys and girls and not only for the hearing- and speech-impaired. In the Netherlands this ceremony appears to have had an emancipatory function for three groups in the Jewish community—hearing- and speech-impaired children, girls, and poverty-stricken boys, in that it provided them with an alternative rite of passage to a bar mitzvah.

The two articles in the fifth section, which deals with **Jewish Identity and Religiosity**, examine two efforts of different kinds in different areas, to express

Jewish identity and to give significance to Jewish religiosity in the spirit of nineteenth-century intellectual and cultural trends.

Irene Zwiep explores the contours of the concept "religious civilization," when and how the term was adopted by Dutch Jewish bourgeois intellectuals, and how it replaced *hokhmah u-musar*, the indigenous tradition of Jewish learning and morals. She examines the various meanings that the term *Israëlitische godsdienstige beschaving* received in the first half of the nineteenth century and shows how it combined French classicist, Dutch enlightened, and German Romantic connotations, and served to express both the private, individual and public, collective implications of Jewish existence in the young Dutch nation state.

It turns out that the subject of Jewish identity played a considerable role for some of the most prominent Jewish artists who were active in Holland during the nineteenth and early twentieth centuries. **Rivka Weiss-Blok** discusses two central aspects of Dutch Jewish art in that period: religious subject matter in the works of Dutch Jewish artists, and the way in which the audience, including critics and writers, both Jews and Christians, defined and discussed religiosity in these works. Religiosity in art grew out of Romantic, mystical and even poetic feelings toward Jewish heritage. Jewish artists often treated Jewish subjects with true feeling and compassion, and out of a personal sense of obligation. Most of the artists discussed in the article were raised in traditional homes and retained connections with the Jewish community. Interest in Jewish art grew as did interest in Jews and Judaism, especially toward those Jews who had come to the fore in the Dutch cultural scene. While Jewish artists were accepted in the general art scene, the public and the artists themselves were aware of their otherness. The article treats, among others, the works of Maurits Leon, Jacob Meijer de Haan, Jozef Israels, Joseph Mendes da Costa, Eduard Frankfort and Joseph Jacob Isaacson.

The two articles in the sixth section of this volume, **The Master: Images of Chief Rabbi Jozeph Zvi (Hirsch) Dünner** by **Bart Wallet** and **Evelien Gans**, discuss the figure of Rabbi Dünner (1833–1911) whose centennial inspired the theme of the conference. Rabbi Dünner was one of the most central and influential figures in the history of Dutch Jewry. He is seen as the architect of its specific character which succeeded in retaining the unity of the Dutch Jewish religious establishment and infrastructure, despite the division between the Orthodox and the liberals. **Bart Wallet**'s article treats the memory culture around Dünner, as it developed until WW II and the establishment of the State of Israel. Dünner was seen throughout those years as the "Father of Dutch Jewry," and the "Grand Master," and was widely and enthusiastically admired. The author examines Dutch Jewry as a "community of memory," in which metaphor, similes, rituals, and collective memories are formed in order to shape and support a shared Dutch Jewish identity. Dünner was one of those historical figures who became part of the collective memory and gained an honorable place in the roster of "great Dutch Jews."

Only after the Holocaust did critical voices begin to be heard, arguing that he had isolated the Dutch Jews, while some criticized him for not accepting the need for dissimilation from Dutch society. **Evelien Gans** relates at length to the opinions of one of Dünner's most vehement critics, the historian Jaap Meijer, who had studied at the rabbinical seminary after Dünner's death but when it was still heavily influenced by the approach and standards he had set. In 1984 Meijer published a biography of Dünner, praising him as an "outstanding Talmudist" and "excellent didactician," but he expressed reservations about his synthesis between the Talmud and the academy and about his bourgeois personality, which prevented him from attracting the Jewish proletariat.

The section that concludes the volume, **Religious Life after the Catastrophe: Post-1945 Developments,** treats present-day Dutch Jewry. The fate of the Jews of Holland was particularly dire during the Holocaust. The percentage of Dutch Jews who were killed was the highest in Western Europe, 107,000 people, who were 75% of the Jews in the country before the beginning of ww II. Some of the survivors emigrated, especially to the State of Israel, which was established three years after the war. Dutch Jewry recuperated very gradually, but it could not return to its pre-Holocaust dimensions. Many of the Jews living in Holland today are immigrants or the children of immigrants who arrived after 1945. Not all of them belong to the organized Jewish community, and the processes of assimilation, which affects the Jewish community in most of the Diaspora, did not spare the Jews of Holland.

The two articles in this section summarize recent sociological studies of various aspects of contemporary Dutch Jewry and the place of religion in defining the Jewish identity of various groups of Jews. **Minnie Mock-Degen** discusses the phenomenon of Jewish women of various backgrounds who have become Orthodox and analyzes various patterns of their behavior on the basis of both earlier research and a series of in-depth interviews with more than twenty of them. Her article points to the role played by the religious Zionist youth movement in the effort to bring secular Jewish youth back to the religion, as well as the intensive activity of Habad-Lubavitch Hasidism which has not omitted Dutch Jewry in its worldwide activities. **Mock-Degen** takes a post-secular point of view, stating that "Religion and being religious still have a vibrant and vital presence in the Western world."

In her article, **Marlene de Vries** examines the validity of the pessimistic thesis advanced by the historian Bernard Wasserstein in his book *Vanishing Diaspora*, where he prophesied the inevitable decline of European Jewry in the wake of the processes of assimilation. Her investigations do corroborate some of Wasserstein's claims, but at the same time she presents a more balanced prognosis. Intermarriage definitely weakens the Jewish identity of the children, and it is very difficult to bequeath secular Judaism to the following generation. Although these two variables do not always act with the same force, regarding Dutch Jewry, given the demographic data and the conclusions of the research, it seems likely that its numbers will continue to decrease. Only large-scale immigration of Jews from other places can change the picture. If this does not happen, then the decline of the Jewish population in the Netherlands seems inevitable. However, the decline will occur in a different speed in different subgroups, dependent upon the number of mixed marriages taking place.

****

This book is dedicated to the memory of Professor Shlomo Berger, whose sudden death in the summer of 2015 shocked his many friends. Shlomo was a unique scholar, with an excellent background in classics, who became, in the past thirty years, an outstanding historian of Ashkenazi culture in the Netherlands and one of the leading scholars of the Yiddish literature of the early modern period in general. His personality positively glowed, he had a warm and sensitive heart, and he was liked by everyone who met him. He was an excellent speaker and talented teacher, beloved and admired by his many students at the University of Amsterdam. His energy was boundless. He initiated international conferences and workshops, established the journal *Zutot: Perspectives on Jewish Culture*, and edited it for thirteen years. Thanks to him, Amsterdam became a leading center for the study of Yiddish culture and literature. He was a regular participant in the international conferences on the history of the Jews of the Netherlands, and a learned and original article by him appears, as mentioned above, in this volume as well. His untimely departure is a great loss for Jewish Studies in the Netherlands and an inconsolable loss for us, his friends and colleagues. We mourn for him.

Yosef Kaplan and Dan Michman

Acknowledgments

We would like to thank all the institutions and individuals that provided essential support for the organization of the Twelfth International Conference on Dutch Jewry and the publication of this book: The Royal Netherlands Embassy in Israel and the former Dutch Ambassador to Israel Mr. Caspar Veldkamp, the Hebrew University of Jerusalem, the Stichting Collectieve Marorgelden Israel (SCMI), and the Dr. Henriette Boas Stichting (www.henrietteboas.nl).

In addition, we would like to express heartfelt gratitude to the Foundation for Research on Dutch Jewry in Jerusalem, its chairman Mr. André Boers and all the members of its Board of Directors. We also wish to thank the Friends of the Center for Research on Dutch Jewry in the Netherlands for their cooperation.

Throughout all the stages of preparing this volume, Irene Sommer, the devoted secretary of the center, spared no effort, always managing to inspire us with good spirits. Last but not least, deep gratitude is due to Dr. Sharon Assaf for her careful copy-editing, which assured consistency in spelling and style throughout the volume.

List of Illustrations

Figures

List of Abbreviations

AJHQ	*American Jewish Historical Quarterly*
AJS Review	*American Jewish Studies Review*
BT	Babylonian Talmud
DJH	*Dutch Jewish History*
JJS	*Journal of Jewish Studies*
JSQ	*Jewish Studies Quarterly*
JSS	*Jewish Social Studies*
JT	Jerusalem Talmud
LBI Yearbook	*Leo Baeck Institute Yearbook*
MGJN	*Maandblad voor der Geschiedenis der Joden in Nederland*
MGWJ	*Monatsschrift für Geschichte und Wissenschaft des Judenthums*
NIW	*Nieuw Israelietisch Weekblad*
REJ	*Revue des études juives*
SAA	Stadsarchief Gemeente Amsterdam
SAA, NIHS	Stadsarchief Gemeente Amsterdam, Nederlands-Israëlietische Hoofdsynagoge Amsterdam
SHDJ	*Studies on the History of Dutch Jewry*
StRos	*Studia Rosenthaliana*
ZWJ	*Zeitschrift für die Wissenschaft des Judentums*

List of Contributors

Marion Aptroot
is professor of Yiddish culture, language and literature at Heinrich-Heine-Universität, Dussledorf.

Avriel Bar-Levav
is associate professor of Judaic studies at the Open University of Israel, Raanana.

Shlomo Berger z"l (1953–2015)
held the chair in Yiddish language and literature at the University of Amsterdam.

Chaya Brasz
is former director of the Center for Research on Dutch Jewry at the Hebrew University of Jerusalem.

Marlene de Vries
is a sociologist and was, until her retirement, a senior researcher at the Institute for Migration and Ethnic Studies of the University of Amsterdam.

Evelien Gans
held the Chair for Modern Jewish History at the University of Amsterdam until her recent retirement and was a senior researcher at the Netherlands Institute for War, Holocaust and Genocide Studies (NIOD).

Matt Goldish
is Samuel M. and Esther Melton Chair of History at Ohio State University.

Jonathan Israel
held the Chair in Dutch History at University College London from 1984 to 2000. From 2001 to 2016, he was professor of modern history at the Institute for Advanced Study, Princeton.

Yosef Kaplan
is Bernard Cherrick Emeritus Professor of Jewish History at the Hebrew University of Jerusalem.

Tirtsah Levie Bernfeld
is an independent scholar residing in Amsterdam, The Netherlands.

Dan Michman
is Head of the International Institute for Holocaust Research and Incumbent of the John Najmann Chair of Holocaust Studies at Yad Vashem and is emeritus professor of Jewish history at Bar-Ilan University.

Limor Mintz-Manor
completed her PhD in early modern Jewish history at the Hebrew University of Jerusalem in 2012, and currently is a nurse in the Bone Marrow Transplantation Unit at the Hadassah Medical Center in Jerusalem.

Minny E. Mock-Degen
studied cultural anthropology at the University of Amsterdam and clinical sociology at the University of Texas and completed her doctorate at the Hebrew University of Jerusalem.

Evelyne Oliel-Grausz
is associate professor of early modern history and Director of the Diplôme Universitaire d'Etudes Juives at the Unversité Paris 1 Panthéon, Sorbonne.

Wout van Bekkum
is professor of Middle East studies at the Rijksuniversiteit Groningen, The Netherlands.

Bart Wallet
is lecturer of early modern and modern Jewish history at the University of Amsterdam.

Rivka Weiss-Blok
served as director of the Jewish Historical Museum, Amsterdam and was curator of European art in the Israel Museum, Jerusalem.

Irene E. Zwiep
holds the Chair in Hebrew and Jewish studies at the University of Amsterdam.

PART 1

Messianic Hopes and Redemption

∴

The Phoenix, the Exodus and the Temple: Constructing Self-Identity in the Sephardi Congregation of Amsterdam in the Early Modern Period

Limor Mintz-Manor

One of the first Jewish prayer books published in Amsterdam was financed by Isaac Franco (Francisco Mendes Medeiros), a Jewish merchant who was also one of the founders and leaders of the Jewish community in the city. Published in 1612, this three-volume *siddur* contained the liturgical texts for weekdays, Sabbaths, holidays, and other festive days of the Hebrew calendar in Hebrew with Spanish translation.[1] An emblem at the center of the title page of each volume featured an image of a phoenix (the legendary bird that is consumed in a fiery blaze at the end of its life-cycle and is reborn from the ashes) and the inscription "*Neve Shalom – Mi Kamokha.*" Neve Shalom is the name of the second Portuguese congregation established in the city. "*Mi kamokha*" ("Who is like thee") is from the Song of Miriam from the book of Exodus (15:11): "Who is like thee, O Lord, among the gods? Who is like thee, majestic in holiness?"

Previous studies noted the symbolism of the phoenix as signifying the revival of the Sephardi community in its newly established Jewish congregation in Amsterdam. They did not, however, mention the more obvious Christian allusions and symbolism of the phoenix that connotes Jesus and the Resurrection.[2]

---

* A version of this article was previously published in Hebrew in *Pe'amim* 120 (2009), pp. 9–59.

1 *Segvnda parte del Sedvr contiene las Pascvas de Pesah, Sebvoth, Svcoth, y dia octauo. Con todas las cosas que nellas se suele dezir en casa y en la ysnogua. Stampada por industria, y despeza de Yshac Franco, à 4 de Adar ve Adar* ([Amsterdam] 5372 [1612]). The three separate volumes were published over a period of a few weeks; see S. Seeligmann, *Bibliographie en historie: Bijdrage tot de geschiedenis der eerste Sephardim in Amsterdam* (Amsterdam 1927), pp. 42–43. A.K. Offenberg, "The Primera Parte Del Sedur (Amsterdam 1612)," *StRos*15 (1981), pp. 234–37.

2 J. de Samuel da Silva Rosa, *Geschiedenis der Portugeesche Joden te Amsterdam 1593–1925* (Amsterdam 1925), pp. 42–43. Seeligmann, *Sephardim in Amsterdam*, pp. 42–44. Cf. M. Bodian, *Hebrews of the Portuguese Nation. Conversos and Community in Early Modern Amsterdam* (Indianapolis 1997), pp. 20, 173 n. 50. M. Studemund-Halévy, "The Persistence of Images: Reproductive Success in the History of Sephardi Sepulchral Art," in *The Dutch Intersection: The Jews and the Netherlands in Modern History*, ed. Y. Kaplan (Leiden and Boston 2008), pp. 138–39.

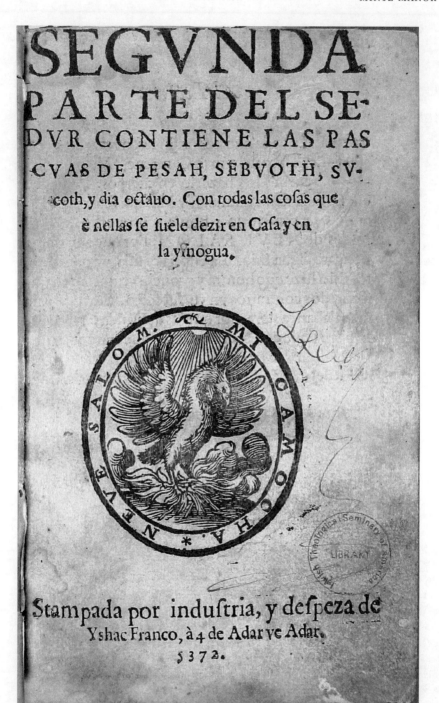

SEGVNDA
PARTE DEL SE-
DVR CONTIENE LAS PAS
CVAS DE PESAH, SEBVOTH, SV-
coth, y dia octauo. Con todas las cosas que
è nellas se suele dezir en Casa y en
la yinogua,

Stampada por industria, y despeza de
Yshac Franco, à 4 de Adar ve Adar.
5372.

FIGURE 1.1   *The phoenix emblem on the title page of the siddur of Neve Shalom congregation,*
published by Isaac Franco, Amsterdam 1612.

Additional texts and images of the phoenix that appeared in the communal sphere might offer a broader perspective on its meaning and use and shed light as well on the significance of the words "*Mi kamokha*" in the emblem. This article sets out to explore the religious and cultural context of the phoenix and related imagery used by the Sephardi community in Amsterdam in the seventeenth and eighteenth centuries. Additionally, it proposes that the biblical narrative of the Exodus was combined with the symbol of the phoenix to form a metaphor for the journey of the members of the Sephardi Jewish community from Christianity to Judaism and from exile (*galut*) in Spain and Portugal to redemption (*geula*) in Amsterdam. Another image that will be considered in this context is the ancient Temple in Jerusalem, which also figured prominently in the construction of the community's revived identity as Jews in the Netherlands.

Latin script on the title page of a prayer book and Spanish translation of the liturgical text were not unusual for the times.[3] Many canonical texts were being translated into Spanish for the benefit of Jews then arriving in Amsterdam. Unfamiliar with Hebrew language and liturgy, the translations enabled them to begin to practice their Judaism publicly. The family roots of these newcomers traced back to the Iberian Peninsula where many Jews, referred to there as *conversos* or *nuevos cristianos* (New Christians), lived either as Christians or crypto-Judaizers for generations in the wake of the expulsion of Jews from Spain in 1492 and forced conversion of the Jews in Portugal in 1497.[4] *Conversos*'

Da Silva Rosa and Seeligmann mentioned that the phoenix was replaced by the pelican and questioned the change, as the latter was a Christian symbol. Seeligmann even suggested that it was a misunderstanding on the part of the Sephardic congregants in Amsterdam, an assumption which doesn't make sense in light of their cultural milieu's general knowledge and deep understanding of the Christian symbolism, as will be demonstrated below. Some scholars confused the two symbols, even though their iconography is different and the pelican became the community symbol only in the nineteenth century. On the pelican as a symbol for the community, see L. Mintz-Manor, "Symbols and Images in the Jewish Sephardic Community in Amsterdam during the Seventeenth and Eighteenth Centuries" (M.A. Thesis, The Hebrew University of Jerusalem 2005), pp. 16–19, 25–28, 49 [Hebrew].

3   This *siddur* was probably one of the first translations of a Jewish prayer book printed in Latin script for Jewish readership. See M. Kayserling, *Biblioteca Española-Portugueza-Judaica* (Strasbourg 1890), pp. 59–63; A.K. Offenberg, "Spanish and Portuguese Sephardi Books Published in the Northern Netherlands before Menasseh Ben Israel (1584–1627)," *DJH* 3 (1993), p. 77.

4   On the history of the conversions in the Iberian Peninsula during fifteenth and sixteenth centuries and the *converso* problem, see Y. Baer, *A History of the Jews in Christian Spain* (Philadelphia 1966), vol. 2, pp. 95–443; H. Beinart, "The Great Conversion and the *Converso* Problem," in *Moreshet Sepharad. The Sephardi Legacy*, ed. H. Beinart (Jerusalem 1992), vol. 1, pp. 346–82; idem, "The *Conversos* in Spain and Portugal in the 16th to 18th Centuries," in *Moreshet Sepharad. The Sephardi Legacy*, vol. 2, pp. 43–67.

affinity for Judaism varied: some completely integrated into Iberian society and Christian life and had no attachment whatsoever to Judaism, some attempted to maintain Jewish practices and customs and others were indifferent to both faiths.[5] When *conversos* did reach Amsterdam, their memory of Jewish life was vague. Their religious practice was characterized by unique crypto-Judaic rituals that were often a syncretism of Jewish and Christian customs. Therefore, those who fled from the Iberian Peninsula during the seventeenth century to the newly established Jewish communities in Western Europe were in need of instruction on normative Judaism as well as translations of the basic Jewish texts and prayers. Through this process of re-education, these "New Christians" who joined the Jewish community in Amsterdam became "New Jews."[6] While they were engaged in the construction of their new religious and communal identity in Amsterdam, they still tried to maintain familial as well as cultural ties to their homeland and often combined their renewed Jewish faith with their Iberian heritage, which was infused with both Spanish and Portuguese culture and Catholic precepts and values.

The pragmatic and relatively tolerant attitude towards minorities in the United Provinces, especially in the city of Amsterdam, contributed to the flourishing there of the Sephardi community. Many of its members were involved in the commercial life of the city, which was then becoming an important economic hub. Amsterdam was also an international center for printing and had more than one Jewish printing house. In addition to commercial ties, Jewish scholars interacted with Dutch theologians and Hebraists, which furthered the Jews' integration into Dutch society and culture.[7]

5   Y.H. Yerushalmi, *From Spanish Court to Italian Ghetto. Isaac Cardoso: A Study in Seventeenth-Century Marranism and Jewish Apologetics* (New York and London 1971), pp. 1–50; idem, "*Conversos* Returning to Judaism in the 17th Century: Their Jewish Knowledge and Psychological Readiness," *Proceedings of the Fifth World Congress of Jewish Studies* 2 (1972), pp. 201–9 [Hebrew]. B.A. Lorence, "The Inquisition and the New Christians in the Iberian Peninsula. Main Historiographic Issues and Controversies," in *The Sephardi and Oriental Jewish Heritage*, ed. I. Ben-Ami (Jerusalem 1982), pp. 13–72; D.M. Gitlitz, *Secrecy and Deceit. The Religion of the Crypto-Jews* (Philadelphia 1996), pp. 35–36, 425–41.

6   About the complex identity of the *conversos*, the process of "returning" to Judaism and the term "new Jews," see Y. Kaplan, "Wayward New Christians and Stubborn New Jews: The Shaping of a New Identity," *Jewish History* 8 (1994), pp. 27–41; idem, "The Intellectual Ferment in the Spanish-Portuguese Community of Seventeenth-Century Amsterdam," in *Moreshet Sepharad. The Sephardi Legacy*, vol. 2, pp. 288–314; idem, *An Alternative Path to Modernity. The Sephardi Diaspora in Western Europe* (Leiden 2000), pp. 1–28. Cf. Bodian, *Hebrews of the Portuguese Nation*, pp. 96–125.

7   Y. Kaplan, *From Christianity to Judaism. The Story of Isaac Orobio de Castro* (Oxford 1989), pp. 235–325. D.M. Swetschinski, *Reluctant Cosmopolitans. The Portuguese Jews of Seventeenth*

"Like the Phoenix that is Born from the Ashes"

Rooted in ancient Egyptian culture, the legend of the phoenix entered the Classical tradition in several versions. The mythical bird was said to dwell in the East and at the end of its lifespan would build a nest atop a palm tree and die in a blaze of fire (while flying directly towards the sun, in some versions), after which a new phoenix would be born from the ashes. Although the phoenix legend was mentioned in late antique Jewish and early Christian sources, it was known mainly through the writings of the Church Fathers. In late antiquity, the phoenix became a symbol of Jesus and the Resurrection in Christian textual and visual sources. The phoenix, often depicted atop a palm tree, appeared alongside the figure of Jesus in church mosaics. Descriptions of the mythical bird were included in medieval allegorical treatises, such as *Physiologus*, and in bestiaries, didactic manuals containing descriptions of animals from which were derived Christian moral and symbolic attributes. In the early modern period, the phoenix was used as a symbol of hope (one of the seven Christian virtues), as well as revival, courage, eternity, martyrdom, sovereignty and nationhood.[8] On the Iberian Peninsula, the phoenix appeared

---

Century Amsterdam (London 2000), pp. 102–64, 278–304. On the legal status of the Jews, see A.H. Huussen, "The Legal Position of the Jews in the Dutch Republic, c. 1590–1796," in *Dutch Jewry: Its History and Secular Culture (1500–2000)*, ed. J.I. Israel and R. Salverda (Leiden 2002), pp. 25–41. On Dutch Calvinism and the different groups, see J.I. Israel, *The Dutch Republic: Its Rise, Greatness, and Fall, 1477–1806* (Oxford 1995), pp. 361–98, 450–77, 637–99, 1019–37.

8 The scholarly literature on the phoenix is immense. For selected bibliography, see *Mythical and Fabulous Creatures. A Source Book and Research Guide*, ed. M. South (New York 1987), pp. 72–74. For the phoenix motif, see S. Thompson, *Motif-Index of Folk-Literature*, rev. ed. (Bloomington 1966), no. B32, also nos. B31.1.0.1, B37, B39, B758. Details about different traditions of the phoenix and visual representations from antiquity to modern times, see R. van den Broek, *The Myth of the Phoenix according to Classical and Early Christian Traditions*, trans. I. Seeger (Leiden 1972); D. Pagis, "The Immortal Bird. The Phoenix Motif in the Midrash and Aggada Literature," in *A Jubilee Book of the Hebrew Gymnasium in Jerusalem*, ed. Ch.-M. Merhavia (Jerusalem 1962), pp. 74–90 [Hebrew]; M.R. Niehoff, "The Phoenix in Rabbinic Literature," *Harvard Theological Review* 89/3 (1996), pp. 245–65; M.F. MacDonald, "Phoenix Redivivius," *The Phoenix* 14/4 (Winter 1960), pp. 187–206; D.J. McMillan, "The Phoenix in the Western World from Herodotus to Shakespeare," *The D.H. Lawrence Review* 5 (fall 1972), pp. 238–67; J.J. Poesch, "The Phoenix Portrayed," ibid., pp. 200–37; *Emblemata. Handbuch zur Sinnbildkunst des XVI und XVII Jahrhunderts*, ed. A. Henkel and A. Schöne (Stuttgart 1978), pp. 795–96; A. Roob, *The Hermetic Museum: Alchemy & Mysticism* (Cologne 2001), figs. 115, 299, 301, 357, 695; S. Orgel, "Gendering the Crown," in *Subject and Object in Renaissance Culture*, ed. M. de Grazia, M. Quilligan and P. Stallybrass (Cambridge 1996), pp. 154–55.

in theological writings, poetry, plays and the visual arts.[9] Members of the Sephardi community in Amsterdam were almost certainly familiar with the image and its varied meanings, as they were well acquainted with Classical and Christian traditions as well as with the work of contemporary Spanish writers, poets and playwrights.[10]

The first appearance of the phoenix in a Jewish context was in the work *Tzemah tzadik* (The Righteous Branch) by the famous Italian Rabbi Leon Judah de Modena, published in Venice in 1599/1600.[11] Modena's book was a Hebrew adaptation of the popular Italian bestiary *Fior di virtù*. The phoenix is

---

9   Such as Francisco de Quevedo, Lope Félix de Vega Carpio, Juan y Sebastían de Horozco
     y Covarrubias, Juan de Pineda. For references to the phoenix in Francisco de Quevedo's
     poetry, see Francisco de Quevedo, *Obra poética*, ed. J.M. Blecua (Madrid 1970), pp. 328–
     31; V. Nider, "La Fenix," *Perinola Revista de Investigación Quevediana* 6 (2002), pp. 61–80.
     In Lope Felix de Vega's play, see T.W. Jensen, "The Phoenix and Folly in Lope's *La noche
     de San Juan*," *Forum for Modern Language Studies* 16 (1980), pp. 214–23. De Vega's nick-
     name was "El fénix de los ingenios." In de Covarrubias's brother's work, see J. Horozco y
     Covarrubias, *Sacra symbola* (Agrigento 1601) ill. 6; idem, *Emblemas morales* (Çaragoça
     1604); idem, (Madrid 1610), where the phoenix emblem appears also on the title pages
     of all three volumes. S. Covarrubias y Horozco, *Tesoro de la lengua castellana*, ed. M. de
     Riquer (Barcelona 1943), pp. 588–89; see also J. Elias Estrugós, *Fénix català, o llibre de sin-
     gular privilegi, favors, gràcies i miracles de Nostra Senyora del Mont del Carme* (Perpinyà
     1644). N. Feliu de la Peña y Farrel, *Fénix de Cataluña. Barcelona 1683*, intro. H. Kamen (Bar-
     celona 1983). For Juan de Pineda's book see in the following. For representations of the
     phoenix in Iberian Art, see for example J. Gallego, *Vision et symboles dans la peinture Es-
     pagnole de Siècle D'or* (Paris 1968), pp. 83–86; P. Burke, "America and the Rewrite of World
     History," in *America in European Consciousness, 1493–1750*, ed. K.O. Kupperman (Chapel
     Hill 1995), ill. p. 34.

10   Kaplan, *From Christianity to Judaism*, pp. 308–25; idem, "El perfil cultural de tres rabinos
     sefardíes a través del análisis de sus bibliotecas," in *Familia, Religión y Negocio. El sefar-
     dismo en las relaciones entre el mundo ibérico y los Países Bajos en la Edad Moderna*, ed.
     J. Contreras, B.J. García and I. Pulido (Madrid 2003), pp. 269–86; idem, "Spanish
     Readings of Amsterdam's Seventeenth-Century Sephardim" in *Jewish Books and Their
     Readers. Aspects of the Intellectual Life of Christians and Jews in Early Modern Europe*, ed.
     J. Weinberg and S. Mandelbrotte (Leiden-Boston 2016), pp. 312–41.

11   The cultural ties between Italian Jewry, especially the congregation in Venice and the Sep-
     hardim in Amsterdam, has been noted by scholars as has the influence of the community
     structures of the senior Venetian Sephardic congregation on the younger one in Amster-
     dam, both of which bear the identical name, Talmud Torah. On the contacts between the
     Jewish communities in Venice and Amsterdam see J.-M. Cohen and J.C.E. Belifante, "The
     Ponentini and the Portuguese: The Influence of Venetian Jewry on the Portuguese Jews
     of Amsterdam," in *Het getto van Venetië – The Ghetto in Venice: Ponentini, Levantini and
     Tedeschi, 1516–1797*, ed. J.-M. Cohen ('s-Gravenhage 1990), pp. 106–24; S. Sabar, "The Golden
     Age of Ketubah Decoration in Venice and Amsterdam," in ibid., pp. 87–105.

mentioned in the thirtieth chapter, "Of fortitude and constancy," as a symbol of loyalty, courage and martyrdom and is compared to the righteous and martyred Jews throughout history. The context evidently presupposed a Christian symbolism, but Modena added midrashic traditions about the legendary bird, quoting the verse from Job 29:18: "Then I thought, 'I shall die in my nest, and I shall multiply my days as the sand'."[12] Modena made significant changes to the original text to suit his Jewish readership, replacing Christian texts with ones from Jewish tradition.[13] This, however, was not usually the case with texts mentioning the phoenix written by Sephardi authors in Amsterdam, which remained, for the most part, infused with Christian symbolism and where the association of the phoenix with courage and martyrdom was standard.

The symbolism of the phoenix was used in martyrological works written in Amsterdam dedicated to *conversos* victims of the Spanish and Portuguese Inquisitions,[14] to praise and sanctify their martyrdom. A book of short poems in Spanish by members of the community, published in Amsterdam in 1655, entitled *Elogios Que zelozos dedicaron A La Felice memorià de Abraham Nunez Bernal*, was dedicated to the memory of Abraham Núñez Bernal and Isaac de Almeida Bernal, who were sentenced to death by the Spanish Inquisition and burned at the stake in Cordoba the same year.[15] The phoenix was exploited here as a metaphor for the two martyrs who chose to die rather than renounce their Jewish faith. In the poem by Daniel de Ribera, Abraham was described as dying gloriously and defeating the Inquisition through his self sacrifice: "And from the burning sacrifice / came out a prodigious phoenix; / So proudly and so piously."[16] In another poem glorifying Abraham who chose the right path,

---

12   Judah Arye Modena, *Tzemah tzadik* (Venice 1599/60), p. 30. Cf. Pagis, "The Immortal Bird," p. 87. On Modena's book see *The Autobiography of a Seventeenth Century Venetian Rabbi. Leon Modena's Life of Judah,* trans. and ed. M.R. Cohen (Princeton 1988), p. 224. On Job 29:18 and the phoenix in early modern Christian interpretations, see below.

13   Modena commented on that issue in his autobiography: "I substituted a saying of the rabbis [of the Talmud] of blessed memory for every reference from their [i.e., the Christians'] scriptures or saints" (Cohen, *Autobiography*, p. 124).

14   Bodian, *Hebrews of the Portuguese Nation*, pp. 80–84.

15   *Elogios Que zelozos dedicaron A La Felice memorià de Abraham Nunez Bernal, Que fue quemado vivo santificando el Nombre de su Criador en Cordova a 3 de Mayo 5415* [Amsterdam 1655]; Kaplan, *From Christianity to Judaism*, p. 332; Bodian, *Hebrews of the Portuguese Nation*, pp. 20, 83. According to the introduction of the *Elogios*, the sermons were given in the synagogue on the occasion of the reading of the names of those who were burned at the stake.

16   "Diosse allí por offendida/ La tiranía frustrada/ Viendo que del polvo y nada/ Saca Abraham immortal vida . . . Y del sacrificio ardiente,/ Salió Phenix prodigioso;/ Tan ufano

meaning the Jewish faith, Semuel de Crasto used the image of the phoenix to
evoke the notion of resurrection: "Like the phoenix, was burned . . . who in the
flame triumphantly went up to the sky."[17]

Some members of the community opposed praising the martyrdom of
conversos, an act they considered overly evocative of Christian conduct. The
debates on such issues also touched on the appropriate attitude towards *conversos* still living in the Iberian Peninsula, the extent to which they could be
considered Jews and mainly the theological question of the fate of their souls
due to their unclear religious status.[18] The martyrological literature composed
by members of the Sephardi community was reminiscent of Christian models
despite attempts by communal leaders to educate new members about Jewish
tradition and distance them from their Catholic past and culture.[19] Although
there are no visual representations of the phoenix in the martyrological texts,
the image of the legendary bird was particularly vivid and clearly incorporated
the Christian essence of its symbolism, as did contemporary emblems featuring the phoenix used within the Sephardi sphere.

After the first visualization of the phoenix in the 1612 prayer book, it appeared for a second time, in 1639, in the emblem of the "Talmud Torah," that
merged into one the three separate Sephardi congregations of Beit Ya'akov,
Neve Shalom and Beit Israel.[20] The seal bearing the inscription: Sello do K.K.
de T.T. de Amsterdam (seal of K[ahal] K[odesh] T[almud] T[orah] in Amsterdam), was probably used on various formal communal documents, such as *ketubbot* (Jewish marriage contracts).

---

y tan zeloso/ Deseó de se abrasar./ Que en el se sacrificar/ Entre el incendio y desvelos/
Dió que notar que admirar" (*Elogios*, p. 41).

17   "El que por justo camino,/ Como el fenix se abraso,/ De a donde resucitó,/ Dexando en el
mundo fama,/ Otro Elias, que en la llama/ Triumphando al cielo subió" (*Elogios*, p. 49).
The phoenix is also mentioned by Jonas Abravanel: "Con animo se arroja, / Al abrasante
incendio, / Que quiere de sus llamas, / Salir un fenix nuebo" (ibid., pp. 55–56), Moshe
Yeshurun Lobo in ibid., pp. 111–12, and by David Yeshurun (Jesurun) in Daniel Levi de Barrios's work *En los caminos de la salvación*, see Heinirch Graetz, *History of the Jews* (Philadelphia 1945), vol. 4, p. 669.

18   Kaplan, *From Christianity to Judaism*, pp. 326–43.

19   On the similarity and difference between the Christian martyrological literature and that
of the former *conversos*, see M. Bodian, *Dying in the Law of Moses: Crypto-Jewish Martyrdom in the Iberian World* (Bloomington and Indianapolis 2007), pp. 182–98. Bodian remarks that one of the differences is the lack of visual martyrological representations in
the literature of the Sephardim in Amsterdam.

20   Da Silva Rosa, *Geschiedenis der Portugeesche Joden*, p. 42., ill. p. 27. See also *Feestelijke
Herdenking van het 250 Jarig Bestaan van de Synagoge der Portugeesch-Israelietische Gemeente te Amsterdam op Vrijdag 10 Menachem 5685 / 31 Juli 1925*, p. 22.

FIGURE 1.2A   *Ketubbah of Moshe Pereira ben Isaac and Lisa Luna bat Moshe, Amsterdam 1795.*
COURTESY OF THE JEWISH THEOLOGICAL SEMINARY OF AMERICA, NEW
YORK.

A small emblem featuring a phoenix was added to the bottom of the most
common type of printed Amsterdam Sephardi *ketubbah* during the eighteenth century. The emblem included an inscription similar to the seal and the
date 1739, the centenary of the unification.[21] The iconography of these three

---

21   "Pertençe ao K.K de T.T. de Amsterdam Roshodes Kislev A 5499." On this type of *ketubbah*, see S. Sabar, *Ketubbah. Jewish Marriage Contracts of the Hebrew Union College* (New
York 1990), pp. 265–70, figs. 154, 157, 169–172; with the phoenix emblem: figs. 171–172.

FIGURE 1.2B   *Ketubbah of Isaac ben Imanuel de Valença and Sara bat Isaac, Amsterdam 1821.*
COURTESY OF THE NATIONAL LIBRARY OF ISRAEL, JERUSALEM.

emblems (on the prayer book, seal and *ketubbah*) was quite similar, though the earliest was the most elaborate. Another, slightly different emblem featuring the phoenix appeared on the title page of the regulations of the Ets Haim yeshiva, published in 1728 in Amsterdam.[22]

The phoenix was combined with the palm as a metaphor of martyrdom, courage and revival in a poem in praise of martyred *conversos* by the prolific author, poet and multifarious figure Daniel Levi de Barrios (Miguel de Barrios): "The Law sent to the brazier / the two youths of Osuna / So in victory (*palma*) like the phoenix / they would be reborn from ashes."[23] The poet condemned the Inquisition's actions and compared the act of martyrdom to the biblical commandment of pilgrimage to the Temple in Jerusalem, a common comparison featured in the writings of other members of the Sephardi community.

S. Sabar, *The Art of the Ketubbah: Marriage Contracts from the Library of the Jewish Theological Seminary* (New York, in press), no. 214; *Joods Historisch Museum*, ed. J.C.E. Belifante, J.-M. Cohen and E. van Voolen (Amsterdam 1995), p. 55. There are twelve *ketubbot* with the phoenix emblem from 1750 to 1835 in the digital *ketubbot* collection of the National Library of Jerusalem.

22   B.N. Teensma, "Van marraan tot jood: 17e en 18e-eeuwse Amsterdamse Sephardim en hun Iberische achtergrond," *Jaarboek van het Genootschap Amstelodamum* 80 (1988), pp. 119, 123. The legendary bird that appears on that book was identified there by mistake as a pelican.

23   *Marrano Poets of the Seventeenth Century: João Pinto Delgado, Antonio Enriques Gómez, Miguel de Barrios*, ed. and trans. T. Oelman (Rutherford 1982), p. 239.

The word *palma*, usually conveying the notions of victory and triumph, carried a multi-layered meaning in de Barrios's poem.

The phoenix and palm tree have shared semantics and symbolism since ancient Roman times, when the palm tree was used as a symbol of victory and eternity.[24] Following the Septuagint translation of the Hebrew word *tamar* (palm) as φοῖνιξ (phoenix) in Psalm 92:12: "The righteous flourish like the palm tree," early Christian literature attached to the palm the meaning of resurrection of the dead, specifically, Jesus. Palm tree and phoenix, widely used in Christian art since medieval times as symbols of eternity and resurrection of Jesus, were used in the same context in literary works by the seventeenth-century Spanish authors Juan de Horozco y Covarrubias and Juan de Pineda.[25] The latter's commentary on Job (printed for a second time in 1612), included an image of phoenix and palm tree as the symbol of resurrection, individual salvation and triumph over death. Christological interpretations of Job 29:18 regarding the legendary phoenix were common in exegetical works on Job written by Catholic and Protestant Hebraists in the seventeenth and eighteenth centuries.[26] Such was the case with an illustration in Juan de Pineda's commentary; one part of Psalm 92:12, in Latin, appeared below the image of a burning phoenix, while the second part, in Greek, was inscribed on a ribbon bound to a palm tree. A similar image of palm tree with ribbon bearing the phrase, in Portuguese, "Justo como tamaral floressera," appears on a family tree by Ishac de Pinto (who served as a *parnas* in the Sephardi community of

---

24   In late antique Jewish literature and art the palm tree was a symbol for renewal, hope, eternity and, at times, redemption, see Pagis, "The Immortal Bird," p. 82. E.R. Goodenough, *Jewish Symbols in the Greco-Roman Period* (New York 1953–1968), vol. 7, pp. 121–34; J. Hall, *Dictionary of Subjects and Symbols in Art*, rev. ed. (New York 1979), pp. 231–32.

25   In Christianity the palm tree was used as a symbol for spiritual victory and at times martyrdom, see G. Schiller, *Iconography of Christian Art*, trans. J. Seligman (London 1971–1972), vol. 2, pp. 18–21, vol. 2a, figs. 1, 53, 110, 355; vol. 2b, figs. 2, 34, 42 46. *Lexikon der christlichen Ikonographie*, ed. E. Kirschbaum (Freiburg 1968–1976), vol. 3, pp. 364–65. On common representations of the phoenix and the palm tree from ancient Egypt to Christian Europe, see Van den Broek, *The Myth of the Phoenix*, pp. 15–17, 51–57, 326–27, figs. xx, xxiv–xxv, xxviii–xxx; McMillan, *The Phoenix in the Western World*, pp. 250–54; MacDonald, *Phoenix Redivivius*, pp. 200–3; Pagis, "The Immortal Bird," pp. 81–82. Covarrubias, *Sacra symbola*, fig. 6.

26   Juan de Pineda, *Commentariorum in Iob* (Antwerp 1612). S. Budick, "Milton's Joban Phoenix in Samson Agonistes," *Early Modern Literary Studies* 11/2 (2005), pp. 1–15. The Hebrew word *ḥol* (Job 29:18), which was translated into Greek as "phoenix" in the Septuagint, already bears the double meaning and was used later in Christian literature, see G. Sajo, "Phoenix on the Top of the Palm Tree: Multiple Interpretations of Job 29:18," *Silva* 3 (8 February 2005); URL: www.studiolum.com/en/silva5.htm.

Amsterdam), printed in Amsterdam in 1758. The identical verse was engraved on the tombstone of Daniel de Pinto (d. 1681) and on a few other tombstones in the Sephardi cemetery in Ouderkerk. In this context, the image of palm tree and biblical verse, together or individually, evoked notions of revival, afterlife and resurrection of the dead, with which members of the community identified. Clearly, the world of ideas of the Sephardim in Amsterdam was rooted in the Iberian and broader early modern Western European theological and cultural milieu.

The association of the phoenix with notions of revival and rebirth can be traced to the Sephardi community's earliest years in Amsterdam. In 1624, the legendary bird was mentioned in this context in the play *Dialogo dos Montes* ("The Discourse of the Mountains"), written in Portuguese specifically for the festival of Shavuoth (the Feast of Weeks) at the Beit Ya'akov synagogue. The play was written by the ex-*converso* Rehuel Yeshurun (Paulo de Pina), who was born in Lisbon and became one of the founders of Beit Ya'akov and Saul Levi Mortera, rabbi of the community and composer of the sermons included in the play.

The play was framed as a debate among seven famous mountains vying for the honor to be the mountain on which the Torah will be given.[27] Every mountain delivered a sermon before the judge Jehoshaphat and the choir, which represented the People of Israel. After a mountain finished its speech, the choir would sing. The play was imbued with motifs of growth and revival as well as images of eternity and resurrection, among them the phoenix. For example, after the sermon of Mount Hor, the choir sang: "What wonder that this fire / Should be prolonged and spread / Till I from the cold ashes like the phoenix / rise again?"[28] At the end of the play, when announcing Mount Sinai as the chosen place, Jehoshaphat also spoke of God having freed His people from the tyranny and cruelty of Egypt, would redeem them from exile, bring them to Zion, rebuild the Temple, an "admirable work [that] will be revived like the phoenix who is born from the ashes."[29] Thus, the phoenix symbolized both the People of Israel and the Temple and its renewal, reflecting the congregants' individual

---

27 On the play and its authors, see Rehuel Jessurun, *Dialogo dos montes*, ed. and trans. P. Polack (London 1975), pp. viii–xxv. More details about Mortera see in the following. The work appeared in a number of manuscripts and was first printed in 1767.

28 "Que muito que este fogo / se dilate eprolongue, / [t]e que das sinzas frias / qual fenix me renoue" (Jessurun, *Dialogo dos montes*, pp. 106–7).

29 "[E] lutozo lamenta de seo Templo/ as gastadas ruhinas, donde ayunda / resuçitar afabrica admirauel / (qual da sinza o fenix se aleuanta) / espero sedo uer, gozoso ealegre," (Jessurun, *Dialogo dos montes*, pp. 144–45).

and collective experience of revival, as former *conversos* and as members of the Sephardi community and the Jewish People.

Dialogo dos montes, similar in form and style to a type of play performed in Catholic ritual ceremonies on the Iberian Peninsula,[30] was performed in the synagogue during the festival of Shavuoth, a central Jewish holiday that marks the People of Israel having been chosen by God to receive the Torah as part of their redemption following their Exodus from Egypt. The freedom of Israel from Egyptian tyranny mentioned at the end of the play, expressed the unification of God and His people. The Beit Ya'akov congregants likely identified with this story of redemption, which conveyed their need to establish their connection to the history of the Jewish People and reinforced their own choice to return to Judaism and join the community in Amsterdam.

The above examples demonstrate that the image of the phoenix served as a prominent symbol of the individual congregant's revival as well as of the revival of Sephardi Jewry in general; just as the phoenix was reborn from the ashes, so the *conversos* revived their Judaism. The fiery phoenix was used as a martyrological symbol for the *conversos* who clung to their Judaism and were burned at the stake, but, at the same time, it was also a symbol for those who had survived "reborn from the ashes" and were "revived" as Jews in their newly established community. These two aspects of the image are indicative of broad boundaries that defined the identity of members of the Sephardi community in Amsterdam, which often was based more on familial and ethnic ties than on religious ones and included not only individuals or members of the Sephardi Jewish community but also *conversos* still living as Christians. Thus, in many community documents, members frequently called themselves *membros da nação* (members of the Nation) or *nação*, a term that originated in Portugal where the *conversos* were disparagingly referred to as New Christians or *homens da nação* (people of the Nation). As Yosef Kaplan has noted, former *conversos* borrowed concepts from their persecutors which they later used to define their own identity, a cultural phenomenon called "mimesis of antagonism."[31]

---

30   J.A. van Praag, "El *Dialogo dos montes* de Rehuel Jessurun," in *Mélanges de philologie offerts à Jean Jacques Salverda de Grave* (Groningen 1933), pp. 242–55. Jessurun, *Dialogo dos montes*, pp. xxi–xxv.

31   Y. Kaplan, "Political Concepts in the World of the Portuguese Jews of Amsterdam during the Seventeenth Century: The Problem of Exclusion and the Boundaries of Self-Identity," in *Menasseh ben Israel and His World*, ed. Y. Kaplan et al. (Leiden 1989), p. 53. The mimesis of antagonism is most relevant to the *conversos* concept of purity of blood, see below. On the term *nação* and its origin, see Yerushalmi, *From Spanish Court to Italian Ghetto*, pp. 12–21. Y. Kaplan, "The Portuguese Community of Amsterdam in the 17th Century:

The story of revival followed by redemption became part of the communal narrative as the life stories of individuals were integrated into the Sephardi Diaspora narrative of liberation. According to this revival-redemption narrative, Sephardi Jewry had survived a potential extinction. When descendants of the Jews of Spain and Portugal fled the Iberian Peninsula and "returned" to Judaism in Amsterdam, they achieved a unique redemption, not only individually, but also, collectively, as members of the Sephardi heritage. Many of them considered this redemption a type of Exodus and it was portrayed as such in the discourse of the congregants on their path to Judaism and in the establishment of their new community. According to Mircea Eliade, "[a]n object or an act becomes real only insofar as it imitates or repeats an archetype. Thus, reality is acquired solely through repetition or participation ... through such imitation, man is projected into the mythical epoch in which the archetypes were first revealed."[32] Using the redemption archetype of the Jewish people of which the Exodus was a part, the newcomers were able to establish a connection with the Jewish People and its biblical-mythical past to which they now wanted to belong. Viewed in this light, the implication of the phrase "*Mi kamokha*" on the Neve Shalom emblem becomes clearer: it identified the biblical Exodus with the historical Sephardi one, bridging time and place and reconnecting them to the Jewish tradition from which they had been cut off for several generations.

"With a Mighty Hand and an Outstretched Arm"

In the writings of *conversos* and members of the Sephardi community in Amsterdam, Spain was compared to Egypt and the escape of *conversos* from the Iberian Peninsula to the Exodus. Early testimonies of the Inquisition show that the Exodus story served as an image of personal and collective experience among the *conversos*, as for example, in a prayer included in the testimony of the *converso* Juan de Fez at the Inquisitorial Court in Ciudad Real in 1484: "[The person under sentence] said that the Creator who exists in the heaven and who created the heavens and the earth and parted the sea into twelve

---

Between Tradition and Change" [Hebrew], *Proceedings of the Israel Academy of Sciences and Humanities* 7 (1985), pp. 166–67. Swetschinski, *Reluctant Cosmopolitans*, pp. 163–67.

32   M. Eliade, *The Myth of the Eternal Return. Cosmos and History*, trans. W.R. Trask. Intro. J.Z. Smith (Princeton 2005), pp. 34–35.

paths and saved the people of Israel from the rule of King Pharaoh, so Lord, help me and free me."[33] The imprisoned *converso's* prayer concealed a parallel between the tyranny of the biblical Pharaoh and the tyranny of Spain and the Inquisition and God's salvation of the People of Israel and his hope for freedom and salvation from Spanish captivity. The Exodus story was used as a source of inspiration in a time of trouble and enabled the supplicant to construct a link to Judaism and the Jewish people that was otherwise forbidden. It is, therefore, interesting to read what the Castilian priest Andrés Bernáldez, who studied the Inquisitional documents at the time, had to say about this image in *converso* discourse:

> All of them [the *conversos*] were Jews and clung to their hope, like the Israelites in Egypt, who suffered many blows at the hands of the Egyptians and yet believed that God would lead them out from the midst of them, as He did with a mighty hand and an outstretched arm. So, too, the *conversos* looked upon the Christians as Egyptians or worse and believed that God had them in His keeping and miraculously preserved them. They held steadfastly to their faith that God would guide and remember

---

33   "[Q]ue el Criador esta en el çielo e crio el çielo e la tierra e partio el mar por doze carreras e saco el pueblo de Ysrael de poderio del Rey Faraon, asi Señor, Tu me apiada e me libra," in *Records of the Trials of the Spanish Inquisition in Ciudad Real*, ed. H. Beinart (Jerusalem 1974–1983), vol. 2, p. 102. On this testimony and other similar prayers, see H. Beinart, *Conversos on Trial. The Inquisition in Ciudad Real* (Jerusalem 1981), pp. 256–59, 283–84. Beinart remarks that this format of prayer could be found in other *converso* prayers. Cf. Bodian, *Hebrews of the Portuguese Nation*, pp. 15–17. On more prayers that contain this format, see C. Amiel, "Les cent voix de Quintanar: Le modèle castillan du marranisme," *Revue de l'histoire des religions* 218 (2001), pp. 195–280, 487–577. E. Cunha de Azvedo Mea, "Orações Judaicas na Inquisição Portuguesa: Século XVI," in *Jews and Conversos. Studies in Society and the Inquisition*, ed. Y. Kaplan (Jerusalem 1985), p. 168. Gitlitz, *Secrecy and Deceit*, p. 100. Beinart, The Conversos in Spain and Portugal, pp. 64–65. P. Amílcar, "O ritual dos criptojudeus portugueses," *Jews and Conversos. Studies in Society and the Inquisition*, ed. Y. Kaplan (Jerusalem 1985), pp. 145–47. The twelve paths motif is found in Jewish midrashic literature, in Jewish and Christian iconography and was also known in Spain through Sephardi Passover Haggadot and bibles from Pamplona dated to the thirteenth and fourteenth centuries. See for example B. Narkiss, *Hebrew Illuminated Manuscripts* (Jerusalem 1984), p. 16 [Hebrew]; S. Shalev-Eyni, "Jewish Art and Christian Art: Interactions," *Mahanayim* 10 (1995), pp. 40–49 [Hebrew]; K. Kogman-Appel, "The Iconographic Models of the Illuminated Haggadot from Spain," *Pe'amim* 50 (1992), pp. 29–68 [Hebrew].

them and bring them out from the midst of the Christians and lead them
to the Holy and Promised Land.[34]

According to his report and other transcripts of *converso* testimonies, the Exodus narrative—begun in slavery under a foreign and idolatrous rule, followed
by hope for redemption and liberation from Egypt, to be completed by reaching the Promised Land—was construed by *conversos* in a novel and real way:
they did not simply identify with the redemption of the Israelites from Egypt,
they structured the narrative so that it became their own individual and collective story of redemption.

Miriam Bodian noted an echo of this narrative in a passage from Ishac de Pinto's above-mentioned family history, where he recounted his great-grandfather
Gil Lopes Pinto's revelation of the family's Jewish origins to one of his children
while they were still in Spain. He expressed his wonderment at God's preservation of the decedents of the Jews in Iberia as a greater miracle than the
Exodus.[35]

This motif was also present in poetry written by *conversos* who eventually
joined the community in Amsterdam during the seventeenth century, such as
João Pinto Delgado. Born in Portugal, Delgado made his way to Amsterdam
where he eventually became a *parnas* in the Talmud Torah congregation. In
his poems, he described God's salvation of the People of Israel through the
biblical narratives of the Exodus and Queen Esther.[36] One of his poems was
titled "Song in which the poet relates the divine mercies granted him and his
own failings to the departure from Egypt to the Holy Land." Similar to a genre
of Spanish Baroque poetry, this poem was formulated as a personal spiritual allegory where the narrator described his feelings while enslaved in sinful Egypt
and asked God to illuminate the darkness around him.[37] Christian notions of
salvation echo in this poem, where the Exodus was a metaphor for Jesus' path

34   Bodian, *Hebrews of the Portuguese Nation*, p. 16. For the Spanish original text, see *Memo-
     rias del Reinado de los Reyes Católicos que escribió el bachiller Andrés Bernáldez, Cura de los
     Palacios*, ed. M. Gómez-Moreno and J. de M. Carriano (Madrid 1962), p. 102.
35   H.P. Salomon, "The Pinto Manuscript: A 17th-Century Marrano Family History," *StRos* 9/1
     (1975), p. 47. See Bodian, *Hebrews of the Portuguese Nation*, pp. 16–17, 40.
36   Oelman, *Marrano Poets of the Seventeenth Century*, pp. 49–52. On the significance of
     Queen Esther in *converso* literature, see for example Gitlitz, *Secrecy and Deceit*, pp. 116–17,
     378–79, 470; Bodian, *Hebrews of the Portuguese Nation*, pp. 10, 15.
37   For the poem's text see Oelman, *Marrano Poets of the Seventeenth Century*, pp. 122–25.
     For example: "En este fiero Egipto / de mi pecado, donde el alma mía / padece la Tirana
     servidumbre / del tesoro infinito / de tu divina lumbre / a mi noche, Señor, un rayo envía"
     (p. 122). On the similarity to Luis de Granada's "Journeys of the Soul," see ibid., p. 136. On
     other poems mentioning Passover and Exodus, see ibid., pp. 54–82.

and the believer's personal salvation. The crossing of the Red Sea represented triumph over death, baptism and renewal of life, which were also among the symbols of the phoenix.[38] A poem by Daniel Levi de Barrios, devoted to the theme of the divine providence of the Jewish People, also used the analogy of Egypt, Christianity and the Inquisition. In it, the narrator described the idolatry in Egypt from which God freed His people, and he called Egypt *tiranía* (tyranny), a word that *conversos* commonly used to refer to the Inquisition.[39]

Indeed, one of the main characteristics of crypto-Jewish tradition, as Israel S. Révah has shown, was the rejection of Catholicism as idolatry.[40] According to this view, the Iberian Peninsula and other Catholic countries where practice of Judaism was forbidden, was perceived as *terras de idolatria* (lands of idolatry). Traveling there was prohibited by the Sephardi communal regulations, because the former *conversos* would have had to hide their identity and appear as Christians, which would have made it impossible for them to practice normative Judaism. Members of the community who went to Spain, Portugal or southern France in spite of the ban, were often punished by the *Mahamad* when they returned and were sometimes even excommunicated.[41]

In his sermons, Rabbi Saul Levi Mortera expressed the idea that the exile in Egypt was not only a Jewish historical event, but also a prototype of all Jewish exiles.[42] In his homily on the weekly Torah portion "Korah," Mortera compared the favorable economic conditions of the *conversos* in Spain and Portugal and their fear of the Inquisition to the experience of the Israelites in Egypt, remarking that just as the Israelites wished to leave Egypt despite the good conditions, so the *conversos* should leave Spain and Portugal despite their comfortable life there. In another sermon, he drew a parallel between the few *conversos* who

38 On Christian symbolism regarding the crossing of the Red Sea, see for example J. Danielou, *The Bible and the Liturgy* (Notre Dame 1956), pp. 6–7, 86–98 and 303–4. For summary and bibliography on that topic, see Mintz-Manor, "Symbols and Images," pp. 29–32.

39 Oelman, *Marrano Poets of the Seventeenth Century*, pp. 242–50.

40 I.S. Révah, "Les Marranes," *REJ* 118 (1959–1960), pp. 29–77.

41 Y. Kaplan, "Amsterdam, the Forbidden Lands and the Dynamics of the Sephardi Diaspora," in *The Dutch Intersection. The Jews and the Netherlands in Modern History*, ed. Y. Kaplan (Leiden and Boston 2008), pp. 33–62.

42 On this notion in Mortera's sermons, see M. Saperstein, *Exile in Amsterdam: Saul Levi Morteira's Sermons to a Congregation of New Jews* (Cincinnati 2005), pp. 235–36, 311–12, 339. Saul Levi Mortera (d. 1660) was born in Venice and arrived in Amsterdam in 1616. Two years later he was appointed to serve as the rabbi of Beit Ya'akov and after the unification of the three congregations, he was appointed the rabbi of Talmud Torah. Some of his sermons were printed in Amsterdam in 1645 entitled *Giv'at Sha'ul*. On Mortera's life and work see for example, H. Prins Salomon, *Introduction to Mortera's Tratado da verdade da lei de Moisés* (Coimbra 1988), pp. ix–cxxvii; Saperstein, ibid., pp. 4–35, 36–66.

expressed a desire to return to the Iberian Peninsula and the Israelites who lamented having left Egypt, pointedly commenting that those who were taken from Iberia by God "with a mighty hand and an outstretched arm," and then complained and wished to return, were already represented in Scripture.[43] In another sermon, dated to 1641, three years before the "lands of idolatry" regulation was announced, Mortera preached that returning to Iberia was worse than the Israelites returning to Egypt.[44] He constructed an analogy between biblical Egypt and the Iberian Peninsula and the enslavement of the Israelites and the condition of the crypto-Jews in order to highlight the problematic issue of the *conversos*. Elsewhere, he remarked that Jacob and his sons went to Egypt for their own comfort just as many *conversos* chose to stay in Portugal.[45]

Other authors also referred in their writings to the difficulty *conversos* had in leaving their comfortable lives in Spain and Portugal. While generally critical of this trend, they used the image of biblical Egypt and the Exodus to explain why many *conversos* chose not to leave the Iberian Peninsula or to return there, but they also emphasized the Iberian "idolatry." For example, Abraham Pharar and Abraham Idaña were more tolerant of the *conversos* who stayed in Spain for economic reasons, although they reprimanded them for remaining in "idolatrous lands" rather than leaving for lands of freedom where they could openly and fully practice Judaism.[46] Immanuel Aboab was sympathetic to the difficulties experienced by *conversos* adjusting to their new lives as Jews, but still rebuked those who lived as Christians, especially in countries where Jewish practice was permitted.[47] However, few went as far as Immanuel Aboab did to

---

43   On this sermon given in 1638, see Saperstein, *Exile in Amsterdam*, pp. 301–3.

44   Mortera refers in that sermon to the "lands of idolatry," see Saperstein, *Exile in Amsterdam*, pp. 303–6.

45   Saperstein, *Exile in Amsterdam*, pp. 278–81; *Jewish Preaching 1200–1800: An Anthology*, ed. M. Saperstein (New Haven 1989), pp. 271–72, 275–80.

46   Abraham Pharar, *Declaracaõ das 613. Encomendancas de nossa Sancta Ley, conforme á Exposissaõ de nossos Sabios, muy neçessaria ao Iudesmo* ... (Amsterdam 5387 [1627]), p. 10. H. den Boer, "Exile in Sephardic Literature of Amsterdam," *StRos* 35 (2001), p. 135. For details on the term *terras de libertad* (lands of freedom), which is the opposite of *terras de idolatria*, see Kaplan, "The Forbidden Lands."

47   C. Roth, "Immanuel Aboab's Proselytization of the Marranos (from an unpublished letter)," *Jewish Quarterly Review* 23 (1932–1933), pp. 129–30, 143–45. The sin of returning to Egypt was emphasized clearly there, ibid., p. 151. Immanuel Aboab was born to a *converso* family and served as a rabbi in Venice. His work *Nomologia o Discursos Legales* in Spanish, which was printed in 1629 in Amsterdam, was widespread in the Western Sephardic Diaspora. In one of his letters, which were copied and quoted by Daniel Levi de Barrios and Menasseh ben Israel, he criticized the *conversos* for staying in Iberia. He tried to convince them to leave and advised them how to adjust to Jewish life, see ibid., pp. 121–62. Compare to Mortera's words and see references in n. 42 above.

condone the *conversos* in his Pentateuch commentary in an analogy between the temporary emigration of Abraham to Egypt and the life of the *conversos* in Iberia. There, he remarked that God directed Abraham "to go down to Egypt because it was there that the sciences were in a more flourishing state than anywhere else" and Abraham "occupied a professorial chair (Cathedra) in Egypt and evinced his great competence in philosophy, astrology and the other liberal arts."[48] Erudition and acquiring knowledge, especially philosophy and the sciences were important values for many Sephardi families in Western Europe and considered part of the Sephardi heritage from medieval times.[49] Aboab used this in his commentary as a way to justify the continued habitation of *conversos* in Iberia, drawing a parallel between the obscure purpose of Abraham's exile in Egypt and *conversos* still living in Spain.

As Harm den Boer has shown, representations of exile in these texts referred to the Iberian Peninsula and not the Dutch Republic, as one might expect.[50] The analogies between Egypt and Iberia contributed to this binary dichotomy between congregants' past in Spain and Portugal, marked by idolatry, evil and death and their present situation in Amsterdam, marked by devotion to God, goodness and life. This dichotomy benefited members of the community who had to cope with parting with their homeland and adjustment to a different country and life, while constructing their identity as "new Jews." However, this dichotomy was sometimes vague when congregants tried to explain the difficulties of the *conversos* to leave their homeland or justify those who chose to remain behind. This polarity expressed not only the supposed feelings of the *conversos* who still lived in Iberia, but, to a great extent, the sentiments of those who had left. The symbol of the phoenix, drawn from their Spanish Catholic cultural heritage, thus, demonstrated their attachment to and longing

---

48   "[S]e professavā las sciencias mas que en otras partes ... leyó Cathedra en Egipto, manifestando en ella su mucha erudicion de la Philosophia, Astrologia, y demas artes liberales" (Ishac Aboab, *Parafrasis comentado sobre el Pentateuco* [Amsterdam 5441 (1681)], p. 33). The English translation is quoted from Kaplan, *From Christianity to Judaism*, p. 312. The view of Abraham as a philosopher and astrologist was first found in Hellenistic literature and became better known in medieval Christian and Jewish literature see A. Melamed, *The Myth of Jewish Origins of Science and Philosophy* (Jerusalem 2010) [Hebrew]. Cf. idem, "A Legitimating Myth: Ashkenazic Thinkers on the Purported Jewish Origins of Philosophy and Science," *Jahrbuch des Simon-Dubnow-Instituts* 8 (2009), pp. 305–6.

49   See for example, Y.T. Langermann, *The Jews and the Sciences in the Middle Ages* (Aldershot 1999), pp. 1–54. M. Idel, "Jewish Thought in Medieval Spain," in *Moreshet Sepharad. The Sephardi Legacy*, ed. H. Beinart (Jerusalem 1992), vol. 1, pp. 261–81. E. Romero, "Literary Creation in the Sephardi Diaspora," in ibid., vol. 2, pp. 438–60.

50   Boer, "Exile in Sephardic Literature," pp. 192–99.

for their homeland and their deep-rooted connection to the Iberian Peninsula.[51] Together with the portrayal of Iberia as a place of harsh exile, the symbol of the phoenix and the Exodus story articulated the ambivalent attitude of the congregants towards Spain and Portugal, which fluctuated between affection and rejection.

This ambivalence is apparent in Jacob Judah Leon's Hebrew commentary on Psalm 77:16: "Thou didst with thy arm redeem thy people, the sons of Jacob and Joseph. [Selah]," where he used the image of the Exodus to explain the difficulties of *conversos* in leaving their comfortable life in Spain: "It is possible that the reason why [the psalmist] refers to the sons of Joseph as a class apart was because they were *Hidalgos*, the most stout-hearted (*brisos*) of all the people; consequently, they were reluctant to leave Egypt, and God [had to] take them all out together with His outstretched arm."[52] In his use of the term *Hidalgos*, which referred to the Spanish nobles of his time, Leon created an analogy between the difficulties encountered by the sons of Joseph to leave Egypt and the *conversos* to leave Iberia. According to the comparison, the former *conversos* were the nobles among their people and had received God's help when they fled Spain. This concept of nobility was common in the writings of many other members of the community who stressed the uniqueness and supremacy of the Jewish people over the other nations.[53] The former *converso* physician Isaac Cardoso, who settled in Italy, expressed this clearly in his work *Las excelencias de los Hebreos*, written in Portuguese and published in Amsterdam in 1679, "The Hebrews are of the most noble blood, and their family was is

51   Boer, "Exile in Sephardic Literature." Kaplan, *From Christianity to Judaism*, pp. 308–13. Kaplan mentioned Van Praag's definition of the *conversos* as "souls in dispute." See J.A. van Praag, "Almas en litigio," *Clavileño* 1 (1950), pp. 14–26. Cf. J.N. Hillgarth, *The Mirror of Spain 1500–1700. The Formation of a Myth* (Ann Arbor 2000), pp. 172–94.

52   "Puede ser que nombra los hijos de Joseph a parte, por ser ellos los Hidalgos, y de todo el pueblo los mas brisos, por cuya razon no devian de querer salir de Egypto, y con todo, Dios los saca a todos, con mano fuerte juntamente" (Yahacob Yehuda Leon Templo, *Las alabanças de santidad* [Amsterdam 1671], p. 209). The English translation is quoted from Kaplan, *From Christianity to Judaism*, p. 312.

53   Yerushalmi, *From Spanish Court to Italian Ghetto*, pp. 352–58, 385–87; Kaplan, *From Christianity to Judaism*, pp. 171–78, 324–25, 353–58; idem, "The Self-Definition of the Sephardic Jews of Western Europe and Their Relation to the Alien and the Stranger," in *Crisis and Creativity in the Sephardic World*, ed. B.R. Gampel (New York 1997), pp. 121–45, (republished in idem, *An Alternative Path to Modernity: The Sephardi Diaspora in Western Europe* [Leiden 2000], pp. 51–77); idem, "Political Concepts in the World of the Portuguese Jews"; Hillgarth, *The Mirror of Spain*, pp. 183–85.

extremely ancient . . . because of the antiquity, their election, their purity and their isolation, the Jews are the most noble nation on the face of the earth."[54]

Not only was the religious aspect of the concept of the "chosen people" present in Cardoso's words, but also the social-ethnic aspect, which praised a chosen group according to nobility and purity of blood. The notion of purity was stated more explicitly by Menasseh ben Israel in his *Humble Addresses*, which was sent to the Lord Protector Oliver Cromwell in 1655, "*Three* things, if it please your highnesse, there are that make a *strange* Nation well-beloved amongst the Natives of the land where they dwell . . . *Profit*, they may receive from them, *Fidelity* they hold towards their Princes; and the *Noblenes* [*sic*.] and purity of their blood . . . All these three things are found in the Iewish [*sic*.] Nation."[55]

The *conversos'* perception of their superiority drew heavily on their Spanish heritage expressed in the *excellencias* literature and their respect for the *limpieza de sangre* (purity of blood). For Spanish Catholics, lineage was judged according to religious as well as social criteria, with tremendous importance placed on "pure" Christian origin, honor and nobility (*hidalgía*), which affected the confirmation of an "honorable name" (*honroso nombre*). The importance of these concepts in the Iberian world led to discrimination of New Christians in relation to Old Christians (*cristianos viegos*). In analyzing the writings of prominent Western Sephardi Diaspora authors, it is clear that they perceived themselves to be not only part of the chosen people, in a manner similar to the ancient Jewish concept, but also a noble and unique nation unto themselves and a select group within the Jewish People. These ideas were articulated not only in their writings, but were manifested through their exclusionary

---

54   "[S]iendo los Hebreos noblisimos de sangre, y antiguissimos de linage de tres, ò quatro mil años de antiguedad, siendo pueblo escogido de Dios entre todos los del mundo . . . sino es que su virtud, y su sapiencia los ilustrasse, y por ellas se hiziessen estimados, la dignidad Real, y el Centro no lo podian tener ni aun los mismos Judios, sino solo aquellos que fuessen decendientes de la Real casa de David . . . con que los Hebreos por su antiguedad, por su eleccion, por su pureza, y separacion son la gente mas noble de la tierra" (Ishac Cardoso, *Las excelencias de los Hebreos* [Amsterdam 1679], pp. 364–65). The English translation is quoted from Kaplan, "Political Concepts in the World of the Portuguese Jews," p. 54. On Cardoso and his perceptions, see Yerushalmi, *From Spanish Court to Italian Ghetto*.

55   Menasseh ben Israel, *To His Highnesse the Lord Protector of the Common-Wealth of England, Scotland, and Ireland. The Humble Addresses of Menasseh Ben Israel, a Divine, and Doctor of Physick, in behalf of The Jewish Nation* (London 1655), p. A. On the quote, see Kaplan, "Political Concepts in the World of the Portuguese Jews," pp. 50–51. On the work, see for example D.S. Katz, *Philo-Semitism and the Readmission of the Jews to England, 1603–1655* (Oxford 1982).

behavior, such as in their attitude and behavior towards the Ashkenazi and Polish Jews in Amsterdam.[56] Former *conversos*, who had been shunned in their native homeland, assumed Iberian notions of nobility and supremacy in their new place of residence and exerted their status similar to the mimetic process regarding the term *nação*, as mentioned above.

These concepts were clearly subsumed into the phoenix symbolism, signified in the uniqueness and exclusivity of this wondrous bird, the only one of its kind in the world. The phrase "*Mi kamokha*" appended to the symbol of the phoenix in the emblem on the Neve Shalom prayer book might also have alluded to the idea of uniqueness in terms of God and the monotheism of Judaism as opposed to "idolatrous" Iberian-Catholicism, or perhaps to the uniqueness of the Neve Shalom congregation itself.

"Jerusalem of the North"

Though the roots of Amsterdam's Sephardi community were entrenched in the Iberian sphere, the growth of the newly established community was taking place on Dutch soil. Concurrently, the nascent Dutch Republic, which had triumphed in its revolt against Spanish rule, was engaged in constructing its own emergent nationhood. This process was expressed in the visual arts as well as in the patriotic writings of statesmen, thinkers and Calvinist preachers.[57] The prominence of biblical imagery in this context is noteworthy, in particular, the developing mythical narrative of the Dutch nation as the New Israel. In this scenario, the Dutch were portrayed as the Israelites and their country as the Promised Land. The biblical story of the Exodus was a central motif, with

---

56   See references in n. 53 above. See also Y.H. Yerushalmi, "Assimilation and Racial Anti-Semitism: The Iberian and the German Models," *Leo Baeck Memorial Lecture* 26 (1982), pp. 3–38. Cf. G.M. Weiner. "Sephardic Philo- and Anti-Semitism in the Early Modern Era: The Jewish Adoption of Christian Attitudes," in *Jewish Christians and Christian Jews. From the Renaissance to the Enlightenment*, ed. R.H. Popkin and G.M. Weiner (Dordrecht 1994), pp. 189–214.

57   J.I. Israel, *The Dutch Republic and the Hispanic World, 1606–1661* (Oxford 1982). On the Dutch negative attitude towards Spain, see especially *idem*, pp. 400, 435–41. On the process of nationhood and its articulations, see S. Schama, *The Embarrassment of Riches. An Interpretation of Dutch Culture in the Golden Age* (New York 1987), pp. 37–125. Cf. J.I. Israel, *The Dutch Republic: Its Rise, Greatness, and Fall, 1477–1806* (Oxford 1995), pp. 563–64. M. Bodian, "The Biblical 'Jewish Republic' and the Dutch 'New Israel' in Seventeenth-Century Dutch Thought," *Hebraic Political Studies* 1/2 (2006), pp. 186–90. For more bibliography on that topic, see in ibid., 186–202.

King Philip II of Spain imagined as Pharaoh, the tyrannical Spanish regime as the oppressive Egyptian rule, the water of Leiden as the sea in which Pharaoh's army was drowned and the liberation of the Dutch from Spanish rule and Catholicism akin to the Israelites' deliverance from slavery and idolatry.[58] Textual and visual descriptions of Spanish cruelty in Dutch martyrological literature emphasized the killing of many Dutch citizens at the hands of Spanish soldiers. This literature, in turn, inspired descriptions of the suffering of the indigenous peoples of America at the hands of the Spanish, with the Dutch portrayed as the allies of the natives.[59] Besides their religious context, these descriptions and images contributed to the construction of Dutch national identity and unity.[60]

The exploitation of biblical motifs in service of the country's budding nationhood was also, apparently, reflected in the writings of the Sephardi community influencing the construction of their Jewish identity in the new Dutch Republic. This, likely, was the context for the extraordinary story of the mythological origins of the Dutch people and their historical bond with Sephardi Jewry in Daniel Levi de Barrios's 1683 work *Triumpho del govierno popular y de la Antiguedad Holandesa*. De Barrios traced the ethnic origins of the Dutch to Yoktan, a descendent of Shem, who fought the Babylonian King Nimrod in order to rescue Abraham. According to this myth, Yoktan's father, Eber, migrated from Kedem (identified as Spain), to Masah (the Netherlands), and his decedents settled in Amsterdam. De Barrios added that the "latest Hebrews," meaning the Sephardim, also left Spain in order to escape the Inquisition and came to the Dutch Republic because of its freedom of conscience. De Barrios based the ethnic bond between the Dutch and the Sephardim on the identity

---

58 G. Groenhuis, "Calvinism and National Consciousness: the Dutch Republic as the New Israel," in *Britain and the Netherlands. Church and State since the Reformation*, ed. A.C. Duke and C.A. Tamse, vol. 7 (The Hague 1981), pp. 118–33. Schama, *Embarrassment of Riches*, pp. 42, 44–45, 51, 53–54, 93–125. T. Dunkelgrün, "*Neerlands Israel*: Political Theology, Christian Hebraism, Biblical Antiquarianism, and Historical Myth," in *Myth in History, History in Myth*, ed. L. Cruz and W. Frijhoff (Leiden 2009), pp. 201–36. On these images in art, see for example S. Perlove, "An Irenic Vision of Utopia: Rembrandt's *Triumph of Mordecai* and the New Jerusalem," *Zeitschrift für Kunstgeschichte* 56 (1993), pp. 38–60.

59 Schama, *Embarrassment of Riches*, pp. 83–93. Hillgarth, *The Mirror of Spain*, pp. 309–27. B. Schmidt, *Innocence Abroad. The Dutch Imagination and the New World 1570–1670* (Cambridge 2001), pp. 21–23, 303–10; idem, "The Hope of the Netherlands: Menasseh ben Israel and the Dutch Idea of America," in *The Jews and the Expansion of Europe to the West 1450–1800*, ed. P. Bernardini and N. Fiering (New York 2001), pp. 86–106.

60 Schama, *Embarrassment of Riches*, pp. 96–97. Cf. Bodian, "Biblical 'Jewish Republic'," pp. 190–98.

of Yoktan's wife as a Jewish woman who expounded the seven Noahide Laws to the sons of Eber. These "Noahide" beliefs were inherent, according to De Barrios, in the doctrines of the Calvinists, the modern descendants of Eber. He further stressed the difference between Spanish idolatry and Dutch monotheistic belief through analogy with the biblical story of Nimrod and Abraham: "The Babylonians burned to death those who did not worship the statue they raised to King Nebuchadnezzar. In the same way, the Inquisitors [i.e., in Spain] burn to death those who do not worship images. But the States of the United Provinces [i.e., the Dutch Republic], show favor to them [i.e., the Jews who do not worship images], just as prince Yoktan did to the patriarch Abraham and his companions."[61]

De Barrios related the struggle of the biblical fathers of the Dutch nation against Nimrod and his idol worship to the war the modern Dutch nation waged against the tyrannical rule of Spain and Catholic idolatry, a comparison that suited the contemporary Dutch discourse. De Barrios's mythology constructed a common origin for the Dutch people and the Iberian Jews that linked their ancestry and history. In so doing, he integrated Sephardi Jewry into the mythical history of the Dutch nation and included their Jewish descendents living in the Republic.[62] Moreover, he used the Dutch discourse of biblical imagery to build a new founding story, albeit different from the widespread myth of the Batavians, the ancient European ancestors of the Dutch who fought the ancient Romans in order to free their land.[63]

As Miriam Bodian remarked, De Barrios probably did not hold the view that the Dutch nation was the true Israel,[64] but he clearly incorporated the contemporary Dutch discourse of biblical imagery and analogies into his writing. This mythology promoted a shared notion of idolatrous Spain as part of their common history, as well as a possible alliance between the Hebrews/Jews and Eber's decedents, the Dutch Calvinists. The contemporary Dutch discourse served the Sephardi community in creating a bond with their new homeland. De Barrios also praised the Dutch for providing the Jews with a safe haven where they could freely practice their faith: "Nowhere else in the world, do

---

61   Daniel Levi de Barrios, *Triumpho del govierno popular y de la Antiguedad Holandesa* (Amsterdam 1683), p. 421; the translation is quoted from Bodian, *Hebrews of the Portuguese Nation*, p. 74.

62   Bodian, "Biblical 'Jewish Republic'," pp. 218–20.

63   I. Schöffer, "The Batavian Myth during the Sixteenth and Seventeenth Centuries," in *Geschiedschrijving in Nederland: Studies over de historiografie van de nieuwe tijd*, ed. P.A.M. Geurts and A.E.M. Janssen ('s Gravenhage 1981), pp. 84–109. Schama, *Embarrassment of Riches*, p. 54.

64   Bodian, "Biblical Jewish Republic'," p. 220.

[the Jews] have less to worry about than in Amsterdam, thanks both to the freedom of conscience that prevails in the seven United Provinces and to the big-heartedness of her quick-witted inhabitants."[65]

The Sephardi Jews' sense of security in Amsterdam was expressed not only in their writings, but was also demonstrated, such as in the inauguration of their new synagogue on *Shabbat Nahamu* (lit. Sabbath of comforting) in summer 1675. Selomoh de Oliveira, in his sermon on that occasion, said, "[It has been] seventy years or more that [God]—in His devotion—favors us in this place [i.e., Amsterdam] together with the benignity of those who protect us [i.e., the city and the Republic]."[66] A similar sentiment infused Romeyn de Hooghe's etchings of the new synagogue in Amsterdam, which were executed mainly for members of the congregation. One of the etchings shows the interior of the building during the inaugural celebration, with the reading of the Torah prominently depicted. Four allegorical figures appear at the top of the etching: the female figure kneeling on the right is an allegory of the Seven Provinces of the Dutch Republic and next to her is the Maid of Amsterdam holding the shield of the city. Two allegorical figures face them: the high priest, probably Aaron, with a Torah scroll and a seated old woman with the tablets of the Law, who might represent *Synagoga*, although here she is portrayed without the traditional blindfold, perhaps to stress the tolerance of the Dutch towards the Jews.[67] This etching clearly underscored the sense of belonging

---

65   De Barrios, *Triumpho del govierno popular*, p. 24. The English translation is quoted from Kaplan, *From Christianity to Judaism*, p. 360.

66   "Setenta annos ha & mais, q'nos favoresce sua piedade neste Lugar, com a benignidade dos q'nos protegem" (*Sermoẽs que pregarão os doctos ingenios do K.K. de Talmud Torah, desta cidade de Amsterdam no alegre estreamento publica celebridade da fabrica que se consagrou a Deos, para Caza de Oração, cuja entrada se festejou em Sabath Nahamù Anno 5435* [Amsterdam 1675], p. 36). For other examples, see Kaplan, *From Christianity to Judaism*, pp. 360–61. Perlove, "An Irenic Vision of Utopia," pp. 51–52. The notion that the Jews in Amsterdam were greeted with kindness by the Low Countries appears also in Simone Luzzatto's work, see Simone Luzzatto, *Discorso circa il stato de gl'Hebrei* (Venice 1638), p. 91: "tutta via ne Paesi Bassi sono con grandissima carità, & amoreuolezza trattati, come in Amstradamo, Retrodamo, & Amburgo di Olssatia."

67   On the allegorical figures, see S.L. Stuart, "The Portuguese Jewish Community in Seventeenth Century Amsterdam: Images of Commemoration and Documentation" (Ph.D. Dissertation, University of Kansas 1993), pp. 48–71. According to Stuart, the different languages found on the various etchings of the inauguration made by Romeyn de Hooghe, point to the varied readership. The above-mentioned etching was made for Spanish speakers, who were mainly members of the Sephardi community, see ibid., pp. 52–59. Cf. R.I. Cohen, *Jewish Icons. Art and Society in Modern Europe* (Berkeley 1998), pp. 37–38. On the new observation of the Jews by Christians in Early Modern Europe, see ibid., pp. 10–61.

felt by the Sephardi community in Amsterdam, as it seemingly combined the
historical narratives of the Sephardi Jews of Amsterdam and of the Dutch
Republic and made a case for the place of the Jewish community in the city
and the Republic. The poems attached to the etchings declared the great appreciation for the new building. The new synagogue became the subject of
etchings and paintings by other artists of the period and was included in descriptions of buildings, a genre that developed in response to the emergent
Dutch nation.[68]

David de Castro Tartaz published a collection of sermons delivered at the
synagogue's inaugural celebrations, together with eight etchings of the synagogue specially commissioned from Romeyn de Hooghe.[69] In the prologue,
Tartaz related the circumstances that led up to the building of the new synagogue and the preparations that were undertaken in order to complete the
project. He described the interior design of the synagogue and commented
on various aspects of the celebrations: "The entire prayer was accompanied
by hymns and the most famous songs and for the imitation of the inauguration of the sacred Temple, which lasted eight days of festivities . . . I attest to
you, kind reader, that [this celebration] seems more like the days of Passover
[celebrated] with liberty in the Temple, than the celebrations of captivity in
an Esnoga [i.e., synagogue]."[70] In this passage Tartaz correlated the inauguration of the Sephardi synagogue with the celebration in the Temple in Jerusalem on the festival of Passover that commemorated the Exodus and liberation

---

On the observation of Jews by Christians in Dutch culture, see Y. Kaplan, "For Whom Did
Emanuel de Witte Paint His Three Pictures of the Sephardic Synagogue in Amsterdam?"
StRos 32/2 (1998), pp. 133–54.

68   Stuart, "Images of Commemoration," pp. 25–45. Of the five poems attached to the etching,
      three were written by Romeyn de Hooghe and the two others by Daniel Levi de Barrios
      and Selomoh de Oliveira, respectively, see ibid., pp. 58–59, 90–91, nn. 129–130.

69   *Sermoẽs*, pp. 1–4. Two of the etchings are depicted in a smaller scale on the top por-
      tion of the above-mentioned etching. Each day of the celebrations, a different person
      preached one sermon, see Kaplan, *From Christianity to Judaism*, p. 205, n. 116. L. and
      R. Fuks, "The Inauguration of the Portuguese Synagogue of Amsterdam, Netherlands, in
      1675," *Arquivos do centro cultural português* 14 (Paris 1979), pp. 496–505.

70   "Toda a oraçaõ acõpanharaõ hymnos, & Cantos mais celebres, & por imitar o Estreamento
      do Sagrado Templo, se tomou 8 dias de festividade, sempre com a mesma solemnidade
      . . . Certificote Benevolo lector q 'mais parecia o estes dias Pascuas com liberdades de
      Templo, q'Festas de cativade em húa Esnoga" (*Sermoẽs*, p. 3). The term Esnoga was used
      by the Sephardim in Amsterdam to refer to the new synagogue, not to synagogues in
      general. For the translation of Tartaz's prologue see, URL: http://www.earlymodern.org/
      workshops/2007/mintz_manor/texto2/intro.php?tid=82.

of the Israelites from Egyptian captivity. The period of the Jews' captivity in Egypt was the antithesis of the celebrations surrounding the inauguration of the new synagogue. Though Tartaz used the word "captivity," a traditional term commonly used by the Sephardi Jews to describe the state of the Jews' exile (*galut*) in the Diaspora, by using the mimetic device of the inaugural celebrations, he implied that the celebration of the new synagogue resembled a holiday celebration in the Holy Land, in the holy city of Jerusalem, in the holy Temple. This device suited the Exodus narrative of those former *conversos* who had left their "Egypt"—the Iberian Peninsula—and for whom being in Amsterdam was equated with reaching the Holy Land and celebrating the holiday of the Exodus in the Temple.

Interestingly, the post-exilic concept of the synagogue as *mikdash me'at* was not invoked in the sermons celebrating the new Sephardi synagogue, which was compared instead to the Holy Temple itself.[71] For example, in the sermon by Eliahu Lopes, published in the above-mentioned collection, the author conjured the motif of the synagogue as the Temple in Jerusalem by giving precise calculations for the Esnoga's dimensions in order to show that its length matched that of the Holy Temple.[72] In the prologue, Tartaz remarked that the celebrations in the synagogue continued for eight days, the same number of days as the festival of Passover was celebrated in the Temple in Jerusalem. Around the time of the synagogue's inauguration, Daniel Levi de Barrios expressed a similar sentiment in a poem: "The temple (*El Templo*) that

---

71   On the notion of the synagogue as *mikdash me'at*, see for example E. Reiner, "Destruction, Temple and Holy Place: On the Medieval Perception of Time and Place" in *Streams into the Sea. Studies in Jewish Culture and Its Context, Dedicated to Felix Posen*, ed. R. Livneh-Freudenthal and E. Reiner (Tel Aviv 2001), pp. 138–52; B. Kühnel, "Jewish Symbolism of the Temple and the Tabernacle and Christian Symbolism of the Holy Sepulchre and the Heavenly Tabernacle: A Study of Their Relationship in Late Antique and Early Medieval Art and Thought," *Jewish Art* 12/13 (1986/1987), pp. 147–68. See also the articles that appeared in *Jewish Art* 24/25 (1997/1998), dedicated to representations of Jerusalem, including the Temple. Cf. G. Sed-Rajna, "Images of the Tabernacle/Temple in Late Antique and Medieval Art: The State of Research," in *The Real and Ideal Jerusalem in Jewish, Christian and Islamic Art: Studies in Honor of Bezalel Narkiss on the Occasion of His Seventieth Birthday*, ed. B. Kühnel (Jerusalem 1998), pp. 42–53. S. Shalev-Eyni, "Jerusalem and the Temple in Hebrew Illuminated Manuscripts: Jewish Thought and Christian Influence," *L'interculturalità dell'ebraismo: Atti del Convegno internazionale*, ed. M. Perani (Ravenna 2004), pp. 173–91.

72   *Sermões*, p. 86. This mimetic motif is present in other sermons in Tartaz collection. On Isaac Aboab, Selomoh de Oliveira and Isaac Saruco's sermons, see Fuks, *The Inauguration of the Portuguese Synagogue*, p. 499. Mintz-Manor, "Symbols and Images," pp. 45–46.

stands in Amsterdam resembles in beauty and greatness the one that stood in Jerusalem."[73]

Over the last fifty years, scholars have pointed to the influence of the model of the first Temple by Jacob Judah Leon on the new Sephardi synagogue.[74]

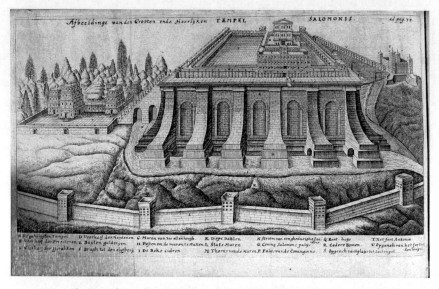

FIGURE 1.3   *The Second Temple in Jerusalem as depicted in Jacob Yehuda Leon Templo's book on Solomon's Temple, Amsterdam 1650, pp. 34–35.*
COURTESY OF THE JEWISH THEOLOGICAL SEMINARY IN AMERICA, NEW YORK.

73   "El Templo Amstelodamo se parece / al de Jerusalén en la hermosura / y en la grandeza"
       (Oelman, *Marrano Poets of the Seventeenth Century*, p. 249). In the poem is ... gatory
       portrayal of Spain along with the depiction of the Sephardi synagogue as the Temple, as
       in Romeyn de Hooghe's poems added to the above-mentioned etching. See above n. 67.

74   The similarities between Leon's model and the Esnoga are evident especially in the bal-
       ustrades at the roofline, the arched apertures and the curved buttresses at the ground.
       Additionally, the courtyard and the two entrances of the synagogue relate to the Temple
       model's yard structure as well. On the architecture of the Sephardi synagogue and the
       influence of the first Temple model, see R. Wischnitzer, *The Architecture of the European
       Synagogue* (Philadelphia 1964), pp. 90–97. J.J.F.W. van Agt, *Synagogen in Amsterdam* (Am-
       sterdam 1974), pp. 36–53, 92–93. A.K. Offenberg, "Jacob Jehuda Leon (1602–1675) and His
       Model of the Temple," in *Jewish-Christian Relations in the Seventeenth Century: Studies and
       Documents*, ed. J. van den Berg and E.G.E. van der Wall (Dordrecht and London 1988), pp.
       95–115. D. Ph. Cohen-Paraira, "A Jewel in the City: Architectural History of the Portuguese-
       Jewish Synagogue," in *The Esnoga: A Monument to Portuguese-Jewish Culture*, ed. J.C.E.
       Belifante (Amsterdam 1991), pp. 41–67. G. Schwartz, "The Temple Mount in the Lowlands,"
       in *The Dutch Intersection: The Jews and the Netherlands in Modern History*, ed. Y. Kaplan
       (Leiden and Boston 2008), pp. 111–22.

THE PHOENIX, THE EXODUS AND THE TEMPLE

The extensive work of Leon on this subject, which earned him the nickname "Templo," comprised two main projects: a book on Solomon's Temple, which included a few engravings and went through many editions in several languages and a wooden model of the Temple, which he exhibited in his house in Amsterdam. In addition to Dutch and English scholars who were interested in Leon's work and were in constant contact with him, a large audience of Christians and Jews visited his home in order to see the Temple model.[75] Leon's model of the First Temple and the engravings in his book were heavily influenced by the work of two Spanish Jesuits, the architect Juan Bautista Villalpando and the theologian Jerónimo Prado. Their work was well known in Western Europe and influenced many other works, images and biblical maps, including Dutch maps of Jerusalem.[76] The Spanish authors prepared a Latin commentary of the biblical book of Ezekiel, which contained textual and visual descriptions of the Temple, combining the description of Solomon's Temple with the prophetic one from Ezekiel. As Gary Schwartz noted, Villalpando's model of the Temple, which was also linked to the construction of the Escorial, the palace of King Philip II of Spain, had a significant impact on the architecture of Dutch buildings, including Calvinist churches.[77] This trajectory reveals a historical irony, where a Spanish model migrated and was implanted in a country that harbored great hatred for the Spanish crown. The image of Amsterdam and the Dutch Republic as a New Jerusalem and Promised Land were central in the religious, political and cultural spheres of the nation, as was

---

75 R.H. Popkin, "Some Aspects of Jewish-Christian Theological Interchanges in Holland and England 1640–1700," in *Jewish Christian Relations in the Seventeenth Century: Studies and Documents* ed. J. van den Berg and E.G.E. van der Wall (Dordrecht and London 1988), pp. 7–11. Offenberg, "Jacob Jehuda Leon," pp. 101–8. Offenberg mentioned that the wooden model probably reached England after Leon's death. On Leon's life, see ibid., pp. 96–99.

76 R. Rubin, *Image and Reality: Jerusalem in Maps and Views* (Jerusalem 1999), pp. 41–45, 110–48. On Villalpando's model and its influence on Romeyn de Hooghe's map, see ibid., pp. 123–35, ill. 8. Offenberg, "Jacob Jehuda Leon," p. 100. Schwartz, "The Temple Mount in the Lowlands," pp. 114–17. On the interest and influence of Villalpando's model and the discourse on the Temple in Western European culture during that time, see P. von Naredi-Rainer, "Between Vatable and Villalpando: Aspects of Post Medieval Reception of the Temple in Christian Art," *Jewish Art* 24/25 (1997/1998), pp. 218–25. L. Kantor Kazovsky, "Piranesi and Villalpando: The Concept of the Temple in European Architectural Theory," ibid., pp. 226–44. Y. Pinson, "The Iconography of the Temple in Northern Renaissance Art," *Assaph: Studies in Art History* (1996), pp. 147–74. J. Sheehan, "Temple and Tabernacle: The Place of Religion in Early Modern England," in *Making Knowledge in Early Modern Europe: Practices, Objects, and Texts, 1400–1800*, ed. P.H. Smith and B. Schmidt (Chicago and London 2007), pp. 248–72.

77 Schwartz, "The Temple Mount in the Lowlands," pp. 116–20.

the mimetic motif of the Temple. The Calvinist writer and preacher Jacobus Lydius expressed this clearly when, in relating to the Dutch triumph in the second Anglo-Dutch War, he offered a parallel between the Dutch, who achieved victory over their enemies and the Israelites who succeeded in their battles, thanks to the eternal covenant of God: "Above all else I thank Him / Whom Holland made Jerusalem."[78]

Conclusion

The designation "Jerusalem of the North," which Daniel Levi de Barrios and others used to refer to Amsterdam, alluded not only to the feelings of his fellow community members, but also to the entire cultural environment in which they functioned, wherein was created the whole symbolic spectrum that accompanied them throughout the formation of their identity and the creation of their new congregation. Their integration into Dutch society and construction of a new communal identity in Amsterdam was also reflected in the play *Dialogo dos montes*. The choice of Jehoshaphat for the role of judge was not coincidental. Among Remonstrant circles, the biblical king Jehoshaphat was the model of a leader who cared for the welfare of his people and subordinated ecclesiastical institutions to his sovereignty. Such a just ruler, who eliminated false religious doctrines such as idolatry, suited the outlook of the Sephardi Jews and of the Dutch who repelled Spanish rule and Catholicism.[79] In the last scene of the play, Jehoshaphat remarks that Mount Zion cries for the People of Israel's long exile and the Temple's ruin, but hopes that it will revive like the phoenix. The hope for the rebuilding of the Temple was a definitive part of normative prayer service in traditional Judaism, to which the former-*conversos* wished to belong. At the same time, however, the Dutch culture inspired a parallel model for perceiving the Promised Land. While the traditional Jewish motif of exile stressed the gap between the reality of the Diaspora and

---

78   Schama, *Embarrassment of Riches*, p. 100. On Lydius's work, see ibid., p. 26. On representations of the Dutch Republic, Amsterdam or Leiden as Jerusalem, see bibliography at n. 58 above as well as ibid., pp. 46, 51, 100–3, 123–24. Cf. Bodian, "Biblical 'Jewish Republic'," pp. 187, 192 and 194. Schwartz, "The Temple Mount in the Lowlands," pp. 120–21. Perlove, "An Irenic Vision of Utopia," p. 49.

79   On Jehoshaphat as a model of a leader by the Remonstrants, see Bodian, "Biblical 'Jewish Republic'," pp. 195, 198. See the words of the Humanist preacher Caspar Barlaeus on the Sephardi synagogue's inauguration and the tyrannical Spanish inquisition in Perlove, "An Irenic Vision of Utopia," p. 51. On his attitude towards Jews, see Schama, *Embarrassment of Riches*, p. 592.

the hope for future redemption and ingathering of the exiles (in Heb. *kibbutz galuyot*), the situation of the Sephardi community in Amsterdam drew on the mimetic device of the Jews' return to the Promised Land and rebuilding the Temple in Jerusalem to underscore the fortuitousness of their circumstances in Amsterdam and the hope for their post-exilic future. This became part of the former-*conversos* narrative, which included their exodus from the Iberian Peninsula and arrival in their new homeland in the Dutch Republic, where they could live openly as Jews and revive their unique Sephardi tradition. Their narrative concluded with their redemption, which was clearly referenced in the celebrations orchestrated for the new synagogue and commenced, by design, on the first Sabbath after the fast of the Ninth of Av, which commemorated the destruction of the Temple in Jerusalem and the hope for the revival of the Jewish People and restoration of the Temple in the End of Days. The parallel between the construction of the Sephardi community's new synagogue in Amsterdam and the Temple in Jerusalem helped to cement the Sephardi community's sense of belonging in their new homeland. By recasting the biblical story of the Exodus as their personal story of redemption, the community forged their own special link to the mythical past of the Jewish People as well as to their new life in the Dutch Republic.

In the construction of a new self-identity, the Sephardi community employed images such as the phoenix to symbolize its revival and redemption. The symbolism of the phoenix encompassed notions of uniqueness and martyrdom, which were also important and meaningful components of the new Sephardi identity. Their choice of the phoenix, however, also demonstrated their continued connection to the culture, values and religion of their Iberian homeland. Although the phoenix was a well-known Christian symbol and evoked connections to institutions and values they had escaped, the Sephardi Jews were comfortable using it as a metaphor for and symbol of their unique experience. The phoenix became a symbol of the revival of the Sephardi *nação* as a unique group within the evolving Dutch nation. Additionally, the symbol of the phoenix, the Exodus narrative and the image of Solomon's Temple, were elements shared by Jews and Christians, especially in Amsterdam in the seventeenth century, where inter-faith dialogue and other kinds of cooperation were taking place. Through these images, we witness the attempt of the Sephardi Jews in Amsterdam to integrate their Christian and Iberian past, the mythical past of the Jewish People and their present as "New Jews" and new residents of the Dutch Republic.

CHAPTER 2

In the Land of Expectation: The Sense of Redemption among Amsterdam's Portuguese Jews

Matt Goldish

The deep interest of the seventeenth-century Dutch Sephardim in the messiah and messianic movements is well known. There is little doubt that Amsterdam's Jews were awaiting the messiah as eagerly as any community in the world. My intention here, however, is to discuss a type of messianism common among both Jews and (in somewhat different form) Christians in seventeenth-century Amsterdam that is easy to miss: a widespread sense that the messianic age had already begun to dawn and that their home—Amsterdam, and the Dutch Republic more generally—was a center of this fortunate new world. Amsterdam would incubate the messianic gestation until the messiah appeared in person to return the Jews to the Holy Land, carrying out judgments and redemption. Historians have long noted this mode of thought but have not put it into a clear ideological framework. They are apparently loathe to calling it messianism though they are aware that it has some relationship to messianic thinking. I will endeavor to place it in its appropriate messianic context.

This sort of messianic strain, which we might call *pre-messianic redemption consciousness*, lacks the spectacular manifestations of an identified messiah figure or a prophet of the imminent end of history. Some scholars would say that the absence of a messiah removes this phenomenon from the category of messianic movements, but others have made the case that more quietistic forms of messianism are also a historically significant messianic phenomenon.[1] In the model I propose, a messiah (as yet anonymous for the Jews; Jesus for the Christians) was still expected to come in the near future and lead the world, but God's salvation was already palpable on earth. Such beliefs were probably heretical in many religious contexts, but their existence was amorphous and inexplicit so as to be almost impossible to distinguish.

---

1 For an example of the former, see H. Lenowitz, *The Jewish Messiahs, From the Galilee to Crown Heights* (Oxford 1998), Introduction. For an example of the latter see M. Idel, *Messianic Mystics* (New Haven 1998), Introduction.

Origins

In order to understand pre-messianic redemption consciousness in the Jewish community of Amsterdam it is helpful to understand its analog in the Christian community; and to do that, we must reach far back into history before we come to the seventeenth century.

The New Testament tells a more or less coherent story about the future: Jesus will return to fight off the antichrist, rule the world from Jerusalem, judge the quick and the dead and either usher in or complete a thousand-year reign of peace and spiritual fulfillment culminating in the End of Days. The Church Father Origen and some of his colleagues felt that this hope was too much oriented to the physical world and thus smacked of Judaism. They taught that the Millennium would be spiritual in nature rather than physical.[2]

We thus enter the Middle Ages with a Christian concept of the Second Coming that is increasingly abstract and spiritual, but essentially coherent and centered on the person of Jesus. It is rather amazing, therefore, that by the time we leave the Middle Ages, not only has the interpretation of the Second Coming been partially returned to a more original historical notion, but a whole host of ancillary stages, human actors and geographical locations have been added to the scenario. These include the revival of prophecy; the Last World Emperor; the Christ-bearer; the harbinger of Christ; the Secret One or Secret King; the New Jerusalem; the New Babylon; the Fifth Empire; and so on. Most of these concepts have a basis in Scripture, but the detailed elucidation of a messianic scenario in which the respective roles of each of these is worked out is largely a product of the late Middle Ages.[3]

This shift has often been attributed to the impact of the medieval Calabrian Abbot Joachim of Fiore, whose prophetically-oriented writings focused

2   Of the enormous literature on these issues see, e.g. S. Mowinckel, *He That Cometh: The Messiah Concept in the Old Testament and Later Judaism*, trans. G.W. Anderson (Grand Rapids 2005; original English edition, Abingdon Press, 1956); J.J. Collins, *The Scepter and the Star: The Messiahs of the Dead Sea Scrolls and Other Ancient Literature* (New York 1995); N. Cohn, *The Pursuit of the Millennium*, rev. ed. (Oxford 1970); *The Encyclopedia of Apocalypticism, Volume 1: The Origins of Apocalypticism in Judaism and Christianity*, ed. J. Collins (New York 1998); L.E. Froom, *The Prophetic Faith of Our Fathers*, vol. 1 (Washington, D.C. 1950).

3   A particularly clear and detailed discussion of these phenomena can now be found in M.A. Travassos Valdez, *Historical Interpretations of the "Fifth Empire": The Dynamics of Periodization from Daniel to António Vieira, S.J.* (Leiden 2011). See also *The Encyclopedia of Apocalypticism, Volume 2: Apocalypticism in Western History and Culture*, ed. B. McGinn (New York 1998); Froom, *Prophetic Faith*, vol. 2; Cohn, *Pursuit of the Millennium*.

on an historical and imminent Second Coming.[4] Joachim certainly played
a large role, but it is likely that elements of Humanism, with its philological
and historical emphasis on ancient texts, were even more responsible for the
return to chthonic and concrete conceptions of the Second Coming. Some of
late medieval Christianity's ideas about additional actors and locations in the
process of the Second Coming appear to draw on ideas from Judaism—such
as the double-messiah, Messiah Son of Joseph and Messiah son of David—
and from Islam, which has its own cast of supporting actors in addition to
the Mahdi.

One of the most significant results of the increased focus on concrete messianic scenarios was the very widespread belief in the late fifteenth and sixteenth
centuries that specific kings and their respective countries would be central
to the impending process of the return of Christ. At some point during this
period almost every major European monarch was hailed by someone—often
by the masses of his subjects—as the Last World Emperor or the king who
would bring the Second Coming. This adulation often bled over into an actual
messianic identity for the king himself.

The Spanish and Habsburg kings were especially involved in this messianic identification. Ferdinand and Isabella, the Most Catholic Monarchs, were
deeply occupied with the purification of their kingdom of infidels such as Jews,
Muslims, Protestants, heretics and witches. The purpose of this purification
appears to go beyond a simple Catholic imperative. Even the papal lands, after
all, remained home to some Jews and other non-Catholics. Sixteenth-century
chroniclers described Ferdinand as a "new David," detailing the miracles that
were performed for him and identifying him as the legendary "*el Encubierto*"
the "hidden king" who would appear near the End of Days to bring godly blessings and peace to his subjects.[5] The support given by Ferdinand and Isabella
to the voyage of Christopher Columbus also had heavily messianic overtones.[6]
Following Ferdinand, even more extravagantly miraculous and messianic roles
were given to Charles V, Philip II and other Habsburg monarchs.

---

4   See M. Reeves, *The Influence of Prophecy in the Later Middle Ages: A Study in Joachimism*
    (Oxford 1969); ead., *Joachim of Fiore and the Prophetic Future: A Medieval Study in Historical
    Thinking* (London 1976).
5   On all this see the previous two notes and G. Parker, "The Place of Tudor England in the
    Messianic Vision of Philip II of Spain," *Transactions of the Royal Historical Society* 12 (2002),
    pp. 167–221, esp. p. 170.
6   See A. Milhou, *Colón y su mentalidad mesiánica en el ambiente franciscanista español* (Val-
    ladolid 1983); and for a negative evaluation, D. Kadir, *Columbus and the Ends of the Earth:
    Europe's Prophetic Rhetoric as Conquering Ideology* (Berkeley 1992).

In Portugal the role of *el Encubierto* was widely assigned to King Sebastian, who died very young in the ill-conceived battle of Alcazarquivir. Sebastian was widely believed to have survived and remained in a secret location awaiting the moment in which he would reappear to manifest his messianic role. This movement was known, of course, as *Sebastianismo* and it had a long life indeed.[7]

These messianic roles for kings came along with ideas about how their respective lands would become the launch-site for the Second Coming, or play some other role in the events of the End of Days. This was true not only of Spain and Portugal, but also of France, Italy, England and other European countries.

Pre-Messianic Redemption Consciousness in the Dutch Republic

I would like to suggest that this image of the messianic future featuring the role of a Catholic king in a pure Catholic land fighting the wars against antichrist and preparing the way for the Second Coming are one model of historicized Millenarianism that existed in the early modern world. Its origins were medieval, Catholic and steeped in the certainty that religious (and perhaps racial) purity was a key to their success.

This Iberian model of purity and race, however, had competition from another model of the messianic future that was essentially Protestant rather than Catholic, Renaissancian rather than medieval, and interested in the success of Christianity through worldly accomplishment and (sometimes, at least) loving persuasion rather than violent purification. This is the messianic model we find often in England, New England, some German states, the Polish-Lithuanian Commonwealth and, especially, in the Dutch Republic. These two models would come into direct conflict in the sixteenth and seventeenth centuries.

The Dutch Republic, perhaps even more than other states, often viewed itself as the New Jerusalem, a place in which God takes a unique interest and treats with special providence.[8] (I would note that the concept of a New Jerusalem

---

7   See J. Lúcio de Azevedo, *A evolução do Sebastianismo* (Lisbon 1947); H.E.R. Olsen, *The Calabrian Charlatan, 1598–1603: Messianic Nationalism in Early Modern Europe* (Houndmills, Hampshire 2003); M.E. Brooks, *A King for Portugal: The Madrigal Conspiracy, 1594–95* (Madison, WI 1964).

8   For an extensive though by no means exhaustive discussion of the concept of the New Jerusalem in the early modern period, see C. Bernet, *"Gebaute Apokalypse": Die Utopie des Himmlischen Jerusalem in der Frühen Neuzeit* (Mainz am Rhein 2007). For the application of this concept to America (and other lands at times) see T.J. Saxby, *The Quest for the New Jerusalem: Jean de Labadie and the Labadists, 1610–1744* (Dordrecht 1987); A. Zakai, *Exile and Kingdom: History and Apocalypse in the Puritan Migration to America* (Cambridge 1992).

implicitly recognizes that there remains an original Jerusalem which may yet be the center of the future redemption.) This self-image is tied up specifically with the detriment and decline of Spain. Dutch success in gaining military and political freedom from the yoke of Spanish control were in large part the instigation for a strong Dutch sense of messianic identity. This identity found expression particularly in the concept of 't Neederlandts Israel—an identification with the Hebrew nation of the Old Testament, its prophets, miracles, Temple, and intimate relationship with God. Professor Bodian quotes the following verses from the Dutch Reformed preacher Jacob Revius (1586–1658), upon the Twelve Years' Truce with Spain, to illustrate the point:

> The Jews marched through the desert forty years
> In trouble, danger and want of everything;
> But in the end and after that sad time
> Joshua led them into the Promised Land.
> The war forced us to march through the desert for forty years;
> Now the Truce opens to us the Promised Land.[9]

A Dutch predikant such as Revius may view his country as the new Promised Land, but the poem suggests as much a temporal as a geographical sensibility. The moment of redemption is at hand and the Dutch are the people chosen by God as its vanguard. They stand at the threshold.

While a few scholars have expressed doubts about the depth of this ideology, Dr. Groenhuis's work on 't Neederlandts Israel in his book De Predikanten cites overwhelming evidence about the importance of this idea in the seventeenth century. This sense asserted itself in popular music, church architecture, botanical gardens, literature, sermons, politics and numerous other areas of life.[10]

---

9   M. Bodian, "The Biblical 'Jewish Republic' and the Dutch 'New Israel' in Seventeenth-
     Century Dutch Thought," *Hebraic Political Studies* 1/2 (2006), pp. 186–202, quotation from
     p. 188. In this very important article, Bodian has pointed out that the idea of the Dutch
     Israel in the sixteenth and seventeenth centuries was seen in a very different light by the
     Remonstrants and the Counter-Remonstrants. Her analysis of this situation is far more
     detailed than the one I am presenting here and serves as important background. I am not
     certain, however, how much the distinctions in the functions of the Dutch Israel thesis
     made by theologians and clergy were relevant to the ordinary person.
10   See G. Groenhuis, *De Predikanten: De sociale positie van de gereformeerde predikanten in
     de Republieck der Verenigde Nederlanden voor 1700* (Groningen 1977), Ch. 3; S. Schama, *The
     Embarrassment of Riches: An Interpretation of Dutch Culture in the Golden Age* (Berkeley
     1988), pp. 93–125; Bodian, "The Biblical 'Jewish Republic.'" A more recent and expansive

There may be another element in this idea of the Dutch Israel and Amsterdam as the New Jerusalem that goes beyond the larger messianic proclivity of
the time and the competition with Spain. While Jean Calvin did not believe
that there was any way to identify the few elect on earth, his followers, who
could not live their entire lives of devotion without any hint of salvation, qui-
etly established a method for identifying the saints. If one observes someone
who is God-fearing and lives a holy life and, at the same time, has success in his
business, it is a sign that the person has God's grace and is destined for heaven.
The seventeenth-century Dutch felt themselves to be very holy as a group and
their commercial success was obvious to all. How could they, then, be anything
except God's elect, the residents of the New Jerusalem, enjoying God's special
providence?[11] We will see shortly that something of this sense apparently en-
croached into the Dutch Jewish consciousness as well.

Messianic consciousness in the Dutch Republic could have expressed itself,
as it did in so many other communities throughout history, strictly as acute
apocalypticism. Some smaller groups among the Dutch populace were indeed
Millenarians of this sort.[12] Figures such as Petrus Serrarius and Adam Boreel
were certain that the Second Coming was about to occur, based not just on the
usual interpretations of scriptural prophecy in the books of Daniel and Revelation, but also on the sense that the events of history and nature in their time
indicated that the End of Days was nigh.[13]

The Wars of Religion, however, had soured many people on the glories of
the battle of Gog and Magog and the destruction predicted in the Bible for the
End of Days. They preferred to focus not on the apocalypse but on the scenario
of the New Heavens and New Earth. The Renaissance interest in utopias was
closely related to messianism and Millenarianism in the sense that the utopia could be conceived as the state of being in that new world. At the same
time, the technology products and great hopes associated with the scientific
revolution made that utopian state more than a dream. In the Dutch Republic

treatment is found in T. Dunkelgrün, "'Neerlands Israel': Political Theology, Christian Hebraism, Biblical Antiquarianism, and Historical Myth," in *Myth in History, History in Myth*,
ed. L. Cruz and W. Frijhoff (Leiden 2009), 201–36.

11   See e.g. Schama, *Embarrassment of Riches*, 329–43.
12   See e.g. G.H. Williams, *The Radical Reformation*, 3rd ed. (Kirksville, MI 2000), Chaps. 12, 19,
     30; *Millenarianism and Messianism in Early Modern European Culture, Volume IV: Conti-
     nental Millenarians: Protestants, Catholics, Heretics*, ed. J.C. Laursen and R.H. Popkin (Dor-
     drecht 2001), Chaps. 3, 4, 5; A.C. Fix, *Prophecy and Reason: The Dutch Collegiants in the
     Early Enlightenment* (Princeton 1991), Pt. I.
13   See *Jewish-Christian Relations in the Seventeenth Century: Studies and Documents*, ed. J.
     van den Berg and E.G.E. van der Wall (Dordrecht 1988).

we may cite the additional blessings of peace (for much of the seventeenth century), wealth based on trade and significant medical advances. People really were living longer, happier lives with security and comfort unknown to their ancestors.[14] This was a kind of living utopia, as if God had begun to redeem his preferred people in preparation for the messianic advent rather than doing it only when the Savior had already appeared.

Pre-Messianic Redemption Consciousness among Dutch Jews

Now, what about the Jews in this entire picture? The former-*conversos* who made up the bulk of the community were in a unique position because of the following factors: first, they were Spanish and Portuguese and, thus, had been exposed to the Iberian-style Millenarian tendencies. Many had suffered at the hands of the Inquisition and had been subject to the Iberian attempt to purify the land of infidels and bad Catholics. Second, they now constituted one of the non-Christian minorities in the Netherlands which enjoyed freedom there on the one hand, but was the subject of ongoing conversionary interest on the other. Third, they were new to Judaism and thus came to it with an unusual amount of residual Iberian Christian identity, including a particular fascination with the role of the messiah. Before considering the Jews' pre-messianic redemption consciousness, we may benefit from a short review of more active messianic activity in the Portuguese community.

The messianic activity among the Portuguese Jews of seventeenth-century Amsterdam is more or less as follows. There was a messianic pretender who is reported to show up there in 1623, an Ashkenazi by the name of Ziegler, but we know almost nothing about him or his movement, and the little we do have is from Christian sources.[15] Not long afterward, the Portuguese physician Jacob Bocarro Rosales was active in the community. He was a complex figure because, at the same time that he left his Catholic life in Portugal, where he was persecuted by the Inquisition and came to Amsterdam to live as a Jew, he remained a leading figure in the Sebastianist movement—that group which continued to believe in the messianic mission of the late King Sebastian of Portugal. Bocarro Rosales's interpretations of the *Verses* of António Gonçalves

---

14   See Schama, *Embarrassment of Riches*.
15   See A.Z. Aescoly, *Jewish Messianic Movements*, 2nd ed. (Jerusalem 1987), pp. 438 ff. [Hebrew].

Annes Bandarra were essential reading among the Sebastianists.[16] We do not know about Bocarro Rosales having a significant following in Amsterdam.

In the 1640s, the leading Amsterdam Jewish messianist was Rabbi Menasseh ben Israel, whose activities in this area are very well known. Highlights of his career include his book *Piedra Gloriosa*, an interpretation of the messianic prophecy of the Book of Daniel, with illustrations by Rembrandt; his book *Hope of Israel*, discussing the Ten Lost Tribes and the imminent coming of the messiah; his publication of the famous messianic tracts written by his wife's ancestor, Rabbi Isaac Abarbanel; his mission to Oliver Cromwell, in which he attempted to convince the English to re-admit the Jews, partly out of messianic reasons; his participation in messianic projects with Dutch Millenarians, such as the translation of the Mishnah and the establishment of a Jewish college in preparation for events soon to come; and his extensive discussions with the Portuguese Jesuit António Vieira, a central figure in Portuguese messianism, who believed the Portuguese *conversos* had an enormous part to play in the End of Days then unfolding.[17]

The Amsterdam Jews were deeply—even centrally—involved in the movement of Shabbetai Tzvi, the messiah from Izmir, which peaked in 1665–6 and remained active underground long thereafter. Dutch Jews were very active in supporting Shabbetai, spreading the news about his mission and even preparing to move to the Land of Israel in some cases. A number of them were involved with the secret underground movement well into the eighteenth century. Petrus Serrarius, the Dutch Millenarian, was also caught up in the Shabbetai Tzvi movement, spreading the news and translating documents for Christian audiences.[18]

---

16   See F. Moreno Carvalho, "On the Boundaries of Our Understanding: Manuel Bocarro Francês – Jacob Rosales and Sebastianism," in *Troubled Souls: Conversos, Crypto-Jews, and Other Confused Jewish Intellectuals from the Fourteenth through the Eighteenth Century*, ed. C. Meyers and N. Simms (Hamilton NZ 2001), pp. 65–75.

17   For the enormous literature on Menasseh, grown since the publication of this work, see J.H. Coppenhagen, *Menasseh ben Israel: A Bibliography* (Jerusalem 1990). See also Menasseh ben Israel, *The Hope of Israel*, ed. H. Méchoulan and G. Nahon (Oxford 1987); M. Dorman, *Menasseh Ben-Israel* (Tel Aviv 1989); *Menasseh ben Israel and His World*, ed. Y. Kaplan, H. Méchoulan and R.H. Popkin (Leiden 1989); C. Roth, *A Life of Menasseh ben Israel: Rabbi, Printer and Diplomat* (Philadelphia 1945).

18   See G. Scholem, *Sabbati Sevi: The Mystical Messiah* (Princeton 1973), Chaps. 5: iii, 7: v; Leyb ben Oyzer, *Beshraybung fun Shabasai Zvi*, ed. and trans. Z. Shazar, S. Zucker, R. Plesser (Jerusalem 1978) [Hebrew]; E. Carlebach, *The Pursuit of Heresy: Rabbi Moses Hagiz and the Sabbatian Controversies* (New York 1990), Chaps. 4–5; R.H. Popkin, "Christian Interest

Another quasi-messianic enterprise among the seventeenth-century Jews was the construction of a scale model of the Temple in Jerusalem by Rabbi Jacob Judah Leon, thereafter known as Leon Templo. This project was undertaken partly under the prompting of the Christian Millenarian Adam Boreel, and it is abundantly clear that the audiences who came to see the model were mainly Christians. The construction and popularity of the model were not merely antiquarian in nature, but included an element of interest in the reconstruction of the Temple which was expected by many in the near future.[19]

A noteworthy element of these phenomena is that almost all of them occur in connection with Christian Millenarians and their movements. Bocarro-Rosales was a Sebastianist; Menasseh worked constantly with Christians, such as Boreel, Serrarius and Rembrandt, on his messianic projects; the Temple model was apparently proposed by Boreel and certainly supported by Christians; and even the Shabbetai Tzvi movement included the participation of Serrarius. A great deal of Christian thinking about the messiah certainly remained deep within the recently returned *conversos*, which aided in the mutual outlook behind messianic thinking in Amsterdam.[20] Jews and Christians were actually able to put aside some of their differences and work together toward the realization of messianic hopes because their visions of the immediate future were so closely related. This is a point that was made often by my late teacher, Dick Popkin, of blessed memory.[21]

No great ideological chasm separates these activist messianic activities and pre-messianic redemption consciousness. Acute messianism could easily mutate into quietistic messianism and vice versa. The only question was where

and Concerns about Shabbatai Zevi," in *Millenarianism and Messianism in Early Modern European Culture, Volume I: Jewish Messianism in the Early Modern World*, ed. R.H. Popkin and M. Goldish (Dordrecht 2001), pp. 91–106.

19   See A.K. Offenberg, "Jacob Jehuda Leon (1602–1675) and His Model of the Temple," in *Jewish-Christian Relations*, pp. 95–115. Other papers in that volume deal with Leon in various contexts.

20   Aspects of this issue are discussed e.g. in Y. Kaplan, *From Christianity to Judaism: The Story of Isaac Orobio de Castro* (Oxford 1989), Ch. 8; Y.H. Yerusahlmi, *From Spanish Court to Italian Ghetto: Isaac Cardoso—A Study in Seventeenth-Century Marranism and Jewish Apologetics* (Seattle 1971), Ch. 7; J. Barnai, "Christian Messianism and the Portuguese Marranos: The Emergence of Sabbateanism in Smyrna," *Jewish History* 7 (1993), pp. 119–26.

21   See e.g. Popkin, "Introduction" and Ch. 4, "Christian Jews and Jewish Christians in the Seventeenth Century," in *Jewish Christians and Christian Jews, from the Renaissance to the Enlightenment*, ed. R.H. Popkin and G.M. Weiner (Dordrecht 1994), pp. 1–9, 57–72; idem, "Jewish Messianism and Christian Millenarianism," in *Culture and Politics from Puritanism to the Enlightenment*, ed. P. Zagorin (Berkeley 1980), pp. 67–90.

a believing individual felt matters stood at a specific moment. Jews were perfectly willing to wait for the messiah while they enjoyed the fine life they had built along the Amstel. Amsterdam was a place that had never expelled its Jews. Its attitude towards them was increasingly liberal. Their community was wealthy by the standards of the day. They had freedoms that were unimaginable almost anywhere else in Europe. Even more, the Dutch, like the Jewish former-*conversos*, had just thrown off the yoke and cruelty of the Spanish, and they welcomed, or at least tolerated, those same reviled *conversos* who came to live among them openly as Jews. These factors led the Portuguese Jews to share a sense with their Christian neighbors that Amsterdam was a kind of New Jerusalem and that their own period was the hinge of the messianic epoch.[22]

Some Examples

While examples of this pre-messianic redemption consciousness appear to me to be visible in many areas of Amsterdam Sephardi life in the seventeenth century, I will give just a few examples from three sources. One is the symbolism used by the Amsterdam Portuguese to represent their community, recently studied by Limor Mintz-Manor. A second is the collection of sermons delivered by Amsterdam rabbis at the dedication of their grand new synagogue in 1675. The third is the collection by Daniel Levi (Miguel) de Barrios called *The Triumph of Democratic Governance* (*Triumpho del govierno popular*; 1683). Each of these sources contains hints at the messianic strain I have attempted to sketch out above.

---

22   See Bodian, "Jewish Republic'," pp. 198–202. This sense sometimes extended as well to Amsterdam Jewry's satellite communities in the New World. See N. Zemon Davis, "Regaining Jerusalem: Eschatology and Slavery in Jewish Colonization in Seventeenth-Century Suriname," *The Cambridge Journal of Postcolonial Literary Inquiry* 3/1 (2016), pp. 11–38; J. Vance Roitman, "Economie, imperium en eschatology: de mondiale context van de joodse immigratie in de Amerika's tussen 1650 en 1670," in *Joden in de Cariben*, ed. J.-M. Cohen, A. Ben-Ur, and A. Mulder (Zutphen 2015), pp. 40–53; L. Leibman, *Messianism, Secrecy and Mysticism: A New Interpretation of Early American Jewish Life* (London 2013). While some of the messianic and eschatological notions proposed by these authors appear to me to be rather weak, to the degree that they do exist and represent something beyond "normal" Jewish messianic expectation, they seem to have been brought to the New World from Amsterdam Jewry. I view them as essentially distinct from the kind of Puritan Hebraic eschatology that saw America as a Promised Land in itself. I am grateful to the anonymous press reader of this volume for the first two of these references.

Mintz-Manor focuses on two symbolic themes that are common throughout the writings of seventeenth- and eighteenth-century Amsterdam Sephardim: the phoenix as a symbol of the Amsterdam Portuguese community and the centrality of the biblical exodus from Egypt in the community's self-image. Both of these interlinked themes admirably demonstrate the pre-messianic redemption consciousness in that society.[23] The mythical phoenix, which periodically burns up and then rises from its own ashes, was a popular symbol of Christ, well known in the Iberian Peninsula. At the hands of the Amsterdam Portuguese, however, it represents the *conversos* themselves, whose collective presence as Jews was snuffed out in Spain and Portugal. Like the phoenix, some were literally burnt to ashes, in this case by the Inquisition. Then, as if by a miracle, they were reborn as Jews—particularly in Amsterdam, their new home. Just as there can be only one phoenix, so too are the Amsterdam Sephardim unique in their odyssey of destruction and rebirth.

Mintz-Manor points out how often the Amsterdam Sephardim used this symbol to represent themselves. It has a clearly messianic connotation, though one that retains a whiff of the Christian background. The phoenix, however, also represents the specific situation of these Jews in a particular way. For Christians, the phoenix represents Jesus partly because it is destroyed and reborn not once, but multiple times, just as Jesus is reborn once in the New Testament and will be reborn again in the messianic future. For the Portuguese Jews, the cyclical nature of the phoenix's journey may represent the idea that, as wondrous and beautiful as it is now, the abode in Amsterdam can be, at most, the penultimate station in the journey to complete salvation. It is, nevertheless, a station that already comprehends the *beginnings* of redemption.

This consciousness of being within the era of redemption, if not yet fully redeemed, is embodied even more significantly in the other symbol of the Amsterdam Portuguese explored by Mintz-Manor: the exodus from Egypt. She points out numerous places in the literature of the community in which authors view the situation of the Amsterdam Sephardim as analogous to the Hebrews leaving Egypt and entering the Sinai desert, freed by God from the destructive clutches of Pharaoh. For the Amsterdam Sephardim, the symbolism precisely reflected their own escape from the persecution of Spain and Portugal.

An aspect of this discussion that is particularly important is the fact that Dutch Christians saw themselves in exactly the same light as the Hebrews

---

23　This discussion, unless otherwise noted, is based on L. Mintz-Manor, "The Phoenix, the Exodus and the Temple: Constructing Self-Identity in the Sephardi Congregation of Amsterdam in the Early Modern Period," in this volume.

whom God had freed from enslavement and was now shepherding with His special providence. The poem cited above is but one sample of this theme in Dutch writing.[24] This sense, as was noted above, came partly from the material success of the Dutch Republic, partly from the efficacious resistance to Spanish rule, partly from the perception of having the best possible government and religion, and partly, as I have suggested, from the better life created by discoveries in medicine and technology. The important point for our purposes is that the Dutch felt much as the Jews did about the special, quasi-redeemed status of their land and society, including the conscription of the same biblical symbols.[25] We are thus able to see that this form of messianic consciousness, like the other messianic activity among the seventeenth-century Dutch Sephardim, occurred in tandem, if not in partnership, with a related view among some of their Christian neighbors.

The significance of the analogy between the Portuguese Jews' pre-messianic redemption consciousness in Amsterdam and the situation of the Hebrews after the exodus from Egypt is especially instructive. The Hebrews in the desert had been redeemed from the horror of their enslavement in Egypt, but they had not yet reached the full salvation of life under Godly rule in the Promised Land. They were, however, under the direct and immediate providence of God, who intervened at every step to advance their progressing salvation. They did not yet have the Temple in Jerusalem, but they had a smaller version of it in the form of the Tabernacle, which served many of the functions of the future Temple. The Amsterdam Sephardim, too, had escaped the horror of repression and Inquisitions in the Iberian Peninsula and were now living in a setting that was understood by both them and their Christian neighbors as an almost perfect society, protected by God's providence. If, furthermore, the desert Hebrews had the Torah and the Tabernacle, the Amsterdam Portuguese had the Torah and the Esnoga, their magnificent synagogue built in 1675, to which we shall return presently. In the astute formulation of Mintz-Manor, referring to a passage by the poet Daniel Levi de Barrios, in which he expresses hope for the building of the Temple in Jerusalem:

> The designation "Jerusalem of the North," which Daniel Levi de Barrios and others used to refer to Amsterdam, alluded not only to the feelings of his fellow community members, but also to the entire cultural

24 See n. 10 above.
25 On this see also Bodian, "Jewish Republic." According to Bodian's careful distinction, it is more specifically the Remonstrants' reading of the biblical parallel that accords most closely with that of the Amsterdam Sephardim.

environment in which they functioned, wherein was created the whole
symbolic spectrum that accompanied them throughout the formation of
their identity and the creation of their new congregation ... The hope for
the rebuilding of the Temple was a definitive part of normative prayer
service in traditional Judaism, to which the former-*conversos* wished to
belong. At the same time, however, the Dutch culture inspired a parallel model for perceiving the Promised Land. While the traditional Jewish
motif of exile stressed the gap between the reality of the Diaspora and
the hope for future redemption and ingathering of the exiles (in Heb.
kibbutz galuyot), the situation of the Sephardi community in Amsterdam
drew on the mimetic device of the Jews' return to the Promised Land and
rebuilding the Temple in Jerusalem to underscore the fortuitousness of
their circumstances in Amsterdam and the hope for their post-exilic future. This became part of the former-*conversos* narrative, which included
their exodus from the Iberian Peninsula and arrival in their new homeland in the Dutch Republic, where they could live openly as Jews and
revive their unique Sephardi tradition.[26]

From the perspective of the present study, it is important to recognize the messianic context for this model or approach, which essentially placed the Amsterdam Portuguese community inside a redemption *process* that had already
begun—and begun with them. They have left Egypt and not yet arrived in the
Promised Land. Meanwhile, however, they are in the desert where the Torah is
given and taught, and miracles occur every day. Redemption has commenced.

Mintz-Manor is entirely justified in drawing our attention to the dedication
of the new Esnoga in 1675 as a focal point for the unique Amsterdam sense of
redemptive providence. In some ways this sense reached its peak at that time
and in the ceremonies marking the opening of the great synagogue. The volume
of sermons delivered over seven days in honor of the occasion is a fascinating
record of the community's self-image.[27] The occasion of a synagogue opening
naturally inspires the preacher to call to mind passages about the dedication of

---

26   Mintz-Manor, "The Phoenix, the Exodus and the Temple," pp. 32–33.
27   *Sermoẽs que pregarão os doctos ingenios do K.K. de Talmud Torah desta Cidade de Amster-
      dam no alegre estreamento publica celebridade da fabrica que se consagrou a Deos, para
      Caza de Oração, cuja entrada se festejou em Sabath Nahamù Anno 5435* (Amsterdam 1675).
      On this topic see L. Fuks, "The Inauguration of the Portuguese Synagogue in Amsterdam
      in 1675," in L. Fuks, *Aspects of Jewish Life in the Netherlands: A Selection from the Writings
      of Leo Fuks* (Assen 1995), pp. 81–99 (giving a very brief overview of the sermons); Mintz-
      Manor, "The Phoenix, the Exodus and the Temple," pp. 28–29.

the Tabernacle or Solomon's Temple in Jerusalem from Scriptures. The concept of God dwelling among the exiles as a *mikdash me'at*, a miniature Temple, is a *locus classicus* for such discussions.[28] The preacher in the Diaspora, however, would need to be careful with such allusions in order to avoid any confusion: exile is exile, a "miniature Temple" is not *the* Temple and, despite the lovely new synagogue wherever it might be, nothing changes meaningfully until God brings the messiah. *Hakham* Saul Levi Mortera of Amsterdam (who had long since passed away before the erection of the new Esnoga) had been careful in this respect, extolling the condition of the Jews in Amsterdam but warning that it was still exile, still the Diaspora.[29]

The seven preachers at the dedication of the Esnoga in 1675, however, consisted of Mortera's competitor and sometime nemesis, *Hakham* Isaac Aboab and members of his circle.[30] Aboab was a mystic who may not have shared Mortera's sense of caution.[31] One of the striking characteristics of these sermons is how consistently they blur or even disregard the distinction between the Amsterdam synagogue and the Temple of Jerusalem, between their days and those of the Judean Commonwealth, between the conditions of exile and those of redemption. Some of this blurring was built into the very fabric of the building, which was self-consciously modeled on the Jerusalem Temple structure.[32]

The new Esnoga is referred to repeatedly in the sermons as the *Temple* rather than by the traditional terminology of "synagogue," a linguistic innovation that would be repeated by the founders of the first Reform temple in Hamburg in 1817–1819. Many scholars have understood the Reformers' motive to be a declaration that they did not believe that a messiah would come to return them

---

28   See Ezekiel 11:16; BT *Megillah* 29r.

29   M. Saperstein, *Exile in Amsterdam: Saul Levi Morteira's Sermons to a Congregation of "New Jews"* (Cincinnati 2005), pp. 132–39 and Ch. 9.

30   On the tension between these two figures see A. Altmann, "Eternality of Punishment: A Theological Controversy within the Amsterdam Rabbinate in the Thirties of the Seventeenth Century," *Proceedings of the American Academy for Jewish Research* 40 (1972), pp. 1–88.

31   Indeed, Aboab was an enthusiastic supporter of the Sabbatai Zevi messianic movement a decade earlier. See Scholem, *Sabbatai Sevi*, pp. 520–23; Y. Kaplan, "The Attitude of the Sephardi Leadership in Amsterdam to the Sabbatian Movement, 1665–1671," in idem, *An Alternative Path to Modernity: The Sephardi Diaspora in Western Europe* (Leiden 2000), pp. 220–24. The evidence of these two authors indicates that Aboab was a believer at the height of the movement in 1665–66 but abandoned it immediately upon the news of Sabbatai's apostasy.

32   See Fuks, "Inauguration," pp. 84–85 and n. 10 there.

to Jerusalem and rebuild the Holy Temple there. Germany, rather, was their homeland with their temple and that is where they would stay.[33] The motives of the Amsterdam rabbis when they refer to the new Esnoga as a temple seem almost diametrically opposed to those of the later Reformers. These rabbis saw their edifice as a stepping stone toward the return to Jerusalem and the rebuilding of the Temple there. They almost certainly had in mind the Talmudic passage (BT *Megillah* 29r) which says that the synagogues of the exiles will be miraculously transferred to the Holy Land when the messiah comes. The Esnoga was not a symbol of any abandonment of the messianic dream, but rather of its ascendancy. Even this simple matter of terminology, then, indicates the sense that Amsterdam and its Esnoga were somehow closer to the state of redemption than they were to that of exile.

Hakham Aboab's sermon sets the tone for the entire group.[34] The *nosé*, the biblical passage with which a traditional sermon structure opened, is taken from Deuteronomy 4:4. Moses is retelling the story of the Hebrews' sojourn in the desert and has just recounted (4:3) the terrible destruction God visited on the Jews who had practiced the *Ba'al Pe'or* idolatry. Aboab quotes the following verse, "But you who did cleave to the Lord your God are alive every one of you this day." One does not need a doctorate in semiotics to understand the significance. The *conversos* who had become sincere Catholics and remained in Spain or Portugal were analogous to the biblical idolaters—dead in spirit if not in body—while the Amsterdam Sephardim were analogous to the faithful Hebrews who all lived. It is, furthermore, no accident that Moses' speech occurred at the end of the desert sojourn immediately before the Hebrews entered the Land of Israel. The implication for Aboab's audience was again that they, like their biblical ancestors, were on the cusp of complete redemption.

The next stage of Aboab's sermon, again following traditional sermon structure, is the *ma'amar*, a passage from the Talmud to which the speaker would connect the *nosé* as well as his larger subject. Aboab went immediately to a passage concerning the Temple—in this case from BT *Yoma* 39 (41v in today's standard Vilna edition). There Rabbi Hoshaiah is quoted as stating that a wealthy person who brings the type of offering allowed for a poor person does not fulfill his obligation.[35] It is no stretch to see that he is alluding to the

---

33   See M.A. Meyer, *Response to Modernity: A History of the Reform Movement in Judaism* (Oxford 1988), p. 42. See the comments of *Hakham* Lopes in *Sermoẽs*, p. 83.

34   *Sermoẽs*, pp. 1–13.

35   The case concerns someone who has become ritually impure and appears at the Temple to become purified. The Torah states that a wealthy person must bring a larger animal while a poor person could bring modest birds.

generosity of Amsterdam's Portuguese Jews and perhaps to the stinginess of certain individuals in supporting the expenses of the new building. This, too, is a common trope throughout the sermons. Aboab then raises the popular notion of man as a microcosm, whether of the Temple or the universe.[36] He shifts to a discussion of the dedication of the Temple of Jerusalem, the synagogue as a miniature Temple and again the generosity of the donors. Here he adds a telling side note based on the passage (Leviticus 26:4), "[If you walk in My statutes, and keep My commandments, and do them;] then I will give your rains in their season, and the land shall yield her produce, and the trees of the field shall yield their fruit." The implication is that just as the biblical Hebrews, under God's direct providence, saw their material success affected immediately by their obedience to God, so too do the Portuguese Jews of Amsterdam enjoy wealth and success because of their obedience to Jewish law. Aboab indeed continues the discussion about divine providence, citing biblical passages teaching that the connection between observance and material success is made in the Temple. Failure to observe the law would bode material disaster, since God is provident now as then and here as there. "But the Lord God solemnly promises that we will be restored, as it is attested by the proclamation of all our prophets."[37]

Aboab's speech is far from the most blatant expression of pre-messianic redemption consciousness among the Amsterdam Portuguese, but the elements are clearly here. The Esnoga is conflated with the Temple in Jerusalem. God's providence hovers over Amsterdam and its temple just as it did over Jerusalem and its Temple. Material success, the hallmark of Dutch achievements in the seventeenth century, depends on piety, and for the Jews it is tied to their synagogue. The Portuguese Jews who are "alive this day" are those who left idolatry and came to practice the law in obedience, just as was the case with their Hebrew ancestors.[38] Their arrival in Amsterdam was like their ancestors' sojourn in the desert, and their next stop on the train of redemption would be the restoration to the Holy Land.

I will not attempt to trace these themes through the other sermons, but they are present in almost all of them. I will just point out a few more noteworthy ideas that support the sense of redemption consciousness among them. The second speaker, *Hakham* Solomon de Oliveira, emphasizes a sort

---

36   This theme is particularly central again in the sermon of *Hakham* Solomon de Oliveira, pp. 23–24, and that of Yshac Saruco, p. 45.

37   *Sermoēs*, p. 13. This paragraph is drawn from Aboab's sermon, pp. 1–13.

38   Rashi on Exodus 13:18 cites a Midrash stating that four-fifths of the Hebrews fell into the idolatry of Egypt and never left.

of two-pronged view: how good things are in Amsterdam, but how much one must still hope for and look forward to the return to Zion.[39] In speaking of the community and Esnoga he explicitly uses the terminology of a flower that has been planted here but is destined to be *transplanted* in the future to the Holy Land.[40] *Hakham* Ishac Saruco heavily emphasizes the analogy between the Esnoga and the Jerusalem Temple, blurring the lines considerably.[41] In his dedication between the sermons of Saruco and *Hakham* Yshac Netto, the editor, David de Castro Tartas, emphasizes the suffering of the Jews all over the world, and especially in Portugal, for the sake of the holy law. Amsterdam, of course, represents salvation from that legacy of anguish.[42]

Hakham Netto takes up the theme of suffering and dispersion. He also suggests that if the Esnoga is a miniature Temple, the Temple itself is a microcosm of the heavenly Temple. While we offered sacrifices in the Temple, we offer prayers in the synagogue. Rabbi Elazar, however, states in the Talmud that prayer is superior to sacrifices. This concept in the present context pointedly privileges the synagogue over the Temple in at least one way. Related ideas emerge when he suggests that the situation in Amsterdam is like the Garden of Eden with everything one could want. This is dangerous ground for a rabbi who needs to keep his listeners oriented towards a future in Jerusalem as well as to their present in Amsterdam. (It is interesting that Netto and other rabbinic speakers at the event have Christian phrasing sprinkled in their sermons, including the ideas of grace and "real presence" of God.[43])

The sermon of *Hakham* Eliahu Lopes has elicited comment because of his detailed comparison of the Esnoga and the Temple.[44] He suggests the novel and creative etymology of the term Esnoga as deriving from the Hebrew *esh nogah*, a radiant light. He presents charts comparing the dimensions of the Temple and those of the Esnoga to show how closely the latter imitates the former. He next invokes the images of the phoenix and the palm tree, commenting that the ruins have turned into the glory. He recalls the suffering of the Jews, citing the cases of Joseph, Mordecai and Hananiah, Mishael and Azariah. This is an odd combination until we examine the implicit symbolism. All three cases occur in the exile. Joseph is taken from his land, forced to live in Egypt as a servant among idolaters and faced with the most severe temptation.

---

39   *Sermoẽs*, pp. 17–36.
40   *Sermoẽs*, p. 36.
41   *Sermoẽs*, pp. 39–56.
42   *Sermoẽs*, p. 57.
43   *Sermoẽs*, pp. 59–74.
44   *Sermoẽs*, pp. 77–97; Fuks, "Inauguration," pp. 92–93.

He overcomes all and ends up a viceroy. Mordecai must use all his will to resist the power of an idolatrous existential enemy, while his niece, Esther, must
hide her identity—she is the first *conversa*.[45] Mordecai too triumphs over his
enemies as a result of his faithfulness to God. Hananiah, Mishael and Azariah,
Daniel's friends, were thrown into a fiery furnace for refusing to worship an
idol. The furnace is an obvious symbol of the Inquisition. The Esnoga represents the Amsterdam former *conversos'* victory over idolatry, temptation and
fiery persecution. They are raising the horn of the messiah and enjoying the
light of God's providence. The entire speech exudes the sense of pre-messianic
redemption consciousness.

The young *Hakham* Yshac Velozihno speaks at length about the perfection
of the new structure, citing as his *ma'amar* a statement from the *midrash* (exegetical text) that God created many worlds before ours but destroyed them
because they lacked perfection.[46] Moses built a tabernacle that was as perfect
as he could make it; then Solomon built the first Temple as perfectly as he
was able. The Amsterdam *Mahamad* followed suit, making the Esnoga as perfect as it could be. They thus imitate God in crafting their work as perfectly as
possible. He points out the problems of war and failures of fortune that had
plagued the period in which the Esnoga was built. He speaks of the community, which contains rich, middling and poor people, all of whom participated
in the building. Providence, however, was also necessary for the construction
of the synagogue. While he waxes eloquent about the perfection of the Temple
and the Amsterdam community, however, Velozinho is somewhat more careful than his colleagues about conflating biblical Israel and its structures with
his own community and synagogue. Finally, in the seventh sermon, David Sar-
phati offers a colorful and emotional history lesson about ancient Israel and
its Temples.[47] His discussion of the government of biblical Israel suggests an
implied parallel with the Dutch government of his own day. He returns to the
subject of providence as well.

Taken as a group, then, these sermons present an amazingly consistent sense
among the rabbis of a city and community that benefit from God's direct providence; a congregation whose great generosity in building the Temple emulates
that of the biblical Hebrews; and an era that resembles the generation of the
Exodus, enjoying God's beneficence as an almost-realized redemption in exile.

The poet and community chronicler Daniel Levi Barrios (ca. 1625–1701) composed poems in honor of the Esnoga and the law as well, though some of these

---

45   See C. Roth, *A History of the Marranos* (New York 1974), pp. 186–88.
46   *Sermoẽs*, pp. 101–29.
47   *Sermoẽs*, pp. 133–55.

appear to have been edited if not written later than the dedication of the new building. He speaks of the *converso* martyrs of the Inquisition, referring specifically to autos da fé of 1680 and 1682. He then, however, talks of the law (i.e., the Torah) vanquishing the Inquisitors. The martyrs emerge in victory like the phoenix, reborn from the ashes of their own slaughter. The people are saved by the synagogue and the law. While he does not explicitly mention Amsterdam in these poems, the imagery of Iberian *conversos* avenged and returned to the good life by the law and the synagogue is clear enough. The atmosphere of the poem is redolent with themes of redemption.

De Barrios presents an even more striking conception of redemption consciousness when he writes overtly of Amsterdam. While it would require a large monograph to discuss the nature and extent of de Barrios's treatment of the Amsterdam Portuguese community and congregation, a few comments will suffice to gauge his general attitude. In many ways one would think that de Barrios had little reason to extol Amsterdam. His adjustment to life there as a Jew must have been difficult after his upbringing in Spain and its colonies. He found the *Mahamad* to be critical of some of his poetic projects, one of whose publication they actively blocked. Whereas de Barrios had been a captain of the Spanish garrison in Brussels, in Amsterdam he lived in much less prestigious and affluent circumstances. Nevertheless, there was no author more effusive in his praise for the Amsterdam Portuguese community, including its lay and rabbinic leadership.[48]

De Barrios's collection of writings, *Triumph of Democratic Governance*, contains every kind of praise for the city of Amsterdam, Holland in general, the Portuguese community of Holland, the *hakhamim* of every community and institution, the institutions themselves, the synagogue, the Torah and the lay leaders. The degree of de Barrios's commitment to the importance of the Netherlands in the history of the Jewish people is revealed by his strange euhemeristic genealogy of the Dutch people. They are, he avers, descendants of the biblical Eber, making them cousins of the Jews. It is, therefore, particularly appropriate—and part of God's plan—that the last Jews of Spain found refuge from the Inquisition in Holland, which offers them liberty of conscience. This is providential history at its clearest.[49] De Barrios goes on to explain how the

48   On de Barrios see W. Ch. Pieterse, *Daniel Levi de Barrios als geschiedschrijver van de Portugees-Israelietische gemeente te Amsterdam in zijn "Triumpho del govierno Popular"* (Amsterdam 1968).

49   Note how Bodian ("'Jewish Republic'," pp. 198–202) reads de Barrios with great subtlety to be commenting upon the Dutch Israel concept of both the Remonstrants and Counter-Remonstrants.

six days of creation in the Bible correspond to the six functionaries (*parnassim*) of the community and the Sabbath corresponds to the overseer (*gabay*). Again, then, with de Barrios, we have a very clear sense of Amsterdam as a special place, blessed by providence, populated by people with a close and positive relationship with the Jews and upheld by the practice of Torah law.

Conclusion

The Portuguese Jews of seventeenth-century Amsterdam, then, had a very specific sense of their place in history at the dawn of the messianic era. Amsterdam was like the desert after the Exodus from Egypt—a providentially rewarded haven from the horrors of persecution and the sufferings of exile. The only members of the nation who were privileged to enjoy this exalted sanctuary were those who girded their loins to deny the allure of Iberian life and risk everything to follow God's path. These brave souls were like the fifth of Egypt's Hebrews who broke free with Moses to escape the fleshpots of Egypt. They were now in a state of *pre-messianic redemption consciousness*: they felt that the messiah had not yet come, yet the era of redemption had already dawned. The Dutch Republic, whose citizens identified so thoroughly with the experience of the ancient Hebrews, granted almost unprecedented freedoms and privileges to the escaped *conversos*. They shared with their newly arrived Iberian Jewish neighbors the experience of Spanish tyranny and the glory of deliverance from it. While the Jews and Christians of that land had fundamentally different conceptions of their redeemed future, they shared a luminous sense of impending salvation. This messianic strand of Amsterdam *converso* thought is easily detected in many writings, sermons and symbols of that community.

Having put forward this thesis, I would like to point out an ironic but important consequence of the redemption-conscious mindset. In the conception of the rabbis and probably most Jews, the Netherlands was a penultimate destination, a last stop *before* the final redemption and return to the Holy Land. It is easy to see, however, that the view I have described above has a thin floor which can easily collapse into something else. If things are so good and redemption has already commenced along the Amstel, why should this not be the *ultimate* destination? What more redemption could one want? What more would the messiah do? I do not want for a moment to suggest that most of Amsterdam's Portuguese Jews in the seventeenth century did not believe in an actual messiah, but as life improved, the longing for renewal and the rebuilding of the Temple in Jerusalem could fade. While a living messianic candidate like Shabbetai Tzvi could swing the Dutch Jews into ecstasies of expectation for the immediate future, his failure as a messiah could as easily return them to complacency and satisfaction with the present. This is one way in which a messianic mindset can turn into a secular one, as it may well have done for many Dutch Jews in the long term.

PART 2

Aspects of Daily Religious Life

∴

CHAPTER 3

Religious Life among Portuguese Women in Amsterdam's Golden Age

Tirtsah Levie Bernfeld

Introduction

The Portuguese Jewish community in Amsterdam in the seventeenth century celebrated its reunion with each member of the nation who managed to escape persecution on the Iberian Peninsula. Individual members could not forget the cruelty of the Inquisition, not only because of the personal suffering he or she had endured, but also because family and friends were still caught in its net. In 1692, Lope Dias was reunited with his wife, Doña Isabel Henriques, in Amsterdam. Both had been victims of the Inquisition.[1] In 1718, Semuel Mendes de Solla delivered a special sermon in Amsterdam on the occasion of the deliverance to safety of his mother and siblings.[2] Members of the community would often pray for the fate of their loved ones, as did Abraham Gabay Isidro in a sermon he gave in the Amsterdam Esnoga in 1724, where he spoke with great emotion of his wife and brothers imprisoned by the tribunal and prayed for their release and eventual arrival in the free Jewish world.[3]

In the seventeenth and eighteenth centuries, women comprised an important sector of the migration streams from the Iberian Peninsula to the various Jewish communities throughout the world, including Amsterdam. What was the motivation of these former *conversas*[4] to reach the free Jewish world? One theory is they were prompted to leave because of their strong desire to embrace normative Judaism. Many *conversas* showed extreme loyalty to Jewish

---

1 Lope, imprisoned by the Inquisition, was set free in 1681, after three years. When his wife Isabel was caught five years later, Lope fled the Peninsula and settled in Amsterdam: SAA 5075, no. 2942, pp. 889–90, Not. P. Padthuysen, 5 October 1703; ibid., p. 897, 8 October 1703.

2 Semuel Mendes de Solla, *Sermam moral em acçam de Graças Pregado na Sta Esnoga* (Amsterdam 1718).

3 Abraham Gabay Isidro, *Sermon Predicado neste K.K. de T.T. En Sabat Vaikrà en R.H. Nisàn del año 5484* (Amsterdam 1724), p. 29.

4 *Conversos* and *conversas* is the term used here for those men and women, respectively, whose ancestors, from the end of the fourteenth century, converted—willingly or by force—from Judaism to Catholicism.

tradition. With the expulsion of Jews from the Iberian Peninsula at the end of the fifteenth century, the home became the center for the clandestine transfer of Jewish tradition to the next generation. Thus, because of their role in the home, women were increasingly instrumental in transmitting Jewish religion, values and practices to the next generation. In view of the fact that secret practice of Judaism was a punishable offense by the Inquisition, these women put their own lives and the lives of their families at risk.[5] Critical study of Inquisition records offers proof of the judaizing activities of many *conversas*. Women's religious committment was also acknowledged by the communities of the Sephardi Diaspora. *Hakham* Yom Tob Zahalon from Safed (1559–after 1638), for example, emphasized the steadfastness of *conversas* in Portugal.[6] Salomon Ayllon, *hakham* of the Amsterdam Portuguese community in the eighteenth century, said in a sermon in 1722/3, that "even during the persecutions in Spain and Portugal these women held fast to their faith and risked their lives and possessions by instructing their children in the word of God."[7] Therefore, any study of the religiosity of Portuguese women in seventeenth-century Amsterdam must take into account the role of *conversas*.

Another factor that spurred women to leave the Peninsula was fear of the Inquisition. Some historians indeed point to such a phenomenon.[8] A.J. Saraiva, for example, cites the eighteenth-century Portuguese writer Francisco Xavier de Oliveyra's *Discours pathétique*, which describes the cruelty of the Inquisition and makes the claim that many people fled the Peninsula and joined Jewish

---

5 R. Levine Melammed, *Heretics or Daughters of Israel. The Crypto-Jewish Women of Castile* (Oxford 1999); idem, "Medieval & Early Modern Sephardi Women," in *Jewish Women in Historical Perspective*, ed. J.R. Baskin, 2nd edition (Detroit 1998), pp. 128–49; H. Beinart, *Conversos on Trial. The Inquisition in Ciudad Real* (Jerusalem 1981), esp. Ch. 7 on Jewish life; Y.H. Yerushalmi, *From Spanish Court to Italian Ghetto. Isaac Cardoso: A Study in Seventeenth-Century Marranism and Jewish Apologetics*, 2nd edition (New York 1981), p. 25. On the "religion" of the *conversos*, also ibid., pp. 31–42; also F. Frade Veiga, "Portuguese 'Conversas' Home Circle: The Women's Role in the Diffusion of Jewish Customs and Traditions (16th and 17th centuries)," *El Prezente. Studies in Sephardic Culture* 3 (2009), pp. 63–81.

6 Yerushalmi, *From Spanish Court*, p. 25, n. 37.

7 Cited in T. Levie Bernfeld, *Poverty and Welfare among the Portuguese Jews of Early Modern Amsterdam* (Oxford 2012), p. 101.

8 For an overview of scholars arguments including his own on the identity of *conversos* see D.L. Graizbord, "Religion and Ethnicity among 'Men of the Nation': Toward a Realistic Interpretation," *Jewish Social Studies* 15/1 (2008), pp. 32–65; also Y. Kaplan, *From Christianity to Judaism, The Story of Isaac Orobio de Castro*, trans. R. Loewe (Oxford 1989), pp. 326–77; and F. Soyer, "It Is Not Possible to Be Both a Jew and a Christian: Converso Religious Identity and the Inquisitorial Trial of Custodio Nunes (1604–5)," *Mediterranean Historical Review* 26/1 (2011), pp. 81–83.

communities simply out of fear of the Inquisition. Oliveyra gave an example of one woman who, despite the fact that she lived in a Jewish community, refused to give up her affiliation with Catholicism.[9]

Economics may also have been an inducement, particularly if there were family and friends already in Amsterdam they believed could be relied on for financial assistance. Ethnicity should also not be ruled out as a motivating factor: the desire to join members of their group, the nation, *a nação* or *la nación* as the Portuguese of Jewish ancestry referred to themselves, with whom they shared similar experiences and memories. Peer pressure may also have played a part.

This study sets out to trace the motivation of *conversas* to reach the Portuguese Jewish community in Amsterdam in the period known as the Golden Age and to follow their adjustment to the open profession of Judaism. The role of the lay and spiritual leadership of the Amsterdam Portuguese community in bringing these women back to the path of normative Judaism, the methods they used and their success or failure will also be examined. We will attempt to determine how successfully the women adapted to their new religious environment and how they coped with the more modest role they were given in normative Jewish life, especially after they had often played such a prominent role in Jewish practice in Spain and Portugal. We will also look at some of the lingering effects of the Catholic environment in which they grew up.

Due to the paucity of written sources regarding women, the researcher is faced with the daunting task of bringing to light the emotions, religious feelings and commitment of a seventeenth-century Portuguese woman in Amsterdam and how she may have translated these sentiments into a normative Jewish lifestyle. Though women made up the majority of the community in the Amsterdam, they lived withdrawn and home-bound lives reminiscent of the place they inhabited in Iberian society and culture and in keeping with contemporary mores of European upper-class society. Moreover, in the patriarchal structure of the Amsterdam Portuguese Jewish community in the Golden Age, women were relegated to the traditional role in the home, while men engaged with the outside world as communal administrators, merchants,

---

9   F.X. de Oliveyra, *A Pathetic Discourse on the Present Calamities of Portugal Addressed to His Countrymen and in Particular to His Most Faithful Majesty Joseph King of Portugal*, translated from the French, 2nd ed. (London 1756), p. 43; also cited in A.J. Saraiva, *The Marrano Factory. The Portuguese Inquisition and Its New Christians*, 1536–1765, trans., rev. and augmented by H.P. Salomon and I.S.D. Sassoon (Leiden 2001), p. 164. For an Amsterdam *responsum* concerning a rosary see M.M. Hirsch, *Frucht vom Baum des Lebens. Ozer Peroth Ez Chajim* (Berlin and Antwerp 1936), p. 84, no. 269.

doctors, authors or spiritual leaders. Nevertheless, digging deeper into archival sources we do come across women's voices also on matters of religion. Let us try to listen carefully.

Making the Journey

It takes courage to leave family, friends and the country of one's birth for an unfamiliar, cold, rainy city in Northern Europe. To judge from the epitaph on the tombstone of Sara Pereira from 1692, it was indeed her religiosity that brought her to Amsterdam: "I was born in Lusitania [Portugal] and prayed to God to be buried in a liberated country. And so I came eighty-seven years of age, old and crippled, to enjoy the privilege of that which I had dreamt."[10] Felipa de Saa made a stop in Amsterdam on her way to the Holy Land, a final destination that showed her strong Jewish identity and desire to fulfil the commandment to live and be buried in the Promised Land.[11] The religious factor must have been equally vital for Leonarda Nunes who brought with her "a young daughter named Gana," born "to Christian parents" from Spain to "over here," [Amsterdam] and "brought her to Judaism."[12] The incentive for many of these women to leave the Iberian Peninsula for the Jewish world in general and Amsterdam's Portuguese community in particular, therefore, must have been the urge to find a safe place where they could adhere to the faith of their forefathers in an openly Jewish environment.[13]

Fear was another reason. Documentary evidence attests to the fact that quite a few women left Spain and Portugal out of fear of arrest by the tribunal that had taken family members prisoner and/or put them to death.[14] Socio-economic opportunity could have been an equally compelling motive

---

10   Cited in T. Levie Bernfeld, "Sephardi Women in Holland's Golden Age," in *Sephardi Family Life in the Early Modern Diaspora*, ed. J.R. Lieberman (Waltham, MA 2011), p. 106.

11   SAA 5075, no. 645B, p. 1499, Not. S. Cornelisz., 28 April 1621; also published in *Stños* 19/1 (1985), pp. 79–80, no. 2397.

12   Levie Bernfeld, *Poverty and Welfare*, p. 23.

13   Y. Kaplan, "Between Christianity and Judaism in Early Modern Europe. The Confessionalization Process of the Western Sephardi Diaspora," *Judaism, Christianity and Islam in the Course of History: Exchange and Conflicts*, ed. L. Gall and D. Willoweit (Oldenburg 2011), pp. 323, 328.

14   Gracia Senior explicitly mentioned she came out of fear from the Inquisition: SAA 334, no. 826, p. 1, 30 August 1673: "Y como me vine por temor de la inquisicion"; Sara Rodrigues Ferois and her son must have both fled to Amsterdam in fear, after her husband and his father was burnt at the stake in Coimbra, Levie Bernfeld, *Poverty and Welfare*, p. 83.

for women to try to reach Amsterdam. It is worth remembering that Amsterdam not only became a well-known center of relative religious tolerance, it was also a rising world economic power, and the Portuguese community quickly established a reputation of wealth and benevolence that attracted Jewish refugees from all over the world. An elaborate system of public and private welfare was established, which also served female refugees in need of aid.

In many cases, whole families managed to flee,[15] and sometimes, women must have been the driving force behind a family's leaving.[16] Many *conversas* also fled the Peninsula alone, in the company of other women or as part of divided or broken families, taking with them whichever members they managed to bring along.[17]

Often, these women received help for their journey from family and friends or from *converso* and Jewish communities. The Portuguese Jews living in Amsterdam sent ships to rescue relatives and members of the nation and bring them to Amsterdam.[18] Some even returned to the Iberian Peninsula themselves in an effort to bring remaining family members to safety.[19]

The Amsterdam Portuguese community, as the official representative of the city's Portuguese Jews, also played a part in getting people out of Spain and Portugal. Besides its commitment to helping fellow Jews worldwide and members of the *nação* in particular, the Amsterdam *kahal* had a special interest in bringing *conversos* to the Jewish free world. Therefore, it was very much inclined to finance efforts for that purpose.[20] The *kahal*, for example,

---

15 See for example, the families of Andre Nunes da Costa and Francisco Gomes making the trip from Lisbon to Amsterdam in 1620 (SAA 5075, no. 645B, Not. S. Cornelisz., p. 1124, 19 November 1620); see more on family migration to Amsterdam in Levie Bernfeld, *Poverty and Welfare*, p. 23.

16 H.J. Zimmels, *Die Marranen in der Rabbinischen Literatur* (Berlin 1932), p. 53.

17 Levie Bernfeld, *Poverty and Welfare*, pp. 23, 54, 122.

18 For ships dispatched to take refugees from the Iberian Peninsula at the initiative of Amsterdam Portuguese Jews, Levie Bernfeld, *Poverty and Welfare*, pp. 28–31. When the above-mentioned Isabel finally was liberated, her husband Lope Dias, once safely settled in Amsterdam, made all the logistical arrangements to get her out of Spain. Accompanied by her aunt and grandmother, they traveled from Toledo to Cadiz, where a ship with a Dutch captain was waiting for them. In addition, three men were instructed to help the women with all their needs on the voyage (for source see above n. 1).

19 Y. Kaplan, "Abraham Franco de Silveyra alias Cristobal Mendez: The Adventures of a Seventeenth-Century Converso," in *Studies in Jewish History Presented to Joseph Hacker*, ed. Y. Ben-Naeh, J. Cohen, M. Idel and Y. Kaplan (Jerusalem 2014), pp. 424–25.

20 Levie Bernfeld, *Poverty and Welfare*, pp. 28–30, 180–84.

responded favorably to the request of Moses Levy, a member of the nation, to save his family from the claws of the Inquisition. Levy had traveled ahead to Amsterdam and successfully appealed to the Amsterdam Portuguese *kahal* for the funds to free his mother and sister in Lisbon and help them come "to the Jewish world."[21]

Requests to the Amsterdam Portuguese community to save victims of the Inquisition also came from people living in other centers of the Sephardi Diaspora. Moses Nunez Xabe, for example, appealed from London to the Amsterdam Portuguese board of governors for help in getting his daughters from Lisbon to London. In 1729, the Amsterdam Portuguese community assisted a Portuguese in Bordeaux who asked for funds to free his wife, daughter and (female) cousin from the prisons of the Inquisition, "where, as martyrs they are doing penitence without being able to free themselves from *idolatría*."[22]

Community support did not end upon the newcomer's arrival in Amsterdam. It was of major importance to the leaders of the Portuguese Jewish community to assist former *conversos* with their absorption into the Jewish community, familiarize them with the laws of normative Judaism and turn them into "New Jews,"[23] and prevent them from returning to Catholicism or other churches in the city or elsewhere.

Conditions for Acceptance: Ancestry, Marriage and Divorce

To become a member of the Amsterdam Portuguese community, newcomers had to prove their Jewish descent from the Spanish-Portuguese nation.[24] Naturally, the matter of proving such an identity was not limited to Amsterdam; it was an important issue for all leaders of Sephardi communities at the time. *Hakhamim* must have been key figures in this process in which many issues

21 Ibid., p. 30.

22 For the request of Moses Nunez Xabe, ibid., p. 30; for that of the Portuguese in Bordeaux in 1718: SAA 334, no. 25, pp. 187–88, 24 Adar II 5489.

23 For the term "New Jews," see Y. Kaplan, "An Alternative Path to Modernity," in idem, *An Alternative Path to Modernity. The Sephardi Diaspora in Western Europe* (Leiden 2000), p. 27.

24 For example, E. Oliel-Grausz, "Mobilité, identité et procédures d'identification dans la diaspora séfarade au XVIIIe siècle," in *L'Écriture de l'Histoire Juive. Mélanges en l'honneur de Gérard Nahon*, ed. D. Iancu-Agou and C. Iancu (Paris 2012), pp. 419–41; see also Levie Bernfeld, *Poverty and Welfare*, pp. 81, 83–86, 107, 133.

were at stake.[25] Quite a few contemporary rabbinical authorities were divided on the Jewishness of *conversos* living on the Peninsula.[26] The majority, though, seemed to have accepted *conversos* as Jews,[27] and preferred their smooth absorption into the Jewish community.[28] The Amsterdam based dowry society *Dotar* offers an example of this lenient attitude: it accepted *conversos* and *conversas* as members or candidates for the lottery on condition that they believed in the oneness of God and identified spiritually with Judaism.[29] Thus, many *conversos*, men and women, living in cities in the Catholic world, such as Lisbon or Antwerp, who complied with this condition could, after balloting, register as members of *Dotar*, while girls living in similar areas could apply for participation in the lottery.[30] Of course, the girls were only able to claim a dowry if they could prove they had married a (circumcised) Jewish partner in a ceremony performed by a rabbi.

25　See discussions among rabbis mentioned in Zimmels, *Die Marranen*, for example pp. 21–35, pp. 101–3, nos. 24 and 27, p. 105, no. 34, p. 107, no. 35a, p. 150, no. 58, p. 152, nos. 61 and 62; for the Eastern Sephardi Diaspora, R. Lamdan, *A Separate People. Jewish Women in Palestine, Syria and Egypt in the Sixteenth Century* (Leiden 2000), pp. 192–93, 203.

26　On the division of opinion among rabbis within the Portuguese community of Amsterdam over the Jewish identity of *conversos* still living on the Peninsula, Y. Kaplan, "The Portuguese Jews in Amsterdam. From Forced Conversion to a Return to Judaism," *St Ros* 15/1 (1981), pp. 40–41; see also idem, "The Portuguese Community of Amsterdam in the Seventeenth Century. Between Tradition and Change," in *Society and Community*, ed. A. Haim (Jerusalem 1991), pp. 150–53; and see the discussion on the issue of Jewishness of *conversos* in the Ets Haim yeshiva in Hirsch, *Frucht vom Baum des Lebens*, pp. 145–47, no. 449; for an overview of opinions on the identity of *conversos* among the different rabbis in the Sephardi Diaspora, Yerushalmi, *From Spanish Court to Italian Ghetto*, pp. 24–31. For the earlier period, B. Netanyahu, *The Marranos of Spain. From the Late 14th to the Early 16th Century* (New York 1966), Ch. 2.

27　Kaplan, "An Alternative Path to Modernity," p. 18 and the literature mentioned in n. 44.

28　See the words of the Amsterdam *Hakham* Moses Raphael de Aguilar appealing to the *conversos* of Bayonne in Kaplan, "Portuguese Jews," p. 42; Zimmels, *Die Marranen*, pp. 57–58.

29　SAA 334, no. 1322, Caput VIII, p. B2, 16 Adar I 5375.

30　For membership of women living in Lisbon, to the Amsterdam based *Dotar* society, SAA 946, no. 84, p. 94, 3 Kislev 5419; for those in Antwerp, ibid., [n.p.], 7 July 1616; see for the entry of these female members from Antwerp as "duas pecoas secretas" also SAA 334, no. 1141, p. 43/58, 20 Tamuz 5376. In fact, one of the women from Antwerp apparently moved to Amsterdam seventeen years later, in 1633: Izabel de Pax, then widow of Duarte Dias de Frandes and now Zara Aboab widow of Duarte Dias de Frandes (SAA 334, no. 1142, p. 180, 1 Elul 5393); for girls from places such as southern France applying for participation in the lottery of *Dotar*, D.M. Swetschinski, *Reluctant Cosmopolitans: The Portuguese Jews of Seventeenth-Century Amsterdam* (London 2000), p. 179.

The leniency of rabbis towards *conversos* could also be inferred from the fact that a *converso*'s Judaism was not always defined according to halakhah (Jewish religious law), that is by matrilineal descent; patrilineal descent was also considered, as in the above example of candidates for the *Dotar* bridal fund. Some women might have been from Old Christian stock, but they seem to have been welcomed if they were married to men of New Christian background.[31] Likewise, a girl could apply for a dowry even if only her father was a *converso* of Jewish descent.[32]

Regardless of their status, the testimonies of anyone entering the community was debated and most certainly those without any local Jewish relatives. Witnesses, including women, were summoned for confirmation; genealogies were presented to prove Jewish ancestry from the *nação*.[33]

Newly arrived couples throughout the Sephardi Diaspora who had married on the Peninsula or elsewhere in a Catholic ceremony were required to remarry in a Jewish ceremony.[34] Testimonial procedures and circumcision of the groom was to be completed before a Jewish wedding could be performed.[35]

---

31   Graizbord, "Religion and Ethnicity," p. 46; in London it turned out to be a problem in case
      Gentile wives joined their *converso* husbands; see Y. Kaplan, "Wayward New Christians
      and Stubborn New Jews: The Shaping of a Jewish Identity," *Jewish History* 8/1–2 (1994),
      p. 37. In Amsterdam, there was talk of persons who came from non-Jewish stock along the
      female line who needed to undergo ritual immersion to be considered Jewish according
      to Jewish law (SAA 334, no. 1, p. 56).

32   SAA 334, no. 1322, p. A, 16 Adar I 5375.

33   See, for example, the testimonies noted down in the different requests for circumcision
      and admission to the Amsterdam Portuguese community in SAA 334, no. 381. For women
      accepted as witnesses testifying to the Jewish background of men who, upon arrival, re-
      quested to be circumcised and accepted as members of the Portuguese community, SAA
      334, no. 381, p. 17 [s.d.]; see further SAA 334, no. 381, p. 4, 25 June 1732; concerning the legal
      position of Jewish women to act as witnesses, SAA 334, no. 118, file 1, pp. 4–5; see also the
      examples of declarations written in petitions by Rachel Desaldaña and Rachel Rodrigues
      Ferois in Levie Bernfeld, *Poverty and Welfare*, pp. 83–84. Rachel Desaldaña stressed her
      Jewish roots on both father and mother's side, realizing this information was important
      to prove her Jewish identity.

34   The Spanish community of Venice is one more example of a *kahal* in which Jewish mar-
      riage ceremonies were offered to couples already married in a Catholic ceremony (Yerush-
      almi, *From Spanish Court to Italian Ghetto*, p. 27, n. 39). Some rabbis in the Sephardi world
      deemed it unnecessary for newly arrived couples to undergo a Jewish wedding ceremony.
      They claimed marriages performed on the Peninsula were valid, ibid.; see also Zimmels,
      Die Marranen, pp. 59, 162.

35   *Hakham* Saul Levi Mortera, in a sermon of 1625/26, stressed the fact that marriages were
      not allowed between Jewish women and uncircumcised *conversos* arriving to the Jewish
      community: M. Saperstein, *Exile in Amsterdam: Saul Levi Morteira's Sermons to a Congre-
      gation of "New Jews"* (Cincinnati 2005), p. 200.

Usually, there was a month-long interval between circumcision and the Jewish wedding ceremony.[36]

Little information is available with regard to the extent to which lay and spiritual leadership imposed its views and indoctrinated newcomers to have Jewish law applied in cases of marriage, though, it seems it did.[37] Males who did not want to undergo circumcision and a Jewish wedding ceremony would not be allowed to perform special duties in the synagogue; without circumcision they would not be allowed to hold any official position within the *kahal*, or receive charity or be buried in the Jewish cemetery.[38] Similar sanctions applied

---

36   For specific examples: the case of Francisco de La Penha who arrived with his wife in Amsterdam in 1699 (SAA 334, no. 220, p. 13, 11 Tishri 5460) and underwent a religious wedding ceremony according to the Jewish law as Abraham and Sara de la Penha around one month later (SAA 334, no. 386, p. 49, 24 Kislev 5460); see also the *huppa* of Jacob Nunez Ferro with Rachel Nunes Ferro on 9 Kislev 5463 (SAA 334, no. 407, p. 101; ibid., no. 387, p. 44); Jacob was circumcised at the age of twenty-nine, one month earlier (SAA 334, no. 377, [n.p.], 30 Hesvan/20 November 5463); for the *huppa* of Abraham Fernandes and Sara Fernandes: SAA 334, no. 407, p. 5, 3 Elul 5482; for the circumcision of Abraham Fernandes one month earlier: SAA 334, no. 377, [n.p.], 6 Ab/10 July 5482. Abraham apparently came from Seville and was by then thirty years old. A *responsum* of the yeshiva Ets Haim mentions a Jewish wedding ceremony to be held three months after circumcision. Hirsch, *Frucht vom Baum des Lebens*, p. 80, no. 251. Zimmels talks about the practice of a period of six months (Zimmels, *Die Marranen*, p. 59).

37   In general, the leadership issued many sanctions on disobedience. In fact, people complained the Amsterdam Portuguese community acted quite severely towards deviants and like an Inquisition: "Il semble que ces petits Juifs veulent établir une Inquisition à Amsterdam," attributed to Juan/Daniel de Prado according to his student Jacob Marchena cited by I.S. Révah, "Aux origines de la rupture spinozienne: Nouveaux documents sur l'incroyance dans la communauté judéo-portugaise d'Amsterdam à l'époque de l'excommunication de Spinoza," *REJ* 123 (1964), p. 371.

38   See for example the case of Francisco López Capadosse, who refused to be circumcized as mentioned in Y. Kaplan, "The Social Functions of the Herem in the Portuguese Jewish Community of Amsterdam in the Seventeenth Century," in *DJH* (1984), p. 118. See also on this theme, idem, "On the Burial of Spinoza's Grandfather and Grandmother," *Zutot* 13 (2016), pp. 26–39. For the prohibition of *conversos* from countries outside of the Jewish world to be buried in the Portuguese Jewish cemetery in Ouderkerk aan de Amstel without being circumcised, SAA 334, no. 19, p. 191/276, 4 Sivan 5405; ibid., p. 377, 17 Kislev 5415; in London *Hakham* Sasportas did not allow any uncircumcised men to participate in synagogue functions as well (M. Goldish, "The Amsterdam Portuguese Rabbinate in the Seventeenth Century: A Unique Institution Viewed from Within and Without," in *Dutch Jews as Perceived by Themselves and by Others*, Proceedings of the Eighth International Symposium on the Jews in The Netherlands, ed. Ch. Brasz and Y. Kaplan [Leiden 2001], p. 18).

to women: unless they complied with the procedures according to Jewish law, they would be barred from entering community life and, consequently, would be even more isolated in their day to day lives. No dowries would be distributed,[39] and they would not be eligible for other forms of charity. Burial in the Jewish cemetery would be prohibited; their children would not be accepted in the educational institutions of the community and so forth. Thus, it seems that the Portuguese leadership played an influential and coercive role in bringing *conversas* back to the path of normative Judaism and did everything in its power to overcome obstacles posed by Jewish law to accommodate these women within the community.[40]

Most *conversos* and *conversas* appear to have voluntarily complied with the communal dictates. We only need consult the community's extensive *ketubbah* (marriage contract) registry to see that many Portuguese solemnized their marriages through a Jewish ceremony.[41] Also quite a few *ketubbot* as well as Jewish wedding rings have surfaced in inventories.[42] Moreover, in marriage settlements or wills signed before a notary, mention was made of Jewish ceremonies and agreements, such as a Jewish marriage contract or the *halitza* ceremony that would release the spouse from levirate marriage. For the division of property, Jewish law was often followed as well.[43] Moses de Daniel Pinto

---

39   See for example the case of Clara de Almeida: her dowry was paid only after information that a Jewish wedding ceremony had taken place, in this case on the basis of a letter written by the *Hakham* of Bayonne (Levie Bernfeld, *Poverty and Welfare*, p. 104 and p. 354, n. 234); for an example of a dowry paid by *Dotar* after a *huppa* in Padua, SAA 334, no. 1142, p. 164, 24 March 5492 (Josef Aboab marrying Ester de Abraham Gaon de Vitoria); for Amsterdam see, for example, SAA 334, no. 1143, p. 76/31, 8 Elul 5402 (David Lopes marrying Rachel de la Cuesta).

40   See also on force exerted on people arriving from outside the Jewish world that they embrace Judaism in Amsterdam and elsewhere, Y. Kaplan, "Wayward New Christians and Stubborn New Jews," pp. 31, 34–36; idem, "The Portuguese Jews," pp. 41–42.

41   For the *ketubbah* registry of the Amsterdam Portuguese community, in SAA 334, no. 382. Most of the marriage contracts date from the latter part of the seventeenth century.

42   See the inventory of Ester, Viuva de Mosseh de Daniel de Pinto. There, in 1707, "hua ketuba en ebraico" was localized, belonging to Sara Pinto mulher de Ab^mo de Ishac Bueno: SAA 334, no. 518, [s.d.] 5467, p. 63. For Jewish wedding rings, see the last will of Sara Alvares (SAA 5075, no. 2237, p. 1107, Not. A. Lock, 23 December 1671).

43   See, for example, the case of Abigail Abarbanel, legitimate wife of Pincas Abarbanel: she divided her dowry leaving half to her family (she apparently died childless), according to the stipulations in her *ketubbah* SAA 5075, no. 2895B, pp. 1378–79, Not. P. Padthuysen, 28 September 1666; see further the last will of Rachel Pinta alias Leonor Torres (SAA 5075, no. 2895B, p. 978, Not. P. Padthuysen, 22 July 1666); for the will of Moses de Oliveira: SAA 5075, no. 2891B, pp. 1204–6, Not. P. Padthuysen, 16 September 1662.

stipulated that Jewish law govern the execution of his will: "comforme Nossa Santa Ley de Mosseh excluyndo quais quer Leys ou Justisa."[44] Often, as a Jewish principle, Jewish law was followed so long as it did not conflict with the laws of the country.[45]

On the other hand, there were also some who preferred to ignore Jewish law in cases of marriage or inheritance and opt for Portuguese or Dutch law instead.[46] Marriage according to Portuguese or Dutch law enabled division of property after the death of a spouse, thus leaving a widow not just with her dowry, but also with half the communal property.[47]

In all, it is difficult to draw conclusions about what motivated people to ignore Jewish law in cases of marriage and inheritance. Financial concerns, ideological or religious sentiment,[48] and even the fate of family members still living on the Peninsula were all possible reasons. When Antonio Fernandes Homem married Paula Brandão in 1605, the marriage contract was based exclusively on Portuguese law. There was no reference to Jewish law even though Antonio's father was known to be one of the founders of the Amsterdam based dowry society *Dotar*. Perhaps any reference to Judaism in this case would have been too dangerous as the groom was in Lisbon when the marriage was contracted.[49]

44   SAA 334, no. 518, p. 66, [n.d.] 5467 [1696–7]: "Copia do testamento de Moseh de Daniel Pinto" (the original will was dated 22 October 1692 and drawn up before Notary P. Padthuysen); see also the marriage contract between Samuel Levy Rezio and Rachel de Morales with references to Jewish law only (SAA 5075, no. 7356, no. 1958, Not. J. Valkenburg, September 1710, pp. 296–99).

45   Apparently in certain cases choosing between Jewish law and the laws of the country the principle "the law of the kingdom is law" (*dina de-malkhuta dina*) was followed: on this principle see *Encyclopaedia Judaica*, ed. M. Berenbaum and F. Skolnik, 2nd ed. (Detroit 2007 [1971]), vol. 5, p. 663–69; see for example the last will of Jose and Ester Pinta (SAA 5075, no. 397a, Not. J. and N. Jacobs, 20 June 1628, pp. 149–50); see also a marriage contract like the one of Juda Vega de Prado and Eliseba de Pinto, in which the law of the country gets priority (SAA 5075, no. 7493, no. 89, Not. J. van den Ende, 6 July 1718).

46   Brites Tomas, widow of Luis Gomes d'Avero, is also a case in point: in Amsterdam she insisted that Portuguese law be applied after her husband died since her marriage was performed according to that law (SAA 5075, no. 646, p. 576, Not. S. Cornelisz., 26 June 1623: last will of Brites Tomas, wife of Luis Gomes d'Avero).

47   On marriage according to Portuguese law, see discussions in Zimmels, *Die Marranen*, pp. 49–50.

48   On similar matters, see the discussions in Hirsch, *Frucht vom Baum des Lebens*, index under "Erbrecht."

49   SAA 5075, no. 61, p. 643, Not. D. Mostart, 15 February 1605; also published in *St Ros* 3/2 (1969), p. 241. For registration of the marriage before the civil authorities in Amsterdam three months earlier, see SAA Doop-Trouw-Begraafregisters (henceforth: DTB) 665, p. 380,

Little is known about the decisions of the community's rabbis regarding the complex legal matters of marriage and divorce that resulted from migration in times of persecution and expulsion. In the matter of levirate marriage, widows without children who had managed to leave Spain or Portugal for Amsterdam could not remarry because they were still tied through levirate bonds to the *converso* brothers of their deceased husbands who had remained behind on the Peninsula. These *conversos* usually had no desire to emigrate so that they could either marry their sisters-in-law or perform the *halitza* ceremony.[50] This may account for the decision of Isaac Franco, alias Francisco Mendes de Medeiros, an important *parnas* and founder of Amsterdam's Neve Shalom congregation, to ignore Jewish law on this point. As he and his wife were childless, he stipulated in his will of 1623, that she have the freedom to remarry any man of her choice without being bound to anyone or the *halitza* ceremony.[51]

No cases have come to light of married women living in Amsterdam who were eager to divorce husbands who had remained behind on the Peninsula or elsewhere.[52] However, the inclusion of an article on bills of divorce in the community regulations of 1639 does suggest that the matter was of topical interest, especially since there is evidence that Portuguese illegally practiced giving a *get* (divorce), which included signatures of witnesses, without communal leadership approval.[53]

---

7 November 1604: Paula Brandoa and Antonio Fernandes Homem; the groom was not present at this ceremony, but in Lisbon; see further on him and his family E.M. Koen "Duarte Fernandes, Koopman van de Portugese Natie te Amsterdam." *StRos* 2/2 (1968), pp. 178–93. Apparently, Antonio moved to Hamburg (........, p. 184).

50   The problem of levirate marriage is mentioned in a sermon of *Hakham* Saul Levi Mortera of c. 1630, Saperstein, *Exile in Amsterdam*, p. 322; on levirate issues, H.T. Adelman, "Custom, Law and Gender: Levirate Union among Ashkenazim and Sephardim in Italy after the Expulsion from Spain," in *The Expulsion of the Jews: 1492 and After*, ed. R. Waddington and A. Williamson (New York 1994), pp. 107–25: Netanyahu, *Marranos of Spain*, Ch. 2.

51   SAA 5075, no. 615a, Not. P. & S. Ruttens, 31 May 1623, p. 435, last will of Isaac Franco alias Francisco Mendes de Medeiros. On Isaac Franco, R.G. Fuks-Mansfeld, *De Sefardim in Amsterdam tot 1795. Aspecten van een joodse minderheid in een Hollandse stad* (Hilversum 1989), pp. 50–52; J. d'Ancona, "Komst der Marranen in Noord-Nederland. De Portugese gemeenten te Amsterdam tot de vereniging (1639)," in *Geschiedenis der Joden in Nederland*, ed. H. Brugmans and A. Frank (Amsterdam 1940), p. 218; also W. Chr. Pieterse, *Daniel Levi de Barrios als geschiedschrijver van de Portugees-Israelietische gemeente te Amsterdam in zijn "triumpho del govierno popular"* (Amsterdam 1968), pp. 48, 95.

52   See a *responsum* on this issue in Hirsch, *Frucht vom Baum des Lebens*, p. 673, no. 671; for discussions among rabbinic leaders in the Sephardi Diaspora, Yerushalmi, *From Spanish Court to Italian Ghetto*, pp. 24–29; for similar problems in the Levant, Lamdan, *Separate People*, pp. 218–20, 223.

53   SAA 334, no. 19, p. 25/110, 22 Tamuz 5399, art. 46; ibid., no. 13, p. 133/65, 1 Shevat 5397.

Furthermore, in a community where so many men were either traveling abroad or whose whereabouts on the Peninsula were unknown, there must have been many cases of *agunot*, abandoned wives, who could not remarry.[54] The names of many women appear on the charity lists of the Amsterdam Portuguese community without any additional details about the locations of husbands.[55] Many women's status was changed from married to widow without a husband ever appearing.[56] The Portuguese community would sometimes even give women money in order to help them to search for their husbands.[57]

The Re-Education of *Conversas*

How much did *conversas* know about normative Judaism when they reached Amsterdam?[58] Rabbi Menasseh ben Israel hinted that *conversas* had only fragmentary knowledge of Judaism.[59] Born generations after the forced conversions on the Peninsula, these *conversas* had very few resources at their disposal to transfer Jewish tradition from one generation to the next, even if they so wished.[60] Documentary evidence shows that *conversos* who took refuge in France knew very little about normative Judaism.[61] On the other hand, seventeenth-century testimonies at Inquisition tribunals appear to suggest

---

54 The *responsa* collection of the Ets Haim yeshiva includes many discussions concerning the *agunah* within the Amsterdam Portuguese community, Hirsch, *Frucht vom Baum des Lebens*, index "agunah"; also Zimmels, *Die Marranen*, p. 58. More in Levie Bernfeld, *Poverty and Welfare*, pp. 37, 53, 55–56; see for the case of Louis da Fonseca, who left his wife for almost twenty years and it was not clear whether he was still alive, SAA 5075, no. 942, p. 295, Not. D. Bredan, 7 April 1633; in a port city such as Amsterdam many non-Jewish women were left alone for years not knowing whether their husbands were alive or dead, and they were eager to remarry, H. Roodenburg, *Onder Censuur, de kerkelijke tucht in de gereformeerde gemeente van Amsterdam, 1578–1700* (Hilversum 1990), pp. 283–84.

55 See for example SAA 334, no. 172, pp. 61–62, 13 Adar 5400; ibid., no. 176, pp. 202–3, 1 Iyar 5455.

56 See examples in Levie Bernfeld, *Poverty and Welfare*, pp. 54–55.

57 Y. Kaplan, "Moral Panic in the Eighteenth-century Sephardi Community of Amsterdam: The Threat of Eros," in *Dutch Jewry: Its History and Secular Culture (1500–2000)*, ed. J.I. Israel and R. Salverda (Leiden 2002), pp. 110–11; on the case of Ester Menasseh see Levie Bernfeld, *Poverty and Welfare*, p. 37.

58 This was an ongoing topic of discussion among rabbis, Zimmels, *Die Marranen*, pp. 78–81.

59 Menasseh ben Israel, *Thesovro dos Dinim* (Amsterdam 5407 [1647/8]), Part v, p. 116.

60 Kaplan, "Between Christianity and Judaism," pp. 313–15.

61 D.L. Graizbord, "Becoming Jewish in Early Modern France: Documents on Jewish Community-Building in Seventeenth-Century Bayonne and Peyrehorade," *Journal of Social History* 40/1 (2006), pp. 153–55.

that *conversas* were engaged in considerable Jewish activity.[62] At any rate, with their arrival in Amsterdam, most of these women had to comply with stricter observance of Judaism than they had practiced in Portugal or Spain. Moreover, they had to adjust to a more modest role in Jewish life than they had been accustomed.

The lay and spiritual leadership was aware of the necessity to provide women with instruction in the basic laws of normative Judaism even though there was no institutional setting in the form of religious schools, academies or study societies comparable to the ones set up for men.[63] Women were barred from such institutions because of the restrictions placed on their freedom of movement in the public space,[64] and because higher Jewish learning by women was believed to be contrary to Jewish law.[65] Following this line of thinking, Menasseh ben Israel maintained, as did many rabbis before him, that women along with slaves and small children were exempt from learning Jewish law.[66] However, since family life was a basic value in Judaism and women were instrumental in its upkeep, the Portuguese leadership understood the importance of finding ways to introduce *conversas* to Judaism's basic tenets.

For this purpose, compendia of Jewish laws were published in Spanish and Portuguese throughout the Sephardi Diaspora and extensive space was devoted in them to the laws pertaining to women acknowledging their important

---

62   For literature see above n. 5.

63   Benjamin Fisher suggested that there was a place for girls to follow the lessons at the Talmud Torah since there was a *mehizah* that separated the sexes and that the Keter Sem Tob society would have provided study opportunities for girls. I am not convinced by Fisher's claim: sisters ("las hermanas") mentioned by Daniel Levi de Barrios must have formed part of the government of this society together with the brothers, while only boys ("los mancebos") studied there one hour every Sabbath (for "las Hermanas con fervor y con union los Hermanos," [Daniel Levi de Barrios, *Triumpho del Govierno popular y de la Antiguedad Holandesa* (Amsterdam, 5443 [1683]); copy the University Library Amsterdam, Biblioteca Rosenthaliana RON A 5252, p. 152/370; for the students, "los mancebos," see De Barrios, *Triumpho*, p. 366; for "veinte Mancebos prudentes," De Barrios, *Triumpho*, p. 367); B. Fisher, "The Centering of the Bible in Seventeenth-Century Amsterdam: Jewish Religion, Culture and Scholarship" (Ph.D. Dissertation, University of Pennsylvania, 2011), pp. 43–44. For a discussion of youth societies like *Keter Sem Tob* see also Levie Bernfeld, *Poverty and Welfare*, pp. 127–30.

64   Levie Bernfeld, "Sephardi Women in Holland's Golden Age," pp. 177, 189–90.

65   Deuteronomy 11:19. Yosef Karo, *Shulhan arukh, Yoreh de'ah*, 246, 6; see for further approaches on this issue the literature mentioned in Lamdan, *Separate People*, p. 110, n. 1.

66   Menasseh ben Israel, *Thesovro dos Dinim* (Amsterdam 1645), Part II, "Do Aprendimento da Ley," p. 94.

role in Jewish family life.[67] One such work in Spanish by the Venetian Rabbi Isaac Athias titled *Thesoro de preceptos*, was first published in Venice and later in Amsterdam.[68] Another Spanish manual, *Compendio de Dinim* by David Pardo, was published in Amsterdam but was apparently meant for the Portuguese community in London.[69] Also in Spanish was the *Arbol de vidas* by Abraham Vaez, printed in Amsterdam in 1692 but meant for instruction of the Portuguese in southern France (Bayonne).[70]

The final part of Menasseh ben Israel's *Thesovro dos Dinim* (1647; reprinted in Amsterdam in 1710), which he addressed to the "very noble and honest *Senhoras*," was probably used for the instruction of the *conversas* in Amsterdam,[71] which the author lamented was not readily available to them. Rules for keeping a kosher household and the laws of matrimony, including the three *mitzvot* [commandments] for married women: separating a portion of dough (*hallah*), observing the laws of purity (*niddah*) and lighting candles (*hadlakat ha-ner*), were laid out in its pages in detail, along with the recommendation that they read his book rather than the ususal idle books.[72]

Menasseh also instructed the women on moral precepts,[73] as well as on matters of dress and demeanor, such as covering their hair and behaving with respect and humility towards their husbands, a plea echoed by David Pardo.[74] He also included certain Hebrew prayers, often in transliteration in Latin characters, followed by Spanish or Portuguese translation, a presumption that some

---

67   On the role of Sephardi women in Jewish family life, Levie Bernfeld, "Sephardi Women in Holland's Golden Age," pp. 191–93.

68   I. Athias, *Thesoro de preceptos, adonde se encierran las joyas de los seis cientos y treze preceptos que encomendò el Senor à su pueblo Israel; con su Declaracion, Razon y Dinim, conforme a la verdadera tradicion, recibida de Mosè y enseñada por nuestros Sabios de gloriosa memoria* (Venice 1627; Amsterdam 1649); more in Y.H. Yerushalmi, *The Re-Education of the Marranos in the Seventeenth Century* (Cincinnati 1980), p. 8.

69   D. Pardo, *Compendio de Dinim Que todo Israel Deve Saber y Observar. Compuesto por Estilo Fasil y Breve* (Amsterdam 5449).

70   A. Vaez, *Arbol de vidas en el qual se contienen los dinim mas necessarios que deve observar todo Ysrael/sacados de varios graves autores* (Amsterdam 1692; copy in Koninklijke Bibliotheek, The Hague, 485L 20).

71   Menasseh ben Israel, *Thesovro dos Dinim*, Part V (Amsterdam 1647), not numbered [v–vi].

72   Ibid., p. vi.

73   Ibid., p. i: dedication to Abraham and Isaac Israel Pereyra.

74   See for example his instructions concerning the obligations of the wife towards her husband (ibid., pp. 72–77); David Pardo also stressed the superiority of husband over wife, which in his view should always be recognized (Pardo, *Compendio de Dinim*, pp. 214–15, 225–29).

readers had not or might not learn to read the Hebrew.[75] In fact, an eighteenth-century *responsum* underlines the fact that women in Amsterdam prayed in foreign languages and did not understand Hebrew.[76] In general, this last part of Menasseh's *Thesovro* dealt with proper management of the household. Divided into three parts, the first part concerned conjugal life and all the laws and moral precepts on the matter, the second instructed fathers on the education of their children, and the third part related to household possessions, including the treatment of slaves.[77]

Menasseh's instructions to his female readers were not all that unique; in fact, he made reference to sixteenth-century printed manuals for women written in Yiddish and Italian.[78] He was probably also familiar with the Christian moral conduct books for women that were widely disseminated throughout Europe in the sixteenth and seventeenth centuries, such as *De Institutione Feminae Christianae* by Juan Luis Vives or *Houwelick, dat is Het gansche Beleyt des Echten-Staats* by Jacob Cats.[79]

75 See for prayers: the prayer for the ritual bath (Hebrew transliterated in Latin characters and Spanish: Menasseh ben Israel, *Thesovro dos Dinim*, Part V [Amsterdam 1647], p. 93); for the prayer in Spanish for separating out the portion of dough (*hallah*) see ibid., p. 111; for prayers relating to the lighting of the candles before the Sabbath and holidays in Spanish (ibid., pp. 112–13); ibid., p. 113 a prayer in Portuguese is included to be recited after the blessing for the lighting of the Sabbath candles, expressing the wish that the woman's sons will be true in their observance of the Law.

76 Hirsch, *Frucht vom Baum des Lebens*, p. 87, no. 283. In a responsum of Samuel Aboab about the question from former Marranos whether it is permitted to pray in a foreign language (i.e., not Hebrew), the answer was in the affirmative, Yerushalmi, *Re-Education*, p. 7.

77 Menasseh ben Israel, *Thesovro dos Dinim*, Part V (Amsterdam 1647), pp. i–ii: "O segundo, da Paternal, e contem o que se observa no bom regimento entre paes a filhos. O terceiro, finalmente os Dinim que tocaõ a parte Senhoril e Possessoria, que he tudo o que o homem possue na vida, de escravos, bems de raiz e movens."

78 Menasseh ben Israel, *Thesovro dos Dinim*, Part V (Amsterdam 1647), p. vi. On the sixteenth-century Yiddish versions see, *My Dear Daughter: Rabbi Benjamin Slonik and the Education of Jewish Women in Sixteenth-century Poland*; with a transcription of Benjamin Slonik's *seder mizvot ha-nashim* (The order of women's commandments) translated by E. Fram and A. Romer Segal (Cleveland 2007) and the different editions (Krakow 1577, 1585, 1595) in the bibliography on p. 314. On the Italian version, B. Slonik, *Mizvot nashim melumadah, Precetti d'esser imparati dalle donne Hebree / composto per Biniammin d'Arodono in lingua todesca; tradotto . . . nella volgare per Giacob Alpron* (Venice 1616).

79 J.L. Vives, *De Institutione Feminae Christianae* (1523), ed. C. Fantazzi and C. Matheeussen, trans. C. Fantazzi, 2 vols. (Leiden 1996); J. Cats, *Houwelick, dat is Het gansche Beleyt des Echten-Staats* (Middelburg 1625); also P. Wittewrongel, *Oeconomia Christiana ofte Christelicke Huys-Houdinghe*, 2 vols. (Amsterdam 1661); it is interesting to note that Menasseh

Menasseh's *Thesovro*, like other similar compendia, included instruction about Jewish dietary laws and kosher food preparation.[80] In his *Compendio de Dinim*, David Pardo was obviously thinking of a female readership in his extensive discussion of food preparation according to the dietary laws, which went into great detail about salting meat in order to draw out the blood and what to look for in order to determine whether meat met the requirements for *kashrut* and how to make plates and crockery kosher for use on Passover.[81] He especially urged women not to excuse themselves from the work related to maintenance of a kosher household.[82] Apparently it was clear to him and probably to his readers in London that many women were not too keen on scrupulous observance of the dietary laws. In addition to these compendia, Spanish translations of ethical works were made available to women, such as *Almenara de la luz* based on the fourteenth-century Hebrew work of Isaac Aboab *Menorat ha-maor*, published in Spanish in Livorno in 1656 and in 1708 in Amsterdam.[83] Interestingly, almost none of these compendia or ethical books appear on inventory lists of Portuguese women. Nevertheless, Juda Obediente apparently had a copy of *Almenara de la luz* in his home, since he brought such a work to the pawn bank, though we do not know whether he studied its content or had his wife read from it.[84]

Sephardi women in Amsterdam and women in the Jewish world at large owned few books.[85] Yet, despite the fact that women in general and Jewish

---

titled the last part of his *Thesovro* (Amsterdam 1647) "Perfeyta Economica"; for secondary literature on the above-mentioned Dutch authors see *Jacob Cats Huwelijk*, ed. A.A. Sneller and B. Thijs (Amsterdam 1993); J. Breevoort, *Vader Cats en de Vrouw* (Kampen 1915); also J.J.H. Dekker, "Moral Literacy: The Pleasure of Learning How to Become Decent Adults and Good Parents in the Dutch Republic in the Seventeenth Century," *Paedagogica Historica* 44/1–2 (2008), pp. 137–51. On Menasseh's Iberian view of running a household and his understanding of the term economics, which in contemporary Iberia also related to the management of the household, J.R. Lieberman, "Childhood and Family among the Western Sephardim," in *Sephardi Family Life in the Early Modern Diaspora*, ed. J.R. Lieberman (Waltham, MA 2011), pp. 131–32.

80   Menasseh ben Israel, *Thesovro dos Dinim* (Amsterdam 1645), table of contents, pp. v–xiv.

81   Pardo, *Compendio de Dinim*, pp. xxi–xxii.

82   Ibid., pp. xxii–xxiii.

83   H. den Boer, *Bibliografia de los impresos en lenguas española y portuguesa de Holanda c. 1600–1800* (Leiden 1985), p. 130 (for the Amsterdam edition of 5468 [1708]).

84   SAA 334, no. 1027, p. 48/15, 15 Hesvan 5449 (no. 177): *f* 1:4. On pawns brought into the Portuguese Jewish pawn bank, see my "Making Ends Meet in Early Modern Amsterdam: People and Pawns at the Portuguese Jewish Loan Bank," (forthcoming).

85   Howard Adelman also reflects on the lack of books among women in Italy: H.T. Adelman, "Jewish Women and Family Life, Inside and Outside the Ghetto," in *The Jews of Early*

women in particular hardly owned any books, many Jewish women in early modern Europe did read the Bible and were taught to say prayers, either in Hebrew, Judeo-Italian, Ladino, Spanish or Portuguese.[86] Some female members of Amsterdam's Portuguese community did own Hebrew books;[87] some even owned Bibles in Spanish or French.[88] A book by Maimonides, in French, was listed in one woman's inventory.[89] Prayer books, some in Hebrew, mostly in Spanish or Portuguese, frequently bound in leather with silver or gilt clasps, are often recorded in inventories of women.[90] Also, we know that Portuguese

---

Modern Venice, ed. R.C. Davis and B.C.I. Ravid (Baltimore 2001), p. 151. Gérard Nahon mentions the case of one woman in southern France (Rachel Carvallo Frois) who left three small books as a legacy; further on the larger libraries of western Sephardi men, see Levie Bernfeld, *Poverty and Welfare*, pp. 126, 160–61; also Swetschinski, *Reluctant Cosmopolitans*, pp. 291–92.

86   For women in Rome reading from the Bible and prayer books (often in Judeo-Italian written with Hebrew characters), H.T. Adelman, "Rabbis and Reality: Public Activities of Jewish Women in Italy during the Renaissance and Catholic Restoration," *Jewish History* 5/1(1991), pp. 30–31. For sixteenth-century Ladino prayer books, O. (Rodrigue) Schwarzwald, "Two Sixteenth-Century Ladino Prayer Books for Women," *European Judaism* 43/2 (2010), pp. 37–51. For books read by *conversas* in Spain, V. Parello, "Inquisition and Crypto-Judaism: The 'Complicity' of the Mora family of Quitanar de la Orden (1588–1592)," in *The Conversos and Moriscos in Late Medieval Spain and Beyond*, ed. K. Ingram (Leiden, 2009), pp. 198–99.

87   Inventory of Mordecai Semah Aboab (SAA 5075, no. 13543, pp. 2v.–3, Not. D. Geniets, 28 August 1755).

88   Out of the legacy of Jeudit Rodrigues Carrion, widow of David de Daniel Rodrigues, a Bible in French and several prayer books in Ladino were found (SAA 334, no. 119 bb, p. 793, 54 June 1739). For the Spanish Bible of Hana de Jacob de Moses Pereira, a single woman, see her inventory in SAA 334, no. 787, pp. 108, 111, Not. J. Klinkhamer, 25 February 1788.

89   Inventory of Ribca Susarte, widow of Eliseu Pereyra (SAA 334, no. 518, p. 250, Not. J. Snoek, 31 May 1722/17 October 1724). It could have been left over from her husband.

90   In the inventory of Ester Barrocas we find five books in "Ladino" (Levie Bernfeld, *Poverty and Welfare*, p. 190); Rachel Medina Chamis had two "*kerkboeken*" (churchbooks) of tortoiseshell with silver clasps (SAA 334, no. 658, Not. J. Barels, inventory of Rachel Medina Chamis, widow of Joseph Henriques Medina); for a "*kerkboek*" with silver locks in a bag with a silver brace, the inventory of Ester Arias, widow of Joseph Abraham Capadoce (SAA 334, no. 632, 22 July 1746); in the inventory of Sara Namias de Castro, widow of David Namias de Castro, we find two prayer books with silver clasps (SAA 334, no. 668, p. 12, Not. J. Barels, 18 April 1747). Hebrew books were found among the belongings Ribca Jessurun brought to her marriage: SAA 334, no. 609, n.d. [beginning 18th century]; see also the last will of Miriam del Sotto alias Miriam Alvares, in which she left her prayer books to her niece (SAA 334, no. 628: "Papeis tocantes a caza mortuoria de Miriam Alvarez que Ds tem. Miriam Alvarez, N° 4," last will, written and signed by Miriam Alvares, 28 October 1678; handed over to Not. F. Tixerandet on 21 November 1678; opened by Not.

women owned *mahzorim* for Yom Kipur, which, evidently, they brought to the pawnbank.[91] Secular books were also found in inventories, most pertaining to theater.[92] One woman had two box-fulls of Spanish comedies.[93]

If they did not derive their knowledge about Judaism from books, then Sephardi women in Amsterdam must have learned about the theory and practice of normative Jewish life from people. According to the *Sefer hassidim* a father is obliged to teach his daughter, a man his wife.[94] In *Sefer shulhan ha-panim* based on the *Shulhan arukh* of Joseph Karo, the Venetian Rabbi Gershon urged husbands to teach their wives family purity and dietary laws, as well as the three religious obligations expected of married women.[95] The editor-translator of a sixteenth-century Ladino prayerbook reiterated Maimonides' command in the *Mishneh Torah* that it was the duty of the father to educate his wife and household.[96] Portuguese women in southern France apparently gathered knowledge on normative Judaism and prayed based on what they had learned from and heard when their husbands and sons read to them.[97] Inquisition records show that both men and women were accused of instructing their family in Jewish law and practice.[98] The leadership of the Amsterdam Portuguese

---

D. van der Groe, 29 August 1685); in the inventory of Ester de Ab^m Keyzer, widow of Guidon Labat we find a golden memorbook and five prayer books with silver bands (SAA 334, no. 719, pp. 69–70, 9 May 1776); see also above n. 88.

91   For example SAA 334, no. 1027, p. 48/14, 12 Tishri 5449, "Ester Nunez . . . livroz . . . outro de kipur." See my forthcoming article on the pawnbank as cited in n. 84.

92   Menasseh ben Israel, *Thesovuro dos Dinim*, Part V, p. vi. Sephardi women poets in Amsterdam might have read some of the "profane books" Menasseh ben Israel referred to; see on Portuguese women poets in Amsterdam, Levie Bernfeld, *Poverty and Welfare*, p. 101. Judith de Souza Machado left a coffin with some printed books (SAA 334, no. 726, p. 59, Not. J. Barels, 5 April 1755). We do not know the titles or the language in which they were written.

93   Inventory Aron Uziel Cardoso: SAA 5072, no. 670, p. 315, 26 September 1754. On Dutch Sephardim and their love for theater, Swetschinski, *Reluctant Cosmopolitans*, pp. 286–89, 312–13.

94   Cited in J.R. Baskin, "Jewish Women in the Middle Ages," in *Jewish Women in Historical Perspective,* ed. J.R. Baskin, 2nd edition (Detroit 1998), p. 115; see also ead. "Ritual Immersion in Medieval Ashkenaz," *Jewish Law Association Studies* 17 (2007), pp. 14–16: it deals here with fathers giving instruction to their daughters (about to marry) on the laws of ritual purity.

95   Yerushalmi, *Re-Education*, p. 9.

96   Schwarzwald, "Two Sixteenth-Century Ladino Prayer Books," p. 42 and Maimonides, *Mishneh Torah*, Hilkhot Sota, 4:19.

97   Cited in Graizbord, "Becoming Jewish," pp. 156–57.

98   For example Beinart, *Conversos on Trial*, p. 214; here he cites the example of the wife of Juan González Panpán, who declared before the tribunal of the Inquisition that it was her husband who influenced their children and brought them up to observe *mitzvot*; also

community turned men into the educators of its female constituency: it often addressed its male members to keep order at home and ensure that their wives and daughters abide by Jewish law.[99] In his *Thesovro*, Menasseh ben Israel called on husbands to instruct their wives.[100]

Because of the frequent absence of husbands and fathers, it is possible that women took on the role of instructors in the ways of normative Judaism for the newcomers. Most likely, the wives of *hakhamim* played an important role in the education of *conversas* as probably other women did, who were born and bred into the observant Jewish milieu.

With more knowledge at their disposal, these female newcomers might also have resumed the task of teaching Judaism, as they had done back in Spain and Portugal. There is a case of a woman in Amsterdam who was paid for home instruction, though no further details are known regarding the substance of the instruction.[101] Another is a mother or teacher in the eighteenth-century girls' orphanage Mazon Abanot.[102] The orphanage statutes required that she provide the girls with instruction on basic Jewish concepts, though the specific details of the curriculum remain vague. It is probable that the Jewish education taught in the orphanage was normally given in a home setting.

Documentary evidence suggests that such Jewish education at home, for girls and boys, was performed by women as well as men: in last wills, for example, husbands instructed their wives or other female family members to continue to instil in their children, a "fear of God" and to teach them to live according to "the Laws given through Moses to Israel."[103] In his *Thesovro*, Menasseh also implied that women were to be involved in the Jewish education of their children, repeating the age-old plea of Jewish mothers that their children

---

ibid., pp. 266–67; and further M. Bodian, *Dying in the Law of Moses. Crypto-Jewish Martyrdom in the Iberian World* (Bloomington, IN 2007), p. 49; Parello, "Inquisition and Crypto-Judaism," p. 197.

99   See for example the warning by the Portuguese community meant for women of the community but addressed to them through male members, not to sit at the door and not to do household work during Christian holidays (SAA 334, no. 24a, p. 41v., 20 Sivan 5437); see also the warning to men to maintain order at home and restrain the style of their wives' dress in order that it will be in accordance with the notions of modesty (SAA 334, no. 21, p. 257, 8 Hesvan 5482).

100   Menasseh ben Israel, *Thesovro dos Dinim*, Part V (Amsterdam 1647), p. 70.

101   SAA 5072, no. 751, no. 7, 21 August 1749, estate of David German; credit owed to Ribca de Mattos for remaining teaching fees.

102   SAA 334, no. 120, file 81, p. 896, para. 6, 8 Adar I 5494. On women teachers in Spain before the expulsion of the Jews, Lamdan, *Separate People*, p. 110.

103   SAA 334, no. 613, Not. C. van Achthoven, 28 May 1722, last will of Moses Abrabanel.

recite particular prayers at home and their sons study in the *beit midrash*.[104] We may conclude therefore, that Portuguese women and girls not only received Jewish education at home, but were at some point also instrumental in the dissemination of knowledge of normative Judaism.[105]

Nevertheless, *conversas* were mostly excluded from official tasks involving various rituals within the community while those women born into the normative Jewish tradition and in many cases related to famous *hakhamim* of the *kehilla* (community), were chosen by *parnassim* and *hakhamim* to perform those tasks. Consequently, these women assisted at births and the *mikveh* (ritual bath); they were assigned the task of separating the dough in bakeries, delivering the meal for matzot, preparing the *haroset* and *verduras* for Passover, printing *ketubbot* and working as *mortalhadeiras*, making shrouds and preparing the female corpses for burial.

Clara and Rachel Belilhos, the orphan daughters of Rabbi Daniel Belilhos and granddaughters of *Hakham* Isaac Aboab da Fonseca, were granted permission to print *ketubbot*.[106] Abigail de Leon, the daughter of Rabbi Jacob Juda Leon Templo, was paid to separate the portion of dough during the preparation of baking kosher bread.[107] Simha de Campos, the granddaughter of *Hakham* Isaac Uziel from North Africa was a midwife and her descendant was appointed a *mortalhadeira*.[108] Rachel and Ribca Pardo, in charge of the *mikveh*, belonged to the Pardo rabbinical family.[109] Also women producing and

---

104 Menasseh ben Israel, *Thesovro dos Dinim*, Part V (Amsterdam 1647), p. 118; see the famous Talmudic saying: "By what means do women acquire merit? By sending their sons to learn in the synagogue and their husbands to study in the school of the rabbis and waiting patiently for them to return home" (BT *Berakhot* 17a).

105 For more on private instruction at home, also Lieberman, "Childhood and Family," p. 158.

106 SAA 334, no. 25, p. 243, 27 Hesvan 5499.

107 SAA 334, no. 174, p. 610, Rosh Hodesh Tevet 5424.

108 SAA 334, no. 1329, carton 24: "Sª da Simha Partera da nacaº mulher q foi de Ymanuel do Campos fº em 16 bemaventurada Yiar Aº 5458" (see on her also Levie Bernfeld, *Poverty and Welfare*, p. 442, n. 104); for appointment of a *mortalhadeira* see that of Simha de Campos (SAA 334, no. 25, p. 170, 10 Kislev 5488); Sara de Aguilar was related to *Hakham* Moses Raphael d'Aguilar (SAA 334, no. 25, p. 308, 23 Hesvan 5507); for gifts to *mortalhadeiras* see SAA 334, no. 612, Not. D. van den Brink, 20 May 1754, last will of Ester Abrabanel widow of David of Samuel Pinto: "aan de vrouwen die mij sullen kisten (*as mortalhadeiras*)."

109 SAA 334, no. 24a, p. 64ᵛ, 13 Tishri 5444; on the aspect of purity among female Ashkenazim in Altona, D. Kaplan, "'To Immerse Their Wives': Communal Identity and the 'Kahalishe' *Mikveh* of Altona," *AJS Review* 36/2 (2012), p. 276. In Jewish society mostly widows were appointed to administer ritual baths: ead., "Women and Worth: Female Access to Property in Early Modern Urban Jewish Communities," *LBI Yearbook* 55 (2010), pp. 99–100.

repairing ceremonial objects were related to rabbinical families such as Juda Leon or Habilho.[110]

The rabbis may have accepted *conversas* as Jews but they avoided assigning them important ritual tasks, which suggests that they distrusted the newcomers' knowledge of Jewish law. This can also be deduced from the fierce tone used by the leadership forbidding women to replace their husbands as assistants making kosher bread, a practice carried out despite the warnings.[111] The Jewish leadership evidently preferred that women's duties in religious communal life be performed by women who they knew were familiar with the laws of normative Judiasm and could be relied on. Thus, most *conversas* newcomers were not empowered by the leaders to assume the functions connected to Jewish law allowed to be performed by women.[112] This state of affairs not only sheds light on the attitude of the leadership towards *conversas*, but also suggests that *conversas* were not informed enough on the laws of normative Judaism.

Applying Their Knowledge

After being taught the fundamentals of normative Judaism, women were expected to apply their newfound knowledge in the home. One woman, Sara Sarfati, had apparently mastered the Hebrew tongue.[113] In order to learn even

---

110   Levie Bernfeld, *Poverty and Welfare*, p. 195 and pp. 440–41, n. 98. In addition to local production, ceremonial textiles might have been imported. I did come across specific indications of the import of Torah mantles and bindings from Italy: T. Levie Bernfeld, "No matter. Matter: Material Culture of Dutch Sephardim (1600–1750)," *StRos* 44 (2012), p. 200 n. 32. Other mantles or covers seem to have been made in Italy as well: J.M. Cohen, "The Migration of Ceremonial: The Case of the Amsterdam Portuguese Jewish Torah Mantle," *StRos* 35/2 (2001), pp. 206–7; for Italian women making Torah binders, H.T. Adelman, "Italian Jewish Women," in *Jewish Women in Historical Perspective*, ed. J.R. Baskin, 2nd edition (Detroit 1998), p. 153; idem, "Rabbis and Reality," p. 32; for Italian women making synagogue and home textiles for ceremonial use: V.B. Mann, "The Arts of Jewish Italy," in *Gardens and Ghettos. The Art of Jewish Life in Italy*, ed. V.B. Mann (Berkeley 1989), pp. 55–57.

111   SAA 334, no. 24a, p. 6, 24 Hesvan 5425.

112   Some exceptions were made like those relating to the women coming from France in 1639 appointed to work at the new *mikveh* (Levie Bernfeld, *Poverty and Welfare*, p. 441, n. 99). Also a Spanish woman was put in charge of another *mikveh*, the so-called "Castellana do banho" (SAA 334, no. 215, p. 92, 18 Tishri 5425). These women must have been aware of and instructed about Jewish rules in their countries of birth or in places en route to Amsterdam.

113   Engraved on her gravestone in Hebrew is that she studied the Holy tongue and daily prayed the morning, afternoon and evening prayers (SAA 334, no. 1329, p. 134, no. 10, Sª de Sara Sarfatim q faleceo em 5 de Sivan 5457).

more about Judaism than she was allowed, Abigail Dias da Fonseca secretly listened in on the sessions of a study society held in her house, as other women likely did as well, perhaps in the Talmud Torah or in one of the other *hevrot* (study societies).[114] Miriam Alvares seems to have meticulously followed halakhah as she concluded her will with the request that her family live as God instructs them and for God to bless his creatures with His love and holy fear.[115]

Nevertheless, the community's leaders often had to warn women against transgressing particular laws. *Hakham* Saul Levi Mortera, for example, was very critical about women's observance of the laws of ritual purity, despite the many available ritual baths.[116] We know very little, as well, of the extent to which the religious dietary laws were observed. Sources from southern France tell of laxity in this area.[117] In the New World, Portuguese Jews were also known for their slack observance of Jewish dietary laws. In Georgia in 1738, Reverend Bolzius observed that "the Spanish and Portuguese Jews are not so strict insofar as eating is concerned as the others are. They eat, for instance, the beef that comes from the warehouse or that is sold anywhere else. The German Jews, on the other hand, would rather starve than eat meat they do not slaughter themselves."[118] While some *conversos* made every effort to refrain from eating meat on trips to Spain and Portugal, others apparently cared little while there about consuming forbidden food.[119]

---

114   Levie Bernfeld, "Sephardi Women in Holland's Golden Age," p. 197. For Benjamin Fisher's assertions on women's education see above n. 63; on women listening to study sessions while men were learning in Jerusalem, Lamdan, *Separate People.* pp. 110–11.

115   Last will of Miriam Alvares (for source see above n. 90).

116   Saperstein, *Exile in Amsterdam*, pp. 187, 189.

117   Graizbord, "Becoming Jewish," p. 167; idem, "A Historical Contextualization of Sephardi Apostates and Self-Styled Missionaries of the Seventeenth Century," *Jewish History* 19 (2005), p. 302: "they did not buy kosher meat when it was available to them since it was more expensive than the non-kosher variety"; for the lack of observance of *kashrut* among the Portuguese in Bordeaux, also C.L. Wilke, "Un moraliste rabbinique parmi les marranes de Bordeaux: Abraham de Oliveira et son *Celo del Temor de Dios*," in *L'écriture de l'histoire Juive*, ed. Iancu-Agou et Iancu, p. 365.

118   Cited by Reverend Bolzius, who led a group of Lutherans from Salzburg in Georgia, in a letter of 21 February 1738, addressed to Johann Heinrich Callenberg, head of a mission to Jews and other "non-believers" at Halle as a description of Jewish life in Savannah, in M.H. Stern, "New Light on the Jewish Settlement of Savannah," *AJHQ* 52/3 (1963), pp. 185–86; in Amsterdam, Ashkenazim were also found to eat forbidden meat or other products such as non-kosher cheese and milk: T. Rädecker, *Schuld en Boete in Joods Amsterdam. Kerktucht bij de Hoogduitse joodse gemeente 1737–1764* (Amsterdam 2012; Menasseh ben Israel Instituut Studies nr. 8), pp. 18–19, 21, 23–24, 26–27.

119   Saperstein, *Exile in Amsterdam*, pp. 158–59; Y. Kaplan, "The Travels of Portuguese Jews from Amsterdam to the 'Lands of Idolatry' (1644–1724)," in *Jews and Conversos. Studies in*

Some scholars argue that the dietary laws were generally followed within the Amsterdam Portuguese community.[120] However, the leadership did issue various warnings to safeguard the dietary laws. One explicitly directed at women, ordered that they no longer take bread from the ovens and walk with it in the streets after the start of the Sabbath.[121] Members of the community were rebuked for eating so-called "*craquelinges*" (Dutch cookies called "*krakelingen*"), "*cuquos de especias*" (spiced gingerbread) and other sweet pastries made with lard by local bakers, which were deemed a "violation of our Jewish law" and "*treife*" (non kosher).[122] *Hakham* Saul Levi Mortera alluded to the lack of observance of *kashrut* in Amsterdam and elsewhere in the 1620s and 30s and tried to encourage his public to change its habits.[123] In 1645, he castigated his public once more comparing their behavior to non-Jews: "we are like them in consuming their cheeses and their wine."[124] By 1750, Lea Curiel, widow of Moses Jezurun da Cunha, for example, not only ordered bread and pastry from non-Jews, but also wine.[125] There were some Dutch Sephardim and Ashkenazim who did not abide by the laws of the Passover festival and ate *hametz* (leavened bread).[126] In fact, there were cases where some Portuguese Jews bought *matzot* from non-Jewish bakers through Jewish intermediaries, a practice strongly disapproved of by the communal leaders.[127] Portuguese Jews in Amsterdam also bought their meat from Ashkenazi or private slaughterers. Apparently meat slaughtered by ritual slaughterers not authorized by the Portuguese communal leadership was cheaper and, therefore, more attractive. In an attempt to stem the loss of communal revenue and to salvage the livelihoods of the community's own ritual services providers, the leadership went so far as to designate

        Society and Inquisition, ed.Y. Kaplan (Jerusalem 1985), pp. 197–224; Graizbord, "Historical Contextualization," p. 297.

120   Daniel Swetschinski is convinced of an overall tendency to keep kosher, but he cites few sources to prove his point: Swetschinski, *Reluctant Cosmopolitans*, pp. 213–14, 271.

121   SAA 334, no. 19, p. 15/100, 10 Sivan 5399; see also an earlier regulation, ibid., no. 13, p. 64v./ 132, 25 September 5396.

122   SAA 334, no. 13, p. 140, 15 Shevat 5398.

123   Saperstein, *Exile in Amsterdam*, pp. 183–84, 186, 321–22.

124   Ibid., p. 190.

125   SAA 5072, no. 752, no. 35, 14 April 1750: "1749: Christoffel Scholten broodbakker f 1080; denselven voor geleverd broodt *f* 32; Burghard Keppel Banquetbacker *f* 127:10; Jan Pelletier banquetbakker *f* 5:8." In the purchase of wine, Lea seemed to be equally unattentive, sometimes buying the wine from Jews, sometimes from non-Jews, ibid.: "1748–1750: Jozeph Montel en David Valabrega voor wijnen *f* 98:7"; "1749 : Jan Berts wijnkoper *f* 216:5."

126   Rädecker, *Schuld en Boete*, pp. 27–29.

127   SAA 334, no. 10, p. 185/270, 4 Adar 5405.

the the competition's meat *"treife."*[128] The communal leadership tried to offer kosher products at competitive prices to the non-kosher market,[129] and provided a wide range of kosher staples to the community including meat, bread and cheese.[130] Special holiday foods such as *simurim* and *haroset* were distributed during the Passover holidays, as were matzot to those who could not afford

---

128   On an early sermon (1620) by *Hakham* Saul Levi Mortera not to buy meat slaughtered by non-Jews see Saperstein, *Exile in Amsterdam*, pp. 183–84; for the ban on buying meat from Ashkenazim, calling it *"terephah,"* see SAA 334, no. 19, p. 15/100, 10 Sivan 5399; ibid., p. 36/121, 13 Tevet 5400; see on the threat of *herem* (excommunication or ban) for buying meat anywhere else but in the Portuguese community, Kaplan, "Social Functions of the *Herem*," p. 122 and there note 24; the Ashkenazi community likewise prohibited their members from buying at the meat hall of the Portuguese Jews, calling meat slaughtered by Portuguese Jews *"treife"* as well (Rädecker, *Schuld en Boete*, p. 19); for the complaint of the Portuguese community concerning their members who sent their servants to the Ashkenazim to have their poultry slaughtered ritually (it was cheaper there) SAA 334, no. 25, p. 38, 6 Av 5456; for the warning in 1703 made by the Portuguese community—through a warning put out by the Ashkenazi community—that a certain *shokhet* (slaughterer) was active in different places in town, especially in the so-called Kaasmarkt and that this meat slaughtered by him was distributed by a *giyoret* (convert to Judaism), the widow of David Hamis, who used to bring home kosher meat to members of the Portuguese community, SAA 334, no. 25, p. 80, 19 Adar 5463; on the notification in synagogue not to buy meat brought in from abroad and sold to the members of the Portuguese community, SAA 334, no. 25, p. 99, 23 Tevet 5468; on income of the Portuguese community through the sale of kosher meat, Levie Bernfeld, *Poverty and Welfare*, pp. 142, 147, 387, nn. 20 and 21. On the foundation of the Portuguese Jewish meathall, A.M. Vaz Dias, "Losse Bijdragen tot de oudste geschiedenis der joden in Amsterdam," *De Vrijdagavond* 9/25, pp. 396–97, 16 September 1932. Among the Amsterdam Ashkenazi Jews we find similar tendencies to avoid buying meat offered through their meathall because of lower pricing offered outside of it and efforts by the same community to restrict such actions by punishing their members (Rädecker, *Schuld en Boete*, pp. 18–25; Levie Bernfeld, *Poverty and Welfare*, pp. 392–93, n. 54).

129   SAA 334, no. 24a, p. 21, 14 Tamuz 5429. For a similar situation among *converso* expatriates in France, Graizbord, "Historical Contextualization," p. 302; Ashkenazim also seem to have made and bought non-kosher cheese and milk (Rädecker, *Schuld en Boete*, pp. 25–27).

130   For instructions to buy kosher food products from the Portuguese community only, SAA 334, no.19, p. 24/109, 22 Tamuz 5399, art. 35; ibid., art. 36; for different instructions by the leadership to Portuguese assistants to bakers, SAA 334, no. 24a, p. 18, 19 Iyar 5428; ibid., no. 24a, p. 30v., 28 Tamuz 5433; ibid., no. 66a, 1 Kislev 5439; ibid., no. 25, p. 71, 15 Menahem [Av] 5462; ibid., no. 25, p. 92, 7 Av 5466; ibid., no. 912, pp. 1–2, 5495; for delivery of kosher cheese, SAA 334, no. 914; further for kosher cheese SAA 334, no. 25, p. 309, 19 Tevet 5507; for a common effort by the rabbis of the Portuguese and Ashkenazi communities to produce kosher cheese: SAA 334, no. 87, 1759.

them.[131] Clara Musaphia née Salom, who was born in Livorno, was one of the persons contracted by the community to deliver matzah meal and prepare *haroset* and *verduras* for the Passover celebration.[132] Special meal for the baking of *matzot* was even sent to Dutch Brazil for the Portuguese Jews living there.[133]

Documentary evidence shows that at least some women did make an effort to maintain a kosher home.[134] Many households apparently employed Jewish and non-Jewish servants, as did the household of Isaac Franco de Medeiros, which employed two servants, Sara and Maria.[135] Household tasks requiring knowledge of Jewish dietary laws were usually assigned to the Jewish maids. A poem written by a Sephardi girl, newly arrived in Amsterdam, tells of her role as a kitchen maid.[136] Lea Curiel employed an Ashkenazi kitchen maid.[137] Gracia Senior specifically left money in her will to the "*tudesquita*" who served her.[138] According to Menasseh ben Israel, Jewish law did not permit a non-Jewish servant to cook for a Jewish family unless assisted by a Jewish woman.[139] In fact, Inquisition records described *conversas* on the Peninsula instructing

131   *Simurim* is matzah that is made under strict rabbinical supervision from the time of harvest through the production process; widely used on the night of the *seder* and throughout Pesach by the more strictly observant. For the production of *haroset* and *simurim* see for example SAA 334, no. 218, p. 1, 13 Nisan–13 Sivan 5445; for the purchase of matzot, SAA 334, no. 218, p. 26, 13 Adar–10 Nisan 5445; for the distribution of matzot to the Jewish staff of the community and recipients of welfare, SAA 334, no. 218, pp. 63–70, 5446.

132   SAA 334, no. 217, p. 55, 26 Iyar 5437. For her place of origin, SAA, DTB 680, p. 82, 19 March 1649.

133   SAA 334, no. 174, p. 85, 20 Adar II 5415.

134   On the use of kosher food abroad and a kitchen by an Amsterdam Portuguese woman on a trip from Amsterdam to Le Havre in 1651, A.M. Vaz Dias, "Een blik in de Marranenhistorie: Gegevens uit het notarieel archief van Amsterdam," *De Vrijdagavond* 9/8 (1932), pp. 121–22.

135   Last will of Isaac Franco alias Francisco Mendes de Medeiros (for source see above n. 51); for a variety of people serving Portuguese families, Levie Bernfeld, *Poverty and Welfare*, pp. 199–200.

136   Cited in H. den Boer, "Exile in Sephard Literature in Amsterdam," *StRos* 35/2 (2001), pp. 198–99. The girl seemed to be descended from a rich family, but was left without means and forced to do kitchen work in her new abode.

137   SAA 5072, no. 752, no. 35, 14 April 1750: "1748–1750: Lea Isaacqs keukenmeyt voor 7 jaaren meijde loon tot mey 1750 *f* 390."

138   Levie Bernfeld, *Poverty and Welfare*, p. 200.

139   Menasseh ben Israel, *Thesovro dos Dinim*, Part IV (Amsterdam 1645), pp. 557–59: "Tratado dos cozinhados feitos por gentios." Also, it was forbidden for non-Jewish servant girls to take kosher meat from the meat hall or kosher slaughtered chickens without a Jewish person to assist: SAA 334, no. 19, p. 25/110, 22 Tamuz 5399, art. 41.

their maids to cook "kosher style."[140] Menasseh also alluded to the custom of Sephardi *Senhoras* hiring Jewish servants for their households.[141]

Despite inconsistencies in practice, Portuguese women, whether or not they knew any of the basic tenets of Judaism upon arrival, must have internalized the laws of normative Judaism to some degree, as we find Sabbath and Hanukkah lamps and Esther Scrolls listed in inventories among the contents found in the kitchen, dining area and best rooms of their homes, suggesting they were regularly used on the Sabbath and Jewish holidays.[142] Eighteenth-century prints show women of the Portuguese community engaged in preparations for and celebrating Jewish holidays.[143]

Thus, despite some lapses, most women aimed to live according to normative Judaism. Their religious fervor and pride in their Jewish identity was reaffirmed in the artwork that decorated their homes; for example, the homes of Amsterdam's Portuguese Jews contained significant numbers of paintings and tapestries featuring Jewish and biblical scenes, though paintings with scenes from the Hebrew Bible were also found in the homes of their Calvinist neighbors.[144] Still, the presence of these paintings, as well as of ceremonial objects, Bibles and prayer books in many homes of women suggests that most women were eager to express their allegiance to Judaism and show a strong and proud sense of their Jewish identity inside the home.[145]

A phrase frequently found in the testimonies of Portuguese women in Amsterdam asserted that they belonged to "the Portuguese and Spanish Jewish nation and believe in the Law of Moses, given on Mount Sinai by a powerful God." This same phrase was found as well on *converso* documents from Spain

---

140   Frade Veiga, "Portuguese 'Conversas' Home Circle," p. 71.

141   Menasseh ben Israel, *Thesovro dos Dinim*, Part IV (Amsterdam 1645), p. 497.

142   Levie Bernfeld, "Matters Matter," pp. 207–9.

143   B. Picart, *Cérémonies et coutumes religieuses de tous les peuples du monde, représentées par des figures dessinées de la main de Bernard Picart, Avec une explication historique, & quelques dissertations curieuses* (Amsterdam, 1733–1743); On Picart's portrayals of Jews, R.I. Cohen, *Jewish Icons. Art and Society in Modern Europe* (Berkeley 1998), pp. 43–52; also S. Baskind, "Bernard Picart's Etchings of Amsterdam's Jews," *Jewish Social Studies* 13/2 (2007), pp. 40–64. In the household of Eliasar de Leon special crockery for Passover was found, Th. Wijsenbeek-Olthuis, "Wooncultuur en sociale verschillen," in *Den Haag, Geschiedenis van de stad*, ed. Th. Wijsenbeek-Olthuis, vol. 2 (Zwolle 2005), p. 282.

144   As elsewhere in the Dutch Republic, these decorations with religious themes were alternated with those of non-religious ones like portraiture, landscape or vanitas paintings: Levie Bernfeld, "Matters Matter," pp. 210–13.

145   On *sifre torah* (Torah scrolls) in Portuguese households and other types of Judaica in early modern Amsterdam, Swetschinksi, *Reluctant Cosmopolitans*, p. 289 and Levie Bernfeld, "Matters Matter," pp. 207–9.

and Portugal.[146] In fact, the phrases "the Law of Moses given on Mount Sinai" and "the Holy Law that God gave to Moses on Mount Sinai," were expressions frequently found in the oaths and confessions of *conversos* before the Inquisition tribunal.[147] *Conversos* on the Peninsula also used this terminology in the belief that only observance of the Law of Moses could lead to their salvation.[148]

Once settled in the Jewish free world, *conversos* felt that they must atone for their sins, especially the transgressions they committed living as *conversos* in Spain and Portugal. Their anxiety surrounding sin was certainly influenced by the Iberian Catholic world in which they had been raised.[149] Portuguese women also seemed obsessed with Jewish laws surrounding death and mourning. The last wills of Portuguese Jews in Amsterdam often read like Jewish versions of the wills of Spanish Catholics, which began with a supplication and confession of faith, followed by judgment before God and a plea for mercy and salvation.[150]

After the obligatory remarks of repentance and salvation, the wills of Portuguese women included various instructions for ensuring that Jewish law is followed in all the rites and ceremonies surrounding their death and burial. In most of the wills consulted for this study, a strong desire was expressed for burial in the Jewish cemetery of "their nation and religion" (in Ouderkerk aan de Amstel or in a suitable manner should they die elsewhere or while on their journey to the Holy Land), not unlike the Catholics in Spain who explicitly stressed in their wills the importance of a religious burial.[151]

146 Kaplan, "Between Christianity and Judaism," p. 314.
147 For example Beinart, *Conversos on Trial*, index "Law of Moses"; Bodian, *Dying in the Law of Moses*, e.g. pp. 47, 49, 109; Levine Melammed, "Judaizers and Prayer," p. 274.
148 For example Beinart, *Conversos on Trial*, p. 266, n. 119; Levine Melammed, "Judaizers and Prayer," p. 286 n. 8: the confession of Isabel de Vega.
149 The widow Abigail Semah Cortiços alias Clara Gomes defined it thus: "I commend my soul always when it goes out of my body to the very powerful God and Lord of the world Who for His mercy will recollect me at the hour of salvation with complete repentance of my sins allowing my body a funeral among the Jews of my nation and religion hoping for beatitude and a blissful resurrection (last will of Abigail Semah Cortiços alias Clara Gomes: SAA 5075, no. 2890B, p. 1217, Not. P. Padthuysen, opened 10 March 1661); Miriam Alvares wrote down she commends her soul to God . . . to Whom she asks forgiveness for her sins in the hope He will apply to her His immense mercy (last will of Miriam Alvares; for source see above n. 90); see also the last will of Gracia Senior (for source see above n. 14), p. 1.
150 C.M.N. Eire, *From Madrid to Purgatory. The Art and Craft of Dying in Sixteenth-century Spain* (Cambridge 1995), pp. 68–86.
151 Ibid., pp. 91–105; for Amsterdam Portuguese women, for example the last will of Abigail Abarbanel, wife of Pinchas Abarbanel, who requested to be buried in "Beth Haim a place

The custom of distributing alms to the poor on the day of burial was a common practice in Spain.[152] Among the Portuguese in Amsterdam the distribution of alms at the funeral was followed by alms-giving at the end of the *shiva* (seven day Jewish mourning ritual), the *sheloshim* (thirty day post-burial commemoration) and at the end of the first year of mourning.[153] *Escavot* (special prayers for the repose of the soul of the dead) prayers were requested to be said in the synagogue or various yeshivot, similar to the Spanish Catholic practice of perpetual mass.[154] In exchange for the prayers, charitable donations were made to the synagogue, the synagogue's charity box, the poor, yeshivot and charitable organizations.[155] The urge to repent (especially in the seventeenth

    dedicated to the Jews in the village of Ouderkerk" (for source see above n. 43). Since Refica Barug meant to leave for Jerusalem, she did not specify the place of burial, but only the way of burial "according to the style of the Jews": SAA 5075, no. 2895A, p. 282, Not. P. Padthuysen, 27 February 1666).

152   Eire, *From Madrid to Purgatory*, pp. 141–48.

153   For Amsterdam the last will of Abigail Semah Cortiços (for source see above n. 149), p. 1218; the last will of Sara Torres (SAA 5075, no. 3720, p. 13, Not. F. Tixerandet, 23 June 1693); the last will of Johebet de Casseres (SAA 5075, no. 3280, no. 74, Not. H. Outgers, 21 November 1685).

154   Eire, *From Madrid to Purgatory*, pp. 200–10; for Amsterdam, the last will of Felipa de Saa in 1621(for source see above n. 11), p. 1501; further for gifts in exchange for saying the *kaddish* and *escavot* prayers and the lighting of a *ner tamid* (lit. eternal light), the following examples: Dona Sara Cahanet, who left money, among other things, for a *ner tamid* (SAA 334, no. 19, p. 175/260, 23 Av 5404); the heirs of Sara Dona Judique Miriam Soares, who donated a copper lamp for the same purpose (SAA 334, no. 19, p. 323, 28 Iyar 5412); that of Hana Aboab, who left a gift of *f* 1000, for the lighting of a *ner tamid* (SAA 334, no. 19, p. 234, 18 Kislev 5408); Dona Lea Abeniacar who left *f* 1000, for *escavot* prayers for her husband and a *ner tamid* (SAA 334, no. 19, p. 251, 29 Elul 5408); Ribca Mendes de Castro who left *f* 200, for *escavot* prayers in memory of her daughter (SAA 334, no. 19, p. 569, 15 Shevat 5427); Ribca Gabai Enriques who left *f* 200 for *escavot* prayers for her husband Isaac Gabai Henriques (SAA 334, no. 19, p. 800, 24 Elul 5438); Rachel Diaz Brandao, who gave *f* 500, for *escavot* prayers for her husband Abraham Diaz Brandao (SAA 334, no. 19, p. 807, 17 Kislev 5439); Abigail Semah Cortiços, who left money for her nephew to say *kaddish* (for source see above n. 149; p. 1218); Gracia Senior who made a bequest of two hundred guilders to the synagogue so that *escavot* prayers would be held permanently all *rashe hodes* (the first day of every new month) and on Yom Kippur. Moreover she gave fifty guilders to say *escavot* on Mondays and Thursdays and most likely also on the Sabbath (the text is quite unreadable here; it says "sauas" of the first year; for source see above n. 14) p. 2; see also the gift of Ester Mendez, who bequeathed two thousand guilders to the "*sedaca* [charity] box of her nation" in exchange for *escavot* prayers for her and her brother (SAA 5075, no. 2939, p. 100, 17 November 1698, Not. P. Padthuysen).

155   For example below (n. 161), the example of Abigail da Silva Pimentel, widow of Jacob da Silva.

century) was the predominant motive for charitable gifts.[156] Likewise, in Spain, there was a similar pattern of donations to the Church, charities, the poor, orphans and for dowries, redemption of captives, schools and confraternities.[157]

In Amsterdam, women mostly granted legacies to the yeshiva Ets Haim, the dowry society *Dotar* and the boys' orphanage Aby Jetomim. Twenty-seven percent of the gifts to the religious academy Ets Haim in the seventeenth century came from women, evidence of their strong commitment to the perpetuation of Jewish tradition.[158] Their grants to orphan girls, *Dotar* and other private dowry foundations were not just acts of benevolence, but stemmed from ethnic and religious concerns: these dowries made it possible for girls to marry men from their own Spanish and Portuguese nation in a free Jewish community enabling the strengthening and perpetuation of the nation and of Jewish family life. Orphan boys who received support through women's donations to Aby Jetomim were able to study, establish themselves within the Jewish community and raise a family.[159] Women's charity also benefited the Spanish and Portuguese nation worldwide and was used chiefly to help ransom captives and aid the poor in the Holy Land. Giving charity expressed the Spanish Portuguese nation's bond with the Jewish people everywhere and its embrace of the principles of Jewish welfare.[160]

Many of the above-mentioned aspects crystallized in the will of Abigail da Silva Pimentel, widow of Jacob da Silva: she not only asked pardon for her sins, but also detailed all the ceremonial arrangements around her funeral and burial. She set money aside to pay for the coffin, the boat to transport her body to

156 Levie Bernfeld, *Poverty and Charity*, pp. 124, 159–66, and 169; on the theme of repentance in the sermons of *Hakham* Saul Levi Mortera, Saperstein, *Exile in Amsterdam, index.*

157 Eire, *From Madrid to Purgatory*, pp. 134–41, 232–47.

158 Levie Bernfeld, *Poverty and Welfare*, p. 399, n. 125; Zimmels also mentions women elsewhere in the Sephardi Diaspora, supporting scholars and students of Jewish law: Zimmels, *Die Marranen,* pp. 59–60. For examples of Portuguese women bequeathing gifts to Ets Haim, Abigail Semah Cortiços: "Item deixo mais florins vinte e çinco a es Haim" (for source see above n. 149), p. 1218. For the gift of Sara Cohen de Herrera to Ets Haim, SAA 334, no. 1052, pp. 9v–10, 20 Elul 5404.

159 More on female involvement in charitable activities in Levie Bernfeld, *Poverty and Welfare*, pp. 105, 174, 179, 183, 398–99 n. 125.

160 For example the last will of Johebet de Casseres, who besides giving to the yeshiva Ets Haim, also took care of people in captivity as well as those living in Eretz Israel (for source see above n. 153); also Rica de Leon gave, besides a gift of three hundred guilders to the *sedaca* funds of the Amsterdam Portuguese community, one of thirty guilders to the Cativos fund and one of thirty guilders to the "*tierra santa*" or Jerusalem (last will of Rica de Leon, alias Maria Pereyra, wife of Moses de Leon, alias Roque de Leon: SAA 5075, no. 7533, p. 1198, Not. J. van Vilekens, 31 October 1710).

the Jewish cemetery and the lamp to be lit in the synagogue and in her house, day and night, during the seven-day mourning period. People were assigned to recite the memorial (*kaddish*) prayer at her grave. She left money for the community charity box to have the *escava* prayer recited in the synagogue on Yom Kippur and on the first day of the new month throughout the year. Money and goods were also left to be distributed among the poor, orphans and the women who washed her corpse. Finally, alms were given to different institutions, such as Ets Haim (also on condition the *escava* be said), Aby Yetomim, Cativos and Terra Santa.[161]

Not only widows showed their independence of thought, action and pride in their Jewish identity in their final requests, as the last will and testament of Sara Alvares illustrates. Contrary to the instructions of Menasseh ben Israel to married women to behave humbly towards their husbands, Sara acted quite to the contrary: on her deathbed, and without consulting her husband who was residing at the time in London, she apportioned sums from her husband's estate to be donated to pious works upon her death.[162] In so doing, and in the traditional wording used in her will, "I am a Jew of the Portuguese nation and believe in the Law as God gave it to Moses on Mount Sinai, through which I hope to be saved," she showed herself to be in control of her own convictions and wholly committed to her Jewish faith.[163] The women of Amsterdam's Portuguese community demonstrated their trust in the leadership by naming *parnassim* and *hakhamim* as executors of their wills.[164] In addition to leaving the

---

161   SAA 5075, no. 2209, Not. A. Lock, pp. 1034–35, 19 December 1660. Also cited by L. Hagoort, *Het Beth Haim in Ouderkerk aan de Amstel: de begraafplaats van de Portugese Joden in Amsterdam 1614–1945* (Hilversum 2005), pp. 60–61.

162   For Sara Alvares' gift of *f* 1000 to the synagogue, her last will (for source, above n. 42), p. 1108; also SAA 334, no. 19, p. 818, 14 Menahem [Av] 5439; the gift was part of a whole package of gifts which amounted to a total of 1940 guilders, which Sara gave away. They included, besides legacies to the building of the synagogue, also those for oil (*f* 40) and to the charity box of the community on condition *escavot* be said on the usual days, Ets Haim (*f* 200), Dotar (*f* 200) and Aby Yetomim (*f* 100). The Portuguese leadership, however, did not accept her gifts only after the approval of her husband.

163   Last will of Sara Alvares (for source see above n. 42), p. 1106.

164   For example, the last will of Gracia Senior. The *Mahamad* was appointed as executors of her last will (for source see above n. 14; p. 1); Miriam Alvares appointed the *Mahamad* in the company of her brother Joseph Alvarez to be the executors of her testament (for source see above n. 90); Ester Mendez, a single woman, also made the leaders of the community the executors of her testament (SAA 5075, no. 2939, p. 101, Not. P. Padthuysen, 17 November 1698); Sara Torres was a widow and also made the leaders of the community the executors of her will (for source see above n. 153). For the appointment of *hakhamim* as executors of women's last wills, see last will of Miriam Alvares who reserved a gift to

community monetary endowments, often extremely large sums, some women also bequeathed beautiful ceremonial objects to the synagogue including Torah mantles and silver and silver-gilt plates and jugs and even Torah scrolls.[165] Women requested in their wills for particular *hazanim* (cantors) to recite the *kaddish*, setting aside sums in their wills for that purpose.[166] The communal leaders also channeled funds to the poor. When Sara Lumbrosa returned to Judaism in 1667 following her conversion to the Reformed Church, *Hakham* Aboab intervened to have her placed on a monthly welfare list.[167] Likewise, in

Hakham Isaac Aboab da Fonseca and requested from him to distribute money among the poor of her *nação*—separate from the poor among her family (for source see above n. 90); on priority of gifts to poor family members, Levie Bernfeld, *Poverty and Welfare*, pp. 171–75; Sara Alvares also appointed *Hakham* Isaac Aboab da Fonseca as the executor of her testament and charged him with distribution of two hundred guilders to whom he saw fit (for source see above n. 42; pp. 1106–8).

165 Last will of Ester Pinta (SAA 5075, no. 414, p. 542, Not. N. Jacobs, 16 December 1636). Ester left her community the wooden box, presently in her house, in which pieces for her synagogue (Beit Israel) were kept. She also granted the *kahal* other pieces, used in her synagogue for Yom Kippur and at the cemetery of Beth Haim. Dona Sara Cahanet bestowed upon the synagogue two silver pieces, a plate and a can, to be used in the service for the *cohanim* (SAA 334, no. 1074, pp. 1–2, 5404 [1644]). Abigail Dias da Fonseca, on her deathbed, bequeathed the synagogue what she already gave in life, namely a *sefer torah* with embroidered mantles and silver *rimmonim* (SAA 334, no. 700, p. 4, 30 March 1703); Ester Morena, widow of Jacob Morena also granted the Portuguese community a *sefer torah* with all the ornaments and silver *rimmonim* and two mantels—a white one with flowers and one with silk flowers, including the *faxas* (ribbons used to wrap around the torah scroll to tie it) (SAA 334, no. 24, p. 22 22 Elul 5409) on condition that *escavot* will be recited. Gifts were even given to their (Jewish) community of origin: the case of Ribca de Granada, widow of Joseph Bueno de Mesquita. In her testament written in Amsterdam, she left the sum of eight hundred guilders to fulfill her vow to bequeath a *sefer torah* to a synagogue in "Tetuan in Berberia" (SAA 5075, no. 8820, no. 363, Not. J. Barels, 6 June 1731); further Levie Bernfeld, "Matters Matter," p. 208; for donations of ceremonial objects by Ashkenazim: J.-M. Cohen, "Donation as a Social Phenomenon: Synagogue Textiles of the Ashkenazi Community of Amsterdam in the Eighteenth and Nineteenth Centuries," *StRos* 32/1(1998), pp. 24–42.

166 Gracia Senior reserved an amount of fifty guilders to pay *hazzan* Faro, or in his absence, his son, *rubi* Faro, to say *kaddish*: last will of Gracia Senior (for source see above n. 14; p. 2); Miriam Alvares requested *hazzan* Abenatar to help her pray at her deathbed and for orphans to say *kaddish*: it would all be paid for (for source see above n. 90); Sara Alvares requested R. Daniel Belilhos to say *kaddish*, for which she reserved money (for source see above n. 42; pp. 1106–8).

167 Levie Bernfeld, *Poverty and Welfare*, pp. 120–21; ibid., p. 221, pp. 474–75 n. 390, p. 476 n. 398, p. 479 n. 415, p. 481 n. 420, p. 484 n. 442.

1670, he transferred a sum of around nineteen guilders to Judith Henriques de Sanlucar—her son had been excommunicated around 1661—so that she could marry off her daughter.[168]

Women's Activities in the *Kahal*

The lives of women in Amsterdam's Portuguese community were not only centered around the management of home and family. Women also ventured outside the home to participate in the religious and social life of the community, so far as they were allowed.

Judging from the several edicts that emanated from the *Mahamad*, it seems that women were frequent synagogue goers. Some wealthy women promised gifts (*promessas*) to the synagogue during prayer services.[169] Women also contributed funds toward the building of the famous Esnoga.[170] Moreover, many women gave generous donations on condition that prayers will be recited in the synagogue in memory of their loved ones. It is possible that these women went to synagogue to hear them being said. The English diarist John Evelyn described his visit to the synagogue in Amsterdam in 1641 and mentioned especially the presence of women in the upper galleries.[171] Good seats in the women's section were apparently in high demand as servants (*moças, mulattas* and *negras*) were ordered to sit from the fourth row in the women's section, and *tudescas* were told to go to their own synagogue.[172] Women's attendance in synagogue at night and in the early morning was frowned upon and at a certain point even forbidden, though the admonishment does show their desire to attend.[173]

---

168   SAA 334, no. 216, p. 2, 4 Tamuz 5430: f 18:18; also on her and her son, Levie Bernfeld, *Poverty and Welfare*, p. 121.

169   SAA 334, no. 175, p. 316, 1 Nisan 5440.

170   SAA 334, no.19, pp. 623–26, 9 Kislev 5431. Around ten percent of the contributors at that time were women (fifty-seven in total); further, ibid. no. 172, p. 32, 28 Tishri 5400; ibid., no. 175, p. 111, 1 Nisan 5440. For other contributions to the building of the new synagogue, the gift of Rachel Gomes Porto (SAA 334, no. 19, p. 670, 12 Adar 5433); for the gift of four hundred guilders by Miriam Alvares to the synagogue see her last will (for source see above n. 90).

171   *The Diary of John Evelyn,* ed. E.S. de Beer (Oxford 1959), p. 25; also cited in Kaplan, "For Whom did Emanuel de Witte Paint His Three Pictures in the Sephardi Synagogue in Amsterdam?" *StRos* 32/2 (1998), p. 137.

172   SAA 334, no. 19, p. 80/165, 18 Elul 5401.

173   Levie Bernfeld, "Sephardi Women in Holland's Golden Age," p. 182 and p. 205 n. 44.

In addition to restricting their attendance in synagogue, women were also not permitted a prominent role in the management of the community or in any of its welfare organizations. Limiting the role of women accorded with the patriarchal nature of the community and the Iberian culture of secluding women from the public sphere. Unlike their female counterparts in other Jewish communities in Europe, women in the Portuguese community in Amsterdam never initiated the establishment of any new societies, but sometimes they were permitted to hold minor roles in the administration of existing ones.[174] On the other hand, their communal role was not completely ignored. In fact, women became very dedicated members of different societies and charitable organizations in the Amsterdam Portuguese community and, as noted above, were also eager financial supporters. The earnestness with which they undertook these roles suggests that many *conversas* must have been in the habit of participating in different social and charitable organizations in Spain and Portugal. Indeed, female participation in confraternities was a common phenomenon in southern Europe during the Middle Ages and the early modern period.[175]

Though Portuguese women in Amsterdam joined these societies and gave to charities out of a sense of religious conviction, they also did it for social reasons. By becoming a member of such a society, a woman was assured of help and financial assistance if she were ever to find herself in need of aid.[176] In fact, many organizations and private endowments were established specifically for girls, women and widows, to provide them with shelter, dowries or monies for food and clothes.[177] By joining these *hevrot* or setting up foundations of their own intended specifically to alleviate the plight of women, those more fortunate Portuguese women showed their solidarity with their sex, at home and

---

174   Ibid., pp. 194–96; Debra Kaplan mentions many such initiatives by women for Prague and the German Lands, ead., "Women and Worth," p. 105.
175   For women involved in confraternities in Spain see M. Flynn, *Sacred Charity. Confraternities and Social Welfare in Spain 1400–1700* (Hampshire and London 1989), pp. 23–24, 56; for Italy, G. Casagrande, "Confraternities and Lay Female Religiosity in Late Medieval and Renaissance Umbria," in *The Politics of Ritual Kinship. Confraternities and Social Order in Early Modern Italy*, ed. N. Terpstra (Cambridge 2000), pp. 48–66; for France, N. Zemon Davis, "City Women and Religious Change," in *Society and Culture in Early Modern France*, ed. N. Zemon Davis (Stanford 1975), p. 75.
176   *Temime Darekh* was such a mutual aid society, very useful and helpful for women. Johebed de Casseres had belonged to it and left it a legacy in exchange for prayers in their yeshivah in her memory and in that of her husband and her mother (for source see above n. 153); more on mutual aid societies and women as their members in Levie Bernfeld, *Poverty and Welfare*, pp. 125–27.
177   Levie Bernfeld, *Poverty and Welfare*, pp. 130–32.

abroad.[178] Poor women sought help from these organizations when they first arrived in Amsterdam or at later points in their lives. In fact, the appeal of such a vast network of available charitable organizations was factored into women's decisions whether to choose Amsterdam as their migration destination. The communal leadership viewed women's involvement in charitable organizations as a way for them to reinforce their supervisory role over their female constituents: women's activities within these societies helped them become familiar with Judaism, not only as a religion, but as a comprehensive way of life.

Peer Pressure

While the majority of Amsterdam's Portuguese *conversas* in the Golden Age returned to normative Judaism without much persuasion and willingly took up the traditional roles designated for women in their new society, quite a few sources suggest that some form of coercion was exerted on *conversas*, not only by the leadership, but also by their peers to bring them into the fold. Women who turned their backs on their ancestral heritage and adopted another were often shunned or isolated.[179]

Many former *conversos* took their newly acquired identity quite seriously and reacted fiercely towards those who chose a different spiritual path or preferred to remain in Catholic areas or even to convert. Conversion in early modern Europe was a very sensitive issue that aroused tremendous anger towards the defectors. For the Portuguese Jews, the animosity was directed against Christianity and the Christians who had made *conversos* into outcasts on the

---

178   Abigail Semah Cortiços, for example, left her simple daily clothes and linen to widows and poor orphan girls (for source see above n. 149), p. 1218; as mentioned earlier, Ester Abrabanel, widow of David de Samuel Pinto, left money to be divided among the women who will wash her corpse and dress it (for source see above n. 108); for charity among Ashkenazi women in Germany, the examples given by Debra Kaplan in "Women and Worth," pp. 98, 103–5.

179   For unconditional legacies of Portuguese Jews in Amsterdam to their family and friends on the Peninsula see for example SAA 5075, no. 2261A, Not. A. Lock, 29 January 1655, p. 591: Inventaris van Sr Henrique Mendes da Silva and Isabella Perera; for efforts to convince *conversos* to leave the Peninsula see for example the efforts of Eliahu Montalto in C. Roth, "Quatre lettres d'Elie de Montalte," REJ 87 (1929), pp. 137–65; also the efforts of Abraham Idaña to convince *conversos* to leave the Peninsula in B.N. Teensma, "Fragmenten uit het Amsterdamse convoluut van Abraham Idaña, alias Gaspar Méndez del Arroyo (1623–1690)," St Ros 11/2 (1977), pp. 126–56; for the attitude of Saul Levi Mortera on *conversos* preferring to stay on the Peninsula in Saperstein, *Exile in Amsterdam*, pp. 278–97.

Iberian Peninsula. It should not be surprising, therefore, that in Amsterdam they directed their rage towards *conversos* who chose differently.[180]

Some women tried to extert pressure on family members by excluding them from legacies if they did not comply. The conditions these women set in their wills were mostly, but not always, cloaked in religious terms. Lea Henriques encouraged her nieces, still living in Spain, to come to live in Amsterdam as an explicit condition for a legacy, though no other conditions were set that might infer religious motives.[181] Miriam Alvares's last will on the other hand, shows a strong aversion to Catholicism: she refused to leave money to a niece in Italy who had become a nun.[182] Many women's wills had religious motives, with potential heirs being informed that in order to inherit they must join the Jewish world. Ribca Carneira, for example, left one thousand guilders to her nephews, who at the time were in the Indias as it is noted, on condition that they return to this country or any other country of *judesmo*.[183] Rachel Pinta left a similar sum to her brother in Madrid, as a gift in case he will come to Amsterdam, to the Jewish world: "*aqui al judaismo*."[184] Also Rica de Leon made her legacy to her family conditional, her family in this case being her niece Maria Gomes who was then a nun in Toulouse, insisting that she come to live in a place in which she could publicly observe the Jewish religion as she described it.[185]

The women of Amsterdam's Portuguese community sought not only to influence family members living abroad, but were as involved as the men in the religious fervor pervading the town,[186] and engaged in discussions on religious matters with the local non-Jewish population. Starting in 1630, the Portuguese leadership in Amsterdam periodically admonished male and female members

---

180 See for verbal abuse by members of the Portuguese community of a Portuguese Jewish woman who joined the Reformed Church in 1695, Levie Bernfeld, *Poverty and Welfare*, p. 472, n. 371.

181 SAA 5075, no. 4246, p. 579, Not. D. van der Groe, 5 February 1698.

182 Last will of Miriam Alvares (for source see above n. 90).

183 It deals here with the sons of her brother Mendo Lopez del Campo. It seems they never showed up in Amsterdam (SAA 334, no. 19, pp. 301–2, 8 Adar 5411; ibid., no. 174, p. 505, 13 Nisan 5422).

184 He would not get anything if he decided to stay; last will of Rachel Pinta (for source, above n. 43), pp. 978–79.

185 "[A] vivir ij observar publicamente la Religion judaica em parte donde lo puedo hazer libremente"; five hundred guilders was promised as a reward if she would do so, four years after Rica's death: last will of Rica de Leon (for source see above n. 160), p. 1199.

186 On social pressure to embrace normative Judaism in southern France, see Graizbord, "Becoming Jewish," p. 165.

for endangering the freedom they enjoyed there by debating religion with the city's Christian inhabitants.[187]

Indeed, the strong reactions of women to those persons who decided to join the Reformed Church reveals much about their attitude towards Christianity.[188] No wonder many converts to Christianity—rich and poor—often bowed under the pressure and returned to the Jewish community, the alternative being isolation.[189] Many defectors were overwhelmed by loneliness and regretted their conversion.[190] Others did not. Gracia Baruch, for example, managed to withstand the pressure and went through with her conversion to Catholicism, even though she was aware, as she stated, it would not meet with the approval of her Jewish friends.[191]

Moral Behavior

Since much of the Portuguese community was made up of women who were either alone or on their own while their husbands were traveling abroad, the leadership strictly supervised their moral conduct. They instituted measures that would prevent unpleasant incidents, keep order in the community and present *bom judesmo* (proper Judaism) to the outside world.[192] To ensure that women showed "*bom modo*" (proper behavior), women were prohibited from visiting synagogue at night to listen to sermons or in the early morning hours, except for the nights of Tisha b'Av, Yom Kippur and Taanit Esther (the fast day

---

187   See the example of 1640, based on an earlier one from 1630 not to discuss religious matters with Christians in order not to endanger the freedom Portuguese Jews enjoyed in Amsterdam, cited in Y. Kaplan, "'Gente política': The Portuguese Jews of Amsterdam vis-à-vis Dutch Society," in *Dutch Jews as Perceived by Themselves and by Others*, pp. 32–33; idem, "Social Functions," p. 122; and SAA 334, no. 13, p. 61, 5391[s.d.]; ibid., no. 19, p. 25/110, 22 Tamuz 5399, art. 38. On Jews performing tasks in front of their homes on Christian holidays, SAA 334, no. 24a, p. 41v., 20 Sivan 5437.

188   See the case of the above-mentioned Sara Lumbrosa in Levie Bernfeld, *Poverty and Welfare*, pp. 215–16.

189   On facing isolation if not embracing Judaism, Graizbord, "Becoming Jewish," pp. 165–66.

190   For example, the case of Sara de Pas: SAA, no. 376, no. 15, p. 82, 14 December 1684; ibid., p. 83, 21 December 1684; ibid., p. 86, 11 January 1685; see also the case of Sara Lumbrosa mentioned before.

191   On her and her different activities Levie Bernfeld, *Poverty and Welfare*, pp. 220–21, p. 475 n. 395, p. 481 n. 420 and p. 484 n. 442.

192   On *bom judesmo*, see Kaplan, "Gente política," esp. pp. 28–30.

before the Purim holiday), and the entrance to the women's section was closed at night and in the early morning.[193]

The leadership also tried to extend its control over other areas of female behavior, including dress. *Hakhamim* repeatedly warned women about their extravagant style of dress, including their abundant jewellery. The admonishment was not well received.[194] Apparently, wealthy women of the community loved to dress conspicuously, and the religious leaders had too little influence in this matter in order to effect any real change. In many Sephardi Jewish communities in the Netherlands and beyond and also in the non-Jewish world, sumptuary laws were threatened and at times applied, though to questionable success.[195] Both the Jewish and Christian clergy in seventeenth-century Amsterdam delivered many sermons to their respective communities against excessive luxury. *Hakham* Saul Levi Mortera lamented that "only those who dress ostentatiously are honored and garments are a prime source of prestige."[196] Besides showy and indecent dress, *hakhamim* also rebuked married women who did not cover their hair. This laxity in dress ran counter, in their words, to the "chastity the daughters of Israel should observe, recommended in our Holy Law, underlined by the prophets, elaborated in good doctrine by our sages."[197]

---

193   Levie Bernfeld, "Sephardi Women in Holland's Golden Age," p. 182.

194   In the seventeenth century repeated efforts were made to reduce excesses in dress, but to no avail (SAA 334, no. 19, pp. 217–19, 2 Tevet 5407/5 Adar 5407); more on this in Kaplan, "Gente política," p. 31. No documentation as been found so far on the prohibition to wear clothing that contained a mixture of wool and linen; among the Ashkenazim we do find such regulations (Rädecker, *Schuld en Boete,* pp. 29–31).

195   For the Amsterdam Portuguese, SAA 334, no. 19, pp. 217–19, 2 Tevet 5407/5 Adar 5407; for Jews in Italy, Adelman, "Italian Jewish Women," p. 153; idem, "Rabbis and Reality," pp. 29–30; for Jews in the Levant, Lamdan, *Separate People,* pp. 106–9; for a review of sumptuary laws in Christian Europe, M.G. Muzzarelli, "Reconciling the Privilege of a Few with the Common Good: Sumptuary Laws in Medieval and Early Modern Europe," *Journal of Medieval and Early Modern Studies* 39/3(2009), pp. 597–617.

196   Saperstein, *Exile in Amsterdam,* p. 193.

197   For the address by the leaders of the Mahamad in the synagogue of 8 Hesvan 5482, see above n. 99; admonitions concerning immodesty of women were not new but were expressed many times in Jewish, Christian and Muslim societies: Grossman, *Pious and Rebellious,* pp. 102–22. Portuguese Jewish ladies do not seem to take the prohibitions of the rabbis too much to heart seeing the presence of many a hoop skirt in Portuguese inventories: Isaak and Menasse Losada (SAA 5072, no. 649, p. 321, 9 January 1731); Isaak Rodrigues Parera (SAA 5072, no. 656, p. 154, 5 June 1738). Ashkenazi women seem to have ignored the eighteenth-century prohibitions on dress equally, as expressed by the Amsterdam Ashkenazi community (Rädecker, *Schuld en Boete,* pp. 48–50). In Protestant milieus there was opposition to the so-called hoop skirt as well (Davis, "City Women," pp. 85–86); on

Their criticism was to no avail. Wealthy Portuguese women continued to dress according to European fashion of the time. Many portraits from the eighteenth century show them in décolletage gowns and with uncovered hair.[198]

Girls were strictly supervised and prevented from engaging in contact outside of home.[199] In order to be able to participate in its lottery, the dowry society *Dotar* demanded a maiden be worthy, as confirmed in the petition by Ester de Chaves, in which witnesses maintained she is "onrada virtuoza y onesta" (a virtuous and honest maiden).[200] Gracia Franka, on the other hand, was anything but and was, therefore, barred from her claim to a dowry from the *Dotar* society because she had given birth to a baby before she was wed.[201]

Despite the various measures to safeguard the community's unmarried and married women, quite a few incidents of indecent conduct came to the leadership's attention and the perpetrators were punished to varying degrees by the community leaders. Punishment ranged from withdrawing welfare benefits to expulsion from the community.[202] Those who were dependent on charity generally followed the new rules in order to not compromise their benefits. A few women who were unable to adjust to the role of the well behaved modest Jewish woman were involved in small conflicts in town.[203] And then there were some women who were not willing to abide by the leadership's strict control and either rebelled or went so far as to turn their backs on the community completely. They preferred to choose what best suited them, either out of religious conviction or love for a person of a different faith. Conversion to Christianity was not exclusive to the Portuguese community.[204] There were also

---

hairstyle and dress in the eighteenth century, H. Michels, *Uiterlijk schoon. Haardracht en opsmuk door de eeuwen heen* (Baarn 1994), Chaps. 6 and 7; also Teensma, "Fragmenten," pp. 26, 33.

198 Levie Bernfeld, "Sephardi Women in Holland's Golden Age," pp. 199, 221 n. 247.

199 Levie Bernfeld, *Poverty and Welfare*, p. 101; eadem, "Sephardi Women in Holland's Golden Age," pp. 177, 182.

200 SAA 334, no. 1153, p. 281, 14 Rosh Hodesh Shevat 5459.

201 Levie Bernfeld, *Poverty and Welfare*, p. 9. In early modern Europe, many girls were found to be pregnant before marriage, Roodenburg, *Onder Censuur*, pp. 255–57.

202 Kaplan, "Threat of Eros," pp. 104–7, 108–9; Kaplan, "Social Functions," pp. 128–29 and there notes 45 and 46, p. 131 and there n. 54; p. 132, p. 133 and there n. 62; p. 136; also Levie Bernfeld, "Sephardi Women in Holland's Golden Age," pp. 182–83; Levie Bernfeld, *Poverty and Welfare*, p. 91.

203 Levie Bernfeld, *Poverty and Welfare*, p. 214.

204 See the case of Sara Jacobs Mettera who maintained she had been a Christian first, became a Jew later but finally chose the Lutheran Church, Levie Bernfeld, *Poverty and Welfare*, p. 221.

cases of conversion among the Ashkenazi community in Amsterdam.[205] A few women from the Portuguese community showed no interest in any religion whatsoever and chose to live independent of the community. They earned their living through crime or prostitution, in defiance of all the rules of normative Judaism.[206]

In the eighteenth century more and more women challenged the boundaries drawn for them by the communal authorities. Admonitions were no longer effective, as greater numbers of women tended not to live according to the strict letter of the (Jewish) law and strayed from what was considered decent, proper and respectable behavior among the Western Sephardim. More cases of adultery surfaced.[207] In *Dotar*, the moral conduct of candidates for a dowry continued to be an issue: in 1747 the *Dotar* board emphasized once more that girls would not be eligible for a dowry through the society and would risk losing one that had already been awarded if "they trespass[ed] the limits of modesty and chastity that the daughters of Israel should observe."[208] Women customarily visited Jewish taverns to eat and drink alongside men. During the Purim holiday masquerades they even dressed up as men and mingled with them.[209] The severe punishments meted out to men and women for deviant conduct points not only to the increasing laxity in conforming to and strictly abiding by the rules of normative Judaism, but also the greater frustration on the part of the leadership to deal with the lack of discipline.[210] Thus, there was an ever growing gap between the intentions of the leadership and the lifestyle of the members of the *nação*.

Conclusion

Not all *conversas* who arrived in Amsterdam came out of a deep desire to embrace Judaism in the free world. There were many other factors. It might be,

205 See the case of Anna Margareta Bon alias Roosje Gabriel Wolf: Haags Gemeentearchief, BNR 351, no. 110, pp. 15–16, 16 December 1781; also that of Samuel Abrahams: SAA 5075, no. 6598, pp. 899–902, Not. G. van der Groe, 6 December 1703.
206 See for example the cases of Sara Olivier and Gracia Baruch in Levie Bernfeld, "Sephardi Women in Holland's Golden Age," pp. 188–89.
207 Kaplan, "Threat of Eros," p. 107. See for example the case of the child of the wife of Abraham de Israel Ricardo, born in 1745: SAA 334, no. 25, p. 291, 30 Tishri 5505. Rabbis were very keen to register such cases as comes to light in this decision of the Beit Din of 5505.
208 Levie Bernfeld, *Poverty and Welfare*, pp. 91–92; see also Levie Bernfeld, *Dowries and Dotar. An Unbroken Chain of 400 Years* (Amsterdam 2015), pp. 41–42.
209 SAA 334, no. 118, file 1, p. 31, 10 Adar 5492.
210 Kaplan, "Threat of Eros"; idem, "Moral Panic," pp. 103–23.

as François Soyer maintained, that their religiosity was fluctuating, adapted to circumstances, as was the case on the Peninsula.[211] Nevertheless, the fact is that many *conversas* in Amsterdam did show a deep commitment to Judaism and Jewish communal life, upon their arrival and later.

Reading all the rules of Jewish law as summed up by Menasseh ben Israel in his *Thesovro dos Dinim*, must have been a daunting undertaking for the newly arrived *conversas*. They likely felt insecure about the maintaining of a kosher household. They may even have resisted being relegated to a Jewish woman's traditional role after having played such an important role in the home in Spain and Portugal. It must have been equally difficult for them to follow all the other regulations of normative Judaism, which were so alien to their daily life. Even those women who were known judaizers on the Peninsula, and did their utmost to conform to a Jewish lifestyle in a hostile environment, had to bridge an enormous gap upon their arrival in Amsterdam.

For its part, the Amsterdam Portuguese community expended great effort to return Portuguese *conversas* to the path of normative Judaism and keep them there. Rabbis were aware of the tremendous gaps in these women's knowledge of Judaism. Menasseh ben Israel and others took up the task of writing compendiums of religious laws for this very purpose. Moreover, husbands and male children, instructed into Jewish law in the different study circles, religious schools and academies of the community, must have encouraged the women at home to become familiar with the wide range of rules pertaining to Jewish law. Jewish servants could also have been a source of valuable information to assist the good governance of the Jewish home and family.

It is difficult to know whether the first generation *conversas* in Amsterdam embraced Judaism as religious belief in the Law of Moses, cognizant that it encompassed a complete way of life. Too few sources provide us insight into the daily routines and religious lives of these women. The leadership remained skeptical about the level of knowledge of normative Judaism among *conversas*. Rabbis refrained from giving them tasks requiring a profound understanding of normative Judaism. In their eyes, apparently, the female newcomers lacked sufficient knowledge to deal with complicated matters involving Jewish law. Therefore, Yosef's Kaplan's view that the belief of *conversos* and New Jews in Moses' law was more important to them than observing halakhah and that their behavior was very far from Talmudic tradition, could be applied to quite a few *conversas* in Amsterdam.[212]

---

211 He relates to a group of *conversas* arrested in Córdoba who were accused of Christiantity and Judaism at the same time. Soyer, "It Is Not Possible," pp. 91–92.

212 Kaplan, "Between Christianity and Judaism," p. 331.

Some did transgress the rules of normative Judaism, intentionally or through
ignorance. Moreover, the strictures and supervision alienated many women
from normative Judaism and the Jewish community. Instead, they tried their
luck elsewhere, in the Reformed Church or in the more familiar Catholic environment. Others detached themselves from all religious frameworks, going so
far as to join the criminal ranks of society.

Nevertheless, it seems that the leadership was quite successful in reaching
its goals. The majority of women were dedicated and active members in the
community, honored for their virtue and charity and complacent with their
traditional role in Judaism.[213] Seventeenth-century sources often reveal a
sense of religious fervor and assertiveness in women's declarations about Jewish religion even if the language they used betrayed the influence of Catholic
concepts and references to Catholic holidays. Links to their former Catholic
affiliation surfaced among items in household inventories of some Portuguese
women, which included paintings with Catholic themes and crosses.[214] The
drive of these women to leave the Peninsula and make the long journey to Amsterdam, taking with them not only members of their nuclear family, but also
persons without any blood connection, suggests a strong religious sentiment,
especially as most of them enthusiastically joined and became active members
of the Portuguese community. Moreover, from their free Jewish base in Amsterdam, many women were strongly motivated to convince other members of
the *nação* still on the Peninsula or in other places, to come and live openly as
Jews in the free world.

However, religion was not the only motive for women's strong desire to leave
the Peninsula or reunite with family in the free Jewish world. The sense of solidarity among the members of the Spanish Portuguese Jewish nation was also
a motivating force. Sharing a common heritage and destiny, this ethnic bond
was vital in maintaining ties on the Peninsula and across the Sephardi Diaspora. It also helps to explain the strong desire of women to settle among other
members of the Portuguese nation. The strong reactions towards those who

213   David Nunes Torres, "Sermam funeral & Panegirico avida &virtudes da muy illustre Sen-
        hora Sara de Pinto, Pregado em 2 de Tebeth do Anno 5446," in *Sermoens de David Nunes
        Torres Pregador da célèbre irmandade de Abi Yetomim* (Amsterdam 5450 [1689/90]).
214   On a painting of rosaries in the house of an Amsterdam Portuguese Jew, Levie Bernfeld,
        "Matters Matter," p. 210 n. 73; Ribca Dias Sanches seems to be in the possession of a chain
        with a diamond-filled cross, apparently an object from her past (for inventory of Ribca
        Dias Sanches alias Samson Dias Sanches: SAA 334, no. 518, pp. 335–37, Not. M. van Son,
        12 May 1728). For the reference to the Catholic festival of All Saints, the memory book of
        Rachel Medina Chamis (SAA 334, no. 658, Not. J. Barels, n. p., last will of Rachel Medina
        Chamis, widow of Joseph Henriques Medina, 12 August 1728).

chose not to join the community or turn their backs on it is suggestive of a strongly knit and committed community, regardless of their original reasons for joining, which ran the gamut from pragmatic to ethnic to religious.

While for the most part, the Portuguese women of seventeenth-century Amsterdam showed either strong will or pragmatism in their decision to adhere to Judaism and join the Jewish community, the situation changed in the eighteenth century and there were more instances of women flagrantly defying religious commandments and the community's strict moral rules. In women's wills in the eighteenth-century references to religious motives behind charitable gifts were less pronounced and based more on social and humanitarian grounds.[215]

The early Enlightenment impacted the level of religiosity among Portuguese women, which can be seen in the loosening of morals and the waning influence of the authorities to stem the tide. They could not prevent women from adopting a worldlier lifestyle, though they banned more and more women for disobedience, adultery and other deviant behavior. Other women gave up ties to the community altogether. The majority of Portuguese women, however, settled for a middle path between following the strict rules of rabbinical tradition and leaving the community completely. Thus, they moved forward towards modernity, the way having been paved by their female anscestors who, a century and more before, braved the journey to the free Jewish world in Amsterdam.

---

215   On this phenomenon Levie Bernfeld, *Poverty and Welfare*, pp. 169–71.

CHAPTER 4

The Amsterdam Way of Death: R. Shimon Frankfurt's *Sefer ha-hayyim* (The Book of Life), 1703

Avriel Bar-Levav

The use of print became established in Western Europe in the early modern period, and its cultural impact expanded. The process that set in motion the widespread accessibility of books, which began gradually with the first use of print in the middle of the fifteenth century, led to the consolidation of the literary use of languages that until then had been vernacular and at this point transformed into cultural and national languages. This process, known as the "widening of the circle of readers," also impacted the self-awareness of readers and the formation of their identities and values.[1]

Together with the acceleration in the number of Jewish books, the Jewish culture of this period underwent an accelerated process of formulation of rituals. New texts and rituals were added to Jewish life, including the service for welcoming the Sabbath, the Midnight Vigil (*Tikun hatzot*), and additions to the prayer book.[2] In this context, deathbed rituals also developed to a detailed formulation, reflected in a new genre of books and booklets which first appeared in Italy at the beginning of the seventeenth century, referred to as "books for the sick and dying." This paper will analyze one of the important books of this genre, *Sefer ha-hayyim* (The Book of Life), printed in a bilingual Hebrew and Yiddish edition (in two parts, one in Hebrew and one in Yiddish) in Amsterdam in 1703, written by R. Shimon Frankfurt, the rabbi of the Ashkenazi Burial Society in Amsterdam. I will discuss this book against the background of its genre and the phenomenon of the formation of deathbed rituals and

---

* Parts of this paper are based on my Hebrew paper "Dying by the Book: Jewish Books for the Sick and the Dying, and the Ritualization of Death in the Early Modern Period," *Zmanim* 73 (2000), pp. 71–78, and on my Ph.D. dissertation, "The Concept of Death in the *Book of Life* (*Sefer ha-hayyim*) by Rabbi Shimon Frankfurt," The Hebrew University of Jerusalem, 1997 [Hebrew]. I am grateful to my friend Prof. Shlomo Berger z"l for his assistance with the Yiddish.

1 On the Jewish aspects, see Z. Gries, *The Book in the Jewish World, 1700–1900* (Oxford 2007).

2 See: A. Bar-Levav, "Ritualisation of Jewish Life and Death in the Early Modern Period," *LBI Yearbook* 47 (2002), pp. 69–82.

© KONINKLIJKE BRILL NV, LEIDEN, 2017 | DOI 10.1163/9789004343160_005

will examine the significance of the position of the writer as the rabbi of the Amsterdam Burial Society.[3]

The Concept of the "Proper Death"

Mourning rituals in the Jewish religion are mentioned already in the Bible and further developed and clarified in the classical rabbinic literature and subsequent halakhic literature. The laws of mourning focus on the behavior of the mourners, not the dying.[4] The significance of this is that the halakhic literature until the seventeenth century essentially presents a model of *ars moriendi*, "proper mourning" (in other words the proper or correct way to mourn). However, there did not exist a consolidated model for "proper death" or "correct death" (in other words the correct or proper way to die). This situation changed in the seventeenth century with the beginning of the establishment of ritualistic public behavior around the death bed, in books that appeared first in Italy and afterward throughout the Jewish world.

It is important not to confuse the concept of "proper death" with the concept of "tamed death" proposed by the French scholar Philippe Ariès, the initiator of historical research on the concept of death in the West.[5] Ariès presented four stages of the concept of death in Western culture: "tamed death," "personal death," "wild death" and "forbidden death." In the first stage, death is understood as a natural part of life, greeted with acceptance, without arousing any particular emotions. According to Ariès, this approach was typical of rural and agricultural societies. In the second stage, motifs of the Day of Judgment and personal judgment appear until, in the third stage, death is perceived as something awful and terrible, frightening and shocking, cruelly tearing the dead from the fabric of society. This stage leads to the final stage in which the phenomenon of death is pushed outside the boundaries of life. The dying people

---

3   On the meaning of the connection between Hebrew and Yiddish in *Sefer ha-hayyim* see A. Bar-Levav, "Between the World of the Texts and the World of the Readers," *Studies in Ashkenazi Culture, Women's History and the Languages of the Jews Presented to Chava Turniansky*, ed. I. Bartal et al. (Jerusalem 2013), pp. 95–122 [Hebrew].

4   See *Death in Jewish Life: Burial and Mourning Customs Among Jews of Europe and Nearby Communities*, ed. S.C. Reif, A. Lenhardt and A. Bar-Levav (Boston 2014); F. Wiesemann, *Sepulcra Judaica: Jewish Cemeteries, Death, Burial and Mourning from the Period of Hellenism to the Present: A Bibliography* (Essen 2005).

5   See P. Ariès, *Western Attitudes towards Death: From the Middle Ages to the Present*, trans. Patricia M. Ranum (Baltimore 1974); S.A. Goldberg, *Crossing the Jabbok: Illness and Death in Ashkenazi Judaism in Sixteenth- through Nineteenth-Century Prague*, trans. C. Cosman (Berkeley 1996), has used the methods of Ariès for a pioneering study of death in Jewish culture.

are moved to institutions which distance them and isolate them from the rest of society and death becomes a taboo subject. Ariès regarded modern American society as an example of a society that forbids death. According to him, fluctuating interactions between four variables produce changes in the perception of death: the human's awareness of himself, society's defenses against wild nature, the belief in life after death and belief in the existence of evil.

It is possible to use the models proposed by Ariès as phenomenological models without claiming a historical developmental connection between them. The need to control death arose as a reaction to major traumas, internal and external, which shaped Jewish society and Jewish culture and transformed them completely in the modern period.[6] However, it is also possible to see this need as yet another attempt by the human, as a human being, to cope with the oblivion that awaits him or her.

The First Books

The first booklet that initiated the genre of "books for the sick and dying" is *Tzori la-nefesh u-marpeh la-etsem* (Balm for the Soul and Cure for the Bone) compiled by R. Leone (Judah Aryeh) Modena (1571–1648), a rabbi, preacher and prolific and multi-faceted author who lived most of his life in Venice.[7] *Tzori la-nefesh* was printed in Venice in 1626 on behalf of the burial society of the Ashkenazi community in the city. In the introduction to the book, the heads of the society complain about the behavior of the sick and their families who in times of illness do not prepare themselves for the possibility of death. When the sick person becomes bedridden, everyone encourages him and tells him that he will soon recover and return to normal life. The deterioration in his condition therefore comes as a surprise for which the patient and those surrounding him are not prepared. The sick person thus loses the opportunity to improve his status in the next world by confessing his sins before his death. The hope is expressed that the commissioned book would contribute to the solution of the problem by establishing a ritualistic framework for behavior

---

6 On early Jewish death rituals see N. Rubin, *The End of Life: Rites of Burial and Mourning in the Talmud and Midrash* (Tel Aviv 1977) [Hebrew]. On modern ones see H.E. Goldberg, *Jewish Passages: Cycles of Jewish Life* (Berkeley 2003); S.C. Heilman, *When a Jew Dies: The Ethnography of a Bereaved Son* (Berkeley 2001). L. Wieseltier, *Kaddish* (New York 1998), has a lot of interesting material.

7 See A. Bar-Levav, "Leon Modena and the Invention of the Jewish Death Tradition," in *The Lion Shall Roar: Leon Modena and His World*, ed. D. Malkiel (Jerusalem 2003), pp. 85–102.

around the sickbed, a framework including prayer and confession before death (the deathbed confession).

The heads of the society go on to mention an additional problem which they hope to solve by the publication of the booklet:

> An additional consideration is that when the turn comes for one of our members to go to watch over the sick person and stay with him, as is our practice, we do not have a custom (*seder*) as to what to say and what to talk about in order to accompany the soul of this dying person, to return his soul to God who gave it (*Tzori la-nefesh*, introduction).

According to this description, the framework preceded the content. The charitable activity of the members of the society, visiting the sick, sitting beside the bedside of the sick and dying, was carried out before there existed a ritual that gave form to the practice. Apparently, the members of the society came to the sickbed and asked themselves: "What do we do now?" With the booklet in their hands they would know what to do—to read the "order of things" (the ritual) written in the book beside the sickbed and to act accordingly.

The introduction to the book contains several essential points: first, the aspiration to ritualize the act of dying; second, the refusal of the sick person and his family to cooperate, because they prefer to deny the terminal nature of the illness and to act as if all were as usual; and third, the arrival of the members of the philanthropic society at the sickbed and their desire to conduct a ritual there, although the content of the ritual was still unclear. From this description it is clear that tension and even conflict existed between the families and the members of the society. Around the sickbed a process was taking place in which a certain amount of authority was expropriated from the personal and familial sphere and transferred to the public and religious sphere. The Hebrew language played a key role in this process of expropriation. The members of the society knew what to say. The personal language of the family was pushed aside in favor of the established religious language of the members of the society, holding in their hands a booklet which contained Psalms, prayers and the text of the confession.

The preface of the author, Leone Modena, reveals that the ritualistic formulation of the end of life is connected to another, inter-cultural and inter-religious sphere in which one culture examines another and, on the basis of the comparison, turns back and examines itself. Leone Modena explained: "Why should our community do less than the people around us by not taking care that when someone is on his deathbed he should meet his Maker in a state of supplication and confession of his sins and transgressions." Proper religious behavior at death is specifically that of the "people around us," in other words the Christians. In order not to lag behind, the Jews must correct their ways and behave according to the "procedure" formulated by Leone Modena. It is interesting to note that this serene comparison to Christianity was in fact conducted within the constricted physical space of the ghetto in which the Christian rulers of Venice, the home of Leone Modena, confined the Jews.

Tzori la-nefesh u-marpeh la-etsem initiated the genre of "books for the sick and dying" but in fact did not leave upon it a strong impression. The book that shaped the genre and continued to influence it is *Ma'avar yabok* (The Ford of the Jabbok, see Genesis 32:23) the work of a relative of Leone Modena, R. Aaron Berekhiya of Modena. It was printed in Mantua in 1626, seven years after *Tzori la-nefesh*.[8] *Ma'avar yabok* is a thick and very scholarly tome which had a tremendous impact. The practical part, prayers to be said beside the sickbed, comprises only one of the 112 chapters (the name of the book derives in part from the number 112, the numerical equivalent of the Hebrew letters y-b-k). The rest of the book deals with various different matters, among which much attention is given to the subject of death, among other subjects, including the synagogue, prayer and holidays.

The introduction to *Ma'avar yabok* also explains the need for deathbed ritual:

> Why should the spark of our fire burn out and our candle die out (God forbid) in the heart of darkness and there should not appear within it the light of Torah ... Why should we not end our days in increasing the light of Torah? (*Ma'avar yabok*, introduction)

The extinguishing of life should take place specifically in light, the light of Torah that shines from the death rituals and from the presence and activity of the members of the society. Like his relative Leone Modena, Aaron Berekhiya met members of a philanthropic society who also felt the lack of "a fixed liturgy in which to raise their voices in song and prayer at the hour of the departure of the soul." This occurred during a visit to the Jewish community of Mantua and the members of the society encouraged him to prepare for them such an "order of prayers." The rite that Aaron Berekhyia of Modena formulated was a great success and became much more widely circulated than that of Leone Modena. Already during the lifetime of the writer it was in use in various communities in Italy and even in Safed. The book was so influential that

---

8 See A. Bar-Levav, "Rabbi Aaron Berekhiya of Modena and Rabbi Naftali Hakohen Katz: Founding Fathers of Books for the Sick and the Dying," *Asufot* 9 (1995), pp. 189–233 [Hebrew].

its name became synonymous with matters relating to preparation for death and many booklets of the genre were entitled after it *Kitzur ma'avar yabok* (A Concise Ma'avar Yabok). In traditional Jewish literature the word *"kitzur"* refers to a paraphrase and, as Ze'ev Gris has shown, the various books entitled *Kitzur ma'avar yabok* were a vehicle for the transfer of local traditions in the creation of death rituals.[9]

The genre that began in Italy spread throughout the entire Jewish world, east and west. An important stage in this development was *Sefer ha-hayyim*, printed in Amsterdam in 1703. The author, R. Shimon Frankfurt, a native of Poland, was the rabbi of the Ashkenazi burial society in Amsterdam. For the first time in the history of the Jewish books for the sick and the dying, in addition to the Hebrew text, the author added a separate volume in Yiddish, the spoken language of most of the Ashkenazi Jews of Europe during this period. This section was intended for readers who were not well enough educated to understand a text in Hebrew, the holy language. Included in this category were women, the primary target group of the old Yiddish literature, but not only them. The poorer members of society and those living in remote rural areas also read Yiddish books, just as their social counterparts among the peoples of Europe read books printed in the vernacular. The Yiddish section of *Sefer ha-hayyim* is not a translation of the Hebrew section but rather a parallel work, a supplementary, different composition intended for a different readership than the Hebrew section and adapted for this readership. *Sefer ha-hayyim*, printed and summarized many times, reflects both the proliferation of books for the sick and the dying and the widening of the circle of readers to which they were directed.

R. Shimon Frankfurt, the Author of *Sefer ha-hayyim*

Only a few details are known about the life of Shimon Frankfurt and their sources are his own words and those of his son Moshe. Shimon was born the son of Israel Judah in 1634[10] in Schwerin an der Warthe, not the capital of

---

9   See Z. Gries, *Conduct Literature (Regimen Vitae): It's History and Place in the Life of Beshtian Hasidism* (Jerusalem 1989), pp. xvi–xvii [Hebrew].

10   This can be seen from the words of R. Shimon quoted in the book of his son, *Zeh yenahamenu*, Amsterdam 1712, which reveal that he was seventy-eight years old. On *Zeh yenachamenu*, a new edition of the *Mekhilta* with a commentary by R. Moshe, see L. Elias, *"Mekhilta* of Rabbi Ishmael according to an Excellent Copy from the Geniza," (MA Thesis, The Hebrew University 1997), p. 95, n. 405 [Hebrew].

the duchy of Mecklenburg in Germany, but rather the Schwerin on the river Warthe, in the area of Poznań in Poland (in Polish, Skwierzyna).[11] Shimon left the city in 1656 when it fell to the Swedish army invading Poland. He adopted the family name of his father-in-law, Benjamin (the son of Moshe) Frankfurt. We have no knowledge of any connection of him or his family with the city of that name. His father-in-law, who was active in the Ashkenazi burial society in Amsterdam, brought him into the society and R. Shimon served as its rabbi for more than thirty years, during which time he taught a daily class on a regular basis in the *beit midrash* (study hall) of the society. R. Shimon merited a long life and died in Amsterdam on 10 Kislev 5363 (9 December 1713).

The extant literary works of R. Shimon include the bi-lingual (Hebrew/Yiddish) *Sefer ha-hayyim* printed in his lifetime (Amsterdam 1703), and *Sefer yitnu*, a book of customs and halakhah which remains in manuscript,[12] as well as poems for special occasions which he wrote for his son, Moshe, printed in those of his son's books published in the father's lifetime. His literary style is clear and pleasant both in Hebrew and Yiddish. His writings reflect great scholarship and profound halakhic knowledge and in *Sefer ha-hayyim* he also reveals narrative skill in the stories which he occasionally weaves into his discussion.

The son of R. Shimon, R. Moshe Frankfurt (1678–1768), held public positions more important than those of his father.[13] R. Moshe was one of two Ashkenazi *dayanim* (religious court judges) in Amsterdam and, after the death of his father, took over his position as the rabbi of the Ashkenazi burial society.[14] R. Moshe wrote important books and commentaries in Hebrew and in Yiddish, edited the Babylonian Talmud that R. Judah Aryeh Leib prepared for

---

11   See A. Heppner and J. Herzberg, *Aus Vergangenheit und Gegenwart: der Juden und der jud. Gemeinden in den Posner Landen* (Koschmin-Bromberg 1909), 2, pp. 966–71. I am grateful to R. Isaac Yudlov, formerly the director of the Institute for Hebrew Bibliography, who kindly brought this to my attention.

12   See Bar-Levav, *The Concept of Death*, pp. 274–79, 284–91.

13   See M. Horovitz, *Frankfurter Rabbinen*, ed. J. Una (Kfar Haroeh 1969), p. 110; and n. 14 *infra*.

14   See the ordinances of the Burial Society, Amsterdam 1742, ordinance 5, 1b, in which was established the daily lesson (with a minimum length of a quarter of an hour) of the rabbi of the society, Moshe Frankfurt; clause 70, 8b, in which it is stated that the rabbi is in charge of the register of the names of the dead and their place of burial and a guest who wants to know the burial place of their dead must pay one schilling to the society and one schilling to the rabbi. In clause 99, 11b, it is stated that R. Moshe Frankfurt is appointed rabbi of the burial society for the remainder of his life. Clause 100 describes the procedure for choosing a new rabbi if one should be required. A schilling (or "schilong") is thirty Dutch cents; I. Markon, "Ordinances of the Community of Polish Jews in Amsterdam from 1672," *Tziyunim: Memorial Volume for J.N. Simhoni* (Berlin 1929), p. 167 [Hebrew].

publication at the printing press of Solomon Markis in Amsterdam, and afterward was himself the owner of a printing press in which he printed several works including (during the years 1724–1727) *Mikraot gedolot kohelet Moshe*, the largest and most comprehensive version of *Mikraot gedolot* (Biblia Hebraica Magna, Bible with traditional Jewish commentaries) ever printed (which he also edited).[15] He was also one of the first printers to distribute quires to subscribers.[16] R. Moshe Frankfurt is important to the history of Hebrew printing in general and to the history of Hebrew printing in Amsterdam specifically by virtue of his being a "learned printer," a printer who was both a rabbi and *dayan* in his city, an author and a translator. In this he is similar to the first Jew to open a printing press in Amsterdam, Menasseh ben Israel, who was also a learned printer.

The Thirty Years War, the revolt of the Cossacks (which reached its climax for the Jews in the Chmielnicki Massacres) and the Swedish Wars, all traumatized the Jewish communities of central and Eastern Europe. Communities were destroyed and many Jews were uprooted from their homes and fled west. Amsterdam was one of the most important destinations of the German and Polish refugees.[17] In this regard, the path of R. Shimon was not rare at that time. Among the factors that led refugees to Amsterdam were the tolerance of the Dutch authorities towards the newcomers and the aide offered to them by the wealthy Sephardi community.

From the beginning of the seventeenth century, Amsterdam served as the primary destination for the emigration of New Christian merchants from Spain and Portugal.[18] The tolerance that they were shown enabled them to take part in the economic prosperity of the city, which reached its zenith in the middle of the seventeenth century.[19] The Jews did not enjoy this level of tolerance in any other place in Europe during this period. They were not obligated to live in a ghetto, to wear a distinctive badge or to pay a special tax. They enjoyed ex-

---

15   See the entry "Bible: Editions of the Bible" by Ch. Rabin in the *Biblical Encyclopedia*, vol. 5 (Jerusalem 1968), p. 374 [Hebrew].

16   See A. Bar-Levav, "Amsterdam and the Inception of the Jewish Republic of Letters," *The Dutch Intersection: The Jews and the Netherlands in Modern History*, ed. Y. Kaplan (Leiden 2008), pp. 225–37.

17   See Y. Kaplan, "Amsterdam and Ashkenazic Migration in the Seventeenth Century," *StRos* 23 [special issue] (1989), pp. 22–44; idem, *An Alternative Path to Modernity: The Sephardi Diaspora in Western Europe* (Leiden 2000), pp. 78–107.

18   See idem, "'Bom Judesmo': The Western Sephardic Diaspora," *Cultures of the Jews: A New History*, ed. D. Biale (New York 2002), pp. 639–69.

19   See J.I. Israel, *The Dutch Republic Its Rise, Greatness, and Fall, 1477–1806* (Oxford 1995), pp. 610–27.

tensive autonomy and their status was higher than that of the Catholics, whose rites were forbidden in Amsterdam. The city became the largest Jewish center in Western Europe and the members of the Sephardi community included both very wealthy people and prominent intellectuals.[20] Amsterdam was one of the most important centers for printing in Europe, both in European languages and in Hebrew. Christian printers published a few books in Hebrew[21] even before Menasseh ben Israel opened a Hebrew printing press in 1626.[22] However, the opening of his press ushered in a new era in the history of Hebrew printing. Hebrew printers became numerous and the high technical and professional level of their work was renowned throughout the Jewish world.

The Ashkenazi Jews arrived in the city a bit later, in the second decade of the seventeenth century.[23] An Ashkenazi community was founded in the city in 1635.[24] The members of the Sephardi community considered themselves superior to the Ashkenazim and kept themselves apart from them.[25] In 1642, they forbade the Ashkenazim to bury their dead in the cemetery in Ouderkerk but lent them money to purchase a plot of land for a cemetery in Muiderburg, an area further from the city.[26] Along with the cemetery, they founded an Ashkenazi charitable society.

20   See the introduction of Méchoulan and Nahon to the English version of *Mikveh Israel* of Menasseh ben Israel: *The Hope of Israel / Menasseh Ben Israel*; the English translation by Moses Wall, 1652, edited, with introduction and notes by Henry Méchoulan and Gerard Nahon; introduction and notes translated from the French by Richenda George (Oxford 1987), pp. 1–21.

21   See L. Fuks and R.G. Fuks-Mansfeld, *Hebrew Typography in the Northern Netherlands, 1585–1815: Historical Evaluation, and Descriptive Bibliography* (Leiden 1984–1987), pp. 94–99.

22   On Menasseh ben Israel, see *Menasseh Ben Israel and his World*, ed. Y. Kaplan, H. Méchoulan and R.H. Popkin (Leiden 1989); Méchoulan and Nahon, *Mikveh Israel*; M. Dorman, *Menashe ben Israel* (Tel Aviv 1989) [Hebrew].

23   See D.M. Sluys, "The High-German Jewish Community in Amsterdam from 1635 to 1795," *SHDJ* (1975), pp. 69–121. The article surveys the history of the Ashkenazi Jews mainly from the point of view of the lay leaders of the community. It was written originally in Dutch and translated to Hebrew for inclusion in the anthology. It appeared originally in the collection *Geschiedenis der Joden in Nederland* (Amsterdam 1940).

24   On the beginning of the Ashkenazim in Amsterdam See Kaplan, *An Alternative Path*, pp. 78–107.

25   See Y. Kaplan, "The Portuguese Community in 17th-Century Amsterdam and the Ashkenazi World," *DJH* 2 (1989), pp. 23–45.

26   See Sluys, "The High-German Jewish Community in Amsterdam," pp. 74, 101–2. Because of the distance of the cemetery from the city, another cemetery was founded in 1714 in Zeeburg, closer to the city, on arid ground, for cases of death occurring on the eve of the Sabbath or a holiday in which case it was undesirable to take them to the cemetery

The arrogance of the Sephardi Jews towards their Ashkenazi brethren in Amsterdam did not affect their sense of responsibility for them or their sense of national solidarity. When catastrophe struck the Jewish world in Eastern Europe, the members of the Sephardi community took it upon themselves to redeem captives[27] and to aide and assist the refugees who fled to Amsterdam. Amsterdam served the refugees as both a way station[28] and as a new center for resettlement. There were refugees who left the city because of the high cost of living there[29] and also because the Sephardim encouraged the Polish refugees to leave, first to central Europe and afterward to return to Poland. However, many of the refugees settled in Amsterdam, among them R. Shimon, who, as we have seen, fled his hometown of Schwerin in the wake of the riots of 1656.[30]

It is possible that when R. Shimon arrived in Amsterdam he witnessed the Sabbatian turmoil which continued until reaching its breaking point with the conversion of Shabbetai Tzvi in 1666.[31] However, I have not found references to these events in his extant writings, which were written more than thirty-five years later.[32] His writings, which reflect his scholarship as well as his position

---

a long distance away in Muiderburg. The relative inferiority of this cemetery is reflected in the fact that the poor, children and non-members were buried in it. See J.C.E. Belinfante, "The Ideal of Jewish Tradition versus the Reality of the Jewish Poor: The Dilemma of the Ashkenazi Jewish Nation," *StRos* 30 (1996), pp. 213–24.

27   See I. Heilprin, *Jews and Judaism in Eastern Europe* (Jerusalem 1969), pp. 72, 230 [Hebrew].

28   See Kaplan, *An Alternative Path*, p. 79.

29   See, for example, the words of R. Moshe Rivkash, the author of *Be'er ha-golah*, who fled from Vilna in 1655, in his introduction to the *Shulhan arukh, Orah hayyim,* the edition of Yosef Atias, Amsterdam 1697: "We set out for Amsterdam and when we arrived here, the mercy of the Sephardi rabbis and benefactors, may God protect them, was roused particularly, and they showed us charity and mercy and invested a lot of money to provide each of us with food and lodging. Because the city, though very large, could not absorb everyone because of the high cost of rent and food, they sent some people, at their expense, to the Jewish community of Frankfurt and provided them with food for the journey."

30   Yosef Kaplan has delineated four periods in the relations between the Portuguese and the Ashkenazi communities in Amsterdam. See his "The Portuguese Community and the Ashkenazi World," p. 26. According to this periodization, R. Shimon arrived during the third period, between 1648 and 1670.

31   See G. Scholem, *Sabbatai Sevi: The Mystical Messiah, 1626–1676*, trans. R.J. Zwi Werblowsky, (Princeton 1975); Y. Kaplan, "The Attitude of the Sephardi Leadership in Amsterdam to the Sabbatian Movement, 1665–1671," in idem, *An Alternative Path*, pp. 211–33; idem, *From Christianity to Judaism: The Story of Isaac Orobio de Castro,* trans. R. Loewe (Oxford 1989), pp. 209–34.

32   As it is well known, writers in the generation after the Sabbatian crisis rarely mentioned the event. See the words of Gershom Scholem at the beginning of his article "A Mitzvah

as the rabbi of the burial society, attest to the rabbinic learning that he acquired in Poland and continued to develop in Amsterdam. The Polish Jews in Amsterdam were, for the most part, more learned than the Ashkenazi Jews and the Sephardi Jews respected them more. Relations between the Polish and Ashkenazi Jews were often tense and between the years 1660–1673 the Poles established a separate community, though the two communities subsequently reunited.

The differences between the Sephardi and Ashkenazi communities in Amsterdam were not merely economic and social. With regard to the nature of the rift, it is perhaps possible to say that from a spiritual point of view it is as if each community lived in its own world, although these worlds were not completely cut off from each other. Among the Sephardim were those who possessed general and philosophic knowledge, some of whom were former New Christians. There were also those who wrestled with the burning theological questions of the time and arrived at positions of skepticism.[33] The most outstanding among them was Baruch Spinoza, a member of the Sephardi community who was excommunicated in 1656[34] and whose importance as a philosopher lies outside the context of traditional Jewish society. The intellectual world of the Sephardi community was anchored of course in the world of tradition,[35] as taught by its rabbis and in its lively *beit midrash*, Ets Haim, whose magnificent Jewish library was one of the most important in Europe.[36] The scholars of the *beit midrash* published the very first anthology (in the entire Jewish world) of

---

Performed in Sin," *Studies and Sources in the History of Sabbatianism and Its Development* (Jerusalem 1984), pp. 9–64; Kaplan, "Attitude of the Sephardi Leadership in Amsterdam to the Sabbatian Movement," pp. 211–33.

33 See idem, "The Intellectual Ferment in the Spanish-Portuguese Community of Seventeenth Century Amsterdam," in *Moreshet Sepharad: The Sephardi Legacy*, ed. H. Beinart, 2nd ed. (Jerusalem 1992), pp. 288–314; on the general context of skepticism in this period see R.H. Popkin, *The History of Skepticism from Erasmus to Descartes* (New York 1964); J.I. Israel, *Radical Enlightenment: Philosophy and the Making of Modernity, 1650–1750* (Oxford 2001).

34 On excommunications in the Sephardi community in Amsterdam, see: Y. Kaplan, "The Social Functions of the Herem in the Portuguese Jewish Community of Amsterdam in the Seventeenth Century," *DJH* I (1984), pp. 111–55. On the excommunication of Baruch Spinoza, see idem, "The Intellectual Ferment," p. 611; idem, *From Christianity to Judaism*, pp. 115–16.

35 See idem, *An Alternative Path*, pp. 1–28.

36 See, for example, *Treasures from the Library, Ets Haim Livraria Montezinos of the Portugees Israelietisch seminarium Ets Haim Amsterdam*, exhibition, April 1980, ed. R. Weiser, Y. Kaplan, English translation, M. Plotkin (Jerusalem 1980).

traditional Jewish scholarship, *Pri etz hayyim* (The Fruit of the Tree of Life)[37] which became a model for other anthologies of its kind, including responsa and halakhic discussions. However, in addition to the activities of traditional establishments such as the *beit midrash*, as we have said, some of the members of the community were open to the winds of change blowing in the wide world and the beginning of the Enlightenment in the seventeenth century.[38] Regardless, it would appear that the Ashkenazi Jews remained for the most part a traditional community, connected to the world of the past, a characteristic reflected also in the nature of their intellectual productivity.

Although Amsterdam was, as we have said, a center for trade, commerce and printing,[39] the Ashkenazi Jews did not create there a center for Torah learning in the traditional sense,[40] but remained dependent intellectually on Torah centers in Central and Western Europe.[41] It can be said, perhaps, that in comparison to the vibrant intellectual creativity of the Sephardi Jews in Amsterdam,[42] the intellectual creativity of the Ashkenazim in Amsterdam in the seventeenth and eighteenth centuries had its own unique character. It emphasized the appeal to the wider community, including members who had not acquired Torah scholarship. We can see examples of this in the translations to Yiddish, among them Moshe Frankfurt's translation of *Menorat ha-ma'or* and Menahem Mann Amelander's translation of *Josippon*.[43] The pinnacle of this

37 See Y. Kaplan, "Eighteenth-Century Rulings by the Rabbinical Court of Amsterdam's Community and Their Socio-historical Significance," *SHDJ* 5 (1988), p. 9, n. 25 [Hebrew]. *Pri Ets Hayyim* was first published in Amsterdam in 1730 and it was printed on and off until 1801. An index entitled *Otzar pirot etz hayyim* was published in Berlin in 1936. I would like to thank my friend R. Aaron Ausubel who brought this to my attention. Some of the volumes were published as a photo offset in New York in 1997.

38 See H. Méchoulan, "A Portrait of the Jewish Community in Amsterdam in the Seventeenth Century," *Pe'amim* 48 (1991), pp. 104–16, esp. pp. 109–10 [Hebrew]. The "Jewish Community" discussed in the article is the Sephardi community.

39 On the economic activity of the Jews in Amsterdam, see H.I. Bloom, *The Economic Activities of the Jews of Amsterdam in the Seventeenth and Eighteenth Centuries* (New York 1937). On Jewish printing presses and the book trade, see ibid, pp. 44–60.

40 See J. Michman, "Between Sephardim and Ashkenazim in Amsterdam," in *The Legacy of the Jews of Spain and the Eastern Lands, Studies*, ed. I. Ben Ami (Jerusalem 1982), pp. 39–40 [Hebrew].

41 See Kaplan, "The Portuguese Community and the Ashkenazi World," p. 25, where it is explained that for Ashkenazim the move to Amsterdam cut them off from their spiritual centers.

42 See Kaplan, "The Intellectual Ferment."

43 On the influence of Dutch on Yiddish in books printed in Amsterdam, see Sh. Berger, *Producing Redemption in Amsterdam: Early Modern Yiddish Books in Paratextual Perspective*

genre were the translations of the Bible into Yiddish.[44] *Sefer ha-hayyim,* especially its Yiddish section, can be seen in this context. Another example can be found in educational materials which were not only published in the city but in some cases also written there.[45] It is possible that the differences between the Jewish communities in Amsterdam and the fact that many different kinds of Jews passed through the city were among the reasons for the development of this type of cultural productivity. In other places as well, people dedicated themselves to the guidance of the general public. However, while this phenomenon was not unique to Amsterdam, it would seem that it was especially pronounced there. The printing presses of Amsterdam distributed throughout the Jewish world not only works of Torah scholarship but also ethical literature, Yiddish literature and popular works, some of which were written in the city itself. It is possible that the existence of an important printing center in Amsterdam created an awareness of the needs of new circles of book buyers. This awareness perhaps also influenced the direction of the intellectual and spiritual output of the city's Jews, including *Sefer ha-hayyim.*

The Ritual in *Sefer ha-hayyim*

Both the sick and the ritual experts participate in the death rituals. (The expert is sometimes referred to as "*baki*," or the knowledgeable one.[46]) The experts are usually the members of a charitable society, specializing, by virtue of their role in society, in ritualistic behavior beside the sickbed. As we have seen, the upshot of the matter is the removal of the family from beside the

(Leiden 2013); M. Aptroot, "Dutch Impact on Amsterdam Yiddish Prints," *Dialects of the Yiddish Language,* ed. D. Katz (Oxford 1988), pp. 7–11.

44   M. Aptroot, "'In galkhes they do not say so, but the taytsh is as it stands here': Notes on the Amsterdam Yiddish Bible Translations by Blitz and Witzenhausen," *StRos* 27 (1993), pp. 136–58.

45   See Ch. Turniansky, "On Didactic Literature in Yiddish in Amsterdam 1699–1749," *SHDJ* 4 (1985), pp. 163–77 [Hebrew]; Sh. Dotan-Ofir, "History, Books and Society: Yiddish Didactic Books Printed in Early Modern Amsterdam," (Ph.D. Dissertation, The Hebrew University of Jerusalem, 2010); Michman, "Between Sephardim and Ashkenazim," p. 32; for a collection of textbooks from Amsterdam see the catalogue of the Exhibition of Jewish Textbooks, The National Library (Jerusalem 1988), p. 4.

46   See E.S. Horowitz, "The Jews of Europe and the Moment of Death in Medieval and Modern Times," *Judaism* 44 (1995), pp. 271–81; idem, "Giotto in Avignon, Adler in London, Panofsky in Princeton: On the Odyssey of an Illustrated Hebrew Manuscript from Italy and on Its Meaning," *Jewish Art* 19–20 (1993–1994), pp. 98–111.

sickbed. The most important aspects of the ritual formulated in the books for the sick and dying are passages to be read (especially verses and chapters of the Bible), prayers, the confession and declarations of faith. Although there are differences in details between the various books, it is nevertheless possible to characterize a type of basic model. Let me analyze schematically the main ritual presented in *Sefer ha-hayyim*.

Deathbed rituals can be divided according to two parameters, the medical condition of the patient and his religious status. A short and concise ceremony is held beside the bed of one who is dying, its length varying according to the dictates of time and the declining strength of the patient. If death is not imminent there is time for a more comprehensive service. The long ritual has two versions: the basic version and the expanded version used when the dying man is a rabbi or scholar. Those gathered around the deathbed read passages or recite prayers, verses or chapters from the Bible. If the patient has strength he participates in the reading, if not, then only those standing around his bed read and study. The ritual can be conducted in two cycles, long or short. In the long cycle, the members of the society present in the room of the patient study passages from holy texts, primarily the Bible but also the Mishnah, the Talmud and the *Zohar*. This study is essentially the recitation of the passages out loud rather than a discussion of their contents. (*Sefer ha-hayyim* is unusual in this regard as some of the study passages in it are comprised from the sermons of the author.) These same passages are studied also in the mourning period, during the *shiv'ah* [the first seven days of mourning]. Study might be the most important religious activity in traditional Jewish culture and thus the house of the sick becomes a center for study. It was also believed to be possible that the very presence of those studying would cause the illness to abate or at least reduce somewhat the existential loneliness of the patient. In addition, the content of the prayers and study passages is for the most part messages of comfort and encouragement.

In the short cycle, the ritual conducted beside the deathbed is focused and occupied primarily with the patient himself and his condition and the patient participates in it to the extent that he is able. The ritual progresses according to the stages of the illness and the transitions from stage to stage are gradual, among other reasons, in order to weaken the possible resistance of the patient and those around him to acknowledge his condition. The ritual in *Sefer ha-hayyim* begins with the prayer of the patient for himself, which is basically the recitation of a collection of verses (copied into the text). This prayer is to be recited "immediately, when one feels a pain in his head or another part of his body or when his wife or one of his children falls ill and also for any distress or misfortune that comes to him whether in his body or his property in which the divine judgment comes upon him."[47] The perception reflected here is that the source of illness, or any other misfortune, is divine decree. This decree is a part of a dynamic divine system, in which the forces of mercy and kindness fight against the forces of pure justice. The strengthening of the forces of pure justice in the upper world results in afflictions in this lowly world. The solution to the crisis lies in repentance: "Therefore he should immediately examine his actions and pray to Him to tell the angel to lessen his grip. He should not resist the divine decree but rather [accept] His Providence, because He is very meticulous with his pious ones." Along with the opportunity for moral development that comes with the illness, expressed in soul-searching and spiritual growth, there is also danger, if the spiritual response is not correct. However, the moral struggle is accompanied by a different struggle whose aim is to help the forces of benevolence (*hesed*) to overcome the forces of strict justice (*din*). This, among other things, is the aim of the prayers and especially the recitation of verses, which have the power to assist the forces of good. This is a metamorphosis of ancient magical beliefs in the power and efficacy of scriptural verses. One of the central ideas of the deathbed rituals is the recitation of a set number of verses. In *Tzori la-nefesh u-marpeh la-etsem*, seventy-two verses are cited, in *Ma'avar yabok*, 112 verses, and in *Sefer ha-hayyim*, one hundred verses. The verses contain positive content of comfort and hope.

If the patient continues to weaken, the transition is made to the next stage: "and if he takes to his bed and becomes ill he should say this prayer immediately." The prayer contains a direct plea for recovery:

> May it be your will, O Lord, my God, to pity me, please, and show me mercy. Send me and all of your people Israel a full and speedy recovery. Diminish my pains and suffering as the moon diminishes and renew the health of my body as the moon is renewed and renew my youth like an eagle . . . Heal me completely, a healing of the body and soul, and send me a lasting cure, a blessed cure, a cure of healing and elevation, a cure of pardon and compassion, a recognized and manifest cure, a cure of mercy and peace and life, a cure of a good and long life.

At this stage the sick person recites the confession. The text of the confession is fixed, not personal, and is based on the version of the confession said in the liturgy of the Day of Atonement (based on the confession of the High Priest in the Temple). Confession does not help in the case of a transgression

---

47   *Sefer ha-hayyim*, Hebrew section, 12b.

committed by one man against another. For sins of this kind the sinner must ask forgiveness from the person he wronged.

If the illness intensifies, the ritual precedes to the next stage. The sick person recites a special prayer of supplication and another confession called the "Deathbed Confession." This is a short confession whose fundamental principle ("May my death be an atonement for all my sins") appears in the Mishnah (*Sanhedrin* 6:2). The version in *Sefer ha-hayyim* is based on the version of *Torat ha-adam* of Nachmanides, and other halakhic works (*Sefer ha-hinukh*, *Sefer kolbo*, *Arba'ah turim* and the *Shulhan arukh*, *Yoreh de'ah* Section 338). This is the text of the confession:

> I acknowledge unto Thee, O Lord my God and God of my fathers, that both my cure and my death are in thy hands. May it be Thy will, my God and God of my fathers, to send me a perfect healing and that my memory and my prayer will rise up before Thee like the prayers of Hezekiah in his illness [2 Kings 20] and if the time designated for me to die draws near – let my death be an atonement for all my sins and iniquities and transgressions that I have committed before You from the day I arrived in this world until today. Give me my portion in heaven and grant me the afterlife reserved for the righteous. "Thou makest me to know the path of life; in Thy presence is fullness of joy, in Thy right hand bliss for evermore" [Psalms 16:11].

The deathbed confession expresses acceptance of the impending decree and submission to divine will, even as the moment of truth approaches. Precisely because the hour of death is perceived as a time of truth in which a person removes the masks that he wore in his lifetime and reveals his true identity and authentic self, there is great meaning in expressions of acceptance of the values upheld by his society. From this aspect the role of the deathbed confession is similar to the role of the *kaddish* prayer, recited by the grave, which praises God precisely at the hour of crisis.

There are two possible conclusions of the ritual. *Sefer ha-hayyim* brings the text of prayers of thanksgiving and praise to be recited by a recovering patient. The book also provides guidance in the case of the second possibility, the death of the patient:

> When the sick person realizes that his hour of death is approaching, he should give himself to heaven with love, and give praise and thanks to His name that he merited to die in his bed, and he should remember His kindnesses to him from the day that he came into the world until that

very day and should turn his thought and contemplation to the world to come until the departure of his soul upon reciting the word "one" . . . and he should spread out his hands and feet and gather them to the bed so that none of his limbs will be outside the bed when his soul departs, as it is written [Genesis 49:33] ". . . [Jacob] gathered up his feet into the bed, and expired . . ." and he should not put his hands or his feet on top of each other nor fold his hands. He should turn his face to the people around him and close his eyes and his mouth and think about the love of God until the cessation of feeling with the departure of his soul, upon reciting the word "one" . . . It is forbidden to leave a person who is about to die, so that he should not die alone. It is a *mitzvah* [commandment] to be with a person at the moment of his death and a *mitzvah* to pray for him to die when one sees that in the process of dying he is suffering.[48]

The departure of the soul upon recitation of the word "one," that is at the time that the person dying or those around him conclude the recitation of "*Shema yisrael*," the verse "Hear, O Israel: the LORD our God, the LORD is one" (Deuteronomy 6:4), is based on the Talmudic description of the death of Rabbi Akiba (BT *Berakhot* 61b) The specific instructions about the position of the body are based on the conceptualization of the *sefirot* [the divine emanations] in the form of the human body, according to which the crossing of the limbs inhibits the flow of the divine emanation. In general, these instructions are based on the belief that a connection exists between the condition of the body on earth and the condition of the soul which has just left the body and is beginning its journey to the celestial world. Such beliefs exist in many cultures. Death, the final separation from the society of the living, must not occur in a state of solitude and thus the living need to stand beside the bed of the dying person until his soul departs.

Traces of Personal Knowledge Acquired by R. Shimon in the Course of His Activity in the Burial Society

The vast experience accumulated by R. Shimon during the many years of his service to the Ashkenazi burial society in Amsterdam are reflected in *Sefer ha-hayyim* in several comments of a practical nature.

---

48   *Sefer ha-hayyim*, Hebrew section, 28b.

It is forbidden to move the dying person from his place or take the pillow from under his head because it is forbidden to hasten his death even if the process of dying is prolonged and death is delayed.[49] Therefore, one should not move him from his place, put anything under him, take anything from him, give him medical treatment (because it has no purpose) nor put anything in his mouth. If anyone does so, it is as if he shed blood because he hastened his death. But if he has enough strength to drink, and he asks to drink, he should be given a drink, because I have seen cases in which people asked to be given a drink close to the moment of death and they drank like a healthy person and then died.[50]

The instruction to exercise caution around the dying person and to avoid approaching his bed or touching him at all has an early source,[51] and appears in all relevant halakhic works. The addition of R. Shimon concerning the dying who immediately before their deaths asked to drink is unique to him and based on personal experience.

Sefer ha-hayyim contains interesting information on temporary burial in Amsterdam at the time of the French siege in 1672. After the siege was lifted, the remains were moved to the cemetery at Muiderburg, an area further from the city. R. Shimon mentions this incident not as an historical event, but in order to illustrate the differences in the levels of preservation of the bodies, differences which attest to their respective spiritual levels.[52]

> Said the writer: in the year 1682, here in the holy community of Amsterdam, when the city was sieged by the French, we buried the dead inside the city [and not in the regular cemetery]. Later, we took out the bodies and buried them in the cemetery outside the city. I was an officer (*gabbai*) in the burial society, and we took out more than two hundred bodies. Some of them were lying in the coffins, as if they were buried for the

---

49 The word used for death here is "*lehipared*," literally "to separate," referring to the separation of the soul from the body. This is one of the euphemisms used for death in the books for the sick and dying and in the registers of the burial society.

50 *Sefer ha-hayyim*, Hebrew section, paragraph 23, 27b.

51 See the sources brought by Nachmanides in *Torat ha-adam*, (the section on the deathbed), *The Writings of Nachmanides*, 2, ed. Ch. Dov Chavel (Jerusalem 1964), p. 50 [Hebrew].

52 On the connection between the spiritual status of the deceased and the condition of the body in the grave, see A. Bar-Levav, "Death and the (Blurred) Boundaries of Magic: Strategies of Coexistence," *Kabbalah: Journal for the Study of Jewish Mystical Texts* 7 (2002), pp. 51–64; A. Bar-Levav, "Jewish Attitudes towards Death: A Society between Time, Space and Texts," in *Death in Jewish Life*, pp. 3–16.

first time. And they were buried more than a year, and were not touched by worms. And some of them had all their two hundred and forty eight organs in their coffin put together as human beings are. [Usually] it does not take a long time till the brain decays. And the beard also grows in the grave. However, some of the coffins were full with worms, like beans. The worms were still living and were in the shape of beans; and they were big and brown. And the worms came out from inside the bodies. But the worms which are outside and lay on the body are as worms made of pieces of meat, like white tapeworms.[53]

This incident is also mentioned in the name of R. Shimon in the book *She'erit yisrael*[54] by R. Menahem Mann Amelander, who was a student of R. Moshe Frankfurt, the son of R. Shimon.

A matter to which R. Shimon devoted a great deal of thought was the performance of the purification of the dead, *taharat ha-met*, the ritual washing of the deceased, on a religious holiday. Outside the Land of Israel, the Jewish festivals are observed for two days,[55] which causes a significant delay in burial. The question of preparation of the dead for burial on a holiday is thus more relevant in the Diaspora than in the Land of Israel. Rabbi Shimon had an interesting halakhic solution to the problem of performing ritual washing on a holiday. The prohibitions of various actions on a holiday, including for example the prohibition of the act of wringing, limited the ability to perform the ritual washing. R. Shimon discussed the suggestion of R. Moses Isserles, in the name of the author of the halachic work, *Terumat ha-deshen*,[56] to cleanse the body by the use of straw:

I tried both these things, to cleanse the body with straw and with grass called "*haya bella*," and discovered that neither of them is effective because one breaks and tears the straw and also if one dips it in water in order to clean with it, one immediately comes to wring it, and even more so with grass. Also, it is a beastly thing to cleanse the body of the dead and to rub and scrape his skin with straw like an animal. Above all, the chaff,

53   *Sefer ha-hayyim*, Yiddish section, paragraph 31, 16a.
54   *She'erit yisrael*, Amsterdam 1743, Ch. 34 (this chapter deals with the history of the Ashkenazim in Amsterdam). The second section is from the book *Josippon* in Yiddish, 134b.
55   It is interesting that in that period the second festival day of the Diaspora was the subject of a halakhic controversy in Jerusalem. See M. Benayahu, *The Second Festival Day of the Diaspora* (Jerusalem 1987) [Hebrew].
56   *Arba'ah turim* and *Shulhan arukh, Orah hayyim,* paragraph 526.

the straw and the hay stick to the body until the whole body is covered in it, so that if one even wipes the body with it, parts of it remain stuck to it, and who would be able to gather up each and every piece or remove them from every orifice or crevice in the body, and it is certainly a disrespect to the dead that this material should remain stuck to his body. Even worse, if one covers the body with grass or straw and then comes to clean it, it falls off of it over and over until the body lies exposed, in great disgrace. We have been strictly cautioned to care for the dead with modesty, as is hinted in the verse "to walk humbly,"[57] which is interpreted with reference to the dead,[58] and the *Shekhinah* [the Divine Presence], with several souls of the holy ones and angels, leads the soul of the righteous one with them, and it is possible that this is the meaning of the words [in the continuation of the verse] "with thy God." And it is not possible to prevent this as I have seen with my own eyes, even though the men are very dedicated and all the more so the women.[59]

Criticism of *Sefer ha-hayyim* in the Book *Simhat ha-nefesh* by R. Elhanan Henle Kirkhhan and the Response of R. Moshe Frankfurt

At the end of the second edition of *Sefer ha-hayyim*, Amsterdam 1716, which was printed after the death of its author, R. Moshe Frankfurt added responses to a critical commentary on the book written by Elhanan Henle Kirkhhan, the author of *Simhat ha-nefesh*.

Elhanan Henle Kirkhhan wrote the following comment on the method of washing the body on the holiday presented in *Sefer ha-hayyim*: "In the first day of a holiday it says that the purification of the dead is done with a sheet. This is not right."[60]

R. Moshe Frankfurt responded to this critique by saying that the words of the critic are vague and that they do not refute the proofs brought by his father in *Sefer ha-hayyim*. This comment is one of the critical comments by the

---

57   Micah 6:8: "and to walk humbly with thy God."

58   See for example, BT *Sukkah* 49b: "'to walk humbly with thy God' – this means to bury the dead and to accompany the bride to the bridal canopy."

59   *Sefer ha-hayyim*, Section 1, paragraph 65, 67a. The correspondent Yiddish discussions in the second section, paragraph 49, 28a.

60   See *Sefer ha-hayyim*, second edition, Amsterdam 1716, at the end of the book, comment 9. All of the comments are quoted in Bar-Levav, *The Concept of Death*, pp. 297–302.

author of *Simhat ha-nefesh*, Elhanan Henle Kirkhhan,[61] which Moshe Frankfurt included at the end of the second edition of *Sefer ha-hayyim*, Amsterdam
1716, to which he added his responses. The comments themselves are quoted
in brief in Yiddish with references to *Sefer ha-hayyim* (according to the pagina-
tion of the second edition). I have been unable to find the original source of
the critical commentary; perhaps it has been lost.[62] However, within *Simhat
ha-nefesh* itself the author criticizes *Sefer ha-hayyim,* if only briefly: "There are
many printings and some of the rules are translated into Yiddish with many
mistakes. And people might fail because of that. Especially *Sefer ha-hayyim*
which was printed in Amsterdam includes many mistakes and therefore nobody could follow them. Those rules everyone can check in this book [i.e., *Simhat ha-nefesh*]."[63]

The critical commentary was written after *Simhat ha-nefesh*, as we learn from
the reference to the book in the nineteenth comment. Perhaps the comments
were written in order to substantiate the general criticism in the introduction
to *Simhat ha-nefesh*, criticism mentioned in the introductory comments of
R. Moshe to his responses to the critical commentary:

> Moshe Frankfurt, the son of the rabbi, the author, may the memory of
> the righteous be a blessing, says: Not long ago,[64] I received an essay of
> the author of the book *Simhat ha-nefesh* and I saw in it several critical
> comments on the book *Sefer ha-hayyim* by my master, my father, may
> the memory of the righteous be a blessing. He also wrote in the introduc-
> tion to *Simhat ha-nefesh* that it is not proper to rely on the words of *Sefer
> ha-hayyim*. Therefore I said that in these circumstances the son absolves
> his father and it is my duty to be concerned for the honor of my blessed
> father, and come to his defense according to my limited abilities. Because
> I know full well that a man as pure and righteous as my blessed father,
> would certainly not write something if he had not seen it and did not
> know its source, and it is worthy to rely upon him and his proofs. I also
> know that my blessed father, the author had all of the books of halakhic

61   About the author, see the introduction of Jacob Shatzky to the second section of his edi-
      tion of *Simhat ha-nefesh* (New York 1926), pp. 11–46. This section includes songs and tunes
      accompanied by musical notation.
62   R. Moshe indicated that the commentaries were written in a special pamphlet. These
      pamphlets are rare and many of them have not survived the ravages of time. Ironically, it
      was the desire of R. Moshe to defend his father that left in our hands the only evidence of
      the criticism leveled against him.
63   R. Elhanan Henle Kirkhhan, *Simhat ha-nefesh* (Frankfurt am Main 1707), Introduction.
64   These words were written around the year 1716.

judgments and responsa and did not lack any information as he himself
wrote in his introduction to his worthy book *Sefer tinui,* which he wrote
on the book *Arba'ah turim.*[65] When I examined the few books in my possession, I found that the contents of his book are straightforward and true
and it is worthwhile to rely upon them, and the words of the critic are
empty and false and cannot be upheld or maintained. I saw that in several places the critic did not understand the words of the rabbinic scholars or the contents of the book, and in several places copied words that
were not written in the book, as the reader can see for himself, with the
help of God. Thus, the contents of the book are valid and there is nothing
in them that is crooked or perverse. Even though in one or two places I
couldn't exactly corroborate his words, in any case we will understand
that which is concealed from that which is revealed, because the author
(may the memory of the righteous be a blessing) certainly did not write
anything that he had not seen in a book of law or responsa. In any case,
I allowed myself to bring corroboration and proof for his words, according to my humble opinion. I also saw that my blessed father, the author
(may he rest in peace) wrote some things according to the custom that
is spreading among the Jewish people. It is right to rely upon my master,
my father (may the memory of the righteous be a blessing) and his book.
May God save us from error and enlighten our eyes with his Torah. Amen.

The critical commentary of the author of *Simhat ha-nefesh* is quoted in the
original Yiddish while the responses of R. Moshe are written in Hebrew. The
comments deal mostly with the particulars of the customs and laws in *Sefer
ha-hayyim*, for example the chapters of Psalms said in the house of mourning
(the first comment), the obligation of the mourner to learn the laws of mourning (the second comment), special cases in which it is permitted for mourners
to cut their hair (the third and fourth comments), customs of mourning on
holidays (comments 10, 17, 24, 29, 30), a distant rumor of a death (that is death
that is heard of only after the time of mourning; comment 15) and so forth.

The controversy is halakhic and substantive but it must be noted that the
general approach of the author of *Simhat ha-nefesh* stresses the observance of
the *mitzvot* from joy and is opposed to intimidation and to excessive occupation with the matters of the world to come. Although *Sefer ha-hayyim* is not

---

65   About this book (which is also called *Sefer yitnu*), see Bar-Levav, *The Concept of Death,*
      pp. 270–91. R. Moshe is referring to the following words written by his father: "God has
      given me the privilege of having many books and I have hardly lacked any." *Sefer yitnu,*
      Birnbaum manuscript, the author's preface.

necessarily intimidating in comparison with the material found, for example, in books such as *Reshit hokhmah* or *Kav ha-yashar*, it nevertheless deals directly with death.

The Meaning of the Deathbed Rituals

In his classic article, "The Bare Facts of Ritual," Jonathan Z. Smith suggested that ritual creates reality as it should be, although not as it is in actuality. It is, therefore, possible to learn from ritual more about what there is not, than about what there is. The ritual design of death (one could even say: its staging) in fact reflects the loss of control and helplessness in the face of death. Why precisely at the beginning of the modern period do we find attempts to fashion death with their accompanying literature?

It is possible to see in this a question about reality, about ritual or about literature. The existence of the literature does not necessarily indicate that people performed the rituals that appear in it, just as not all of the prayers found in the prayer books are actually said in practice, and vice versa, there are prayers that are said although they do not appear in the prayer books.

The literature is new, and the texts include many new dimensions, yet the essence of the phenomenon of attempts to control and ritually shape the hour of death is not new. The death of Rabbi Akiba, for example, is a ritual death shaped by design and control, even in a difficult situation of torture and repression. Another very influential model is the description of the death of Rabbi Shimon bar Yochai in the *Zohar*. Examples of designed death appear also in stories about the death of scholars in the classical rabbinic period and in the Middle Ages. However, until the beginning of the modern period this model was limited to the spiritual elite, special people whose intensive spiritual and religious lives were reflected in all their actions and, predictably, in their deaths. The books for the sick and dying did not create a new ritual reality, but rather expanded it and presented it as a model of ideal behavior to new classes who previously had not been able to form a ritual of their own. This is one of the indications of the widening of the circle of readers.

The deathbed rituals must be seen in the larger context of the "ritualization of Jewish life," a general process taking place in Jewish society at the beginning of the modern era. Many aspects of Jewish life at that time underwent a process of ritualistic formation, the most prominent example of which, mentioned earlier, is the service of welcoming the Sabbath, which became the apogee of the Jewish liturgical week. The new rituals reflect the needs of new readers who wanted to join the community of those who perform rituals and were intended to fill a social need as much as a religious one. Ritual expresses, of course, the religious principles of its society, though this does not mean that the motivation for its performance can only be religious. This theory contradicts the opinion that new rituals were formed in the sixteenth and seventeenth centuries only under the influence of various new ideas, in particular the Lurianic kabbalah. It would appear that myth serves the needs of ritual as much as ritual is created from myth.

We should not ignore the role of rituals, including deathbed rituals, in the creation of identity. Rituals unite their performers in a community of doers. Moreover, Jewish faith-based identity is particularly emphasized in the deathbed rituals which often include declarations of faith, for example the recitation of Maimonides' thirteen principles of faith. Acceptance of death with love also establishes and strengthens the identities of both the dying and those around him participating in the ritual. The need to emphasize Jewish identity is perhaps connected to the response to the beginning of the process of challenging traditional society, as it had taken shape by the end of the Middle Ages. It is possible that this must be seen against the backdrop of the Sabbatian crisis, which challenged traditional conceptions of Jewish identity. If so, it is possible to perceive in the ritualization process and the Enlightenment two aspects of the attempt to cope with the disintegration of patterns of traditional Jewish life. Not coincidentally, some of the polemics of the enlightened intellectuals were aimed at Jewish death customs, for example the attempts to encourage a delay of burial (in order not to accidently bury a live person) as well as the calls to permit cremation.[66] One can see in the ritualistic design of death in *Sefer ha-hayyim* an attempt to shape Jewish life and to unite the Jewish community by means of ritual, presented within the very medium which Amsterdam so excelled in producing—the printed book.

---

66   See M. Samet, *Chapters in the History of Orthodoxy* (Jerusalem 2005), pp. 157–227 [Hebrew]; Horowitz, "The Jews of Europe and the Moment of Death"; D. Malkiel, "Cremation: Technology and Culture, a Historical and Phenomenological Analysis," *Italia* 10 (1993), pp. 37–70 [Hebrew].

CHAPTER 5

Reading Yiddish and *Lernen*: Being a Pious Ashkenazi in Amsterdam, 1650–1800

Shlomo Berger

Torah study is a fundamental duty, a *mitzvah* that every Jewish male is required to fulfill.[1] It is a *mitzvah* which, besides advancing the attainment of knowledge, may also help a person to improve his spiritual and mental prowess; and, ultimately, by becoming a *talmid hakham*, a scholar, he may earn respect and status within the community.[2] The ideal is to dedicate oneself to the study of Torah day and night, to engage continuously with the holy text, its commentaries as well as rabbinic writings.[3] Although in principle one can study individually, Torah study, or in Yiddish *lernen*, was predominantly a group activity (usually within a communal society dedicated to Torah study[4]) that was conducted orally: a rabbi teaching a class on a text to the male members of his community. The pupil may have prepared the lesson (the weekly portion or a rabbinic exegesis) at home before attending the class and afterwards can re-read the text upon returning home. The role of the rabbi-teacher was essential and almost necessary; he was the person who explained matters and virtually sanctioned an interpretation of the text.

The text being studied is usually a *loshn koydesh* one: a text written in Hebrew, Aramaic or a combination of the two. In principle and in practice, a Yiddish text could not serve as a text intended for study. A Yiddish text was primarily written, printed and distributed for individual study, that is private

---

1 On the duty of Torah study or *mitzvat limud Torah*, see the basic command in Deut. 6: 7; the duty of every community to teach the children (rich and poor) was formulated by Rabbi Joshua ben Gamla: BT *Baba Batra* 21a.

2 On the term, see BT *Shabbat* 114a.

3 Joshua 1:8; on "day and night" and the study of Greek in ancient Israel, see S. Lieberman, *Greek in Jewish Palestine*, 2nd ed. (New York 1965), p. 16; the study of secular disciplines is tolerated in Jewish writing for historical, scholarly and practical reasons: see D. Rapel, *The Seven Wisdoms: The Debate on Secular Studies in Judaism* (Jerusalem 1990) esp. pp. 46–66 [Hebrew]; see also Maimonides, *Mishne Torah, Madda: Hilkhot Talmud Torah* I, 11–12.

4 During the eighteenth century, the Ashkenazi community of Amsterdam had several Torah study groups, for instance, *Talmud Torah, Hesed ve-emet, Shomrei mishmeret*. I would like to thank Tehila van Luit for the information.

© KONINKLIJKE BRILL NV, LEIDEN, 2017 | DOI 10.1163/9789004343160_006

reading or study in an informal gathering in someone's household. A Yiddish version of a text originally composed in the holy tongue was considered an auxiliary tool that supported Torah study in the Ashkenazi lands and, therefore, it may also have served as a "modern" development of the שמו"ת or *Shemot* practice: reading a biblical text twice in Hebrew and once in translation, originally the Aramaic *targum* text, or now an effort to understand the original and difficult Hebrew text while reading it twice, facilitated by a translation of the text into the Ashkenazi and more easily understandable vernacular.[5] Nevertheless, during the early modern period we encounter Yiddish texts whose producers went one step further claiming that such books were, in fact, suitable replacements of Hebrew ones and not only auxiliary tools. Thus, why and how could a Yiddish text eventually become a legitimate tool for Torah study?

A Jew living in Amsterdam had to confront and overcome serious challenges in his daily life and, in particular, worries regarding breadwinning. Preoccupation by such anxieties exerted pressure on Ashkenazim wishing to fulfill the *mitzvah* of Torah study day and night. Yet, as Arnold Eisen has shown, Torah was the sole meaningful territory of Jews in exile; and diasporic life was steered and guided by keeping to the holy text. Living within this "holy textual territory" (a metaphorical and yet a real territory) and accepting its overall validity, Jews had to consider Torah (in its widest meaning) as their basic instrument to guide an individual from the moment he woke up in the morning to the moment he fell asleep at night.[6] Therefore, a way had to be found that would mediate between the effort to lead a solid Jewish life and private worries regarding breadwinning. Moreover, calling on Jews to study Torah was a scepter that rabbis could sway before community members attempting to keep them within the fold of rabbinic Judaism and guide them (back) to the righteous path. Still, although Ashkenazi culture was in essence bilingual,[7] Ashkenazim faced ever

---

5   On reading translations of Torah in other languages and not the traditional Aramaic *Targum*, see *Turei zahav* by David b. Shmuel Halevi Segal (Lublin 1646: see M. Steinschneider, *Catalogus Librorom Hebraeorum in Bibliotheca Bodleiana* [Berlin 1852–1860] 886, no. 4844, 4) who advises those people who cannot read Hebrew to take up Yiddish books like the *Tsene rene*: "אבל מי שאינו בר הכי ודאי ראוי לקרות בפי' התור' שיש בל' אשכנז בזמנינו כגון ספר צאנה וראנ' וכיוצ' בו כדי שיבין ענין הפרש" (ט"ז על שולחן ערוך אורח חיים, הלכות שבת, סימן רפ"ה, סעיף ב) ("[B]ut the one who is not educated, it is certainly advisable that he reads current Torah interpretations in the Ashkenazi language as the *Tsene-rene* and suchlike books in order to understand the weekly lessons").

6   A. Eisen, *Galut: Modern Jewish Reflections on Homelessness and Homecoming* (Indiana 1986), pp. 35–56.

7   Ch. Turniansky, *Language, Education and Scholarship among Eastern European Jews* (Tel Aviv 1994), pp. 81–87 [Hebrew]; ead., "Yiddish and the Transmission of Knowledge in Early Modern Europe," *JSQ* 15 (2008), pp. 5–18.

growing complications in their attempt to follow this ideal, because the masses
had a poor or restricted education and could not usually (fully) understand
Hebrew texts, which comprised this meaningful diasporic spiritual territory.
They encountered difficulties grasping the Hebrew liturgy they were reciting
in synagogue; reading rabbinic literature presented an even higher hurdle and
the majority could not follow the legal arguments as well as the language of
Jewish Law. Thus, although refusing to openly recognize the problems, as time
passed the language barrier became practically insurmountable.

Subsequently, rabbis and intellectuals felt that by addressing the public in
their own vernacular, Ashkenazim would be offered a literature that might
help them to be constituents of the diasporic Torah territory. Indeed, rabbis
delivered sermons and discussed halakhic matters in Yiddish, but when putting texts of sermons in writing or compiling texts of responsa, they published
them in Hebrew. Nevertheless, authors were also ready to begin to translate,
adopt and compose explanatory tracts and commentaries in Yiddish and embrace other strategies and modes of argumentation that the masses would be
able to follow, grasp and, more importantly, internalize. Gradually and sporadically, the gap between the oral and written presentation of rabbinic texts began to close. Of course, the idea of reading the original Hebrew texts of Torah
and prayers was not ignored and could not be abandoned. Public liturgy was
conducted in Hebrew and when in the first decade of the eighteenth century
efforts were made to introduce Yiddish liturgy in synagogue, they failed. Public
liturgy was still recited in Hebrew and the custom did not change throughout the ages.[8] Still, other genres of text (including Torah commentaries) began to receive their own mode of Yiddish adaptation or translation. Yiddish,
the universal Ashkenazi vernacular up to the end of the eighteenth century,
subsequently assumed the position of Aramaic and became the translation
language of Torah, prayers and rabbinic literature to all Jewish dwellers north
of the Alps.[9] The process was protracted and never linear. The adoption of

8   See the case of Ahron ben Shmuel: I. Zinberg, *The History of Jewish Literature 6* (Vilnius 1935),
    pp. 255–58 [Yiddish].

9   Indeed, for the Ashkenazi Yiddish speaker, Aramaic was considered a layer of the *loshn
    koydesh*, and thus, a traditional text may have included Hebrew and Aramaic segments
    that formed a Jewish text. Recently scholars, for instance, Dovid Katz (*Words on Fire: The
    Unfinished Story of Yiddish* [New York 2004], pp. 46–47), has forwarded the idea that Ashke-
    nazim were, in fact, trilingual, and therefore, consider Aramaic to be a third language that
    Ashkenazim employed. Katz's conclusion is exaggerated. It can be argued, as Katz does,
    that there were intellectuals who could distinguish between Hebrew and Aramaic and were
    aware of the fact that the *Zohar* was composed in Aramaic. Still, this phenomenon cannot
    describe the masses' linguistic state of knowledge. Ashkenazim did not "know" Aramaic and

Yiddish was carried out on different levels and diverse methods and procedures were employed.[10]

Translations of prayers into Yiddish were considered a means that would help Ashkenazim to understand what, in fact, they were reciting in synagogue. The often used maxim that justified such translations was: תפילה ללא כוונה כגוף ללא נשמה or "prayer without intention is like a body without a soul."[11] Full intention can be achieved when someone understands what his mouth is uttering, and language proficiency is central to any understanding. Thus, the producer of a prayer book published in Amsterdam in 1721[12] admits that people already possessed Hebrew prayer books and, therefore, the new Yiddish volume was printed in quarto, the format typical of Hebrew prayer books, and it should be bound together with the Hebrew book. Consequently, attending a synagogue service an Amsterdam Ashkenazi would be able to leaf through the translation and grasp what was printed in the Hebrew prayer book and understand what he was reciting.[13] Moreover, in moments of intermission during the service, the Ashkenazi male would be able to go on reading the Yiddish text and refrain from chatting with his neighbor.[14] The Yiddish text, then, was intended for reading and a sort of *lernen* and also reflected the act of praying.

Reading Torah was another matter and yet presented similar consequences. As an integral section of the Sabbath day service, the weekly portion was of course recited in Hebrew, and the Ashkenazi was encouraged to prepare himself for the occasion. Still, as the Ashkenazi annals show, further steps were taken and Yiddish also assumed a more substantial role in this department of Jewish liturgy and ritual. One such Yiddish text turned to the supreme bestseller of Yiddish literature up to date, and it demonstrates the process whereby Yiddish occupied a more central and profound position within Ashkenazi Jewish religious culture. The *Tsene rene* is a commentary on the five books of the Torah and also includes translations (with a high measure of adaptation) of

did not consider it a separate linguistic entity. For Ashkenazim, the "holy tongue," which may have occasionally included Hebrew and Aramaic segments, was one linguistic unit. Therefore, it is advisable to go on describing Ashkenazi society as bilingual.

10   S. Berger, "Functioning within a Diasporic Third Space: The Case of Early Modern Yiddish," *JSQ* 15 (2008), pp. 68–86; idem, "Jiddisch und die Formierung der aschkenasischen Diaspora," *Aschkenas* 18–19 (2009–2010), pp. 509–27.

11   Isaac Abrabanel, *Avot* 2:13.

12   *Makhzor bilshon Ashkenaz ke-minhag Ashkenaz u-Polin, Krovets*: see M. Gutschow, *Inventory of Yiddish Publications from the Netherlands, c.1650–c.1950* (Leiden 2007), p. 66 n. 236.

13   It is, indeed, an awkward mode of reading and it may be assumed that usually Ashkenazim did not follow the advice.

14   See another such advice below: the 1713 prayer book.

the five scrolls and the weekly portions composed of texts from the Prophets.[15] Of course, it did not replace the synagogue's liturgy, but Ashkenazi men and women alike were encouraged to read the text and get acquainted with the narrative of the Torah and its messages. Moreover, women, who could never be a partner of a quorum in the synagogue, were advised to read the Yiddish weekly portion of the *Tsene rene* on the Sabbath when the men were in synagogue. Thus, although being strictly connected with the annual liturgical cycle, the book also functioned as the medium of reading for the sake of reading for men and women alike; and reading here is also understood as *lernen*. Moreover, those who could not read at all could listen to the text recited by others and, therefore, could be considered "readers" as well. In scholarly research it is defined as the aural function of reading.[16]

Yet another development can be detected here which signals the process of change within the Ashkenazi world during the seventeenth and eighteenth centuries. Reading (and listening to) the *Tsene rene* demonstrates the gradual development of individual, private reading. Indeed, the book was never read in synagogue or at any other official public event. It was usually read at home and within the circle of family and friends. The presence of listeners still indicates a public forum of reading, but it was an informal gathering and the listener was not encouraged to learn the text by heart in order to recite it in the future. The *Tsene rene* was too long for that purpose anyway. A person may also have read the book in his own room and silently.[17]

The *Tsene rene* was, and still remains, the supreme bestseller of Yiddish literature, but other books that adopted the same and similar strategies were published in Yiddish and Amsterdam, being the center of the Hebrew book industry in Europe during the seventeenth and eighteenth centuries, produced a bulk of such books. Undeniably, local book agents were ready to produce and disseminate Yiddish texts, which actually heralded the changing of the times and the introduction of "modern" modes of practicing Judaism. The Amsterdam Ashkenazim were the first group of consumers for whom these books were prepared. Indeed, it is imperative to notice that in the area of book production there is no difference between an Ashkenazi living in *Mokem Alef* and

---

15   The *Tsene rene* was most probably written and printed during the last years of the six-
      teenth or the first years of the seventeenth century; the first known edition of the book
      is its fourth edition published in 1622. On the book, see Ch. Thurniansky and J. Elbaum,
      "Tsene-Rene" in YIVO *Encyclopedia of Jews in Eastern Europe*, ed. G.D. Hundert (New Ha-
      ven 2008), pp. 1912–13.

16   B. Stock, *Listening for the Text: On the Use of the Past* (Baltimore 1990), pp. 20–23.

17   Ibid., pp. 101–3.

an Ashkenazi from Lvov. The necessary existence of dissimilar conditions in both cities affected Ashkenazim's daily life in both geographical regions, but the books they consulted while deliberating and structuring their Jewish life were practically the same. Still, the Amsterdam Ashkenazim were the local and instant consumers of these books.

The most important genre of Yiddish literature that emerged, developed and flourished during the seventeenth and eighteenth centuries is that of *Muser sforim* or ethical books. Of course, ethical books were based on the Hebrew genre of *Musar* which was already known and popular during the Middle-Ages.[18] However, authors of the equivalent Yiddish books paved their own ways and directed their texts in another direction, attempting to conquer the Ashkenazi reading public and cater to their preoccupations. Thus, the local Amsterdam, as well as European, Ashkenazim were offered another variety of texts, which, according to scholars, actually defined Yiddish literature and culture of the period.[19] Even when medieval Hebrew ethical tracts were translated into Yiddish, besides the fact that the philosophical argumentation was minimized or eliminated, the Ashkenazi setting served as the narrative background; and when original Yiddish ethical texts were published, these actually described Ashkenazi historical realities and preoccupations.[20]

Defining the genre and its boundaries may indeed teach us about these books' strength, effectiveness and popularity. Ethical literature in Yiddish may

18   Y. Tishbi and J. Dan, *Hebrew Ethical Literature: Selected Texts with Introduction, Notes and Commentary* (Jerusalem 1970) [Hebrew]; J. Dan, *Hebrew Ethical and Homiletical Literature (The Middle Ages and Early Modern Period)* (Jerusalem 1975) [Hebrew].

19   M. Erik, *History of Yiddish Literature from Its Earliest Times to the Enlightenment Period* (Warsaw 1928), pp. 207–420; see Introduction, 207–9 [Yiddish].

20   Ibid., p. 245: "they (i.e., ethical books) not only include a myriad of details on Jewish internal life of the period, and not only enable those with a keen eye to chart a picture of these generations' internal static and frozen life. They also delineate lines of dynamic, psychological movement and spiritual life of the folk (in Yiddish: *folksmasn*). And precisely here the Yiddish ethical books are more important: the Hebrew books are more abstract, theoretical, detached from life, while Yiddish ethical books are mostly based on concrete details, real and daily questions; the books are more intimate and anyhow less pious (*farfrumt*), they are positive (*gutmutiker*), restricted and more persuasive – in short earthlier (*erdisher*). But also linguistically the Yiddish ethical books are of great value. Because of obvious reasons the books' language is popular, and by far more natural than the artful (*gekintslter*) 'language of literature' of our romances from the same period" [author's translation s.b.]. The condescending tone reflects Erik's modern and secular preoccupations and, therefore, he harshly judges the early modern Ashkenazi way of life. Nevertheless, although romantic in tone, his account still gives a plausible historical picture of the genre.

be outlined within an inclusive or exclusive framework. The genre may refer to books and texts the sole task of which was to offer spiritual guidance to readers. While Hebrew medieval ethical texts occasionally aimed at philosophizing and, therefore, pertained to learned men and their intellectual interests, their Yiddish counterparts were mainly interested in questions of ethics on a daily and practical level, in providing moral guidance to a larger public of readers. The books usually offered advice in the form of easily understood principles, rules, sayings and maxims explaining duties to be performed and stressing the Ashkenazi's individual responsibility towards himself, his family and community and the people of Israel in general. Yiddish *muser sforim* usually and deliberately avoided a theoretical discourse on Jewish law,[21] and their authors preferred to chart modes of behavior by elucidating matters on the basis of examples and tales rather than presenting hypothetical and speculative arguments.[22] Thus, there is also good reason to include within this genre books like *Minhagim* or custom books,[23] whose aim it was to register local usages of texts of prayer, modes of ritual and issues of conduct and which allowed the individual Ashkenazi to lead a righteous life as well as become an upright member of his community. The correct performance of duties was seen as a proven method to achieve moral excellence. Ethical books were individually read and not studied within a group and, thus, the act of reading became a significant act of *lernen*. The equation between reading (in Yiddish) and *lernen* can be interpreted as an introduction of a new diasporic and "modern" mode of Torah study, which perhaps is less sophisticated than the traditional one but more "democratic," advocating and encouraging another level of *lernen*. Subsequently, Torah study was divided into two segments: the scholarly engagement carried out in the *yeshiva* and at least theoretically encouraging a scholarly

---

21   See also *Sefer emunas yisroel* below.

22   A gratifying example is the book *Simkhes ha-nefesh* (Frankfurt a/M. 1707; Amsterdam 1723). The book's first part includes exemplary stories on questions of behavior and custom, while the second part is dedicated to the presentation of rulings mainly concerned with daily Jewish practices, beginning with items referring to the rules a person should follow in the morning from the moment he wakes up. Both sections offer similar advice: the first part in the form of storytelling and the second in the form of maxims. To a certain extent, the book may function as an encyclopaedia of Ashkenazi daily life; on the book, see Zinberg, *History*, pp. 235–43, 245–46; J. Baumgarten, *Introduction to Old Yiddish Literature* (Oxford 2005), pp. 210–12.

23   Custom books were printed in each and every city where Jewish printers were active from the sixteenth century on. On Amsterdam editions of Yiddish custom books, see Gutschow, *Inventory*, p. 12, no. 3; p. 21, no. 44; p. 30, no. 83; p. 36, no. 103; p. 37, no. 109; p. 50, no. 162; p. 70, no. 243; p. 75, no. 264.

study of texts within the boundaries of faith and the popular education in Judaism as offered by the *beit midrash* (study house) as well as individual reading at home. Yiddish earned another measure of legitimization within, at least, an Ashkenazi popular cultural setting.

The mere employment of the Yiddish language was always a decisive factor of communication. Ethical maxims written down in Yiddish were easier to understand. Moreover, writing in Yiddish enabled authors to express themselves without too many restrictions and granted them a space within which they were released from the shackles of rabbinic forms of argumentation. Authors were usually exempt from rabbinic criticism because Hebrew books were "important" and Yiddish books merely a necessary evil.[24] Indeed, it is possible to describe a cultural development in the use of Yiddish in ethical books: justifying the use of Yiddish as a necessary means in the first place,[25] then claiming that for the simple person a Yiddish book may replace a Hebrew equivalent as a text of study,[26] later arguing that even intellectuals can, at least occasionally, enjoy a Yiddish written book,[27] and finally practically admitting that there are more genres of Yiddish books which may serve the purpose of Torah study.[28] The process was always tied up with arguments about the nature of Ashkenazi daily life and the Jew's individual situation on the one hand and arguments regarding the value of texts and books on the other. While customarily being defined as "People of the Book," the Ashkenazim were now "People of Yiddish books."

Rabbinic literature and culture praises the study of Torah and rabbis attach different values to this *mitzvah*. Thus, the study of Torah outweighs other duties like visiting the sick and honoring one's parents (BT *Shabbat* 127a). A number of sages consider Torah study more important than the rescue of human life (BT *Megillah* 16b). According to Rabbi Meir, when one studies Torah for its own sake the creation of the entire world is worthwhile (*Avot* 6:1). As a child

---

24   Indeed, Moshe Frankfurt admits in his preface to the Yiddish translation of *Menorat ha-ma'or* (Amsterdam 1722) that there were intellectuals who opposed the translation of the book because it included "difficult ideas" that Ashkenazim could not understand, but he apparently disregarded their criticism and completed the translation. He goes one step further and argues that brilliant intellectuals like Maimonides have written texts of fundamental importance to Jewish culture in other languages and not in Hebrew. Does he want to convince the readers or the rabbis and intellectuals who objected to the project?

25   S. Berger, *Producing Redemption in Amsterdam: Early Modern Yiddish Books in Paratextual Perspective* (Leiden and Boston 2013), pp. 93–116.

26   As in the case of *Menorat ha-ma'or*, see n. 24.

27   Berger, *Producing Redemption in Amsterdam*, p. 97.

28   See discussion on *Beys yisroel-Beys bkhiro* below.

must quench his hunger day by day, so must the grown-up person busy himself with the Torah each hour (JT *Berakhot* 9). Whoever learns Torah at night is granted grace during the day and whoever neglects it will be fed burning coals in the world to come (BT *Avodah Zarah* 3b). Even lepers and the ritually unclean are required to study Torah (BT *Berakhot* 22a). All such maxims do not refer to the question of the language of study, but to the act of study itself. Perhaps the reading of Hebrew is taken for granted, but the fact that questions of language do not play a role gradually allowed the case to be put for studying in different languages. Indeed, only one such piece of advice does refer to the question of language: the recommendation to read the weekly portion twice in Hebrew and once in *Targum* (Aramaic), which thus acknowledges that the Torah may usefully be read in another language for the sake of comprehension.[29] In Ashkenazi society, Yiddish replaced Aramaic as the daily vernacular and it, therefore, became advisable to use it for the same purposes. Indeed, almost all published Yiddish books in the early modern period, in Amsterdam too, regularly mentioned the license to print books in the vernacular. The need to assist the Ashkenazi masses was accepted as a primary legitimizing measure and, in the course of time, it turned into a useful and repetitive *topos* which appeared on the title pages of most Yiddish books.[30] Though it was a *topos*, this does not weaken the strong sense of urgency felt by all book agents and readers when employing Yiddish.

Yiddish books printed in Amsterdam provide overwhelming evidence for the above-described process that turned Yiddish into a meaningful tool of Torah study. The duty of *lernen* is always voiced in the texts and, although primarily advocated on practical grounds, reading Yiddish becomes an instrument that supports qualitative Torah study. Evidently an Ashkenazi householder who was not a *lerner* by nature was to be encouraged to engage in reading in whatever form and at any given time. A case in point is the above-mentioned *Krovets* (1721), when the producer admits that people already possess Hebrew prayer books, and when he advises the men to read the Yiddish version during intermission of prayer and thus refrain from chatting with their neighbors, which is a faux pas. Clearly, although not in so many words, the *Mokemer* Ashkenazi is pushed towards reading and *lernen* at every possible moment. *Lernen* is here practically combined with the adoption of appropriate modes of behavior in synagogue.[31]

---

29   See above.

30   Berger, *Producing Redemption in Amsterdam*, pp. 26–29, 96–107.

31   Correct and appropriate behavior was a recurrent issue within the Amsterdam Ashkenazi community. A *Seder hanhagot beit ha-kneset* ("The Order of Customs in the Synagogue")

Other situations also presented opportunities to read Yiddish and learn. In a prayer book published in 1713 we read that "this beautiful prayer book with many new items has now been printed in order to delight people's hearts. Everything was set in orderly fashion, and the like of it has never been seen in the world. Nobody has to look for [the correct place of prayer] and ask somebody else. And also the weekly portions were translated into Yiddish, which is also a new phenomenon. It will provide pleasant and good learning as happened when it helped me on sleepless nights. And when others are chatting in the synagogue with each other and making an upheaval, the pious man can find in it many good things to read." Besides being useful in synagogue, this prayer book is apparently profitable in cases of insomnia as well, and for private reading occasions at home. The prayer book with Yiddish additions in whatever form is not only a ritualistic object to be used in synagogue (or at home), but a Yiddish book that an Ashkenazi may study in his living room or, indeed, bedroom. The prayer book is to be employed in public gatherings and under specific conditions and also within one's own house at moments chosen by the individual Ashkenazi. A prayer book is not only intended for prayer but also for *lernen*.

The economic necessity to earn one's living created a distinct set of problems. Ashkenazim were busy with work and refrained from learning and, therefore, a limited plan could be set up which would encourage men to engage in *lernen* at least during the Sabbath. This is minimalistic in essence but, again, conceived out of practical considerations. In *Tikun Shlomo* (1731), the publisher declares that "at the present time I find that the majority of the people, including simple householders who are not learned, are busy all week long making a living in order to feed their wives and children and, therefore, have no time to learn the Torah and only on the Sabbath do they deal with the Torah." The message here indicates that *lernen* is a duty to be fulfilled by learned and uneducated persons even if it is restricted to the Sabbath. But even on the Sabbath Ashkenazim turned idle and frivolous and, thus, special songs were written in order to dissuade Ashkenazim from singing *goyish* melodies among other things, as

was published in 1716 and reissued in 1759 and 1776 (Gutschow, *Inventory*, p. 61, no. 209; p. 96, no. 344; p. 113, no. 410). As the preface of the booklet's first edition shows, the community was preoccupied with disorder in the synagogue before and during prayers. The regulations attempted to forge a system that would decide about the local custom regarding the recitation of prayers, and also the system that organized the division of privileges to community members concerning the recitation of, for instance, the *kaddish* prayer or *haftorot*: see also Berger, *Producing Redemption in Amsterdam*, pp. 167–68; and idem, "Hanhagat beit ha-kneset 1716," in *Ze'ev Gries Jubilee Book*, ed. O. Israeli, et al. (Jerusalem, forthcoming).

is suggested in *Shirei Yehuda* (1693).[32] On other occasions, Ashkenazim would
take a nap after consuming the *sholet* (or *tsholent*), as suggested in the preface
to the 1736 Yiddish edition of *Pirkei oves* (Ethics of the Fathers) and, therefore,
a new edition of the Mishna tract in Yiddish may persuade them to dedicate
time to Torah study during the Sabbath.[33] Moreover, the songs were composed
in Hebrew in order to bestow on them an aura of prayer, but the Hebrew text
was accompanied by lengthy Hebrew and Yiddish commentaries that made
the book attractive to those who knew Hebrew and to others who could read
Yiddish only. In the second case of *Pirkei oves*, the book includes the Yiddish
translation (or indeed adaptation) of the mishnaic text and the detailed preface locating the tract within a contemporary Ashkenazi worldview.

What, then, is the nature and value of *lernen* in Yiddish? In *Sefer emunas yisroel* (Amsterdam 1764), it is claimed that "there is the pillar of belief, the pillar
of ritual and the pillar of Torah study. I collected practical notions from books
of giant Jewish sages which may animate hearts. And they expanded [their
arguments] with testimonies from Talmud which would here demand an additional hundred quires. [Therefore], in this booklet I included all these notions
without testimonies (= arguments), because I have noticed that God [also]
loves believers who do not inquire and do not look for proof." *Lernen* is here
understood in terms of belief combined with the act of reading; and because
no discussions of subjects are included and no thorny argumentation is dealt
with, *lernen*, the act of reading, should lead the Ashkenazi reader to repeat
maxims and to internalize ethical rules. Subsequently, reading, equivalent to
studying, equivalent to believing, will lead the Ashkenazi to the righteous path.
One must accept the rulings, "the conclusions," and act according to them. The
Yiddish book operates as a personal guidebook for modes of behavior, which
also imply spiritual training and correct notions of belief.

Yet, as suggested above, Yiddish ultimately could also be fruitful for scholars.
Prefacing *Kohelet Shlomo* (1743), the compiler, editor and translator Shlomo

---

32   דא ווערין גירעט פיל דברים בטלים אונטר דעסין אונ טאן אן חורבן הבית פֿאר געשין. אונ׳ ווען
     זיא הלטין אין טרינקן דא זינגן זיא לידר דיא מען ניט זאל גידענקן. ("[I]n the meanwhile trivi-
     alities are widely said and the destruction of the Temple is forgotten. And when they are
     drinking they sing songs which are better not remembered").

33   איין טייל לייט, אזו בלד אז זיא אן שבת אויף געסין האבין, טונין זיא זיך שלאפֿין ליגן. אונ דר נאך
     רידן זיא דברים בטלים. אז וויא דיא צייט פר גיט דיא זענין גלייך אז דיא בהמות.
     אזו בלד אז דער שאליט אדר דיא קוגל גיגעסין איז, גיבט קיינר אונזר גאט קיין גוט ווארט. דער
     ליגט זיך שלאפֿין, דער גיט רידן דברים בטלים. ("[I]mmediately after eating on Shabbat,
     some people go to sleep and thereafter speak about trivialities. As the time passes they
     resemble beasts. As soon as the *Tsholent* or *Kugl* is eaten, nobody expresses a good word
     towards God [bless God]. They are off to sleep and speak about idle matters").

Zalman London argues that "also the scholar who knows more than I do will not be offended by taking this book in hand. He will find in the book many good things to see [read], which he would have to look for in many other books and now, looking only through the Hebrew text of the book, he will be able to enjoy them. And he will save a lot of money in addition, [by not having to] buy small books, which are necessary in any household on a daily basis." The arguments are particularly oblique. The book includes Hebrew and Yiddish texts. Therefore, London suggests that a scholar may consult the Hebrew section only and be satisfied with the book. Thus, London mollifies the intellectual reader by stressing the possibility of reading Hebrew texts only, while in fact indirectly pointing him to the reading of the Yiddish texts as well. The door is open for scholars to get acquainted with texts in the vernacular, while the less educated may improve their Hebrew proficiency. The combination of Hebrew and Yiddish texts within one volume underlines the ongoing existence and relevance of Ashkenazi bilingualism.[34] Options for individual *lernen* in both Hebrew and Yiddish are suggested, involving diverse methods and levels of reading and study within Ashkenazi society.

The act of individual and informal *lernen* is also organized in cycles, which are different from the liturgical cycle but, of course, imitate its logic; a cycle may ensure a regular engagement with Torah. The Yiddish version of Ibn Gabirol's *Keter malkhut* published in Amsterdam in 1671 is divided into seven sections, each of which should be read on another day of the week.[35] This daily division could be put forward because the medieval poem was included in Sephardi prayer books and had the value of a prayer. Still, it is impossible to discern any content-based logic for this particular division. The division is clearly arbitrary. Thus, the publishers wished to support daily reading activity that carried the value of prayer. A textual rationality of division is of no importance; repetition is advisable and to be praised. In *Sefer hen tov* (1756) the publisher suggests a monthly division: "every householder, in order to find grace in the eyes of God, will read [recite] the book to his wife and children around the family table in a cycle of thirty days." Indeed, *lernen* here is advocated as a family activity and, thus, expands the circle of potential readers in an informal gathering to include females and the younger generation. It is also logical to assume that the text was eventually discussed and examined, albeit on a lower level. Torah

---

34   See above.

35   S. Berger, "From Philosophy to Popular Ethics: Two 17th-Century Yiddish Translations of Ibn Gabirol's *Keter Malkhut*," in *Sepharad in Ashkenaz: Medieval Knowledge and Eighteenth-Century Enlightened Jewish Discourse*, ed. R. Fontaine et al. (Amsterdam 2007), pp. 223–33.

study is conceived here as a common and less professional activity, rather than as a religious duty, and *lernen* is directed towards the accumulation of basic knowledge that may enrich an Ashkenazi Yiddish reader.

Ultimately, one further and last step was taken by Yiddish publishers. They began to justify the printing of books which do not belong to the genre of liturgy or classical rabbinic literature by claiming that these serve the cause of *lernen* as well. For instance, in *Beys yisroel-beys bkhiro*,[36] the author strives to organize the biblical narrative in a chronological order and then claims that he is imitating strategies of studying history among the gentiles. The book's preface indicates the importance of studying Jewish history, considering it a legitimate and rewarding Torah study. In fact, the preface's author promotes a study of the Bible, albeit within its correct chronological order, and promotes it as a new, "modern" desideratum that is justified by diasporic realities. The nations are interested in their history and Ashkenazim should follow their example; knowing one's history is essential to understanding one's situation and eventual survival.[37] The Amsterdam Ashkenazi Menahem Mann Amelander could eventually launch an original Yiddish project by writing and publishing the first ever Jewish history in Yiddish, *Sheyris yisroel* and describing the Jewish diasporic annals from the destruction of the Second Temple to the date of publication (1743). By recounting the Jewish past, the efforts to locate

---

36   The first edition was published in Offenbach in 1719 and the second edition in Amsterdam in 1724: on the book and especially on the second part *Beys bkhiro*, see Ch. Shmeruk and I. Bartal, "'Contemporary Jerusalem' by R. Alexander b. Moses Ethausen," *Shalem* 4 (1984), pp. 445–58 [Hebrew].

37   ערשטליך וייל איך גיזעהן האב דאש אלי אומות גרושי ליב האבר זיין פון (דברי הימים), דען איטליכר מלך אונ' שר אזו ווייט אלש זיא נאך זוכן אונ' זעהן קענן וואז איר הער קומן איז וויא וואול איטליכי מדינה, איטליכש מקום האלטן איר קראנקי, וויא וואול דש אלש בישטיט אין מעננשן זכרון. אבר מיר בני ישראל אונזר הער קומן איז אויז דברי הימים דיא אלי זיין (ברוח הקודש) גירעט וואָרן אונ' אונזר חכמים דיא דא האבן קבלה אמיתית גיהאט (איש מפי איש) ביז משה רבינו ע"ה. ניט מער עש איז אייגינטליך קיין ספר דרויף גימאכט וואָרן...דארום האב איך מיך בימיאט אונ' האב אויז אלי ספרים דער שורש ארויז גינומן וואש צו דער זאך פון ניטן איז, דש איין. איטליכר אלש וואול פר שטין קאן. ("[F]irstly, I have noticed that all nations are lovers of history, because each king and minister investigates as much as possible and as far as human memory exists their ancestry as well as [the history of] each land and location that is confronted with its problems. We, the people of Israel, our ancestry is found in the Books of Chronicles which were delivered by the holy spirit and our sages received the truth mouth to ear until the days of Moses. But practically speaking, no book was written about it ... therefore, I took the trouble and collected from all other books the roots [basics] which are necessary for the issue and with which everyone can fully understand [the matters]").

the lost tribes were underscored and the subsequent coming of the Messiah forwarded.[38] Reading *Sheyris yisroel* was an act of *lernen* that was to enhance the Ashkenazi's understanding of his Jewish life and support religious daily practices of prayer and ritual.

Lernen in Yiddish transformed Torah study from a, mainly, study group event into a private, or semi-private, occasion. On a basic level, the Yiddish texts came to parallel the Hebrew ones and, therefore, the language change should have not involved any radical movement away from the study of the Bible, commentaries and rabbinic literature. Still, significant changes surfaced in the way these texts were appreciated and the targets that were attached to reading Yiddish texts were different. Authors, publishers and readers were less concerned with a highly intellectual handling of theoretical questions of Jewish Law. The importance of rabbinical argumentation was curtailed. In turn, questions of belief and conduct were highlighted. Rabbinic Judaism in Yiddish aimed at keeping the Ashkenazim on the righteous path and showing them the way to live a solid daily Jewish life within the diasporic setting. Indeed, consciously or not, the employment of Yiddish offered an opposite route to *pilpul*.[39] The naive believer was encouraged to follow a route that God would approve. Thus, it may also signify a movement towards an increasingly personal interpretation and democratic treatment of texts and books and belief. The individual Ashkenazi was now responsible for his own choices. Men and women had to find time and create occasions to engage in the study of Torah by reading a Yiddish text at home. Yiddish, then, assisted with the formation of another community within the Ashkenazi textual territory, which influenced different areas of Jewish life.

First and foremost, the linguistic shift that started in around the tenth century,[40] now secured Yiddish a far more stable position in Ashkenazi culture. Following Eisen's formulation, Yiddish printed books formed an ever expanding and meaningful territory for religious and subsequently secular culture in the Ashkenazi world.[41] Claiming that a history book is meaningful and important to read, Ashkenazi Yiddish culture stretched the boundaries between the religious and the secular. Moreover, in a city like Amsterdam, a

---

38   B. Wallet, "Links in a Chain: Early Modern Yiddish Historiography in the Northern Netherlands, 1743–1812," (Ph.D. Dissertation, University of Amsterdam 2012), pp. 109–61.

39   D. Rapel, *The Debate over the Pilpul* (Tel Aviv 1979) [Hebrew].

40   M. Weinreich, *History of the Yiddish Language* (New Haven 2008).

41   Indeed, the boundaries of the Ashkenazi world are defined by the presence of Yiddish speaking Jews: see, J. Davis, "The Reception of the *Shulhan Arukh* and the Formation of Ashkenazic Jewish Identity," *AJS Review* 26 (2002), pp. 251–78.

seaport by nature,[42] Yiddish successfully operated as a buffer language that
kept the Ashkenazi within the fold of his religion and community.[43] The Ashkenazi did not read Hebrew but he did not switch to Dutch and remained loyal
to the Ashkenazi vernacular.

Second, targeting a larger public defined as the uneducated, the simple-
minded masses or the ignorant, producers of Yiddish books could circumvent
potential competition with Hebrew and criticism by rabbis and intellectuals.
Yiddish went on to serve as the Ashkenazi language *par excellence* and Hebrew
as the marker of Jewish identity.[44] Yiddish book producers adopted a sense of
modesty that prevented detractors of Yiddish from launching an overall assault on its usage; indeed, most if not all Ashkenazim used Yiddish as a spoken
language on a daily basis and they were able to read it, though clearly not all
could write it.[45]

Third, as far as modes of composition are concerned, the emphasis on questions of belief and conduct rather than rabbinic argumentation and the insistence on ethical conduct and daily morals advanced a personal diasporic
approach to Jewish life. This may be regarded as a hesitant and unintended
step towards bolder movements of change that would eventually characterize
the period after the 1750s, in Western Europe towards Enlightenment and in
Eastern Europe towards Hasidism.

Lastly, an apparent lowering of the level of *lernen* enabled a larger segment
of the Ashkenazi population to take up this duty. The learned Yiddish texts may
have been easier to grasp and follow, the lessons were practical and the barriers
between men and women were actually broken down. *Lernen* in Yiddish offered

---

42   D. Sorkin, "The Port Jews: Notes Towards a Social Type," *JJS* 50 (1999), pp. 87–97; *Port Jews:
      Jewish Communities in Cosmopolitan Maritime Trading Centers 1550–1950*, ed. D. Cesarani
      (London 2002); *Jews and Port Cities, 1590–1990: Commerce, Community and Cosmopolitan-
      ism*, ed. D. Cesarani and G. Romain (London 2006); L. Dubin, "Introduction: Port Jews in
      the Atlantic World," *Jewish History* 20 (2006), pp. 117–27.
43   On the difference between Amsterdam and Prague as manifested in a particular Yiddish
      text, see S. Berger, "The Jewish Community of Cochin in Ashkenazi Worldview," *Pe'amim*
      135 (2013), pp. 105–24 [Hebrew].
44   J. Myhill, *Language in Jewish Society: Towards a New Understanding* (Clevedon 2004),
      pp. 32–53.
45   Up to 1800, countries in north and north-western Europe achieved "something as mass
      literacy in terms of reading skills" and only after 1800 "a decline in illiteracy, which . . .
      may be taken as an inability to sign the marriage register"; see D. Vincent, *The Rise of Mass
      Literacy: Reading and Writing in Modern Europe* (Oxford 2000), pp. 8–11. It is generally
      assumed that the level of literacy among Jewish boys was higher, but it was certainly not
      universal or close to universal.

a novel trajectory that could be partially controlled. Authors, editors and publishers of Yiddish texts usually produced "trustworthy" texts, but Yiddish *lernen* mainly became a matter of reading. Indeed, in his preface to *Orkhes tzadikim* (Amsterdam 1735), Shlomo Zalman London complains that people tend to buy books as ornaments for their living rooms and shelve them as a sign of the household's pretensions in areas of Torah study and social standing.[46] Reading Yiddish was meant to redirect this negative trend and it should have penetrated Ashkenazim's minds.

In sum, the notion of *lernen* in Yiddish is tied up with the notion of reading and thus it expands the idea of Torah study on several levels. First, it allocates a legitimate position to Yiddish within Ashkenazi Jewish culture. Yiddish is certainly not canonized as a Jewish language, but it is recognized as a genuine and justifiable carrier of religious tradition within the Ashkenazi diasporic territories. Second, *lernen* in Yiddish took on a larger individual dimension. Because it is a reading activity not (always) controlled by rabbis, the Ashkenazi is encouraged to assume more autonomy and responsibility; this reflects modernizing effects on Ashkenazi culture in Amsterdam and Europe, in general. Third, reading in Yiddish turns *lernen* into a rather general mode of education instead of only an occupation for talented scholars dealing with intellectual questions and ideas. Moreover, reducing the intellectual claim attached to *lernen* enabled an expansion of the *lernen* public. Therefore, Yiddish reading and/or *lernen* transforms Torah study into a daily and "practical" phenomenon and thus assisted rabbis in their effort to keep the Ashkenazi masses within the fold of Judaism. Offering the public the possibility to read in Yiddish, rabbis could impose demands concerning behavior and conduct in individual life.

Because Amsterdam was a Jewish book production center, the availability of Yiddish books turned the local Ashkenazim into the first European community that was widely exposed to these new modes of study. And because rabbis were imported from central and Eastern Europe until the nineteenth century, and a local *yeshiva* was not established until well into the nineteenth century,[47] the absence of a local authentic Ashkenazi intellectual elite made

---

46   דר וייל ער האט מיט זיין חכמה גיזעהן דז זיין מענכי לייט דיא דא ספרים קויפן און לאזן זיא שין
     בינדן און שטעלן זיא פר איין צירראט אין אירן שאנק גיהיט צו ווערן. ("[B]ecause in his wisdom
     he has seen that some people buy books and let them to be beautifully bound and, then,
     put them on the shelf as ornaments").

47   On the history of the Amsterdam Ashkenazi community, see D. Sluys, "Hoogduits Joods
     Amsterdam Van 1635 Tot 1705" in H. Brugmans and A. Frank, *Geschiedenis der joden in
     Nederland* (Amsterdam 1940); revised version in *Studies in Dutch Jewry* 1 (1975), pp. 307–81
     [Hebrew].

these Yiddish books significant messengers of Jewish tradition and custom. It is however important to emphasize that the above-described developments cannot be interpreted as clear signs of an early phase of Enlightenment. The advancement of Yiddish reading and *lernen* may, at best, represent an evolutionary process within the Ashkenazi conservative society that reluctantly drove European communities towards modernization and change.

CHAPTER 6

From Yiddish to Dutch: Holiday Entertainment between Literary and Linguistic Codes

Marion Aptroot

Ashkenazi Jews who settled in the Netherlands from the seventeenth century onward were speakers of Yiddish. Their descendants were to become speakers of Dutch. The language shift from Yiddish to Dutch took place over a longer period but mainly during the nineteenth century.

The reasons for the abandonment of Yiddish by the majority of its speakers in any country for the language of the majority society are usually thought to be self-evident. Some of the reasons for the linguistic acculturation away from Yiddish seem logical because we can recognize the practical and pragmatic reasons and understand the speakers who adopted a language other than their mother tongue as their main means of expression. Nevertheless, it seems incongruous that one can argue for the emergence of Yiddish stressing the importance of a culture distinguishing itself from its surroundings by means of language use,[1] only to dismiss the aspect of group identity a few hundred years later.[2]

Religion and language were cornerstones of the group identity of Dutch Jewry. Texts in the vernacular, some of them reprinted for several generations of readers, also played a part. Some traditional genres from the early modern period, which were still being printed into the nineteenth century, were stylistically highly formalized, e.g. *mayses* (short prose stories, e.g. Talmudic legends, stories about exceptional feats of famous Rabbis) and *tkhines* (supplicatory prayers, often in Yiddish). Yiddish literary codes connected with traditional genres and styles were eventually abandoned in the Netherlands. Their influence on Dutch Jewish literature in the nineteenth century, if it exists, is unknown.

---

1   This argument is one of a number of models used to explain the emergence of Yiddish in the Middle Ages. The importance of language to signal and express social and religious identity in the present, among Jews who have grown up as speakers of English in the United States, is discussed in S. Bunin Benor, *Becoming Frum: How Newcomers Learn the Language and Culture of Orthodox Judaism* (Baltimore 2012).

2   Indeed, Yiddish can still function as a symbol of group identity even as it is no longer the vernacular of most Ashkenazi Jews; see J. Shandler, *Adventures in Yiddishland. Postvernacular Language and Culture* (Berkeley 2005).

It may be fruitful to study phenomena of linguistic shift and literary contact in Dutch Jewry together as part of one complex of developments influenced by contact and acculturation. Texts written as light entertainment on the occasion of Purim or other Jewish holidays may provide clues for developments in the linguistic and cultural assimilation of Dutch Ashkenazim. They are useful sources for a first exploration of questions of language and genre since they were written both in Yiddish and in Dutch and were subject to similar cultural influences, and produced and read within the same multilingual community. Furthermore, they were part of a living tradition of written popular culture, not the bowdlerized recording of a defunct oral culture for another audience.[3]

The Ashkenazi Jews who came to the Netherlands in the seventeenth and eighteenth centuries brought with them Yiddish which served them for everyday oral communication, but which was also an important written language for them. From the moment they set foot on Dutch territory, they began learning Dutch and the contact between the two languages influenced their Yiddish. Dutch words and expressions became part of their Yiddish,[4] a normal phenomenon of language contact. The contact with Dutch was probably a contributing factor in the breakdown of the Yiddish case system and the related inflection of articles and adjectives among Ashkenazim in the Netherlands.[5] We don't have records of the spoken language, but from written sources we can surmise that the case system was no longer stable: in writing, some Jews did not bother with systematic case endings, others did but weren't certain what the grammatical rules of Yiddish outside the Netherlands were, and yet others adopted the rules of German grammar because they gave them a foothold for lack of Yiddish grammar books.

This is not to say that their Yiddish gradually mutated into Dutch. Language change is a process that takes place over a long time, language shift is

3 Cf. P. Burke, "Introduction," in *Language, Self, and Society: A Social History of Language*, ed. P. Burke and R. Porter (Cambridge 1991), p. 10. Examples of such publications can be found later, e.g. in Berlin, see R. Gruschka, "Von Parodien deutscher Dichtung, dem Nachleben von Isaak Euchels 'Reb Henoch' und anderen Lesestoffen der Berliner Juden: Die Kolportagereihe 'Gedichte und Scherze in jüdischer Mundart'," *Ashkenas* 13 (2004), pp. 485–99.

4 See, e.g. A. Zwiers, *Kroniek van het Jiddisj. Taalkundige aspecten van het achttiende-eeuwse Nederlands Jiddisj* (Delft 2003), pp. 469–97.

5 Cf. e.g. M. Aptroot, "Yiddish, Dutch and German among Late 18th-Century Amsterdam Jewry," in *Dutch Jewry. Its History and Secular Culture (1500–2000)*, ed. J.I. Israel and R. Salverda (Leiden 2002), pp. 201–11.

6 R. Fuks-Mansfeld presumed a "gradual, almost imperceptible Hollandization of Yiddish." R. Fuks-Mansfeld, "Yiddish Historiography in the time of the Dutch Republic," *StRos* 15 (1981), p. 9.

not; they are distinct processes, even though phenomena of language contact may blur the picture. One person may switch his primary language within his own lifetime, depending on his circumstances and linguistic abilities. In general, a generation suffices. If language shift is necessary or wanted, or both, minorities can give up their own language in favor of the majority language within a generation or two. We have seen this among Ashkenazi Jews in the United States: for many children of immigrants, English became their main language as soon as they had acquired a command of it, whether at school or at home. Becoming American (*zikh amerikanizirn*) was encouraged by the older generation, which, in general, adopted the new language too. Because of a constant flux of immigrants, there was a market for Yiddish books, newspapers and radio programs into the 1950s, but numbers were falling despite the new immigration, and in recent decades Yiddish survives only in minority groups within American Jewry: Hasidim and Yiddishists (mainly secular proponents of the use of Yiddish as a language of Jewish culture). Within the Hasidic communities in the United States we see big differences: some groups are English speaking, others—notably Satmar, Skver and Stolin-Karlin—insist on the in-group use of Yiddish. The fact that their Yiddish is influenced by English is not an issue with them, but they resist linguistic acculturation.

On the European continent, the attractiveness of acculturation in the eighteenth and nineteenth centuries is often linked to bourgeois culture and legal rights.[7] A culture to aspire to and equal social and economic possibilities to those open to members of the majority culture, as well as the simultaneous loss of status of dialects and minority languages, made language shift an attractive option. Before those circumstances were in place, knowledge of the surrounding language was of importance and some Jews had an excellent command of the majority language both as a spoken medium and in writing, but there was no necessity or wish to abandon Yiddish, which served as a symbol of cultural belonging.

The language shift from Yiddish to Dutch was a complicated process[8] which has received little scholarly attention.[9] Bart Wallet has discussed the

---

7   See D. Sorkin, *The Transformation of German Jewry* (New York and Oxford 1987); N. Roemer, *Tradition und Akkulturation: Zum Sprachwandel der Juden in Deutschland zur Zeit der Haskalah* (Munich 1995); S. Lowenstein, "The Complicated Language Situation of German Jewry, 1760–1914," *StRos* 36 (2002–2003), pp. 3–31.

8   Because of the distance in time, research has to be based on written sources, which have to be used with caution and give distorted information on the spoken language, so even if patterns emerge, they can only be partial.

9   For a comparable linguistic situation, see Sorkin, *The Transformation of German Jewry*; Roemer, *Tradition und Akkulturation*; Lowenstein, "The Complicated Language Situation of German Jewry, 1760–1914."

administrative coercion to give up Yiddish as part of the process to establish Dutch as the standard language in the Netherlands.[10] Yiddish speakers were subjected to the same pressure as those who spoke Frisian and Dutch dialects. In the course of her research on Yiddish materials in Dutch archives,[11] Tehilah van Luit noticed that Yiddish had a certain status among members of the secondary Jewish intelligentsia in the Dutch provinces in the nineteenth century that still considered a command of Yiddish as a hallmark of a good Jewish education and lifestyle.[12] When Jews in the Netherlands abandoned Yiddish as their vernacular, they continued using Yiddish words and expressions in their Dutch, and the Dutch of some Jews, especially those living in larger Jewish communities, also showed traces of Yiddish syntactic structures well into the twentieth century.[13]

Just like Dutch words and expressions had entered their spoken and written Yiddish before the language shift, their literature in Yiddish shows the influence of Dutch songs, anecdotes, pamphlets, dramas, and books.[14] This kind of influence is a universal contact phenomenon. Former Yiddish speakers who started writing Dutch could also transfer stylistic elements and genre conventions from their old to their new language.

The simultaneous use of Yiddish and Dutch among Ashkenazim in Amsterdam is illustrated in the so-called *yontev-bletlekh*, small publications on the occasion of holidays, which were written and printed there. These publications do not only give clues as to language use and the function and status of the languages involved, they also give pause to reflect on text genres as means of a cultural group to define itself.

---

10   B. Wallet, "'End of the Jargon-scandal' – The Decline and Fall of Yiddish in the Netherlands (1796–1886)," *Jewish History* 20 (2006), pp. 333–48.

11   T. van Luit, *Mediene Remnants: Yiddish Sources in the Netherlands Outside of Amsterdam* (Leiden 2009).

12   Personal communication.

13   "Ook vermijde men Amsterdamsch-hebreeuwsche zinsconstructies als b.v.: Ik heb gelezen het boek, dat . . . enz. in plaats van: Ik heb het boek gelezen, dat . . ." (Amsterdam-Hebrew syntactic structures should be avoided, e.g.: I have read the book that . . . [in word order different from standard Dutch] etc. instead of: I have read the book that . . . [in standard Dutch word order]), in Anon., *Taalkundige en andere wenken voor medewerkers en correspondenten van de Nieuwe Rotterdamsche Courant*, 3rd ed. (Rotterdam 1935, http://www.dbnl .org/tekst/_taa013taal01_01/), p. 5. I first came across this example in a newspaper column by E. Sanders, "Taalkundige en andere wenken," *NRC Handelsblad*, 16 March 2009.

14   L. Fuks, "Zum Einfluß der niederländischen Kultur auf die jiddische Literatur des 17. und 18. Jahrhunderts," in *Fragen des älteren Jiddisch. Kolloquium in Trier 1976. Vorträge*, ed. H.-J. Müller, W. Röll (Trier 1977). This article gives a concise general overview. Studies of individual Yiddish texts written in the Netherlands provide detail.

Yiddish, Dutch, and bilingual *yontev-bletlekh* from Amsterdam, which were probably printed around 1800 and in the early decades of the nineteenth century, do not only provide us with information about a particular type of holiday entertainment and the connection of Dutch Jewry with Ashkenazi culture in other regions of Europe. These entertaining broadsheets and brochures may provide clues about the way authors who did not exclusively belong to the scholarly elite, maybe not even to the secondary intelligentsia, moved between languages and their linguistic and cultural codes. Since the texts are often parodies and burlesques of established text genres, these publications can also be used as sources for the inquiry into stylistic "code switching" in an "unsophisticated" genre that draws on the authors' and their audience's knowledge of specific types of Yiddish and Dutch texts.

The corpus on which I am basing my observations consists of small broadsheets (about our standard A4 size) and small brochures in octavo or duodecimo, printed in Amsterdam. Most of them are currently held in Ets Haim, the library of the Sephardi community of Amsterdam, others in the Bibliotheca Rosenthaliana, which is part of the library of the University of Amsterdam.

These ephemeral texts were known among Dutch Jews as *purim-krantn* ("Purim papers") and thus considered by their audience as belonging to a genre. They were meant to be consumed in a certain season and to be discarded afterwards. There is no reason to doubt that they were printed in Amsterdam, although, in general, the place of publication is often not indicated. Most *purim-krantn* are undated, but all that have come down to us must have been published around 1800 and in the early decades of the nineteenth century. Lajb Fuks and Mirjam Gutschow provide dates for a number of the texts.[15]

All of the publications in the small corpus can be considered *purim-krantn*, with the exception of one *Nayen yors un simkhes-toure krant* (a paper for Rosh Hashana and Simhat Torah).[16] A few actually are entitled *purim-krant* or *purim-kurant*. *Courant* and *krant* are two variants of the same word in Dutch, the former being more formal, the latter more colloquial.[17] The publications

---

15   L. Fuks, "Van Poerimspelen tot poerimkranten," *MGJN* 1/vi–vii (1947–1948), pp. 162–76. M. Gutschow, *Inventory of Yiddish Publications from the Netherlands c. 1650–c. 1950* (Leiden 2007), Nos. 450, 471–472, 477–480, 483–484, 486–487, 489–491, 494–495, 497–498, 500, 513, 519, 522–523, 525. The dated texts are: Nos. 450 (1793, date uncertain), 471–472 (1799), 513 (1802), 519 (1804), 522–523 (1805), 525 (1806).

16   For a discussion and edition of this broadsheet, see M. Aptroot, "Wie zal dat betalen, zoete lieve Gerritje? – A Popular Song in Cultural Transformation," *StRos* 42–43 (2010–2011), pp. 107–27.

17   Nowadays, the variant *Courant* survives in the name of many Dutch newspapers, e.g. *Haagsche Courant*, *Leeuwarder Courant*, and *krant* is the word used to designate a newspaper.

may be subsumed for practical reasons under the title *yontev-bletlekh*, "holiday papers,"[18] since they are (superficially) related to similar publications on the occasion of Purim which are published in different countries and languages to date. These Dutch-Yiddish publications are a local expression of a general Ashkenazi tradition and they may be the first instances of this age-old tradition finding its way into print. Maybe other similar, contemporary Yiddish ephemera were lost or haven't been rediscovered yet; maybe Amsterdam was the first city in which *yontev-bletlekh* were printed. Up to the mid-eighteenth century Amsterdam had been a major, if not *the* major center of international Hebrew and Yiddish publishing. By the late eighteenth century, the Amsterdam presses no longer served the large Jewish readership in Eastern Europe. There must have been an overcapacity for Yiddish and Hebrew printing and this, combined with cheaper paper being more readily available because of new production processes, created ideal circumstances for starting to publish works which may, up to that point, not have been thought worth printing.

On an earlier occasion, I discussed a group of twenty-four *yontev-bletlekh* from Ets Haim—twenty-three in Yiddish, one bilingual.[19] These works, which are no creations of great literary craftsmanship, were a form of popular literature, varied in content and form. They were not published for aesthetic purposes or to spread new ideas, but simply to entertain and—and this is mentioned explicitly in some of them—for economic profit. The broadsheets and small brochures are nearly all humorous. Most of them contain pastiches of well-known literary or sub-literary printed genres or of popular songs. These texts could be religious or secular in nature. Purim entertainment is often in a carnivalesque vein and nearly all these publications conform to the tradition of the grotesque, typical of most carnivalesque literature. Purim offered a set time in the Jewish calendar, like carnival (Mardi Gras) in Christian culture, to make fun of religious and communal authority and to express criticism. A distinctive feature of these Yiddish and bilingual *yontev-bletlekh* is a fear of poverty and destitution and a preoccupation with social justice.

These latter preoccupations with economic and social justice can be detected in the form of anxiety and anger, which emerges through the generally humorous surface. The subtext expresses a fear of sliding into destitution and anger about social injustice. Some of the authors are preoccupied with the hardships of Jewish daily life caused by the costs of keeping the commandments,

18   This designation has become popular in Yiddish literary history because of publications with this title by the modern Yiddish author Yitskhok Leybush Peretz (1852–1915).

19   M. Aptroot, "Western Yiddish *yontev-bletlekh*: Facing Modernity with Humor," *JSQ* 15 (2008), pp. 47–67.

which accumulate at feasts such as Passover and the High Holidays. Next to human failings and injustices, Jewish law and custom are identified as causes for the poverty of many Jews. In the humorous, anonymous and unassuming *yontev-bletekh*, subversive ideas and attitudes, the questioning of certain costly customs and sometimes even of the tenets of religion were printed.

One of the texts in the corpus studied earlier is bilingual.[20] It is the only text explicitly published not on the occasion of Purim, but for Rosh Hashana and Sukkot. The text of *Nayen yohrs und ekstra Simkhes Toure-kurand be-nign lekre Kherritkhe. Dialogue tusschen Rebe Henokh en eyshes-khayil Gerritje* (New Year's and Simhat Torah Paper to the tune of *lekkere Gerritje*. Dialogue between Mr. Henokh and his "woman of valor" Gerritje), is a song in thirty stanzas of four verses. Six stanzas are in Yiddish, the others are bilingual. The Yiddish is printed in Hebrew characters, the Dutch in roman letters. It is thus, even at the level of the graphics, an example of code switching and implies that the publisher knew there was an intended audience which, in all likelihood, was that of the other Amsterdam *yontev-bletlekh*, namely *dos gemayne folk* (common people), peddlers and other small tradesmen and their families, who must have had a good command of both spoken and written Yiddish and Dutch. This bilingual text shares some of the characteristics of Yiddish *yontev-bletlekh* printed in Amsterdam, including references to Yiddish, Hebrew and Dutch texts and traditions as well as a criticism of the requirements of a Jewish way of life as financially crippling. In this case, aspects of daily life and small luxuries are also blamed for the financial penury in which Henokh, one of the two speaking characters, finds himself. His wife, Gerritje, would rather have her husband give up his seat in synagogue than make her scrimp on clothing and the accouterments of a bourgeois lifestyle she aspires to. The two main characters are rooted in Jewish, Yiddish-speaking traditional life, but are well versed in Dutch and aspects of the majority culture. The author and his intended audience obviously were, too. The song is set to a popular melody, that, at the time, was a new and exciting Dutch dance song and which has come down to us in fragmentary form as the song "Dat gaat naar Den Bosch toe, zoete lieve Gerritje" (We are going to Den Bosch ['s-Hertogenbosch], sweet, dear Gerritje) and the dialogue was, I think, influenced by a particular Amsterdam literary tradition, namely the topical dialogue of Thomasvaer and Pieternel for the New Year, which used to be recited at the end of the comedy *De bruiloft van Kloris en Roosje*. This short, light-hearted play was performed every year after Vondel's historical drama *Ghysbrecht van Aemstel* in the Amsterdam Theater on or close to the first of January, and the characters of the parents of the groom,

---

20　Aptroot, "Wie zal dat betalen, zoete lieve Gerritje?"

Thomasvaer and Pieternel, would recite New Year's wishes with references to local current affairs at the end of the performance.

The existence of this bilingual broadsheet can be seen as an indication that we cannot simply assume that the Yiddish *yontev-bletlekh* precede the Dutch ones. The bilingual nature of this broadsheet is not the expression of inadequate knowledge of the "new," Dutch language, or a gradual loss of the "old," Yiddish language that is not capable of expressing new concepts, but a playful use of two languages, each in their own alphabet, of which the author and his reader have a good command.

Since broadsheets and brochures are often not catalogued separately, I have thus far only found four (or five) Dutch texts that are related to the Yiddish *purim-krantn* in form and content.[21] Sometimes even the same jokes and techniques can be found in both languages. In the course of my research, I have come across more Dutch broadsheets and brochures that were published during the first half of the nineteenth century on the occasion of Purim, but they are either simple collections of jokes or entertaining stories that are very different in content and style from the traditional *yontev-bletlekh*. One author, who uses the initials D.C.P. instead of his full name, writes in a modern Purim-booklet published in 1857, "dat ik niet gaarne in de term van de zoo reeds lang bekende Poerim-Courant wilde vervallen," he does not want to write in the style of the long-established *purim-couranten*.[22] From this, we can conclude either that *purim-krantn* with their traditional coarse humor and a love of the absurd were still published and read in Amsterdam in the 1850s or, that the author and his audience were familiar with a recently extinct genre.

These four (or five) Dutch *yontev-bletlekh* are:

(1)   Extra / Joodsche / Purim Courant. / No. 6600 't tweede Jaar, N° 20. Maandag, den 59ste van Jobmaand. / Waar op uitgenodigt wordt, alle uit de vier hoeken, daar onder begrepen word: kromme, Bochels, Scheven, Lammen, Blinden, Zwartinnen, Molattinnen, Hot-/ tentotten en al wat onder de Jooden Buurten Gebooren en gemaakt is.[23]

---

21   I have located these at Ets Haim/Livraria Montezinos of the Portuguese Israelite Community of Amsterdam and the Bibliotheca Rosenthaliana, Special Collections, University Library of Amsterdam, with the kind assistance of the librarians. At present they cannot be found in a public access catalogue.

22   *Luimen/ van een/ oude rijmer./ Lectuur/ bij gelegenheid van het/ Purim-Feest./ Door D.C.P./ Gedrukt en te bekomen bij/ S. Mendes Coutinho Jbz./ Muiderstraat, V 239. /1857.* Amsterdam 1857. Ets Haim 20B67[33].

23   "Extra Jewish Purim Paper. Nr. 6600, year two, No. 20. Monday, Month of Job, 59th. From where all from the four corners are invited. Understood by 'all' are: stooped, hunchbacked,

Broadsheet. Ets Haim 20867[30] (30B332).

The text of this broadsheet is a burlesque newspaper with different news items. At the top of the page are three coarse woodcuts, roughly the same size. On the outside left a man's head with a visor cap, on the right hand side a woman's head in a cap in profile, in the center a scene with two full-length male figures with top hats.

(2)   2178 9e Jaargang. Hamans-Feest 5011. No. 71834. / Vermakelijke Poerem-krant / van Dorstdag den 46 van Hongersmaand.[24]

Dit blad verschijnt geregeld elke avond na het sluiten der Herbergen. – Men abonneert zich voor niet minder dan 25 jaren, tegen den prijs van 100 gulden per dag. – Adres in de Vlooijenbuurt, bij den Uitgever-Direkteur Mortje Pintnees.[25]

Gedrukt voor rekening van L.H. Broekhuizen.

Broadsheet, Bibliotheca Rosenthaliana, Ros. Ebl. C-40.

Burlesque Newspaper. Many similarities with the next paper, which is considerably shorter; the contents are in part almost identical.

(3)   101e Jaargang Hamans-Feest 20.109 No. 4444 / Vermakelijke Poeremkrant / van Dorstdag den 32 van Hongersmaand.[26]

Dit blad verschijnt geregeld elke avond na het sluiten der herbergen. – Men abonneert zich voor niet minder dan 50 jaar, tegen den prijs van 1 gulden per dag. – Adres in de Vlooienbuurt, bij den Uitgever-Direkteur Morttje Pintneus.[27]

---

crooked, lame and blind people, black and mulatto women, Hottentots and all who were born and conceived in the Jewish quarters." The enumeration of physical disabilities and different racial and national groups, in fact any elaborate list of uncommon people, animals, occurrences or objects is considered humorous. Similar listings are found in other humorous literature of the early modern period (cf. Rabelais), Yiddish *yontev-bletlekh* from Amsterdam included, see, e.g. Aptroot, "Western Yiddish *yontev-bletlekh*," pp. 56–58.

24   "2178 9th year. Haman's Feast 5011. No. 71834. Entertaining Purim paper of Thirst-day, Hunger Month, 46th."

25   "This paper appears regularly, every evening after the closing of the inns. One subscribes for no less than 25 years for the price of 100 guilders per day. Address in the Vlooijenbuurt [Flea's Quarter, a wordplay on Vlooienburg, the main Jewish quarter of Amsterdam at the time] at the publisher-director's Mortje Pintnees [Mordecai Pint-nose]."

26   "101st year. Haman's Feast 20.109. No. 4444. Entertaining Purim paper of Thirst-day, Hunger Month, 32nd."

27   "This paper appears regularly, every evening after the closing of the inns. One subscribes for no less than 50 years for the price of 1 guilder per day. Address in the Vlooienbuurt [Flea's Quarter, see fn. 25] at the publisher-director's Morttje Pintneus [Mordecai Pint-nose]."

Broadsheet, Bibliotheca Rosenthaliana, Ros. 9822–3 (old number, new number unknown).

Burlesque Newspaper. Many similarities with the previous paper, which is more extensive; the contents are in part almost identical.

(4) Korte schets van de / Hagadah[28] / in Zang / Ernstig / En M. Calö's, Privaat Hagadah in Prosa, Boertig.[29]

Broadsheet, Dutch in roman letters with Hebrew in square script, Yiddish words in roman letters as part of the second Dutch text. Bibliotheca Rosenthaliana, Ros Ebl B-11.

(5) Gedachten over Purim. / Gekheden, ten voordele des schrijvers.[30]

16pp., Ets Haim 20B67.[37]

This brochure contains texts representing different genres: poems, a dialogue, jokes. On p. 8, at the end of a poem, Salomon Cohen, a.k.a. Rodrigues[31] Jzn. is mentioned as author. Because the author was probably a Sephardi Jew, this brochure has to be used with caution in the present context and a direct link with the Yiddish publications less likely.

Obvious similarities between Dutch *purim-krantn* and the Yiddish ones that were printed in Amsterdam point to immediate influences. One of the most popular text-types among the Yiddish brochures was the *purim-luekh* (Purim calendar), of which several copies are extant. They start with impossible dates, e.g. two similar publications with the title *Vermakelijke Poeremkrant* (entertaining Purim paper) boast a date set in the future, namely 20.109[32] and 5011,[33] which is reminiscent of the Yiddish title *Evn nav purim-luekh, mi-shnas*

---

28 In Hebrew.

29 "Brief sketch of the Haggadah in [the form of a] song, serious. And M. Calö's private Haggadah in prose, farcical."

30 "Thoughts on Purim. Pleasantries for the [financial] advantage of the author."

31 The name Rodrigues implies that the author is probably a Sephardi Jew. The word "segnoeda" also points in this direction; otherwise there are similarities with the Yiddish *yontev-bletlekh*, e.g. the combination of disparate texts, sometimes with loose and contrived connections to Purim or Passover. One of the jokes, told as part of a more serious anecdote, is widely known among Ashkenazim too (p. 6). Seeing Haman and his sons having been executed, someone asks why they are hanging. Another answers: Because the rope was too short. Apart from the direct mention of Haman and his sons, this must have been a well-known joke among the general population.

32 This broadsheet is part of the collection of the Bibliotheca Rosenthaliana (9822–3) and appears not to have received a new inventory number since it is on loan to the Jewish Historical Museum of Amsterdam as part of the permanent exhibition.

33 Bibliotheca Rosenthaliana, Ros Ebl C-40.

shmounim alofim 585 le-f"k (A new Purim calendar from the year 80,585 in the abbreviated count).[34] Not only the date is impossible, the world in these Purim calendars and papers is topsy-turvy: Purim, according to the Dutch name used in the broadsheet purportedly printed in 20.109, is not the holiday for celebrating Esther and Mordecai, but is *"Hamans-Feest,"* the holiday of Haman.[35] The day on which the broadsheet is published is described in both as *"Dorstdag"* (thirst day), which is both a reversal of Purim as we know it, when men are supposed to drink enough alcohol to make it impossible to distinguish Haman from Mordecai and like the month *"Hongersmaand"* (hunger month), a reference to economic hardship, a central topic in the Yiddish *purim-krantn.* Plain and simple absurdity is present here too, not just in the year, but also in the mentioning of the thirty-second or even the forty-sixth day of a month.

The parodic calendar appears to have been popular in Yiddish and Dutch Purim leaflets. In both languages different ones have come down to us and in both cases, the later version used a previous one and introduced some changes and additions in order to advertise themselves as "never printed before." In the first two Yiddish *purim-lukhes,*[36] for example, a reference to red Jews, familiar from Yiddish folklore and modern Yiddish literature,[37] is made. In the elaborated version red *and green* Jews are mentioned.[38] The reference to green-haired Jews is an original (and absurd) embellishment. In the Dutch Purim calendars we also see that small changes are made to justify the self-advertisement that such has "never been printed before," for example by changing the numbers

---

34   Gutschow, *Inventory,* no. 477.

35   This designation of Purim is one I have not been able to find in Yiddish sources, but it was used by Christians writing about Jews and their customs, e.g. in German, J.J. Schudt, *Jüdische Merckwürdigkeiten* (Frankfurt and Leipzig 1714; reprint, Berlin 1922), vol. XI, Ch. 4, p. 55; in Dutch, review of Jz. de Jongh, *Esther en Mordechai, of het Purim der Israëliten. Treurspel* (Amsterdam 1817) in *Vaderlandsche Letteroefeningen* (1818), p. 713. The Dutch author of this review refers to Jews with the derogatory term *mousjes* (derived from Moushe, the Western Yiddish pronunciation of Moses). I would like to thank Oren Roman for informing me about Schudt's use of this term.

36   Gutschow, *Inventory,* nos. 477 and 479.

37   Cf. R. Voß, "Entangled Stories. The Red Jews in Pre-Modern Yiddish and German Apocalyptic Lore," *AJS Review* 36/1 (2012), pp. 1–41. Although this article focuses on the pre-modern era, Voß also refers to works of modern Yiddish literature in which (stories about) red Jews play a part, such as Sholem-Yankev Abramovitsh's *Kitser masoes Binyomin hashlishi* ([Abbreviated Travels of Benjamin the Third], 1878) and Sholem Aleichem's *Di royte yidlekh* ([The Little Red Jews], 1900).

38   Gutschow, *Inventory,* no. 495.

(year and day of the month, see above). In these calendars, for all their absurdity and light humor, poverty is the central theme.

Most texts in the *yontev-bletlekh* are burlesques, for example, fictitious newspaper advertisements and burlesques of the *Haggadah shel Pessah* (the Passover Haggadah). The following lines from a fictitious personal announcement is enough to get the gist: "Na een kortstondig, doch welverdiend lijden van 13 jaren zal mijn Henkie Leepoog, morgen tusschen licht en donker de laatste snik geven" (After a short, but well-deserved illness of thirteen years, my Henry Sly will breathe his last at twilight).[39] The absurd, cruel humor is put in a more nuanced light by means of the rest of the sentence: "allen die mij dikwijls met een blauw oog hebben zien loopen, zullen begrijpen hoe zijn dood mij eens uit de brand helpt" (all who have often seen me go around with a black eye will understand how his death helps to get me out of a predicament). However, we do not need to feel much sympathy: the advertisement is signed "Hessie Mansiek, toekomende weduwe Leepoog" (Esther Nymphomaniac, future Widow Sly) and in a post-script the sixty-two-year-old imminent widow welcomes marriage proposals from ten o'clock on the evening of her husband's funeral.

Although these leaflets are published on the occasion of Purim, Passover is an important topic in quite a number of *yontev-bletlekh*. It is the next Jewish holiday after Purim and is an elaborate and expensive affair, fueling fears of sliding into poverty. The house has to be cleaned, food has to be kosher for Passover, the plates, cutlery and utensils that can be used on Passover often have to be taken out of the pawnbrokers' shop at great expense, no money can be earned during the first and last two days of the holiday and often not in between either, because of the difficulties for peddlers and other businessmen to travel with even greater dietary restrictions than usual (bread and beer, both forbidden during Passover, being two important sources of sustenance for Jewish travelers at the time). Burlesque or parodic *hagodes* (pl. of Haggadah) have come down to us in both languages. An excerpt from a Yiddish text reads as follows:

Ma nishtano – vos iz frendirt – *halaylo hazey* – di nakht fun peysekh – *mikol halayles* – meyn veder andre nakht fun gantsen yor. Ayn gans yor hob ikh tsu esn gelen rihbn, vayzn ribn, mit ehrdepel, hayte ovnt hob ikh nokh nikhts tsu esen. Ayn gants yohr hob ikh gor nikhts ayn tsu tunkn, hayte ovnt hobe ikh tsvey mohl ayn tsu tunkn. Ayn gants yohr ese ikh ayn

39 Bibliotheca Rosenthaliana 9822–3 (old number). In Bibliotheca Rosenthaliana, Ros Ebl C-40 the husband's name is Joppie Leepoog (Joseph Sly).

shtik broht ous der hant, ikh zits nisht, ikh geh nikht, ikh lige nikht, ikh
shteh nisht – *halaylo hazey* – zaan mir kulonu meshuge.⁴⁰

Ma nishtana – what is different – *halayla haze* – this Passover night –
mikol halelot – from all other nights of the year. All year long I eat yellow
beets, white beets, with potatoes, tonight I don't have anything to eat yet.
All year long I don't have to dip anything, tonight I have to dip twice. All
year long I eat a piece of bread which I hold in my hand, I don't sit, I don't
go, I don't lay down, I don't stand. *Halayla ha-ze* – this Passover night –
we've all gone mad.

The following Dutch burlesque is similar, but more subdued. It is part of a
broadsheet with two texts. The first is a serious song about the Exodus from
Egypt. It is followed by a very short burlesque on parts of the Haggadah, which
is described as "M. Calö's private Haggadah in prose."⁴¹ In contrast to the "ernstig" (serious) song at the top of the broadsheet, this text is characterized as
"boertig" (coarse and humorous).

Ma nishtano – Calo vraagt: Waarom is deze avond verschillend van andere avonden. Alle avonden om dit uur drink ik een half glaasje bitter
om appetijt te krijgen (begaijes niet meer) – vanavond vier glazen wijn
kasere Malaga. Andere avonden best roggebrood – vanavond beste simoerim. Andere avonden ingelegde lemmetjes – vanavond bittere
kruiden. Andere avonden zittende of leunende – vanavond leunen wij de
ellebogen aan stuken van de vermoeienissen.

---

40   Gutschow, *Inventory*, no. 490, f. 1b. The transcription maintains some of the idiosyncratic
     forms of the original. I have added to the punctuation of what in the original is one long
     sentence, made easier to read by the use of (modern!) commas. In the original Yiddish, the
     literal Hebrew quotations from "*Ma nishtana*," the four questions asked by the youngest
     participant at the beginning of the *seder*, are printed in Hebrew square script in contrast
     with the Ashkenazi semi-cursive letters of the Yiddish text. Here they are represented in
     italics characters in the transcription and in the English translation.
41   Bibliotheca Rosenthaliana, Ros Ebl B-11. "En M. Calö's, Privaat Hagadah in Prosa, Boertig"
     is part of the title. Below the horizontal line separating the serious from the humorous
     text, the heading reads: "Nu iets pour la grap" (Now something for the fun of it). The use of
     French words *pour la* in and of itself was deemed to be an expression of humor which can
     be found in cliché-ridden Dutch writings and performances during the early modern and
     modern period. Calo is a historical family name of Amsterdam Jewry and occurs in an-
     other leaflet, *Gedachten over Purim* (see above) as "the famous philosopher Moses Calo."
     (This epithet is not to be taken at face value, for contemporaries in Amsterdam the name
     may have had humorous connotations that are now lost.)

Ma nishtana – Calo asks: Why is this night different from other nights. Every evening at this hour I drink half a glass of [gin and] bitters (upon my life not more) – tonight four glasses of kosher Malaga wine. Other evenings best rye bread – tonight best *shmure matses*. Other evenings preserved lemons – tonight bitter herbs. Other evenings sitting upright or leaning – tonight we lean so heavily for exhaustion, we wear our elbows out.

Whereas the first, serious text is written in flawless Dutch, this "boertig" one uses typical Jewish expressions and pronunciations (in this quotation: *begaijes* ["upon my life"], *kasere* ["kosher"], *simoerim* ["vegetables"], *shmura matzeh*, *lemmetjes* ["preserved lemons"], elsewhere *mangel-koekjes* ["almond cookies"], *dalfonem* ["poor people"], etc.).

In comparison with their Yiddish counterparts, the Dutch texts are more subdued. This may be a cultural development: authors who were writing in the language of the majority may have wanted to conform to "higher" literary standards and provide less coarse entertainment. Some, but by no means all, of the later Dutch publications don't contain any criticism, coarseness or absurdities. It may also be because these texts could be read by members of the majority culture and, therefore, authors and publishers felt less free, but the range of Jewish publishing in Dutch from the second half of the nineteenth and early twentieth century makes it more likely that this was related to personal sensibilities rather than to general pressures felt by all Jewish authors and publishers. It can be said though, that the earlier Yiddish publications make use of literary forms and strategies gleaned from publications and performances in the majority culture, and that these are used freely and combined with Yiddish and Jewish traditions. Some of these traditions are also used in Dutch ephemera, but here we find more texts that try to emulate the formal and aesthetic genres of Dutch—primarily Calvinist—literature.[42]

Few *yontev-bletlekh* have come down to us from the time around 1800 and most of them are undated. Some are in Yiddish, others in Dutch and one is bilingual, so one must be very cautious when making conjectures about developments. Because of this and because we have the one bilingual text in both scripts, it is impossible to say whether first there were the Yiddish *yontev-bletlekh* and, subsequently, they were made in Dutch. This corpus may be an expression of a culture that was in the process of a language shift. As far as Yiddish in Western Europe is concerned, we know that the period of language shift was dependent on individual and familial circumstances that started in

---

42   E.g. *Luimen/van een/oude rijmer.*

the eighteenth century and lasted well into the nineteenth and, in some areas, into the twentieth century.[43] If these brochures were printed more or less simultaneously during the period of a few decades, later occasional vernacular literature for Purim in the Netherlands was printed in Dutch, we see here how some authors were exploring new linguistic possibilities while maintaining literary conventions with which they and their audience were familiar. There were enough reading materials available in Dutch, a market in which these authors and publishers may not (or not yet) have been able to compete, and they may have hoped that the familiar held a certain appeal for a Jewish audience. Since the Yiddish texts of the period and older ones already demand a knowledge of non-Jewish text forms, such as dance songs, theatrical plays, play bills, newspapers and ferry timetables, it is not so much the world outside and its literary codes that are an impetus for a shift from Yiddish to Dutch for the genre of *yontev-bletlekh*.

Through the analysis of Yiddish, bilingual and Dutch *purim-krantn*, a heterogeneous pattern in the acculturation of Dutch Jewry in the time around 1800 emerges. With time, the publication of Yiddish ceases and Dutch texts or Dutch texts with some Hebrew and/or Yiddish take their place. Neither the Yiddish language nor the traditional genre of the *yontev-bletlekh* were abandoned abruptly. Rather, the Yiddish, Dutch, and biblingual *yontev-bletlekh* printed in Amsterdam indicate a transition period characterized by linguistic and literary code switching. Changing tastes among Jewish authors and readers would lead to new developments in Dutch Purim publications in the following decades, but these remain to be explored.

---

43   Cf. the literature mentioned in fn. 7.

PART 3

Jewish Religion in Troubled Waters:
The Dutch-Sephardi Diaspora Overseas

∴

CHAPTER 7

A Tale of Caribbean Deviance: David Aboab and Community Conflicts in Curaçao

Evelyne Oliel-Grausz

[A]nd it [Curaçao] was the Mother city of all the Islands of the Americas.

DAVID ABOAB, *Sefer emet ve-yatsiv*

∴

While this quote extolling the grandeur of Curaçao is often associated with Caribbean Jewish history, its author David Aboab remains an elusive and marginal figure in that island's chronicles and in Dutch Jewish history as well, though he was not Dutch himself and may not have remained Jewish throughout his life.[1] Following his biographical trail, this contribution will also open a window upon Curaçaoan community life and strife. Aboab was described as an Italian *talmid hakham*, a scholar who wandered among the Sephardi communities in the Caribbean in the 1740s trying to make a living from his Jewish expertise. In the records of the community of Curaçao he was referred to as *"forasteiro,"* a poor foreign vagrant in need of assistance. A minor character in Curaçao's history, he was also an ephemeral figure in the archival documentation, appearing in the records in the years 1746 to 1747 and then vanishing. During this short period, however, he was at the center of a conflict that ripped apart the

---

*   *In memory of J. David Grausz z"l, who loved Caribbean tales.*

1   "וְהִיא הָיְתָה עִיר וָאֵם בְּכָל אִיֵּי הָאַמֶּרִיקָא," David Aboab, *Sefer Emet ve-yatsiv*, 1746, preamble. This manuscript, belongs to the Ets Haim collection, EH 47C44 (38577), see L. Fuks, *Hebrew and Judaic manuscripts in Amsterdam public collections*, vol. 2: *Catalogue of the manuscripts of Ets Haim-Livraria Montezinos Sephardic community of Amsterdam* (Leiden 1975), p. 187, where it also appears under n°349. I used the copy of the manuscript available in the manuscript department of the National Library, Jerusalem, and am most grateful to the archivists for their help. As well, I want to express my deep gratitude to Omri Shasha for his help in deciphering this manuscript and to Odette Vlessing for her friendly help and support in navigating the Amsterdam municipal archives. Last, I thank the Central Archives for the History of the Jewish People, for allowing me to use their copy of the Amsterdam *copiador de cartas*.

island's Portuguese community Mikve Israel. Proclamations for Aboab's expulsion were read aloud no less than six times in the Curaçaoan synagogue during the month of September 1746. The repercussions affected more than just his personal fate: the first proclamation, read three times, stipulated that all persons connected to the unrest surrounding Aboab were under penalty of *herem* (excommunication) and were to seek absolution from the *hakhamim*.[2] Rather than calming things down, this announcement added to the turmoil. A public appeal from the governor aimed to appease the matter by proclaiming a general pardon and an end to the collective ban, while also reiterating Aboab's expulsion.

The interference of the governor in this episode shows that the historical relevance of the Aboab affair goes beyond the fate of a raucous itinerant Italian scholar who was expelled from the island. The episode was deeply enmeshed in the bitter and enduring conflicts of mid-eighteenth-century Curaçaoan Jewry that involved *hakhamim*, *parnassim*, much of the community's social elite and the *kahal* itself, the governor, as well as the lay and rabbinic leaders of the Amsterdam community's Talmud Torah, administrators of the West India Company, the States General and, ultimately, the Prince Stadholder himself. The unique archival culture of Amsterdam's Portuguese Jewish community and the thoroughness of its chancellery, whether regarding conformity or dissent, ensured the preservation of a wealth of sources concerning all communal matters, and the Aboab affair was no exception.

It has been recently suggested in a stimulating article that the historiography of Curaçaoan Jewry is heavily modeled after narratives of conflictuality, to the point of dismissing alternative analytical paths.[3] For the eighteenth century, at least, the historiographical emphasis on conflict is unavoidable in most references to Curaçaoan Jewry, including general encyclopedias.[4] A combination

---

2   24, 25, 27 Elul 5506 (9, 10 and 12 September 1746), and 28 Elul 5506, 5 and 8 Tishri 5507 (13, 19, 22 September 1746), SAA 334-1028B, f°362–5.

3   See C. Kaiser, "Islets of Toleration among the Jews of Curaçao," in *Toleration within Judaism*, Oxford, Littman Library of Jewish Civilization, ed. M. Goodman, J.E. David, C.R. Kaiser, S. Levis Sullam (Cambridge, MA 2013), pp. 130–60. Dealing mostly with nineteenth-century issues and material, but offering also very interesting insights into eighteenth-century history, the author ponders on the centrality of conflictuality in the classical historical narratives and proposes to read the history of the Jews of Curaçao "against the grain," shifting the questioning and emphasis from conflict to modes of coexistence.

4   A rather precise relation of the conflict between the Jewish factions in the 1740s occupies most of the section devoted to the history of early modern Curaçao Jewry in the *Encyclopedie van de Nederlandse Antillen*, ed. J.P. de Palm (Zutphen 1985), vol. 2, *s.v.* Joden-Curaçao, pp. 252–56.

of historical and heuristic factors explain, in my view, this emphasis: first and foremost, the majority of the documentation used to write the history of Curaçaoan Jewry prior to the nineteenth century stemmed from the correspondence between Curaçaoan Jews and their metropolitan Jewish and non-Jewish correspondants in Amsterdam, not local community records.[5] Second, these conflicts, which perdure long after the Aboab affair, together with detailed relations of their most spectacular quarrels, become a sort of *cause célèbre* that ultimately reach the directors of the West India Company, the States General and the Statholder himself, for resolution and appeasement. It is important to bear in mind that the Jews in Curaçao were a major entity within the island's history. From initial attempts by Portuguese Jewish merchants to establish a settlement in Curaçao in the early 1650s, followed by the granting of official privileges by the West India Company in 1659, the Jews developed into a major demographic and economic group on the island.[6] Throughout most of the eighteenth century, despite variations in demographic estimates, they constituted the majority of the white population.[7]

In his classic work, *History of the Jews of the Netherlands Antilles*, which remains the most important secondary source to date on the history of Curaçaoan

---

5   On the links between Curaçao and Amsterdam, see Y. Kaplan, "The Curaçao and Amsterdam Jewish Communities in the 17th and 18th Centuries," *American Jewish History* 72 (1982), pp. 193–211. The communal registers of the Mikve Israel community have not been preserved for the eighteenth century, but the abundant correspondence sent to the Amsterdam *parnassim* and rabbis, in this case by all the important actors in the local conflicts, allows for a precise reconstruction. The only important source we have not been able to consult so far is the *Memorias Senior*, a manuscript kept in the Maduro Library in Curaçao, which chronicles eighteenth-century community life and crises on the island.

6   I.S. and S. Emmanuel, *History of the Jews of the Netherlands Antilles* (Cincinnati 1970), pp. 38–50; on the establishment of the Jewish presence in Curaçao see also Y.H. Yerushalmi, "Between Amsterdam and New Amsterdam: The Place of Curaçao and the Caribbean in Early Modern Jewish History," *American Jewish History* 72 (1982), pp. 185–92, and W. Klooster, "Networks of Colonial Entrepreneurs. The Founders of the Jewish Settlements in Dutch America, 1650s and 1660s," in *Atlantic Diasporas: Jews, Conversos, and Crypto-Jews in the Age of Mercantilism, 1500–1800*, ed. R.L. Kagan and P.D. Morgan (Baltimore 2008), pp. 33–49.

7   Though no reliable population data exists prior to the nineteenth century, estimates of the Jewish, almost exclusively Sephardic, population place it between 1500 to 2000 persons in the mid-18th century when it reached its demographic peak. See J. Hartog, *History of the Netherlands Antilles*, Vol. 3, *Curaçao. From Colonial Dependance to Autonomy* (Aruba 1968), p. 133. For a comparison of the various estimatations, see F.P. Karner, *The Sephardics of Curaçao. A Study of Socio-Cultural Patterns in Flux* (Assen 1969), p. 29. On the Caribbean and Atlantic networks of Curaçaoan Jews, see J. Israel, *Diaspora within a Diaspora* (Leiden 2002), pp. 511–32.

Jewry, Isaac Emmanuel devotes significant attention to these conflicts.[8] Yet, despite his thorough knowledge of the Amsterdam sources and of Aboab's own vindictive writings, he remains very cautious in his portrayal of the Aboab story. In the appendices, he includes a few excerpts from Aboab's manuscript *Emet ve-yatsiv*, to which a later section of this essay is devoted. But Emmanuel's digest of this document is the result of a process of edulcoration of Aboab's prose, since he leaves out the harshest sections and removes from his quotations those words that could be construed as offensive. Emmanuel's selection is but a tame echo of Aboab's critical, often insulting, text and reads like the product of an ambivalent writer who was torn between his desire to quote from this fascinating manuscript and the constraints under which he wrote his book. In a preliminary section to the work entitled "censorship," Emmanuel, who was the acting rabbi of the Mikve Israel congregation in Curaçao, tells how his manuscript was subjected to the careful scrutiny of the *parnassim* before its publication. He describes their filiopietist attitude as an overall desire "to omit anything that might cast a shadow on the established good reputation of the people portrayed," and describes the editorial struggle over the chapter covering the twentieth-century merger between the Portuguese and Reform congregations.[9] While Emmanuel does not mention active intervention of the board of censors concerning the contents of the sections of his book dealing with the eighteenth century, he takes it upon himself to sift through the Aboab story and material with a similar filiopietist approach: he justifies his editing and self imposed censoring of the excerpts he presents as the respect that is due to the *hakhamim* and *parnassim* of Aboab's time and their descendents, thus carrying the ideals of *bom judesmo* well into the twentieth century.[10]

The purpose of this essay is twofold: it first aims at reconstructing the Caribbean leg of David Aboab's life story as part of a work in progress that is a more comprehensive study of his biography and spiritual journey. Paradoxically,

8   See the chapter entitled, "Bitter Conflicts of 1744–1750," pp. 181–212.

9   Emmanuel, *History of the Jews of the Netherlands Antilles*, vol. 1, pp. 8–10. Alan Benjamin, an anthropologist who in the early 1990s began a dissertation on the Jews in Curaçao, spent the first few months negotiating a contract with the local community and its lawyers. He had to agree to full supervision of his work before publication. Serious financial penalties would be incurred for any material published without permission and previous supervision. If his experience echoes Emmanuel's, he chose to weave this seeming technicality, the negotiation of his publication contract, into his research, devoting a section of his book to the analysis of the process and its impact on his representation and writing, A.N.F. Benjamin, *Jews of the Dutch Caribbean: Exploring Ethnic Identity on Curaçao* (Routledge 2002), pp. 23–33.

10   Emmanuel, *History of the Jews of the Netherlands Antilles*, vol. 2, pp. 1020–23.

instead of deepening our understanding of his intellectual and religious mind-set, the abundance of sources and the necessity to reconcile them cause us even greater puzzlement because they do not add up to a consistent portrait. Secondly, this study intends to contribute to the history of community life and conflict in the Caribbean, which has attracted much attention of late.[11] It will posit that Aboab's story is a relevant entry point into the history of the social and religious dynamics of an eighteenth-century Sephardi Caribbean *kehillah*. Above and beyond the particular details of the episode, the ongoing conflicts highlight several key issues, such as the continuous struggle for authority between lay and rabbinic figures, the status of rabbinic knowledge as a source of authority, the social and cultural implications of these struggles for communal control, when, in other Western Sephardi communities, increasing secularization often led the elite to distance themselves from the communal institutions.

Aboab's Arrival and Curaçaoan Jews

The island of Curaçao was captured by the West India Company from a small colony of Spaniards in 1634, at about the same time as the first Jews settled in Surinam. Whereas the Guyanese settlement quickly grew to be a prosperous colony of planters, the rocky and poorly endowed soil of the Curaçaoan island did not allow the same option. However, prosperity would eventually accrue from the advantageous situation of the island relative to the American coast, and before long, it became a major Caribbean entrepot and smuggling hub. The Jewish population grew rapidly and enjoyed extensive religious freedom under the protection of the West India Company and the rule of the local governor. Around the middle of the eighteenth century, the Jewish inhabitants made up half the white population of the island, numbering around 2000 people. The Jews, in their vast majority of Portuguese or Spanish descent, were most active in trade, with an elite group of merchants and ship owners sending

---

11   Since this article was completed, two very relevant publications have appeared: J. Roitman, "'A Flock of Wolves instead of Sheep.' The Dutch West India Company, Conflict Resolution, and the Jewish Community of Curaçao in the Eighteenth Century," in *The Jews in the Caribbean*, ed. J. Gerber (Oxford 2013), pp. 85–105. This article bears in part on the same conflict being analyzed here, bringing a welcome complementary outlook from the archives of the West India Company. See also A. Ben Ur, J. Roitman, "Adultery Here and There. Crossing Boundaries in the Dutch Jewish Atlantic," in *Dutch Atlantic Connections, 1680–1800: Linking Empires, Bridging Borders*, ed. G. Oostindie, J. Roitman (Leiden 2014), pp. 185–223.

shipments of cacao, tobacco and hides to Amsterdam, local traders and a size-able group of local or vagrant poor who were assisted by the community. The Mikve Israel community was an offshoot of the Amsterdam Talmud Torah community, upon which the *parnassim* relied for guidance in matters of self government and assistance in times of conflict; the Amsterdam *parnassim* and rabbis were entrusted with the mission of selecting and electing, when needed, rabbis, cantors, school teachers, and sometimes doctors, to be dispatched to Curaçao, as was the case with other daughter communities such as Surinam's Beraha Vesalom.[12] The circulation of rabbinical and para-rabbinical person-nel between Amsterdam and the Caribbean and the steady intercommunal and private mercantile correspondence, which allowed for a permanent flow of information and requests, resulted in a close connection between the two communities and their leaders, despite the distance.[13]

When David Aboab arrived in Curaçao in 1745 or early 1746, he found a com-munity rife with social and communal tensions between factionsthat had been brewing beneath the surface for some time. He came on the scene just when the unrest was developing into open conflict. Two issues brought the friction to a head: one was the founding of a second synagogue in Otrabanda, on the other side of the canal on St. Ann's Bay. The community's main synagogue, which still stands today, was constructed in the years 1730–32, to replace the 1703 building, in order to accomodate the growing community.[14] However, al-ready in the early decades of the eighteenth century, Jews, including some from prominent families, had started building homes in Otrabanda, outside the city walls. They initiated a secondary *minyan* called Neve Shalom in a private house there. In 1734, Mosseh Penso, one of the wealthiest and most powerful Jews in Curaçao as well a prominent member of the island's governing elite, as the official deputy of the Jewish nation with the Island authorities and a *parnas*

---

12   W. Klooster, "The Jews in Suriname and Curaçao," *The Jews and the Expansion of Europe to the West, 1450 to 1800*, ed. P. Bernardini, N. Fiering (New York 2001), pp. 350–56.

13   G. Nahon, "Amsterdam and the Portuguese 'naçao' of the Caribbean in the Eighteenth Century," in *The Jews in the Caribbean*, ed. J. Gerber (Oxford 2013) pp. 67–83 E. Oliel-Grausz, "La circulation du personnel rabbinique dans les communautés de la diaspora séfarade au XVIIIe siècle," *Passages et transmissions en monde juif*, ed. E. Benbassa (Paris 1997), pp. 313–34.

14   The present edifice, inaugurated in 1732, was actually the sixth synagogue, if one includes the early constructions close to the plantations: see Emmanuel, *History of the Jews of the Netherlands Antilles*, vol. 1, pp. 51, 59, 88, 93–4, 120–24. See also R.D.L. Maduro, *Congrega-tion Mikvé Israel-Emanuel, Our "Snoa" 5492–5742, Published to Commemorate the 250th An-niversary of the Consecration of Synagoge Mikvé Israel (since 1964: Mikvé Israel-Emanuel)* (Willemstadt 1982).

during part of the Aboab conflict, offered to host the services in his house. Another faction, around the important figure of Selomoh Nunes Redondo, competed with Penso for the right to finance and sponsor the new Otrabanda synagogue, while the rest of the *parnassim* viewed the establishment of a new synagogue as a threat to the full authority of the *Mahamad*. A violent incident took place in the synagogue on Yom Kippur 1745 that pitted the factions against each other and led to the temporary suspension of services.[15]

The second issue was a dispute about marriage and inheritance laws that erupted between the Leao and Pereira families in 1744. The widower argued that the mutual will that he and his childless wife had signed shortly before her death takes precedence over their *ketubbah* (marriage contract) and, therefore, he should be allowed to keep his wife's dowry.[16] Mosseh Penso headed the faction that held the law of the land over Jewish law and custom and refused to sign a general statement upholding the *ketubbah* and declaring the mutual wills invalid. As was customary, these issues were submitted to the Amsterdam *parnassim* and *hakhamim* for arbitration and guidance.[17] In December 1744, just as these conflicts were gaining momentum, a new *hakham*, Semuel Mendes de Solla, arrived in Curaçao to assist the elderly *Hakham* Jessurun. De Solla, a native of Portugal who was trained at the Ets Haim rabbinical seminary in Amsterdam, was known for his riveting oratory skills and unusually irascible temperament, whose distinctive disposition did not help to quell the situation in Curaçao. In fact, it did the opposite. His sharp and vindictive sermons, as well as his easy resort to *herem* fueled the conflicts throughout the next year.[18]

---

15   Emmanuel, *History of the Jews of the Netherlands Antilles*, vol. 1, pp. 184–85. See also the letters and documents sent by the leaders of the Otrabanda factions on the synagogue issue, then and at later stages, SAA 334-1028B, fº442–52, 492–503.

16   Emmanuel, *History of the Jews of the Netherlands Antilles*, vol. 1, pp. 181–83.

17   On the links with Amsterdam see Y. Kaplan, "The Curaçao and Amsterdam Jewish Communities," pp. 207–11; on Amsterdam's guidance and arbitration of local conflicts, see E. Oliel-Grausz, "*Patrocinio* and Authority: Assessing the Metropolitan Role of the Portuguese Nation of Amsterdam in the Eighteenth Century," in *The Dutch Intersection. The Jews and the Netherlands in Modern History*, ed. Y. Kaplan (Leiden 2008), pp. 149–72.

18   On de Solla, see Emmanuel, *History of the Jews of the Netherlands Antilles*, vol. 1, pp. 178–80, 242–48 and Y. Kaplan, "The Curaçao and Amsterdam Jewish Communities in the 17th and 18th Centuries," *American Jewish History* (1982), pp. 208–9. A letter to the Curaçao community dated June 1744 and sent together with Semuel de Solla's rabbinical contract, praises at length his orthodoxy and outstanding rhetorical gift : "alem de ser sugeito temeroso de Dˢ & observante de Sua Santa Ley, tem feito tao boms progresos no studio della, q. foy avansado p. seu saber a primeira clase dos Baale tora de nosso insigne medras de Eshaim, e com aplauso de todo este kahal tem o louvor de ser hum dos melhores pregadores q. ao

Hakham de Solla joined the ranks opposing the Penso faction on the matter of the Otrabanda synagogue and the *ketubbah* issue, advocating strict adherence to the conditions of the marriage contract, as well as personally opposing Mosseh Penso.

Conflicts and Feuds within the Community

Such was the situation in Curaçao when David Aboab arrived there from Jamaica where he had spent the last four years. Little is known about his origins, though he was said to have come from Italy and described himself as the son of "*kedoshim ve-tzadikim*" (holy and righteous persons).[19] As to his social status, he was portrayed as a wandering *talmid hakham*, a scholar of some sort, looking for employment.

Mapping out the conflicts at the time of Aboab's arrival is crucial to understanding his place in the communal conflict. Aboab quickly found himself allied with the Penso faction, which was busily employed during spring of 1746 in competing with Selomoh Nunes Redondo for the honor of building the new Otrabanda synagogue on a plot bought through a community subscription, as well as in backing the preeminence of the will over the *ketubbah*.[20] In this enterprise, each party sought whatever support could be gained, on the island and beyond, with the governor, the Council of Ten, the Curaçao and Amsterdam *parnassim* and the officials of the West India Company. Throughout Aboab's stay in Curaçao, the Otrabanda issue remained active, with periods of quiet and flare-ups. The synagogue was inaugurated in Elul 1746, a few days before Aboab's expulsion.[21]

---

presente temos, tanto pella sua boa e ortodoxa doctrina quanto pella natural eloquencia q. possua q^{to} pella escolhida rhetorica com q. sabe ornar os seus discursos."

19   David ben Semuel Aboab could plausibly be the son of the Venetian Rabbi Semuel Aboab, born in 1692, himself a grandson of the famed Talmudic scholar and rabbinical authority, Semuel Aboab (b. Hamburg 1610–d. Venice 1694), in which case, his assertion about his scholarly ascendance would be true, his father, uncles and great-grandfather all having been distinguished rabbis. See L. Löwenstein, "Die Familie Aboab," *MGWJ* 48 (1904), pp. 661–701 and C. Roth, "Aboab," *Encyclopaedia Judaica*, ed. M. Berenbaum and F. Skolnik, 2nd ed. (Detroit 2007 [1971]), vol. 1, p. 265.

20   Emmanuel, *History of the Jews of the Netherlands Antilles*, vol. 1, pp. 185–86.

21   Ibid., p. 187. It is to be noted that the confrontation between the Penso, Redondo and de Solla factions peaked in 1748; on the fights in Otrabanda in 1748 see ibid., pp. 194–96. For the permission granted by Governor Isaac Faesch to build a synagogue in Otrabanda on

The distribution of the various players and their roles in these conflicts sheds much needed light on the fact that *Hakham* Semuel Mendes de Solla was the main target of Aboab's pamphlet *Sefer emet ve-yatsiv*. There is an abundance of documentation covering the communal feuds as well as Aboab's sojourn on the island. Since Mikve Israel's eighteenth-century community records have disappeared, most of the available documentation comes from correspondence between the Amsterdam metropolis and Curaçao. The majority of the extant documents were written by the parties to the conflict in order to explain their narratives and to advance and defend their positions with the authorities in Amsterdam.[22] Standard practice for important transatlantic mail was to send the same item twice, sometimes even three times, because of the dangers at sea, the "*segunda via*" always being noted on the sent letter. Due to the idiosyncratic archival culture of the Portuguese communities, not only were documents preserved, but despite the redundancy, several copies of the same letter could be preserved. All parties thus composed their own narratives of the conflicts, sometimes in installments. The *parnassim* of Mikve Israel related the history of the discords in a thirty-six-page report, called *epitome* or *deduccao*, composed in November 1746 and augmented in January 1747. This was sent to the Amsterdam *parnassim* together with other documents concerning the conflicts inside a special locked chest bearing the seal of the *kehillah* "MI" (Mikve Israel).[23] Another vivid account of the matter was given by *Hakham* Semuel de Solla in his protracted letter to the Amsterdam *parnassim* sent in the same chest.[24] Then, there is David Aboab's manuscript pamphlet, *Sefer emet ve-yatsiv*, which narrates these conflicts in literary form, from the time of the arrival of *Hakham* de Solla until October 1746 when Aboab is forced to leave the island.[25] Each faction presented its own etiology of the conflicts: while the Curaçaoan *parnassim* and *Hakham* de Solla ascribed the origins of these conflicts to the *ketubbah* dispute and the role played by Mosseh Penso,

14 July 1746, see Z. Loker, *Jews in the Caribbean: Evidence on the History of the Jews in the Caribbean Zone in Colonial Times* (Jerusalem 1991), pp. 88–89.

22   SAA 334–1028B *passim*.

23   SAA 334–1028B, f°339–436 (hereafter, *Epitome*). The Portuguese nations of Curaçao and Surinam had their own mark or stamp used to identify shipments, as was the case with all merchants.

24   SAA 334–1028B, f°459–471 and second copy f°521–534, dated 6 July and updated 4 November 1746.

25   See above n. 1.

further aggravated by David Aboab, the Penso faction placed the source of all the trouble in the person of *Hakham* de Solla and his associates.[26]

Aboab's Life and Deeds: Rumors and Investigations

Upon Aboab's arrival in Curaçao, rumors started circulating about his deviant conduct back in Jamaica. As recounted by the *parnassim* and de Solla, in spring 1746, the Curaçaoan *beit din* (rabbinical court), which included *Hakham* Jessurun and *Hakham* de Solla, summoned Aboab in secret, out of respect for his knowledge and his impoverished situation and informed him of the rumors about his Jamaican past. The *beit din* had hoped, in this way, to bring him to confess and repent, but Aboab squarely denied every accusation. Subsequently, the *beit din* summoned witnesses who had been previously living in Jamaica and recorded their testimonies on 4 Iyar 5506 (24 April 1746). Aboab was called again, and the declarations of three witnesses were read to him, but he rejected these as inconclusive, saying, according to de Solla's telling, that the *beit din* could not punish him because the testimonies were not corroborative.

At the same time, the *parnassim* requested the leaders of the Kingston *kehillah* to conduct an investigation and gather additional testimonies about Aboab.[27] Thus, there were parallel "*inspeççao*" (inquiries) conducted in Jamaica and Curaçao on the matter of the young Italian teacher-preacher. On 4 July 1746, the letter of the Curaçao *parnassim* was made public in the synagogue in Kingston just before the reading of the Torah. Anyone who had heard or seen things regarding David Aboab was asked to come forward and testify.[28] The testimonies collected in Jamaica were sent to Curaçao. The fate of these documents reveals a great deal of information about the nature, as well as the dangers, of Caribbean life. The ship carrying these documents was overrun by a Spanish privateer and brought to Porto Cabelo on the coast of Caracas.[29]

---

26   *Epitome*, f°413, *Sefer emet ve-yatsiv*, f°5: for David Aboab the beginning of trouble on the island dates back to precisely 2 Tevet 505 (7 December 1744) i.e., the arrival of *SH-Me-Ts pissul*, Sh(emuel) M(endes) Ts(olla). See further below for the nickname.

27   *Epitome*, f°413, Semuel de Solla's letter to the Amsterdam *parnassim*, 1746, SAA 334–1028B, f° 464–69.

28   SAA 334–1028B, f°349–58.

29   Puerto Cabello, about two hundred km. west of Caracas, a favorite location for Dutch smuggling due to the short distance to Curaçao. On the geography of contraband, see A. Ramón, *Curazao y la costa de Caracas: introducción al estudio del contrabando en la provincia de Venezuela en tiempos de la Compañía guipuzcoana, 1730–1780* (Caracas 1993), pp. 41–51.

There, the papers were spotted by a monk who was involved in a smuggling operation with some Jewish merchants in Curaçao. Surmising that these papers belonged to Jews, he sent them on a boat to Curaçao, which was, in turn, seized by the British, who ultimately forwarded the documents to Curaçao![30] By the time the testimonies finally reached their destination, the *parnassim* of Mikve Israel had already decided to ask the governor to expel Aboab, but this "providential" material strengthened the evidence of his misconduct.

These fascinating testimonies reveal another side of Aboab's character. People reported that his attendance at the synagogue was scarce, at best, and that he openly transgressed the Sabbath. Several persons testified to seeing him on Friday evening or Saturday carrying a stick, walking into stores, purchasing merchandise and smoking a pipe. He was said to be living openly with an Englishwoman, and one witness testified to seeing him all dressed up entering a church with an Englishman on a Sunday morning. Not only did the testimony from Kingston show Aboab to be lax in his observance of Judaism, he was also reported to be publicly critical of the commandments, deriding *tefillin*, the *lulav*, calling himself a *naturalista*. When pressed on this last assertion by the witness and asked whether he believed that Moses had received the Holy Law, Aboab said that he did believe that, but he also believed that Moses had added to what God had commanded. However, his deviant words and slack religious observance are not enough to sum up his character. His relations with the community also became conflictual because of his deeds: he had taken the liberty to grant a local couple a letter of divorce and, additionally, when the Jamaican *parnassim* rejected his request for aid when he was ill and in great need, he took upon himself the authority to excommunicate them.

These testimonies, which were later used to build the case against Aboab for the Dutch authorities and the Amsterdam community, were not available when Aboab arrived in Willemstad and joined in the local conflicts in late 1745 or early 1746. However, his "island hopping" from Jamaica to Curaçao did not ensure him immunity with regard to his previous misdemeanors, since witnesses to his misconduct in Jamaica had also "hopped" their way to Curaçao, which illustrates the intensive Jewish mobility in the Caribbean.[31] The Mikve

---

30   *Epitome*, f°419. On Caribbean smuggling and the Jews, see W. Klooster, "Contraband Trade by Curaçao's Jews with Countries of Idolatry, 1660–1800," *StRos* 31/1 (1997), pp. 58–73; C.A. Monfante, *El contrabando holandés en el Caribe durante la primera mitad del siglo XVIII* (Caracas 1984), vol. 1, pp. 46–67.

31   Intra-Caribbean mobility was intense. Johan Hartog describes the movement of those who try out their luck on successive islands as "island hopping," *History of the Netherlands Antilles*, p. 131.

Israel leaders were suspicious of Aboab and his outstanding rabbinical knowledge, but yet, were not unwilling to help him. After warning him that he was not
to meddle in the business of the *Mahamad* and the *beit din*, Aboab was even
hired by the *parnassim* to serve as a teacher in *Hakham* de Solla's *beit midrash*
for which he was paid a small stipend by the community. He was also recruited
as a preacher in the mutual aid society *Tovat Marhe,* also called "Companhia
de pasiantes," recently established under Penso's influence, which focused on
assisting travelers and Torah study.[32]

Clashes: Troublemaker versus Irate Rabbi

The first confrontation with the Jewish authorities in Curaçao, according to
both De Solla's and the *parnassim*'s report, occurred when Aboab undertook to
write a halakhic decision on a matter submitted to the local *beit din* concerning
a family dispute between Benjamin Moreno Henriquez and his brother-in-law
with regard to who was repsonsible for the expenses for the funeral and tombstone for their deceased mother and mother-in-law.[33] For this encroachment
upon the domain and prerogatives of communal leaders, Aboab received a
second warning from the *parnassim*. According to de Solla, "the said Aboab,
seeing that we had closed the way to his spreading discord, he tried (as an Italian would do) to raise an accusation against my fellow [*hakham*]."[34]
    Matters next escalated into a near brawl on the patio of the Mikve Israel
synagogue, when Aboab, together with several members of Penso's mutual aid
society, turned up after a rumor was circulated that *Hakham* Jessurun had spoken ill of the confraternity. Upon hearing the dispute and witnessing it from
his window, *Hakham* de Solla came running from his own lodgings and confronted Aboab, who accused *Hakham* Jessurun of lying. De Solla threatened to
muzzle Aboab if he did not cease to offend the elderly *hakham*. He then had
him forcibly removed from the patio and placed under ban (*niduy*).[35]

---

32   Very little is known about this confraternity, one among many charitable societies es-
     tablished in Curaçao. See the chronological list of foundations in Emmanuel, *History of
     the Jews of the Netherlands Antilles*, pp. 125–28. For a comprehensive study of Amsterdam
     Sephardic charitable institutions after which most Curaçaoan confraternities were mod-
     eled, see T. Levie Bernfeld, *Poverty and Welfare among the Portuguese Jews in Early Modern
     Amsterdam* (Cambridge, MA 2012).
33   Emmanuel, *History of the Jews of the Netherlands Antilles*, p. 188.
34   SAA 334–1028B, f°466, Semuel Mendes de Solla's letter to the Amsterdam *parnassim*.
35   Ibid.: de Solla's account is very vivid and conveys the sharpness of the exchange between
     the two fiery characters, "(lhe disse eu) sinao for medido em suas palavras lhey porey hua
     mordasa na lingoa."

In the subsequent meeting of the communal leaders and rabbis, it was decided that Aboab should publicly ask forgiveness from the *hakham* and the community by going barefoot to the pulpit the next day, in accordance with the rite for public penance. When Aboab was told of the *parnassim*'s resolution, a heated discussion and negotiation ensued regarding the contents of his apology and the details of the "rite." Aboab wanted to add to the text he was given and Mosseh Penso wanted to spare his *protégé* the humiliation of being barefoot and suggested that he might be allowed to wear cloth shoes. *Hakham* de Solla rejected the latter's proposition, replying that it was neither Yom Kippur nor the Ninth of Av, referring to the custom of wearing cloth shoes on those days of atonement and contrition. Aboab was finally called up to the pulpit on the next day following the afternon service. When he was first summoned by the beadle, he refused to stand up, but then changed his mind and approached the pulpit, though he kept his shoes on in an act of defiance. With the beadle as intermediary, *Hakham* de Solla ordered the offender to take off his shoes. Aboab, in mock compliance, left the shoes dangling on his feet like slippers until de Solla forced him to remove them completely. Once at the pulpit, according to de Solla's description, instead of reading the apology with contrition, Aboab sang the text. At the end of the reading, after the ban was lifted, Aboab refused to obey the *beit din*'s order to sit on a low bench, as was required in the repentence ceremony and acted, according to de Solla, as if he had committed no crime.[36] Following the exit from the synagogue of the members of the Tovat Marhe society on that day, fighting broke out in the streets. The *parnassim* and *hakhamim* were infuriated by Aboab's public defiance of their authority and the community rules and turned to Governor Isaac Faesch to have him expelled from the island as a troublemaker.[37] In early September 1746, Governor Faesch ordered Aboab to leave the island within eight days and never return.

---

36   Ibid., f°467–68. On excommunication in the Sephardi Diaspora see Y. Kaplan, *An Alternative Path to Modernity: The Sephardi Diaspora in Western Europe* (Leiden 2000), Ch. 6 and, in particular, p. 147 n. 11, the author mentions two eighteenth-century cases in which the transgressors were spared actual excommunication but were still required to remove their shoes when asking forgiveness in a semi private or private setting, the chamber of the *Mahamad* or the home of the *hakham*.

37   Epitome, f° Semuel Mendes de Solla, f°464–49. Though the initial privileges granted to the Jews have not been preserved in the original, but only through nineteenth-century summaries, we know that based on the 1659 charter, the Jewish community could expect support of the island's authorities in disciplining its members ; article 13 of the first extant *Ascamot* (1688) drawn up by congregation Mikve Israel stipulated that in case of a member of the Nation leading an indecent life, he will be warned twice and, therafter, a report shall be sent to the Governor to request his banishment, see Emmanuel, *History of the Jews of the Netherlands Antilles*, vol. 2, pp. 544–45.

Arguing that the Jewish New Year was approaching, Mosseh Penso and his co-
horts petitioned the governor for Aboab to be allowed to remain on the island
until the next ship for Amsterdam and provided him with affidavits.[38]

The Aboab affair turned into an open confrontation between the factions.
The initial proclamation read in the synagogue to announce Aboab's expulsion implied that those who sided with him and Penso were also under *herem*
and were to seek absolution from the *hakhamim*, which caused much confusion and strife. It necessitated a second proclamation, this time formulated
by the governor himself, annoucing the expulsion and lifting of the collective
ban to restore some peace. Aboab lingered on the island for some time and
even found a measure of toleration from the *parnassim* after his promise of
good behavior. At the end of October, he attended services in the Mikve Israel
synagogue, where his misconduct during two subsequent Sabbath services led
the *parnassim* to, once again, call for his expulsion. From the description in
de Solla and the *parnassim*'s version and from an official complaint sent to
Governor Faesch it appears that he purposely showed signs of disrepect to the
rabbis by repeatedly walking by their seats instead of using the back entrance
to the synagogue and refusing to salute them.[39] The *parnassim*'s request was
granted and Aboab was supposed to be kept under arrest until his departure.
After a game of hide and seek, with Aboab allegedly abbetted by the Penso
faction, he finally departed Curaçao for Eustatius and surfaced in Amsterdam
in early 1747.[40]

In *Hakham* de Solla's and the *parnassim*'s account, Aboab was widely condemned, while Penso was blamed as the puppeteer manipulating the Italian
forasteiro. In Aboab's pamphlet *Emet ve-yatsiv*, the archenemy was *Hakham* de
Solla along with his accomplices.

A Sulfurous Manuscript: *Sefer emet ve-yatsiv*

Only in light of these rivalries does Aboab's unique and sulfurous manuscript
become intelligible. Though it is deserving of more attention than Emmanuel's

---

38   SAA 334–1028B, fº374–80: request for banishment by the *parnassim* and decree of expul-
      sion, dated 5 September 1746. The Amsterdam file also contains a copy of Aboab's request
      to suspend the execution of the ban until after the imminent New Year and of affidavits
      provided by Mosseh Penso and Abraham Belmonte.

39   SAA 334–1028B, fº468–69, Semuel de Solla's letter.

40   SAA 334–1028B, fº359–60, request sent to Governor Faesch, 31 October 1746, by the *parnas-
      sim*, recounting Aboab's provocation and disturbance of the service on 22 and 29 October
      1746. When summoned afterward by the *Mahamad*, he stated that he refused to obey the
      parnassim and elders, recognizing only the Governor's authority.

terse and cautious treatment, due to the brevity of this present contribution, I will merely offer a cursory analysis of its contents. *Sefer emet ve-yatsiv* is a twenty-four-page manuscript written in the style of an allegorical dialogue between a mother, *Emet*, meaning Truth and her son, *Yatsiv*, meaning steadfast, firm or enduring. The words of the title *emet ve-yatsiv* (Truth and Enduring) are also the first words of the benediction that immediately follows the reading of the morning *Shema* prayer, a text composed of a series of laudatory attributes of the Divine. Aboab's manuscript is brimming with biblical and rabbinical expressions sharpened into rhetorical weapons. It is not a mere patchwork of quotations, but reveals, on the contrary, a true mastery of the Hebrew language and biblical and rabbinical literature. The original verses are reformulated to match the author's polemical and satirical pupose. It bristles with puns, some quite offensive and definitely fits the definition of a libel. The dialogue is divided into three parts, with each part representing one day during which the son questions his mother about what happened in Curaçao. In a long prologue, after praising the grandeur of Curaçao and the Dutch government—the source of the oft-quoted sentence about Curaçao being the mother city of the Caribbean—the mother explains how the island was idyllic, full of good people and Torah until the arrival of the evil de Solla who became involved with two other evil men, Mordecai Haim Senior and Selomoh Nunes Redondo.[41] Aboab's inventive and scholarly mind produced a roster of nicknames meant to mask the identities of, as well as to insult, his three enemies. De Solla's Hebrew initials—Shlomo Mendes Tsolla—were slightly modified to match a Talmudic expression—*SheMeTs Pissul*, which became de Solla's nickname throughout the pamphlet. The usual rendering of this rare Talmudic expression is "blemish of unfitness," but, in the present context, the meaning is even more precise and "unfitness" points to dubious ascendance or forbidden unions. Thus, a faithful rendering in English of the sniping pun could be "a scent of illegitimacy."[42] The re-ordered initials of Mordecai Haim Senior become *Ish HaMaS*, a "violent man,"[43] and Selomoh Nunes Redondo, *ShuNRa bisha*, or "bad cat." The combined names of all three: Senior–Redondo–Tsolla, becomes *SheReTs*, meaning vermin. The prologue concludes with a formula of *herem* imposed

---

41   Mordecai Haim Senior was a *parnas* in 1744 and Selomoh Nunes Redondo was Penso's competitor in the project to build the new synagogue in Otrabanda.

42   See BT *Megillah* 25b, where the expression "*shemets pissul*" is used to refer to a man whose ascendance is stained, born of a forbidden union; in *Pessahim* 3b, it refers to genealogical flaws that disqualify the *Kohen* (Priest) from serving in the Temple. It could well be that the violent criticism intended in this nickname combines the two notions of unfit to serve as a *Kohen*/rabbi and of dubious birth. Commentators often use that expression in the context of a suspicion of adultery.

43   Proverbs 16:29: "A lawless man misleeds his friend making him take the wrong way."

on these three characters and a group of their followers. The libelous nature of the text is evident in its overall architecture; Aboab is less concerned with a precise chronological rendering of events than with constructing a genuine anti-*Hakham* de Solla device.

The dialogue for each of the three days, in the form of questions and answers between *Emet* and *Yatsiv*, intended to restore the truth, contains accusations pertaining to three different categories: the first day and first line of attack, which will be pursued throughout the dialogue, centers round personal slander of de Solla and the terms of his rabbinical appointment in Curaçao. As a literary satirical work, the dialogue in *Sefer emet ve-yatsiv* intertwines factual information about de Solla with seemingly fictitious elaborations, such as the long list of the *hakham*'s parents' despicable professions, which were intended to shock and emphasize his family's lowly origins. A lengthy passage deals with the *hakham*'s bloated ego, which led him to disregard the original terms of his contract stipulating that he was to be an "assistant" to the "old man" (*Hakham* Jessurun). De Solla is depicted as neglecting his teaching and rabbinical duties, embracing instead profane pastimes such as hunting and dancing.

The second series of accusations addressed in the second day's dialogue points to de Solla's alleged ignorance, lax observance and hypocrisy. Aboab made two claims: first, that the *hakham* taught the commandments and expected his congregants to follow them without actually following them himself; second, the rabbi tried to convince the congregation of the exclusive legitimacy of his ways, as for example, the proper manner to perform the *lulav* ceremony, or shaving during the counting of the *omer* (the forty-nine days between the first day of Passover and the festival of Shavuot).

Lastly, in the third part, Aboab presents a halakhic discussion criticizing all of de Solla's decisions from the time of his arrival on the island: regarding the *ketubbah* vs. the civil law dispute, Aboab argued against de Solla's opinion, that there was indeed a legal way for the husband to be relieved of his commitment in the *ketubbah*. He referred to the collective petition in which 235 members of the *kahal* supported the preeminence of the *ketubbah* in order to reinforce the argument that the majority cannot impose its opinion on the minority if the decision incurs financial loss. As to the other issues—the matter of the payment for the mother-in-law's tombstone, opposition to the new synagogue in Otrabanda and de Solla's contention about the appropriate movements of the *lulav*, which de Solla wanted to reform according to what he had learned from *Hakham* Aylion in Amsterdam, or even the way he handled the *tsitsit* during the reading of the *Shema*—these provide colorful occasions for revealing De Solla's malice. His stubbornness and conceit are exemplified by his refusal to perform the commandment of the *lulav* simply because he does not agree with the type of *arava* (one of the four species of the *lulav*) used in Curaçao.

According to Aboab's description, he simply appeared in the synagogue with only three out of the four species, leaving out the *arava*. Each of de Solla's decisions, endeavors or behavior is discussed and invalidated with a vast array of halakhic references. This last part also contains numerous anecdotes about de Solla's misconduct on the island, such as his public affair with a young servant he had brought with him and his family from Holland, and back in Amsterdam, such as the alleged acts of indecency that justified his temporary suspension from the *beit midrash*. Altogether, it's a true character assassination and a depiction of a *hakham* deeply engrossed in heterodoxy, heteropraxis, debauchery and more. A very puzzling passage relates his inappropriate relation with a widow involved in spells and magic.

Through a skillful "mise en abîme," Aboab placed himself within the dialogue, in the guise of a young *talmid hakham* the old rabbi tries to subvert. Depicting his own predicament as a victim of the *hakham*'s associates, Aboab portrayed himself as a sheep among wolves, a righteous character loyal to those who had come to his aid, in this case, the *Tovat Marhe* society and a victim of de Solla's malice and schemes, which lead to his excommunication and expulsion.

It is difficult to reconcile Aboab's self-portrayal in *Sefer emet ve-yatsiv* as a champion of orthodoxy with the image of him from the testimonies that painted him as a deviant character who was negligent in his religious observance. One possible explanation for this disparity is to consider the pamphlet not as an expression of Aboab's viewpoint, but rather, as a work commissioned by Mosseh Penso himself. In this scenario, Aboab's knowledge, imagination and wit would have been used to produce a very elaborate form of ammunition in the battle between the two factions and, more specifically, between Penso and *Hakham* de Solla. As already mentioned, Aboab was shown to be Penso's protégé on many occasions throughout the conflict, with Penso arguing on Aboab's behalf to reduce his humiliation during the pardon ceremony in the synagogue, interceding for him with the governor, supporting him financially through the mutual aid society and, lastly, paying for his passage to St. Eustatius and from there to Amsterdam.[44] A letter in Portuguese, written by *Hakham* de Solla and which Penso was accused of stealing from the communal papers and circulating, was embedded in the middle of Aboab's Hebrew pamphlet, with the contents intended to illustrate de Solla's conceit and disregard for his congregants.[45] While the sharpness of mind and pen were Aboab's, the issues,

---

44 *Epitome*, f°434.

45 De Solla's letter appears in *Emet ve-yatsiv*, f°14–16, and in the incoming letters from Curaçao in SAA PA 334–1028B f°556–58. In the said letter adressed to the *Mahamad* after his opinion on the correct movements of the *lulav* had been rejected in a communal

battles and enemies were Penso's, an adamant advocate of the law of the land and the new synagogue.

The pamphlet's contents indeed seem to point, first and foremost, to the personal war between Penso and de Solla. The repeated assertions about de Solla's bloated ego and ignorance—in Aboab's words the *hakham* thinks Semuel equals Moses plus Aaron—echoes a violent confrontation that took place between Penso and de Solla mentioned in de Solla's letter and which reads like a transcript of the conversation: during the said clash, de Solla brought up "Rav Beit Yosef," Yosef Karo, author of the extensive codes of Jewish law *Beit Yosef* and *Shulhan arukh*, in order to establish that he was entitled to follow his own custom for the *lulav* movements. Penso, de Solla related, mocked him with a sniggering remark to the effect of, how could "this little piece of *Hahaozinho*" (or tiny *hakham*) compare himself to Beit Yosef?[46] De Solla's words about Penso were not much kinder, as he depicted him as "a seditious malevolent and agitated troublemaker to the public good and above all an obstinate enemy of the law of God."[47] The fact that Penso's name is nowhere mentioned in the pamphlet is, of itself, suspicious and might be an indication that, *deus ex machina*, he was behind the pamphlet's composition and orchestration.

Conflict Resolution and Interpretation

Besides personal enmity, fueling this war of words were the complex social and cultural communal dynamics that were common to Sephardi *kehillot* and also specific to the circumstances in Curaçao. In an early study, Yosef Kaplan had emphasized two distinctive socio-religious features of Curaçaoan Jewry:

---

ordinance, de Solla complained that he was sent away from his homeland "a ser pastor de lobos em lugar de ovelhas," and wrote sharp words about the ignorance of Curaçaoan Jews and of those appointed to be his judges. He agreed later to apologize in front of the offended *Mahamad*, and it was decided that his letter will be burnt and destroyed. Penso, then *parnas*, was accused of stealing a copy of that letter and circulating it to expose de Solla's character in Curaçao as well as in Amsterdam, see SAA 334–1028B, *Epitome*, f°421–22.

46   Letter of *Hakham* de Solla, Amsterdam, 3 November 1746, f°470: "dizendo eu … eque em couzas de Din, nao estava hum H.H. sogeito a seguir o costume do outro eque assim hera Din cortado pello Rab Bet Josseph, aoq^e Ditto hipocrita respondeu com despreso: Olhem q.authorid^des nos alega o H.H. com o Beth Joseph; o Bet Joseph hera ou foy mais q. hum pedaço de Hahaozinho."

47   Ibid., f°460: "homem sediciozo malevolo torbulento perturbador do bem publico y sobretudo enemigo aserimo da ley de D^s."

"the clear oligarchization of the leadership of the community and its pattern of conduct; and the uninterrupted attachment to the Portuguese community of Amsterdam and the willingness to accept, at all times and under all circumstances, the leadership and authority of that community."[48] These assertions, while insightful and accurate, call for some qualification. The "absolute domination by the wealthy-oligarchic stratum,"[49] went hand in hand with ruthless struggles within the ruling élite that mirrored the fierce commercial and maritime competition. As appears clearly, the ruling élite in Curaçao was divided and organized into factions and systems of patronage. In the case of Curaçao, classic patterns of tension and competition for authority within the community, as well as between lay and and rabbinical leaders, were made more complex because they were interwoven with very strong factions and sharp social competition for power and respectability.

The first issue of consequence for us is that of lay versus rabbinical authority within the community. In Curaçao, as was the case in Surinam a few years ealier in the controversy around *Hakham* Abraham Gabay Isidro, these tensions were greatly exacerbated by the personality of the *hakham*,[50] and exemplified in *Hakham* de Solla's obstinancy in imposing his version of *netilat lulav* (lit. lifting of the *lulav*) and the protracted controversy he initiated over the conformity of the local *arava* for Sukkot. In his opposition to the *parnassim* on halahkic issues, de Solla battled for recognition and for a definition of *bom judesmo* that was slightly different from that of the *parnassim*, with a greater emphasis on halakhah and on the halakhic teaching he received in Ets Haim under the tutelage of Selomoh Aylion. He strove not only for recognition of his own expertise and superior knowledge—which came, it seems with much condescension for his congregants—but also greater respect for the authority and role of the *hakham* in all communal matters, which he refused to confine to an ancillary position.[51] The question of the *ketubbah* shows, however, that beyond the confrontation between lay and rabbinic authority, these were multiplex conflicts. The dispute about the precedence of civil law over Jewish matrimonial law, serves merely as the pretext for crystallizing and mobilizing the main factions.

---

48   Kaplan, "The Curaçao and Amsterdam Jewish Communities," p. 203.

49   Ibid., p. 206.

50   On Abraham Gabay Isidro and Mendes de Solla, see Oliel-Grausz, "Patrocinio and Authority," pp. 155–58.

51   See Kaplan, "The Curaçao and Amsterdam Jewish Communities," p. 208: "Rabbi Mendes de Solla managed, during his term of office (1744–1761) to convert the chair of the community rabbi into the central and decisive post in the life of the community."

The second issue here is the scope of communal autonomy and authority within the local political and juridical context. Bedeviled by his adversaries, Penso undertook to fend off the calumnies by writing to the Amsterdam *parnassim* a number of letters in which he explained that encroaching upon the civil authority and jurisdiction in matters of wills would only damage the Jews' situation. Undoubtedly, he encouraged Aboab to develop that line of argumentation in his pamphlet, with the relevant halakhic grounds, where he proposed a secularized view of the same reasoning. Himself a former *parnas* and official deputy of the Nation with the island authorities, he devoted much effort and resources between the years 1746 and 1750 to curbing the prerogatives of the *parnassim* and the *hakham* and to limiting the use of excommunication, repeatedly taking the *parnassim* to court in Curaçao and Amsterdam and was repeatedly called "*pleitista*" (extremely litigious) by his opponents.[52]

Lastly, whatever confrontations developed, in Curaçao even more so than in Surinam, they rarely remained a "face à face," two-party affair: the factions, *parnassim* and *hakhamim* systematically fell back on the Amsterdam metropolis. Here again, I concur with Yosef Kaplan on the importance of the link, but differ somewhat as to the processes involved in the conflict resolution. The Amsterdam metropolis, as a potential source of support and legitimation for the various parties, was a central actor in these controversies. But, as emphasized in a previous symposium, requesting the *patrocinio* (patronage) of K.K. Talmud Torah did not necessarily mean taking their advice or complying with their decision.[53]

Turning to the Dutch metropolis was often a strategic move, rarely followed by straightforward compliance and not necessarily effective. In the Curaçaoan conflicts of the mid 1740s, Amsterdam's intervention was both frequent and cautious. The Amsterdam *parnassim* repeatedly warned the leaders in Curaçao against excessive use of the *herem*, enjoining them to conform strictly to the *ascamot* (the ordinances of the Portuguese Jews), and reminding them that the ban was not a solution for conflicts between goups or individuals. Their support of the Curaçao *parnassim* whose authority was being challenged was far from unconditional, even though they defended communal authority and provided their support to prevent Aboab from publishing his slanderous manuscript. They had to reckon with the powerful Penso faction that had many friends in Amsterdam close enough to the *parnassim* there to be able to offer to procure copies of all the documents sent to Amsterdam.

---

52   Penso's ideas on the subject were clearly expressed in his letter to the Amsterdam *Mahamad* dated 1 July 1746, SAA 334–1028B, f°537–39, letters to Amsterdam; about his character, f°47–49, Selomoh Nunes Redondo's letter to K.K. Talmud Torah, 21 May 1748.

53   Oliel-Grausz, "Patrocinio and Authority," pp. 149–72.

Cautiousness and divided loyalties in Amsterdam proper might explain the relative leniency with which the Amsterdam *parnassim* dealt with Aboab. After being informed by Joshuah de Cordova, a would-be-candidate for a rabbinical position in the Caribbean, in Curaçao in particular, that Aboab was badmouthing *Hakham* de Solla, they summoned Aboab and confronted him about it. Aboab apologized and was persuaded to sign a declaration in which he promised that he would not publish anything without the permission of the Amsterdam *parnassim*, a very benign punishment considering the evidence they possessed of his misconduct.[54] In a letter to the Curaçao *parnassim*, the Amsterdam *parnassim* justified their leniency in consequence of Aboab's sorry state.[55] Their caution was also voiced in the letters they sent to all the parties on the same day, 23 April 1747, in which they did not clearly take one side over another, or rather, were unable to side clearly with the Curaçao *parnassim*, because they could not agree with them on the *ketubbah* issue. On this matter, they advised the Caribbean community to take a different course, because they did not wish to reach a point where they would have to oppose it should the issue ever land in front of the superior civil authorities. The Amsterdam *parnassim* saved their harshest words for *Hakham* de Solla whom they chastised for overstepping the boundaries in his sermons and his excessive use of the *herem*. As to Penso, they criticized his bad judgment in supporting such a character as Aboab.[56] The role of the leaders of the Portuguese community of Amsterdam and, for that matter, of the West India Company, which showed similar caution and was an essential part of the Curaçao community dynamics, cannot be factored in as a simple metropolitan arbitration because of the specific

---

54 See the resolution of the *parnassim* recorded for that same day: "Em 7 Jiar. Havendose feito queixa aoss[rs] do M.M. p. Josua de Cordova & Ishac Rod. Penamacor contra a pessoa de David de Samuel Aboab, que ultimam[te] chegou de Curaçao aesta, sobre diversas particularidades implicantes a boa reputaçao do H.H. Mendes de Solla, hum dos *Hahamim* de d° K.K. e havendo feito compareser diante doss[res] do M.M. ao d° Aboab, p[a] dar sua descarga confesou de plano ser verdadeira a queixa, & como foi levado de paixao declarava retractarse, oq.fez for escrito p. elle firmado neste dia, pello qual confesa ser contra a verdade o q. dixe, & se obrigou de nao escrever nem fazer escrever nem imprimir recta ou indirectam[te] papel ou livro algum sem q. antesipadam[te] aya sido aprovado pellos S[res] do M.M. em falta e transgredir firmou de submeterse ao rigor das ascamot deste K.K. e ajusta indignasao dos S[res] do M.M., & o d° papel se guardou nos archivo dos papeis de K.K. n° 49," SAA 334, 25, Livro de memorias, 1688–1751, f°310.

55 SAA 334–92, f°174, Copiador de Cartas, letter from the *parnassim* of Kahal Kados Talmud Torah to Mosseh Penso.

56 Ibid., f°170–76, letters to the *parnassim* of Kahal Kados Mikve Israel, to the *hakhamim* of the same, separate letter to *Hakham* Semuel Mendes de Solla, to Mosseh Penso, to Jacob Jeuda Leao, to Selomoh Nunes Redondo, i.e., to all the main actors and parties involved in the above mentioned conflicts, all letters dated 23 April 1747.

parameters of these conflicts. A challenge of this magnitude to the authority of the *parnassim* would have been met with greater and speedier support from both entities had the leader of the opposition not been Penso, who was soon joined by the richest merchant in Curaçao, Mordecai Alvares Correa. Thus, the question of authority and the quest for legitimation, in this case, defies simple models of interpretation and support from the metropolis.

The Penso–Aboab–de Solla conflict raises another issue associated with authority, that of the communal involvement of the island's elites. As we know from studies about the London and Amsterdam Sephardi Jewish communities in the eighteenth century, social integration and secularization entailed a relative distantiation from community involvement. These processes were also a part of the Jewish Caribbean experience, despite some heightened social and religious control due to the insular context. If any of *Hakham* de Solla's testimony about Penso is true, it would seem that he was hardly capable of reading his prayers and scorned the daily donning of *tefillin*. De Solla related that when he and Mosseh Penso were still on good terms, he tried to explain to Penso the relevance of the commandment to lay *tefillin*, to which the latter retorted, that as *parnas*, he did not need a lecture. Because of the specificities of colonial and insular society, it was not only the Orthodox kernel, as Yosef Kaplan called it, which remained at the core of the *kehillah* in Curaçao. Prominence in the institutions of the Jewish community remained a sought after source of prestige and notability and, therefore, communal involvement may well have thrived while disconnected from religious fervor or traditional observance.

Aboab: From Misfit Scholar to Convert?

Turning again to David Aboab, it appears that he and *Hakham* de Solla shared a number of similar characterisics, even though the former was merely a *forasteiro*, while the latter was an established *hakham*. They both had exentsive rabbinical training, sharp tongues and easily flared tempers, high self-esteem and an image of their own capabilities as *talmid hakham* and *posek* (a halakhic scholar who decides legal rulings based on Jewish law). They even resorted to the same imagery, a sheep among wolves, which was equally unsuitable to both. They both struggled to gain public and formal acknowledgement of their rabbinical expertise. Despite their divergent social status, both could be viewed as embattled scholars craving recognition and authority.

Aboab's rabbinical knowledge was his main intellectual and social capital. He did not seem to gain much benefit from it in Jamaica and when he told a witness that he wanted to get rid of his books in a public sale and depart for

Portugal, he was, primarily, voicing his dissatisfaction with the uselesness of his rabbinical training in helping him to earn a living.[57] In Curaçao, his knowledge did earn him some regard, helping him to find an odd job as well as the protection of a powerful member of the community. His sharp pen and capacity to defy the *hakham* made him a valuable asset and instrument for Mosseh Penso. Undoubtedly, he was a very puzzling and ambivalent character. Not simply remiss in his observance or purely a deviant, his was a complex personality that combined a measure of behavioral secularization and religious laxity with fierce pride in his rabbinical abilities and deep contempt for ignorance.

The fate of David Aboab, after confessing his errors and submitting to the conditions of the Amsterdam *Mahamad*, is half mired in mystery. In 1748, an English pamphlet by one David Aboab was published under the title: *Sefer hesed ve-emet. The mercy and truth Or, a brief account of the dealings of God with David Aboab, A native of Venice: born and educated a Jew, but now converted, from the darkness and blindness of Judaism, to the glorious light of the Gospel of Christ. To which is subjoined: A compassionate Expostulation to his brethren the Jews concerning many of their superstitions; with sevral proofs from the Old Testament that the Messiah is already come: with other doctrines and particular remarks upon ancient prophecies concerning their conversion.* Although this is not the place to present a full analysis, I have many reasons to believe that the converted David Aboab is none other than our Curaçaoan Aboab, who following his conversion, became active as a Christian Hebraist in the circle known as the Hutchinsonians,[58] a movement that took part in the Enlightenment debate on the status of the Old Testament and was intent on showing through Hebraic studies the Old Testament roots of the Trinitarian doctrine.[59]

The conversion narrative in the booklet seems to fit the biographical and chronological events in the life of the Caribbean David Aboab: the character, originally from Italy, went to Jamaica for several years, then to Curaçao in 1745 and to Holland in 1747. However, it also raises a number of questions: there was nothing about his being a *talmid hakham* or his conflicts with Jewish authorities. He simply presented himself as a merchant or a smuggler. If they

---

57 SAA 334–1028B, f°340, testimony of Abraham Lopez Penha in Curaçao, formerly from Jamaica.

58 Cecil Roth hinted at that possibility, which still calls for a thorough examination and analysis: "He [the convert] is possibly identical with the David, born in Italy, who was excommunicated in Curaçao in 1746 after a bitter controversy with the rabbinate," see *Encyclopaedia Judaica*, ed. M. Berenbaum and F. Skolnik, 2nd ed. (Detroit 2007[1971]), *s.v.* "Aboab," vol. 1., p. 265.

59 See D. Ruderman, *Jewish Enlightenment in an English Key: Anglo-Jewry's Construction of Modern Jewish Thought* (Princeton 2000), pp. 65–68.

are indeed one and the same person, as I am inclined to believe, the silence and the discrepancy regarding particular aspects of his biography may be attributed to the fact that this conversion narrative may bear, as was often the case, the intervention of his church mentor or may even be a version of the baptismal sermon preached when he became Christian.[60] Besides the matter of the different languages of the two pamphlets, the change in tone is notable, as if conversion had taken away the sting and humor; it is impossible to recognize in this bland recounting, any of the biting, rabbinical, poetic style of *Sefer emet ve-yatsiv*. In many ways, *Hesed ve-emet* follows the conventions of the conversion narrative genre, with its insistence on providential episodes during an idyllic childhood and pre-conversion life that foreshadowed the ultimate conversion. It is, obviously, an accumulation of *topoi* and, therefore, many of the apparent discrepancies need not be taken as such.

If I am correct in assuming that this is the same David Aboab, did any of his past actions give an inkling of how things would eventually turn out for him? Apart from the episode where he was allegedly seen by a witness in Jamaica entering a church, which could be explained in many ways, from the various accounts of his behavior in the Carribean, one could attempt to draw a psychological portrait of him that might offer some existential continuity. David Aboab would then be a frustrated intellectual and religious misfit, craving intellectual recognition and social status, neither of which he could attain in the course of living as a Jew.[61]

Aboab's Caribbean tale was just one episode in the protracted conflict that tore apart Curaçaoan Jewry and that came to a head around 1750 with violent fighting inside the synagogue and outside on the streets and in the cemetery, until appeasement was achieved through the involvement of the highest autorities of the West India Company and even the Stadtholder himself. As the historian of the Dutch Caribbean Cornelis Goslinga put it, "because of their noisy manifestations and ebullient spirits they gave the incorrect impression of being more numerous than the non-Jewish residents."[62] The Dutch model of a Jewish community imposing social control within its ranks in the promotion of *bom judesmo*, a respectable Judaism, was greatly undermined by the discord in Curaçao.

---

60   See E. Carlebach, *Divided Souls: Converts from Judaism in Germany, 1500–1750* (New Haven 2001), pp. 88–105.

61   About the allegedly Chrisitan leg of David Aboab's journey, see my article, "David Aboab, ou l'itinéraire frustré d'un converti juif au XVIIIe siècle, entre lacunes et certitudes," *Revue de l'Histoire des Religions*, 2017 (in press).

62   C. Ch. Goslinga, *The Dutch in the Caribbean and in the Guianas* (Assen 1985), p. 115.

CHAPTER 8

The Dutch Jewish Enlightenment in Surinam, 1770–1800

Jonathan Israel

The Dutch Jewish Enlightenment in Surinam was the short-lived project of a tiny group of enterprising young men. Although the Jewish community of Surinam was, by any standard, small and remote (in 1786 consisting of 1,311 persons out of a total population of whites of only 3,356, hence amounting to well over one third of the white population of the colony[1]), this group believed, not without some justification, that Surinam Jewish history, viewed from a certain perspective, represented an unparalleled experiment of a special significance for the entire world, Jewish and non-Jewish. In Surinam, both the Portuguese and the Ashkenazi Jews, as the leading figure David de Ishac Cohen Nassy (1747–1806) expressed it, were placed on a footing "happier and more favorable than any other place in the universe."[2] During the second half of the seventeenth century, the Sephardim found themselves placed on the same level as the Protestant colonists, without any significant distinction in status or rights, first by the English and, after the Dutch conquest in 1667, by the States-General.

"Nowhere in the world," wrote Nassy at one point, "there exists a place where religious toleration has such scale and is more strictly observed, without any discussion or controversy, than in Surinam." So favorable was the Jewish position in Surinam compared with that in eighteenth-century France, Germany or Italy, that even those Jews helped most by the advance of the Enlightenment thus far, such as those of Tuscany under the rule of the Habsburg grand duke Leopold, one of the foremost of the so-called enlightened despots, could not consider themselves to be either so favorably positioned or so equal in status to the rest of the citizenry, as Surinam Jewry.[3] The Ashkenazim had not formally

---

1 Of these, 1,045 lived in Paramaribo, among them 615 Sephardim and 430 Ashkenazim; see, David de Ishac Cohen Nassy, *Essai historique sur la colonie de Surinam*, 2 vols. (Paramaribo 1788), vol. 2, p. 39.

2 "[P]lus heureux et plus favorable que dans aucun endroit de l'univers," Nassy, *Essai historique*, vol. 1, p. 78.

3 "Il n'y a peut-être dans aucun lieu du monde, un endroit ou la tolérance religieuse ait plus d'étendue, et soit plus strictement observée, sans qu'il y ait eu jamais une discussion ou controverse quelconque, qu'en Surinam," ibid., p. 81.

become a separate community from the Sephardim in Surinam, until September 1734. But ever since, their community had enjoyed equivalent privileges, communal autonomy and status. Besides the Jews, the Moravian Brethren and Lutherans had their churches and, privately, other religions were present without anyone concerning themselves with this at all. "Gentle philosophers, come together to pray to the Being of beings for the salvation of a government which, without losing track of the regard due to its cult, could bring about and protect the opposite of what causes the shedding of rivers of blood in Europe."[4] Full untrammeled religious toleration was the first of the principles of Nassy's Enlightenment.

The Surinam Jewish Enlightenment was also of very fleeting duration. It was created by a few friends borrowing each other's books, researching and debating intensively. It was a movement that emerged from an, in the Guyanas, unprecedented and unparalleled literary ferment and book-buying craze beginning around 1750,[5] afterwards strengthened by the remarkable enthusiasm for the theater that gripped the Sephardi communities of Paramaribo and Joden Savanneh in the 1770s. Within a short space of time, during the 1770s and 1780s, the intellectual group's intense bibliophilia generated an abundance of books, zeal for reading and awareness of recent developments in publishing in Europe that provided the momentum and essential basis without which no Enlightenment movement can be possible.[6] But it is also striking that top Dutch colonial officials, in particular Jan Gerhard Wichers, who eventually became Surinam's *gouverneur-generaal* (1784–90), were the prime movers in setting up *Het Collegie van Natuur-Onderzoekinge*, the Surinam society for naturalist research in February 1780, with himself as its president, as well as a treasurer and secretary and the Surinam Enlightenment's other main institutions, including the circle of *Surinaamse Lettervrienden*, a poetry reading group set up in 1786.[7] *Het Collegie van Natuur-Onderzoekinge* gathered monthly with mixed success

---

4 "Philosophes aimables, réunissez-vous pour implorer l'Etre des êtres pour le salut d'un gouvernement qui sans perdre de vue les égards dus à son culte, sut mettre en vogue, et protéger le contraire de ce qui a fait verser des ruisseaux de sang en Europe. Que l'intolérance civile, et le préjugé national puissent être bannis de la terre à perpétuité," Nassy, *Essai historique*, vol. 2, pp. 27–28.

5 Ibid., p. 77.

6 R.G. Fuks-Mansfeld, "Verlichting en emancipatie omstreeks, 1750–1814," in *Geschiedenis van de Joden in Nederland*, ed. J.C.H. Blom et al. (Amsterdam 1995), pp. 177–203, here p. 185; R. Cohen, *Jews in Another Environment. Surinam in the Second Half of the Eighteenth Century* (Leiden 1991), p. 105.

7 Nassy, *Essai historique*, vol. 2, pp. 77–79.

and continued at least until 1789. Its greatest glory was the tropical garden, the *Hortus Surinamensis* that it laid out near Kwatta.[8] It is striking that these societies, in contrast to their equivalents in the United Provinces, posed no obstacle to admitting Jews, a point in which Surinam was, again, a remarkable forerunner.[9]

By 1786, there were two reading societies meeting monthly, "to pass on to each other the content of the works they receive from Holland for their society."[10] Nevertheless, there were very few serious readers among the native-born in the colony, whether Christians or Jews and the budding Enlightenment there was, in many ways, extremely limited. Nassy gives the example of the famous collection of and illustrations of Surinam's insects compiled by Madame Merian, celebrated throughout the world since 1690. An illustrious early Enlightenment achievement and model of systematic research into nature, no-one living in Surinam had tried to follow her method in other branches of nature or even add further to her study of Surinam's insects.[11] Furthermore, the flourishing Surinam Enlightenment was very brief. After a quarter of a century, the movement had vanished. "By 1810 they were all gone," observed Robert Cohen, "leaving behind a Surinam that looked, intellectually speaking, in the 1830s, very much as it did in the 1760s."[12]

It was a movement partly the result of cultural separation. The original *Hollandsche Schouwburg* (Dutch theater), established in Paramaribo in 1775, did not admit Jews. In response, the Jewish urban and planter elite established their own Dutch-language theater in Paramaribo, which proved rather successful. In 1784, the latter theater moved into a refurbished building, which remains today one of the principal historic landmarks of Paramaribo. According to the *Essai historique*, in 1786 this theater, at that time, put on plays at the rate of twelve per year. Meanwhile, the library, which was to become the main seedbed of the Surinam Enlightenment, had been founded by Salomon de Montel. who also played the leading part in building up the library's holdings. "Monsieur de Montel," reports the *Essai historique*, "a Portuguese Jew and a great lover of French literature, had begun a steady correspondence with Marc-Michel

8   M. van Kempen, *Een Geschiedenis van de Surinaamse literatuur*, 5 vols. (Paramaribo 2002), vol. 3, p. 87.

9   Ibid., p. 94.

10   "[P]our se communiquer le contenu des ouvrages qu'ils reçoivent de la Hollande pour leur société," Nassy, *Essai historique*, vol. 2, p. 79.

11   Ibid., p. 82.

12   Cohen, *Jews in Another Environment*, p. 106.

Rey, publisher and book-seller in Amsterdam, who furnished works to all the book-lovers of Surinam."[13]

Several high Dutch officials of the colonial administration and senior army officers, together with the physicians Van Wiert and Godfried Willem Schilling and a handful of young cultivated Jews comprised the Surinam Enlightenment. Nassy had strong medical interests. Schilling, who ran the military hospital in Paramaribo and was a friend of Nassy's, was one of the world's leading experts on leprosy about which he had published a Latin treatise, *De Lepra commentationes*, at Leiden in 1778.[14] Schilling also possessed a "vast collection" of medical and optical instruments as well as curiosities and rarities and abundantly illustrated the fact that this was a specifically Dutch Enlightenment, the impulse for which, even if enriched by several French visitors, came overridingly from Holland.[15] Several Surinam-born Dutchmen who became professionals, most notably the lawyer Abraham Verheul (Paramaribo 1770–Amsterdam 1817), whilst still very young, were decisively shaped in Surinam by this wave of Enlightenment enthusiasm and, subsequently, made their mark back in the United Provinces. Between them, this group amassed in Paramaribo a "library that was so large and so filled with works on all subjects that it yields in no respect to any other in all the Americas and equals several of the large libraries in Europe."[16] Of the eight qualified physicians in the colony in 1786, four were (Ashkenazi) Jews, four Christians; of eight apothecaries, two were Jews, one Ashkenazi and one Portuguese.[17] Doubtless, also several more of these medical practitioners were actively involved in the Enlightenment movement.

The first irregular meetings in this library resulted, on 16 February 1785, in the founding of the Jewish literary and learned society *Docendo, docemur* ("By teaching we are taught"), with the newly arrived governor of the colony Wichers, who had earlier been "First Fiscal in Surinam" in the years 1772–80, as its chief patron.[18] The society's surviving prospectus was drawn up in the house of Montel and signed by the leading figures of the Surinam Jewish Enlightenment, Montel, Emanuel de Anavia, David Nassy, Moseh Pereira de Leon and others such as Isaac de la Parra, S.G. Soares and Samuel Hoheb Brandon.[19] The prospectus of this "collège de littérature" identified as its chief objective the urgent task of countering the "crasse ignorance" characterizing both the

---

13   Nassy, *Essai historique*, vol. 2, pp. 78–79.
14   Ibid., p. 22.
15   Ibid., p. 80.
16   Ibid.; Cohen, *Jews in Another Environment*, p. 98.
17   Nassy, *Essai historique*, vol. 2, pp. 63–64.
18   Nassy, *Essai historique*, vol. 1, p. 180.
19   Nassy, *Essai historique*, vol. 2, pp. 182–83.

youth and the older generation of the Surinam Jewish community.[20] Interestingly, it was proposed that women would be admitted to the society. Sessions were to be held in French and Dutch alternately, with interjections in Spanish and Portuguese where passages were not readily understood. For a short time, it proved rather successful and was attended by both prominent Jews and Christians. The leading role was played by David Nassy who was later, in 1792, the first Jew to be made a member of the Philadelphia-based American Philosophical Society.[21] It drew in several of the same prominent members as the aforementioned Natural History Society at Paramaribo established some years prior to this, in the 1770s, when Wichers and some friends had already admitted Jews on the same basis as Christians. The éloge which Wichers had devoted to the memory of the Jewish physician, Anavia, a member of the body who died in 1781, "gave honor as much to Mr. Wichers' philosophy," wrote Nassy, "as to the memory of the late Jewish doctor."[22]

Docendo, docemur, under its prospectus, gathered twice a week on "Sundays and Wednesdays from six o'clock in the afternoon until nine o'clock," at the residence of the elderly Salomon de Montel, who was described in the *Essai historique* as "an old man as amiable in his virtues as unfortunate in his kindnesses," and who offered the society the use of his house and magnificent library, which besides containing many rare books and classical texts, included works on every subject.[23] *Docendo, docemur* planned to begin with a course of reading and debate on the history of ancient Rome, which included Montesquieu's *La grandeur et la décadence,* followed by a course on commerce and agriculture with Condillac and Raynal among their guides.[24] Subsequently, it was proposed to study "philosophy in general," taking among the main guides, rather daringly, *La philosophie du bon sens* and again, boldly but also appropriately, since this work cited and discussed a vast number of relevant French works, the radical and highly controversial *De la philosophie de la nature, ou traité de morale pour l'espèce humaine,* by Jean-Baptiste Delisle de Sales (1741–1816), originally of 1770 but complete only in the six-volume Amsterdam edition of 1777.[25]

---

20 Ibid., pp. 175–76.

21 R. Bijlsma, "David de Is. C. Nassy, Author of the *Essai historique sur Surinam,*" in *The Jewish Nation in Surinam. Historical Essays,* ed. R. Cohen (Amsterdam 1982), pp. 65–73, here p. 65.

22 "[F]it autant d'honneur à la Philosophie de Mr Wichers qu'à la mémoire du feu médecin juif," Nassy, *Essai historique,* vol. 1, 165–66.

23 "[V]ieillard aussi aimable par ses vertus, que malheureux par ses bontés," ibid., p. 181; Cohen, *Jews in Another Environment,* p. 99.

24 Nassy, *Essai historique,* vol. 2, p. 179.

25 Ibid., p. 180; on the place of Delisle in the Enlightenment, see J.I. Israel, *Democratic Enlightenment. Philosophy, Revolution and Human Rights, 1750–1790* (Oxford 2011), pp. 675–83.

Since Marc-Michel Rey (1720–1780), Montel's chief supplier and, apparently, chief supplier to Surinam generally, was among other things, a leading publisher of Radical Enlightenment texts (as well as of Rousseau), it is unsurprising that the Surinam Enlightenment was familiar with the most daring and clandestine texts then to be found in Europe.[26] Intriguingly, Rey, a Genevan who had moved to Amsterdam in 1744, was married to Elisabeth Bernard, daughter of the radical enlightener Jean-Frederic Bernard (c. 1683–1744), who was the first to compile a kind of encyclopedia of religion subversively treating all religions on an equivalent basis and presenting Judaism in a relatively dignified light.[27]

An economic failure, Nassy, son of the notary or "jurator" of the Jewish nation Isaac de Joseph Cohen Nassy, evidently found solace in reading and enlightenment. He was a man of some standing in the Sephardi community, having been trained as a communal notary adjunct to his father and, in 1772, became *gabay* (treasurer) of the Joden Savaneh congregation. But in 1770, he had used all his capital to purchase the coffee plantation Tulpenburg on the Surinam River for 93,000 guilders, equipping it and increasing its number of slaves by taking out a mortgage loan of around 117,000 guilders with a firm in Amsterdam at 6 percent interest. This was the undertaking which ruined him financially. Things went wrong virtually from the outset. His labor force was struck by a high death rate, presumably some kind of epidemic, the plantation deteriorated through shortage of labor, partly becoming flooded and the coffee bushes fell into a bad state. By 1773, he was bankrupt. The estate, subjected to a forced sale at a time of financial crisis in Amsterdam, brought him only 40,000 guilders at its disposal. He was a ruined man and, as such, was suspended, in 1775, from the community juratorship to which he had succeeded after the death of his father.

He was also by the age of thirty, in 1777, which is when the French official Pierre-Victor Malouet visiting Surinam from neighboring Cayenne met him, a most extraordinary person. He had, within a short time without any other help than his native genius, learned several ancient and modern languages, wrote French "purement" and had explored historical literature to the point that he could thoroughly detail the errors of Boulanger on the subject of antiquity. He had corresponded with the Royal Society in London and also with Voltaire, with whom he had remonstrated over his attacks on the Jews in his writings and his questioning of the antiquity and chronology in Genesis. As to the latter, noted Malouet, "Nassy argued more as a chronologist than . . . theologian, for

---

26   Ibid., pp. 137–38, 667, 806–7.

27   R. van Vliet, *Elie Luzac (1721–1796). Boekverkoper van de Verlichting* (Nijmegen 2005), p. 232.

there was neither pedantry nor fanaticism in his erudition."[28] And this man, who spent eight hours a day studying and corresponded "with the famous men of Europe," supported himself during these years, much to Malouet's amazement, selling second-hand goods like many of the poorest of his community, until his decision to move to Philadelphia, in 1792.

This "very learned Jew of Surinam" impressed Malouet, among other things, as an expert on the local Amerindindians and their language, Galibi. Apparently, he had composed a short dictionary of their language, giving the equivalents in French, Latin and Hebrew, which he showed to Malouet. After expounding to Malouet the basic rules of Galibi syntax, Nassy had explained that his studies on the construction and origin of languages and on the character of that of the Indians "led him to believe in the existence of a primitive language, which had been altered through the dispersal of families and tribes, thus resulting in various dialects," a view which fitted well with Malouet's own conception of human history. Both men apparently believed in an original primitive human type that had subsequently become dispersed across the globe, bringing many related word roots as well as similar tools, weapons and other objects to all parts.[29]

Given the strongly French orientation of his books and interests, it is impossible not to suppose that he must, at least in some degree, have been influenced in his early development as Surinam's foremost *philosophe* by the model of the Sephardi philosopher towering over the supposed prejudices of rabbinic Judaism and tradition and surveying the world "with a philosopher's eye" peopling works such as the marquis d'Argens' *Lettres Juives* (6 vols. [The Hague 1738]) and other radical French writings of the early eighteenth century. These imagined philosophers, which d'Argens nevertheless claimed also corresponded to certain actual Jews of wide reading and discernment who he had met in Holland and at Venice, were designated as "Spinosistes," and there is good reason to suppose this is precisely how Nassy viewed himself.[30]

Remarkably enough, one of the imagined Sephardi philosophers of the first half of the century, a veritable cross between "Spinoza" and Isaac Orobio de Castro, the model of the Jewish philosopher who remains within and helps

28   "Nassy défendait en chronologiste plus qu'en théologien, car il n'y avait ni pédanterie, ni fanatisme dans son érudition," P.-V. Malouet, *Mémoires*, 2 vols. (Paris 1868), vol. 1, p. 158.

29   "[L]'avaient conduit à croire à l'existence d'une langue primitive, dont l'altération, par la dispersion des familles et des peuplades, avait produit divers dialectes," ibid., pp. 158–59.

30   J.I. Israel, "Philosophy, Deism and the Early Jewish Enlightenment (1655–1740)," in *The Dutch Intersection: The Jews and the Netherlands in Modern History*, ed. Y. Kaplan (Leiden 2008), pp. 173–201, here pp. 174–84.

steer his community, was supposedly nurtured and acquired his reading in
Surinam. This is the fictitious Sephardi Jew, Moise Aboab, who the English
nobleman "Mylorde Bolingbroke" encounters in the *Entretiens sur divers sujets*
(Amsterdam 1711) of Mathurin Veyssiere de La Croze (1661–1739), a work admired by d'Argens and the "Jewish" part of which was separately published in a
curious Dutch "conversionist" version in Amsterdam in 1757, deleting Aboab's
rejection of Christianity. La Croze's "Moise Aboab" had fervently read philosophy, theology, Latin and Greek while whiling away his ample spare time on his
plantation in Surinam and who, on his travels in Europe, finds himself disgusted with both most Judaism and most of the Christianity that he encounters.
Having rejected traditional Judaism and finding that both the endless feuding
among the Christian churches and their collective persecution of the Jews "has
disgusted me," seeks salvation in philosophy instead.[31]

As an additional prop to his difficult financial circumstances, Nassy taught
himself pharmacy, a field in which he became a celebrated expert, and considerable medical knowledge, and became partners with a community doctor
practicing medicine in the community and in running a dispensary. It was in
this capacity that he observed that the Jews in Surinam, being less addicted
to strong drink than non-Jewish whites, were also more resistant to tropical
fevers.[32] In Philadelphia, where he arrived in 1792, after a short stay on the then
Danish Caribbean island of Saint Thomas, he was the first Jewish physician to
practice.[33] He was an admirer of both Benjamin Franklin and the celebrated
Philadelphia "universalist" and enlightener Benjamin Rush and on first meeting him, presented him with a copy of the *Essai historique*. Rush paid him the
compliment of describing him as an "ingenious physician," but that was before
their disagreement on the correct cure for yellow fever. During the yellow fever
epidemic of 1793 which struck Philadelphia hard, Rush, the leading physician
of Philadelphia at the time, advocated "drastic bleeding" and violent purges as
the best way to combat the disease. Nassy, familiar with yellow fever from his
homeland, siding with an opposing faction among the local medical fraternity,
recommended rather stimulants, quinine and a light diet. It was fitting that the
paper that he delivered to the society on 20 February 1794 was on the subject of

31   "[M]'en a dégouté," MM.V. de La Croze, *Entretiens sur Divers Sujets d'Histoire et de Reli-
      gion entre Mylord Bolongbroke, et Isaac d'Orobio, Rabin des Juifs Portugais a Amsterdam*
      (London 1770), p. 38; Israel, "Philosophy, Deism," pp. 184–85.

32   Nassy, *Essai historique*, vol. 2, p. 59.

33   H. Bloch, "Dr David d'Isaac Nassy," *Journal of the American Medical Association* 207 (1969),
      p. 1228.

botany, for he was certainly one of the most knowledgeable men alive on the subject of the plants and natural products of Surinam.

Generally speaking, modern historians of the Enlightenment greatly underestimate the decisive role of philosophy as its driving force, being much misled by vague notions of sociability and unconscious cultural shifts. This inevitably leads to both confusion and inaccuracy. Hence, it is necessary here to begin by insisting on Nassy's conception of Enlightenment as the "century of enlightenment of philosophy," as he called it, for otherwise one cannot really understand anything about the Surinam Jewish Enlightenment (or indeed any other kind of Enlightenment). Nassy possessed a library consisting when it was inventoried in 1782, of 433 books, only a few of which were Hebrew or prayer books. It contained portraits of Voltaire and Rousseau and French philosophy and literature dominated his collection. Among his books were copies of Bayle's *Dictionnaire*, a seven-volume set of the works of Montesquieu, Hobbes's *Leviathan* in Dutch, Fontenelle and Voltaire, much the best represented author in his library, as well as Hume's philosophical works in a two-volume French translation published at Amsterdam in 1764 and much of the rest of the French Enlightenment.

Of course, he was bound to possess a copy of the most influential of all eighteenth-century "philosophical" works dealing with the world outside Europe, the *Histoire philosophique des Deux Indes*, attributed to Raynal. Other major works dealing with the role of the Europeans in the Indies composed in an enlightened context that figured in his personal library were a French rendering of Bartolomé de Las Casas, William Robertson, *Histoire de l'Amérique*, *La Legislation Orientale*, the major work by Anquetil Duperron championing Hindu, Zoroastrian and other Indian and Persian learning and traditions and subjecting European colonialism in India to a devastating critique, Marmontel's *Les Incas*.

Among his various ancient classics, he also had Lucretius's great poem against religion, the *De Rerum natura*. More unusual and notable, was his possessing d'Holbach's *La Morale universelle* (3 vols. [Amsterdam 1776]), one of the century's most subversive and important works of moral and general philosophy, along with d'Holbach's *Ethocratie*.[34] Since he also had Toland's *Le Nazarenéen*, a four-volume set of Fréret and a copy of Isaac de Pinto's *Précis des arguments contre les matérialistes* besides de Pinto's *Essai sur le luxe* and several of the works of the marquis d'Argens, including his famous *Lettres Juives* (6 vols. [The Hague 1738]) and *La Philosophie du Bon Sens* (3 vols. [Amsterdam

---

34   See Appendix A: "Catalogue of the Nassy Library," in Cohen, *Jews in Another Environment*, pp. 203–4.

1737]) and Baculard d'Arnaud and also Voltaire's attempt to refute d'Holbach's atheism in his *Dieu, Réponse au* "Système de la Nature," it is certainly no exaggeration to say that he possessed a broad knowledge of the Enlightenment generally and also of materialism and the anti-religious Radical Enlightenment specifically.[35] He also possessed Richard Price's *Observations sur la nature de la liberté civile* (Rotterdam 1776). A further notable item here was the *Bekeerings-Geschiedenis van den Graaf J.F. Struensee uit het Hoogduitsch vertaald* (Amsterdam 1772), recounting the dramatic Struensee episode in the kingdom of Denmark.

Listed no. 235 in Robert Cohen's catalogue of Nassy's library, intriguingly, is the *Entretiens Sur divers subjects d'histoire et de religion entre Mylorde Bollingbroke, et Isaac d'Orobio, rabin des Juifs portugais a Amsterdam* (London 1770), one of the outstanding clandestine texts of the Enlightenment and one with a particular connection with Surinam. Indeed, it would be fascinating to know, were this possible, how early on in his intellectual career Nassy first read this important text and how far it might have first suggested to him the model of the Surinam Jewish enlightener of surpassing penetration, scope and enlightened grasp of our world, mankind and its religions.

David Cohen Nassy had been intellectually outstanding and a man familiar not just with the moderate but also with the Radical Enlightenment since his youth. We know this from the account of a French official (and later royalist leader during the Revolution), Pierre-Victor Malouet, who visited Joden Savanneh from French Cayenne in 1776 (not 1777 as sometimes stated).[36] While there, Malouet encountered two Jews, "whose erudition and wisdom greatly astonished me; one is called Joseph Barrios and the other Isaac Nassy. The latter is an extraordinary man, if one considers that never having left Surinam where he was born, he managed at thirty years of age, without any other help than his genius, to rise above the errors of his sect, to go deep into its history, to pick out Boulanger's mistakes in what he wrote about antiquity, to learn methodically Arabic, Chaldean, rabbinic Hebrew and most modern languages which he speaks and writes purely."[37] This was doubtless rather exaggerated;

35   Bijlsma, "David de Is. C. Nassy," p. 68; Cohen, *Jews in Another Environment*, p. 113.
36   Nassy, *Essai historique*, vol. 2, p. 57.
37   "[D]ont l'érudition et les lumières m'ont fort étonné; l'un se nomme Joseph Barrios et l'autre Isaac Nassy. Le dernier est un homme extraordinaire, si l'on considère que n'étant jamais sorti de Surinam où il est né, il a parvenu à trente ans, sans autre secours que son génie, à s'élever au dessus des erreurs de sa secte, à en approfondir l'histoire, à relever les fautes de Boulanger dans ce qu'il a écrit sur l'antiquité, à apprendre méthodiquement l'arabe, le caldéen, l'hébreu rabbinique, et la plupart des langues modernes, qu'il parle et écrit pûrement," Bijlsma, "David de Is. C. Nassy," p. 67.

but certainly he possessed an excellent knowledge of French and Spanish as well as Dutch and Portuguese. The reference to Boulanger relates to Nicolas-Antoine Boulanger (1722–1759), the ally of Diderot and d'Holbach who became notorious for his highly subversive *L'Antiquité Dévoilée dans ses usages* (1766), one of the classics of eighteenth-century radical thought. Joseph Barrios died young, regretted by his friends, in 1786, shortly after being entrusted by Governor Wichers with a responsible position, in charge of food supplies for the military cordon running through Joden Savanneh.[38]

The Jewish population of Surinam in the late eighteenth century, estimated in 1791 as consisting of 834 Sephardim and 447 Ashkenazim (in 1849 the corresponding figures were 683 and 681), was small by Jewish and general standards. Nevertheless, it represented a rather important outpost of the Enlightenment both in Jewish and general terms. In the outlying parts of the world—outside, that is, Europe, the United States and Canada—there were very few significant outposts of Enlightenment as an organized, conscious movement of intellectual enterprise and social amelioration and most of what there was—as in the two most important examples, the British Asiatic Society and its circle in British India, the Batavia Society in the Dutch East Indies—had no Jewish connection. An Enlightenment outpost in a remote part of the world, where Jews and non-Jews joined together in debate, research and discussion, hence, stands out as a somewhat unique phenomenon.

The study of *la philosophie*, modern enlightened thought, was a solace for Nassy. But the Jewish Enlightenment in Surinam also had a profoundly social and practical orientation, being deeply preoccupied with the steadily worsening economic and general situation of the colony's Jews. In 1760, the Jews still possessed 115 out of the 591 sugar, coffee and cotton plantations in Surinam, but by 1788 this figure had shrunk to no more than forty-six.[39] The community was facing a full-scale socio-economic emergency. By the 1780s, it was obvious to all, not least to Nassy, that the entire community was rapidly sinking into what he called "dire poverty and decay." Thus, the Jewish community's own communal tax on its congregants' incomes, the *finta*, suffered a catastrophic shrinkage of more than two-thirds between 1770 and 1790.[40] One of the community leaders and militia captains on guard duty at Joden Savanneh, Abraham Rafael Curiel, for instance, saw his *finta* assessment fall from 246 guilders in 1770 to only eighty guilders in 1778 and eighty-three in 1787; yet, at the same time, he

38   Nassy, *Essai historique*, vol. 1, p. 182.
39   R.A.J. Van Lier, "The Jewish Community in Surinam. A Historical Survey," in Cohen, *Jewish Nation in Surinam*, p. 23.
40   Cohen, *Jews in Another Environment*, p. 74.

rose from twenty-fourth to eleventh richest of the Surinam Sephardim, in 1778 and fifteenth in 1787.[41] As prospects for reversing the decline and diminishing profitability of the plantations were not good, saving the community socially and economically inevitably implied re-educating it and re-orientating to take up new professions and occupations. This was all the more so in that the community's decreasing affluence tended to intensify discrimination and hostility against them, in Paramaribo, on the part of Christian whites and the colonial authorities.[42]

As Nassy saw it, notably in a memorandum urging a thorough revising of the community regulations or *ascamot*, composed and submitted to the *Mahamad* in 1785, the general ignorance, lack of education and lack of culture characterizing the community consequently figured among the most serious hindrances and difficulties that it faced. The Jewish community, Sephardi and Ashkenazi, was seriously deficient in education beyond basic literacy and numeracy and also too prone to superstition.[43] In the *Essai historique*, complimenting them on their looks, he refers to the ignorance of the Ashkenazi women in these terms: "These women only lack education and the knowledge of high society to equal the most distinguished European women." The women suffered in particular from "l'ignorance des langues."[44]

One of the root causes of this prevailing ignorance, he argues in this submission, was that during the more affluent and successful era of the first half of the eighteenth century, the Jews of Surinam had experienced an ease of living and abundance which had led them totally to neglect the need to educate their offspring and introduce them to modern knowledge and science.[45] It was an urgent matter, he contended, that this educational deficit should be reversed: "we consider it our duty, so as not to leave our nation in blind ignorance, to introduce a public school here in Paramaribo." In particular, over a period of years, he continually urged the need to establish a Jewish school in Paramaribo based on enlightened principles.

With the drift away from Joden Savanneh, where the Jews lived apart from others, to Paramaribo, where they needed to integrate with the rest of the colony's society and preoccupations to a much greater extent, the evolution of

---

41   Algemeen Rijksarchief, The Hague, archives of the Surinam Sephardic community (NPIG)
      vol. 1, res. 20 July 1778.

42   Van Lier, "The Jewish Community in Surinam," pp. 24–25.

43   Nassy, *Essai historique*, vol. 2, pp. 76–77.

44   "[I]l ne manque à ces femmes que l'éducation, et la connoissance du grand monde, pour
      qu'elles n'ayent en rien à céder aux plus distinguées des femmes Européennes," ibid., p. 60.

45   Bijlsma, "David de Is. C. Nassy," p. 69.

Surinam Jewish society itself called in question the tight control of the community that the *parnassim* (as the synagogue elders were called) had traditionally exerted. One prominent strand of the Surinam Jewish Enlightenment, therefore, was a drive to curtail the religious authority of the *Mahamad* in the name of equality and individual liberty. In this area, what has aptly been termed the "emancipatory universalism," making all equal on the basis of the same human rights of the Radical Enlightenment, was to prove far more useful than the moral relativism and particularism of Montesquieu, Rousseau or Hume. Release from the constraints of organized religious authority had been a deeply personal matter for Montel since he had become involved in a long and ugly dispute with the congregation.

In 1761, a quarrel had arisen between Montel and another Jew, Aron de Fonseca, over a 5,000 guilder loan that the colony's civil court had directed, in August 1750, should be repaid with interest. But Fonseca, having discovered that he could appeal to Jewish law to evade the agreed interest, appealed to the *parnassim* who duly ordered Montel to repay the interest Fonseca had paid him. He was eventually accused of unlawful usury and threatened with the community ban of *herem*, causing Montel to appeal, in 1761, to the colony's governor, claiming he was being subjected to a form of religious coercion incompatible with the freedoms and practices of the United Provinces. There was no question that the *parnassim* had acted in accordance with the privileges and regulations of the Jewish community. The issue was whether the congregation could exercise the kind of religious authority over Montel's life and activities that it was claiming. "Under the appearance of privilege," protested Montel, the *parnassim* "seek to introduce a religious coercion and inquisition contrary to all liberty." By endorsing the decision of the *Mahamad*, the governor would be restoring "the auto-da-fe whose flames would be kindled once again and could pass to other persuasions."[46] It seemed to the governor that existing Dutch law did in fact endorse the principle of excommunication from religious communities and that the *Mahamad* was, in any case, acting within the terms of the community's specific privileges.

The *Mahamad* had made it clear in 1761 that it was proceeding in this rigorous manner against Montel chiefly owing to his attitude. Quite apart from the question of usury, he was flouting the authority of the community in the most overt and contemptuous manner. He was reported as saying: "Yes, even if one wanted to excommunicate him thus daily, he could not care less." He was setting a ruinous example to the entire community. The *Mahamad* now wanted Montel banished from Surinam until he had submitted to the congregation's

---

46   Cohen, *Jews in Another Environment*, pp. 131–32.

authority and repaid the interest paid by Fonseca. Expelled, Montel returned to Holland where he appealed directly to the States-General in The Hague. On 20 July 1764, the States-General found in favor of Montel asking the governor of Surinam to readmit him to the colony and "effect a speedy reparation of the in-justice done." Consequently, Montel returned in triumph to Surinam and Jew-ish religious authority in the colony suffered a famous and long-remembered defeat.

But the Surinam Jewish Enlightenment was not just concerned with releas-ing individuals from the close oversight of the congregation in matters regulat-ed by law but also in advancing and securing freedom of thought. Here, again the obstacle to be surmounted was traditional Jewish religious authority. The Sephardim who settled in Surinam in the late seventeenth century may have been in an exceptionally favorable position and had the energy and enterprise to take advantage of their situation, but they also brought with them some-thing of the "*bigotisme*," as Nassy calls it, that spirit of intolerance, punishing the slightest fault in religious observance that stemmed from the Portugal of the Inquisition. Nassy was not a religious man and although, whilst in Philadel-phia, later, he became a member of the Mikveh Israel synagogue and meticu-lously supported its charities, reducing religious authority over the individual was clearly one of the most essential parts of his Enlightenment ideology.

Those who had escaped the flames of the "hideous tribunal of the Inqui-sition" were the very men, he laments in the *Essai historique*, who instituted "the religious despotism" among the Sephardim of Surinam. Exactly the same spirit of persecution and fanaticism reigned in the Jewish congregations of late seventeenth-century Cayenne and Surinam, he contends, as drove the Jews of Holland to persecute Spinoza and Uriel da Costa "before their atheism could spread."[47] This "dangerous passion" for persecution, joined to the lack of gen-eral education prevailing generally among the whites of Surinam, gave rise to a continual theological wrangling among the Jews, preoccupation with "super-stitious ceremonies," and a most regrettable bigotry that they had entirely in common with the devotees of other religions.

But there was a still more urgent issue. The three-year period Montel spent in Holland coincided with a lively discussion among the intellectual circle of Amsterdam Sephardi Jewry over Voltaire's attacks on rabbinic tradition and books and on the character of Jewish society and on the harm he alleged Jew-ish tradition had over the centuries inflicted on the Jews themselves and on humanity generally. Since 1762, the Portuguese Jews in the Netherlands—or rather Isaac de Pinto (1717–1787) and their intellectual leadership—had been

47   "[A]vant que leur athéism eut éclaté," in Nassy, *Essai historique*, vol. 1, p. 157.

protesting to and against Voltaire in a vigorous manner. In his "Réflexions critiques" on Voltaire's standpoint of 1762, de Pinto, the model of a modern enlightened Jew to many young Portuguese Jews of Montel's generation, had taken the great Voltaire to task for his remarks about the Jews in manner later amplified in the well-known publication *Lettres de quelques juifs Portugais et Allemands à M. de Voltaire* (1769).[48] In his *Sermon du Rabbin Akib* (1761) and numerous other places in his works, Voltaire had maintained that the Jews had, in ancient times, been "a barbaric, superstitious, ignorant and absurd people." All this doubtless made a powerful impression on the French literature-loving Montel. One only need turn to the pages of the Surinam Enlightenment's most important book, the *Essai historique sur la colonie de Surinam*, completed in 1786 but not published until 1788, most of which was composed by Nassy, to appreciate that among the Surinam Jewish Enlightenment's principal aims was that of marshalling a powerful armory of enlightened ideology with which to assert the general and civil equality of the Jews, justifying their demand that society assign the Jews equal status as intellectually independent and mature men of integrity and as citizens. To this end, they consciously set out to use Radical Enlightenment emancipatory universalism as a weapon against the rooted anti-Semitism, the centuries of prejudice, discrimination and religious bigotry directed at the Jews inherent at the time in all Christian societies. This burden of discrimination and oppression, physical and moral, was something of which Nassy was acutely conscious and frequently complained.

Combating such prejudice with its roots in religious credulity, whether by non-Jews or Jews, was itself a quintessentially Enlightenment concern and required an effective grasp of developments in recent Enlightenment literature. At the outset of the *Essai historique*, we discover that this remarkable book had emerged from a lively discussion among the Jews (and presumably non-Jews) in Surinam prompted by the appearance of a French *précis* of the contents of Dohm's *Über die Verbesserung der Juden* (1781) published in the *Gazette Littéraire* of May 1784 and then, after a long and frustrating wait, the appearance of the first copy of the book itself in the colony in February 1786.[49] Christian Wilhelm von Dohm (1751–1820), who had served the Prussian crown as an archivist in Berlin where he had become friendly with Moses Mendelssohn, the foremost of the Jewish enlighteners and a campaigner for the modernization of Jewish society and religious institutions, which included a vigorous plea to quash all

---

48   I.J.A. Nijenhuis, *Een joodse philosophe. Isaac de Pinto (1717–1787)* (Amsterdam 1992), pp. 18, 26; H. Chisick, "Community and Exclusion in Rousseau and Voltaire: The Case of the Jews," in *L'Antisémitisme éclairé*, ed. I.Y. Zinguer and S.W. Bloom (Leiden 2003), pp. 84–85.

49   Nassy, *Essai historique*, vol. 1, p. ix.

notion of a communal right to ban or expel, all idea of a *jus excommunicationis* of the kind that had been used in Amsterdam in 1656 against Spinoza.[50] In this respect, especially in urging the complete elimination of communal autonomy in the legal sphere and with regard to individual liberty of thought and action, Mendelssohn actually went further than Dohm who proposed retaining at least some remnants of communal autonomy.[51]

Dohm had won a Europe-wide reputation for being the first enlightener seriously to raise the question of how to integrate Jewish society into general society in an effective and positive manner and, despite his considerable reservations about the Jewish religion and the character of Jewish society in Germany and Poland, had gained a world-wide reputation as a friend of the Jews and champion of their cause. Nassy and the other intellectual leaders of the Surinam community were so impressed with and grateful for Dohm's book that the *parnassim* wrote him a letter of thanks dated 10 March 1786, which was signed by Nassy and several other leading figures of the Surinam Jewish Enlightenment such as S.H. de la Parra and Moseh Pereira de Leon.[52]

But theirs was not just a movement to combat prejudice and discrimination. At bottom, the Surinam Jewish Enlightenment was part of the wider trans-Atlantic debate at its height during the 1780s, especially in Germany where Mendelssohn imparted to its greatest momentum and Holland, about the modernization and integration of Jewish society and Judaism itself.[53] Enlightened Jews such as Moses Mendelssohn as well as enlightened non-Jews such as Dohm had become increasingly worried since the anti-Jewish riots in Alsace in 1780 regarding the divisive effects in general society of certain traditional traits of Jewish society. In the minds of men like Dohm and Cloots, Christian tradition and attitudes may have been overwhelmingly the cause of the frightful disparagement and oppression of the Jews over the centuries, indeed unquestionably they were. Nevertheless, European Jewish society's historically heavy emphasis on retailing, peddling and usury, along with its lack of awareness and understanding (understandable though this was) of the common good and strict communal separateness, was insidiously feeding the

---

50   W. Goetschel, *Spinoza's Modernity. Mendelssohn, Lessing and Heine* (Madison, WI 2004), pp. 135, 139.

51   D. Sorkin, *The Religious Enlightenment. Protestants, Jews and Catholics from London to Vienna* (Princeton 2008), pp. 198–99.

52   Nassy, *Essai historique*, vol. 1, p. xxi.

53   G. Heinrich, "Die Debatte um 'bürgerliche Verbesserung' der Juden 1781–1786," in *Appell an das Publikum. Die öffentliche Debatte in der deutschen Aufklärung 1687–1796*, ed. U. Goldenbaum, 2 vols. (Berlin 2004), vol. 2, pp. 813–95, here pp. 816–19.

ideological reconstitution and resurgence of popular anti-Semitism, all too evident at the time in Alsace as in Germany and elsewhere.

The solution, to the minds of these men, was to determine under what circumstances and conditions the moral character of Jewish society could be "improved," that is, purged of its alleged defects and excessive preoccupation with money and business, stripped of strong rabbinic and communal religious authority and equipped with a more positive sense of citizenship and respect for the common good.[54] The hallmark of the movement to secure Jewish emancipation and equality in Germany was the idea that society's laws and traditions have an essentially historical character and should be regarded as in every respect subject to fundamental modification in the interests of amelioration. This was the view of Dohm and those other *Aufklärer* supporting this campaign in Prussia, such as Christoph Gossler and Heinrich Friedrich Diez (1751–1817), the orientalist and biographer of Spinoza determined to see Christian religious authority weakened and justice done to the Jews.[55] Spinoza's first sympathetic biographer Diez, incidentally, went even further than Dohm in rejecting the demand for conversion to Christianity as a central demand or condition for according equality to the Jews. Diez pushed for Jewish emancipation, rehabilitation of Spinoza and was also, in 1781, the first writer in central Europe, rather than Bahrdt, to publish a general plea for full freedom of thought and the press. But Diez could push for Jewish emancipation without conditions, it is crucial to bear in mind, only because he was a radical enlightener who thought that the Germany of his time was a land in fetters weighed down with absurd prejudice and credulity based on harmful religious authority.[56]

Here was an Enlightenment campaign up against considerable odds for most of the *philosophes* and *Aufklärer* either hesitated to pronounce the Mendelssohn–Dohm–Diez extension of civil rights to the Jews immanently feasible or else, like Fichte, rejected the idea out of hand.[57] Only radical enlighteners pushed for this outcome, not moderate Enlightenment enlighteners. In the Netherlands, where a number of lively Enlightenment reading societies and associations were set up in the 1770s and 1780s, there was a particular emphasis on the specifically Christian character of what was regarded as respectable forms of Enlightenment, so that by definition deists, atheists and materialists, but also Jews, were excluded. Thus, in Amsterdam, prestigious Enlightenment

54   J. Carp, *The Politics of Jewish Commerce. Economic Thought and Emancipation in Europe, 1638–1848* (Cambridge 2008), pp. 97–98.

55   Heinrich, "Die Debatte um 'bürgerliche Verbesserung'," pp. 828, 877–78.

56   Israel, *Democratic Enlightenment*, pp. 20, 188, 701–2.

57   Heinrich, "Die Debatte um 'bürgerliche Verbesserung'," p. 821.

clubs, like the *Felix meritis* established in 1777 with strict rules, principally
by Mennonites and other Protestant dissenters rejecting the theology and
traditions of the Dutch Reformed Church, excluded Jews. The Sephardim responded to this situation by setting up their own reading society "Concordia
crescimus" established in 1789 which, despite conducting its debates in Dutch
and stressing the need for Jews to assimilate contemporary Dutch culture, was
purely Sephardi in character.[58] Reducing the hold of rabbinic tradition and the
congregation and weakening religious authority, but also closing the cultural
gap between the Sephardi and Ashkenazi worlds in other words, were not just
integral components of the Jewish Enlightenment program in Surinam as in
Holland and Germany, but highly subversive in terms of Jewish religious tradition as well as generally in the wider trans-Atlantic context; it was, indeed,
this major turning-point in the history of Jewish thought that marks the true
beginning of the ceaseless war between modern Jewish reform and orthodoxy.

   Nassy and his circle were closely familiar with the work of Dohm from early
1786 and there they subsequently pursued "in our Literature College (known
as Docendo Docemur) . . . a sustained reading" and found it to be "filled with
solid reasoning and with a lucid impartiality."[59] They must also, already before
that, have been familiar with Raynal's *Histoire philosophique des Deux Indes*
(1770), the most famous European work concerning the Indies East and West of
late Enlightenment and the European colonial empires and a work which had
appeared in an exceptionally large number of editions and is cited by Nassy
in the *Essai historique* in its Geneva edition of 1771.[60] Quite apart from the
fact that the *Histoire philosophique*, much admired by Diez, was a significant
source for his and Dohm's own thinking about social oppression and about
colonial empires, about which the latter published an important work,[61] the
Histoire philosophique was, by far, the most authoritative and, perhaps, the only
well-known Enlightenment work contending that at some point in the future
Jewish emancipation, to become fully effective and complete, would require
some secure spot in the world, perhaps the island of Jamaica or some other

---

58   M. de Vries, *Beschaven! Letterkundige genootschappen in Nederland, 1750–1800* (Nijmegen
     2001), pp. 165, 385.

59   "[D]ans notre Collège de Littérature (connu sous le nom de Docendo Docemur . . .), une
     lecture suivie remplie de raisonnements solides, et d'une impartialité lumineuse," Nassy,
     Essai historique, vol. 1, pp. ix–x.

60   Ibid., pp. 3, 27, 191 and vol. 2, pp. 34, 61.

61   C.W. von Dohm, *Geschichte der Engländer und Franzosen im östlichen Indien* (Leipzig
     1776).

Caribbean island, where the Jews would be left alone to rule themselves and could dwell "free at last, quiet, and happy in a corner of the universe."[62]

If historians in general have underestimated the importance of the *Histoire philosophique* in the history of the Enlightenment and of anti-colonialism generally, they have certainly underestimated its importance in shaping the Enlightenment's view of Jews and Judaism. It is cited more often and more centrally in the *Essai historique* than any other Enlightenment source and with good reason. The *Histoire philosophique* was concerned with the emancipation of all humanity generally, the Jews no less than others. Nassy cites verbatim the passage where the *Histoire* declares, in reference to Surinam:

> There may be no other empire on earth where this unfortunate nation (the Jewish one) is treated so well; not only we have allowed it the freedom to proclaim its religion, to own land, to resolve by itself the disagreements which arise among its members, but it also enjoys the right common to all citizens to take part in the general administration, to contribute to the choices of public magistrates; the advances in the spirit of commerce are such that they silence all the prejudices of nations or of religion, in the face of the general interest that must bind all men. What are these vain denominations of Jews, Lutherans, Frenchmen, Dutchmen? Unhappy inhabitants of a land so hard to cultivate, are you not all men?[63]

Nassy can only applaud "la philosophie impartiale" that he finds in this fundamental text and regret that this passage, for whatever reason, was omitted by Raynal from some later editions, specifically that published at Geneva in 1781.

Nassy and his circle agreed with Raynal's thesis that less protectionism and a shift to free trade, in particular to the new United States, would benefit Surinam and benefit the metropolis.[64] But they were especially grateful for the

62   "[E]nfin libres, tranquilles et heureux dans un coin de l'univers." Israel, *Democratic Enlightenment*, p. 495.

63   [I]l n'est peut-être d'empire sur la terre où cette malheureuse nation (la juive) soit si bien traitée, non seulement on lui a laissé la liberté de professer sa religion, d'avoir des terres en propriété, de terminer elle-même les différens qui s'élèvent entre ses membres; elle jouit encore du droit commun à tous les citoyens, d'avoir part à l'administration générale, de concourir aux choix des magistrats public; tels sont les progrès de l'esprit du commerce, qu'il fait taire tous les préjugés des nations ou de religion, devant l'intérêt général qui doit lier les hommes. Qu'est ce que ces vaines dénominations, de Juifs, de Luthériens, de François, d'Hollandois ? Malheureux habitants d'une terre si pénible à cultiver, n'êtes-vous pas tous des hommes? Nassy, *Essai historique*, vol. 2, p. 34.

64   Ibid., p. 44.

thesis developed by Dohm and, after him, other works attributing what all Enlightenment writers saw as the perverse stress on trade in Jewish society to the disabilities, prohibitions and restrictions heaped on them by Christian rulers and churchmen.[65] The idea that the particular characteristics of the Jews were the consequence of their circumstances and, in particular, the discrimination to which they had been subjected over the centuries, was not just a product specifically of the emancipatory universalism of radical thought which was the chief feature of Dohm's book on the Jews, but this discrimination could (as is still the case) only be fought by using the revolutionary emancipatory, universalist ideology.[66] Dohm's campaign on behalf of the Jews was rooted in the logic of the *Histoire philosophique des Deux Indes* and was followed by an entire revolutionary literature building on the principle he was the first to develop in detail specifically in relation to the Jews. The Franco-German materialist-atheist Anarcharsis Cloots (1755–1794), for example, in his *Lettre sur les Juifs à un ecclesiastique de mes amis* (Berlin 1783), another work with which the Sephardi reading group in Paramaribo was familiar (though this item was not in Nassy's library),[67] warmly praised the intellectual capacities of the Jews, insisting that the highly unfortunate distortion of Jewish society over the centuries was a distortion imposed by Christianity, beginning with the heavy pressure exerted by the late Roman Christian emperors.[68]

This radical, strongly anti-theological, but also subversive, social and political thesis became the chief instrument of Nassy and the Surinam Jewish Enlightenment in countering the influence of Voltaire whom they held responsible for introducing a strain of virulent anti-Semitism into the (moderate) European Enlightenment, which remained all too current in the 1770s and 1780s and was being propagated in supposedly enlightened contexts by his many disciples. But provided one sufficiently knew one's *Histoire philosophique*, Dohm, Cloots and Mirabeau, the author of *Sur Moses Mendelssohn, sur la réforme politique des juifs* (1787), one could confront Voltaire's standpoint, effectively demonstrating that, notwithstanding Voltaire's immense prestige, his claims and theses about the Jews were entirely contrary to the true spirit and moral universalism of the European (Radical) Enlightenment. According to Nassy, Voltaire had gone all out to "crush the Jewish nation and make it hideous to the eyes of the universe," not least in his *Traité de la Tolérance* (1763), of which

---

65   A. Cloots, *Lettre sur les Juifs à un ecclesiastique de mes amis* (Berlin 1783), pp. 45, 53–54.

66   J. Hess, *Germans, Jews and the Claims of Modernity* (New Haven 2002), pp. 35–41.

67   Nassy, *Essai historique*, vol. 1, p. xxxii; Cohen, *Jews in Another Environment*, p. 242.

68   Cloots, *Lettre sur les Juifs*, pp. 53–54, 72–73.

there were two copies in Nassy's personal library, "which must only be considered as a complete treatise of philosophical fanaticism."[69]

Defaming the Jews had been converted into a general feature of the Western Enlightenment by Voltaire and, paradoxically or not, systematic prejudice buttressed by Voltaire and the wrong kind of Enlightenment was also a specific threat to the position of the Jews in the Guyanas. The magistrates of Demerary and Essequibo in western Guyana, despite being equally subjects of the Dutch Republic as the inhabitants of Surinam, had recently endorsed a published assault on the reputation and standing of the Jews in Dutch America under the title *Brieven over het bestuur der colonien Demerary en Essequibo, tusschen Aristodemus en Sincerus* (12 vols. [Amsterdam 1785–89]), which Nassy and his colleagues regarded as a veritable scandal.[70] Like Dohm, the Sephardi reading circle of Paramaribo regarded Enlightenment and still more Enlightenment the only answer.

The point of the *Essai historique*, explains Nassy at the end of his introduction, is to join forces with Dohm and contribute to a situation in which *philosophes*, generally, would learn to follow his lead and unite their efforts "to achieve the happy revolution of banishing all distinction toward a nation hated and persecuted for eighteen centuries."[71] And in order to contribute as much as they could "to this happy revolution" to proving that Jews can become just as good citizens as Christians, the Jewish enlighteners of Surinam were offering their text.

The views of Dohm, Cloots and Mirabeau, the future French revolutionary leader who had formed a close relationship with Dohm while staying in Berlin in 1786–7 and became one of the principal voices calling for both general emancipation and Jewish emancipation in Europe, on the need for and the future mechanics of Jewish emancipation and their stress on Enlightenment as the only solution, were embedded in a complex theologico-political and social argument. It was a claim about the nature of social oppression and monarchical despotism in the world which characterized the adverse moral, psychological and social effects of prolonged oppression as a system capable of persisting over many centuries and drawing its logic and seeming justification from the very effects of its operation. By depressing a whole people into misery,

69   "[É]craser la Nation Juive et de la rendre hideuse aux yeux de l'univers "qui ne doit être regardé que comme un traité complet de fanatisme philosophique," Nassy, *Essai historique*, vol. 1, p. xxv; Cohen, *Jews in Another Environment*, pp. 113–14.

70   Ibid., p. xxxvii.

71   "[P]our opérer l'heureuse révolution de bannir toute distinction envers une nation haïe et persécutée depuis 18 siècles," ibid., p. xxxviii.

humiliation and degradation, such a system itself generates the appearance of inherent inferiority and negative attitudes which then, in turn, appears to provide justification for disabilities, subordination and official discrimination. But exactly the same system of theology, monarchical rule and discrimination had been employed for centuries to enslave the black peoples of Africa and their offspring transported to the New World, including the Guyana colonies, and this poses the question of how far the logic of the *Histoire philosophique*, Dohm, Cloots and Mirabeau relating to Jewish emancipation and also to black emancipation was understood actively at work among and disseminated by the Enlightenment in Surinam.

The *Essai historique* itself shows that Nassy had thought long and hard about the relationship between whites and blacks and was troubled by it. On arriving in the United States (of which he became a citizen in 1795), he had promptly set free the two personal slaves that he had brought with him. Since the two enlighteners whom he met and admired in Philadelphia, Franklin and Rush, were committed abolitionists, he can hardly have failed to feel the force of abolitionist arguments. The "Pennsylvania Society for Promoting the Abolition of Slavery," set up in 1787, was the foremost abolitionist organ in the United States. When he knew them, Franklin was its president and Rush its secretary.[72]

Certain remarks of Nassy suggest, and this becomes a significant question when we consider that he was steeped in works such as the *Histoire philosophe*, Cloots and Mirabeau, that it not only marked the real beginning of modern anti-colonialism and the war on slavery as an institution, but directly laid the ground for the *Declaration of the Rights of Man* and the Brissotins' campaign to emancipate the free blacks during the early and middle stages of the French Revolution, suppress the slave trade and work towards the final abolition of slavery. It is often maintained that the "Enlightenment did not provide a source of antislavery ideology" either in general or in the specific case of Surinam.[73] But when we consider the role of the *Histoire philosophique* in the Netherlands, where it powerfully impressed such key democratic writers as Pieter Vreede and Bernard Nieuhoff,[74] and in the Dutch colonial empire, as well as in France and Germany and the centrality of the writings of Raynal, Cloots and Mirabeau in Nassy's argumentation on behalf of Jewish emancipation, it becomes

72   Bloch, "Dr. David d'Isaac Nassy," p. 1228.
73   G. Oostindie, "Same Old Song? Perspectives on Slavery and Slaves in Suriname and Curaçao," in *Fifty Years Later. Antislavery, Capitalism and Modernity in the Dutch Orbit*, ed. G. Oostindie (Pittsburgh 1996), pp. 148, 150.
74   M.R. Wielema, "Het verlichtingsbegrip van Bernard Nieuhoff," *Geschiedenis van de wijsbegeerte in Nederland. Documentatieblad van de Werkgroep "Sassen"* 5 (1994), pp. 189–90.

obvious that this claim is incorrect. The real explanation of weakness of anti-slavery ideology in late eighteenth-century Surinam is rather different.

He was certainly in a position to comment extensively on the tense and often violent relations between whites and blacks in Surinam. Nassy is devastating, for example, in his characterization of the French Code Noir, the code relating to slavery and the blacks in the French colonies proclaimed in the name of Louis XIV in 1680. "A work has never received," commented Nassy, "a title more appropriate to its contents than this one. It seems to designate more the blackness of fanaticism and religious intolerance than the color of the Negroes from which it got its title."[75]

Somewhat curiously, there was a direct connection between the project of emancipating the Jews and the highly problematic issue of black slavery. For as the *Essai historique* indignantly points out, the start of the large-scale flight of runaway slaves into the Surinam forests and beginning of the maroon communities living in open rebellion against the Dutch during the opening years of the eighteenth century and especially in the years around 1750, were widely blamed by the Christian whites in the Guyanas on the alleged excessive harshness of the Jews towards their slaves.[76] Nassy insisted that there was no basis at all for accusing the Jews in Surinam "of more tyranny toward their slaves than is attributed to the other inhabitants of the colony." But the myth that the running away of large numbers of slaves from the plantations and the eighteenth-century Surinam slave revolts were caused by the cruel treatment that the slaves received especially at the hands of Jewish slave-owners remained a powerful one even into the nineteenth century.[77] In addition to the total of white Jews, 1,311, there were also one hundred Jewish mulattoes and free blacks out of a total of 650 in this group.[78]

Although we do not know why Nassy returned to Surinam after only three years in Philadelphia (where he had only just become a United States citizen), it is interesting to note that his return to his native land coincided with the French revolutionary conquest of the United Provinces and the setting up of the Batavian Republic in 1795. This was a moment of particular hope and promise for all Dutch enlighteners marking the onset of a period of intense constitutional debate and reform and the drawing up of plans for the reconstitution

75   "Jamais ouvrage n'a reçu un titre plus analogue à son contenu que celui-ci. Il semble qu'il désigne plutôt la noirceur du fanatisme et de l'intolérance religieuse, que la couleur des Nègres qui lui a fait donner ce titre," Nassy, *Essai historique*, vol. 1, pp. xxxvi–xxvii.
76   Ibid., pp. 59–61.
77   Van Lier, "Jewish Community in Surinam," pp. 23–24.
78   Nassy, *Essai historique*, vol. 2, p. 39.

of every aspect of Dutch public life and law, including the colonial empire. Very possibly, Nassy hoped to participate in the reorganization and reconstitution of Surinam under the first Dutch democratic republic. Whatever the truth of this supposition, it is evident from the *Essai historique* that Nassy felt strongly about the traditional institutionalized discrimination against Jews in the political and legal establishment of the United Provinces, as we see from the passage where he recounts the exclusion of one of the Surinam *parnassim* and pillars of local enlightenment Moseh Pereira de Leon, with exceptional experience as a lower advocate in the Surinam courts, as a senior procurator, on the grounds that there was no precedent in Holland for the appointment of a Jew to such a position.[79]

In any case, it is certain that the Radical Enlightenment, in general and as represented in the thought-world of David Nassy and other products of the Surinam Enlightenment, rejoiced not only in the American Revolution but also in the core principles of the French Revolution and were full of renewed hope at the time of the French conquest of the Netherlands in 1795 and the setting up of the Batavian Republic. There were several celebrations and banquets in Surinam to mark the alliance between France and the Dutch Republic, in 1795 and the adoption by the Dutch of the Declaration of the Rights of Man and Citizen. At one of the banquets, one toast being to Abraham Verheul who, in February 1795, delivered his *Redevoering over de gelijkheid der menschen* in the famous *Felix Meritis* assembly hall in Amsterdam and later that year became president of the *Comité tot de zaaken der colonien ende bezittingen op de kust van Guinee ende in Amerika*, bring to bear his Enlightenment principles and legal expertise in the hope of bringing about far-reaching political social, legal and educational reforms.[80]

---

79   Nassy, *Essai historique*, vol. 1, pp. 183–84 and vol. 2, pp. 194–95.
80   Van Kempen, *Een Geschiedenis*, vol. 3, pp. 91–92.

PART 4

Ceremonial Dimensions

∵

Jewish Liturgy in the Netherlands: Liturgical Intentions and Historical Dimensions

Wout van Bekkum

In 1853, the Christian Reverend Alexander M'Caul composed his book *Nethivoth Olam, Old Paths, or, the True Israelite, Modern Judaism in Comparison to the Law and Religion of Moses and the Prophets*. M'Caul was rector of the Church of St. Magnus, St. Margaret and St. Michael at London Bridge and prebendary of St. Paul's Cathedral. His curious work was soon after publication translated into Dutch.[1] In his so-called "Voorloopig Berigt" ("Preliminary Message"), the anonymous translator/editor states that the author wished to focus on synagogue prayer texts as the most reliable source for the argument that one should make a distinction between Judaism as a religion and the Jews as a people. Judaism is simply to be considered as an errant faith and, therefore, the contemporary Jews are the innocent victims who cannot be blamed personally, because their prayer books have led them into confusion. Throughout the centuries, synagogue prayers had been corrupted by the tales and legends of the rabbis who manipulated both liturgical and poetic passages and so deceived the worshipping Jew.

It is not so much this observation which catches our attention, because the Reverend M'Caul also for some time served as Head of the London Society for Promoting Christianity among the Jews. It is, rather, his deliberate effort to impress upon the reader that synagogue prayers and poems are the ultimate reflection of *Torah she-be'al peh*, the Oral Torah, which represents the intolerance of contemporary Judaism as contrasted with an ever tolerant message of the Christian New Testament. How could it otherwise be explained that Jewish prayer contains allusions to the Gentiles by the employment of appellations such as Edom or Edomites, a consistent reference to the Christians who should

---

* First published in *Judaica, Beiträge zum Verstehen des Judentums*, 68. Jahrgang, Heft 4, Stiftung Zürcher Lehrhaus: Judentum Christentum Islam (Zürich 2012), pp. 374–87.

1 London 1834; Dutch translation: *De oude paden, of, de ware Israëliet, Het hedendaagsche Jodendom vergeleken met de leer en godsdienst van Mozes en de Profeten, door Rev. Alexander M'Caul, D.D., Professor der Godgeleerdheid, aan het Koninklijke Collegie, te London, Prebend. van de St. Pauluskerk, Predikant, enz. enz.*, London 1853.

be put to the sword according to a Passover hymn.[2] It is not just this text, recited only once per year, but also the daily prayers which equally condemn the
Epicureans, as M'Caul phrases it, without any sense of compassion and forgiveness, such as *ve-la-malshinim al tehiy tikvah*, etc. As a matter of fact, M'Caul's
misinterpretation is part of a long tradition of textual adaptations in statutory
prayer, varying from *malshinim* ("slanderers") to *meshummadim* ("apostates"),
minim ("heretics," hence, the name of the prayer is *birkat ha-minim*) and *zedim*
("the arrogant").[3] Religious pressures and historical realities were taken into
account even into modern times, when prayer reform began to make apologies
for this benediction, which was often perceived as an ugly malediction and,
therefore, modified or even omitted.

The history of *birkat ha-minim* is only one example of how the intentions
of synagogue *tefillot* and *piyyutim* were misunderstood, a phenomenon of all
times. This is a continuing problem in the study of the transmission of Jewish
liturgical materials up to and including the nineteenth and twentieth centuries. The history of Jewish liturgy and poetry involves a perennial process of
preference and selection, moving from variety in more ancient times to fixity
in later days. The existence of a statutory and obligatory set of prayers, *Shema*
and *Tefillat shemoneh 'esreh*, with optional extras was not exclusively a matter
of halakhic authority as reflected in Talmudic or geonic sources, but was also
subject to the cultural spirit and literary taste of Jewish communities in the
Diaspora. Of course, no one was to doubt the centrality of the two aforementioned prayers; they were common to Jews everywhere, as were other forms of
worship, such as the reading of Bible and Prophets.[4] As against this uniformity
from one late antique or medieval synagogue to the next, prayer service varied
in different locales, just as was indubitably the case with types of Aramaic Bible translations, the several *targumim*, or the sermons which were offered, the

---

2 ליל שימורים פסח אכלו ("The night of watching, they ate the Passover lamb hastily"). *Nethivoth Olam*, p. 110 with reference to the words כימי חג / ביד צח ואדום / פסח חרב חדה על אדום
פסח—"Pesach, a sharp sword over Edom, in the hand of God who is radiant and ruddy, like
the days of the Pesach festival."

3 *Nethivoth Olam*, p. 114; see also R.R. Kimelman, "*Birkat Ha-Minim* and the Lack of Evidence
for an Anti-Christian Prayer in Late Antiquity," in *Jewish and Christian Self-Definition*, Vol. 2,
Aspects of Judaism in the Graeco-Roman Period, ed. E.P. Sanders (London 1981), pp. 226–44;
W. Horbury, "The Benediction of the '*Minim*' and Early Jewish-Christian Controversy," *Journal
of Theological Studies* 33/1 (1982), pp. 19–61; J. Marcus, "*Birkat Ha-Minim* Revisited," *New Testament Studies* 55 (2009), pp. 523–51; R. Langer, *Cursing the Christians: A History of the Birkat
HaMinim* (Oxford 2011), pp. 141–55.

4 S. Reif, *Judaism and Hebrew Prayer, New Perspectives on Jewish Liturgical History* (Cambridge
1993), pp. 61–64.

derashot and all the poetic additions and embellishments, the *piyyutim*. The result is a rich tapestry of communal and local preferences, and the picture held by modern researchers of the varied attitudes towards synagogue liturgy in the Jewish world has, therefore, to allow room for considerable nuance.

The best and, the best-known, text of medieval Jewish liturgy, one which tells us much about the institution and adaptation of Jewish prayer in different communal settings, deserves to be mentioned here. It is a beautifully orna-mented and written manuscript, one of the earliest codices of medieval Ash-kenazi liturgy known as the Amsterdam *Mahzor*, mainly because it forms part of the collection of the Jewish Historical Museum in Amsterdam.[5] Close inves-tigation of the liturgical and iconographical aspects of the Amsterdam *Mahzor* revealed that the codex actually originated in Cologne and preserved the order of prayer texts and *piyyutim* according to the rites of the Rheinland district.[6] Numerous marginal annotations proposing liturgical changes give evidence of its use in a diversity of communities, showing that each user had his own pref-erences. The original contents of the Amsterdam *Mahzor* represent the crys-tallized shape of the western Ashkenazi rite, whereas the numerous *piyyutim* often reflect considerable antiquity: some of the latter can be attributed to the seventh-century hymnist Eleazar birabbi Kalir or Kilir, a composer of almost mythical stature and one whose presence in Ashkenazi liturgy can be called canonical.[7] The Amsterdam *Mahzor* is, therefore, a valuable starting point for the study of alternation and adaptation in synagogue worship of the western Ashkenazi branch during the late Middle Ages.

A brief word is also appropriate here concerning the Sephardi liturgical tra-dition in which a variety of rites and customs existed and in which two major trends can be discerned exerting influence on communal prayer practice: one is the application of liturgical guidelines from geonic responsa and the other is the effect of kabbalistic or pietistic devotion. Generally speaking, after 1492 the Sephardi Diaspora tended to look for a more unified form of liturgy as much as Ashkenazi communities, when printing was invented and widely adopted.

---

5   For a comprehensive study of the Amsterdam *Mahzor*, *The Amsterdam Mahzor: History, Lit-urgy, Illumination, Litterae Textuales*, A Series on Manuscripts and Their Texts, ed. A. van der Heide and E. van Voolen (Leiden 1989).

6   See E. Fleischer "Prayer and Liturgical Poetry in the Great Amsterdam *Mahzor*," in *The Am-sterdam Mahzor*, Ch. 3, pp. 26–43. This chapter was translated into English but the original Hebrew version will be published in a forthcoming collection of articles on Hebrew prayer by Ezra Fleischer, edited by S. Elizur and T. Beeri.

7   See, for instance, E. Fleischer, *Hebrew Poetry in the Middle Ages*, supplemented and annotated by S. Elizur and T. Beeri (Jerusalem 2007) [Hebrew]; S. Spiegel, *The Fathers of Piyyut, Texts and Studies toward a History of the Piyyut in Eretz Yisrael*, ed. M.H. Schmelzer (New York 1996).

The printed form of Jewish prayer, both the technical process and the impetus for canonicity, would lead to remarkable liturgical adjustments. Elements of revision and even censorship can be detected in the prayer-texts of Isaac ben Moses ha-Levi Satanow, David Friedländer and Wolf Benjamin Ze'ev ben Samson Heidenheim.[8] Modern Jewish liturgical research has, therefore, to take account of these and other problems of revision and omission. Can we really study these prayer books without preconceived notions about the accuracy of their transmission and ways of standardization or, rather, authorization? To pose the question is tantamount to giving the answer.

Amsterdam was internationally famous because of its Hebrew press in the domain of synagogue liturgy and poetry, but the spirit of modern times asked for new national and religious expressions of worship. There is almost no parallel to the situation of early nineteenth-century Dutch Jewry which left its imprint on the content, appearance and purpose of the *siddurim* and *mahzorim*, both Ashkenazi and Sephardi. The compositors of these volumes were not and did not wish to be in the same position as the *hazzanim*, who in earlier days dominated the cantorial-liturgical directions per community or even per synagogue, each following its own inherited or imported ritual. The great German scholar Leopold Zunz noted, for example, that in Saloniki around the year 1540 there were at least fourteen different Jewish congregations operating more than twenty synagogues and identifying themselves by their places of origin, the latter including Aragon, Catalonia, Portugal or Lissabon, Evora, Italy, Calabria, Apulia, Sicily, Greece and Provence.[9] Strong commitments but also tensions played a powerful role and the question was, whose religious and cultural authority would emerge the strongest?

One of the surprising effects of modern Jewish emancipation in Western Europe was that what was left to the inner religious domain of Judaism—such as synagogue liturgy—was put into the hands of a limited circle of rabbis, compositors and printers. The very few modern studies of Dutch-Jewish liturgy touch on the transformation and printed representation of (Orthodox) prayer-texts, whether or not with the aid of translation into the Dutch vernacular. In this context we may turn to the epoch-making article of the late Joost Divendal, who published a survey of the life and works of one of his own ancestors,

---

8   For instance, Isaac Satanow (1732–1805) in his edition of penitential hymns or *selihot* (1785); David Friedländer (1750–1834) in his prayer book with German translations (1786); Wolf Heidenheim in his numerous editions of *mahzorim* since 1800.

9   L. Zunz, *Die synagogale Poesie des Mittelalters*, Zweite Abtheilung: *Die Ritus des synagogalen Gottesdienstes, geschichtlich entwickelt* (Berlin 1859), p. 146.

Mozes Cohen Belinfante.[10] As early as 1791 or 1793, Belinfante was in charge of a comprehensive translation of Sephardi *tefillot*, with the title *Prayers of the Portuguese Jews Translated from the Hebrew*, four volumes for daily prayer, Sabbath and festivals, fast days and individual events of which the first was published in The Hague by Lion Cohen.[11] The project was not entirely Belinfante's personal enterprise; members of the society *Talmidey Sadic* with reference to Sadic Cohen Belinfante, Moses' father, were involved as well. Their justification of translating religious texts into Dutch is clearly inspired by ideas of Mendelssohnian *Bildung*:

> Jewish knowledge of the Holy Language Hebrew has weakened. Hebrew study is required, but in-depth understanding of Jewish liturgy is lacking, therefore, devotional intention has diminished. Already in earlier times, rabbis and sages were forced to adopt a language like Chaldean (that is, Babylonian Aramaic) for Talmudic expositions. The language of synagogue chants has lost its purity and accuracy, for which poetic devices like meter and rhyme are to be blamed. Previous translations into Spanish and Portuguese were too literal and lack explanatory notes. Translations into antiquated English and French are judged to be of higher quality, but quoting the Bible in English is too much a pro-Christian gesture. The Ashkenazim enjoy the German translation of David Friedländer [in Hebrew characters], but the Sephardim have no valued Dutch prayer book, so the Society *Talmidey Sadic* was to provide this desideratum.[12]

Several instructive pieces about the Jewish calendar and the holidays precede the translated texts, each one introduced with one or two initial words from the Hebrew original. The Dutch rendering is formal and the amount of explicatory notes is surprisingly low. Each of the four volumes followed fixed patterns, omitting most of the non-biblical hymnody.[13]

---

10   J. Divendal, "Mozes Cohen Belinfante, Jew to the Depth of His Soul," *StRos* 31(1997), pp. 94–138. I am indebted to Chaya Brasz for the reference to this important article.

11   In Dutch: *Gebeden der Portugeesche Jooden, door een Joodsch Genootschap uit het Hebreeuwsch vertaalt* ('s Graavenhaage 1791); see J. Divendal, "Mozes Cohen Belinfante," n. 32.

12   *Gebeden der Portugeesche Jooden*, vol. 1, p. 11 (translation into English is mine).

13   The reason for the omission of *piyyutim* is described as follows: "De berymde Zangen zyn allen met vrome inzichten opgesteld; maar by sommigen is de zuiverheid van taale verbasterd, naardien de woorden veeltyds naar den klank en menigte van lettergreepen geboogen zyn" (All rhymed hymns are composed with pious insights, but some have corrupted the purity of language, because words are often adapted according to sound and a large number of syllables).

Obviously, these and other similar translation activities were the result of intellectual developments without much bearing on public Jewish ritual, but such attempts did pave the way for the inclusion of vernacular European languages without any specific association with Jewish tradition in the prayer book. A new and distinct balance of interests was needed in Orthodox texts and practice: vernacular items could be introduced, but the Hebrew original should be retained. By the nineteenth century, the arrangement of vernacular alongside Hebrew became the norm in Western Europe and in the Netherlands. It remains to be seen to what extent Jewish prayer texts in Dutch would ever reach equal validity with their Hebrew counterparts, but surely they were helpful in advocating Jewish goodwill in the non-Jewish world—for instance, the Dutch version of the prayer for the royal family would unequivocally prove general Jewish support for the House of Orange.

Despite this, one should not be led to think that due to the changing historical circumstances the development of Dutch-Jewish liturgy and worship in the modern era follows a linear pattern. Words like tradition, progress and change should be used with caution, given the fact that the nineties of the eighteenth century seem to display more eagerness to internal changes than the twenties or the thirties of the nineteenth century. For instance, in 1793, during a short first invasion of the southern Dutch provinces by the French revolutionary army, the chief rabbi of Rotterdam, Aryeh Loeb ben Hayyim Breslau selected and composed a series of prayers that were translated into Dutch by "learned Jewish men" and edited by a Christian clergyman.[14] Such a local publication may have been intended as an example of interfaith cooperation (although Dominee Scharp's missionary activities are suspect); they also arouse scholarly interest on the part of the Christian Hebraists to come closer to contemporary Jewish prayer texts. By the way, the Dutch word "*plegtig*" (here with a meaning close to the English "decorous") seems to play a major role in many titles and descriptions of how synagogue readings and rituals should be regarded and performed. "*Plegtig*" stands for the forceful guidance of the Jewish worshippers towards an organized and standardized synagogue practice and performance policy, which was in many ways derived from the surrounding Protestant Christian and to a lesser extent from the German Jewish example. The introduction of formalized services was not an entirely Orthodox prerequisite but was also emphasized in the few Reform attempts within modern

---

14   In Dutch: *Plegtige gebeeden voor de joodsche gemeente te Rotterdam* ... *in de Hebreeuwsche taal opgesteld door den eerw. opperrabbijn der joodsche gemeente te Rotterdam. In 't Nederduitsch vertaald, door geleerde joodsche mannen* ... *met eene voorrede,* uitgegeven door Dominee Jan Scharp, predikant te Rotterdam, 1793 [edition Rotterdam 1793].

Dutch Judaism, be it as early as 1796 in the secessionist Adath Yeshurun congregation of Amsterdam, or the *Shoharei De'ah* association of Rabbi Dr. Isaac
Chronik in 1856 (who propagated Reform ideology but was strongly opposed;
he only reached agreement on the introduction of a choir and was then forced
to leave), or as late as 1931 in the developing Union of Liberal-Religious Jews.
Significant liturgical adaptations would not have been realized, were it not for
the sake of enhancement of the decorum of prayer recitation and melodious
chant in the synagogue.

The activities of composers and translators in nineteenth-century Netherlands are aptly described by J.H. Coppenhagen in *The Israelite "Church" and
the Dutch State, Their Relations between 1814 and 1870*.[15] Some of them were
outstanding figures: Samuel Israel (ben Azriel) Mulder (1792–1862), religious
teacher, translator, curator of the Seminary, secretary of the Major Synagogue
and inspector of Israelite schools for many years, was a clear exponent of Jewish orthodoxy in combination with academic scholarship.[16] In 1843, Mulder
received a Ph.D. from the University of Giessen and, in 1844 he published his
Scattered Fruits of Writing in Leiden, a collection of published or unpublished
essays about subjects, varying from a literary study of biblical psalms to a
mathematical study of the number seven. Closest to our theme is his article on
the art of translation, a written up speech from 17 January 1824.[17] The scientific-
historical contents of Mulder's arguments and his discussion of aspects of what
could be defined as comparative linguistics are surprisingly modern. He is well
informed about the new theories considering the classification of the world
languages, despite the fact that they were supposedly all derivatives from the
valley of Sinear, a reference to the biblical Tower of Babel story in Genesis 11.
The art of translation is in Mulder's view always a choice of keeping the middle
way, eschewing either slavish rendering or free paraphrase, both to be considered as the extremes. What is idiomatic for the source language—his meaningful expression is "what is national about the source language"—should be

---

15   In Dutch: *De Israëlitische "Kerk" en de Staat der Nederlanden, Hun Betrekkingen tus-
      sen 1814 en 1870*, (Amsterdam 1988), pp. 82–96. In Coppenhagen's list one comes across
      more or less familiar names, such as S.I. Mulder, G.I. Polak, G.A. Parsser, M.L. van Am-
      eringen, M.S. Polak, S. Heijmans, M. Lehmans, M.M. Cohen, D.J. Lopes Cardozo and
      R.D. Montezinos.

16   See I.E. Zwiep, "A *Maskil* Reads Zunz, Samuel Mulder and the Earliest Dutch Reception
      of *Wissenschaft des Judentums*," in *The Dutch Intersection: The Jews and the Netherlands in
      Modern History*, ed. Y. Kaplan (Leiden 2008), pp. 301–18.

17   *Verspreide Lettervruchten van S.I. Mulder, Doctor in de Wijsbegeerte, en Inspecteur der
      Godsdienstige Israëlitische Scholen* (Leiden 1844). His *Verhandeling over de Kunst van Ver-
      talen* is the first contribution, see esp. pp. 62–64.

transposed into the target language with account of the original intentions and the result should be of good quality. The greatest difficulty is to respect rabbinic opinions and at the same time to reach at a useful and elegant translation.[18]

Mulder's observations are significant when we turn to his Hebrew-Dutch translation work on Bible books, synagogue prayer and hymnody. While scholars like Gabriel Isaac Polak and Moses Loeb van Ameringen initially edited prayer books without the vernacular, in later editions they added Dutch translations of liturgical or poetic segments with the Hebrew *en face*. These prayer books clearly reflect a deeper intrusion of the vernacular into the religious domain. It may seem to us quite puzzling, how these Ashkenazi and also Sephardi prayer books in those generations could contribute to more familiarity, as they were mainly intended to encourage decorum and propriety. Certainly, some standard editions with *haskamot* or rabbinic approbations dominated the Dutch-Jewish synagogue customs, but it is doubtful to what extent printed Jewish liturgy in this respect could have been attractive, had it not been for the melodious cantor or even for the harmonized chant of the choir. The physical representation of prayer texts and particularly *piyyutim* appeared to have been reduced to the minimum needed for marking strophic structures, rhyme schemes and alphabetical acrostics. Annotations are only sporadically inserted, mostly in the form of instructions for cantor and congregation. Source citations and contextual explanations are hardly encountered. A festival *piyyut* which included the name acrostics of the composer would perhaps lead to a short introductory note in very small Hebrew typeface, clearly not meant for historical or devotional clarification.

No wonder that the complex poetry of the earlier mentioned Eleazar birabbi Kilir and other revered hymnists was recited or sung in an abbreviated form or often entirely omitted. An example of a well-known *piyyut* which cannot be ignored from the traditional point of view is the seasonal composition by Kilir (with the opening words *Elim beyom mehussan*), describing the theme of *tal*, dew, to be granted by God during the approaching dry hot summer. This most elaborate poem in rich and flowery Hebrew is recited on the first day of Passover in the *Musaf* prayer. In these verses Kilir combines the name of the twelve months, the twelve signs of the zodiac and the twelve tribes of Israel, featuring multiple acrostics, alliteration, assonance and internal rhyme in twenty-one strophes. By example, the first two strophes in Hebrew original are presented with the Dutch Polak-van Ameringen translation:[19]

18   See *De Nederlandsche Spectator* of 14 February 1863.
19   According to the critical edition of Y. Frankel, *Mahzor le-shalosh regalim* (Jerusalem 1993), p. 225.

אלים ביום מחוסן / חלו פני מנוסן

טל   אורות לנוסן / להטלילם בעצם ניסן

אשאלה בעדם מען / גבורות טל להען

טל   אב הבטח לשען / יתן להמתיק לען

ככתוב בתורתך ויתן לך האלהים מטל השמים ומשמני הארץ ורב דגן ותירוש

בשמך טל אטלה / בילדות טל להטלה

טל   בו איתן מטלה / בדיו ירעו כמו טלה

ברית כרותה לראש אבות / חיליו בטל להרבות

טל   בל-יזיז מבני אבות / להרסיס עם נדבות

ככתוב בדברי קדשך עמך נדבת ביום חילך בהררי קדש מרחם משחר לך טל ילדתיך

De machtigen (Israël), *smeeken op dezen uitstekenden dag voor het aangezicht huns Toevluchts, om hen met lavenden dauw te verkwikken, hen daarmede te omschaduwen in de daartoe bestemde maand Nisan! Ik wil hunnentwege met gebeden smeeken, dat hun de wonderkrachtige dauw geworde, – de dauw, den aartsvader* (Abraham) *als eene ondersteuning toegezegd, verleene Hij* (God) *dien, om der gewassen bitteren smaak te verzoeten.*

Door Uwen naam ben ik als met dauw omschaduwd, door de jeugdige verdiensten van Abraham, die door dauw verheven werd, beschermd; wil ook zijne nakomelingen als een LAM * *weiden. Een verbond immers sloot gij met den eersten der vaderen (bij de ten offer brenging Izaks), om zijne telgen door den dauw te vermenigvuldigen. – De dauw wijke niet van de kinderen der aartsvaderen, hij droppele steeds neder op het volk, gewillig om den Eeuwige te dienen!*

*Het hemelteeken RAM heet in het Hebreeuwsch LAM.

The elaborate structure of Kilir's poetic language deserves to be considered in its own right in spite of the verse mannerisms.[20] Kilir composed in all more

---

20   See my rendering of these first two strophes:

    "The lesser gods" [Israel] *on that very day, / pray to the God of their refuge,*

    To grant them the dew of the morning light, / to let dew descend in the middle of Nisan.

    Let me [Kilir] *ask on behalf of them* [the community] *in reply, / to read the prayer on the power of dew,*

    Dew which was promised to support the patriarch; this is how bitter is made sweet.

    As it is written in your Torah: "May God give you heaven's dew and of earth's richness, an abundance of grain and new wine" *(Gen. 27: 28).*

    In God's name: let Abraham find protection by dew,/ as dew has graced me in my youth; the steadfast [Abraham] *abounded in dew,/ his offspring will graze like a lamb* [Aries];

than 1,500 hymns with wide-ranging stylistic innovations, and these opened new opportunities for enhancing the aesthetic component of Jewish liturgy and worship in his own days and in the subsequent centuries. His work became a formal and thematic model for succeeding generations of Jewish poets in Babylonia, Italy and central Europe and so, entered the Ashkenazi prayer book.

In current Hebrew hymnological research there has been much discussion as to whether and, if so, how these texts were understood by their listeners and readers. Those who were well versed in Jewish literary and folk sources, scholars, preachers, rabbis, other learned men of the community—such people may have caught and understood the paytanic message and enjoyed the playfulness of Kilir's verse; however, they may not have grasped in full all of his references, allusions and connotations and, therefore, needed commentaries.[21] The presence of Hebrew compositions and Dutch translations does not prevent that most communities practiced local customs with regard to what should be or rather should not be recited during public service. The general impression which one gets is that the average visitor of the Orthodox congregations in Amsterdam and *Mediene* was not much inspired by the lyrical intentions and deeper meanings of the poetic insertions; most compositions would simply have been perceived as obligatory by traditional observance: *kinot* (lamentations) for the Ninth of Av, *selihot* for the days preceding New Year and, of course, the lengthy compositions for the High Holidays and other festivals.

During the late nineteenth and early twentieth century, synagogue attendance suffered from a demographic stagnation and congregational life went into decline for a combination of socio-historical reasons which have been explained elsewhere. There was less expectation that the synagogues would be filled with congregants for daily, weekly or annual prayer gatherings. The synagogue as a communal house of prayer and chant had become peripheral to a considerable segment of Dutch Jewry, a simple fact of modern Jewish life in the Netherlands, both prewar and postwar. One of the chief rabbis devoted much of his time and energy to synagogue liturgy, translating all essential texts

---

a covenant was made to the first of patriarchs,/ to multiply his descendants by dew;
dew will not leave the children of the patriarchs,/ to sprinkle a willing people.
As it is written in your holy words: "Your troops will be willing on the day of battle. Arrayed in
holy majesty, from the womb of the dawn you will receive the dew of your youth" (Ps. 110:3).

21   See for medieval *Piyyut* commentaries E. Hollender, *Clavis Commentariorum of Hebrew Liturgical Poetry in Manuscript*, Clavis Commentariorum Antiquitatis et Medii Aevi, vol. 4 (Leiden and Boston 2005); idem, *Piyyut Commentary in Medieval Ashkenaz*, Studia Judaica, Forschungen zur Wissenschaft des Judentums 42, (Berlin 2008); B. Loeffler and M. Rand, "*Piyyut* Commentary in the Genizah," *European Journal of Jewish Studies* 5/2 (2011), pp. 173–203.

and providing extensive commentary in Dutch. This was Lion Wagenaar, chief rabbi of Friesland during the years 1886–1895 and of Gelderland until 1918. Later, he became rector of the Dutch Israelite Seminary until 1930. Wagenaar was a gifted scholar and teacher whose voluminous prayer books appeared during the years 1899 to 1901. He understood that in modern days loyalty to Jewish prayer was under great pressure:

> Our reality is very different; we are occupied by daily concerns; our best moments are taken away by them. Happily so, since ancient times the good God has put in the heart of people the need to leave earthly matters during a number of fixed moments and turn to the highest God in true service of the heart (Hebrew: *'avodah she-ba-lev*).[22]

However, Wagenaar's translations are to such an extent explicative that there is hardly any sense of linguistic or poetic beauty left. In his introduction to the translation of hymns in praise of the Sabbath,[23] he apologizes for the Oriental excessiveness of images and expressions which seem overdone to Western eyes. As late as 1933, the Amsterdam Rabbi Izak Vredenburg (1904–1943), son of Chief Rabbi Joël Vredenburg, produced a *Siddur ngouneg sjabbos* with a syllable-by-syllable translation, also known as the *driestuivertefillo*, a kind of "threepenny-prayer book" possibly intended to be sold to the poor Jews of, mainly, Amsterdam. It remains to be investigated, whether this sympathetic booklet proved ever functional in liturgical practice, but not a single *piyyut* line is included therein apart from the Sabbath eve song *Lekhoh doudi*.[24] The hymnist Kilir was in twentieth-century Dutch-Jewish worship practically on his way to oblivion despite the increasing international scholarly attention given to his oeuvre and that of other early and medieval composers. The 1933 editions of the Liberal Rabbi Dr. Hans Hirschberg for the autumnal festivals are intriguing exceptions: in accordance with common (maskilic-) liberal preference, Hirschberg occasionally included Dutch translations of Sephardi *piyyutim*. Thus we find the *reshut* (lit. permission, a short *piyyut* said by the *hazzan* before certain prayers asking permission from the congregants or from God to

---

22   In Hebrew: עבודה שבלב, see L. Wagenaar, *Gebedenboek met Nederlandsche vertaling en verklaring* (סדר הגיון נפש), (Amsterdam 1901), pp. 2–3; idem, *Orde der gebeden voor den Sabbath-morgendienst* (Amsterdam 1899).

23   Such as מה-יפית ומה-נעמת בתענוגים and מה-ידידות מנוחתך.

24   *Sjabbos-Tefillo genaamd Ngouneg Sjabbos, bevattende alle gewone gebeden voor sjabbos, t.w. van vrijdagmiddag tot en met zaterdagavond, met woordelijke vertaling en aanteekeningen door Izak Vredenburg (met illustraties), uitgegeven door de "Centrale Organisatie tot de Religieuse en Moreele Verheffing der Joden in Nederland"* (Amsterdam 1933).

pray) of Solomon Ibn Gabirol *shahar avakshekha tzuri u-misgabi* ("At dawn I seek You, my Refuge and Rock"), among the morning prayers for New Year. Obviously, the prewar prayer books of the Union of Liberal Jews from the thirties and the postwar *Seder tov lehodot* from the sixties symbolically maintain a few opening lines from Kilir's most prominent works, but large portions are entirely omitted.[25] In our days, the stronger sense of focus and self-consciousness on the part of the Liberal Jewish community and their independence vis-à-vis the Orthodox community has led to the publication of more successful and employable prayer books including Dutch introductions, translations and explanations, with moderate incorporation of Hebrew prayer texts.[26]

Half a century after the war, the Orthodox Dutch-Israelite community (*Nederlands Israëlietisch Kerkgenootschap*, abbreviated NIK) decided to edit a new series of Ashkenazi *mahzorim*.[27] The prewar liturgy of the High Holidays and the three pilgrimage festivals was left intact, but the rabbis and the council of the NIK accepted a radically different typographical presentation of the *piyyutim* in accordance with modern standards of scholarly editing: strophic structures were restored, rhyme schemes and acrostics were made visible, and an explanatory Dutch translation was added to each part of the *piyyut* compositions. Whether this adaptation in fact benefits the modern user,

---

25   One of the earliest prayer books of the Union was published in 1931 by the lay-leaders Levie Levisson and Raphael Jesaja Spitz under the general editorship of the German Rabbi Dr. Joseph Norden of Elberfeld. *Seder tov lehodot* No. 1 was published by Rabbi Jacob Soetendorp and the lay-leader Robert A. Levisson in 1964, see Ch. Brasz, *In de tenten van Jaäkov, Impressies van 75 jaar Progressief Jodendom in Nederland 1931–2006* (Amsterdam and Jerusalem 2006), p. 52. Dutch Liberal congregations also used an abbreviated version of the German *Einheitsgebetbuch* (Munich 1899) in a photo-offset edition, see J.J. Petuchowski, *Prayerbook Reform in Europe: The Liturgy of European Liberal and Reform Judaism* (New York 1968), p. 347. See also D. Michman, *Het Liberale Jodendom in Nederland 1929–1943* (Amsterdam 1988).

26   *Seder tov lehodot* No. 2 was published in recent years by Rabbi David Lilienthal; see J. Frishman, "Who We Say We Are: Jewish Self-Definition in Two Modern Dutch Liberal Prayer Books," in *A Holy People, Jewish and Christian Perspectives on Religious Communal Identity*, ed. M. Poorthuis and J. Schwartz (Leiden and Boston 2006), pp. 307–19. Frishman offers a number of relevant observations on the two versions of *Seder tov lehodot*, the first one published in 1964 and the latter in 2000. *Piyyutim*, either Hebrew or Dutch, are hardly found in both editions.

27   This was after the publication and successful distribution of *Siach Jitschak, Siddoer, de geordende gebeden voor het gehele jaar*, compiled by the physician Jitschak (Izak) Dasberg (1900–1997) and edited by the NIK. in 1977. The series of *mahzorim* was published during the years 1991–1998 with the aid of Izak Dasberg, Abraham Wijler, Rabbi Abraham W. Rosenberg and the author of this article.

remains to be seen. All in all, modern revisions of Jewish prayer hardly promote creativity and spontaneity.

Let me conclude with one final generalization on modern liturgical performance according to Ashkenazi, Sephardi and Liberal Jewish liturgies in the Netherlands: some components are decisively influenced by Israeli and Anglo-American customs but obviously rudiments of distinct Dutch-Jewish liturgical customs survive until this day, most notably in the melodies and songs of the skilled cantor, either by survival in a manuscript or by publication.[28]

---

28   Handwritten document by master B.M. Stern, *Koul Jehoedoh, Chazonoes J.I. Vleeschhouwer* (*1839–1913*), Groningen 5688–1928; H. Bloemendal, *Amsterdams Chazzanoet, Synagogale Muziek van de Ashkenazische Gemeente* [*Amsterdam Hazzanut, Synagogal Music of the Ashkenazi Congregation*], ed. J. Poolman van Beusekom (Buren 1990).

CHAPTER 10

Paving the Way: "Deaf and Dumb" Children and the Introduction of Confirmation Ceremonies in Dutch Judaism

Chaya Brasz

On Sunday morning, the sixth of August 1858, a group of prominent Jews in Groningen came together for a festive religious ceremony. Among them were the members of the local synagogue board and the provincial Great Synagogue Council, the educational committee, the congregation's secretary, the Jewish religion teacher Samuel J. van Ronkel and two other Jewish religion teachers.[1] All the men were invited together with their wives, in other words, women also attended this public religious event. At the center of this gathering were three girls—Aleida, age fifteen, Anna, age thirteen and Maria Esther, age twelve— the daughters of Rebecca Schaap-Hijman and Isaäk Lazarus Schaap.[2] The girls' father was a widely respected attorney as well as prominent Jewish leader. As a "corresponding member," he represented all the Jews living in the province of Groningen in the Hoofdcommissie tot de Zaken der Israëlieten (Supreme Committee for Israelite Affairs), the government-imposed umbrella organization of Dutch Jewry, residing in The Hague.[3] The Schaap daughters were celebrating their confirmation day, the day of their "confession of faith" (*geloofsbelijdenis* in Dutch), followed by their confirmation as members of the congregation. During the ceremony conducted in Dutch, the girls were thoroughly questioned about the Jewish religion. Their answers were clear and intelligent. Speeches praising them were given and in the Jewish weekly of those days, the *Weekblad*

---

*   This article is a partial result of a research project on Judaism in the Netherlands, conducted by the author for the Robert Levisson Institute for the training of Rabbis, Cantors and Teachers in Amsterdam and sponsored among others by the Prins Bernhard Cultural Fund and the Maror Foundation in the Netherlands.

1   *Weekblad voor Israëlieten* 4/3 (1858), p. 3.

2   The names and personal data were retrieved from the population registry in the Groningen archives. Aleida Schaap later married the well-known Dutch Jewish painter Jozef Israëls. I am indebted to Rivka Weiss-Blok for this information on Aleida's later life.

3   Representatives from the periphery were "members by correspondence" in the *Hoofdcommissie* and did not attend meetings.

© KONINKLIJKE BRILL NV, LEIDEN, 2017 | DOI 10.1163/9789004343160_011

voor Israëlieten, the ceremony was depicted as an example to both boys and girls.[4]

Jewish worship and ceremonies underwent fundamental changes during the nineteenth century. Religious reform originated primarily in Germany, but spread to Jewish communities in other countries as well, including the Netherlands. Jewish confirmation ceremonies were introduced as a *rite de passage* in several modern Jewish schools in Germany, the first ones being held in 1803 (Dessau) and 1807 (Seesen and Wolfenbüttel).[5] Their format clearly derived from Protestant Christianity, both as regards the catechism-style educational material and the ceremony itself. However, their appearance in Judaism also was an outcome of the *Haskalah* (Jewish Enlightenment) and the educational views of Naphtaly Herz Wessely (1725–1805). In his *Divrei shalom ve-emet* (1782), Wessely proposed to limit traditional talmudic learning to a small number of eligible pupils, while for all the others he sought to apply a far more practical Jewish education, more in accordance with the children's capabilities: "*hanokh lana'ar al pi darko*." In addition, Jewish education had to give way considerably to the profane subjects these children were in need of in order to make a living in a non-Jewish society, slowly opening up to their integration.

Confirmation ceremonies can therefore be studied as testimonies of a different and modernized understanding of Judaism, as it was adapting to its non-Jewish surroundings.[6] The traditional bar mitzvah ceremony was limited to boys alone and focused on the child's practical ability to perform Jewish traditional rituals and commandments. With the progress of assimilation and the loss of Hebrew proficiency, the bar mitzvah ceremony became subject to criticism. The mechanical learning and public reading of a Hebrew text, in most cases no longer understood, offered the boys little systematic knowledge of Judaism. Moreover, much of the attention, especially in a developing middle-class milieu, no longer focused on the bar mitzvah ceremony itself, but on the boy's new clothes, the presents and the festive meal instead. In the Netherlands, like elsewhere, criticism of the bar mitzvah ceremony was openly expressed halfway into the nineteenth century:

4   *Weekblad voor Israeliëten* 4/3 (1858), p. 3.
5   L. Zunz, *Gesammelte Schriften* 2 (Berlin 1876), p. 214.
6   M. Eliav, *Jewish Education in Germany in the Period of Enlightenment and Emancipation* (Jerusalem 1960), pp. 257–70 [Hebrew]. Also available in German: *Jüdische Erziehung in Deutschland im Zeitalter der Aufklärung und der Emanzipation* (Münster 2001), pp. 330–47; D.R. Blank, "Jewish Rites of Adolescence," in P.F. Bradshaw and L.A. Hoffman, *Life Cycles in Jewish and Christian Worship* (Notre Dame and London 1996), pp. 81–110; I.G. Marcus, *The Jewish Life Cycle, Rites of Passage from Biblical to Modern Times* (Seattle and London 2004), pp. 82–123.

No new clothes, or banquets, or gifts will teach the child! No good wishes or religious ceremonies will change anything for the better—but only religious instruction, performed by competent and suitably assigned teachers, will be of benefit to him. It shocks our souls watching a youngster appear for the first time before the Holy Book, wondering: does he know what is written in it? Has he received thorough instruction in the truths of religion? Is he aware of the manifold obligations imposed on him? And having to reply to those questions in the negative! We deeply regret witnessing that our sublime religion is reduced to a game of imagination, a pompous display of luxury, a farcical—or rather, a dismal—show![7]

Advocates of confirmation ceremonies generally argued that, in contrast with the bar mitzvah ceremony, the confirmation ceremony held in the vernacular, and thus more understandable for a growing number of Jews, was a serious test of the child's theoretical knowledge of Jewish religious principles. When the child confirmed his or her commitment to the Jewish faith, this act did not arise from automatically inherited tradition, but rather, at least in theory, from rational understanding and free choice.[8] The method also had the advantage of equipping youngsters with the ability to defend themselves against Christian missionary activities.

Confirmation ceremonies did not involve major halakhic problems and were not necessarily performed in synagogues. As a result, they were not confined to those circles in Germany pushing for radical reform, but made their appearance in moderate traditional communities as well. An important feature of the ceremonies was that they included girls and, hence, they may be considered as forerunners of nowadays bat mitzvah ceremonies. Confirmations can be found back in a wide variety of forms in most European countries during the nineteenth century, among them England, France, Poland and Russia.[9] In France, the contents of the manuals written for confirmation involved strong aspects of French nationalism, serving the process of French nation building.[10] In several German states and in Denmark, the ceremonies were imposed upon the Jewish population as part of an enforced and regulated assimilation process in

---

7   *Nederlands Israëlietisch Nieuws- en Advertentieblad* 1/ 11(1850), p. 2. The author of these lines was not in favor of confirmation ceremonies either.
8   Blank, *Jewish Rites*, pp. 95–97; Marcus, *Jewish Life Cycle*, pp. 113–14.
9   Blank, *Jewish Rites*, p. 96.
10   I am indebted to Prof. Evelyne Oliel-Grausz for her remark on this aspect of the French manuals.

which both their national identity and their church affiliation were defined.[11] Elsewhere, Jews themselves initiated them for their own purposes.

In France where, similar to the Netherlands, Reform or Liberal Judaism remained absent during the nineteenth century, confirmation ceremonies for boys and girls were known since the early 1840s in traditional synagogues, usually in groups during Shavuot, the festival of *matan Torah*, the giving (and receiving) of the Torah.[12] Jewish confirmation underwent a much broader development in the United States. In American Reform congregations, which formed the majority of American Jewry, the ceremonies even replaced the bar mitzvah. Their popularity diminished only with the renewed interest in bar mitzvah ceremonies in the beginning of the twentieth century, followed by the gradual introduction of bat mitzvah ceremonies for girls from 1922 onwards. Although she read from a book and not from a Torah scroll, Judith Kaplan, at age twelve, is usually mentioned as the first girl to celebrate her bat mitzvah in 1922, on a Sabbath morning in her father's synagogue in New York.[13] She was the oldest daughter of Rabbi Mordecai Kaplan, founder of Reconstructionist Judaism. Bat mitzvah ceremonies remained exceptional for many years after, during which those ceremonies for girls, *if* they were performed, were confined to Friday evening services with the girl reading (part of) the *haftarah* (a selection from the Prophets thematically related to the weekly Torah reading) of that specific Sabbath in the vernacular. The real breakthrough of fully egalitarian bat mitzvah ceremonies only came along during the 1970s and 1980s.[14]

In the Netherlands, Liberal Judaism did not make its appearance until the early 1930s.[15] When it was finally introduced, confirmation ceremonies had already become outdated. Girls belonging to Dutch Liberal congregations had their bat mitzvah ceremony during Friday evening services, which included candle lightning and reading of the *haftarah*, or part of it, in the vernacular,

---

11 M.A. Meyer, *Response to Modernity, A History of the Reform Movement in Judaism* (Detroit 1995), p. 144.

12 Meyer mentions 1841 in *Response to Modernity*, p. 170; J.R. Berkovitz mentions 1844 in *Rites and Passages, The Beginnings of Modern Jewish Culture in France, 1650–1860* (Philadelphia 2004), pp. 224–25.

13 Marcus, *Jewish Life Cycle*, pp. 106–10.

14 Ibid., p. 114.

15 D. Michman, *Het Liberale Jodendom in Nederland, 1929–1943* (Amsterdam 1988); Ch. Brasz, *In de tenten van Jaäkov, impressies van 75 jaar Progressief Jodendom in Nederland, 1931–2006* (Amsterdam and Jerusalem 2006); ead., "Dutch Jews and German Immigrants, Backgrounds of an Uneasy Partnership in Progressive Judaism," in *Borders and Boundaries in and around Dutch Jewish History*, ed. J. Frishman, D.J. Wertheim, I. de Haan and J. Cahen (Amsterdam 2011), pp. 125–42.

FIGURE 10.1   *First independent aliyah for the Torah reading of a bat mitzvah in the Nether-*
lands: Ariane Boeken in the Liberal Jewish synagogue of Amsterdam on 21 No-
vember 1970. Standing from left to right around her: Dr. Maurits Goudeket, Nico
Boeken (her father), Rabbi Jacob Soetendorp, Ludi Boeken (her older brother)
and Sal van Weezel.
PRIVATE COLLECTION ARIANE BOEKEN-RUBIN.

whereas boys had their traditional ceremony with Torah reading on Saturday mornings. The first girl in the Netherlands to receive an independent *aliyah* (being called up to the Torah) during the Torah reading in a Saturday morning service was Ariane Boeken in 1970 in the Liberal synagogue in Amsterdam.[16] She had performed her bat mitzvah ceremony the evening before.

It is clear that, in view of the late introduction of Liberal Judaism in the Netherlands, confirmation never was a custom of Dutch Liberal Judaism, but rather a nineteenth-century development within Orthodoxy.[17] Confirmation ceremonies were part of the acculturation process taking place in the Dutch Jewish community as a direct outcome of the official Emancipation of the Jews in 1796. One of its characteristics was its adaptation to Dutch Protestant church culture. Part of that process was imposed by the authorities and the small enlightened Jewish elite, such as the way rabbis had to dress as Protestant clergymen and the obligatory use of the Dutch language in their sermons.[18] Other aspects developed from within and were initiated by the Jews themselves. Confirmation ceremonies in the Netherlands belonged to the latter category and during several decades they were perceived as a legitimate feature of Dutch Jewish religious culture. Efforts to introduce them mainly took place between the 1830s and 1860s. Occasional confirmations continued to reappear sporadically even in the late 1880s.

The Deaf and Dumb

The Schaap girls in Groningen in 1858 were not the first Dutch Jewish children celebrating this type of ceremony. In the Netherlands confirmation ceremonies started with a very specific category of children, who in those days were still defined as "deaf and dumb." This is the old and humiliating term for what was also once called deaf-mute children and today are referred to as hearing and speech impaired. Until the end of the eighteenth century, deaf-mute

---

16   By "independent" I mean, that she alone was the one who received an *aliyah*, and not as an added person to the *aliyah* of her father. This was introduced under the guidance of Rabbi Jacob Soetendorp. *Laynen* (reading the Torah) by girls and women, directly from the scroll, was introduced later, under the guidance of Rabbi David Lilienthal.

17   Until now only briefly mentioned in B. Wallet, *Nieuwe Nederlanders, de integratie van de joden in Nederland, 1814–1851* (Amsterdam 2007), pp. 167–68; J. Meijers, *Erfenis der Emancipatie, het Nederlandse Jodendom in de eerste helft van de 19e eeuw* (Haarlem 1963), pp. 53–55, 76.

18   Wallet's *Nieuwe Nederlanders* and Meijers' *Erfenis der Emancipatie* offer the most extensive overviews so far.

children were perceived as "dumb" or "stupid," even though most of them had a normal intelligence. The problem was that the tools to educate them simply did not exist. This excluded them from any normal educational process and turned them into outcasts who had great difficulty to communicate with their, usually hostile, environment. Surprisingly, the first Jewish children to hold confirmation ceremonies in the Netherlands were hearing and speech impaired children. To be precise, four boys in the Guyot Institute for the Deaf and Dumb (Guyot Instituut voor Doofstommen) in Groningen were confirmed as early as 1829.

The Guyot Institute, founded in 1790 by a Huguenot clergyman, welcomed children of all creeds and was a pioneer in the education of deaf-mute children.[19] At the Institute they were taught to communicate. They acquired basic skills such as reading and writing and learned a simple profession to provide them with a decent livelihood. Being a clergyman, Henry Daniel Guyot also insisted on their religious education, each child in his or her own religion. Before they left the Institute, most children had confirmation ceremonies in their respective churches or at the Guyot Institute itself. The ceremonies enabled them to join their churches as full members, something never achieved before.

Jewish children had been among the first pupils of this Institute. Deafness was a rather widespread phenomenon in the Jewish community.[20] Many of the Jewish pupils came from Amsterdam and none had parents who were able to participate in the financial costs. At the Guyot Institute they were treated like all other children. In the beginning they stayed with Jewish foster families, among them the home of Chief Rabbi Salomon Rosenbach and his wife.[21] From 1843, they lived in a Jewish boarding facility.[22] Their religious education at the Institute was put in the hands of local Jewish religion teachers. In 1829, Catholic children were emancipated at the Institute by introducing the "Holy Communion" for them. When this happened, Jewish children were to become the only ones without a religious ceremony. Because of their limitation in hearing and in speech, deaf-mute boys could not have a regular bar mitzvah, as it involved the public reading of the Torah and giving of a *derasha*, a sermon. In

19   H. Betten, *Bevrijdend Gebaar, het levensverhaal van Henri Daniël Guyot* (Groningen 1984); I am indebted to Henk Betten for introducing me to the Guyot Institute and for his advice for my research in its archives in Groningen and in Haren.

20   M. Rietveld-van Wingerden and W. Westerman, "'Hear, Israel': The Involvement of Jews in Education of the Deaf (1850–1880)," *Jewish History* 23 (2009), p. 49; W.M. Feldman, *The Jewish Child. Its History, Folklore, Biology and Sociology* (London 1917), pp. 393–97.

21   Groninger Archieven (GA), Het Repertorium Part 1 (detailed list of pupils, 1785–1872) of the Koninklijk Instituut voor Doven H.D. Guyot, GA 1496, inv. no. 933, p. 38.

22   Ibid., pp. 40, 41.

general, traditional Judaism raised many problems with regard to the integration of the disabled in prayer services and a continuous debate existed around the status of deaf and blind people.[23] Disabled persons were not counted in the *minyan* (quorum of ten adult Jewish males needed to perform certain religious obligations) and could not perform any *mitzvot*. In addition, unlike the other religions represented in the Guyot Institute, Judaism offered no equivalent ceremony for girls either.

The existence of Jewish confirmation ceremonies in Germany was no secret to the Jews of Groningen. Since 1815, the local Jewish community had developed the most enlightened Jewish school in the Netherlands. Several of its educators originated from Germany and were closely connected to the leaders of the German Jewish Enlightenment. Therefore, it is not surprising that the bylaws of the school quoted Wessely's *hanokh lana'ar al pi darko* as its educational principle. The school provided its pupils with a basic Jewish education along with good quality general training.[24]

These local circumstances, along with the desire to allow Jewish pupils at the Guyot Institute to hold a ceremony like their non-Jewish peers, must have led Chief Rabbi Salomon Rosenbach (born in Bavaria, 1764) and the prominent Jewish lay leader Mozes van Coevorden to introduce confirmation ceremonies for deaf-mute Jewish boys as an alternative to the bar mitzvah ceremony. The first ceremony was held on 13 June 1829, in the large hall of the Guyot school building. It was based on the catechetical method of questions and answers, combined with lip reading, sign language or, when possible, speech. Van Coevorden asked the questions and the four boys, David IJzerman, Salomon Soesan, Hartog van Wezel and Levi Woudhuizen, who were all from Amsterdam, answered in the presence of the chief rabbi, the *parnassim*, the members of the provincial Great Synagogue Council and a considerable crowd of Jews and non-Jews together.[25]

The first girl to hold such a ceremony in the Netherlands was Leentje van der Klei from Heerenveen, a deaf-mute girl at the same Institute together with

---

23   T.C.R. Marx, *Halakha and Handicap, Jewish Law and Ethics on Disability* (Jerusalem and Amsterdam 1992–3).

24   *Algemeen Verslag en Reglement van het Instituut Tipheret Bachurim ter onderwijzing van de Israëlitische Jeugd te Groningen en deszelfs Plegtige Inwijding op den 1 Augustus 1815* (Groningen 1815); S. van der Poel, *Joodse Stadjers, de joodse gemeenschap in de stad Groningen, 1796–1945* (Assen 2004), pp. 37–54.

25   *Algemeen Verslag gedaan binnen Groningen in de zeven en dertigste Jaarlijksche Vergadering van Contribuerende Leden den 20sten Julij 1829 wegens het Instituut voor Doofstommen, aldaar opgericht in den Jare 1790*, p. 18 (Bibliotheek Koninklijke Kentalis te Haren); Het Repertorium Part 1, GA 1496, inv. no. 933.

the confirmation of three more boys.[26] Their ceremony took place in 1831, the year in which the certainly-not-Reform-minded Rabbi Akiba Eger in Brunswick, Germany, introduced confirmation ceremonies for boys and girls as well. The decisions of the Jews of Groningen thus were quite in pace with German moderate Orthodoxy. Leentje van der Klei was interrogated and confirmed by Chief Rabbi Rosenbach himself.

Official Introduction

The next step was to take these ceremonies out of the Guyot Institute into the Groningen congregation itself, for the hearing and speaking sons and daughters of its members. The first confirmation ceremony ever held in a Dutch Jewish congregation, was celebrated in 1835 by Levie Andries de Leeuw, son of a printer's assistant.[27] Since the boy was born in September 1822 and had his confirmation ceremony in October 1835, we may conclude that the event was somehow combined with his bar mitzvah ceremony. At the request of Chief Rabbi Rosenbach and the educational committee, teacher Samuel van Ronkel even had prepared a small manual. In 1837, Levie de Leeuw was followed by five additional boys.

1837 also was the year in which the Hoofdcommissie in The Hague officially advocated confirmation ceremonies as a desirable innovation for Dutch Jewish congregations countrywide. Obviously unaware of the ceremonies previously held in Groningen and the manual produced there by Van Ronkel, the Hoofdcommissie promised a reward for the Jewish religion teacher who would produce the best manual for confirmation ceremonies.[28] Two teachers, Seligman Susan of Wageningen and Israël Waterman of Kampen took up the challenge and, subsequently, also described their first ceremonies in detail.[29] In Kampen, the whole ceremony for a boy took place in the synagogue and was modeled after German confirmation ceremonies. Waterman had to overcome

26   Het Repertorium, Part 1, GA 1496, inv. no. 933; according to the population registry of Heerenveen in Friesland, Leentje van der Klei was born there in 1815 and she died in Sneek in 1885. She was the only child of butcher Michiel Hartogs van der Kley and Martje Levi van Dam.

27   *Jaarboeken voor Israëlieten in Nederland* 3/2 ('s Gravenhage 1837), p. 115.

28   Wallet, *Nieuwe Nederlanders*, p. 167.

29   NA 2.07.01.05/1. Commissie tot de Zaken der Israëlieten 1814–1817, Hoofdcommissie tot de Zaken der Israëlieten 1817–1870, Ingekomen en minuten van uitgaande stukken betreffende de Israëlietische Kerkgenootschappen 1814–1870, Inv. Nos. 91/155 (Susan) and 93/512 (Waterman).

considerable opposition in his congregation. In Wageningen, the boy was first interrogated by his teacher Seligman Susan in the presence of the congregational board, on a Friday at home.[30] After he proved his impressive knowledge of the Jewish religion, the board confirmed (*bevestigde*) him, congratulated him and invited him to proceed the next morning, during the Sabbath morning service. The customary Torah reading by this bar mitzvah boy—as he was referred to—was replaced by his reading a Hebrew prayer in the form of a poem, especially composed for the occasion. After this, the boy pronounced the usual *berakhot* (blessings) before and after the Torah reading, to which he only listened. This was followed by his *derasha*, a speech in Dutch, in which he again showed his extensive knowledge of Judaism and thanked his teacher and his parents. The entire package constituted the celebration of his confirmation and was regarded as an upgraded bar mitzvah ceremony.

After Waterman and Susan both claimed to have been the first and delivered their handwritten occasional manuals comprising the impressive educational program they had worked through with their pupils, Samuel van Ronkel argued that those ceremonies had existed in Groningen for many years already in the Guyot Institute and that the first confirmation ceremony in his congregation, for which he also had written a manual, had taken place in 1835.[31] In the ensuing discussion, Susan claimed he had in fact, ever since 1830, instructed youngsters according to the educational method in use for confirmations. He had learned about the method and the ceremony from his father in 1825, the year of his own bar mitzvah in Middelburg.[32] Susan's parents originated from Hamburg and he himself was born there as well, which explains their familiarity with the ceremony. Confirmation ceremonies had been introduced there in the framework of a modern Jewish school (1809), while the family was still living there. Later on, in December 1817, the well-known Reform *Neuen Israelitischen Tempelverein* of Hamburg grew out of this school. By then, the Susan family had already moved to Middelburg in the Netherlands, where they apparently created an interest in the new ceremony. A member of the Middelburg Jewish school commission, J.D. Isaacson, eventually visited Groningen in July 1836 and learned more about the subject from observing Samuel van Ronkel's educational methods in the Groningen Jewish school for the poor.[33]

---

30   The Wageningen ceremony is also described in detail in *Jaarboeken voor de Israëliten* 3/1 (1937) pp. 22–24, but by mistake as if it had taken place in Middelburg. This was corrected to Wageningen in the next issue of the *Jaarboeken voor de Israëliten* 3/2 (1937), p. 113.

31   Ibid., pp. 113–15.

32   *Jaarboeken voor de Israëliten* 3/3 (1937), p. 200.

33   *Jaarboeken voor de Israëliten* 3/2 (1937), p. 115.

It is clear that around 1830, some Dutch Jews kept well abreast of developments in Germany. They were not marginal, but included Jewish religion teachers and rabbis. Moreover, the first confirmation ceremonies in the Netherlands had been held spontaneously and well before their official introduction from above by the Hoofdcommissie.

Educational Material

The educational technique of questions and answers, a "catechismus," had first been introduced in Judaism in Italy by Abraham Jagel's *Lekah tov* in the late sixteenth century (Venice 1595).[34] It was based on a Catholic example and remained an isolated case until Protestantism caused great popularity of this method in early modern Europe. This popularity spilled over into Judaism in Amsterdam, when in 1749, the Jewish publisher and bookseller Eleasar Soesman, produced a Yiddish textbook *Mikrah meforash*, following this educational method to simplify Torah education for children.[35] It concentrated on the weekly Torah portions.

In 1816, another far more comprehensive book on Judaism for boys and girls, and written as a catechism in Dutch, was published by Moses Cohen Belinfante with the full approval of the Ashkenazi and Sephardi rabbinates. The book was an adapted Dutch translation of a Hebrew catechism originally published in Berlin by Shalom J. Cohen and several years later in English translation in London.[36] Cohen had visited the Netherlands shortly before and his book was in use in several countries, but its appearance in the Netherlands, in 1816, was premature for the introduction of confirmation ceremonies and may not even have been intended for that purpose. Belinfante's publications always were perfectly in pace with developments in Germany, but permanently ahead of their time in the Netherlands.[37]

Only two decades later, Dutch Jewish teachers produced some first experimental manuals for specific confirmation ceremonies without even referring to it. Waterman mentioned other, more recent German material, including the

---

34   Eliav, *Jewish Education*, p. 257; Marcus, *Jewish Life Cycle*, p. 113.

35   B. Wallet, *Links in a Chain, Early Modern Yiddish Historiography from the Northern Netherlands* (Amsterdam 2012), p. 78.

36   S.J. Cohen, *Shorshei Emunah*, Hebrew Catechism with English translation by J. van Oven (London 1815).

37   See on this prominent representative of the *Haskalah* in the Netherlands: J. Divendal, "Mozes Cohen Belinfante, Jew to the Depth of His Soul," *StRos* 31/1–2 (1997), pp. 94–138.

well-known manual by J. Heinemann.[38] Official Dutch publications followed in print from 1842 onwards. These manuals were compiled by the Dutch Jewish religion teachers Samuel J. van Ronkel in Groningen, Mozes M. Cohen in Oude Pekela and later in Assen and Israël Waterman in Kampen, later Arnhem. It was Van Ronkel, who in the end received the reward, promised by the Hoofdcommissie, but Waterman developed into the most successful author of educational material. His manual of 1842, published in Kampen with the approval of Chief Rabbi Hartog Josua Hertzveld, was improved and republished in Arnhem in 1854 with the approval of Chief Rabbi Jacob Lehmans.[39] These teachers introduced children of both sexes, and in the Dutch language, to subjects like "Man and his destination" and "God and religion in general." Only after having dealt with those universal issues, they proceeded with subjects specifically pertaining to the Jewish religion—the Thirteen Principles of Faith after Maimonides, the Ten Commandments, the Jew's obligations towards God, themselves and their fellow human beings—and they concluded with the "confession of faith" itself. The overall character of the manuals was universal. Concepts like the Jewish People or the Land of Israel played no role in their contents. The Jewish teachers who wrote them perceived themselves and their fellow Jews as belonging to *Mankind*, as emancipated members of the *Dutch Nation*, while Judaism was their religion alone.

> Q: What should, henceforth, constantly and strongly prompt us to serve God with zeal and loyalty?
>
> A: The solemn confession of our faith in God and the commitment related thereto to lead a God-fearing life, should constantly and strongly prompt us to serve God with zeal and loyalty.
>
> Q: How should we regard the day on which one becomes bar mitzvah and performs one's confession of faith?
>
> A: The day on which one becomes bar mitzvah, performs one's confession of faith and is solemnly confirmed as a grown-up member of the Jewish religious congregation is one of the most important days in our

---

38   J. Heinemann, *Die Religions-Lehre der Israeliten in Fragen und Antworten* (Berlin 1829).

39   S. van Ronkel, *Leiddraad bij het Godsdienstig Israëlitisch Onderwijs ten dienste der scholen en tot huiselijk gebruik* (Groningen 1845). This book was awarded by the Hoofdcommisie; M.M. Cohen, ברית ה' of *Geloofsbelijdenis voor Israëliten* (Koevorden 1849); I. Waterman, *Beknopte Handleiding bevattende de Geloofs-Belijdenis van de Israëlitische Godsdienst tot opleiding en bevestiging van kinderen van beiderlei kunne in het Israëlitisch voorouderlijk geloof* (Amsterdam 1842); idem, *Het Israëlitisch Voorvaderlijk Geloof, bevattende de Geloofsbelijdenis van de Israëlitische Godsdienst ter opleiding en bevestiging in de Mozaïsche Godsdienst van Kinderen van Beiderlei Kunne* (Arnhem 1854).

life; as on that day we enter into a closer association with God and all His followers.

Q: What is finally required from those who perform their confession of faith?

A: Those who perform their confession of faith are required to openly confess that they wholeheartedly believe in the religious doctrine which they have embraced and that they vow to always follow and observe it.

Q: Do you now agree to confess that you wholeheartedly believe in the religious doctrine which you have embraced and that you promise to adhere to it with God's help, to refrain from sinning and to always lead a religious life?

A: Yes, I do.

Q: And will you now, in consideration of the Omniscient God, solemnly make this promise?

A: I will!

In this case, please make this confession in the language of our forefathers, loudly and solemnly!

עֵדָה קְדוֹשָׁה וְנִכְבָּדָה!

הִנֵּה בָזֶה אַגִּיד בִּפְנֵיכֶם תּוֹךְ קְהַל וְעֵדָה/ עֲדַת יִשְׂרָאֵל מִי מָנָה/ שֶׁאֲנִי מַאֲמִין
בְּלֵב שָׁלֵם בֵּאלֹהִים יָחִיד וּמְיוּחָד/ הַבּוֹרֵא הַיָּכֹל עַל כֹּל/ הַמּשֵׁל וּמַנְהִיג וּמַעֲמִיד
אֶת הַתֵּבֵל כֻּלָּהּ/ בְּחָכְמָתוֹ וּבְטוּבוֹ/ אֲבִי כָּל בְּנֵי אָדָם/ שֹׁפֵט וְגוֹמֵל עַל כָּל
מַעֲשֵׂיהֶם/ וְהִנְנִי נוֹדֵר לְעָבְדוֹ וּלְכַבְּדוֹ בְּיִרְאָה וּבְאַהֲבָה/ לִשְׁמֹר מִשְׁמַרְתּוֹ וְלִבְטֹחַ
בּוֹ כָּל יְמֵי חַיָּי/ וּלְמַלְּאוֹת תְּעוּדָתִי הָעֶלְיוֹנָה בְּכָל כֹּחִי וְיָכָלְתִּי:
מוֹדֶה אֲנִי בִּפְנֵיכֶם/ כִּי נֶאֱמְנוּ לִי לִמּוּדֵי הָאֱמוּנָה וְהַמִּצְוֹת הַכְּלוּלִים בְּסִפְרֵי
הַקֹּדֶשׁ/ הַנְּתוּנִים וְהַמְקוּבָּלִים הֵמָּה לָנוּ עַל פִּי יְיָ/ וְהִנְנִי נוֹדֵר לְקַיְּמֶם וְלַעֲשׂוֹתָם
כָּל הַיָּמִים/ וְגָמַרְתִּי בְּלִבִּי לִשְׁמוֹר תָּמִיד בְּקִרְבִּי דִּבְרֵי הָאֱמוּנָה הַזֹּאת/ אֲשֶׁר
הוֹדַתִי עֲלֵיהֶם הַיּוֹם/ וּלְהָכִין מַחְשְׁבוֹת לִבִּי וּמַעֲשֵׂה יָדַי כִּרְצוֹן יְיָ וְהַבְּרִיּוֹת/ כָּל
יְמֵי חַיָּי יִהְיוּ קֹדֶשׁ הִלּוּלִים לַיְיָ/ מְקוּדָּשִׁים לְמִשְׁפָּט וָצֶדֶק וּלְטוֹבַת עֲמִיתִי/ וְתָמִיד
אֶתְאַמֵּץ לְהוֹסִיף יוֹם יוֹם אֹשְׁרִי וְהַשְׁלָמַת נַפְשִׁי אָמֵן:

[All diacritical marks are as per the original text.]

And now, please make this declaration also in the Dutch language! Distinguished congregation!

In your presence, which greatly honors me, I now wish to confess that I believe wholeheartedly in the one and only God; in Him, who created the universe and who, through His wisdom and goodness, provides for all creatures present therein. In Him, the Father of human beings, who watches their actions and justly rewards them.

I now vow to love and respect Him to the utmost, to observe His laws, to have faith in Him each day of my life and to fulfill my sublime mission as human being with all my strength and power.

I declare before you that I acknowledge the tenets of the Jewish faith and the commandments of the Holy Scriptures, which were imparted on us according to His supreme request. I vow to always observe them and abide by them.

All the days of my life will be dedicated to honoring God and contributing to the wellbeing of my fellow human beings, so that through these my transient and eternal happiness will be accomplished! Amen.[40]

Like Belinfante's early publication of 1816, these manuals were never published without the consent of the rabbinate. Although teachers usually took the initiative, there is no doubt that several chief rabbis officiating during the first half of the nineteenth century either tolerated or actively supported the ceremonies. Those were Salomon Rosenbach in Groningen, Emanuel Joachim Löwenstam in Rotterdam, Hartog Josua Hertzveld in Overijssel and Drenthe and Jacob Lehmans in Nijmegen (Gelderland). Chief Rabbi Hartog Josua Hertzveld, in 1841, included confirmation ceremonies in his plans for a Rabbinical Assembly, during which he probably hoped to take a countrywide rabbinical decision on the introduction of confirmations and choirs in Dutch congregations. His efforts to organize such an assembly were obstructed however by the ultra-Orthodox, mainly Zvi Hirsch Lehren and Avraham Prins in Amsterdam, and he could not realize his plans.[41] But from 1850 onwards, Chief Rabbi Jeremias Hillesum in Drenthe still was an active supporter, and Hertzveld's successor, Dr. Jacob Fränkel in Overijssel, promoted the ceremonies till the 1870s.[42]

The ceremonies existed mainly in the north-eastern and eastern part of the Netherlands, but as we already saw, they also found support in the congregations of Rotterdam and Middelburg. Opposition was felt in North Holland (dominated by Amsterdam), The Hague and its surroundings, the province of Utrecht (dominated by the very traditional Jewish community of Amersfoort), and they seemed to have been rare in the Catholic provinces of Brabant and

---

40   Waterman, *Het Israëlitisch Voorvaderlijk Geloof*, pp. 53–55.

41   Meijers, *Erfenis*, pp. 51–55; I. Erdtsieck, "The Appointment of Chief Rabbis in Overijssel in the Nineteenth and Twentieth Centuries," *StRos* 30/1 (1996), pp. 167–68.

42   Fränkel published about the subject in *Weekblad voor Israëlieten* 1/33 (1856), p. 1. During the 1870s Jewish religion teachers, using the catechetical method, were opposed "from above," as was remembered with regret by a Jewish religion teacher from Kampen in Overijssel, S.M. Salomons, in a letter to the editor in *Achawah* 14/159 (1907), p. 4.

Limburg, although they may have taken place in Maastricht, at the initiative of lay members.[43]

Rotterdam around 1850 had a Jewish population of some 3,500 souls and was the second largest Jewish community in the country, after Amsterdam. It had a small but very active liberal middle-class and Jewish confirmation ceremonies were held there. They were mentioned by several opponents.[44] A supporter of the ceremonies criticized them for their disorderly character in one of the Jewish newspapers: "Greater solemnity should be introduced during confirmation and the female gender should be subjected to the ceremony as well."[45] From the remark on the female gender, we understand that in Rotterdam the ceremonies were limited to boys. The problems with their disorderly character disappeared rather promptly with the nomination in 1849 of Chief Rabbi Dr. Josef Isaacsohn, who came from Germany and was an opponent of the ceremonies. He simply abolished them.[46]

The establishment, however, of the Rotterdam School for the Deaf in 1853, created the possibility to continue them in that Institute where they soon flourished for boys and girls alike.[47] This was not surprising since the Rotterdam Institute, though aiming at the general population, was founded by liberal Jews and specifically by the local Jewish physicians, Dr. Alexander Symons and Dr. Machiel Polano.[48] They invited a German Jewish teacher, David Hirsch, to become the Rotterdam school's principal. Hirsch had proven to be a great innovator in education of deaf children in Aachen and was a liberal-minded Jew, also when it came to Judaism. Thus, the local Jewish religion teacher Abraham D. Lutomirski, a supporter of the ceremonies, was enabled to continue them in that school. Moreover, the school worked in close contact with a similar institute in London and with like-minded Jewish circles there, who had introduced

43 From an article in *NIW* 12/ 31 (1877), it is clear that not everything was published. Someone who reported on the singing of a "ladies choir" in the synagogue of Maastricht and unsuccessfully sought publication of this report in the *Nieuw Israëlietsich Weekblad*, was instead reprimanded by the newspaper and "should have done better not even reporting on it, since the rabbi—would he have been informed beforehand—of course never would have tolerated a ladies choir in the synagogue, just like he would have disapproved of 'so-called' confirmations" (all this according to the newspaper).

44 D. Hausdorff, "Dr. Josef Isaacsohn en zijn tijd," in *Rotterdams Jaarboekje* (1959), pp. 132–33.

45 *Nederlands Israëlietisch Nieuws- en Advertentieblad* 1/30 (1850), p. 3.

46 Hausdorff, "Dr. Josef Isaacsohn," p. 141.

47 Rietveld-van Wingerden, "'Hear, Israel,'" pp. 41–56.

48 Rietveld-van Wingerden, "Reform in Education of the Deaf: David Hirsch and His School in Rotterdam (1853)," in *Children and Youth at Risk*, ed. C. Mayer, I. Lohmann and I. Grosvenor (Frankfurt am Main/ Bern/ Brussels/ New York/ Oxford/ Vienna 2009), pp. 121–35.

confirmation ceremonies in Reform as well as in Orthodox Judaism. Chief Rabbi Josef Isaacsohn became cooperative in the framework of the Rotterdam Institute for the Deaf, but he insisted on calling the ceremonies "festive public examinations," rejecting confirmation ceremonies as an undesired imitation of a Christian ceremony.

More evidence of the acceptance of confirmation ceremonies in the Netherlands can be found in the reactions to a report on Jewish education published in 1862 by the Society for the Benefit of Israelites in the Netherlands (*Maatschappij tot Nut der Israëlieten in Nederland*). This organization for the improvement of the Jew's cultural and social development was dominated by the secularizing educated middle-class and included several religion teachers as well. The Society made rather radical proposals for Jewish educational reform and, although those proposals were rejected by the rabbinates, there was one exception to this general pattern; the proposal to introduce confirmation ceremonies gained openly expressed approval in the provinces of Groningen and Drenthe, from Chief Rabbi Jeremias Hillesum and the religion teachers in that area: "Performing a solemn confession of faith under guidance of the regional chief rabbi should serve as a creative stimulus for education, as well as an event worthy of remembrance and, as such, should favorably influence the mindset and further life of young Jews of both genders."[49]

An attempt to introduce confirmation ceremonies for boys and girls in Amsterdam remained unsuccessful. The effort was undertaken in 1860 by several members of the Dutch-Jewish liberal elite, among them the prominent jurists and politicians A.S. van Nierop and M.H. Godefroi, together with Rabbi Dr. Isaac Löb Chronik, a German Reform rabbi who lived in the Netherlands for several years.[50] They had founded the society *Shochrei De'ah* through which they strove to achieve synagogue reform, including the introduction of choirs and confirmation ceremonies. They succeeded with the former but not with the latter. That does not mean, however, that something like confirmation ceremonies did not exist in Amsterdam of those years, though under a different name: "festive public examinations," similar to the name Chief Rabbi Isaacsohn had introduced in Rotterdam several years before. Those public group examinations at the end of Jewish religious education for boys and girls, gained

---

49   H. Jacobs, *Bijdrage tot de Geschiedenis van het Lager Godsdienstonderwijs in Nederland* [n.p., n.d.], p. 15.

50   J. Frishman, "Gij Vromen zijt Nederlanders! Gij Onverschilligen, zijt Israëlieten! Religious Reform and Its Opponents in the Mid-Nineteenth Century in the Netherlands," *StRos* 30/1 (1996), pp. 146–50; Brasz, "Dutch Jewry and Its Undesired German Rabbinate," *LBI Yearbook* 57 (2012), p. 80.

popularity and from their description it is clear that they showed similarity with confirmation ceremonies elsewhere in Europe.

On a Sabbath afternoon in 1869, one of Amsterdam's assessor rabbis, Joseph S. Hirsch was the highest authority present during such a ceremony for eight boys and eight girls, all thirteen years old.[51] Other attendants were the children's parents, teachers, members of the school commission and fellow pupils. The children were required to show their knowledge in the "fundamentals of faith" (*gronden des geloofs*), the commandments, religious doctrine (*godsdienst-leer*) and the meaning of the Jewish festivals. It is clear from the description that such a "children's festival" as it was also called, was not an exceptional event. It was emphasized that it should be distinguished favorably from what was happening abroad, where, according to the newspaper, the study of the sources was so easily thrown away. The Dutch celebration concluded a period of serious study by the children as "a crown on the work" of their Jewish education. A significant remark also followed as to this celebration's special importance for poor children "who otherwise enjoyed so little of the pleasure that should accompany the bar mitzvah and who heard barely anything in public of the obligations applying to them when reaching this age."[52] In other words: the bar mitzvah celebration had become too much of a middle-class affair to be enjoyed by boys whose parents were too poor to afford it. The "festive examination" at the end of religion school was taking over that central function for them.

The actual examination was preceded and followed by the singing of psalms. The newspaper explicitly mentioned that during the examination "the girls behaved just as brave[ly] as the boys." Afterwards, the boys conducted a full *minha* (afternoon prayer) service with Torah reading by one of them and at the end all children received a present: Dr. S.M. Mulder's *Bijbel voor de Jeugd* (Youth Bible). The girls received volume one to nine and the boys were given volume ten till seventeen. Whoever chose this as the present may have speculated that one day these children might marry each other and together would be in the possession of a complete set!

Although the location of the event was not mentioned, it is difficult to believe that this ceremony took place in a synagogue, but it definitely was on a Sabbath. A Jewish school building must have been in use for the event. What made it special was the involvement of girls: they were questioned just like the boys and although they had no active role in the *minha* service, they were attending it and they received the same present afterwards. Boys and girls clearly

---

51   *NIW* 5/9 (1869), p. 35.
52   Ibid.

were experiencing a religious group ceremony together and for poor boys, as
for the girls, it functioned as a replacement of the middle-class bar mitzvah
ceremony they could not enjoy. In spite of the obvious efforts to distinguish
the event from confirmation ceremonies abroad, all this was not even so different from what happened in other countries after all. Moreover, in the Netherlands the ceremony had the function of emancipating three groups in the
Jewish community by offering them a serious *rite de passage* as an alternative
to the bar mitzvah ceremony: hearing and speech impaired children, girls and
poverty-stricken boys.

Synagogues and Confirmations

The above descriptions of the ceremonies bring us to the core questions about
their acceptance in the Netherlands: did they ever enter the synagogues and
how frequently were they actually held? A closer look at the confirmation ceremony of the three Schaap girls in 1858 in Groningen, teaches us that it was
not held on a Sabbath but on a Sunday in the beginning of August. In spite
of all the details mentioned about the event, it is not clear where the Groningen ceremony took place. It could have been at home or in a classroom of the
synagogue building. It might even have been in the synagogue itself, but held
on a Sunday, not on a Sabbath day, nor on any festival and thus not in front
of a whole congregation. Those present were the notables and their wives, a
selected and no doubt liberal public. The event also had the character of a re-
introduction of these ceremonies in the Groningen congregation, apparently
because, after the first enthusiasm of the 1830s, they had become forgotten.

It is difficult to estimate the popularity of confirmation in the Netherlands.
Jewish newspapers only appeared from the very end of the 1840s and although
confirmation ceremonies are frequently mentioned in advertisements and articles, some of those announced confirmations might, in fact, have been regular bar mitzvahs for which the parents preferred to use a "modern" name in
Dutch: *kerkelijke confirmatie* or even *kerkelijke aanneming*.[53] In December 1855,
the *Weekblad voor Israëlieten* dedicated its whole front page to confirmation
ceremonies.[54] The reader easily understands from its contents that the ceremonies existed but were barely held in synagogues, as the newspaper would

---

53   See the variety of announcements in *NIW* 2/17 (1866), mentioning a "confirmatie" in Delft,
      and 36 (5 April 1867) mentioning a "בר מצוה (confirmatie)"; ibid., 6/24 (1896) describes a
      "confirmatie" at the home of Portuguese Jews; ibid., 8/35 (1873) a "kerkelijke confirmatie."
54   "De Confirmatie," in *Weekblad voor Israëlieten* 1/20 (December 1855).

Zaterdag, 3 Juni a.s. פרשת נשא zal de geloofsbevestiging plaats hebben van mijne dierbare Pleegdochter MATHILDA.

Wed. SAMSON.

Rotterdam, 1 Juni 1871.

FIGURE 10.2   Announcement of the confirmation of a girl, held at
her home, published in Weekblad voor Israëlietische
Huisgezinnen, 2 June 1871, Vol. 2, no. 18, p. 111. The event
was criticized as an undesired "exception" in
the next issue of the same newspaper.

have preferred. In spite of the enthusiasm of several religion teachers and rabbis, the popularity of the ceremonies seemed to remain limited and, in most cases, did not leave the context of school and home, especially when the participation of girls was involved.

The ceremonies in the Netherlands also remained strongly connected with bar mitzvah age. In other countries, and especially in Reform Judaism in the United States, confirmation ceremonies moved to a later date, several years after bar mitzvah age, thus having the advantage of prolonging Jewish education for boys and girls. In the Netherlands this opportunity was not utilized and Jewish education ended early, at bar mitzvah age. The exception could be found in the Institutes for the Deaf: at the Guyot Institute in Groningen children of all creeds, including Jewish children, had their confirmation ceremony right before they left the Institute, which often happened at a later age, like fifteen or seventeen years old.

Confirmations in synagogues were clearly limited to boys at bar mitzvah age. Apart from the two detailed descriptions of the first individual confirmations of bar mitzvah boys in synagogues in 1837 initiated by Seligman Susan in Wageningen and by Israël Waterman in Kampen, the description of a third one in Hoogeveen in Drenthe in 1851, confirms this pattern of a strong attachment to the bar mitzvah ceremony.[55] The boy first performed his traditional bar mitzvah obligations, including Torah reading by himself. This was immediately followed by a confirmation ceremony in the form of questions and answers in Dutch, after which he was blessed and confirmed as a new member of the congregation. This seems to have been an accepted format for boys at least in the north-eastern provinces: confirmation, if taking place in the synagogue was, in fact, part of their bar mitzvah ceremony (or vice versa). Moreover,

55   Israëlietisch Weekblad 1/15 (April 1851).

confirmations were in all cases the beginning of membership: the confirmand was accepted (in fact "confirmed") as a member of the congregation. Thus, the ceremony also seems to have been an effort to bring Jews in line with the membership model in Protestant churches: full membership with active voting rights and the right to function in the administrative institutions of the Protestant church, was confined to those persons who were not only "members by baptism" (the so-called *doopleden*), but members after "confession of faith," usually performed at young adult age (the so-called *belijdenden leden*).

When girls were involved or when boys and girls received equal treatment, Dutch Jewish confirmation ceremonies did not take place in the synagogue and in those cases boys had a separate bar mitzvah afterwards. I found only one exception to this general pattern. In the congregation of Assen, again in the province of Drenthe and very close to Groningen, confirmations of boys and girls together were described without mentioning their location, but another source mentions the regular custom of "examinations" for boys and girls together *taking place in the synagogue*.[56] The combination of the two makes it most probable that group confirmations of boys and girls together took place in the synagogue of Assen. This also fits the impression that for several decades the Jews of Assen were the most acculturated Jews of the country. At an early stage they successfully turned their chaotic prayer services into most orderly ones by the introduction of a male choir, coordinated praying together and prayers in complete silence in order not to disturb one another, thus clearly copying the atmosphere of the Protestant church. Assen was even nicknamed "Sodom" by other Jews.[57]

In general, the introduction of confirmation ceremonies seems to have met considerable problems countrywide and depended on local religion teachers. Those teachers must have had a difficult time for they had to introduce innovations through the official Jewish schools for the poor, while most well-to-do middle-class families, who could have served an example to others, showed little interest, not because they were so traditional but, rather, because of their complete indifference towards religion. The example of the confirmation ceremony of the Schaap girls in Groningen in 1858 appears to have been an unusual and rare exception to this rule and had to do with the specific liberal Jewish middle-class milieu of that area. It should be noted that Groningen in that period had two different congregations after a conflict over the introduction of a

56   *Nederlands Israëlietisch Nieuws- en Advertentieblad* 1/14 (1850), p. 2; F.J. Hulst and H.M. Luning, *De Joodse gemeente Assen, Geschiedenis van een behoorlijke kille, 1740–1976* (Assen 1991), p. 60.

57   *Nederlands Israëlietisch Nieuws- en Advertentieblad* 1/14 (1850), p. 2.

male choir. The most traditional Jews had established a separate congregation and the liberal lay leadership of the mother congregation must have felt free to introduce innovations.[58]

Growing Opposition

As mentioned before, halfway through the nineteenth century, Rotterdam's new Chief Rabbi Dr. Josef Isaacsohn abolished confirmation ceremonies in his congregation. He had come from Germany (Emden) and was the first rabbi with a doctorate nominated in the Netherlands (1849). That doctorate and the application sermon he delivered in the German language caused the Jews of Rotterdam to perceive him as the modern and liberal rabbi they desired.[59] They were, however, soon to be disappointed. In the Netherlands, traditional Jews, among them the Lehren brothers who dominated the Rabbinical Seminary in those years, vehemently opposed university education for rabbinical students. Therefore, a doctorate in the hands of a rabbi was understood as an expression of liberalism. In Germany, however, the situation was different, since academic studies and rabbis with doctorates enjoyed early acceptance also in Orthodoxy. In defense against Reform tendencies and under the leadership of rabbis like Samson Raphael Hirsch, German traditional Judaism halfway into the nineteenth century was in a process of redefining itself. In this process of creating what was soon to be named Neo-Orthodoxy, it was also deciding upon which customs were to be considered Jewish and which were not. Confirmation was one of the issues where they drew a clear line: those ceremonies were doomed to disappear from Judaism.

Isaacsohn was closely related to these developments. Contrary to what Rotterdam's Jews expected, his doctorate and modern appearance were no guarantee for a liberal attitude. In his eyes, the ceremonies were "completely in conflict with the Israelitic faith."[60] Although he tolerated them in the Institute for the Deaf in Rotterdam, he insisted on calling them "festive examinations," a final public exam concluding the child's Jewish education at elementary school level, but not a religious ceremony.

58   Van der Poel, *Joodse Stadjers,* pp. 55–72; W.J. van Bekkum, "De afgescheiden Gemeente Teschuat Jisraël te Groningen," in *De Folkingestraat: Geschiedenis van de joodse gemeenschap in Groningen,* ed. L. Ast-Boiten and G. Zaagsma (Groningen 1996), pp. 63–69.
59   Brasz, "Dutch Jewry," p. 78.
60   *NIW* 2/48 (1867), p. 3.

Isaacsohn was supported on this issue by the chief rabbi of Limburg Dr. Salomon Cohn, nominated in 1853.[61] Isaacsohn and Cohn were personally related, since their wives were sisters, daughters of the influential Rabbi Jacob Ettlinger of Altona, who was an early and dominant defender of traditional Judaism. These two young German rabbis, in fact, were the first ones to express a well-defined modern Orthodox opposition against what they recognized as undesirable Reform in Dutch Judaism and, in the absence of a chief rabbi in Amsterdam, their influence cannot be underestimated. They desired to eradicate the ceremonies not only by changing their name to "public examinations," but also by changing their character, rejecting the catechetical method and by confining those examinations to the strict domain of the school.

Somewhat later in the century, other rabbis, especially Dr. Louis Landsberg, who was Cohn's successor in Limburg from 1860, continued their opposition against the ceremonies. Landsberg criticized the educational method of questions and answers in the vernacular, which could so easily be learned by heart and detached pupils from the Jewish sources. He and his only nine-years-younger colleague Dr. Jozeph Hirsch Dünner, chief rabbi of Amsterdam and North Holland from 1874, joined forces on educational issues and actively strove to preserve the knowledge of Hebrew in education.[62] They preferred children to learn about the contents and meaning of Judaism by reading directly from the Torah and understanding its Hebrew text. As a result, from the 1870s onwards, confirmation ceremonies eventually started to disappear.

Conclusion

When compared to surrounding countries, Dutch Jewish religious culture as it was created during the second half of the nineteenth century lacked the further development of liberal customs in Judaism. Choirs were introduced in Dutch synagogues, even excellent ones, but they remained male choirs. Confirmations of boys and girls had made their appearance earlier in the century, but they did not enter synagogues as independent ceremonies for both sexes and detached from the bar mitzvah ceremony. Moreover, they were repressed before the end of the century.

61   Brasz, "Dutch Jewry," p. 79; S. Cohn, "Een woord over de confirmatie," in *Weekblad voor Israëlieten* 1/30 (1856), pp. 2, 3.

62   N.L. Dodde, "Jewish Education in Schools in the Netherlands from 1815 to 1940," *StRos* 30/1 (1996), p. 83.

In most countries mixed choirs in Liberal or Reform synagogues and confirmations of boys and girls—mostly group confirmations even in Orthodox
synagogues—functioned as tools to introduce girls and women in the public
domain of synagogues. In the Netherlands that opportunity was suppressed
and Liberal Judaism also remained absent until the 1930s. This probably is
one of the reasons why Dutch Judaism showed a particularly long absence of
women in synagogue life, not only on the ceremonial side but also when it
came to their place on synagogue boards. In Germany and England women
were permitted to enter Orthodox synagogue boards during the 1920s, but Rotterdam's Chief Rabbi Dr. Bernhard Ritter took a different position.[63] He made
an in-depth study of the subject and his conclusions not only strongly opposed
voting rights and board membership for women, but also gained great international respect. That obviously made it impossible for Dutch Jews to follow
other rabbinical conclusions.[64] Ritter was considered a great scholar and he
was one of their own respected chief rabbis, after all.

Only when some fifty years later, after the *Shoah*, when small communities
of survivors in the Dutch countryside lacked the manpower to continue their
existence, did they, out of necessity, fall back on women as board members.
In the Orthodox community in Amsterdam this process took much longer
and was only completed in 2009, when the first woman was chosen to join the
board of the Nederlands Israëlietische Hoofd Synagoge.

Therefore, in the end, the "deaf and dumb" seem to have gained most from
the existence of confirmation ceremonies in the Netherlands, for their ceremonies, transformed into "examinations," remained popular in the Institutes
for the Deaf, with the warm support of the chief rabbis and for boys and girls
alike. When a boy or girl had such an "examination," even in the 1930s, this
was still perceived as a special event, though the character had become somewhat less "festive" and less "public." The examination took place in front of the
local Jewish religion teacher and the chief rabbi, who personally blessed the
child, boy or girl. By then, the nineteenth century confirmation ceremonies
were completely forgotten, but the examination still offered a *rite de passage*
to children who could not have a regular bar mitzvah ceremony and girls were
not excluded from this examination. Thus, while "regular" girls, in the end, did

63   "Das Frauenwahlrecht nach der Halacha," in *Jeschurun, Monatsschrift für Lehre und Leben im
      Judentum* 6 (1919), pp. 445–48. The article opposed an earlier *Gutachten*, written by Dr. David
      Hoffmann, Rector of the Rabbiner Seminar für das Orthodoxe Judenthum, ibid., pp. 262–66.
64   See "The Halakhic Debate over Women in Public Life: Two Public Letters of Rav Abraham
      Ha-Kohen Kook & The Responsum of Rav Ben Zion Uziel On Women's Suffrage and Rep-
      resentation," in *The Edah Journal, Halakhic Possibilities for Women* 1/2 (2001).

not benefit from the earlier introduction of confirmation ceremonies, we may conclude that those ceremonies improved the position of hearing and speech impaired children in the community, boys and girls.

Over the years, from 1829 till the late 1930s, some one hundred and sixty Jewish children had such a ceremony in the Guyot Institute alone. The last Jewish boy registered in the large handwritten books of the Guyot Institute, in the column with "confessions of faith," was Isaac Leeraar in July 1937. The last girl, for whom Chief Rabbi Simon Dasberg came to the Guyot Institute was Sophia Betje van Essen, born deaf in Dinxperloo in 1918. Her examination took place in June 1935. Beneath her name was later added that she was murdered in Poland on 27 November 1942.[65]

---

65   Bibliotheek Koninklijke Kentalis te Haren, Het Repertorium Part 2 (detailed list of pupils, 1873–1956) of the Koninklijk Instituut voor Doven H.D. Guyot, nr. 2420 (Isaac Leeraar) and nr. 2377 (Sophia Betje van Essen). This second handwritten Repertorium comprises the later years of the Institute. The one on earlier years is preserved in the Groninger Archieven (GA) as mentioned already in note 21. Chief Rabbi Dasberg's involvement in Sophia Betje van Essen's ceremony is mentioned in the 1936 Year report of the Institute in the library of Koninklijke Kentalis in Haren, *Algemeen Verslag gedaan te Groningen in de Jaarlijksche Vergadering van contribueerende leden, gehouden 8 Juni 1936, wegens het Instituut voor Doofstommen aldaar opgericht in den Jare 1790*, p. 11.

PART 5

Jewish Identity and Religiosity

∵

CHAPTER 11

Religion, Culture (and Nation) in Nineteenth-Century Dutch Jewish Thought

Irene E. Zwiep

Introduction: A Brief Conceptual History of Nearly Everything

In this paper I propose to explore the contours of a concept that featured prominently in nineteenth-century Dutch-Jewish discourse and motivated virtually all efforts at preserving, amidst processes of rapid acculturation, the Jewish flavor of the Israelite presence in the Low Countries: "religious civilization" or, in Dutch, *godsdienstige beschaving*. I shall begin by determining when and how the term "civilization" was adopted by Dutch Jewish intellectuals, and how it replaced *hokhmah u-musar*, the indigenous tradition of Jewish learning and morals. Thereupon we shall trace how the connotations of individual *politesse* and sophistication (which were inherent in the original conception of civilization) were transformed into a collective cultural-religious content and how the result was put to task in the creation of a new Jewish civic identity.

Zooming in on three representative texts from the period, we will then try to establish to what extent the idea of an Israelite *godsdienstige beschaving* implied a departure both from the universalistic mentality of the Batavian Republic (1795–1815) and from the German *Wissenschaft des Judentums* (1820 and after), whose efforts at mapping the historical *Cultur der Juden* provided our authors with a steady source of inspiration. Freely fusing Dutch enlightened master narratives with a variety of *Wissenschaft* themes and sources, these authors exhibit a degree of eclecticism that was at once puzzling and productive and thus deserves further consideration. In passing, we will encounter different conceptualizations of religion, culture and nationality, three modern key-concepts that remained, despite the Dutch Jews' unequivocal civic status, shifting categories in the hybrid discourse on "Dutch-Israelite religious civilization" during the first half of the nineteenth century.

A Linguistic Jewish Identity or: Redefining the *Tongeleth* Society

Between 1796 and the 1830s, when the (German) notion of culture entered the debate on post-emancipation Jewish identity, Jewish difference in the Low

Countries was articulated almost exclusively in terms of religion and its language, in *casu* Hebrew. The foundation of the Hebrew *Tongeleth* confraternity
in 1815 may serve as a case in point.[1] Amsterdam-based, short-lived, counting
fifty members at best and devoting all its energy to the cultivation of pure biblical Hebrew, the *Tongeleth* confraternity can hardly be considered representative of the early nineteenth-century Dutch-Israelite mindset.[2] Still, a closer
look at this Hebrew *Sprachgesellschaft*, its roots, aims and scope, will help us
gain a better understanding of the universalist, ecumenical mentality of the
decades following the emancipation decree of 1796—a mentality that determined the earliest Jewish steps on the road to Dutch citizenship. As common
opinion has it, *Tongeleth*'s primary goal was to advance Jewish emancipation
(though one cannot help wondering how the study of ancient Hebrew grammar will have contributed to the consolidation of Jewish civic equality). The
fact that this modest Hebrew salon was credited with such ambitious political
aspirations may well have been inspired by the belief that *Tongeleth*'s primary
source of inspiration had been the Berlin *Haskalah*.[3] In scholarly literature,
this Jewish branch of the European Enlightenment, which had prepared the
ground for the linguistic and cultural integration of Jews in the Habsburg
Empire, was generally identified as *the* intellectual role model of Dutch Jewry
at the turn of the century.[4] Yet although the two cultural spheres certainly
shared such preoccupations as the discovery of secular knowledge, the exploitation of Hebrew-vernacular bilingualism, and a staunch veneration of Moses

---

1   Witness the emphasis on Hebrew proficiency in the two publications (*Bikkure Chinnukh*
    [1809] and *Yesodot ha-Miqra* [1810]) that were issued by the educational society Chanoch
    Lannangar ngal pie darkoo, instigated by Louis Napoleon in 1809. See also D. Michman, 'Jew-
    ish Education in the Early Nineteenth Century. From Independence to Government Supervi-
    sion', *Studies on the History of Dutch Jewry* 2 (1979), pp. 89-138 [Hebrew].
2   In present-day scholarly literature, *Tongeleth*'s demise is usually located sometime during
    the 1830s. Significantly, the society stopped issuing volumes after its debut *Bikkure Tongeleth*
    (1820) and its successor *Peri Tongeleth* Part 1 (1825). On these volumes, see A. van der Heide,
    "Problems of Tongeleth Poetry," *StRos* 19/2 (1985), pp. 264–74. A not always entirely favor-
    able exposé on the society can be found in I. Maarssen, "Tongeleth. Een joodsche letterkun-
    dige kring in de xixe eeuw," *De Vrijdagavond* 1/25 (1924/5), pp. 390–93; 35, pp. 135–37, 146–48,
    199–201.
3   See especially, P. Tuinhout-Keuning, "Kitve ha-chevrah ha-amsterdamit 'Tongeleth' ve-ha-
    haskalah be-germanyah," *Studies on the History of Dutch Jewry* 5 (1988), pp. 217–77.
4   Most explicitly, F. Hiegentlich, "Reflections on the Relationship between the Dutch Haskalah
    and the German Haskalah," in *Dutch Jewish History* 1 (1984), pp. 207–18, and, of course,
    the tell-tale chapter "The *Reception* of the Haskalah – The Initial Period" (italics mine) in
    J. Michman, *The History of Dutch Jewry During the Emancipation Period, 1787–1815: Gothic Tur-
    rets on a Corinthian Building* (Amsterdam 1995), pp. 162–67.

Mendelssohn, the sheer parallelism of course hardly proves direct, exclusive maskilic influence.

The idea of a German-Jewish blueprint reflects the tendency dominant up until the 1990s, to over-interpret the impact of the Berlin *Haskalah*. In Dutch-Jewish historiography this trend was paired to a post-*Shoah* ideology that valued autonomous Jewish development over the possibility of gentile-Jewish cultural exchange. Yet upon closer inspection both the timing of the supposed "Dutch *Haskalah*" and its intellectual concerns point at a local Dutch rather than German complex of factors and stimuli. In ardent response to the prevailing political atmosphere, Jewish intellectuals in the Batavian Republic chose to model their activities upon immediate Dutch examples rather than distant Jewish initiatives. The result, which I have described elsewhere, was an almost cosmopolitan, emphatically non-confessional type of Jewish public discourse that endorsed the generically Christian values of the Dutch Enlightenment, while simultaneously striving to minimalize all recognizably Israelite content. The Jews of the Batavian Republic indeed had been quick to internalize the enlightened universalism which, in the name of Tolerance and Natural Law, had welcomed them into Europe as potential equals, as fellow-human beings rather than as Jews.[5]

It has been observed that the name *Tongeleth*, meaning "[For the Common] Good," was chosen in deliberate allusion to the Dutch *Maatschappij tot Nut van 't Algemeen*, which had dominated the Dutch educational scene ever since its foundation in 1784. Yet we should realize that this influential Christian society for popular education merely served as an overall source of inspiration. Some eight years prior to the birth of *Tongeleth*, a more immediate ancestor presented itself, when Tzvi Hirsch Somerhausen (1781–1853), a Berlin Jew who had moved to Amsterdam and would later settle in revolutionary Brussels, enriched the city's cultural tapestry with yet another literary confraternity.[6] Combining contemporary society's two most urgent ideals, he proudly named his *Letteroefenend Genootschap Tot Nut en Beschaving*, i.e., "For the [Common] Good and *Civilization*."[7]

---

5   I.E. Zwiep, "Jewish Enlightenment (almost) without Haskalah. The Dutch Example," *Jewish Culture and History* 13/2–3 (2012), pp. 220–34.

6   For Somerhausen's Belgian period, see B. Wallet, "Belgian Independence, Orangism, and Jewish Identity. The Jewish Communities in Belgium during the Belgian Revolution," in *Borders and Boundaries in and around Dutch Jewish History*, ed. J. Frishman et al. (Amsterdam 2011), pp. 167–82.

7   Emphasis mine. For a survey of Jewish literary societies before 1850, see P. Buijs, "Tot nut en eer van 't jodendom: Joodse genootschappen in Nederland 1738–1846," in *De gelykstaat der joden: Inburgering van een minderheid*, ed. H. Berg (Zwolle 1996), pp. 15–24; for the

In tune with the spirit of the times, Somerhausen's *Tot Nut* was devoted to such general pursuits as art, science, and *zedelijke beschaving*, the ideal of "ethics and civilization" to which I shall return shortly in somewhat greater detail. In the spirit of contemporary enlightened universalism, the society was explicitly non-denominational and open to all. Though mainly run by its Jewish members, it avoided "all association with existing religious or political systems," lest "it should become an Israelite confraternity."[8] Given the predominantly Jewish membership, *Tot Nut*'s publications were conspicuously devoid of Jewish themes; its biographical sections, an immensely popular genre at the time, were devoted to Christian rather than Jewish celebrities.[9] The early volumes of *Collected Essays*[10] reverberate with the universal aesthetics of French classicist writings rather than the *divre hokhmah u-musar* of the Hebrew-German *Ha-Me'assef*. Somerhausen's essay on education, Moses Leman's elaborate musings on how to distinguish an adjective from an adverb, or even Samuel Mulder's prize essay on the art of translation—they all reveal a primary affinity with contemporary European themes, at the cost of Jewish language and content.

Yet the society's uncompromising embrace of general knowledge and culture should not tempt us into believing that its members consciously tried to obscure, let alone obliterate their Jewish heritage. Their cheerful universalism was merely a logical correlate of the enlightened notion of civilization so eagerly adopted in the society's name. In current social and political thinking, civilization was put forward as an important tool of universalism, a virtue that, once it was shared by all, would forever unite mankind and bring world peace and brotherhood. As the Dutch Lutheran minister Hendrik Justus Matthes (1780–1854), summarized in an exemplary text from the period, *beschaving* would eventually conquer the vicissitudes of nature, class and state, and render meaningless all individual, social, national and religious differences.[11] For

---

participation of Jews in Dutch non-Jewish societies, cf. A.J.A.M. Hanou, "Joden en Nederlandse genootschappen, 1750–1850," ibid., pp. 25–34.

8   "[V]erhoede ... dat het zou zijn een Israëlitisch genootschap," quoted from a speech held at the society's fiftieth anniversary, in A.J.A.M. Hanou, *De sluier van Isis: Johannes Kinker als voorvechter van de Verlichting, in de Vrijmetselarij en andere Nederlandse genootschappen* (Deventer 1988), vol. 1, p. 463, and cf. vol. 2, p. 115 n. 3.

9   Cf. Zwiep, "Jewish Enlightenment," pp. 223–24.

10   The *Werken van het Letteroefenend Genootschap Tot Nut en Beschaving*, vols. 1–3 (Amsterdam 1821, 1825 and 1831).

11   H.J. Matthes, *Redevoering over de zedelijke en godsdienstige beschaving beschouwd als den voortreffelijksten band van vereeniging der menschen* (Amsterdam 1821), esp. pp. 13–19, 24–26. See also immediately below.

the new Jewish devotees to this egalitarian ideal there was thus little need to articulate their Israelite particularity, however long and illustrious its pedigree.[12]

If this interpretation of civilization strikes us as idealistic but straightforward, we should not forget that in nineteenth-century Dutch usage *beschaving* had become a slightly more intricate concept. Not only do we encounter "civilization" as the unifying principle of all mankind, the term also connoted the process of sophistication that should lead *towards* that blissful state. Not only entire states and societies participated in this ongoing process of spiritual refinement, there was also such a thing as personal *beschaving*, a highly commendable property that combined manners and erudition and was located somewhere between the French concept of *politesse* and the German idea of *Bildung*.[13] Alongside these general applications, we also encounter references to a more narrowly-defined *zedelijke en godsdienstige beschaving*. In Dutch pedagogical texts of the period, this combination of "moral and religious civilization" was promoted as the backbone of all human and divine association and exchange. In the words of teacher-preacher Matthes, it constituted nothing less than a modern "holy covenant" between man, his fellow-men and God.[14] In Dutch enlightened compositions of the early nineteenth century, the concept of *beschaving* could thus be credited with personal *and* communal, horizontal as well as vertical dimensions.[15]

In the context of the late Dutch Enlightenment, this final "transcendent" aspect deserves further consideration. For if God as an abstract divine force was quite prominent in Dutch enlightened discourse, the rest of his heavenly as well as earthly entourage was not. In Matthes's *Address*, for example, hardcore Protestant ingredients such as faith, grace and the church are noticeably absent. His portrayal of God, too, never mentions the omniscient, loving Father of Christianity. In Matthes's anthropocentric ethics, God is presented as the alpha and omega of the universe[16] and as the abstract, impassionate medium through which all private ambitions (the famous *verum, bonum, pulchrum*

---

12   For a recent reconstruction of the late eighteenth-century Dutch political debate on radical egalitarianism, see M. Rutjes, *Door gelijkheid gegrepen. Democatie, burgerschap en staat in Nederland, 1795–1801* (Nijmegen 2012).

13   R.A.M. Aerts and W.E. Krul, "Van hoge beschaving tot brede cultuur, 1780–1940," in *Beschaving. Een geschiedenis van de begrippen hoofsheid, heusheid, beschaving en cultuur*, ed. P. den Boer (Amsterdam 2001), pp. 213–54, esp. 214–24.

14   Thus Matthes, *Redevoering*, p. 26.

15   This vertical, religious dimension stood in stark contrast to the exclusively *national* (and thus social-horizontal) approach to culture as adopted by the early *Wissenschaft des Judentums*, cf. the following section.

16   Matthes, *Redevoering*, p. 7.

of the nineteenth century) may be actualized.[17] In other enlightened texts, too, the confessional contents of religious civilization were phrased in such generic terms as to strike the modern reader as vaguely Christian at best. Needless to say, this mildly secularizing trait made it easier for Jewish intellectuals to join the Dutch enlightened endeavor. Significantly, the mission statements of both *Tot Nut en Beschaving* and *Tongeleth* emphasize a commitment to the ideal of *zedelijke verbetering en beschaving* (moral edification and civilization), but remain utterly silent on such Jewish concerns as Israelite religion, civic equality and emancipation. Consistent as this may seem, it does raise the question why Samuel Mulder (1793–1862), himself a member of the semi-neutral *Tot Nut* society, felt prompted to create its Hebrew namesake *Tongeleth*, whose Hebrew bias limited its membership and thus seemed to contradict the enlightened universalism that lay at its root.

The answer lies in the timing of Mulder's initiative. Together with his friend Moses Loonstein, he founded *Tongeleth* in the spring of 1815, just as the Kingdom of the Netherlands was beginning to take shape under William I of the Orange and Nassau dynasty. The new political order did not pose a threat to Jewish emancipation, nor did it demand greater stringency and devotion from the new king's Israelite subjects. It did, however, instigate a grand-scale *cultural* reorientation, when the hitherto divided provinces were gradually gathered into one distinctive *vaderland*. The spirit of enlightened ecumene that had characterized the Batavian Republic of course did not disappear, but from now on it was supplemented by new expressions of Dutch linguistic awareness, of national etiquette and shared custom. In the wake of these cultural revaluations, and in a similar vein, the recognizably Israelite *Tongeleth* society now complemented the passionately neutral *Tot Nut* confraternity. In 1815 the founding of *Tongeleth*, one might say, had been a very Dutch-national thing to do.

In an attempt at joining the latest developments, Mulder *cum suis* proposed to pursue the fashionable theme of *beschaving* through the study of hoary Hebrew sources.[18] Superseding Dutch and French as the language of civilized discourse, Hebrew thus served as a *cultural* marker. However, given the language's extensive track-record as the medium of Jewish religion and tradition, the result of *Tongeleth*'s activities inevitably turned out pious and conservative. One

---

17 Ibid., p. 11.
18 "[D]it Genootschap heeft ten doel de beoefening der Bijbeluitlegkunde, der Misne, des Talmuds en der Hebreeuwsche Taal- en Letterkunde in het bijzonder en ... zowel de bevordering van zeedelijke beschaving en veredeling van hart en geest," quoted in Maarssen, "Tongeleth," p. 391.

easily understands Jozeph Michman's oft-quoted intuition that the Dutch-Jewish Enlightenment was a "Haskalah, *but Orthodox*."[19] In the case of *Tongeleth*, however, that apparent Orthodoxy was perhaps more a consequence of the return to the Jewish sources than a deeper motive behind their rediscovery. Indeed one feels that, in 1815, Mulder had precious few alternatives. The German *Wissenschaft des Judentums* had yet to be invented and its—soon dominant—historicist conception of Jewish culture was still to be formulated. Accordingly, something as avant-garde as Dutch-Israelite civilization could not yet be expressed in the national-historical terms to which we have grown used today. Instead, it was cast in a linguistic Hebrew mold—with all the pious overtones that accompanied the ancient biblical and rabbinic legacies.

Summing up we may conclude that Mulder's *Tongeleth* was a logical "parallel successor" to Somerhausen's Tot Nut en Beschaving, which was only eight years its senior. In response to the newly kindled Dutch national spirit, *Tongeleth* catered for a budding sentiment of Israelite nationality, or rather, for the wish to offer a distinct Israelite contribution to Dutch nationality. Not yet equipped with the historical means that were soon developed to carry out the European cultural-nationalist agenda, its members relied on Hebrew for shaping that contribution, which as a result took on a markedly religious hue. As we have seen, this devout direction tied in neatly with the religious element in the contemporary Dutch conception of "civilization."

Yet, timely though they were, *Tongeleth*'s Hebrew forays into Jewish civilization proved but a transitory strategy. In the early 1820s, the Berlin *Wissenschaft des Judentums* developed a revolutionary, historicist rather than linguistic approach to Jewish identity that seems to have outclassed *Tongeleth*'s efforts almost immediately.[20] Within a decade, Leopold Zunz's *jüdische Philologie* had reached the Netherlands, where it was quickly, and not seldom unrecognizably, absorbed into existing modes of thought.[21] The result was a typically Dutch branch of *Wissenschaft* that was at once deceptively conservative and aptly innovative. Freely fusing historicist insights with Jewish tradition, the

---

19   Cf. the seminal chapter of that title in his 1995 *History of Dutch Jewry*, pp. 158–83 (emphasis mine).

20   Cf. above, fn. 2.

21   Witness especially Samuel Mulder's *Iets over de verdiensten van R. Salomo ben Izak, bij verkorting genaamd Ras'si als verklaarder van de Heilige Schrift en Talmudische werken en verbreider van Hebreeuwsche taal- en letterkunde* (1826), which was an (indeed highly idiosyncratic) adaptation-cum-plagiarization of Zunz's article on "Rabbi Salomon ben Isaac, genannt Raschi," ZWJ 1/2 (1822), pp. 277–384. A survey of other examples can be found in Zwiep, "The *Haskamah* of History, or: Why Did the Dutch *Wissenschaft des Judentums* Spurn Zunz's Early Writings," *European Journal of Jewish Studies* 7/2 (2013), pp. 131–50.

Dutch-Jewish intellectuals forged a conception of culture that was both deeply indebted to, and functionally different from the *Wissenschaft*'s academic take on the Jewish corpus. In the following sections we shall discuss a few testimonies on *Israëlitische godsdienstige beschaving* in the light of the *Wissenschaft*'s notion of an, only remotely religious, *Cultur der Juden*. This comparison will allow us to monitor the eclectic Dutch-Jewish use of the new scholarly sources, to better recognize the inconsistencies that came with that eclecticism, and perhaps even draw some preliminary conclusions regarding the nineteenth-century Dutch-Israelite perception of the delicate balance between nation, religion, and culture.

Beschaving/Cultur – The German Perspective

As we have seen, the founding of *Tongeleth* marks a shift in the Jewish understanding of civilization from the enlightened-universal to the (as yet only vaguely) ethnic or national, without ever relinquishing the vertical, religious orientation of Dutch *zedelijke beschaving*. By contrast, the definition of culture as employed by the founding fathers of the *Wissenschaft des Judentums* was explicitly national and emphatically horizontal, lacking almost all points of contact with the realm of the divine. Jewish culture, the German-Jewish historians conceded, had ultimately been inspired by an abstract *religiöse Idee*, a divine revelation that had been closely bound up with the enigmatic tetragram of the Bible.[22] All further expressions of that transcendent revelation, however, had been an exclusively human affair, together subsumed under the label "culture."

In Leopold Zunz's polemical debut *Etwas über die rabbinische Literatur* (1818), for example, we find *Cultur* defined as the interaction between the literature— a typically nineteenth-century term for *all* cultural manifestations—and the civic existence of a people.[23] This two-fold identification of *Cultur* as

---

22 "[I]n einer doppelten Gestaltung, einmal enthalten in historisch-litterarischen Documenten . . . zweitens, als noch lebendes Prinzip," I. Wolf, "Über den Begriff einer Wissenschaft des Judenthums," *ZWJ* 1/2 (1822), pp. 1–24, esp. pp. 1f.

23 Cf. *Etwas über die rabbinische Literatur*, p. 4, where Zunz wrote: "Nicht um einen Knäuel zu entwirren, an der geschicktere Finger sich versuchen mögen, sind wir von der Litteratur eines Volkes in seine Existenz abgeschweift. Wir kehren vielmehr, nach dem wir *beider Wechselwirkung aufeinander* mit einem Paar zügen gezeichnet" ("Not in order to dissolve a knot, which more adroit fingers should attempt [to unravel], did we veer from the literature of a nation into its existence. Instead we turn, having sketched *their respective influence on each other*"; emphasis mine). For an analysis of the concept's subsequent *Werdegang*, see I.E. Zwiep, "Scholarship of Literature and Life. Leopold Zunz and the

"literature and human experience" was ratified by Immanuel Wolf, who in the movement's first research agenda repeated that the abstract idea behind Judaism had revealed itself "in a two-fold sense, one preserved in historical literary documents . . . the other as a living principle."[24] Encompassing both the Jewish historical library *and* the everyday life of ordinary Jews, this conception of culture was thus both diachronic and synchronic. The diachronic part of culture could be accessed through national philology (*in casu* Zunz's *jüdische Philologie*); its synchronic counterpart was to be tackled with the help of *statistische Judenthumskunde*, i.e., through a set of sociological and demographical methods that remained to be developed.[25] Something as otherworldly as "the religious," we may conclude, inevitably fell beyond the scope of either realm or discipline.

One source for this conception of culture as an essentially human phenomenon can be found in the writings of the philosopher Moses Mendelssohn (1729–1786). In his famous essay on the nature and meaning of Enlightenment he was one of the first to venture a positioning of the word *Kultur* in the German lexicon:

> *Bildung* can be divided into culture and enlightenment. The former seems to evolve from the practical . . . enlightenment, by contrast, refers to the theoretical . . . Language acquires enlightenment through the sciences, and acquires culture through social engagement, poetry and eloquence.[26]

Here we encounter "*Kultur*" alongside "*Aufklärung*" as one of the two core ingredients of that other virtually untranslatable German concept: *Bildung*. Where

---

Invention of Jewish Culture," in *How the West Was Won. Essays on Literary Imagination, the Canon, and the Christian Middle Ages for Burcht Pranger*, ed. W. Otten, A. VanderJagt, H. de Vries (Leiden 2010), pp. 165–73.

24   Wolf, "Über den Begriff," pp. 15–18.
25   In the closing section of the *Zeitschrift*, Leopold Zunz punctually provided a set of methodological "Grundlinien zu einer künftigen Statistik der Juden" (pp. 523–32), which was not picked up by following generations of Jewish historians.
26   "Bildung zerfällt in Kultur und Aufklärung. Jene scheint mehr aus das Praktische zu gehen . . . Aufklärung hingegen scheinet sich mehr auf das Theoretische zu beziehen . . . Eine Sprache erlanget Aufklärung durch die Wissenschaften, und erlanget Kultur durch gesellschaftlichen Umgang, Poesie und Beredtsamkeit." "Über die Frage: was heißt Aufklären?" *Berlinische Monatsschrift* 4 (1784), pp. 193–200; the passage is quoted from *Was ist Aufklärung? Beiträge aus der Berlinischen Monatsschrift*, ed. N. Hinske (Darmstadt 1977), pp. 445–46 (emphasis mine).

Aufklärung was primarily associated with theoretical enquiry, *Kultur* seems to have had more everyday practical implications. In human traffic, Mendelssohn argued, *Aufklärung* expressed itself in the sciences. Being slightly more prosaic, *Kultur* would realize itself through human communication and social exchange, with poetry and eloquence as its two most sublime manifestations. "Social engagement, poetry and eloquence," reading these words through the eyes of his later Berlin interpreters, one might say that for Mendelssohn too, culture came close to the sum of *Literatur und Bürgerleben*,[27] i.e., of "literature and human, civic, life."

Unlike Mendelssohn, who had defined culture in general *social* terms, Zunz by 1818 had learned to partition society into various different *nations*. In doing so he followed Johann Gottfried Herder (1744–1803), who in his *Ideen zur Philosophie der Geschichte der Menschheit* (1784–1791) had introduced and defended the nation as a category for classifying human collectives, their ways and customs.[28] Within the universal pool of civilization, each nation distinguished itself by a shared indigenous culture, which more often than not was expressed in a common tongue. Language thus became the key to all historical interpretation, just as literature became the object of almost every historical study. The divine and the natural, those two other worlds which every human being occasionally touches upon, constituted two additional realms, to be traveled via different routes. Untouched by the *Kritik* and *Interpretation* of national philology, the human involvement in nature was classified by Zunz as technology, commerce, industry, and art. The human understanding of God and his creation was articulated, he added, in such genres as theology, halakhah and ethics and, in the case of God's creation, through a broad range of natural sciences.[29]

Thus we find that, in stark contrast to its Dutch equivalent, the early *Wissenschaft*'s definition of Jewish culture was strictly national and lacking a personal religious dimension. Of course this did not stop Jewish scholars in the Kingdom of the Netherlands from adopting the *Wissenschaft*'s historicist perspective on Judaism as a collective cultural legacy. Simultaneously, however, they put great stress on the immediate, everyday importance of that legacy for individual piety and devotion.[30] Contrary to the critical *Wissenschaft*, they

---

27   *Sic* Wolf, "Über den Begriff," p. 23.

28   See, e.g., F.M. Barnard, *Herder on Nationality, Humanity and History* (Toronto 2003).

29   *Etwas über die rabbinische Literatur*, pp. 16–20.

30   As such, *godsdienstige beschaving* was an obvious conflation of Dutch-French *beschaving* and German *Kultur*. In Germany an interesting, if politically rather remote, parallel can be found in the thought of Friedrich Julius Stahl (1802–1861). In his *Der christliche Staat und sein Verhältniß zu Deismus und Judentum* (Berlin 1847), this spokesman of German

never openly questioned the Jewish religious past. In their writings, moral edification always got the better of *Kritik und Interpretation*, the alpha and omega
of Jewish-national philology. Historical scrutiny served to sanction, not to re-
consider the time-honored traditions and customs.[31] Needless to say, the fact
that Zunz's Dutch readers had never received any training in academic philology only strengthened this edifying turn, as did the fact that they were working
from rather than *towards* political emancipation.

Three "Dutch" Approaches to Israelite Civilization

In 1815, Samuel Mulder had relied on Hebrew as the cornerstone of his hyphen-
ated Dutch-Israelite identity. From the 1830s down to the Interbellum, a group
of teachers, rabbis, journalists and dilettante scholars chose to ground that
identity in the "holy trinity" of *godsdienst-letterkunde-geschiedenis* (religion,
literature and history). Unlike early modern authors, they approached these
Jewish foundations with a healthy dose of historicism; unlike the exponents
of the German *Wissenschaft*, however, they never allowed the deconstructive
force of modern *Kritik* to nibble away at Judaism's theological basis. When
asked whether there was such a thing as a *Wissenschaft des Judentums* in the
Netherlands, I guess the answer would be a cautious "yes." At times it may have
looked precious little like the German original, but in its own, pious and intro-
verted way it was just as innovative and effective, given the particular Dutch
circumstances.

In "The Haskamah of History," I have explored the interplay between traditional ethics and historicism in Dutch-Jewish edifying literature of the 1840s
and 50s.[32] In the present section, we shall approach the issue from a slightly
different, more conceptual angle, by looking at the representation of *beschaving* in three Jewish texts from the period. The first, the *Hartelijk woord*
that Abraham van Lee wrote "to all [his] fellow-Israelites" in 1841, was an attempt at civilizing Israelite religious practice, to help it conform to what was

---

conservatism (who had converted from Judaism at the age of 17) likewise defined Judaism
as both a *religiöse* and a *nationale Gemeinschaft*. In Stahl's conception of Jewish nationalism, however, territoriality, though essentially eschatological, played a much more prominent role than in Dutch-Jewish discourse; cf. D. Avraham, "Nationalism and Judaism in
the Conservative Thought of Friedrich Julius Stahl," *Zion* 77/2 (2012), pp. 67–94 [Hebrew].

31   Cf. I. Schorsch, *From Text to Context. The Turn to History in Modern Judaism* (Hanover, NH
1994), who identified the debunking of traditional myth as a prominent marker of the
early German *Wissenschaft*'s scholarly ethos (esp. Chapters 8 and 9).

32   "The Haskamah of History," see above, fn. 21.

considered bon ton in the Dutch public sphere. The other two publications
were adaptations of German-Jewish classics, a genre that took up quite some
space on the mid nineteenth-century Dutch Jewish bookshelf. In both cases,
the German authors had relied on conceptions of Jewish religion and culture
that differed, to varying degrees, from the Dutch notion of *Israëlitische godsdienstige beschaving* and its importance for Jewish life and continuity. In either
case, this raises the question as to how their Dutch adaptors read the German
sources, and whether they recognized the at times awkward tensions that
emerged from their eclectic readings.

(a)   *Religious Civilization Equals Civilized Religion: Van Lee's* Hartelijk
       woord aan alle mijne mede-Israëliten zonder onderscheid ter
       overdenking toegevoegd (1841)
Van Lee's *Cordial Address* to his fellow Israelites had been triggered by the attempts of Hartog J. Hertzveld (1781–1846), chief rabbi of Zwolle, to initiate a
"verbetering van de openbare godsdienstoefening," a revision of the religious
service in the Dutch synagogues. Where the other rabbis had rejected Hertzveld's plans, journalist and newspaper editor Abraham van Lee (1804–1869)
heartily concurred, claiming that to reach "een bekoorlijke trap van godsdi-
enst-beschaving" (a graceful degree of civilized religion) had become an urgent desideratum.[33] In support of Rabbi Hertzveld, he even indulged in some
straightforward body politic, dismissing traditional religious practice as "illness and rot," and recommending the Rabbi's suggestions at improvement as
cures, remedies and, significantly, palliative medicine. Among these indeed
rather standard palliatives were the weekly sermon in Dutch ("de schoone
moedertaal"), the appointment of knowledgeable *hazanim*, the confirmation
of boys and girls and the purging of the liturgy from the "horrendous and in-
comprehensible" medieval *piyyutim*, which the "new, admirable critical theological literature" of the *Wissenschaft des Judentums* had exposed as "weirdly
fantastic."[34]

    Needless to say, Van Lee's concern for decorum reflects similar preoccupa-
tions within the German-Jewish Reform—which, it should be added, never
developed a Dutch equivalent prior to the twentieth century. Simultaneously,
however, his preoccupation with a civilized liturgy was indebted to the French
notion of *politesse* as well as to the *verligte godsvrucht*, the well-informed piety

33   *Hartelijk woord*, p. 6, fn. *, in reference to the report in *Algemeen Handelsblad* no. 3103,
      18 October 1841.
34   *Hartelijk woord*, p. 19. On this final point, Van Lee anticipated Abraham Alexander Wollf's
      Die Stimmen der ältesten glaubwürdigsten Rabbinen über die Pijutim (Leipzig 1857).

that featured so prominently in contemporary enlightened Dutch *beschaving*.[35] In combination, these supplementary notions of civilization led to an—in the Dutch context at least—unprecedented rejection of traditional Jewish form and content, justified by the historical verdict of what Van Lee characteristically labeled the "critical *theological* literature" of the German *Wissenschaft*.

In Van Lee's *Address*, as in other related texts on the topic, *godsdienstige beschaving* equaled *godsdienstbeschaving* (with the German term "Gottesdienst," i.e., religious service looming large in the background). Religious civilization thus became synonymous to "civilizing religion," especially in the semi-public domain of the synagogue, where religious custom was felt to interfere with modern decorum and enlightened devotion. As we have seen in the quotations from Matthes, the latter were essential ingredients of contemporary Dutch Christian discourse; simultaneously, via Prussian-born Hertzveld there can be little doubt of additional German inspiration. Our next example was an even more straightforward adaptation from the German: Izaak Jacob Lion and Moses Mijers's Dutch translation of Isaac Jost's *Allgemeine Geschichte des jüdischen Volkes*, written between 1820 and 1829. Even when recast in moderate Dutch terms, Jost's radical critique of rabbinic Judaism was of a much more fundamental nature than Van Lee's bourgeois renunciation of ancient ritual, and had much more severe implications for Jewish religion and culture. In the following section we shall try to imagine how his iconoclastic message was met by the Dutch-Jewish audience, whose Israelite identity was beginning to be shaped by Jewish history, but who may not have been fully equipped to grasp the ideological potential of historiography.

(b) *Jews without Religion and Culture? Mijers and Lion's* Algemeene geschiedenis (1842–43)

According to Leopold Zunz, Isaac Jost's comprehensive *General History of the Jewish People* had been written way ahead of its time. Completed in 1829, it could only anticipate, not build on the groundbreaking results Zunz expected his critical *Wissenschaft* to yield. However, through a careful reading of Jost's *magnum opus* Ismar Schorsch has shown that, rather than anticipating the outcome of *Wissenschaft* research, Jost's narrative in fact questioned its fundamental premises.[36] In opposition to Zunz's romantic cultural-nationalist paradigm, the enlightened rationalist Jost chose to follow an older model, which stressed the universal political dimensions of history at the cost of national

---

35   See above, pp. 252 and 254 of this article.
36   I. Schorsch, "From Wolfenbüttel to *Wissenschaft*. The Divergent Paths of Isaak Markus Jost and Leopold Zunz," *LBI Yearbook* 22 (1977), pp. 109–28.

culture and religion (which in his view were closely intertwined). One is almost tempted to think that Jost felt so little affinity with the Jewish past precisely *because* it seemed to coincide with the hey-day of religious, rabbinic
Judaism. In contemporary *Wissenschaft* theory, the rabbinic movement was
believed to have safeguarded the Jewish *Geist* and legacy after the destruction
of the Temple. In Jost's paradigm, however, there was no redeeming role for the
rabbis, whose teachings he considered irrelevant for the modern Jew. "One volume of Goethe contains more reason and learning than three hundred folios
of Talmud," he would write, twenty years later, in a letter to his life-long friend
Samuel Ehrenberg.[37]

It was of course no coincidence that in this quotation the Spinozist Jost
chose the Spinozist Goethe to outmanoeuvre Talmudic wisdom. The *Allgemeine Geschichte*, too, resonated with Spinoza's radical critique of religion. It was
no accident, for example, that Jost began his survey with the Maccabean revolt
and surge for power in Seleucid Palestine. For him (as for Spinoza), the true
turning point in Jewish history had not been 70 CE but 586 BCE, when exile to
Babylon had brought an end to the Jewish state, the Mosaic political program
and the chosenness of the Jewish people.[38] The Maccabean reign between
167 and 63 BCE was but a brief revival of Jewish sovereignty, a minor bleep
on the radar of Jewish nationalism. Still, for Jost, it constituted a much more
congenial starting point than the birth of rabbinic, spiritual-religious Judaism.
Equally obvious was his choice to conclude the survey in the year 1815, when
the European balance of powers had been decided and history, certainly Jewish history, seemed to have come to an end. Continuing this line of reasoning
into the future, the messianic era was quickly reduced to a political metaphor.
For Jost, the Coming of the Messiah, that all-time Jewish utopia, was little more
than an allegory for achieving full assimilation into the German here and now.

In 1829, Jost's *Allgemeine Geschichte* had not only anticipated the results
of Leopold Zunz's historical forays into Jewish culture, but also the much
later call, ascribed to Moritz Steinschneider, to "decently bury the remains"
of that culture.[39] In Steinschneider's late nineteenth-century view, the

37   Ibid., p. 121.
38   *Tractatus Theologico-Politicus*, Ch. 3; cf. also Schorsch, "From Wolfenbüttel to
      Wissenschaft," p. 117.
39   "Wir haben nur noch die Aufgabe die Überreste des Judentums ehrenvoll zu bestat-
      ten," quoted in M.A. Meyer, "Jüdische Wissenschaft und jüdische Identität," in *Wissen-
      schaft des Judentums. Die Anfänge der Judaistik in Europa*, ed. J. Carlebach (Darmstadt
      1992), p. 15. N.B., Steinschneider's own conception of *Kultur* was emphatically free of po-
      litical overtones, witness his definition in *Allgemeine Einleitung in die jüdische Literatur
      des Mittelalters* (Berlin 1901), pp. 10f.: "Die Kultur is die Thätigkeit des Geistes selbst . . .

cultivation of national cultures undermined true cosmopolitanism; in Jost's early nineteenth-century prefiguration, it got in the way of beneficial, enlightened universalism.

The radicalism of Jost's message makes one wonder how it was received by his more temperate Dutch readers, who by 1842 could buy Izaak Lion and Moses Mijers's heavily annotated translation, the *Algemeene Geschiedenis des Israëlitischen Volks*.[40] We do know that Jost's ideas were uncomfortably far removed from contemporary Christian expectations *vis-à-vis* the Jews' role in history. Witness, for example, the anonymous review that was published in the *Vaderlandsche Letteroefeningen* two years after the translation's appearance.[41] The Protestant reviewer heartily disapproved of the authors' (*sic*) choice to write (*sic*) a political, not a religious, history of the Jews. He renounced their explicit "anti-theological stance," their debunking of divine miracles, and frequent anti-Christian polemics. Religious teacher Mijers, who had been responsible for the translation from the German, was even accused of "arid Deism" (*droog Deïsme*). His mistaking the Coming of the Messiah for Jewish assimilation was considered an improper negation of Christian theology, "for the Rationalist, the continued existence of the Jewish people is but an anachronism," the reviewer rightly concluded. This may have held true for arch-rationalist Jost, but I must confess that I am less sure about Jost's Dutch editors. Eager to supply the Dutch audience with a comprehensive history of the Jews, were they entirely aware of, and ready to endorse, the radical message they had just translated into their new mother tongue?

The controversial journalist Izaak Jacob Lion (1821–1873), who annotated the text and wrote the general preface to the first volume, indeed seems to have embraced Jost's negation of Jewish religion and its civic and cultural implications.[42] In fact, he appears eager to see them exploited. In several passages

Kulturgeschichte is das eigentliche Ziel der Weltgeschichte . . . Die Geschichte ist nicht philosophischer Schematismus (Hegel) oder politischer Pragmatismus" (Culture is the activity of the spirit itself . . . cultural history the true aim of world history . . . History is not philosophical *Schematismus* (Hegel) or political pragmatism).

40   *Algemeene Geschiedenis des Israëlitischen Volks, uit het Hoogduits vertaald door M. Mijers onder toezigt en medewerking van, met eene voorrede, aanteekeningen en chronologische tafelen voorzien door Iz. J. Lion* (Leeuwarden 1842).

41   *Vaderlandsche Letteroefeningen* (1844), pp. 642–47.

42   On Lion, who became associated with the Dutch daily press and frequented conservative government circles, see *Nieuw Nederlandsch Biografisch Woordenboek* 5, ed. Molhuysen and Blok (1921); R. Vos, "Izaak Jacob Lion (1821–1873), een omstreden joods journalist," *Misjpoge* 17/1 (2004), pp. 1–9, and idem, "Clamorous, Controversial, Competent. Izaak Jacob Lion: Journalist, Mediator in Politics, and 'Politician', 1853–1873," in *Mediatization*

he extolled the original author's "national and religious impartiality,"[43] claiming that history should always "be completely divorced from religion."[44] He confessed that the book's primary addressees were not his fellow-Israelites but the general Dutch audience, to whom he offered his work "as proof of the [Jews'] profound love of their fellow-countrymen *and their civilization*."[45] Judging by the *Wortlaut* of these and other passages, we may conclude that Lion envisaged a Jewish past, present and future divorced from religion and infused with modern European culture. The ideal was perhaps a trifle too novel for his Christian readership, who continued to pose religious demands.[46] Yet ironically, in the hands of Isaac Jost and Izaak Lion, Jewish historiography proved the perfect medium for expressing precisely the opposite *political* agenda.

The case of translator Moses Mijers is slightly more complex. If anything, it suggests that by the 1840s historiography could serve multiple Jewish agendas. Unfortunately for us, translator Mijers executed his task in humble silence. The only testimony on his participation is given by co-editor Lion who mentions that, true to contemporary translation theory, his colleague had produced a faithfully literal translation. Though bent on reproducing the German author's original ideas, he had tried to avoid all ugly Germanisms, Lion assures us.[47] Circumstantial evidence, however, suggests that religious teacher Mijers, of whom otherwise little is known, was a staunch champion of religion. In 1833, he had published a *Godsdienstig en zedekundig handboek gegrond op de Bijbelse geschiedenis* (Religious and Moral Handbook Grounded in Biblical History), at the request of the Hoofdcommissie tot Zaken der Israëlieten in Nederland. It had turned out an impressively bulky manual, intended to fill a gap in the curriculum of the more advanced Israelite pupils. Essentially a translation of Herz Homberg's *Bene Zion, ein religiös-moralisches Lehrbuch* (1812), it merged maskilic ethics with directions for a modern Jewish civic identity.[48] As Mijers acknowledged in his preface to the *Handboek*, the spirit of Homberg's teacher

---

of Politics in History. Groningen Studies in Cultural Change 35, ed. H. Wijfjes and G. Voerman, (Louvain 2009), pp. 137–50.

43 *Algemeene geschiedenis*, p. v; also pp. viii–ix, where Lion stated that the "history [of the Jews] should be both philosophical and impartial . . . The great Jost, putting aside all love for his people . . . has proven that one can be judge of one's own history."

44 Ibid., p. xv.

45 Ibid., p. x, italics mine.

46 Cf. the anonymous review in the *Vaderlandsche Letteroefeningen* of 1844, above, p. 263.

47 *Algemeene Geschiedenis*, p. xi.

48 On Homberg, see most recently D. Sadowski, *Haskala und Lebenswelt. Herz Homberg und die jüdischen Deutschen Schulen in Galizien 1782–1806* (Göttingen 2010).

Mendelssohn still hovered over his attempt at enlightening the Israelite youth and helping them become modern Dutch citizens.[49]

As I have indicated above, soon after the publication of the *Handboek* in 1833 maskilic modes of education were superseded by a new paradigm that used historical narrative as an additional means of Dutch-Israelite edification. This edifying trend was founded in 1836, when Samuel Mulder published a short *Chronological Handbook for the History of the Israelites*, in an attempt at fortify-ing the "newly aroused spirit of *Israelite religious civilization*."[50] Though claim-ing original historianship, Mulder had mainly relied on Jost, to whose book he kept referring as a *Geschichte der Juden*. As on other occasions, he had freely revised Jost's more controversial findings with the help of traditional authori-ties that ranged from Rashi to the recent Dutch Van der Palm Bijbel, translated and annotated by Johannes Henricus van der Palm (1763–1840) to replace the outdated Staten Bible. Likewise, Mulder had tacitly "corrected" Jost's Spinozist periodizations, in order to prolong the Jewish national era from the creation of the world to the destruction of the Temple in the year 70 CE. This correction was in neat accordance with mainstream *Wissenschaft* historiography and be-came the standard for all Dutch-Jewish historians, with the obvious exception of Lion and Mijers in 1842.

Mulder's pioneering reliance on Jost and Van der Palm proved him an early adaptor to nineteenth-century historicism. His *Chronologisch Handboek* was soon followed, however, by a veritable outburst of edifying Jewish historiogra-phy in Dutch.[51] Given his track-record as a *godsdienstonderwijzer*, one might assume that Moses Mijers viewed his translation of Jost's *Geschichte* as part of

---

49   Mijers, "Voorberigt," pp. i, vi.

50   S.I. Mulder, *Chronologisch handboekje voor de Geschiedenis der Israëliten, van de schepping der wereld tot op onzen tijd* (Amsterdam 1836), *Voorrede*, unpaginated (italics mine).

51   Following Lion and Mijers's *Algemeene geschiedenis* (1842), we encounter S. Keijzer's *Reize van Benj. van Tudela in 1160–1173 door Europa, Azië en Afrika* (Leiden 1846); I. Waterman's *Tijdrekenkundige tafel voor de geschiedenis der Israëliten, van de vroegste tijden tot op onze dagen, in zeventig lessen* (Kampen 1849); L. Borstel's *Schets van de algemeene geschiedenis der Israëliten en die der Nederlandse Israëliten* (*van den vroegsten tot den tegenwoordigen tijd*) (1853, see below); and G.I. Polak and L. Goudsmit Azn., *Seërith Jisrael of lotgevallen der Joden in alle werelddeelen van af de verwoesting des Tweeden Tempels tot het jaar 1770* (Amsterdam 1855). In Christian circles we find the prize-winning monograph *Geschie-denis der Joden in Nederland* (Utrecht 1843), written by Hendrik Jakob Koenen (possibly in collaboration with Samuel Mulder, see J. Meijer, *H.J. Koenen/Geschiedenis der Joden in Nederland 1843. Historiografische analyse* [Heemstede 1982]), and I. da Costa's messianic *Israel en de Volken* (Utrecht 1848; Eng. translation 1850, German translation 1855). Signifi-cantly, this *hausse* of historical surveys subsides after 1860.

this collective attempt at spreading Israelite *godsdienstige beschaving*, which by the 1840s had become as much an individual, enlightened ideal as a collective historical legacy. This would imply that Mijers had joined Lion's enterprise with a different audience in mind, writing not for his Dutch compatriots but for an Israelite readership eager to bolster their new "religious civilization" with historical knowledge. It also raises the question whether Mijers had recognized the radical message of Jost's *Allgemeine Geschichte*, to which he may have resorted for want of other comprehensive surveys. Are we right in surmising that, in this early stage of Dutch-Jewish historicism, Mijers was not yet equipped to distil the politics of history from amidst the wealth of chronological data? Is that what happens at the interface of paradigms? Or, having grown sadder and wiser, had he perhaps changed his mind on which road to follow to Jewish emancipation, and accordingly embraced Jost's radical political program?

(c)   *Leman Borstel on History, Religion (and Nation)*

Of all early Dutch-Jewish historians, Leman Borstel (1827–1911) strikes us as the most erudite by far.[52] Already before 1855, when he and his colleagues could (and did) join Ludwig Philippson's Institut zur Förderung der israelitischen Literatur, Borstel's work reveals a striking acquaintance with *Wissenschaft* research. No doubt he had benefited much from the library of Doktor-Rabbiner Joseph Isaacsohn (1815–1885), who in 1850 had been appointed chief rabbi of Rotterdam, where Borstal acted as communal secretary.[53] Borstel's annotated Dutch translation of Jedaiah ha-Penini's *Bechinat Olam* (1855), for example, reveals equal acquaintance with traditional rabbinic sources and contemporary *Wissenschaft* studies.[54] When reading the latter, Borstel of course could not escape their cultural-nationalist rhetoric, some of which he (subconsciously?) reproduced in his own work. Thus we find that the preface to his historical

---

52   Concise bibliographical information on Borstel is found in J.G. Frederiks and F. Jos. van den Branden, *Biografisch woordenboek der Noord- en Zuidnederlandsche letterkunde* (Amsterdam 1888–1891), and D. Hausdorff, *Jizkor. Platenatlas van drie en een halve eeuw geschiedenis van de joodse gemeente in Rotterdam van 1610–1960* (Baarn 1968), 134f.

53   I thank Bart Wallet for the suggestion.

54   *Bespiegelingen over de wereld, van den wijsgeer en dichter Jedaja ha-Penini ben Rab. Avraham Bedersi in 't Nederduitsch vertaald, met aanteekeningen en eene inleiding voorzien door L. Borstel* (The Hague 5615–1855). In the annotations, Borstel referred to recent studies by Zunz, Munk, Luzzatto, Dukes, Jost, Frankel, Fürst and Wiener, alongside the usual Christian classics by De Rossi, Wolf, Michaelis and Delitzsch.

Schets of 1853 features both the customary Dutch ideal of a personal-collective religious civilization *and* the German notion of a Jewish *Kulturnation*. In 1853, i.e., half-way between the 1795 Emancipation Decree and the rise of territorial Zionism, Jewish nationality was somewhat of an anomaly in Dutch-Israelite discourse—enough of an anomaly, at least, to take a closer look at Borstel's conception of civilization and its sources.

Borstel's *Schets van de algemeene geschiedenis der Israëliten en die der Nederlandse Israëliten* was written in response to an essay-contest instigated by the Maatschappij tot Nut van de Israëlieten in Nederland, a society founded in 1849 to "promote morality, virtue *and civilization* among the Israelites in the Netherlands."[55] In the spirit of the times, the Maatschappij hoped to advance that civilization through historical literature, preferably via a popular exposé (*volksleesboek*) or a specialist school manual. No less stylishly, Borstel responded to the challenge by writing an historical introduction that addressed both audiences in one go. As his point of departure he chose Moses Elkan's *Leitfaden beim Unterricht in der Geschichte der Israeliten* (1850³), which he supplemented with his own readings of the Old Testament, rabbinic literature, the apocrypha, Josephus, and more recent historical authors, including Samuel Mulder. The result, he hoped, would satisfy not only Jewish teachers and *Israëlitische huisgezinnen*, but also an adult Christian readership fascinated by Jewish religion and culture.

Ever the enlightened educator, Borstel began his *Schets* by explaining the functional relationship between history and religion—no doubt, a novel combination for many of his readers. He assured them that learning about the past would bring them greater knowledge, and thus a better understanding, of religion. In the case of their own religion, it would provoke a more rational, and thus more sincere gratitude towards God. Where it touched upon other religions, it was bound to inspire greater tolerance among men.[56] Within this context, the memory of Judaism as a grossly undervalued nation almost naturally entered Borstel's text. He expressed the hope that knowledge of Judaism would also help to "arouse love for *a nation* venerable because of its antiquity, honorable because of its teachings, institutions and fate, and *important for all humanity* because of its impact in past *and present*."[57] On reading these lines,

---

55   "[D]e bevordering van goede zeden, deugd *en beschaving* onder Israëlieten in Nederland, alles overeenkomstig den Israëlitischen *godsdienst*" (italics mine).

56   *Schets van de algemeene geschiedenis der Israëliten en die der Nederlandse Israëliten* (*voor en tijdens hun volksbestaan*) (The Hague 1853), p. xx.

57   "[O]pwekken liefde voor *een volk*, eerwaardig door zijne oudheid, belangrijk door zijne leer, instellingen en lotgevallen, *gewigtig voor gansch het menschdom*, door den invloed

which resound with the romantic-nationalist apologetics of the *Wissenschaft des Judentums*, the Christian reader may well have nodded approvingly: with or without emancipation, the Jewish nation continued to play an important role in the Christian *Heilsgeschichte*. Borstel's Israelite fellow-reader, however, will have interpreted them as a reference not to the present but to the past; a past that had ended in the year 70 CE when, according to most historians, the Jewish national existence (*volksbestaan*, in Borstel's words) had come to an end. For while in Germany Heinrich Graetz had reintroduced Jewish politics as early as 1846, the dominant horizon of Dutch Jewry remained staunchly Dutch. In the early 1850s, Dutch-Israelite culture was still framed in purely religious terms, and would remain so for decades to come.

Concluding Remarks

In the Low Countries where, in 1795, the corporate nation had been dissolved in a spirit of enlightened universalism, Jewish nationality had lost its political urgency. When, after 1815, it became opportune to express a modest degree of ethnic difference, it was first the Hebrew language (as cultivated in the Hebrew *Tongeleth* society), followed by *religious civilization* that was chosen to distinguish Dutch Jews from their Christian neighbors. Jewish nationality, however, was never proposed as a distinguishing trait. Thus we may conclude that in our final example, i.e., in Leman Borstel's exposé on the blessings of Jewish history, praise of the Jewish *Kulturnation* was an accidental Germanism, inspired by the author's exhaustive readings of Zunz, Fürst and Frankel. Yet, by the same token, it's almost natural appearance suggests that at the interface of paradigms, the term civilization had become somewhat of a floating signifier, an empty yet meaningful term whose reference wavered between personal religious sentiment and shared "secular" culture, depending on the eyes (and erudition) of the beholder.[58]

---

die het . . . op het wereldtooneel heeft uitgeoefend *en nog aanhoudend blijft uitoefenen*"; ibid. (italics mine).

58   Cf. Chief Rabbi Berenstein's (1808–1893) approbation of the *Schets* which, hardly surprising, represents a more narrow religious conception of *godsdienstige beschaving*. Having tested its contents "against the principles of our religious doctrines," Berenstein was convinced that Borstel's book would strengthen the Israelite religion by "enhancing our knowledge, and hence our devotion and loyalty to the beliefs of our fathers," ibid. (unpaginated).

Seamlessly fusing French classicist, Dutch enlightened and romantic German-Jewish connotations, the term *Israëlitische godsdienstige beschaving* served to express both the private, individual and public, collective implications of Jewish existence in the young Dutch nation state.[59] It arose in the mid 1830s and within less than ten years became a household concept. In the wake of such later developments as mass secularization and changing conceptions of nationality and belonging, the original bond between religion and culture inevitably loosened, while the ties between culture and nation were strengthened. In the first half of the century, however, when the scope and content of modern Jewish identity were first defined, the multiple dimensions of religious civilization provided the right margins for experimenting with the Israelite share in Dutch civil society, whether in Hebrew (as advocated by the short-lived *Tongeleth*), or via the Jewish past, as revived by subsequent generations of Dutch-Israelite historians.

---

59   Compare, *mutatis mutandis*, J. Casanova, "Private and Public Religions," *Social Research* 59/1 (1992), pp. 17–57, and idem, *Public Religions in the Modern World* (Chicago 1994), Part I, pp. 1–2.

CHAPTER 12

"Religiosity" in Dutch Jewish Art in the Nineteenth and the Early Twentieth Century

Rivka Weiss-Blok

Religiosity is an elusive term when pertaining to art. In order to give it a firmer grounding in this essay, I will deal with two particular aspects: religious subject matter in works by Dutch Jewish artists and the manner in which audiences, critics and writers, Jewish and Christian, revealed, defined and discussed "religiosity" in Dutch Jewish art.[1]

The beginning of the nineteenth century in Holland saw a revival within Protestantism, with movements such as the Reveil proposing a deepening of religious experience. Among its founders was the converted Jew, Dr. Abraham Capadose (1795–1874), and following in his footsteps was another converted Jew, the poet Isaac da Costa (1798–1874). The tone used for discussions of Jewish art was influenced by this spiritual revival. Criticism and appreciation was voiced, of course, also by Catholics, especially after the restoration of the Catholic hierarchy in 1850.

The Jewish Artists and Tradition

Most Jewish artists, though perhaps not observant themselves, grew up in homes where Jewish tradition was upheld. They knew some Hebrew or could at least read the prayers. Jewish rituals at home and in the synagogue were part of their cultural heritage. The majority still maintained ties with the Jewish community and some kept a few religious rules. Thus, we know that Jozef

---

1 I wish to express my gratitude for the assistance I received from the following people and institutions. I am thankful for the advice they gave me, and their assistance in obtaining material for the writing of this article and permission to use images from their collections: Charles Dumas, Netherlandish Institute for Art History, Rijksbureau voor Kunsthistorische Documentatie (RKD), The Hague; Joel Cahen, Jelka Kroeger, Anton Kras, Jewish Historical Museum, Amsterdam; Prof. Yosef Kaplan, The Hebrew University of Jerusalem; Ahuva Israel, Ruth Feldmann, Tel Aviv Museum of Art, Tel Aviv; Margaret Nab, Kroeller-Mueller Museum, Otterlo; Anke Riesenkamp, Van Gogh Museum, Amsterdam; Willy Lindwer, Jerusalem.

© KONINKLIJKE BRILL NV, LEIDEN, 2017 | DOI 10.1163/9789004343160_013

Israels never painted on the Sabbath, honoring a promise he had made to his father. The sculptor Mendes da Costa, son of a monument cutter, also refrained from work on the Sabbath. It is worth noting that in all of Meijer de Haan's self-portraits as well as in portraits of him by others he is depicted wearing some kind of head covering, leaving us to wonder whether this was for religious reasons.

Traditional ties to Judaism influenced the artists' choice of typical Jewish themes: rabbis learning, Jewish rituals, synagogue interiors, people praying, Jewish historical figures and biblical scenes. Even the subjects, such as homes for the aged, may be considered typically Jewish ones that emphasized Jewish welfare and caring for the elderly. We may assume that the artists considered these subjects romantic, and in the eyes of potential buyers and the general public they may have been viewed as mysterious and exotic.

The artists included in this research are Maurits Leon (1838–1865), a talented and promising artist who died at the young age of twenty-seven; Jacob Meijer de Haan (1852–1895), whose family owned a cracker and *matzo* factory in Amsterdam; Jozef Israels (1824–1911), one of the most prominent Dutch artists of his time; the reviver of Dutch sculpture Joseph Mendes da Costa (1863–1939); Eduard Frankfort (1864–1920); and Joseph Jacob Isaacson (1859–1942), murdered in Auschwitz at the age of eighty-three. Two non-Jewish artists will be discussed as well, Jan Voerman (1857–1941), known mainly as the landscape painter of the IJsel and for his cloud studies, and Vincent Van Gogh (1853–1890).

Not all Jewish artists who fulfilled the criteria for this study are included, and likewise, not every Jewish artist necessarily fit the criteria set out here. For example, the talented artist Isaac Israels (1863–1934), son of Jozef Israels, though known to have painted portraits of prominent Jewish figures of his time, such as the first female physician Aletta Jacobs (1854–1929) and the Zionist banker Nehemia de Lime (1882–1940), had no interest in Jewish subject matter. David Bles (1821–1899), a respected artist of his day, known for his middle-class anecdotal genre scenes that earned him the title "*maître du plesier*" or "The Dutch Hogarth," proffered no Jewish message in his art. Moreover, he did not think much of deep religious contexts. An anecdote attributed to Jozef Israels reveals Bles's thoughts about art: "[Israels] described how honored he felt when, as a promising artist, he was permitted to walk round an exhibition arm in arm with Bles . . . who . . . told him pretty frankly that he did not understand the so-called poetry in Israels's painting, and that, for the rest he had never understood what poetry and painting had in common."[2]

---

2 H.G. Marius, *Dutch Art in the Nineteenth Century* (Philadelphia/London 1909), p. 72.

Maurits Leon – Synagogue Scenes

While living in Amsterdam in 1862–3, Maurits Leon came under the spell of the historic Jewish quarter there. His *Preparations for the Priestly Blessing* also known as *The Washing of the Hands*, takes place in the synagogue, before the priestly blessing over the congregation (Figure 12.1), when the Levites wash the hands of the *kohanim* in a ceremony commemorating the ritual performed in the ancient Temple in Jerusalem.[3]

The work is related to a long poem of the same theme by the poet Estella Dorothea Salomea Hijmans-Hertzveld (1837–1881), also from The Hague.[4] It is not clear whether her inspiration for the poem came from Maurits Leon's painting, or, what seems more probable, that Leon was inspired by her poem,

FIGURE 12.1
Maurits Leon, Washing of the Hands / Preparation for the Priestly Blessing (*Oil on wood, 20 × 16 cm*), *Formerly Collection Willy Lindwer, Jerusalem.*
PHOTO WILLY LINDWER

---

3   This painting was in the collection of Willy Lindwer. It was auctioned at Sotheby's, Tel Aviv on 17 April 2001.

4   The poem is quoted in M.H. Gans, *Memorboek, Platenatlas van het leven der joden in Nederland van de middeleeuwen tot 1940* (Baarn 1971), p. 405. Estella published a bundle of her poetry, *Gedichten van E. Hijmans-Herzveld* (S'Gravenhage 1881), the cover adorned with an embossed drawing by Jozef Israels.

but the message of both is similar. Estella Hertzveld was known for the warm national Jewish feelings expressed in her poetry, as in these lines from the poem: "Still they are blessed, still stays with them the dear word of God—their most precious treasure." That these two artists were linked by common ideas of Jewish identity acquires even more meaning when we consider that lines from a poem of Hertzveld were inscribed on Leon's tombstone.

Leon portrayed another part of the synagogue service in the life-size painting *The Rolling of the Holy Scroll*, also titled *Gelilah*.[5] After the reading of the weekly Torah portion, the scroll is rolled-up and prepared to be returned to the Holy Ark. The people, depicted in three-quarter length view, give the viewer a feeling of nearness and of participating in the scene.

My late friend and colleague Christiaan Roosen, to whom we are indebted for rediscovering the nearly forgotten Maurits Leon, suggested that Leon intended to create a series of paintings dedicated to Jewish ceremonies in the synagogue.[6] Two other of his works that could have fit such a series are a painting (present whereabouts unknown) titled *The Prayer, Het Gebed* and the painting *Interior of a Synagogue*.[7] Roosen writes: "Leon went to synagogue not as an outsider, but as a Jew." He had ambitious plans for creating more Jewish subjects and described to friends his intention to make a large historical painting showing the special events of the first Yom Kippur of the Jews in Amsterdam at the beginning of the seventeenth century.[8] He did not live to complete the project. Following his premature death in October 1865, the writer of his obituary noted that, "the peculiar character of the ceremonies of the ritual of his race enchanted him."[9]

Eduard Frankfort – Religious Themes

Like Leon, Eduard Frankfort was also inspired by Hertzveld's poem describing the priestly benediction, and painted a version of the subject that is known

---

5   It is the property of the NIG in The Hague, on loan to the JHM (Jewish Historical Museum). It has been recently restored for exhibition there.

6   See C. Roosen, "Maurits Leon," *Journal of Jewish Art* 16–17 (1986), pp. 46–52.

7   The painting *Interior of a Synagogue* was auctioned at Sotheby's New York in 2004.

8   J. Meijer, "Om de Verlooren Zoon," *Supplement Sefardicum Neerlandicum* (Heemstede 1988), p. 25. The author quotes J.J. Belinfante on the idea for the historical painting.

9   "Het eigenaardig karakter der ceremonien van de eeredienst zijns geslachts trok hem aan," *Kunstkroniek* (1865), clipping, RKD (Rijksbureau voor kunsthistorische documentatie. Netherlandish Institute for Art History).

only from a preliminary study.[10] Whereas Leon concentrated on the preparation for the blessing, the Levites washing the hands of the majestic figure
of the priest, Frankfort showed the *kohanim* already in front of the Ark, their
heads and faces covered by their prayer shawls according to the custom, with
the hand-washing ceremony being conducted in the foreground. Frankfort's
oeuvre contains many Jewish religious themes, such as *Rabbis Reading, Morning Prayer*, also known as *My Father Praying*, and *The Divorce*, which came to
light recently, in which he used the image of his father for one of the rabbis
(Figure. 12.2). This painting was, at the time, chosen to adorn the meeting hall
of the chief rabbinate in Amsterdam.[11]

At the request of the paper *Het Reformatisch Dagblad*, the art collector
Krijnera Koekkoek was invited to describe a painting from her private collection. She chose *Three Rabbis Learning around a Table* by Frankfort,[12] explaining

FIGURE 12.2
*Eduard Frankfort, The Morning
Prayer / My Father Praying, 1886
(Oil on canvas, 195 × 145.5 cm).*
JEWISH HISTORICAL MUSEUM,
AMSTERDAM, JHM 00640

10   Photo RKD. An oil study of part of the composition was auctioned at Sotheby's in 2000.
11   *Een Kerkelijke Echtscheiding.* Joseph Gompers in *De Vrijdagavond* 6/12 (1929), p. 25, relates
      that at first the rabbis had commissioned a painting of Yehezkeel, from a non-Jewish art-
      ist, with which they were unhappy. The rabbi on the left is a portrait of Frankfort's father.
12   E. de Bruijn, "Mijn Kunstwerk," in *Reformatisch Dagblad* 18 April 2005.

her particular choice of painting thus: "I think in depth because it deals with the word of God. It is good daily to be reminded that Israel is our older brother, and that the promises are relevant in the first place to the Jews . . . I am thankful that I have come to know our Lord through them." Regarding the painting's subject she added: "These three men read the Torah together, they are busy with '*lernen*.' You can see from their pose how deeply they are thinking about the word of God, how respectful they are towards each other and towards the Script." For her, the religiosity of the theme evoked a new kind of religiosity in the spectator. This modern reaction is, no doubt, revealing for the manner in which religiosity and religious ideas are read into the picture and gain relevancy even today.

In some aspects, Frankfort's work may be defined as romantic socialism, especially in scenes such as of the inhabitants of homes for the elderly. For instance, in one of his paintings of a group of women sewing by a window and dressed in the uniform of the institute, these women were construed as making the best use of their time. In these subjects his work is close to that of Jozef Israels and Max Liebermann.[13]

Meijer de Haan – Controversy over His Religious Themes

Meijer de Haan began his artistic career in Amsterdam and later went to Paris and then to Brittany where he was a student of Paul Gauguin (1848–1903). In Amsterdam, de Haan became known for his depictions of rabbis learning or discussing issues of Jewish religious law, such as the painting *Talmudic Anatomy*, known also as *Is This Chicken Kosher?* showing a young woman bringing a slaughtered bird to the rabbis to determine whether it is kosher. The painting can be described as down to earth and even humoristic, as the young woman looks somewhat anxious about how their verdict might affect her dinner. Although this and other scenes of similar mood appear uncomplicated and innocent, one of de Haan's works in this genre, *A Difficult Passage in the Talmud*, also known as *Theological Discussion* from 1878 caused quite a fierce interreligious debate (Figure 12.3).

It began when a print after the painting was inserted as a supplement in the January 1880 edition of the magazine *Eigen Haard*, and Prof. Hendricus Oort (1836–1927) of Leiden University was asked to write an article to accompany

---

13   See for instance Eduard Frankfort *Interieur in het Ouderlieden Gesticht* (*Interior of the Home for the Elderly*), oil on canvas, collection JHM, inv. no. 02280.

FIGURE 12.3   *Pierre-Emile Tilly (after Meijer de Haan),* A Difficult Passage in the Talmud, *1879
                (Woodcut, 32.4 × 48.4 cm).*
                JEWISH HISTORICAL MUSEUM, AMSTERDAM, COLLECTION JAAP VAN
                VELZEN, JHM 07259

it. Oort seized the opportunity and, using the print as a trigger, launched a
battle against the Talmud as a source for Jewish life and behavior. It would be
better, he advised, if Jews did not rely on the Talmud, thereby coming closer
to the truth of Christianity. In his opinion, the ethic value of the Talmud was
like "a spoonful of wine in a pail of water."[14] Rabbi Tobias Tal (1847–1898), a talented and sharp thinker, and student and follower of Chief Rabbi Dünner, took
up the Jewish side of the polemic. Tal brought a counter argument to every

---

14   See H. Oort, "Een moeilijke plaats uit den Talmoed," *Eigen Haard,* No. 1, January 1880,
        pp. 8–12. Oort writes: "Ja een woestijn, want in de Talmoed ontbreken nagenoeg geheel
        warmte van hart . . . Alle poezie is er ten eene male vreemd aan" (Yes a desert, because in
        the Talmud there is no warmth of heart . . . any poetic feeling is strange to it). See about
        the debate Gans, *Memorboek,* pp. 371–78, with a reproduction of the painting.

comparison of the New Testament to Jewish sources. The debate continued up to 1892, with the writer Multatuli (Edward Douwers Dekker, 1820–1887), known for his atheist views, even taking a side in the dispute in favor of Tal and Judaism and what he defined as the truth.[15]

Jan Voerman in Amsterdam

In the years 1883–1884, the non-Jewish artist Jan Voerman studied and lived in Amsterdam, for a time in the former studio of Jozef Israels. Among his Jewish friends was the artist Louis Hartz, a nephew of Meijer de Haan. Like the artists mentioned above, he too came under the spell of Jewish Amsterdam. On Friday nights he would go with his non-Jewish teacher, August Alebee, to watch the prayers at the Esnoga. Alebee was known for his many friendly connections with Jewish artists such as the German artist Max Liebermann, who, for many years had been painting scenes of the Jewish market in Amsterdam. Amsterdam inspired Voerman to make in total five Jewish religious paintings, which are unique in his entire oeuvre. Famous among those is *Shiv'ah* or *The Days of Mourning* (Figure 12.4).

The painting is not only accurate in every detail of the men's Eastern European garb, the *yizkor* (memorial) candle, the *tefillin*, and the Hebrew *Mizrah* (a decorative plaque marking the direction of Jerusalem) on the wall, but also glows with true expression. The detail at right of the widow, with one of her children, seated on a low bench, is a direct quote from a work by Jozef Israels.[16] In 1978, The Jewish Historical Museum in Amsterdam bought another of Voerman's Jewish works, *A Widow at the Pawn Shop*, dated 1884.[17]

In his later life, Voerman never forgot his Jewish friends. When Meijer de Haan returned from Brittany (where he had been studying with Paul Gauguin) to Holland, already ill and knowing that his days were numbered, Voerman supported him in his artist community in the village of Hattem.

---

15   A letter from Tobias Tal to Dekker is kept at the Mediatheek of the JHM, inv. No.00009291 letter. See also D.S. Zuiden, "Naar aanleiding van Meijer de Haan's schilderij," *De Vrijdagavond* 6/16 (1929), pp. 246–49.

16   See *De Schilders van Tachtig, Nederlandse Schilderkunst, 1880–1895*, ed. R. Bionda and C. Blotkamp, exh. cat. (Amsterdam 1991), pp. 318–20, with illustration. See also A. Wagener, *Jan Voerman, Ijselschilder* (Wageningen 1977), p. 21.

17   *Nieuwsbrief JHM* (February 1987), *Een Weduwe bij den Uitdrager*, dated 1884.

FIGURE 12.4   *Jan Voerman, Days of Mourning, ca. 1884 (Oil on canvas, 74.2 × 99.2 cm).*
JEWISH HISTORICAL MUSEUM, AMSTERDAM, JHM 01111

Spinoza and Uriel Acosta

During the second half of the nineteenth century, Holland was engaged in forming its modern national identity and national cultural heroes in the process. One of these national assets was Baruch Benedictus Spinoza (1632–1677), the great seventeenth-century free-thinker and philosopher, who, in 1656, was excommunicated by the Jewish community. Around 1870, two hundred years after his death, there was a resurgence of interest in his writing and philosophical thinking, though in other parts of Europe interest in him had begun even earlier. The liberal Jewish world all across Europe joined in adoration of the great Dutch Jew. With Spinoza came also a revival of interest in Uriel Acosta (1585–1640), another Sephardi Jew of Holland. Both had been excommunicated by the official leadership of the Jewish community, but each reacted in different ways. Acosta was, no doubt, the more tragic figure. His humiliation and desperation at his excommunication led to his suicide.[18] It was in this

---

18   Interest in Uriel Acosta and Spinoza began in the Jewish Enlightenment circles in Eastern
        Europe. The German writer Carel Ferdinand Gutzkow (1812–1882) wrote a play on Acosta

general pan-European interest in Spinoza that the Polish-Jewish artist Samuel Hirschenberg (1865–1908), portrayed the two historical figures in an imaginary scene where the older Acosta is shown teaching the child Spinoza, who is seated in his lap.[19]

Maurits Leon painted *Spinoza before His Judges* in 1865, a work we now know only through a print by Rennefeld (Figure 12.5). Jaap Meijer noted the psychological depth of the work, the inner conflict of the religious teachers who had gathered to judge Spinoza and his restraint. The painting was a revelation. It was as if this Sephardi painter himself had been witness to the historical pronouncement of the ban.[20] Leon likely felt an affinity for Spinoza who was also a resident of The Hague and was buried in the *Niewe Kerk*.

Another Sephardi artist, the sculptor Joseph Mendes da Costa, created a bronze sculpture of Spinoza in 1909 (Figure. 12.6). He portrayed him standing in his house robe and slippers, "*en pentoufles*," hands clasped, head turned up in a moment of revelation and with characteristic grimace. As the word "*Beatitudo*" inscribed on the pedestal shows, he had indeed become the wise and blessed figure. Da Costa read extensively about Spinoza in preparation for the work and even found a model who was a descendant of Spinoza's family. This small scale sculpture creates a monumental impression. It differs from the artist's early work featuring small terracotta figurines that were mainly anecdotal genre depictions of Jewish life in Amsterdam.

The *Spinoza* is part of a series of small scale sculptures of saints, artists and cultural heroes which da Costa was inspired to make by his friend, the writer and artist H.P. Bremmer (1871–1956), himself an expert on Spinoza. In the series, we note a tendency towards a symbolic, more abstract art. Da Costa's

---

in 1846, which in turn inspired the Jewish-Polish painter Maurycy Gottlieb (1856–1879) to paint his *Uriel and Judith* and the small *Uriel Acosta in the Synagogue* at the Israel Museum in Jerusalem. Gutzkow's play was performed in Amsterdam in 1881, where it had great success. Israel Zangwill relates Acosta's story in his 1898 *Dreamers of the Ghetto*. See for Gottlieb, E. Mendelsohn, *Painting a People: Maurycy Gottlieb and Jewish Art* (Jerusalem 2006), pp. 124–27, with illustrations [Hebrew].

19 The artist was influenced by the sculptor Mark Antokolsky, whose *Spinoza* of 1882 was well known, as well as by Gottlieb. The painting is an early work by Samuel Hirshenberg dating from 1888. In 1907 he painted his *Spinoza*. Spinoza himself does not mention Acosta in his writings.

20 J. Meijer, *Om de Verlooren Zoon*, p. 24. The print by Rennefeld, was originally made for the book by J. van Lennep, J. ter Gouw, W. Moll, *Nederlands geschidenis en volksleven in schetsen; staahl gravuren naar de schildereijen van de historische galerij* (Leiden 1868–1872).

FIGURE 12.5   *Johannes Heinrich Rennefeld (after Maurits Leon),* Spinoza Before His Judges,
1865–1867 (Steel engraving, 14.6 × 11.7 cm).
JEWISH HISTORICAL MUSEUM, AMSTERDAM, JHM 03373

personality was close to that of his subject, as he had an air of humbleness,
positivism and work ethic that may be defined as "Spinozist."[21]

---

21   See T.B. Roordra, "Nieuwe beeldhouwkunst in Nederland, Dr. J. Mendes da Costa" (Am-
      sterdam n.d. [1928?]), p. 16. For a comprehensive overview on the sculptor see C.J. Roosen,

FIGURE 12.6
Joseph Mendes da Costa, Spinoza, *1909 (Bronze, 32.5 × 9.7 × 10.2 cm).*
COLLECTION KROELLER-MUELLER MUSEUM,
OTTERLO, KM 121.273, CAT. NO. 640 (SCULPTURE
1992)

Following the trend, and likely inspired by Maurits Leon, Meijer de Haan set to work between the years 1880 and 1888 on a very ambitious large-scale Jewish history painting of *Uriel Acosta before His Judges.* The painting is untraceable, and we can only guess how it looked from a photograph of it in the collection of the Jewish Historical Museum.[22] De Haan organized an exhibition of his works in the Panorama building in Amsterdam with this work occupying a central place. It must have come as a great shock to the aspiring young artist when it was harshly criticized in a review in *De Nieuwe Gids* by J.N. Stemming (a pseudonym for the painter Van der Valk). Stemming, who went so far as to suggest that the creator of the *Acosta* would be better off to quit painting altogether, ridiculed the artist's apparent wish to become a second Rembrandt by misguidedly attempting to achieve this by working in dirty brown colors. He put the question to the artist: "What did you feel for this great tragic figure, Uriel Acosta? [you made him] a sturdy man, without a recognizable head,

"Joseph Mendes da Costa: The Revitalization of Dutch Sculpture," in *DJH* 3 (1993), pp. 261–71.

22   See *Meijer de Haan, A Master Revealed,* ed. J. Kroeger, exh. cat. (Amsterdam, Paris 2009), p. 31, fig. 28.

without any posture."[23] The rabbinical authorities in Amsterdam, also unhappy with the new interest in the tragic figure of Acosta, did not come to De Haan's defense.

However, not all critics were negative in their review of *Acosta*. Jan Zuercher wrote a long article about the painting, the making of which he had followed over the years during several visits to the artist's studio. He saw a Christian message in the painting: "the way of suffering (Via Dolorosa) of a great man, who in his own manner has taken up the struggle with the spirit of the day." His words were relevant not only for the figure of Acosta, the painting's subject, but also for the struggling artist, and the critic indeed directed them to de Haan and his students, to whom we will return later, and Hartz, saying: "Yes, yes, there is only one way to heaven . . . Golgotha." Zuercher also praised de Haan's painting *Talmudic Dispute*, which had caused such uproar.[24]

Still, it is likely that the extreme negative reaction towards what de Haan intended as his ultimate masterpiece, which came on the heels of the vociferous debate about his *Talmudic Dispute*, was the catalyst for his decision to leave Amsterdam for Paris.

Van Gogh

Vincent van Gogh, for whom religiosity was the aim of art, suits the subject of this article in many ways. During his stay in The Hague between 1881 and 1883, Van Gogh used to visit the Jewish quarter. A few years ago, a hitherto unknown portrait drawing by him came to light of the Jewish book-seller Blok, probably Jozef Blok, who was nicknamed the "*Binnenhof* outdoor librarian" (Figure 12.7).

In letters to his brother Theo, Van Gogh described the magazines and prints he would get from Blok's booth. He made the portrait in exchange for these, but expressed interest also in Blok as a model: "I wish I could draw more members of that family, for they are very good models."[25] While in The Hague, Van Gogh expressed great admiration for the work of Jozef Israels, known as the leader of The Hague School. Van Gogh spoke about "de *ziel* (the soul) in art,

---

23   "[T]'s afscuwelijk geschilderd. Wat heeft hij gemaakt van de hoofdpersoon? Wat heeft hij gevoeld voor die groote tragische figuur van Uriel Acosta?" J.N. Stemming, "Meijer de Haan's *Uriel Acosta*," *De Nieuwe Gids* (1888), vol. 2, pp. 435–37.

24   J. Zuercher, *Meijer de Haan's Uriel Acosta*, (Amsterdam 1888). The reproduction on the jacket of this booklet is our only clue to how it looked. "Dat doek is een lijdensgeschidenis van een groot man . . . Ja, ja er is maar een weg ter hemel . . . Golgotha."

25   See http://webehibits.org/vangogh/letter/11/241.htm ed. Robert Harrison.

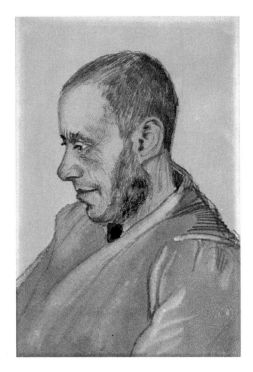

FIGURE 12.7
Vincent van Gogh, Portrait of Jozef Blok,
*11-05-1882 (Drawing and watercolor,
38.5 × 26.3 cm).*
VAN GOGH MUSEUM, AMSTERDAM,
(VINCENT VAN GOGH FOUNDATION),
D1123V/2004 F993

and felt that Israels had grasped just that quality in his art. Indeed, both artists had nurtured religious aspirations in their youth. Van Gogh, possessed of a
strong evangelical streak, wished to become a preacher who would bring light
and consolation to poor miners. Similarly, Jozef Israels, in his youth, had considered becoming a rabbi, having felt drawn to the mystery and poetic feeling
in religion.[26] Van Gogh's *Potato Eaters* of 1885 has been compared to works depicting peasant meals by Israels. Van Gogh was influenced by Israels' scenes of
frugal meals in which peasant families are gathered round a plain table at the
center of which is a simple potato dish from which steam rises. In Jewish tradition, the table is viewed as symbolic and assumes the holiness of an altar, and
the meal is blessed. Similar ideas prevail also in Christianity. The steam rising
from the dish adds to the religious quality of these depictions, and Van Gogh,
stressed this by showing the true piety of humble peasants.[27]

---

26   Israels to Hermann Struck in an unpublished interview in the summer of 1905: "For a
      while I thought to become a rabbi as a young man is impressed by the mystic and poetics
      in religion" (my translation from the German).
27   A. Boime, "A Source for Van Gogh's *Potato Eaters*," in *Gazette de Beaux Arts* 108 (1966), VI,
      67, pp. 249–53. See also C. Moffett, "Vincent van Gogh en de Haagse School, in *De Haagse*

Van Gogh's letters were first published in 1914, and soon after, da Costa made his bronze statue of the artist in the Bremer series (Figure 12.8). Van Gogh is portrayed holding his palette and brushes, his head turned up to the sky in a moment of "ecstasy" (a term much used by da Costa), trying to capture the image of the cruel sun, beseeching God to help him in his heroic artistic struggle, in which da Costa surely saw himself.[28]

When Meijer de Haan went to Paris accompanied by his student and friend, Joseph Jacob Isaacson, his life became intertwined with Van Gogh's. In Paris, De Haan lodged with Theo van Gogh. Through him, De Haan and Isaacson saw works by Vincent who was still fairly unknown. Isaacson, who at that time was the art correspondent for the Dutch magazine *De Portefeuille*, recognized Van Gogh's greatness and expressed his belief in his art, becoming one of the first to recognize his importance.[29] Theo had earlier seen De Haan's *Acosta* and

FIGURE 12.8
Joseph Mendes da Costa, Vincent van Gogh,
1914 (Bronze, 39 × 12 × 13 cm).
COLLECTION KROELLER MUELLER
MUSEUM, OTTERLO KM 122.518, CAT.
NO. 639 (SCULPTURE 1992)

School; Hollandse meesters van de 19de eeuw, ed. R. de Leeuw, J. Sillevis and C. Dumas (Paris, London, The Hague 1983), pp. 137–46.

28   Roorda, *Nieuwe Beeldhouwkunst in Nederland,* p. 17.

29   He wrote: "Hij staat alleen in den grooten nacht, zijn naam Vincent is voor de nageslacht" (He stands alone in the expanse of night, his name Vincent is for posterity). See I. Faber, "Joseph Jacob Isaacson and the Other Students of Meijer de Haan," in Kroeger, *Meijer de Haan,* pp. 76, 77.

wrote to Vincent about it, stressing that de Haan must persevere with his art. These two erudite modern Jews left an impression on Theo, so different were they from the familiar stereotype. He noted in a letter to his sister, "if it were possible one could call them Christian-Jews."[30]

De Haan's Meeting with Gauguin

In Paris, Meijer de Haan met Paul Gauguin and eventually became his student. De Haan followed Gaugin to the small village of Le Pouldu in Brittany, during which time he provided Gaugin with financial support. Under Gauguin's tutelage, de Haan developed a new style that was completely different from his Dutch period. The two became friends, but there was a certain distance in their relationship. Gauguin admired de Haan's erudition, learning and knowledge, but also viewed him as different and exotic, perhaps even an embodiment of the "Wandering Jew." At the same time, he was envious and considered him a rival for the affections of the innkeeper, Marie Henri. Gaugin's pride was most likely hurt when she preferred the Dutch Jewish hunchback to him. De Haan's intellect and philosophical breadth inspired and haunted Gauguin, who painted his likeness on five different occasions, attributing to him diabolical traits in the paintings. As much as seven years after de Haan's death, while living in a completely remote part of the world, in the French Polynesian islands where originally they had planned to go together, Gaugin conjured his dead friend back to life as the Peeping Tom in his 1902 painting *Contes Barbares*. The painting portrays de Haan with slanted green eyes, hair standing up like diabolic horns and claw-like hands and feet, watching two seemingly innocent, pure and half-naked Polynesian girls. Gauguin died the next year, in 1903.[31]

Meijer de Haan returned to Holland around 1892–3 and died soon after. He was buried in Muiderberg, his tombstone carved by Mendes da Costa. As regards Gauguin, it seems that he gave expression to his inner thoughts about his friend and his friend's religiosity through the works in which he repeatedly depicted him in an ominous manner.

30   See J. Kroeger, "Meijer de Haan (1852–1895); From Traditional Painter to Modern Artist," in
      Kroeger, *Meijer de Haan,* pp. 33, 34, and n. 72.
31   The painting is in the collection of Museum Folkwang in Essen. See C. Boyle-Turner,
      "Gauguin's Philosophical Muse: Meijer de Haan," in Kroeger, *Meijer de Haan*, pp. 86–108.
      See also A. Ekker, "Meijer de Haan: 'profeet' in Frankrijk werd in eigen land nog niet geerd,"
      in *Pulchri* 18/1 (1990), pp. 6–9; also E. Denneboom, "Meijer de Haan, Mimi en Gauguin's
      perfide genie," in *Levend Joods Geloof* 56/1 (September 1990), pp. 32–34.

Jozef Israels

Jozef Israels' first religious painting *Hannah in Shiloh* of 1860 is based on 1 Samuel 1. The painting was a commission, however the patron went bankrupt, and the work was sold to a collector from Vienna and remained out of sight for nearly a century until it was auctioned at Sotheby's Amsterdam in 1994.[32] While organizing the Jozef Israels exhibition in Amsterdam and Groningen, we discovered the painting to be the property of C. Kumala of Jakarta, Indonesia, a Chinese Christian. The interest in this painting even across such a great distance testifies to the power of the religious expression sensed in the work of this Jewish Dutch artist. In Jewish tradition, Hannah was one of the first to have grasped the significance of silent prayer. After years of barrenness, her silent prayers are answered by the birth of the son she named Samuel, who she brings to the temple at Shiloh where he will grow up in the service of God. Israels depicts her standing before the Ark holding the naked child while praising God. He portrays the heartbreaking moment when she offers her child to God despite her motherly feelings. Max Eisler, an expert on Israels, commented on "[t]he invisible and silent, consequently the inner religious state of feeling portrayed here."[33] Another Jewish critic, Frits Stahl wrote about Israels' religiosity: "With his art he serves God in his own way."[34] Vosmaer, who had written an early biography on Israels and knew him well, commented on the expression in the painting: "Yet Israels' Hannah evokes a religious awareness ... because he lays aside all traditional form and is only human."[35]

People were continuously inspired by Israels' work, to which they attributed deep religiosity and prophetic powers. Wally Moes in *Heilig Ongedult* described Israels' work thus: "His creations . . . could not be different than they were, because their maker was a willing tool, more or less powerful, as the ancient spirit spoke through him."[36]

---

32   The reappearance of the painting after a century was widely reported in the news. In a clipping from *Magriet Antiek 65*; at the RKD, Evelyn van Oischot of Sotheby's Amsterdam reported this to be one of two exciting findings during her work there. See D. Dekkers, *Jozef Israels 1824–1911*, Groninger Museum, Groningen; Jewish Historical Museum, Amsterdam, Institute of Art and Architectural History, exh. cat. (Zwolle 1999), pp. 148, 149.

33   M. Eisler, *Jozef Israels* (London 1924), p. 13.

34   See F. Stahl, "Jozef Israels," in *Juedische Kuenstler*, ed. Martin Buber (Berlin 1903), pp. 13–40, p. 39: "Auch er ist ein frommen mann. Mit seinem kunst . . . dient er Gott auf seine weize."

35   C. Vosmaer, "De Haagsche tentoonstelling van kunstvoorwerpen," *De Nederlandse Spectator*, 1860, p. 219.

36   W. Moes, *Heilig Ongeduld; Herinneringen uit mijn leven* (Sacred Impatience, memories from my life), reprint (Amsterdam/Antwerp 1961), p. 155. "zijn [scheppingen] konden niet

Jewish themes and biblical subjects make up but a small part of Israels' large oeuvre. Significantly, his non-religious subjects appealed more to Protestant and Reformed preachers, who found in them what they defined as true Christian feelings. Israels, who grew up in Groningen, may have been inspired by the atmosphere in that city where, since 1820, a branch of the Dutch Reformed Church developed and cherished a romantic view of the simple people living in harmony with their surroundings. This romantic religiosity is found in his depictions of peasants and fishermen. It was in these modest, humble folk, seemingly happy with their lot, and not in his biblical themes, that preachers seemed to find the embodiment of their weekly sermon. One extreme case is the preacher, Dr. W. Haverkamp (1851–1917), author of a booklet titled *Jozef Israels, Preaching the Gospel with His Brush*.[37] Haverkamp toured the country with a series of lectures based on the booklet and reproductions of Israels' work, praising him as "this son of the old Israel who has grasped deep in his soul." Further: "Israels like no other knew how to give artistic expression to the good luck of the poor," and: "he draws true richness from material want." The writer then reached the crux of the matter: "Street socialists and those who protest want to turn the thankful and quiet ones into unhappy ones, thinking that they do good work." Haverkamp claimed that Israels himself was aware of the "angelic patience which might be found in eighty percent of our poor." Haverkamp praised the feelings emanating from the painting *Alone in the World*, in which a widower is portrayed seated in front of the bed on which lies his dead wife, a moment after death has struck (Figure 12.9).[38]

He also expresses great admiration for Israels' *From Darkness to Light*, which shows another death-stricken family seated in a dark room, while the coffin of their loved one is carried from the dark abode to the light outside where a church spire rises up in the distance. For Haverkamp, these were the inspiration for a sermon on the eternity of the soul. He mentioned the Bible depicted in these paintings, expressing his appreciation for the artist, who, though: "In the Old Testament there is no mention of the belief in the immortality of the soul, here, this son of an old people, shows us that this hope lives on in his heart."[39] Israels expressed a different view on the issue, as he told Hermann

anders worden dan zij zijn, omdat de maker een willig werktuig was, meer of minder machtig, al naar de oergeest door hem sprak."

37   W. Haverkamp, *Jozef Israels Het Evangelie predikende met zijn Penseel* (Nijmegen 1899). The following quotations will be from this publication.

38   Dekkers, *Jozef Israels 1824–1911*, pp. 198–200. The work is dated 1881, and titled *Nothing Left* or *Alone*. Another painting from 1878 is indeed titled *Alone in the World*. In this period Israels had often treated the subject of death.

39   The paining dates from 1871. It is in the collection of the Tel Aviv Museum of Art. See Dekkers, *Jozef Israels 1824–1911*, pp. 178–80.

FIGURE 12.9   *Jozef Israels,* Alone / (Solo en Mundo), *1881 (Oil on canvas, 125 × 200 cm).*
THE MESDAG COLLECTION, THE HAGUE, HWM 154

Struck in 1905: "Well, I don't believe in *Olam haba* (the afterworld) . . . but he
who does not believe is also a good Jew."[40]

Jozef Israels, Isaac Israels and the Catholic Frans Erens

The Israels family frequently traveled abroad. On one of their visits to Rome
they were invited for an audience with Pope Pius IX. The painter's son, Isaac,
who would become a successful and gifted artist in his own right, joined his
parents and the Pope gave him a special blessing. Jozef Israels later recounted
this anecdote to Frans Erens, a devout Catholic who was a friend of both father
and son. Erens gave an account of the event in his *Vervlogen Jaren,* in his mem-
oirs on Isaac: "The Pope put his hand on the child's head blessing him and said
that he hoped that one day he will see the light of truth. Certainly this blessing
had the good effect directing him [Isaac] to the good." Erens further elaborated
on the idea: "Where Christ the charitable sees and praises the good because
they will do good, I know that my friend, who was charitable (*barmhartig*), has
found mercy with God . . . and that I will meet with his complete personality in

---

40   See above n. 26. These are actually the final lines of the interview.

the eternal bliss ... For me, who still exists in this earthly world, the bond with him remains in my prayers for the rest of his soul."[41]

Jozef Israels was praised for his true Protestant Christian feelings, and after him, his son Isaac, who, as far as I know, did not have any religious belief, was hailed as one of the merciful souls who will find their place in the Catholic Heaven.

In addition to works with explicit Christian content, such as grace before meals, among Israel's works were those bearing lightly veiled Christian iconography. Early in his career he painted a scene of a woman seated at a table feeding porridge to her baby. She is a beautiful young woman clad in blue and red, the traditional colors of the Virgin Mary. She is, moreover, barefoot, and a cross and rosary hang from the shelf above her. Clearly, the artist used familiar symbols of Christian iconography as a means of sanctifying this every-day scene. It is not surprising, therefore, that the painting became known as the *Cottage Madonna*.[42]

Meijer de Haan's *Maternity* of 1889, a portrait of the artist's mistress Marie Henri nursing her first daughter, evokes a similar idea. Marie Henri is dressed in blue and red and the glowing yellows of the haystacks in the background create a kind of halo above mother and child.[43]

Joseph Mendes da Costa

The literature about the sculptor Mendes da Costa describes him as a religious, spiritual and poetic artist and even a prophet (Figure 12.10).

These qualities become apparent in his biblical works, both Christian and Jewish, such as of John the Baptist, Saint Francis, King David and Job. A small group of his works may serve as example. In the 1917 sculpture *Elijah and Elisha*,

---

41   See F. Erens, *Vervlogen Jaren* (Years Flying by) (S'Gravenhage 1983), ed. H.G.M. Prick, p. 277. Quoted here is the entire relevant part: "Waar Jezus de barmhartigen zalig prijst, omdat zij barmhartigheid zullen verwerven, weet ik, dat mijn vriend, die een barmhartige was, in Gods hart barmhartigheid heeft gevonden en dat ik eens zijn volkomen persoonlijkheid zal terug vinden in het eeuwige geluk. Voor mij, die nog in het aardse leven ben, blijve de band met hem van mijn gebeden voor de rust van zijn ziel."

42   See Dekkers, *Jozef Israels 1824–1911*, pp. 167–69. Typically, in F. Stahl's "Jozef Israels," the cross and rosary are cut off in the reproduction, and the painting is titled merely *The Young Mother*.

43   See A. Cariou, "Meijer de Haan and Paul Gauguin at le Poldu," in Kroeger, *Meijer de Haan*, pp. 116–17. Cariou interprets the haystacks as symbolizing fertility and the Eucharist.

FIGURE 12.10
Joseph Mendes da Costa, Self Portrait,
1927 (Terracotta, 23 × 15.8 cm).
JEWISH HISTORICAL MUSEUM,
AMSTERDAM, JHM 01260

the prophets are shown walking together in a state of ecstasy bordering on the theatrical (Figure 12.11).

A contemporary critic commented on the work's deep religiosity, modernity and relevance: "Here Mendes creates a modern idea, showing us how the modern movement keeps the fire. The older person Elijah—the man of God—walks on further together with the younger. These two prophets are moving together, as Elijah had promised the younger [Elisha] not to abandon him. It is in this small group that the Divine path may be perceived. The fire chariot carried the one away, but his soul remained on [in] Elisha, the idealist."[44]

T.B. Roorda also described da Costa's art as deeply religious, venturing a guess as to the artist's state of mind and belief: "Nowhere is anything left to chance, all is planned, mentally meant to be, but at the same time it burns with religious passion, which considered the 'doing' not as the work of a mortal, more or less gifted, but as revelation in him of a 'personality' above the individual self . . . It is these, da Costa's unspoken words, but surely unconsciously felt,

---

44   See T. van Reijn, "De Beeldhouwer Mendes da Costa," in *Elsevier Geilustreerd Maand-schrift,* (19 July 1922), pp. 219–25. See text referring to Elijah and Elisha on p. 224 and a reproduction of the sculpture on p. XLIV.

FIGURE 12.11
Joseph Mendes da Costa, Elijah and Elisha,
1907 (Glazed stoneware, wooden base).
COLLECTION KROELLER-MUELLER
MUSEUM, OTTERLO, KM 118.385, CAT.
NO. 633 (SCULPTURE 1992)

which have given him the power."[45] Da Costa had summed up his artistic credo
in his *Ideas about the Monumental in Visual Ar*t, published in August 1939, a
month after his death. He expressed his belief that works containing the monumental have a religious character. To his friend Anna Egter van Wissekerke
he revealed his artistic goals: "Truth, beauty and belief in a harmonious unity
he craves to achieve. The painterly falls away." And further on: "Religion is no
belief, but if you work the Divine, it becomes religion again."[46]

In his book *The History of Art in The Netherlands*, published immediately after the war, in 1946, van Gelder defined da Costa's art in a similar vein, but with

---

45   Clipping in artist file RKD from *Het Vaderland,* 8 November 1923, which quotes an article
      written by T.B. Roorda for Mendes's sixtieth birthday in *Architectura:* "Nergens wordt ge-
      rekend op toevalllig effect . . . alles is er doordacht . . . maar tegelijk doorgloeid door een
      religieuse passie, die het 'doen' zelf beschouwt . . . als een openbaring . . . van een boven
      individueele 'Persoonlijkheid.'"
46   A. Egter, "Herinneringen aan Mendes da Costa, een gesprek," a booklet in the Mediatheek
      of the JHM (ca. 2009). She quotes da Costa: "Men zegt dat er eenmaal een Godsdienst zal
      zijn voor alle menschen, maar wat voor jou goed zal zijn is het niet voor mij" (It is said that
      there will be one religion for all people, but what is good for you is not so for me).

a Jewish twist: "[His art is] typically Jewish, filled with *'Messias verwachting'*—
Messianic Expectations." This comment indeed seems relevant both for the
artist as well as for the time of the book's publication.[47]

A show of da Costa's work formed the inaugural exhibition of the Jewish
Historical Museum in the restored synagogues complex of the Jonas Daniel
Square, back in 1976. Significantly, it was this free-thinking man of sublime
feeling who was chosen as the first artist to be shown in the renewed museum.
His work symbolized a new beginning, perhaps like the Phoenix that is reborn
from the ashes, emblem of the Portuguese-Sephardi community. Da Costa
passed away just before the war, working full days till his last. He belonged to
the artists who still believed in a peaceful future.[48]

Joseph Jacob Isaacson: Believing in the Mission of Art

Joseph Jacob Isaacson, the last artist to be discussed here, was deported in
1942, at the age of eighty-three, to Auschwitz where he was murdered.

His first mentor was Meijer de Haan, with whom he went to Paris, as mentioned above. He traveled twice to Egypt, in 1896 and 1905, where he fell under
the spell of the Eastern light and color and its human scene. From 1910 onwards, he mainly painted depictions of prophets and biblical heroes. An in-
trovert who led a secluded life, he was especially interested in philosophical
aspects of religion as well as in Jewish mysticism. As described by Zuercher, his
was the embodiment of "the mysterious feeling of a tribe so many thousands
of years old . . . and still clear thinking."[49]

---

47   See M.E. van Gelder, *Kunstgeschidenis der Nederlanden* (Utrecht 1946), pp. 815–22. On
     da Costa's religious mission see also A.M. Hammacher, "Mendes da Costa, de Geestelijke
     Boodschap der Beeldhouw Kunst," (Mendes da Costa, the Spiritual Mission of the Art of
     Sculpture) (Rotterdam 1941).
48   On the exhibition see Joods Historisch Museum, "Dr Joseph Mendes da Costa, 1863–1939
     Beeldhouwer," exh. cat. (Amsterdam 1976). See also, E. van Sraaten, "Op zoek naar het
     'Geestelijke Wezen dat in en achter elke verschijning leeft'," *Vrij Nederland* (17 July 1976),
     clipping, artist file RKD. According to C. Roosen, da Costa received a commission from the
     Portuguese Synagogue around 1890 to carve the pelican feeding its brood with its own fat
     and blood from its chest, symbolizing life and charity. For Christians too it is meaningful
     as a personification of Christ. According to Willy Lindwer, the pelican in the Esnoga is not
     by da Costa.
49   Zuercher, "Meijer de Haan's *Uriel Acosta*": "'t mysterieuze gevoel van een stam zoveel dui-
     zend jaar oud."

Joseph Gompers interviewed him at his home for the *Vrijdagavond*. He described him as very humble, refusing to have his photograph taken for the paper. While there, a reproduction of *Abraham*, a large-scale dreamlike oriental figure with a very expressive face, caught his attention (Figure 12.12).

Isaacson told his visitor how he had learned the bible stories from his grandmother, explaining his attraction to these biblical subjects: "Because we all carry with us the biblical figures since ancient times, because we learn to know these beautiful persons who play such an important role in the oral tradition of our history."[50] The *Telegraaf* of January 1922 reported that the *Abraham* was slated to go to Palestine, but would travel first to the United States until the situation in Palestine will be calmer. Today, the painting is in the collection of the Tel Aviv Museum of Art.[51]

Justus Havelaar, who wrote about Isaacson in 1929, elaborated on his religious beliefs: "Hear O Israel—the *Shema yisrael*—is for him the quintessence

FIGURE 12.12
Joseph Jacob Isaacson, Abraham, *1918*
(Oil on canvas, 75.5 × 56 cm).
COLLECTION OF MR. SIMON
AMSTERDAM, TEL AVIV MUSEUM
OF ART, TAMA 1245

---

50   "Omdat wij de Beeltenis van alle bijbelse figuren van oerouden tijden . . . her in ons
       rondragen," J. Gompers, "De Joodse Schilder J.J. Isaacson," *De Vrijdagavond* 4/5 (1927),
       pp. 72–75, here p. 74.
51   Clipping in artist's file, RKD.

of the Jewish religion. He is driven by the idea of a single metaphysic personality ... His Judaism has become immanently cosmic ... He is no Zionist; he bears
his Jerusalem in his heart, believing in the world mission of the Jewish spirit."[52]

In August 1940, Isaacson answered a questionnaire in preparation for a
prospective artists' lexicon. His answers are testimony to his ideas and convictions: Q. Schooling. His answer: "Autodidact." Q. Subject: "Biblical." Q. To which
group do you belong? "The most non-collective; that of my own calling." Q.
The importance of your work: "To work on without tiring."[53] "*Ongemoed doorwerken*," in Artist's file, RKD. Sadly for him, his belief in Judaism's world mission
came to naught as did his wish to continue to work on in peace.

Conclusion

Though "religiosity in art" remains an elusive term, it acquires more meaning
and substance through the examples of the mainly Jewish artists discussed
here who were active in the nineteenth and the early twentieth centuries and
the cultural relevance of the issue in Holland at the time.

Interest in Jewish art increased over the course of the nineteenth century as
did interest in Judaism and specifically Jews who had stepped into the contemporary Dutch cultural scene. While Jewish artists were accepted in the general
art scene, the public and the Jewish artists themselves remained aware of their
otherness.

This study has exposed the negative criticism against the Talmud and its
study, the deep feelings of fear of the diabolic embodied in the image of the
Jewish artist, and contempt for his endeavors and aspirations. On the other
hand, however, was the persistence of the notion that Jewish art contains spiritual, poetic and religious content along with a positive attitude of the Jewish
artist and of his spiritual world, bordering on veneration. In accordance with
the spirit of the time, the artist was considered a tool or vehicle giving expression to the "ancient spirit," to quote the artist Wally Moes.

Religiosity was not only to be found in Jewish-oriented subject matter
whether it was a genre scene, Jewish ceremony or custom, or a historical or biblical scene, but could be detected in works where the symbolic, often Christian,
content remained hidden. Zealous Christian writers, grasping the essence of

---

52   See J. Havelaar, "J.J. Isaacson," *Elsevier* 39/77 (1929), pp. 218–25, with illustrations, esp. 219,
      220. Havelaar sees his Judaism as that of the "New Born" (according to the terminology of
      William James).

53   "*Ongemoed doorwerken,*" in Artist's file, RKD.

these sentiments, often expressed a real concern for the souls of these Jewish artists, at times offering interpretations beyond the artist's intent. Detected in their writings was the hidden wish for a fellow artist to inhabit the same safe Christian world, both here and in the afterlife. It is in this manner that Frans Erens' words about his dead Jewish friend must be construed, though of course Isaac Israels was not at all concerned with his Jewish identity, or with any other religious definition.

While in The Hague, the young Van Gogh came under the spell of Jozef Israels' work, in which he saw the work of the soul. Later, the sculptor Joseph Mendes da Costa would portray Van Gogh with palette and brush in hand at a soulful moment of spiritual ecstasy and struggle.

Christian Roosen, a non-Jew who dedicated his life to the study of Dutch Jewish art was, no doubt, drawn to these aspects. He used to say that there is *rachmoenes* (compassion) in the work of Jozef Israels and a lot of *neshome* in Dutch Jewish art. *Neshome* means soul, *ziel*, the quality van Gogh was striving for in his art, which he had found in the work of Jozef Israels.

Religiosity in art grew out of Romantic, mystical, and even poetic feelings toward Jewish heritage. Jewish artists often treated Jewish subjects with true feeling and compassion, and from a personal sense of obligation.

Jewish art, in all its aspects and not just the Jewish subject matter, was often described as containing deep religious feelings. Religiosity was felt to emanate from the artist who had put his soul in his work. This quality seems to underline the work and the interpretation of the works discussed here.

From the Jewish point of view, the words of Nathan Birenbaum (1864–1937), an important but lesser-known figure in early Zionism, may seem relevant: "In Judaism there are lines of similarity between the artist, God and religion."[54]

---

54   N. Birenbaum, "Gottesdienst und Art in Judentum," *Menorah* 3 (March 1925), pp. 51–52; the print by Jozef Israels, *An Old Man* (the Blind Man), appears beside the text.

PART 6

The Master: Images of Chief Rabbi Jozeph Zvi (Hirsch) Dünner

∵

"The Great Eagle, the Pride of Jacob": Jozeph Hirsch Dünner in Dutch Jewish Memory Culture

Bart Wallet

On 16 January 1966, a cold snowy Sunday morning in Amsterdam, a group of people assembled on a bridge in the Weesperstraat. Among them was the secretary of the municipality, the Amsterdam and Rotterdam chief rabbis, several other rabbis and members of the board of the Orthodox community. The photos of the event even show a number of children in caps and shawls. All had left their warm houses to attend the unveiling of the Dr. Dünner Bridge, named after Amsterdam's well known former chief rabbi, located in the heart of what had been the city's thriving Jewish quarter. Jozeph Hirsch Dünner, born in Krakow in 1833, had been the dominant Jewish religious leader in the nineteenth-century Netherlands, combining halakhic Orthodoxy with modern scientific methodologies. From 1865 he led the Dutch Israelite Seminary and educated several generations of Dutch rabbis, while from 1874 onwards he guided the largest community in the country, Amsterdam, as its chief rabbi. The acting Chief Rabbi Aron Schuster, praised his predecessor in a short address as a genius and first-class scholar who had left his imprint on Dutch Jewry. Thereafter, one of the grandchildren of Dünner, Miss S. de Paauw, was given the privilege of unveiling the small plaque on the bridge bearing his name.[1]

With this little ceremony on the bridge, the lobby by the administration of the Orthodox Jewish community was successfully concluded.[2] Dünner had finally received a fixed, albeit modest, place on Amsterdam's postwar map, just like many others who had been important in the city's history. But what was the significance of the short ceremony on the bridge? Was it an expression of a living memory culture, a milestone in a continuing admiration or even cult around Dr. Dünner, as he was commonly called? Or should we better interpret

---

* The title "The Great Eagle, the Pride of Jacob" refers to the traditional qualification of Maimonides, which was used for Jozeph Hirsch Dünner in a special prayer recited during the inauguration of Abraham Salomon Onderwijzer as Dünner's successor as chief rabbi of Amsterdam in 1917.

1 J. Weijel, "Naamgeving," *Hakehilla* 11/5 (1966), p. 7.

2 SAA, NIHS, minutes Daily Board (Kerkbestuur) 12 May 1960; 9 November 1961; 26 January 1966.

the ceremony as a conclusion, a definitive mark that Dünner had become history, past perfect tense?

In the years before 1966, since Dünner's death in 1911, the former chief rabbi had been far from forgotten. On several occasions, he was publicly remembered in meetings and synagogue services. Frequently, he was invoked as an authority to stress someone's convictions, while his portrait could be found in a prominent place in the living rooms of a number of Amsterdam Jewish families; it goes without saying that his portrait also posthumously overlooked the offices of the Jewish community and the Dutch Israelite Seminary.[3] In post-Dünner Amsterdam, it seemed that Dünner was still very much present.

Studying Dünner and the ways in which he was remembered is studying Dutch Jewry. Already during his life, Dünner had become one of the main characters in a developing narrative on Dutch Jewish history.[4] After his death, Dünner's memory became part of a larger attempt by religious and administrative elites to ensure religious and cultural continuity between Dünner's period and present times. There are different approaches to research the construction of a Dutch Jewish identity. One could describe the community in institutional terms, concentrating on membership policies, or in terms of adherence to certain convictions, be it religious or national ones, but here I would like to concentrate on Dutch Jewry as a "community of memory" in which metaphors, images, rituals and collective memories were produced in order to shape and support a shared Dutch Jewish collective identity. In this process of identity formation the "social circulation of the past," as Daniel Woolf termed it,[5] served a specific goal: Dutch Jewry had to be given a past which gave meaning to the present, and, therefore, those events and figures were remembered that fitted the identity the "memory managers" wished for. Dünner was one of the historical figures that were memorialized and given a place in a catalogue of "great Dutch Jews."[6]

The focus of this article, therefore, will not be the "historic Dünner," but Dünner as bearer of symbolic meaning. To trace this "memorialized Dünner," I collected pamphlets, newspaper reports, articles in journals, novels, archival

3 J. Meijer, "Amsterdam die joodse stad (III): Herinneringen van een seminarist III," *Hakehilla* 29/5 (March 1948), pp. 11–17, there 11.

4 For the first time analyzed in J. Meijer, *Rector en raw: De levensgeschiedenis van Dr. J.H. Dünner (1833–1911) – Deel I (1833–1874)* (Heemstede 1984).

5 D. Woolf, *The Social Circulation of the Past* (Oxford 2003).

6 The approach chosen here is indebted to P. Nora, "Entre mémoire et histoire: la problématique des lieux," in *Les lieux de mémoire*, ed. P. Nora, 7 vols. (Paris 1984–1992), p. 1; E. Zerubavel, *Time Maps: Collective Memory and the Social Shape of the Past* (Chicago & London 2003), and C. Cornelißen, " Was heißt Erinnerungskultur? Begriff, Methoden, Perspektiven," *Geschichte in Wissenschaft und Unterricht* 54 (2003), pp. 548–63.

material and the like in which Dünner figured sometimes prominently, other times only mentioned in passing, but not with any less significance. In the memory culture around Dünner I roughly distinguish three phases: the first phase was during his life, mainly around special anniversaries, but with the "Master" still present to eventually correct distortions of his image;[7] the second phase started with his funeral in 1911 and continued until the start of the Second World War. As I will demonstrate, the war, and a bit later, the foundation of the State of Israel significantly changed Dünner's memory with which a third phase started. In this paper I will concentrate on the last two phases and show how Dünner's memory changed in the course of time, while continuing to foster a Dutch Jewish collective identity.

Respect for the Great Master, 1911–1940

On a variety of occasions Dutch Jewry took the opportunity to remember publicly the late Dr. Dünner. First, needless to say, when he died in 1911 nearly all Dutch Jewish journals, but also the major newspapers in the country which often had a special reporter for Jewish affairs, published extensively on the life and work of Dünner and his legacy for Dutch Jewry.[8] Dünner's former students, who then occupied nearly all chief rabbinic seats in the Netherlands, played a prominent role, each stressing how much they personally, but also Dutch Jewry collectively, were indebted to the late chief rabbi. A telling example of their veneration for Dünner was provided by Lion Wagenaar, who just a few weeks later celebrated his silver jubilee as the Gelderland chief rabbi and decided spontaneously to dedicate the money he received from his flock to the Dutch Israelite Seminary in memory of Dünner, it being his teacher's most prominent creation.[9]

A year later, Dünner returned to the forefront on two occasions: first, the administrative leaders of the community decided that while Dünner had been such an exceptional leader and, therefore, had been able to combine the functions of rector of the Seminary and chief rabbi of Northern Holland, it could not be expected from any possible successor. Both functions were therefore ultimately split and, eventually, Dünner's pupils, Philip Gobits and Abraham

---

7   See e.g. the series of articles by A. Polak Jzn. in the 1899 volumes of the *Weekblad voor Israëlietische Huisgezinnen*.

8   On the funeral and the commemorative events organized in 1911: SAA, NIHS, inv. nrs. 1346 and 2264.

9   "Israëlietische Kerk," *Nieuws van den dag*, 8 November 1911.

10 *Nieuwe Rotterdamsche Courant* (abbreviated: NRC), 29 February 1912; 22 May 1912.

Onderwijzer, became, respectively, rector and chief rabbi of Amsterdam and the province of Northern Holland.[10] Second, the customary unveiling of the tombstone on Dünner's grave in 1912 was made into a memorial ceremony, with speeches by the presidents of both the board and the council of the Amsterdam Orthodox community. As the lawyer Benjamin Emanuel Asscher put it, the monument was supposed to speak to the present generations about the great works wrought by Dünner.[11]

Every year on Dünner's *yahrzeit* (memorial anniversary of death), the Amsterdam *Beit Hamidrash* organized a special service in memory of the late chief rabbi. In 1916, five years after Dünner's death, the service was given special attention, with official representatives in attendance.[12] Likewise, the Orthodox Zionist *Mizrachi* movement took a special initiative and collected among its adherents a significant sum of money, more than enough to have a tree planted in the Land of Israel by the Jewish National Fund on his *yahrzeit* for the next seventy years. In 1929, a special committee was formed by Chief Rabbi Onderwijzer to publish the hitherto unpublished theological works of Dünner. The first volume, Dünner's annotations to Maimonides' *Mishneh Torah*, was published on the occasion of the eightieth birthday of Dünner's widow, Sara Landauer.[13]

All these events, however, were minor in comparison to the great attention paid to the commemoration of Dünner's one hundredth birthday in 1933. Jewish weeklies and journals were once again filled with articles on the late chief rabbi; a special brochure was printed with collected articles from the *Nieuw Israëlietisch Weekblad* (*NIW*), while in Amsterdam a special meeting and synagogue service were organized.[14] The meeting was held with a large portrait of Dünner surrounded by fresh greenery towering above the attendants, while the uncrowned king of Amsterdam Jewry, Abraham Asscher, delivered a speech. During the synagogue service itself, Chief Rabbi Onderwijzer honored his predecessor in a sermon and special prayer.[15]

11   *Nieuws van den dag*, 28 May 1912; "Monument Dünner," *Nieuws van den dag*, 4 Ju 1912.

12   "Uit onze beweging," *Mizrachie* 1/7 (1916).

13   "Isr. Kerk," *Het Vaderland*, 1 May 1929; E.M. Francès, "Boekbespreking," *De Vrijdagavond* 6/12 (1929), pp. 183–86.

14   *Bij den Honderdsten Geboortedag van Dr. J.H. Dünner. Verzamelde artikelen en redevoeringen verschenen in het Nieuw Israël. Weekblad bij de herdenking van den Honderdsten Geboortedag van Dr. J.H. Dünner op 12 Teiweis 5693 te Amsterdam, met een voorwoord van den Heer E. van Dien, voorzitter der Vereeniging tot steun aan het Nederl. Israëlietisch Seminarium* (Amsterdam 1933); SAA, NIHS, inv. nr. 2386.

15   "Rondom het Meijerplein. Amsterdamsche Brief CCLVI. Opperrabbijn Dr. J.H. Dünner herdacht," *Weekblad voor Israëlietische Huisgezinnen* 64/2 (1933).

Analyzing the speeches, articles and references to Dünner in the pre-war period, a few remarks could be made. First of all, Dünner and his heritage were nearly inviolable: he was referred to as someone who was in a league of his own and, therefore, nearly immune to criticism. The Dutch Israelite Weekly noted, in 1933, that Dünner was such a grandiose figure that no one on earth would be able to fully understand him, and that a study of his personality would have to comprise many volumes of books.[16] Benzion Hirsch, already three years earlier, reasoned that because of Dünner's greatness, any attempt to write a comprehensive biography on him was doomed to fail.[17] For many, Dünner was a person loftier than his contemporaries as well as the present generations. It is telling that, frequently, authors reasoned: "Although Dünner was also a human being, he . . . ," thus stressing his extraordinary, nearly supernatural role. For example, his doctor, Herman Pinkhof, commented that as a human being he must have made mistakes, but that he had always remained faithful to the greater good.[18] Perhaps the most pointed remark came from Dr. David Mozes Sluys, the secretary of the Orthodox community, who stated that, although Dünner had been a human being, if he wouldn't have been here, God would have had to perform another miracle to save Dutch Jewry.[19] In sum, Dünner was a miracle, a gift of God to Dutch Jewry and, therefore, not to be fully understood and immune to criticism.

Influenced by the rise of psychology, most authors devoted some attention to Dünner's personality, describing the great chief rabbi as a serious, strict and critical person, but overwhelmingly, he was viewed as a living embodiment of certain principles.[20] Dünner stood for a solid Orthodox Judaism, a scientific approach to Jewish sources and was considered to be the architect of "decorum" in synagogue.[21] For that reason, after his death in 1911, Dünner was given the posthumous role as Dutch Jewry's "conscience." Though no longer alive, it

---

16   Editors NIW, "Dr. J.H. Dünner–Herdenking (Inleiding)," in *Honderdsten Geboortedag*, pp. 4–5.

17   B.J. Hirsch, "Dr. Dünner's Tosefta-theorie. Bijdrage tot een studie van Dünner's Talmoed-school," (reprint) *De Vrijdagavond* 7 (1930), pp. 5, 8, 10 and 26.

18   H. Pinkhof, "Aan de nagedachtenis van Dr. J.H. Dünner z.g.," in *Honderdsten Geboortedag*, p. 11; Pinkhof's daughter gave a vivid description of her childhood perception of Dünner, his character, and the impact of his death on their family: C. Asscher-Pinkhof, *Danseres zonder benen* (Dommelen1989), pp. 28–31, 43–44.

19   D.M. Sluys, "Hoe ik Dr. Dünner zie," in *Honderdsten Geboortedag*, pp. 14–17.

20   Already during Dünner's funeral this approach became apparent in Rabbi Vredenburg's eulogy; "Uitvaart Dr. J.H. Dünner," NRC, 18 October 1911.

21   In fact, many of the measures Dünner was credited with, were already issued and implemented in the first half of the nineteenth century; B. Wallet, *Nieuwe Nederlanders: De integratie van de joden in Nederland 1814–1851* (Amsterdam 2007), pp. 146–76.

was as if he was still present to guide his flock in the right direction.[22] Chief
Rabbi Onderwijzer expressed it like this: "When difficult matters arise, though
problems, crucial interests are at stake, I consult his spirit, and I ask him, what
he would have done in this case."[23] Elsewhere, he described how "the admoni-
tory voice of the Great Master" guided him and kept him on the right track.
Debates in the Amsterdam community, therefore, could easily be silenced with
a reference to Dünner. When, in 1933, the Permanente Commissie, the highest authorities of Ashkenazi Dutch Jewry, proposed to open up the possibility to have foreigners accepted as candidates for the function of rector of the
Seminary, the lawyer Jeremias Elia Hillesum fiercely opposed it and stated that
if that were to be allowed Dünner's legacy would be spoiled. The committee
withdrew the proposal immediately and stressed that they did not want to do
anything that could possibly harm Dünner's legacy.[24]

    Then what was it, precisely, that Dünner stood for? In many instances, read-
ers were urged to follow the example of Dünner, though often it was not made
clear in what respects Dünner was exemplary.[25] Two main topics, however,
arise when all of the material is looked at together. First, Dünner was perceived
as the architect of Dutch Jewry's specific character, which was described as
completely unique in the Jewish world.[26] Unlike elsewhere, Dutch Jewry was
still a unity, consisting of real *Einheitsgemeinden*: whereas liberal and Orthodox Jews had split elsewhere, in the Netherlands they all remained united in
the national NIK denomination. Dünner had succeeded in this unique project,
by following a consistent middle way, because of which he was attacked from
both the strict-Orthodox and Reform sides. For the best of Dutch Jewry, however, he remained steadfast and did not give in, either to the left, or to the right.
Dünner was credited with the already existing Dutch Jewish tradition in which

22   The *Mizrachi* movement remembered Dünner "as if he were alive," since "great spirits
     don't die" and described its goal to be "bearers of his spirit"; "Jaartijd Dr. J.H. Dünner z"l,"
     Mizrachie 5/7 (1920), p. 45.
23   "Rede gehouden door den WelEerw. Hr. A.S. Onderwijzer," in *Honderdsten Geboortedag*,
     pp. 66–72.
24   "Buitengewone zitting der Centrale Commissie," *Weekblad voor Israëlietische Huis-
     gezinnen* 64/6 (1933).
25   E.g. Dr. E. Slijper, "Bij de jaartijd van Dr. Dünner," *Mizrachie* 2/7 (October 1917); "Rede ge-
     houden door den Heer A. Asscher," in *Honderdsten Geboortedag*, pp. 58–63.
26   A.S. Onderwijzer, "Dr. Dünner's Honderdste Geboortedag," in *Honderdsten Geboortedag*,
     pp. 6–8; Ben-David [J.H. Davids], "De installatie van Opperrabbijn S. Dasberg," *De Vrij-
     dagavond* 5/41 (1929), pp. 234–36; "De beteekenis der Asjkenasische Gemeente te Am-
     sterdam," *Het Vaderland*, 26 September 1935; "Dr. J.H. Dünner," *Het Joodsche Weekblad*, 10
     October 1941.

the administrative leaders of Dutch Jewry did not have to live an Orthodox life-style in order to fulfill representative positions, as long as the Orthodox rabbis were in control of the religious domain. In 1933, Lazar Dünner, the eldest son of the late chief rabbi, urged the leaders of the day not to leave his father's path; elsewhere, there was "hopeless division, conflict and a lack of tolerance," but Dutch Jewry was "an unharmed community, an undivided unity" and, there-fore, the leaders had to be "faithful to this glorious tradition of unity, concord and peace," in which Dutch Jewry was a true example for Jewish communities elsewhere.[27]

Second, Dünner was perceived as someone who had succeeded in bring-ing together, in a fruitful way, secular and religious knowledge, thus opening a viable way for Jews to participate in society on the one hand, and to renew Orthodoxy from within on the other hand. Dünner had reorganized the Dutch Israelite Seminary, brought in classical studies, introduced the historical-critical method to study rabbinic texts and was active in international Jew-ish scholarship.[28] True, many authors acknowledged that Dünner's approach to Talmud study had been controversial in Orthodox circles, but the "Great Master" was not to be blamed for that; the critics simply did not understand him properly or were not as learned as he had been.[29] Furthermore, Dünner was credited with introducing "decorum" in synagogue, thus making Ortho-doxy more attractive for modern Jews. Irrational elements in the liturgy were taken out, in order to create a "purified" synagogue service. Whereas, many argued that for Dünner's scholarly approach to succeed, one needed to be very learned, the more practical synagogal heritage was easier to conserve and keep for coming generations.[30]

Dünner's legacy was so strong, that those who didn't agree with him on a certain point, preferred not to speak about it, rather than publicly distance themselves from him. There were some Dutch rabbis who were cautious with Dünner's approach to Talmud study, being familiar with the severe criticism of some of Germany's leading Orthodox rabbis, but they mostly reasoned: quod licet Iovi, non licet bovi (what is permissible for Jove is not permissible for

27 "Rede gehouden door den WelEerw. Heer L. Dünner," in *Honderdsten Geboortedag*, pp. 64–66; "Rondom het Meijerplein."
28 A.H., "Bij den vijfden jaartijddag van Dr. Dünner zts"l," *Mizrachie* 1/7 (1916); J.H. Sohlberg, "Het Ned.Isr. Seminarium," *De Vrijdagavond* 7/39 (1930), pp. 199–202; 7/40 (1931), pp. 210–12; 7/41 (1931), pp. 226–28; 7/42 (1931), pp. 243–46.
29 *Het Vaderland*, 2 April 1929.
30 B.J. Hirsch, "De halachische voordracht ter Groote Synagoge te Amsterdam," *De Vrijdaga-vond* 3/24 (1926), pp. 370–73.

an ox). Because of the genius Dünner was, he could study the Talmud in such a way, but we, normal people, we are not able to do so, and should, therefore, stick to more traditional ways of studying the Talmud.[31]

There was only one topic on which Dünner's disciples publicly expressed different opinions, namely Dünner's attitude toward Zionism. Dünner had delivered some sermons in favor of Zionism already in the late nineteenth century and had until his death in 1911 been a member of the religious Zionist *Mizrachi* movement. Whereas the Dutch Zionist Organization described Dünner as one of their predecessors, thus using his authority to convince Orthodox Jews to join the Zionist movement, for the *Mizrachi* he was even more than that.[32] Rabbi Simon Philip de Vries wrote: he was our *auctor intellectualis* and our spiritual guide.[33] The *Mizrachi* remembered Dünner every year on his *yahrzeit* in its journal, stressing the Great Master's Zionist convictions and his continuing importance as "example" and embodiment of "the *Mizrachi* idea in its purity."[34] Also pieces of unpublished work of Dünner found their way to the *Mizrachi* journal, most of it not dealing with Zionism in any way, but clearly expressing the *Mizrachi*'s convictions that Dünner belonged to their camp.[35] A major step to underline this reasoning was the publication of the correspondence between the young Dünner and the proto-Zionist Moses Hess, in the time the latter was writing his influential *Rom und Jerusalem*. Although Zionism is barely referred to in these letters, they became an important showcase

31   J.H. Sohlberg, "Twee methoden van Talmudstudie," IV, *De Vrijdagavond* 6/27 (1929); V, *De Vrijdagavond* 6/23 (1929).

32   "Nederlandsche Zionistenbond," NRC, 27 December 1911; "De Joodsche Congresdemonstratie," NRC, 18 February 1918; "De Nederlandsche Zionistenbond 25 jaar," *Het Vaderland*, 13 June 1924; "Geschiedenis van 't Israëlitisch kerkgenootschap," *Het Vaderland*,15 February 1940; G.C. Polak, "Vóór en bij de geboorte van den Nederlandschen Zionistenbond," *De Vrijdagavond* 1/12 (1924), pp. 182–85; S. Ph. de Vries, "Op den terugweg naar Zion," in *Nederlandsche Zionistenbond 1899–1924, 5659–5684. Gedenkboek*, ed. F. Bernstein, K.J. Edersheim, M.J. Simons (Amsterdam 1925), pp. 84–88; "Brieven uit Amsterdam," *Het Vaderland*, 17 January 1920.

33   S. Ph. de Vries, "'n Pikante herinnering. Naar aanleiding van de herdenking van Dr. J.H. Dünner z"l bij den honderdsten verjaardag van zijn geboortedag," *Mizrachie: Maandblad der Nederlandsche Afdeeling der Wereldorganisatie "Mizrachie"* 16/8 (1933), pp. 57–58; cf. also S. Dasberg et al., *Rabbijn De Vries, dienaar des Jodendoms, ter gelegenheid van zijn afscheid als rabbijn te Haarlem* (Amsterdam 1940).

34   "Jaartijd Dr. J.H. Dünner z"l," *Mizrachie* 5/7 (1920), p. 45; "Bij den Jaartijddag van Dr. Dünner z"l," *Mizrachie* 6/7 (1921), p. 56.

35   E.g. J.H. Dünner, "Ursprung, Bedeutung und Abfassungszeit der Esterrolle," *Mizrachie* 15/9 (1932), pp. 10–13; 15/10 (1932), pp. 81–83.

for Dünner's Zionist convictions: even before Theodor Herzl, Dünner had already seen the true light, his *Mizrachi* disciples commented.[36]

Most of Dünner's pupils, however, did not follow their Great Master in his Zionist convictions. Moreover, they became active in the anti-Zionist Agudath Israel movement. Some tried to delegitimize the *Mizrachi* movement's claims and argued that Dünner, toward the end of his life, had distanced himself from Zionism, and even brought in some documentary evidence for that.[37] Most chose, however, a different approach. In the journal of the Agudah, virtually no reference at all was made to Dünner; he was simply ignored. Also, during the official 1933 commemorations, Dünner's Zionism was deliberately left out of the official program. The *NIW* had numerous articles on Dünner's significance for a variety of Jewish institutions and movements, but none on Zionism. It was only in Abraham Asscher's speech that a short mention was made of Dünner's Zionism.[38]

What rhetoric was used to describe Dünner? A number of titles was given to him, the most frequent being "Father," "Great Master" and "Genius." "Father" was a metaphor with which contemporary Jews attached themselves to Dünner, expressing their willingness to continue his path. Dünner's fatherhood was described in Victorian terms: he was a strict father, educating his children in a proper way, doing what was best for them rather than what they would have liked him to do.[39] But Father Dünner could deal with the consequences, and was to be trusted in what he did. Being a father also meant that Dünner was not able to be too loving and caring which was a mother's role, but he expressed his love in his discipline. First and foremost, Dünner was represented as the "Father of Dutch Jewry," a nearly spiritual role that brings to mind the

---

36   "Brieven van Moses Hess aan Dr. Dünner z.g.," *Mizrachie* 7/1 (1922), p. 2; 7/2 (1923), pp. 10–12; 7/4 (1923), pp. 25–26; 7/5 (1923), pp. 34–36; 7/6 (1923), pp. 41–42.

37   These attacks on the Mizrachi movement were answered by the Groningen Chief Rabbi Abraham Asscher Ezn., once again using Dünner's authority to defend their case: "Eenheid," *Mizrachie* 6/6 (1921), pp. 46–47; also fiercely in H. Pinkhof, "Dr. J.H. Dünner z"l," *Mizrachie* 1/7 (1916); disappointment on the attitude of Dünner's pupils is also expressed in L. Asscher, "Jaarverslag v.d. Secretaris aan de 2e Jaarlijksche Algemeene Vergadering der Ned. Mizrachie," *Mizrachie* 8/4 (1924), pp. 36–38.

38   "Rede gehouden door den Heer A. Asscher," in *Honderdsten Geboortedag*, pp. 58–63; "Rondom het Meijerplein," "Dr. J.H. Dünner, 1833–1933," *Het Vaderland*, 10 January 1933.

39   A.S. Onderwijzer, "Dr. Dünner's Honderdste Geboortedag,"in *Honderdsten Geboortedag*, pp. 6–8; telling is A. Polak's recollection of Dünner's arrival at the Dutch Israelite Seminary in 1862 and how he restored order after exclaiming "Ist es hier ein Thiergarten?"; cited after Meijer, "Amsterdam die joodse stad (III)," p. 15.

image of a hasidic rebbe and his followers.[40] The *NIW* wrote in 1933: "A father he was for Dutch Jewry, protecting his children from the spiritual and moral dangers of present times; who countered with his sharp pen and powerful words the attacks on the legacy of the ages and who showed his flock the way to the godly ideal."[41] Jewish leaders, in a move to legitimize their authority, went so far as to attribute to Dünner a role as their father. Moreover, a number of institutions or movements did the same: he was perceived as the "father" of Jewish days-schools, modern Jewish youth movements, the Dutch rabbinate, and Dutch Zionism in general and *Mizrachi* in particular.[42]

Next to "father," he was labeled "the Great Master." This term was given to him predominantly by his former students at the Dutch Israelite Seminary.[43] As Onderwijzer put it in 1917: At the Seminary we had many good teachers, but Dünner was the "nesher ha-gadol," the great eagle (a qualification generally reserved for Dünner's hero Maimonides), because he had a complete overview over Torah and Talmud.[44] All Dünner's students stood in the shadow of their "Great Master," and whatever event took place in their lives, from taking a position as chief rabbi, a jubilee, or their death, always they were referred to as Dünner's pupils.[45] They themselves expressed as well their willingness

40   "Het levenswerk van Dr. J.H. Dünner z.g.," in *Honderdsten Geboortedag*, pp. 55–57.

41   Homiletical article in *NIW* weekly, "Bij den honderdsten geboortedag van Dr. J.H. Dünner z.g.," in *Honderdsten Geboortedag*, pp. 28–31.

42   J.E. Hillesum, in *NRC*, 11 December 1916; idem., "De verordening van den Amsterdamschen kerkeraad betreffende de bijzondere scholen," *De Vrijdagvond* 1/21 (1924), pp. 324–3., "De Joodsche jeugdbeweging," *NRC*, 26 April 1924; "De Joodsche kiesvereeniging, Het *Vaderland*, 9 February 1928; "De Joodsche bijzondere school," *NRC*, 10 February 1928; J.E. Hillesum, "Dr. J.H. Dünner z"l en de Joodsche Bijzondere School," in *Honderdsten Geboortedag*, pp. 25–28.

43   Out of many examples, De Vries, "'n Pikante herinnering"; B. de Vries, "Rector Wagenaar z"l, *De Vrijdagavond* 7/11 (1930), pp. 162–66; A. Druijff, "Een eerelijst: De Moré's, opgeleid aan het Ned. Isr. Seminarium onder het rectoraat van Dr. J.H. Dünner z.g.," in *Honderdsten Geboortedag*, pp. 32–54.

44   *Orde van den dienst ter gelegenheid van de plechtige bevestiging van den weleerwaarden heer A.S. Onderwijzer, als opperrabbijn van het ressort Noord-Holland, op zondag 13 Siwan 5677 (3 juni 1917)* (Amsterdam 1917), p. xiii.

45   E.g. The Hague Chief Rabbi A. van Loen: *Het Vaderland* 9, February 1922; *NRC*, 11 February 1922; or his successor: "Installatie van opperrabbijn I. Maarsen," *Het Vaderland*, 26 October 1925; others, "Opperrabbijn A.B.N. Davids," *NRC*, 1 December 1929; B.J. Hirsch, "In memoriam L. Wagenaar z"l: bij de herdenking van zijn eersten 'jaartijd,'" *De Vrijdagavond* 8/8 (1931), pp. 115–18; "Begrafenis Opperrabbijn A.S. Onderwijzer," *Het Vaderland*, 20 November 1934; "Opperrabbijn J. Vredenburg 75 jaar," *Het Joodsche Weekblad*, 8 August 1941; "Opperrabbijn J. Vredenburg overleden," *Het Joodsche Weekblad*, 19 March 1943.

to continue in the path of their "Great Master."[46] A telling example is Onderwijzer's jubilee, serving the Amsterdam *kehillah* for forty years. In an article Onderwijzer is constantly compared to Dünner. Dünner was described as the architect, he set out the strategy, he made the plans; Onderwijzer was the one to follow him, to bring Dünner's ideas into practice. Whereas Dünner made officers for the army, Onderwijzer popularized the Great Master's ideas and made soldiers for the army.[47] Some within the Dutch rabbinate were also in a more personal way related to Dünner, as his sons, grandchildren and those who married into the family. When A.B.N. Davids took up the Frisian chief rabbinate in 1924, he chose the same day as his grandfather fifty years earlier to be inaugurated, and during the service expressed his reverence for the "Great Master," promising to continue in his grandfather's footsteps.[48]

Finally, Dünner was also frequently termed a "genius." A number of legends located in his Krakow youth were employed to demonstrate that Dünner, from his birth, had been a very special and gifted person.[49] Being a genius meant that Dünner could do things that for normal people, even for normal rabbis and Talmudists, were practically impossible. As a genius Dünner was able to read Talmud without Rashi and, even, could harshly criticize Rashi. Dünner's genius was demonstrated in the fact that he was well-practiced in rabbinic and modern scholarship, bringing both together.[50] Being a genius meant that Dünner worked alone, since there were barely people who could grasp his general work. As Benzion Hirsch put it, the heads of the other Talmudists at the time barely reached Dünner's shoulders.[51] He was considered a genius in every respect, not just as a Talmudist, but no less as a leader and a preacher.[52]

Dünner was frequently compared with two of his contemporaries: Abraham Carel Wertheim and Rabbi Samson Raphael Hirsch. Together with Wertheim, Dünner formed a couple; Wertheim assumed the administrative leadership of

---

46   "Voor het Ned. Isr. Seminarium," *Weekblad voor Israëlietische Huisgezinnen* 64/2 (1933), p. 2.

47   "Opperrabbijn A.S. Onderwijzer," NRC, 31 July 1928; "Jubileum opperrabbijn A.S. Onderwijzer," NRC, 1 August 1928.

48   "Moré A.B.N. Davids," *Het Vaderland*, 30 November 1923; 4 July 1924; "De installatie van den opperrabbijn van het ressort Friesland," *Het Vaderland*, 29 December 1924; "Installatie van den opperrabbijn van Friesland," NRC, 29 December 1924.

49   "Dr. Dünner z.g. als wetenschappelijk onderzoeker," in *Honderdsten Geboortedag*, pp. 12–14.

50   B. de Vries, "Dr. J.H. Dünner z"l," *De Vrijdagavond* 5/52 (1929), pp. 405–09.

51   Hirsch, "Tosefta-theorie," p. 15, cf. p. 8.

52   B.J. Hirsch, "In memoriam Dr. J.H. Dünner z"l: Op zijn jaartijddag 24 Tiesjrie," *De Vrijdagavond* 9/30 (1932), pp. 37–39.

Dutch Jewry, Dünner the religious.[53] Just before the commemoration of Dünner in 1933, Wertheim was also publicly commemorated in December 1932.[54]
Abraham Asscher expressed the opinion that in a time lacking real leadership
Dutch Jewry looked back in admiration to these two giants who were a source
of inspiration for the present. Although Wertheim was a liberal and non-
observant Jew, he fully fitted into Dünner's theory of accommodating such
Jews into nominal Orthodoxy.[55] Both are described by many pre-war authors
as not just collaborators, but intimate friends. The editors of the *NIW* weekly
went even further and, including also Cantor Isaac Heymann, compared the
three men to the three patriarchs and the central values in rabbinic literature
of *Torah* (Dünner), *Avodah* (Heymann) and *Gemilut Hasadim* (Wertheim).[56]

The comparison with Samson Raphael Hirsch is a different story. Most
considered Dünner more successful and greater than Hirsch, the architect of
neo-Orthodoxy. Dünner was the man of unity, Hirsch the man of separation.
Dünner saw that Orthodoxy needed to stay in contact with the wide circle of
Jews around it, whereas Hirsch thought to find his strength in isolating Orthodoxy. Hirsch's critique of Dünner's Talmud approach as being too much
influenced by historical criticism was, according to the Dutch, because he did
not understand properly Dünner's genius. Paradoxically, however, a significant number of Dünner's students fell under Hirsch's influence. Although they
didn't dare to introduce the concept of *Austritt* (an Orthodox split from the *Einheitsgemeinde*) in the Netherlands, they oriented themselves toward Frankfurt
and eventually followed Hirsch in union with Eastern European Jewry in the

---

53   See e.g. "Rede gehouden door den WelEerw. Heer L. Dünner," in *Honderdsten Geboorte-
      dag*, pp. 64–66.

54   "Leven en werken van A.C. Wertheim: 1832 – 12 December – 1932," *Algemeen Handelsblad*,
      4 December 1932.

55   "Rondom het Meijerplein"; "Rede gehouden door den Heer A. Asscher," in *Honderdsten
      Geboortedag*, pp. 58–63; Wertheim's wife Rosalie, in a poem, already pointed at the curi-
      ous relationship between her husband and Rabbi Dünner:

          U die den Kerkeraad met 't levend woord bezielt,
          De Vleeschhal zuivert, en voor Dünners grootheid knielt,
          U, die naar woorden zoekt om Moozes' wet te prijzen,
          Maar toch op Zaterdag Uw Wasch omhoog doet rijzen,
          U, die ik als ware jood vereer, bemin en koester, –
          U zend ik op deez' dag als huldeblijk een . . . oester.

      Cited after, M.H. Gans, *Memorboek: Platenatlas van het leven der joden in Nederland
      van de middeleeuwen tot 1940*, 4th ed. (Baarn 1974), p. 394.

56   *Torah* meaning study, *avodah* meaning work, and *gemilut hasadim*, charity work. Editors,
      NIW, "Dr. J.H. Dünner-Herdenking (Inleiding)," in *Honderdsten geboortedag*, pp. 4–5.

anti-Zionist Agudath Israel movement.[57] Not surprisingly, therefore, in the Dutch Agudah journal Dünner and Hirsch are put on the same level, described as driven by the same convictions, while Hirsch's *Torah im derekh eretz* was equated with Dünner's modern scholarly approach to Talmud study.[58]

Testator of Halakhah, 1945–1984[59]

After the Second World War the reception of Dünner gradually changed and became increasingly critical. The *Shoah* and the foundation of the State of Israel had a huge impact on Dutch Jewry and consequently changed the image of Dünner. In the postwar years, many of the "memory managers" from the prewar period were gone; they either had been murdered in the camps, or had migrated to Israel. Thus, the number of possible "memory managers" was significantly reduced. The Amsterdam Chief Rabbi Justus Tal was widely perceived as the last student of Dünner and, after 1945, he was generally considered to be old-fashioned, representing a world that had disappeared and to which he, nevertheless, remained faithful.[60] When Tal died in 1954, many commentators described it as the definitive end of the prewar period.[61] Tal was buried next to his beloved "Great Master" and the liturgy of his funeral service followed Dünner's from 1911.[62]

There were, however, some who tried to uphold Dünner's memory and direct Dutch Jewry in Dünner's footsteps. The most significant of them was Jaap Meijer, on whom Evelien Gans writes more extensively in this volume. In the 1960s, Jaap Meijer frequently visited the meetings of the board of the Amsterdam *kehillah* and developed a number of proposals to remember Dünner. In 1961, he wished to commemorate Dünner's passing; in 1962 he argued that the arrival of Dünner in the Netherlands one hundred years ago was a fitting event

---

57   De Vries, "Op den terugweg naar Zion," pp. 85–87.

58   "De jongste Agoedo-dag," *Agoedas Jisroeil: Officieel veertiendaagsch organ van de afd. Nederland van den wereldbond der orthodoxie Agoedas Jisroeil* 8/9 (1933), pp. 1–3.

59   1984 is chosen as a symbolic *terminus ante quem* as in this year Jaap Meijer's *Rector en raw* was published, which is to date the most recent study of Dünner.

60   Justus Tal prided himself on being the Great Master's last pupil, and there is even a legend that Dünner's last word had been "Tzodek," Tal's Hebrew name; Meijer, "Amsterdam die joodse stad (III)," p. 16.

61   SAA, NIHS, Eulogy of Rabbi Aron Schuster for Chief Rabbi Justus Tal, 1954.

62   SAA, NIHS, nr. 4282, Report on the death and burial of Chief Rabbi Justus Tal, 16 June 1955; further in B. Wallet, P.l van Trigt, H. Polak, *Die ons heeft laten leven: Geschiedenis van de Joodse Gemeente Amsterdam [NIHS] van 1945 tot 2010* (Amsterdam 2011), pp. 96–102.

to celebrate. Jaap Meijer had big plans: he wished to organize a Dünner month, starting with a halakhic *derashah* (sermon) by Chief Rabbi Schuster, including a public event at the University of Amsterdam, the presentation of a scholarly book, the publication of Dünner's *hagahot* (critical annotations to the Talmud, *Tosefta* and *Midrashim*), a traveling exhibition and a children's book. When one of the board members asked: "Why should we remember Dünner, who is there who still knows him?" Jaap Meijer answered: "Exactly for that reason we need to commemorate Dünner, as he is still significant for present-day Amsterdam Jewry."[63] In the end, two years too late, only a book was published in memory of Dünner, *Moeder in Israël*, written by Jaap Meijer commissioned by the NIHS and offering a short history of the Amsterdam Ashkenazi *kehillah* with specific attention to Dünner's role.[64]

For the scholarly volume, Jaap Meijer had visited Israel and asked the collaboration of Rabbi Benjamin de Vries and Dünner's grandson Sally L. de Beer. Although the book was never published, De Beer had written his contribution, which now was given a place in the community journal *Hakehilla*. For some years, every volume of *Hakehilla* had a contribution of De Beer on Dünner.[65] After some time, board member Herman Musaph complained that *Hakehilla* had become so boring and referred to the Dünner series. Sal Boas, another board member, however, argued that it was of great importance to Amsterdam Jewry to read these articles, given the continuing importance of Rabbi Dünner.[66]

In what way had Dünner's memory changed after the war? First, after 1948, Dünner the Zionist was fully accepted. He was honored as a wise man, who had recognized, very early on, the rightful claims of Zionism.[67] Due to the Zionist ideology and in the wake of the *Shoah* however, also the appreciation of the

---

63   SAA, NIHS, minutes Daily Board, 15 September 1960; 17 October 1960; 9 May 1961; 20 July 1961; 29 August 1961; 28 December 1961; 1 March 1962; 5 June 1962; 9 October 1962; minutes General Board (Kerkenraad) 9 July 1962.

64   SAA, NIHS, minutes General Board, 27 October 1964; J. Meijer, *Moeder in Israël. Een geschiedenis van het Amsterdamse Asjkenazische Jodendom* (Haarlem 1964).

65   S.L. de Beer, "Ha-raav Dr. J.H. Dünner z"l, Een karakterschets (bij het verstrijken van 100 jaren na zijn aankomst in Nederland)," *Hakehilla* 8/1 (1962), pp. 3–5.

66   SAA, NIHS, minutes General Board, 28 October 1963; 14 November 1963.

67   E.D.D., "Een halve eeuw na Dünner," *De Joodse Wachter* 52/11 (1961), pp. 16–18; S.L. de Beer, "Ha-raav Dr. J.H. Dünner z"l, Een karakterschets: Dünner als Zionist," *Hakehilla* 9/10–11 (1964), pp. 2–4; while his Zionism was lauded, Dünner at the same time was criticized on having been critical of the Socialist movement, which should have resulted in an alienation of the working classes from Zionism; A.J. Herzberg, "Een gelukwens en een beschouwing," *De Joodse Wachter* 44 /17 (1953), pp. 4–6.

emancipation changed. In prewar times, emancipation was considered to be a great blessing, but now it became a curse. In the Dünner reception this analysis changed his image in two ways. On the one hand Dünner was presented as the "savior" who had saved Dutch Jewry after the emancipation from complete assimilation. He had given them, once again, a solid Jewish identity. But, unfortunately, he could only do that by isolating Dutch Jewry from world Jewry, thus, in effect, breaking the national unity of all Jews. Whereas before the war Dutch Jews were proud of this distinct identity, and thanked Dünner for that, now they blamed him for precisely the same thing: he was the man who had isolated the Dutch Jews.[68] Already in 1941, J. Melkman argued that in his radical Zionist opinion Dünner, although he accepted Zionism, was still an assimilationist by not accepting the need of dissimilation from Dutch society.[69]

Second, Dünner's unity discourse was, however, not completely lost. Meijer, De Beer, but also others, argued that Dutch Jews should reconnect with world Jewry, in the first place in Israel, but at the same time not lose the *Einheitsgemeinde*. In their Zionist ideology, the *Einheitsgemeinde* was a national structure, a part of Israel outside of Israel. After the war, Dünner's legacy had to be defended in two directions. First, after Jaap Soetendorp took over the rabbinate of the Liberal Jewish Community in Amsterdam in 1954, Reform Judaism became a force to be reckoned with. According to Jaap Meijer, his proposed Dünner commemorations were a way to counter Reform Judaism. Dünner was the one who had saved Dutch Jewry from Reform Judaism in the nineteenth century, and by remembering Dünner Dutch Jews would realize that Reform Judaism was nothing less than "*dilletanten-Jodendom*" (Judaism of dilletantes).[70] De Beer added one more perspective. He saw with growing disquiet, that Dutch Orthodox families developed a tradition of sending their children to yeshivot abroad. In De Beer's eyes, they thus left the creative Seminary route, which led to a solid, but also civilized Orthodoxy and opted for the traditionalist Eastern European Orthodoxy, which didn't fit either the Netherlands or Israel, where De Beer then lived. De Beer's series of articles, therefore, were meant for the Orthodox youth to stick to Dünner's legacy and not give in to Eastern European Orthodoxy. Likewise, because Dutch Jewry after 1945 had

---

68   See for example, J.E. Vleeschhouwer, "Nehemia de Lieme als Jood. Een levensloop als phase van Nederlandsch-Joodsche geschiedenis," *De Joodse Wachter* (1952), pp. 9–18; S.L. de Beer, "Ha-raav Dr. J.H. Dünner z"l. Een karakterschets: Het 'Denkschreiben' (kritisch)," *Hakehilla* 9/1 (September/October 1963), pp. 18–20.

69   J. Melkman, "Dr. J.H. Dünner 1833–1911," in *Menorah 5701. Joods Jaarboek*, ed. H. Heymans and J. Melkman, 2nd edition (Amsterdam 1940), pp. 125–33.

70   SAA, NIHS, minutes Daily Board, 9 May 1961; cf. Meijer, *Moeder in Israël*, p. 134.

to look for foreign rabbis who were no longer trained at Dünner's Seminary, De Beer wanted them to read his articles in order that they understand, appreciate and adopt Dünner's model of Amsterdam Orthodoxy.[71]

In postwar publications, authors try to historicize Dünner, giving growing attention to his psychology, the conditions in Western Europe, Dutch society and the like. Those writing about Dünner, however, remained roughly the same as before: those related to Dünner's family and those tracing their rabbinic genealogy to Dünner. He began to be forgotten, turning into a name rather than a program to adhere to. This process of historicization, however, becomes most clear when we study, once again, how Dünner is referred to and with whom he is compared.

Some, like Chief Rabbi Justus Tal or Rabbi Benjamin de Vries, still used the prewar terminology: Dünner as their father, the "Great Master."[72] Also Jaap Meijer did so, but in his work, the term "Great Master" turns increasingly into an ironic one, as he developed over time a growingly critical appreciation mainly of Dünner's pupils. Meijer, however, introduced a new term for Dünner in correspondence with contemporary historiography: "Testator of the halakhah."[73] The term testator, "erflater" in Dutch, was introduced by his teacher Jan Romein,[74] who, as a Marxist, saw these "testators" as original bearers of the "Zeitgeist," great personalities who embodied their times and connected individual and community. By studying biographies of "great persons," Romein thought to get a grip on Dutch history.[75] Meijer took this concept and presented Dünner as the embodiment of Dutch Jewish nineteenth-century Orthodoxy, the "testator of halakhah." By studying Dünner, Meijer thought one would get a grip on Dutch Jewish history. But Meijer introduced one more aspect. He started to compare and equate Dünner to Rabbi Dr. Meijer de Hond. Meijer took over a contemporary Jewish socialist critique of Dünner and argued that he was too much of a bourgeois, and thus failed to attract the Jewish proletariat. Only the

71   S.L. de Beer, "Ha-raav Dr. J.H. Dünner z"l. Een karakterschets: Het 'Denkschreiben' (kritisch)," *Hakehilla* 8/11–12 (1963), pp. 2–4; idem, "Ha-raav Dr. J.H. Dünner z"l. Een karakterschets: Dünners bijzondere persoonlijkheid (slot)," *Hakehilla* 9/12 (1964), pp. 1–3.

72   M.M. Poppers, "Boekbespreking: Benjamin de Vries: Jozeph Tzevi Halévi Dünner," *Hakehilla* 4/7 (1959), p. 9.

73   Meijer, *Moeder in Israël*, p. 86f.

74   On the relationship between Jan Romein and Jaap Meijer: E. Gans, *Jaap en Ischa Meijer: Een joodse geschiedenis 1912–1956* (Amsterdam 2008), pp. 166–70, 485–86.

75   J. and A. Romein, *Erflaters van onze beschaving: Nederlandse gestalten uit zes eeuwen. 1: 14ᵉ –16ᵉ eeuw*, 5th edition (Amsterdam 1946), pp. 7–11. For an analysis of Romein's "erflater" concept: J. Tollebeek, "Finalisme en anti-finalisme in de geschiedschrijving van de Nederlandse cultuur," *Revue belge de philologie et d'histoire* 68/4 (1990), pp. 922–48.

people's rabbi Meijer de Hond was able to reach them; he was the "testator of *Aggadah*" (the homiletic, non-legalistic part of Jewish tradition), according to Meijer. By bringing together Dünner and De Hond, who had large and enduring conflicts while alive, Meijer at once historicized Dünner, but also added a new ideological, socialist perspective.

How influential Jaap Meijer's new approach was, became apparent on several occasions. When the NIK celebrated its 150th anniversary in 1965, Chief Rabbi Aron Schuster mentioned both together as two "men of stature," who together shaped Dutch Jewry and saved it from serious threats.[76] Moreover, on the same day as the Dünner Bridge was unveiled in 1966, a De Hond Bridge was unveiled not far from there.[77] While some of the attendants might have still thought about Dünner in the prewar categories, the ceremony itself was a clear manifestation of the new historicized Dünner. From that time on, the discussion of Dünner within the Dutch Jewish community nearly completely disappeared. Dünner was, from then on, nearly only mentioned when a new chief rabbi was inaugurated and his great predecessors mentioned. Out of the long list of Amsterdam Ashkenazi chief rabbis, ultimately only three had reached the catalogue of significant, influential rabbis of the past: the early modern halakhic authority *Hakham* Zvi, the famous R. Saul Amsterdam, named after his book the *Binyan Ariel*, whose offspring served as Dutch Jewry's religious leadership well into the nineteenth century, and Rabbi Dr. Jozeph Hirsch Dünner. They remained impressive figures, but had become symbols of the past.

---

76   "Rede van Opperrabbijn A. Schuster," *Hakehilla* 11/1 (1965), pp. 9–11.
77   Weijel, "Naamgeving."

CHAPTER 14

Image(s) of "The Rav" through the Lens of an Involved Historian: Jaap Meijer's Depiction of Rabbi Jozeph Hirsch Dünner

Evelien Gans

Scholarly biographies of leading personalities in the history of Dutch Jewry are scarce, especially biographies of influential rabbis. Rabbi Jozeph Hirsch (Zvi) Dünner, who undoubtedly left a remarkable imprint on religious education, on the raising and shaping of an entire group of Dutch rabbis, on religious practices and on the beginnings of the Zionist movement, was not taken up as a case for historians until ww ii. It was Joseph Melkman (later: Michman) who made a first attempt to do so, remarkably during the first phase of the German occupation. In the year book *Menorah 5701* (1940), published by the Dutch Zionist Federation with the aim to strengthen Jewish identity, he wrote a seven-page article on Dünner. In it he complained that in spite of many hailing and glorifying descriptions that had appeared in Jewish newspapers during his lifetime and after his death in 1911, no critical biography on the person in the context of his time had been attempted, even though almost thirty years had elapsed since his passing away. Melkman's article, which did "not have the intention . . . to provide a much-needed biography," indeed only dealt with Dünner's intellectual path as a deeply committed Orthodox as well as nationalist in coping with modern scholarship and its repercussions (he compared him to Abraham Geiger, Samuel Holdheim and Samson Raphael Hirsch in Germany).[1] A second, more extensive but essentially informative and descriptive biographical article was written in Hebrew by Professor Rabbi Benjamin de Vries, a professor of Talmud at Bar-Ilan University; it was included as an introduction to the republication of Rabbi Dünner's commentaries on the

---

1 J. Melkman, "Dr. J.H. Dünner, 1833–1911," *Menorah 5701* (Amsterdam 1940), pp. 125–33. Melkman was not only a historian, but also married to Frederika de Paauw, a granddaughter of Dünner; he (under his Hebraized name Michman) would return to Dünner in his later studies, such as J. Michman, "The Impact of German-Jewish Modernization on Dutch Jewry," in *Toward Modernity: The European Jewish Model*, ed. J. Katz (New York 1987), pp. 171–87; idem, "De strijd om de benoeming van Dr. J.H. Dunner tot rector van het Nederlandsch-Israelitisch Seminarium," *StRos* 22/2 (1988), pp. 165–85; J. Michman, H. Beem, D. Michman, *Pinkas: Geschiedenis van de joodse gemeenschap in Nederland* (Amsterdam 1999), pp. 98–101.

© KONINKLIJKE BRILL NV, LEIDEN, 2017 | DOI 10.1163/9789004343160_015

Talmud by Mossad Harav Kook in 1984; it lacked a critical historical approach and did not set Dünner in an interpretative historical context.[2] Therefore, historian Jaap Meijer's partial but extensive biography of Dünner *Rector en raw. De Levensgeschiedenis van Dr. J.H. Dünner (1833–1911)*, as well as the many instances where he related to Dünner's personality in his other books, should be seen as the first real attempt to evaluate this influential person in a multifaceted way. But Meijer was a most complex person, as I have pointed out extensively elsewhere,[3] and his evaluation was not *sine era et studio*.

Jaap Meijer had a tendency to interject his very self into the history that he was writing. He did it either openly and explicitly (quite often) or (sometimes) in a subtle way, hiding his involvement between the lines. This was definitely the case with his depiction of Dünner. Consider, for instance, the following anecdote: in the notes in the back of his book *Erfenis der Emancipatie* [Heritage of the Emancipation], when referring to Rabbi Dünner's arrival in Amsterdam, Meijer goes into some detail about Dünner's manuscript *Denkschreiben* (1862), the outline of the rabbi's vision regarding the reorganization and restructuring of the Dutch Jewish Seminary. First, Meijer provides some raw facts: the manuscript, dated 29 January 1862, had been published in Amsterdam in 1917 with an introduction by Lasar Dünner (Rabbi Dünner's eldest son). He then adds a personal dimension to these facts, namely that the original manuscript, in which Dünner himself had made many notes in the margin, had been consulted by him in 1940 but has since gone missing.[4] Thus, Meijer subtly brings several points to the reader's notice. First, the fact that Dünner had made many notes to his own manuscript is interesting for those who wish to have a better understanding of Dünner's scholarly process; it made clear that drafting a policy document like *Denkschreiben* appears to have entailed a thorough process of deep thinking and writing. Second, Jaap Meijer's admitting to having seen the original document gives him a certain authority over the reader who has not seen it and will not be able to see it in the future and, in so doing, makes the reader dependent on his authority. Third, by citing the year 1940, the author makes it clear that he studied the document in an exceptionally dramatic year,

2   B. de Vries, "Harav Dr. Jozeph Zvi Dünner z"l: Toledotav, Mif'alo, Mishnato," in *Hidushei Haritzad* [=*Harav Yozef Tzvi Dünner*] (Jerusalem 1981), pp. 9–32.

3   E. Gans, *Jaap en Ischa Meijer. Een joodse geschiedenis*, vol. 1 (Amsterdam 2008); idem., "Next Year in Paramaribo: *Galut* and Diaspora as Scene-changes in the Jewish Life of Jakob Meijer," in *The Dutch Intersection: The Jews and the Netherlands in Modern History*, ed. Y. Kaplan (Leiden and Boston 2008), pp. 369–87.

4   J. Meijer, *Erfenis der Emancipatie. Het Nederlandse Jodendom in de eerste helft van de 19e eeuw* (Haarlem 1963), p. 78. (The chapters were first published as articles in *Hakehilla*, April/May 1956–February 1957).

which is underlined by the fourth claim, that the precious manuscript was lost during the Nazi occupation.

Meijer on Dünner: Debunking the Myth

As said, in 1984 Meijer wrote the hitherto sole comprehensive, be it only the first part, of Dünner's biography. But that was only the tip of the iceberg: as from his early writings until his posthumously published autobiographical book on his life as a student at the rabbinical seminary, Dünner was omnipresent in Meijer's historiography.[5] So, what were the main points in Dünner's career and personality that interested Meijer?

First, there was the historical moment of Dünner's arrival in Amsterdam in 1862 and nomination as Rector of the Nederlands Israëlietisch Seminarium (NIS), the rabbinical seminary. Several times Meijer stated that that very moment had been turned into some sort of legend reminiscent of the Biblical Flood—an event which had swept away all preceding history. Consequently, Dünner was made a *Deus ex machina*. Meijer recorded how Dünner's coming, as described in the school books he had read, had impressed him as a child: "Then came Dr. Dünner," functioning as a "primitive historical sensation . . . We were saved."[6] From this perspective he dissociated himself now as a historian and turned more to proving that Dünner's elevated intellectual status—as a brilliant academic next to his being an outstanding Talmudist—was partly founded on myths. Dünner's doctorate examination in Heidelberg showed traces of hastiness and left much to be desired. His PhD thesis on the Jewish-Spanish medieval philosopher and linguist Ibn Ezra, famous (and controversial in ultra-Orthodox circles) for his Bible commentaries, was never printed and remained unknown in the academic world.[7]

The watershed importance of Dünner's coming was accentuated by his reform of the rabbinical Dutch Jewish Seminary. However, Meijer wanted to make clear that the educational reforms, of which Dünner was supposed to be

---

5   Except for Dünner's biography (Part 1) *Rector en raw. De Levensgeschiedenis van Dr. J.H. Dünner (1833–1911)* (Heemstede 1984), see also idem, "Dr. Dünner en het sociale vraagstuk," *Habinjan* 6/ 6 (May 1953); idem, *'Moeder in Israël.' Een geschiedenis van het Amsterdamse Asjkenazische Jodendom* (Haarlem 1964); idem, *Hoge Hoeden/Lage standaarden. De Nederlandse Joden tussen 1933 en 1940* (Baarn 1969), pp. 24 ff.; idem, *Rapenburgerstraat 177. In herinnering aan Menachem Bolle* (Heemstede 1993) pp. 18–19, 23, 35 and, 54. Additional instances where Dünner is related to will be mentioned throughout the article.

6   Meijer, *Moeder in Israël*, p. 86; idem, *Rector en raw*, p. 93; idem, *Erfenis der Emancipatie*, p. 7.

7   Idem, *Rector en raw*, p. 60 ff.; pp. 68–70.

the founding father, were, in essence, already formulated before: they were, according to him, the product of a long-lasting fight between progressive reformers such as the jurist J.E. Goudsmit and conservative forces as represented by the brothers Lehren.[8] At stake was the proportion between Talmudic studies, originally the core of the classical rabbinical education and academic training, a modernist development which was, as the Lehren brothers reluctantly realized, unavoidable. Shortly before Dünner's arrival a compromise had already been reached: for the acquirement of a *Moré* (teacher) certificate, a first university degree in the Humanities was made a precondition.

Did this imply Meijer's degradation of Dünner altogether? Not quite so. While disparaging Dünner's academic achievements[9] and reducing the originality of his educational reforms, Jaap Meijer praised Dünner as an "outstanding Talmudist" and "excellent didactician." Moreover, being an "ambitious intellectual" and "first-rate organizer," Dünner had indeed succeeded in implementing three fundamental innovations in the Seminary: he created a gymnasium section, established order and discipline and modernized the teaching of rabbinical literature.[10]

Yet again, these innovations were not all positive. Meijer remains neutral in his evaluation of the first innovation (the gymnasium). But regarding the second one, the enforcement of order and discipline, he is explicitly negative. The student body that Dünner found when he came to the seminary was a motley crew of youngsters. Winning the instant backing of the governors of the seminary, Dünner struck with an iron fist, like a German *Feldwebel*, according to Meijer, who in 1984 was, apparently, inclined to use provocative terminology easily associated with WW II. Underlining that rebellion of any sort was punished, he mentioned one of the rooms on the top floor of the seminary that had functioned as a kind of cell where the worst troublemakers were sent to serve their time, occasionally lasting up to eight days. The room in question had been called the *cachot*, as was revealed to Jaap Meijer by Dr. E. Slijper, who had once been incarcerated in it; Meijer added that Slijper had told him this fact when both were in Westerbork of all places![11] But Meijer had more

---

8   See for example, J. Michman, H. Beem, D. Michman, *Pinkas. Geschiedenis van de joodse gemeenschap in Nederland* (Ede and Antwerp 1999), pp. 98–99.

9   See also: ibid., pp. 129–30; idem, *Moeder in Israël*, p. 99. Jaap Meijer stated too that Dünner had failed in his ambition to make the seminary into a "mini Breslau," referring to the Breslauer Seminarium, the principal exponent of "positive-historical Judaism": idem, *Rector en raw*, pp. 98–99.

10   Ibid., pp. 109, 114.

11   Meijer, *Rector en raw*, p. 112. Dr. E. Slijper must have been Ezechiël Slijper (1874–1953) who, indeed, was a pupil at the Seminary and became a well known classicist. He

to say regarding Dünner's second reform. In the biography published in 1984, he actually accused Rabbi Dünner of abusing the power he held due to the "abject system of bursaries." Quoting from letters that have been preserved, he states that Dünner was well aware of the fact that the poverty-stricken prole- tarian children had no choice but to let themselves be subjected to Dünner's law and order policy. Here, he turns against Dünner completely, calling him a "dictatorial school director."[12] It is not difficult to see the connection between this point of criticism and what he perceived as Dünner's elitist, patronizing attitude towards the Jewish proletariat and socialism.

In *Moeder in Israël*, a study dealing with the history of the Amsterdam Ash- kenazi Jewish community (NIHS – Nederlands Israëlitische Hoofdsynagoge) and published twenty years earlier (1964), Meijer's tone was definitely more mild; yet that is not surprising, as the book was written and published upon the request and under the auspices of the board of that community in memory of the adored Chief Rabbi Dr. Dünner! In that book Meijer emphasized another aspect: Dünner's pro-Zionist outlook and earlier relationship with the proto- Zionist Moses Hess, an attitude which, at the time, had been both remarkable and dissenting in Orthodox circles.

However, even in *Moeder in Israël*, Meijer inserted a critical tone re- garding Dünner, though not in harsh words. Dünner was depicted in the Jodenbreestraat—literally and figuratively—unable to connect with the sim- ple, poor people. His detachment only grew towards the end of the nineteenth century.[13] In *Hoge Hoeden / Lage Standaarden* (1969), which Meijer wrote without any formal request and, therefore, was able to express his own views freely, he gave this issue a clear political interpretation. What had Dünner un- derstood of socialism, the breeding ground for new ideals, Meijer wondered: "What did he sense of the attraction Marx exerted on the thousands for whom Moses could not provide much of an answer anymore?"[14]

Meijer's attempt to evaluate Dünner's influence on the religious level and particularly on rabbinical studies reveals, again, considerable ambiguity. In

---

survived Theresiënstadt; his wife died a natural death at home; his son was deported to and murdered in Auschwitz: www.joodsmonument.nl and: http://www.dbnl.org/tekst/ _jaa003195401_01/_jaa003195401_01_0011.php. As mentioned before, Jaap often referred, between the lines, to his war experiences. In Westerbork he met and talked to a great number of people. If applicable, he incorporated their remarks or information in his work.

12   "Een dictatoriale schoolleider," in Meijer, *Rector en raw*, p. 137.

13   Meijer, *Moeder in Israël*, pp. 93, 97.

14   Idem, *Hoge Hoeden/Lage Standaarden*, p. 21. See also, idem, "Dr. Dünner en het socia- le vraagstuk," p. 8. For Dünner's negative attitude towards socialism, see for example, S. Bloemgarten, *Henri Polak. Sociaal democraat 1868–1943* (Amsterdam 1993), p. 37.

Moeder in Israël he stated that, as a rabbi, Dünner had fought with the Amsterdam City Council for the establishment of a special Jewish school after the school reforms enacted by the state during the second and third quarters of the nineteenth century had abolished the old Jewish school system and channeled all Jewish pupils to the public schools. This, according to Meijer, was "a brilliant notion" of a "proudly acting" rabbi. Therefore, on this issue of preserving at least something of authentic Jewish identity, Dünner scored points.

Another important issue for Meijer, one that particularly caught his attention, was the non-emergence of Reform Judaism in The Netherlands (until the 1930s). Meijer was an everlasting archenemy of liberal Judaism. Therefore, he showed much interest in the attempts that had been made—but failed—to establish a Reform movement inspired by the developments in German Jewry.[15] Meijer made it clear that Dünner was the man who had put an end to the leading Dutch "Reform-dilettantes."[16] He had done so, among other things, by imposing strict honorable (i.e., bourgeois-style) conduct during prayer in the synagogue and more so in the modes of study at the seminary, thus taking the wind out of one of the most important sails of the reformers. While in this regard, at least Dünner may have been considered the rescuer of Dutch Jewry, at the same time, Meijer's praise of Dünner's courage and conscious will to renew must be considered partly ironical. By abolishing the traditional singing, hand gestures and body movements while studying rabbinical literature, Dünner had definitively broken with his origins in Eastern European Jewry and the traditional *Yeshiva*. In *Rector en raw* Meijer displays a certain mistrust regarding Dünner's full-fledged Orthodoxy, alluding to his connections with "Geiger-epigones" like Chief Rabbi of Trier Joseph Kahn; this elicited a characterization of Dünner being "ni l' un, ni l'autre."[17]

Jaap Meijer did not like compromises. And he found signs of them everywhere in Dünner's career: in the cautious formulated motto of the newly founded (in 1865) Dutch Jewish weekly *Nieuw Israëlietisch Weekblad*, in which Dünner played a leading role,[18] in Dünner's liberal views on Bible exegesis, in his, according to Meijer's taste, overly deep respect for the "goyish scholarship"

---

15   The struggle between Orthodoxy and Reform is a main element in Meijer, *Erfenis der Emancipatie*, for example, pp. 13–19, 51–58; idem, *Moeder in Israël*, pp. 68–69.

16   Ibid., p. 102. See also, idem, *Rapenburgerstraat 177*, p. 13.

17   Meijer, *Rector en raw*, pp. 114–17.

18   In its motto the weekly tried to reconcile a moderate conservatism with a temperate progress: "In het privaat-leven op godsdienstig gebied gematigd conservatief, eene rigting, niet in strijd met een matigen vooruitgang, geheel en al in den geest des Jodendoms," ibid., p. 136.

of liberal Christian theologians like Minister Jan Pieter Land.[19] Dünner was also on good terms with the well-known historian Heinrich Graetz who taught at Zacharias Frankl's Breslau rabbinical seminary (the principal exponent of "positive-historical Judaism," which later developed in the United States into the Conservative movement) and even contributed to that institute's scholarly monthly *Monatschrift*, yet at the same time he never became a real *Wissenschaftler des Judentums* himself.[20] Consequently, who was Dünner really? The climax for Meijer was coming across a letter of Dünner's to Professor Goudsmit asking him for his comments and evaluation on some of his studies. This was remarkable because Goudsmit was a Dutch member of "reformist Geigerian circles," the one who, or so Meijer was told when a seminary student, had been Dünner's archenemy who had tried to block his nomination as the new rector.[21] On the last page of Part 1 of Dünner's biography Meijer quotes one of Dünner's (many) foes, Rabbi Joseph David Wijnkoop who, at the time of Dünner's appointment as chief rabbi of the Ashkenazi community of Amsterdam in 1874, registers uncomfortable rumors and questions: "Is he really Orthodox? Is he a scholar?" And, still more in the line of Jaap Meijer, Wijnkoop mentions the doubt of a friend: "Tell me . . . is the man really a *Jehoedie* [Jew]?"[22] Quoting such a comment in a slightly favorable way is, of course, an act expressing deep reservations.

What Motivated Meijer's Depiction of Dünner?

Jaap Meijer (1912–1993) was raised in a very poor family in Winschoten (Groningen) and had been sent to Amsterdam in 1926, at the age of thirteen two

---

19   Ibid., pp. 125, 149–52.

20   Ibid., pp. 137, 140 and further.

21   Ibid., pp. 156–57. In this letter, written in 1872, i.e., ten years after his arrival in Amsterdam, Dünner asked Goudsmit urgently to read and comment on some of his articles on Bible- and halakhah criticism, which were about to be published in Graetz's *Monatsschrift*. Dünner wrote: "I don't want to flatter you, when I state, that you, noble professor ('UEd. Hooggel.'), though not being a professional Bible critic, can claim to pass judgement on such research with the same authority ('met evenveel regt') as the most well-known Christian Bible critics." For Meijer, this request from a former arch-enemy, moreover, a Liberal, was crucial proof of Dünner's inconsequent and unclear position.

22   Ibid., p. 166. For Dünner's unconciliatory behavior towards J.D. Wijnkoop, who was very popular among Amsterdam Jewry, see for example S. de Wolff, *Voor het land van belofte. Een terugblik op mijn leven* (1954; reprint, Nijmegen 1978), p. 272; A.J. Koejemans, *David Wijnkoop. Een mens in de strijd voor het Socialisme* (Amsterdam 1967), p. 30.

years after his father's death, in order to continue his studies at the Nederlands Israëlietisch Seminarium. Assessed as being talented enough to become a rabbi, he completed most of the necessary training, without however, reaching the final stage: the acquirement of the official *Moré*-certificate. His embrace of radical Zionism, his relationship with Liesje Voet who was social democratic and secular and his passion for history at the University of Amsterdam (the subject he had chosen for his obligatory study in the Humanities), explain why his life took a different course than the rabbinical one: he became a historian. He married Liesje Voet in June 1940, several weeks after the occupation of the Netherlands by Nazi Germany and obtained his doctorate in October 1941, one of the last Jewish students to be allowed to do so, with a thesis on the Jewish poet Isaac da Costa and his conversion to Christianity in the early nineteenth century. Meijer, his wife and their newborn son Ischa were deported in June 1943 to Westerbork and from there to Bergen-Belsen. All three survived, but each was, in his or her own way, marked for the rest of their lives by those terrifying years.[23] Meijer himself first became a history teacher, but also embarked on writing an expanded version of his dissertation. He became, in the end, one of the most authentic, conspicuous and productive historians of Dutch Jewish history, though at the same time also hardly ever undisputed.

Meijer was more or less fixated on the monumental figure of Dünner: he wanted to observe him from all possible angles in order to pass historical judgment on him from the perspective of a post-Holocaust historian who shies away from nostalgia and seeks to dissect the Jewry that was and, at the same time, to understand his own history. Meijer undoubtedly admired his object of study, yet he also felt that his personal life had been directly affected by Dünner, even though he was born a year after Dünner's death. These feelings colored his evaluation and depiction of Dünner as we observed above.

From the moment the thirteen-year-old Jaap Meijer entered the Dutch Jewish Seminary, he was confronted with Dünner on a daily basis. Although by then Dünner had been dead for fifteen years, his spirit was still very present in the institution: in the educational program as it was devised in Dünner's *Denkschreiben*, in his portrait that hung in the staff room above the desk and especially, as Meijer would state several times, in his legend.[24] A direct connection to "the Master," as Dünner was respectfully referred to by all, existed through Lion Wagenaar, one of Dünner's prominent pupils and himself a chief rabbi. It was Wagenaar who, in his capacity as rector of the Seminary, welcomed Meijer

---

23   See Gans, "Next Year in Paramaribo," pp. 369–87.

24   J. Meijer, *Het verdwenen ghetto. Wandelingen door de Amsterdamse Jodenbuurt* (Amsterdam 1949, 2nd printing) p. 75; idem, *Erfenis der Emancipatie,* p. 7.

on his first day, handing him his school timetable and the addresses of the
families where the young Meijer would, in a fixed schedule, eat supper. The,
by then, elderly Wagenaar would instruct Meijer and his classmates for several years in religious doctrine. Wagenaar was a fine teacher and though he
sometimes fell asleep in class, Meijer would listen to him "breathlessly," that is
mainly when Wagenaar improvised; yet even then as Meijer noted, Wagenaar
remained cerebral and stiff, as he ought to be in accordance with the code of
behavior that had been shaped by Dünner.[25]

While remaining filled with admiration for Wagenaar and his rabbinical
colleagues, at the same time Meijer was possessed of the spark of youthful
impatience, of rebellion, which was especially associated with the youth of the
interwar years. The ambivalence of the young and penniless seminary student
towards the rabbinical establishment colors the attitude of the adult historian Meijer regarding Wagenaar and Wagenaar's generation,[26] and even more
the one who had modeled them: Rabbi Dünner. The humility that Wagenaar
displayed in his *hesped* (eulogy) for Dünner, did not escape Meijer's notice.
Wagenaar considered himself not up to the task of depicting "the Master in
the sharpness of his genius, in the richness of his talents . . . in the power of
his great personality, in his fatherly love."[27] Meijer would never adopt such a
stance: nowhere would he characterize Dünner with an epithet of "fatherly
love"; instead, he emphasized Dünner's inaccessibility and stiffness.[28] Meijer
benefited from the gymnasium option instituted by Dünner at the seminary,
which allowed him to climb the educational and social ladder.[29] However, in
various ways Dünner symbolized, in Meijer's eyes, even more the obstacles he
had met with in the seminary: as the "Grunninger Jokkob" (i.e., the "Jacob from
Groningen," as he was nicknamed, the simple Jew from the countryside) who
had come to Amsterdam, made to find his way in an unknown city without
any relatives around, mocked for his northern accent and, above all, entirely

---

25 Meijer, *Rapenburgerstaat 177*, p. 18; idem, *Moeder in Israël,* pp. 122–24; Gans, *Jaap en Ischa
    Meijer*, p. 69.

26 An exception was Jaap's attitude towards the Rabbi, classicist and philogist Isaac de
    Jongh: Gans, *Jaap en Ischa*, p. 75.

27 Meijer, *Rapenburgerstraat 177*, pp. 18–19; Gans, *Jaap en Ischa Meijer*, p. 61.

28 See for example: Meijer, *Moeder in Israël*, pp. 96–97; idem, "David Josef Wijnkoop, zoon
    van een rabbijn," in idem, *Zij lieten hun sporen achter. Joodse bijdragen tot de Nederlandse
    beschaving* (Utrecht 1964) pp. 178–81; idem, *Rapenburgerstraat 177*, 37.

29 For Jaap Meijer though, after finishing the gymnasium, the study of history had become
    an alternative for classical studies which had been the one and only option during "the
    age of Dünner," see my own indication of the "Dünner tijdperk," Gans, *Jaap en Ischa
    Meijer*, p. 62.

dependent on Jewish charity and on the strict rules, both pronounced and un-spoken, in the seminary. Thus, Meijer felt deep ambivalence towards the semi-nary and the idea of Jewish Orthodoxy and the way of life it represented. This mind-set found its way into his historiography of Dutch Jewry in general and of Dünner in particular. Add to that his embrace of Zionism as a young adult and later also social-democracy—much of Meijer's choice of historiographical top-ics and the ways he wrote about them become much more comprehensible.

In *Erfenis der Emancpatie* Jaap Meijer reveals, implicitly, one other reason why it was so difficult for him to come to terms with Dünner. In his disserta-tion on the Jewish poet Isaac da Costa (1798–1860), whom he greatly admired, he explained da Costa's conversion to Christianity as the result of the lack of response for his longing to and pursuit of the restoration of Jewish (mainly Sephardic) grandeur and intensity. Disillusioned, da Costa turned away from Judaism and towards the Dutch branch of the Réveil, the European orthodox-Protestant movement which directed itself against the rationalism of the En-lightenment and highlighted the experience of personal piety and harmony between dogma and feeling. The Réveil was a parallel phenomenon to Roman-ticism. Elsewhere I argued that Meijer, "in the depth of his thoughts," was a romanticist.[30] As a "Jewish romanticist," Meijer expressed a certain dismay towards rationality and reason, the forces that had led to Emancipation and assimilation and, intrinsically, to a flat, superficial version of Judaism.[31] In his view, Dutch Jewry had not embraced the man—Da Costa—who had been able to lift it integrally over the threshold of the century, creating "a synthesis of the orthodoxy of the heart and the orthodoxy of the law."[32] Meijer was looking for exactly such a synthesis. He never found it in what he called, with contempt, the "assimilated reformers," but also not in Dünner's synthesis of Talmud study and academia. As long as there was no alternative—a passionate, but "wet-tisch" (law-abiding) Judaism—Meijer theoretically opted for what he consid-ered were "real Jews," the brothers Lehren for whom, strikingly enough, the *meshumad* (convert) Da Costa, at the time, had taken a stand.[33]

---

30   Ibid., pp. 161–62, 427 ff.

31   Ibid., pp. 438–39.

32   Literally Meijer wrote: "It was apparently not possible to achieve so early 'a synthesis of the orthodoxy of the heart [van de orthodoxie des harten] (in the style Allard Pierson characterizes the Réveil) and the orthodoxy of the law,'" Meijer, *Erfenis der Emancipatie*, p. 23. Allard Pierson (1831–1896) was a prominent Dutch professor of theology and art his-tory, belonging to the circles of the Réveil.

33   Ibid., p. 25.

Did Jaap Meijer himself succeed in living according to the synthesis of the heart and the law? Though he was, certainly, in many ways a living contradiction, one could argue that he tried. In a way, he personified exactly the inconsistency, the dissension which can be evoked by a combination of emotion and dogma, in his quest for communion with a human, moody, witty, personal God. The religion he seems to have felt at home with was quite different from the one that Rabbi Dünner nourished. Meijer was, in general, a historian who loved debunking mystifications. This was one of the attractions of writing about Dünner. But, as we have seen, there was much more to it: Dünner had had an enormous impact on Meijer in the crucial years of his upbringing, and he struggled with that heritage throughout his life. Dünner was, therefore, not only a public hero but also a personal symbol; on both levels Meijer strived to dissect, debunk and disparage him and yet, uphold him as a central figure.

PART 7

Religious Life after the Catastrophe: Post-1945 Developments

∵

CHAPTER 15

The Return to Judaism in the Netherlands

Minny E. Mock-Degen

The return to Judaism, or the *teshuvah* movement, had its start at the beginning of the 1960s when young secular American Jews, who had become disillusioned with activist political ideals, began searching for spiritual meaning in
life. In the context of their spiritual search, they happened to come into contact with ultra-Orthodox Judaism in Israel, which they experienced as highly
inspiring and, above all, authentic. Within a relatively short period thousands
of secular Jews in various Jewish communities discovered and embraced Orthodox Judaism.[1] A Jew who returns to Orthodox Judaism is known as a *ba'al
teshuvah*; for a woman the term is *ba'alat teshuvah* (plural forms: *ba'alei* and
ba'alot teshuvah).

Although striving to observe an Orthodox way of life meant a new experience for those involved, the concept of "return" to Judaism was launched to
denote the religious influx. In a later phase of the *teshuvah* movement the idea
of committing oneself to an observant way of life also attracted Jews who were
less alienated from the Jewish community and for whom the Modern-Orthodox
stream offered a more appealing option than ultra-Orthodoxy with its strong
segregate character and anti-Zionist orientation. The phenomenon of secular Jews choosing (ultra) Orthodox Judaism has given a broader meaning to
the concept of *teshuvah*. In Jewish tradition, *teshuvah* refers to repentance for
violations of Jewish religious practice and the endeavor to return to the true,
straight path. This traditional religious notion of *teshuvah* is an essential element in the life of observant Jews. *Teshuvah*, whether in the traditional sense
or referring to the contemporary phenomenon of the return to Judaism, has
at its core the belief that human beings have the power to bring about inward
change.

According to Aviad, the phenomenon of the return to Judaism has a
pronounced neotraditional character and forms "a dramatic and powerful

---

1 J. Aviad, *The Return to Judaism: Religious Renewal in Israel* (Chicago 1983). M.H. Danziger,
Returning to Tradition: The Contemporary Revival of Orthodox Judaism (New Haven 1989). The
middle of the 1960s is considered as the beginning of the *teshuvah* movement as at that time
the first *yeshivot* for *ba'alei teshuvah* were established in Israel. See Aviad, pp. 16–17.

example of Jewish religious resistance to secularization and modernization."[2] Yassif approaches the return to Judaism in the context of Israeli society and notes that it appears to be one of the most profound social and cultural developments during the 1970s and 1980s.[3] For Shapiro, the return to Judaism represents primarily a completely unforseen development, which stands out as a remarkable contrast to the "vanishing Jewish identity in many Jewish communities."[4]

Early research about returnees to Orthodox Judaism has mainly focused on (potential) students of ultra-Orthodox yeshivot/seminaries and the impact of the environment on the newly religious. Davidman and Kaufman were the first to do research among women who had returned to Judaism.[5] From a feminist perspective they were puzzled by the question of why well-educated Jewish women in contemporary society were attracted to Orthodox Judaism, with its very traditional gender roles and patriarchal structure. Sands and Roer-Strier researched how mothers of female returnees viewed and experienced the religious transformation of their daughters and what its impact was on intergenerational and multifamily relationships.[6] While assisting Sands and Roer-Strier in the framework of their research, they suggested to me to do a similar study among Dutch *ba'alot teshuvah* and their mothers. The suggestion resulted in a qualitative study that paid attention to specific aspects of the *teshuvah* phenomenon in the context of family dynamics.[7] These aspects included: how do Dutch returnee women and their mothers participating in the study experience, perceive and interpret the return to Orthodox Judaism; how do they deal with the divergence in lifestyle; did the religious change of the daughter affect family relationships; and how did the involvement of the *ba'alat teshuvah* with Orthodox Judaism originate and develop? In the framework of the study among Dutch returnees and their mothers, the return phenomenon was

---

2 Ibid., ix, x.

3 E. Yassif, "Storytelling of the 'Repentance movement,' Rhetoric, Folklore and Cultural Debate in Contemporary Israel," *Jewish Folkore and Ethnology Review* 14 (1992), pp. 1–2, 26–32.

4 F. Shapiro, "Continuity, Context, and Change: Towards an Interpretation of *Teshuvah*," *Journal of Psychology* 19 (1995), pp. 295–314.

5 L. Davidman, *Tradition in a Rootless World: Women Turn to Orthodox Judaism* (Berkeley and Los Angeles 1991); D. Kaufman, *Rachel's Daughters: Newly Orthodox Jewish Women* (New Brunswick, NJ 1991).

6 R. Sands and D. Roer-Strier, "Divided Families: The Impact of Religious Difference and Geographic Distance on Intergenerational Family Continuity," *Family Relations* 53 (2004), pp. 102–110.

7 M. Mock-Degen, *The Dynamics of Becoming Orthodox: Dutch Jewish Women Returning to Orthodoxy and How Their Others Felt about It* (Amsterdam 2009).

explored in a broader setting as well as in a more specific Dutch context. In this contribution, an overview will be given of the major research findings, supplemented with some recent data from interviews with Dutch returnees.

From the perspective of the sociology of religion, return to Orthodox Judaism represents a manifestation of the many options that exist in the late modern or post-secular society for seeking religious or spiritual existential meaning. By using, in this context, the term "post-secular," I want to refer to what sociologists of religion, philosophers and political scientists have observed about religion and the secularization thesis. The thesis depicts a linear development towards modernity through the secularization process, which would result in religion and religiosity being pushed to the margins of society, probably becoming superfluous. The thesis has exhausted itself. Religion and being religious still have a vibrant and vital presence in the Western world, especially in the United States, whereas Europe has witnessed the emergence and rapid growth of conservative religious groups, the influx of Muslim immigrants and an increasing spirituality outside established churches. Public awareness, according to Habermas, has to adjust itself to the continued existence of religious communities in an increasingly secularized environment.[8]

In the Netherlands, the return to Judaism was actively promoted by the Zionist Orthodox youth movement *Bnei Akiva* (founded in 1948) and by the circle of Dutch followers of Lubavitch Hasidism. Already at the end of the 1950s and in the course of the 1960s, the *Bnei Akiva* movement broadened its scope from targeting youth originating in Zionist Orthodox milieus to also include attracting young people from non-Orthodox backgrounds. That endeavor was based on the conviction that it was essential to retain Jewish youth for Orthodox Judaism in post-war Holland.

An indication that the widening of focus yielded results is shown by the rising number of young people from non-Orthodox families joining *Bnei Akiva* during the 1960s. In an (undated) anniversary edition to celebrate the twentieth anniversary of *Bnei Akiva*, the Israeli *shaliah* (emissary) of the youth movement during the years 1963–1965 in the Netherlands observed that it was the task of the Jews to approach the *rehokim* (those who are far distanced from Orthodox Judaism) and to unite the *Mediene* (areas outside Amsterdam) in a community of Jews.[9] A 1971 interview with one of his successors indicates that about half of the members was estimated to come from non-observant

8   J. Habermas, "Notes on Post-Secular Society," *New Perspective Quaterly* (Fall 2008), n. p.

9   J. Sharir, "Mediene," *Zeraiem*, Jubilee Edition (n. d.), pp. 14–15.

families; it was a high priority for *Bnei Akiva* to bring these youth closer to Orthodox Judaism.[10]

The application of a low threshold by *Bnei Akiva* made Orthodox Judaism accessible to non-Orthodox youth. The youth movement offered them an ideological and social framework in which the process of becoming observant could evolve and develop. An important function of the *madrikhim* (counselors) of *Bnei Akiva* lay in being an inspiring role model of contemporary modern Orthodoxy, especially for the non-observant members. From interviews with former members/*madrikhim* conducted between 2005 and 2010 in the framework of researching the return to Judaism it became clear that the share of *Bnei Akiva* in the return phenomenon can de identified as relatively substantial. During the years 1960 to 1980 approximately one hundred young people became Orthodox through *Bnei Akiva*, most of whom emigrated to Israel.

As far as Lubavitch (Habad) is concerned, this branch of Hasidism emerged in the Netherlands at the beginning of the 1960s to promote the return to Judaism. The initiative to become active in the Netherlands took place at the instigation of the Lubavitcher Rebbe in the movement's world headquarters in New York. The first Dutch adherents organized outreach activities, such as *farbrengens* (meetings) to memorialize historical events in the life of the Lubavitcher rebbes and gave lectures on Lubavitcher Hasidism and philosophy. At the end of 1964, Lubavitch in the Netherlands was formally established by setting up the foundation *Le-Ezrath Chinoech Chabad*. In 1967, Lubavitch launched a campaign to promote the use of *tefillin*, which was highly appreciated in Dutch rabbinical circles and received due media attention.[11] From the Lubavitcher perspective, "return to Judaism" implied not only the new experience of committing oneself to a religious lifestyle, but becoming a follower of Lubavitch Hasidism.

Lubavitch was successful in drawing large-scale attention to the option of returning to Judaism. As for attracting new followers, success was limited. The rise in numbers was mainly through natural growth, the first generation of Lubavitch followers with their large families resulted in a sizeable second generation.

---

10   A former youth leader of *Bnei Akiva*, Mr. U. Cohn, informed me that he considered it as his duty towards the people who had perished during the *Shoah* to interest young people in post-war Holland in Judaism. Personal communication from 7 July 2004.

11   D. Brodman, "Een jaar tefillien-campagne," *Nieuw Israëlietisch Weekblad*, 21 June 1968; M. Just, "Een paar vragen aan de heer A.J. Herzberg," *Nieuw Israëlietisch Weekblad*, 27 September 1968.

Yet, the impact of this Hasidic movement in the context of Dutch Jewry has been significant. For some years now all rabbinical posts in the *Mediene* are held by Lubavitcher Hasidim—who were born in the Netherlands or settled there from abroad—while also the Amsterdam community counts a Lubavitcher rabbi among its rabbinate. Recently, a Lubavitcher rabbi has been stationed in Amsterdam for organizing outreach activities among Jewish tourists. The disproportionately large number of Lubavitchers in the Dutch rabbinical leadership is not characteristic for Holland only. Also elsewhere, Lubavitcher Hasidim have a strong stake in holding rabbinical functions; nearly half of the pulpit positions in England are occupied by Lubavitcher rabbis.[12] This pattern is the result of a targeted policy by the Lubavitch movement to send rabbis and community workers as *shelihim* anywhere in the world in order to activate Jewish life, as well as to obtain and develop a Lubavitch influence.

The phenomenon of the return to religion has been overlooked in circles of socio-demographic scholars interested in Dutch Jewry. In 2000, an extensive socio-demographic study of the Jews in the Netherlands was published based on research among a representative sample of the Jewish population in the Netherlands. The study found that about 6% of Dutch Jews—meaning at the time there were the 30,000 halakhic Jews and some 13,000 so-called "father-Jews"—self-identified as Orthodox. I quote from the study: "About 60% of them have two Jewish parents and about one quarter one Jewish parent (usually the mother), while 13% were not of Jewish origin."[13] Attention is paid to the relatively high percentage of *gerim* (converts), but the significance that about 25% of Orthodoxy comes from a mixed marriage was overlooked. This data implies that a quarter of Dutch Orthodoxy did not grow up in an Orthodox family and has returned to Judaism. In addition to this, it should be noted that it is highly probable that among the Orthodox people who have two Jewish parents, some—an unknown percentage unfortunately—are actually returnees. This justifies the conclusion that the *teshuvah* phenomenon in the Netherlands represents a relatively important strengthening of the Orthodox ranks. Without the influx of returnees, Dutch Orthodoxy would be reduced to a very minimal residual category.

My research among Dutch women who returned to Judaism and the possible implications of the religious return for intergenerational and multigenerational

---

12   D. Berger, "The Rebbe, the Jews and the Messiah," *Commentary* 112 (September 2001), pp. 23–31, here p. 25.

13   M. de Vries, "Mede-joden. De gemeenschap," in H. van Solinge and M. de Vries, *De Joden in Nederland anno 2000. Demografisch profiel en binding aan het jodendom* (2001), pp. 199–225, here p. 223.

relationships was undertaken through in-depth interviews or "conversations." The research involved 21 participants: seven couples of returnees (hereafter referred to as *ba'alot teshuvah*) and their secular mothers, four separate *ba'alot teshuvah* and in two cases separate mothers of *ba'alot teshuvah*. I will focus further on findings which concern the *ba'alot teshuvah* who participated in this research. I will also refer to returnee narratives that were recently collected.

At the time of the research (2000), the returnee women were in the age range of thirty to fifty-eight years old. They had two to five children, were all married (first marriage), most of them had received higher vocational training, some were university graduates, most worked in a part-time job, a few worked full-time and they were involved in volunteer activities. Most returnee women self-identified as Modern Orthodox, a few sympathized with Lubavitch. Some returnees had returned to Judaism over thirty years ago, others about twenty years ago, the most recent return dated back to over ten years. Most returnees came from homes with at least some connection to Jewish observance or rituals, while others had a background characterized by hardly any or no ethno-religious practices and Jewish involvement.

Most returnees were married to husbands who had also become religious, while some found marriage partners from established Dutch Orthodox families. Danzger noted in his 1989 study on the return to Judaism, that *ba'alei* and *ba'alot teshuvah* themselves prefer to get married to a returnee partner. This preference stems from a feeling of joint familiarity with the secular world and a feeling that they will not confront each other with their past lives, which might happen with members of the established Orthodox community. The phenomenon of returnees marrying returnees has also to do with the fact that in the Orthodox world, especially the Ashkenazi one, the newly religious are less acceptable as marriage partners. This did not seem to apply to the Dutch-Jewish ambiance. It was mainly the joint background which was of relevance in this context.

The *ba'alot teshuvah* married at a younger age than their mothers: they were all married before they reached the age of twenty-five. This is remarkable not only in an inter-generational perspective, but also in comparison to the Dutch population and the Jewish population in particular. The marriage pattern of these *ba'alot teshuvah* fits more into the social pattern that is associated with Dutch society from the pre-1960s than the post-modern society in recent decades, which is characterized by a tendency to postpone marriage and raising a family. That the *ba'alot teshuvah* married at a relatively young age was related to the early timing of their becoming observant.

From interviews with the returnee women, four patterns of becoming involved with Orthodox Judaism emerged: the *peer group* pattern, the *partner prompted* pattern, the *wanting-to-connect* pattern and the *by chance* pattern. In the *peer group* pattern, involvement in Jewish observance developed through association with peers. An essential element in this pattern was that the potential returnee was part of a setting in which youngsters of observant and non-observant families interacted, such as the Jewish day school framework, which often resulted in joining *Bnei Akiva* together. In the *partner prompted* pattern, involvement with religious practice unfolds as a consequence of meeting an observant partner. In the framework of recent investigations, I interviewed a woman who fits this *partner prompted* pattern of returning to Judaism noticed in the earlier research. Orit (not her real name), aged thirty-seven, mother of two children, came from a secular home where few ethno-religious practices were observed ("we were two or three day-a-year Jews"). Through a girl she had befriended in the setting of *Moos*, an organization in the Netherlands for young people with a Jewish background, she met her husband-to-be, David (not his real name). His family was traditional; after his parents divorced, his mother became more observant. She sent him to the *heder* (strictly Orthodox) school system. When they met, Orit considered David to be "super-Orthodox"; it became obvious to her that for a marriage to take place there was no other choice than to become observant.

Orit, who self-identifies as Modern Orthodox, describes how she experienced keeping kosher:

> I could not really imagine how it worked in practice. I had some idea about what it might mean, but I think it took at least four to five years before I got used to the taste of kosher food, which is different from non-kosher food ... because in your mind you have certain taste sensations ... such as cheese on spaghetti [Bolognese], it took me years to accept that ... and for instance when making soup, I used to buy ... a small bottle [of] ready-made bouillon and seasoning, whatever. But those times were over.[14]

After their marriage, the couple started observing the family purity laws. Orit covered her hair with a hat or a beret when in *shul* (synagogue) or at outings. In 2010—the couple married in 2003—she decided to put on a *sheitel* (wig) to cover her hair. Orit describes the process of making this decision as follows:

---

14   Personal communication with Dutch *ba'alat teshuvah*, July 2011.

It was not "not wanting" to wear it; when we were first married I said I will do it when I feel okay with it and when I have the feeling that it concerns something between me and up there [points her finger up high], again that spiritual thing, which gives me the feeling that it is good to do it ... Because I wear a *sheitel* I feel much more conscious of who I am and what I emanate ... I wanted to make a statement at a point that I also felt completely comfortable with it ... I wanted to stand firm on my feet, for myself, that I realized what I was doing and that I did it because I wanted it and not chiefly because of David.[15]

One of the returnees who participated in the earlier research about Dutch women returning to Judaism—at that time she was just over 40 years old—spoke about the issue of covering her hair in a way that clearly showed her ambivalence on the subject. She agreed that married women should cover their hair, but struggled with the issue for many years. She might have overcome her hesitation had she been encouraged more. Yet, she would never wear a *sheitel*, which she identified with a group of Orthodox women in Amsterdam she considered snobbish and excessively focused on outward appearance:

I think the women in Buitenveldert, the *sheitel*-wearing group ... although you shouldn't generalize, isn't a group I want to be part of ... women who emphasize outward appearances and don't represent the Judaism that I want ... It's a difficult subject, it's hard for me as a woman to cover my hair. Maybe I just imagine it's difficult. On the one hand I think it's an obligation; on the other hand I'm slightly rebellious, because I think: what about the men? They have *tzniyut* [modesty] rules too ... If I could find a group [women wearing] *sheitels*, head coverings and everything, a more assertive group, then ... I'd feel at home ... What I'd prefer is to cover my head and to wear trousers.[16]

The *wanting-to connect* pattern noticed among the Dutch returnee women is characterized by a desire to seek contact with other Jews and participate in Jewish settings. Sometimes this push is associated with *Shoah*-connected family traumas, feelings of loneliness and an urge to find one's place. In the *by chance* pattern, the trajectory to Judaism is completely accidental and unforeseen. To give an example from the research: a Dutch Jewish post-adolescent looking for an au pair job happens to become employed by an Orthodox family

---

15   Ibid.
16   Mock-Degen, *The Dynamics of Becoming Orthodox*, p. 173.

in London, gets enchanted by the warm family atmosphere and the way they live their traditional Jewish life.

Becoming involved in Judaism and the choice of an Orthodox lifestyle occurred during adolescence and post-adolescence. This distinguished the Dutch *ba'alot teshuvah* who participated in the study from newly religious women elsewhere, for example in America and France.[17] The impression is that becoming observant during these periods of the life-cycle is characteristic for return to Judaism in the Netherlands during the 1960s up to the 1990s. That commitment to Judaism occurred during adolescence and post-adolescence suggests that, for these Dutch *ba'alot teshuvah*, becoming Orthodox was characterized more as a process of growing into Orthodoxy or aging into it during the teenage years than a profound identity transformation typically involving a radical break with the past, as reported in the literature on the return to Judaism. For most *ba'alot teshuvah*, becoming observant occurred in a gradual way; an abrupt turn towards Orthodoxy took place in only a few cases. One of the interviewees of the first research described the gradual process as follows:

> You keep moving one step forward, then another and another. With each step I always kept in mind that everything I took upon me, I had to do with conviction. I wanted to know the background. Of course there are some things you have to do . . . So from around fourteen to fifteen years old, I took my time making each of those decisions . . . continuing with Jewish lessons, keep up and broadening my knowledge.[18]

The *ba'alot teshuvah* were not characterized by a need to construct their own religious truth or to express their religious search in an individualistic way. Neither did they feel inclined to approach Orthodox Judaism from a specific female perspective or to use rhetoric and hyperboles when talking about the traditional role and status of women, which is especially characteristic of American *ba'alot teshuvah*.

Orthodox Judaism appealed to the *ba'alot teshuvah* and continued to appeal because of its meaningfulness, atmosphere, social life and connectedness between people. In particular, the traditional character of Orthodox Judaism was of importance, in the sense of a code of pre-established meaning, to use the

---

17   Davidman; Kaufman; L. Podselver, "La techouva: Nouvelle Orthodoxie juive et conversion interne," *Les Annales* 57 (2002), pp. 275–96.

18   Mock-Degen, *The Dynamics of Becoming Orthodox*, p. 135.

terminology of Hervieu-Léger,[19] passing from generation to generation. Some *ba'alot teshuvah* explicitly, others more implicitly mentioned the *Shoah* as a factor mostly affecting family life in their parental home. The impact of the *Shoah* was apparent in the atmosphere, the style of educating and parental attitudes to the outside world. Even though they did not view becoming religious as motivated by the *Shoah*, the interpretation of the *Shoah* for their own life came to stand for a strong attachment to Jewish continuity. They saw living an Orthodox way of life and founding an observant family as their personal contribution to preserving Jewish life. For some *ba'alot teshuvah*, becoming Orthodox represented a moral obligation towards grandparents they never knew to uphold Judaism. One of the interviewees was informed when a young teenager that her father's parents perished during the *Shoah* and that he was adopted by his aunt and uncle. This interviewee's milieu was totally disconnected from Judaism, no ethno-religious practices were observed, mixed-marriages were and are common in her family. Her only awareness of being Jewish was through stories about the *Shoah*. In her home, "Jodendom was dodendom" ("Judaism was deathism"), she said. She described how she related, from a religious perspective, to her perished grandparents:

> I had this kind of fantasy that proved to be correct. That these people had been observant, I mean my real grandparents. I had an idea that they would not want me to leave Judaism after they had been killed for being Jewish . . . These people would have appreciated my involvement with Judaism. I always felt that this is what they would have wanted.[20]

Returnees did not perceive themselves as newly religious. They expressed a sense of feeling integrated in the local Orthodox community of Buitenveldert and Amstelveen. The only exception was a *ba'alat teshuvah* who initially felt at home in the more lenient synagogue of Amstelveen and, after moving to Amsterdam Buitenveldert, ended up in a *shul* frequented by established Orthodox families.

The impression that emerges from studies about return to Judaism is that a person's choice of a certain version of Orthodoxy is definite and that, once chosen, the way of life is not subject to change. I contend this has to do with the fact that earlier research targeted mostly recent returnees. An interesting

19   D. Hervieu-Leger, "The Transmission and Formation of Socio-Religious Identities in Modernity: An Analytical Essay on the Trajectories of Identification," *International Sociology* 13 (1998), pp. 213–28.

20   Mock-Degen, *The Dynamics of Becoming Orthodox*, p. 116.

finding of the study undertaken in 2000 and also from recent investigations is that changes may occur in the religious trajectory. For example, a returnee may switch from Lubavitch to Aguda-styled Orthodoxy, from middle-of-the-road-Orthodoxy to becoming more tolerant, for instance eating fish in a regular restaurant, or becoming more strictly Orthodox, as is notable in the decision to start covering one's hear, or choosing to wear a *sheitel*. These fluctuations can also occur among religious Jews who come from an observant background.

A sense of the process of finding one's religious niche may be found in the narrative of a recently interviewed male returnee. Simon (not his real name) is a sixty-five year old professional from a family with a strong Jewish awareness. During adolescence and young adulthood, he participated in Jewish clubs, though he was unmotivated to remain affiliated. At a certain moment, realizing that he lacked a Jewish education, he started taking lessons in Judaism and Hebrew and spent a sabbatical in a Jerusalem *yeshivah*.

> From the first experience some fifteen or twenty years, I do not remember, maybe twenty-five years ago it has been a slow but steady development to a more observant attitude and an inner process that still continues. There are two important forces: the acknowledgement of and love for what I learn in Orthodoxy; secondly, the disgust of the *goyishe* and secular way of life. These two forces influence each other to the benefit of Judaism . . . I experienced H. [the Hebrew teacher] as very supportive and stimulating, as far as the rest of the Jewish community, it is enough to make you weep, although some people are well meaning [they] don't have any sense what you are looking for . . . In the meantime, I found, more or less, my place in Amsterdam, very good friends as well . . . The biggest shortcoming is that I did not find a partner, as a consequence I have to undertake everything on my own . . . Looking back at how things developed, it worked out when I came upon good Jewish circles and I could keep up [with them], that gave delight and rejoicing.[21]

What may be relevant in this context is that the small segment of Orthodoxy in the Netherlands is very fragmented. Just to illustrate: in the Amsterdam-Amstelveen area where there are about fifteen hundred Orthodox Jews, there are some fourteen *minyanim* (congregations) of diverse orientations. Returnees were and are confronted with some navigational work in order to find a style of Orthodoxy that suits them and their own religious niche in Dutch Orthodoxy.

21 Personal communication with a Dutch *ba'al teshuvah*, November 2011.

Conclusions

In the framework of research carried out in 2000 among Dutch women who have returned to Orthodox Judaism and the possible intergenerational and multigenerational implications of the religious return, the return phenomenon was explored in a broader setting as well as in a more specific Dutch context. This study as well as later investigations have shown that, in Holland, the return phenomenon became actively pursued at the beginning of the 1960s by the Orthodox-Zionist Bnei Akiva youth organization and the Lubavitcher Hasidism movement. Bnei Akiva's endeavor was based on the conviction of its local leadership that it was essential to maintain Jewish youth within Orthodox Judaism in post-*Shoah* Holland and bring young people from non-observant backgrounds closer to Orthodoxy. The Lubavitch initiative, stimulated by the New York headquarters via personal contacts with a few Dutch adoptees of the movement, was especially focused on attracting Jews in Holland to this branch of Hasidism. While in the initial period, Bnei Akiva was more successful in promoting a return to Judaism, the Lubavitch project was more skillful in drawing large-scale public attention to it.

Evidently, it was characteristic for most Dutch returnees, especially from the 1960s to the 1990s, to become involved with Judaism and interested in choosing an Orthodox lifestyle during adolescence and post-adolescence. This distinguished the Dutch returnees from the newly religious Jews elsewhere, for example in America, France and the former Soviet Union. As far as the Dutch context is concerned, it was, for most, a process of growing into Orthodox Judaism during their teenage years rather than experiencing a radical break with their past involving a profound transformation of their identity, as reported in the literature on the return to Judaism.

Although neither the Dutch women returnees who participated in the research—most of whom self-identified as Modern Orthodox and a few who sympathized with Lubavitch—nor their mothers viewed becoming religious as motivated by the *Shoah*, the *Shoah* was still an important factor in their strong feelings regarding Jewish continuity on a personal and family level.

The results of the interviews with the returnee women pointed to four patterns of becoming involved with Orthodox Judaism: peer group; partner-prompted; wanting to be connected; and by chance. In the peer group, involvement in Jewish observance developed through association with peers; involvement with religious practice for the partner-prompted unfolded as a consequence of meeting an observant partner; the wanting-to connect pattern is characterized by a desire to seek out contact with other Jews and participate in events within Jewish settings; in the by-chance pattern, the trajectory to Judaism is completely accidental and unforeseen.

The Dutch *ba'alot teshuvah* were not characterized by an urge to construct their own religious truth or to formulate their religious search in a very personal, individualistic way. They did not feel the need to interpret Orthodox Judaism from a specific gender perspective or to use female rhetoric when talking about Orthodox Judaism and the role of women—a trend that is reported as especially characteristic of American returnees. Dutch *ba'alot teshuvah* gave the impression of being typically "*nuchter*," or down to earth.

CHAPTER 16

Vanishing Diaspora?
Jews in the Netherlands and Their Ties with Judaism: Facts and Expectations about Their Future

Marlene de Vries

"The Jews are vanishing from Europe—and not only because of Hitler," wrote the British historian Bernard Wasserstein. Twenty years ago, Wasserstein published his study of European Jewry since 1945 under the telling title *Vanishing Diaspora*.[1] Wasserstein argues that the future of Jews in Europe is under threat—not for individual Jews but for the group as a whole. All the misery inflicted by the Second World War did not put an end to their existence, but the present circumstances will.

Wasserstein advances two main arguments for this gradual demise. The first is a demographic one: the number of Jews in Europe will decrease due to aging, low birth rate and an increase of mixed marriages. Second, due to continuous secularization and assimilation, the substance of remaining Jewish culture is being diluted and is therefore difficult to transmit to new generations. Hence, there is little hope for its long-term survival. Wasserstein exempts the small groups of ultra-Orthodox Jews from his claim, citing their high fertility rate and strict adherence to religious prescriptions. The rest of the European Jews, he asserts, will simply fade away.

Wasserstein's prophecy did not make him a popular figure in the Jewish world. He evoked feelings of fear and grief and attracted also a deluge of protests and objections. My intention is to not sing along with any of these choirs. Instead, I want to critically examine to what extent Wasserstein's prediction applies to Jews in the Netherlands by weighing his prophecy in light of recent research. I will argue that he does have a convincing point as for demography, but that his predictions about the future of secular Judaism may be not only premature but also too absolute.

The findings that I will present come from two recent large-scale demographic studies: *De Joden in Nederland anno 2000. Demografisch profiel en binding aan het jodendom*[2] and *De Joden in Nederland anno 2009. Continuïteit en*

---

[1] B. Wasserstein, *Vanishing Diaspora*, rev. ed. (London 1997).

[2] *De Joden in Nederland anno 2000. Demografisch profiel en binding aan het jodendom*, ed. H. van Solinge and M. de Vries (Amsterdam 2001). The sample of this socio-demographic

verandering[3] as well as from additional qualitative research in the 2004 study *Een blijvende band? Niet-religieuze joden en hun binding aan het jodendom.*[4]

In all three studies, a broad definition of "Jew" was being applied: everyone with at least one Jewish parent, regardless of whether this was the mother or the father. The definition was thereby broader than the halakhic definition, since it also incorporated patrilineal Jews, who are not Jewish according to Jewish Law.[5] This made it possible to study influences of partial and full Jewish descent.

The samples of both demographic studies should not be considered as fully representative for the entire Jewish population in the Netherlands. In particular, people who are only marginally, or not at all, tied to Judaism are most likely underrepresented. This means that the outcomes of these studies are flattering in the sense that they offer too rosy a picture of ties with Judaism, including religious ties.[6]

The Estimated Number of Jews in the Netherlands

Let's now first take a look at the current (estimated) number of Jews in the Netherlands.

---

survey published in 2001 was drawn in 1999 and consisted of 1,036 persons aged eighteen or older. The respondents had at least one Jewish parent (in 1% of the cases only one Jewish grandparent) and 1% was not Jewish by birth but had converted to Judaism either through an Orthodox or a non-Orthodox rabbinate.

3   H. van Solinge and C. van Praag *De Joden in Nederland anno 2009. Continuïteit en verandering* (Diemen 2010). The sample of this socio-demographic study published in 2010 was drawn in 2009 and consisted of 665 people, aged between eighteen and eighty-eight. They had at least one Jewish parent (6% only a Jewish grandparent), with the exception of 1% of the respondents who were converts. 65% of the respondents were also in the sample of 1999.

4   M. de Vries, *Een blijvende band? Niet-religieuze joden en hun binding aan het jodendom* (Amsterdam 2004). The qualitative study of 2004 was a follow-up to the survey of 1999. It was conducted among thirty secular, post-war born respondents (born between 1953 and 1974), drawn from the 1999 sample.

5   As already mentioned in notes 2 and 3, the samples of both demographic studies also contained a few converts. In addition, all three samples contained a limited number of people with only one Jewish grandparent.

6   In the study of 2001, however, the ideal of representativeness has been approached somewhat more, at least at some points, because the sample was re-weighted, i.e., adjusted for some aspects: sex, age, Jewish descent (one or two Jewish parents), region and civil state. This most probably increased the representativeness of the Dutch Jews in the sample, but much less of the foreign Jews (mainly Israelis) in the Netherlands. Both samples were biased in favor of religious affiliations, but the sample of 2009 most probably more than the sample of 1999.

TABLE 16.1   *Estimated number of Jews in the Netherlands.*

	2000	2010	2020
Halakhic Jews:	35.665 (70%)	36.924 (70%)	38.255
– 2 parents Jews	47%	45%	
– matrilineal Jews	24%	25%	
Patrilineal Jews	15.060 (30%)	15.727 (30%)	15.970
Total	50.725	52.651	54.225

SOURCE: VAN SOLINGE AND VAN PRAAG, 2010

According to these estimations, there were almost 53,000 Jews living in the Netherlands in 2010. This includes roughly 10,000 immigrants, of whom the vast majority, an estimated 9,000, has an Israeli background.[7] This is a substantial share of no less than 17% of the Jews in the Netherlands. In the last decade, the number of immigrants from Israel and their children has been growing and a further modest growth is expected in the current decade.[8] As a result, the Jewish population in the Netherlands increasingly consists of people with a non-Dutch background.[9] Whether this development will continue or not in the long run is of course difficult to predict. This will depend on both the political and economic situation in Israel and the Dutch policy towards immigration.

The moderate growth of the number of Jews in the Netherlands can also be attributed to an increasing number of Dutch Jews who have only one Jewish parent. Actually, the total number of Dutch Jews has risen slightly since the 1960s as a result of increased mixed marriages. This may sound like a paradox, but it can be explained as follows: if a Jewish man and a jewish woman marry and have two children, they bring two Jewish children into the world. But if they each marry a non-Jewish spouse and if both couples produce two children, then according to the applied definition of "Jewish" (including patrilineal Jews) there will be *four* instead of *two* Jewish children added to the next generation. Thus, the moderate growth of the Jewish population in the last

---

7   This concerns both people of Israeli nationality only and of double nationality (Dutch and Israeli), as well as both first and second generation.

8   Israeli immigrants tend to be quite young and therefore provide for extra growth of the Jewish population in the Netherlands compared to the entire population of Dutch Jews that is relatively elderly. Obviously, this only counts in so far as these immigrants and their children will stay in the Netherlands.

9   At a rough estimate, 14% of the Jewish population in the Netherlands in 1999 were Israelis (people with Israeli nationality and/or born in Israel), as opposed to 17% in 2009 (Van Solinge and Van Praag, *De Joden in Nederland anno 2009*, p. 20).

decades implies a substantial shift in its composition. The percentage of Jews with two Jewish parents has declined and the percentage with just one Jewish parent has increased.[10]

This growing number seems to contradict Wasserstein's prediction. However, he is likely to be put in the right in the long run as future mixed marriages will contribute to the shrinkage of the number of Jews and no longer to growth. That is because mixed marriages tend to work as a self-enforcing mechanism. Persons with only one Jewish parent are more likely to choose non-Jewish partners themselves and so are their children. And so on and so forth. Hence, mixed marriages initially contribute to the growth of the group, whereas they result in shrinkage in the longer term.

In the sample of the latest socio-demographic survey (2010), 38% of the respondents had a Jewish partner at the time of the research, whereas 44% of them had had a Jewish partner in the past.[11] This figure of 44% was used as the basis for extrapolation of the choice of partner that the respondents' children and grandchildren made or will make.[12] The outcome is shown in Figure 16.1 that illustrates to what extent marriages with non-Jews will continue to expand over time.

We see how the chance of a non-Jewish partner is increasing in each subsequent generation. And it is increasing so much that only 11% to 18% of the respondents' grandchildren are likely to end up with a Jewish partner.[13] However, the figures vary depending on someone's descent in terms of one or two Jewish parents, as is illustrated in Figure 16.2.

The chance of a Jewish partner appears to be highest for persons with two Jewish parents. In that sense, ending up with a Jewish partner seems to be hereditary. But only up to a point: almost half of the persons with two Jewish parents end up with a non-Jewish partner. This development will effectively

---

10   We can see that reflected in the different age groups: the proportion of persons with two Jewish parents is largest in the oldest age category, born before 1925. 71% of them have two Jewish parents, as opposed to only 44% of those who were born in 1965 or later (Van Solinge and De Vries, *De Joden in Nederland anno 2000*, p. 35).

11   For brevity's sake, I am speaking of "partners," also when it concerns spouses. As the sample concerned was far from representative and was biased in favor of strong Jewish ties, we should not attach too great an importance to these numbers, though. In the entire population of Jews in the Netherlands, the number of persons having a Jewish partner is almost certainly much lower.

12   If the figure of 38% had been used as a starting point instead (which equals the percentage of respondents that had a Jewish partner at the time of the research), the outcome would have been even stronger in favor of the share of people having non-Jewish partners.

13   The figure of 11% is the most probable one, provided that there is continuous assimilation (Van Solinge and Van Praag, *De Joden in Nederland anno 2009*, p. 110).

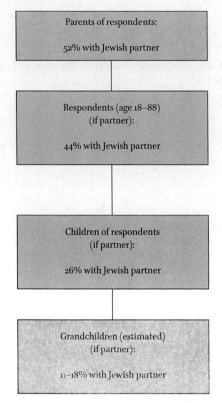

FIGURE 16.1
Choice of partner in four generations:
All respondents.
SOURCE: VAN SOLINGE AND VAN PRAAG, 2010

diminish Jewish identification, for the strength of someone's ties with Judaism proved to be highly dependent on their descent from one or two Jewish parents or on their partner being Jewish.

Ties with Judaism

Persons with two Jewish parents tend to have stronger ties with Judaism than persons with only one Jewish parent; and of the latter, matrilineal Jews have stronger ties than patrilineal Jews. In addition, persons with a Jewish partner are usually more strongly tied to Judaism than persons with a non-Jewish partner. The importance of having a Jewish partner often even overshadows the effect of having two Jewish parents. Many people with one Jewish parent and a Jewish partner express a stronger bond with Judaism than people with two Jewish parents and a non-Jewish partner. But the combination wins: having both two Jewish parents and a Jewish partner gives the greatest chance of strong Jewish ties. And those who were born of two Jewish parents have bigger chances to end up with a Jewish partner.

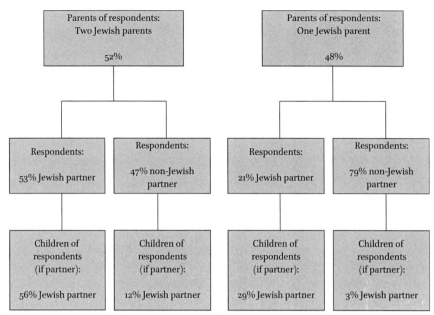

FIGURE 16.2   *Choice of partner in three generations: Respondents with two Jewish parents
compared with respondents with one Jewish parent.*
SOURCE: VAN SOLINGE AND VAN PRAAG, 2010

Children with only one Jewish parent tend to be much less exposed to Jewish influences during their upbringing and this will translate down the generational chain because they are more likely to choose non-Jewish partners. Chances are high, then, that either the one-parent Jews themselves or their offspring will be lost to Judaism.

Obviously, a person's ties with Judaism are not only influenced by their upbringing and choice of partner, but also the spirit of the times in which they grew up. Hence, we also see differences between generations, between parents and children. One of the most striking differences between older and younger generations is the diminishing meaning of both the Second World War and the State of Israel as a source of Jewish identification.[14] However, we see greater continuity between the generations when it comes to Jewish traditions and religion. Or rather, what we see here is continuity and change at the same time: continuity, because a strong bond of the parents themselves and a Jewish upbringing still is a good predictor of the children's ties as for religion and observance of traditions; change, because children tend to be tied in a different way to religion and traditions than their parents, with a stronger

14   Van Solinge and Van Praag, *De Joden in Nederland anno 2009*, pp. 73–74.

emphasis on personal feelings and individual choices and less committed to organizations—a reflection of a more general societal development towards greater individualism.

Returning to Wasserstein, I now want to especially spotlight secular Jews. Secular Jews form the vast majority of the total Jewish population. In both surveys mentioned, about 80% of the respondents were secular Jews,[15] but their share in the real population must be even larger, because the samples were biased in favor of religious affiliations. Is Wasserstein right by claiming that secular Judaism can hardly be transmitted to the next generations so that it contains no potential for the future?

To investigate this, I conducted in-depth interviews with thirty secular, postwar born persons (born between 1953 and 1974; aged twenty-eight to forty-eight at the time of the study). These thirty respondents had different backgrounds in terms of having one or two Jewish parents and whether they were brought up with or without Jewish customs, traditions or religion. Most of them had somewhat different ties to Judaism than their parents, either stronger or weaker, but mostly weaker. Most importantly, their ties had become freer of obligations and more fragmented, with more emphasis on personal feelings and choices and less on behavior. This was especially true for those who had received a traditional or religious upbringing. For them, Judaism was no longer a driving force in their lives, as it had been for their parents.

Growing up in the 1960s and 1970s, the respondents were deeply influenced by the then governing spirit of the times: multiculturalism, individualism and women's emancipation. And in those years, there also was a growing self-assurance among Dutch Jews. All this was reflected in the respondents' desire to determine for themselves, what was important in their personal lives, also concerning Jewish matters, such as the content and extent of their Jewishness.

---

15   The division in the 1999 sample was as follows: non-practicing – 57%; non-religious but observing some Jewish holidays and traditions – 17%; liberal religious – 12 %t; traditional religious – 9%; Orthodox religious – 5%. N=1027 (Van Solinge and De Vries, *De Joden in Nederland anno* 2000, p. 123). The first two categories combined were considered as secular.

The division in the 1999 sample restricted to those born between 1953 and 1974 was as follows: non-practicing– 48%; non-religious but observing some Jewish holidays and traditions – 22% liberal religious – 14%; traditional religious – 9%; Orthodox religious – 7%. N=287 (De Vries, *Een blijvende band?*, p. 14). In the 2009 sample a somewhat different division was being made, and the outcome was as follows: non-practicing – 44%; non-religious but observing some customs – 41%; religious, but not observing all rules – 11%; religious and observing all rules – 4% (Van Solinge and Van Praag, *De Joden in Nederland anno 2009*, p. 57).

Their most striking and shared characteristic was the primacy they gave to personal sentiment above the idea that Judaism places demands on someone. As one of them, (a woman who was raised in quite a traditional-religious way), exclaimed: "Those Jewish rules and prescriptions I was brought up with, I don't feel them. *I just don't feel them!*"

There were important differences, too, among the thirty interviewees, which nuances Wasserstein's implicit suggestion that secular Jews are more or less the same. I identified three subgroups on a continuum of different kinds of Jewish identification.

The first subgroup was made up of people who were the embodiment of a completed assimilation process and therefore were the living proof of Wasserstein's prophecy. Most of these persons had one Jewish parent only and had received little or no Jewish upbringing. Judaism played no appreciable role in their daily lives, either in a religious or traditional sense, or in a social sense, because they scarcely knew any Jewish people outside their family. Their bond with Judaism, or rather with their partial Jewish origin, manifested itself only occasionally in personal sentiments and feelings of loyalty, often deriving from the war experiences of their Jewish family members. They sometimes felt a certain pride, too, about being part of the Jewish people, albeit at a distance. These people tended to consider themselves as "someone with a Jewish background" rather than as "a Jew."

The second group, around the middle of the continuum, was made up of people who had received a somewhat more Jewish upbringing, at least in a cultural sense. Most of them had one Jewish parent. Their bond with Judaism was mainly linked to their family of origin, to cherished family memories and values, along with some remnants of Jewish traditions and customs in family settings and most certainly to emotions they held as a result of their family's war experiences. They were brought up with an attenuated form of traditional Jewish culture, manifesting itself in interaction within the family, like certain types of humor, word usage, "friendly bickering" and also by specific dishes, like the famous chicken soup. They all cherished this typical family atmosphere. The current social environment of these people was predominantly non-Jewish, including their partners. In a certain phase of their lives, a number of these respondents had felt the drive "to do something" with their Jewishness and had tried to find ways for it. Often that had resulted in unpleasant experiences with Jewish congregations or organizations, because these people did not meet the halakhic criterion for being Jewish and were, therefore, refused participation, or because they were treated as outsiders for other reasons. This had been very discouraging to them. In that sense, certain Jewish institutions seem to contribute to Wasserstein's prophecy coming true.

The third subgroup represented the other end of the continuum. The bond that these people experienced was not only restricted to private feelings, but it also found expression in the (selective) attention they devoted to certain Jewish traditions and holidays. They, thereby, expressed their feelings of ethnic belonging and not of religious faith. In fact, they took quite a detached attitude towards religion. Most of these people had two Jewish parents. A number of them had been brought up in traditional-religious families. Only a few of them had a Jewish partner, however. Some of them did not attach a special meaning to having a Jewish partner, but those who did, frequently reported difficulties in finding one. These persons internalized the Jewish legacy they received from their parents, but adapted it in such a way that it was compatible with their personal needs and did not interfere with the rest of their busy lives; for example, no lengthy preparations for the Friday evening meal, but pizza delivery instead and "back to normal" right after the meal. These persons often had Jewish friends and participated (mostly sporadically) in institutionalized Jewish life. They had quite an ambiguous attitude towards the latter, however. On the one hand they considered Jewish congregations and the NIK (the Orthodox denomination) in particular, as the best safeguard for Jewish continuity, but on the other hand they criticized the NIK violently, as being a "closed and inflexible community."[16] They had a similar ambiguous attitude towards Jewish schools. These persons certainly were devoted to Jewish continuity though and tried to raise their children accordingly.

All these various types of identification clearly hold a different potential for continuity. It seems that Wasserstein's rather uniform expectations about the impossibility to transmit secular Judaism can be refined.

His expectations do seem to apply to those whose links with Judaism consist of no more than an awareness of their Jewish origin and their occasional emotional feelings about it. In these cases, it concerns a rather individual bond that usually receives no new stimuli, as it is mainly tied to someone's older or already-deceased Jewish parent or grandparent and there is no viable basis for a Jewish identity to be transmitted to the next generation. Descendants of these people are more likely to carry over no more than a faint curiosity about their Jewish origins that perhaps will motivate them to visit a Jewish museum or so.

---

16   NIK (Nederlands-Israëlitisch Kerkgenootschap), the coordinating Orthodox denomination, is the largest Jewish denomination in the Netherlands, numbering about thirty congregations. Only 26% of its members, however, defined themselves as Orthodox (Van Solinge and De Vries, *De Joden in Nederland anno 2000*, p. 130).

Wasserstein's expectations may also apply to those respondents whose ties with Judaism have largely been reduced to the level of family idiosyncrasies. There usually were no incentives to carry on and transmit the legacy that these people received from their parental home. A number of them, however, did attempt to transmit some sense of Jewishness to their children, even though these respondents were committed to freedom of choice, also in Jewish matters. They were hoping, but less expecting, that a Jewish touch in the upbringing would appeal to their children. Thereby, they often had to face practical problems, such as lack of sufficient knowledge of Judaism or the incentive of a Jewish partner. It is likely that any Jewish identification their descendants may develop will be marginalized even further and associated with the Jewish part of their family only, rather than with Judaism as a collectivity or an agency that gives meaning to one's life. Therefore, it will not carry much potential for Jewish continuity in the long run other than in a very personalized form.

The greatest potential for continuity seems to lie in the attachment maintained at the other end of the continuum, of which loyalty to certain Jewish traditions forms an integral part. This relationship with Judaism is more readily transmitted to subsequent generations as the transmission is accompanied by some rituals, traditions and knowledge and mostly also by some group affiliation with Jews outside the family (a circle of Jewish friends, membership of Jewish congregations or organizations). Respondents that belonged to this subgroup wanted, in their own words, "the best of both worlds": for themselves and for their children they opted for full participation in the non-Jewish world and for Jewish continuity. Almost all of them found it extremely difficult to find the right balance between the two. One of them, a bright young woman, member of the Liberaal Joodse Gemeente (Liberal Jewish Denomination), therefore, labeled this type of Jewish attachment as "the most vulnerable Jewish attachment that exists nowadays."[17]

Conclusion

What can we now conclude when we consider all these findings in the context of Wasserstein's prophecy? As for demography, it seems very likely that the number of Jews in the Netherlands will gradually decline. The only counterforce imaginable would be a continuously increasing influx of Jews from elsewhere. If this will not happen, the decline of the Jewish population in the

---

17   The Liberaal Joodse Gemeente, comparable to Reform congregations elsewhere, numbers
      ten congregations in the Netherlands.

Netherlands seems inevitable. However, the decline will occur in a different speed in different subgroups, dependent upon the number of mixed marriages taking place. As mixed marriages tend to work as a self-strengthening force in subsequent generations, we can establish that Wasserstein offers a very strong and convincing argument here.

Mixed marriages change both the composition of the group and the ways people are tied to Judaism. Does that mean that any basis for a collective Jewish identity will eventually vanish as Wasserstein suggests? Based on the research that I referred to, I find it extremely difficult to answer this question. On the one hand, full assimilation certainly is already a fact for an unknown number of people and will most probably increase in the coming generations. Remnants of a Jewish identity in a strongly diluted and personalized form may indeed endure for several generations, but probably won't offer a sufficient basis for a collective identity and, therefore, are not likely to provide for a substantial continuity. On the other hand, the potential for Jewish continuity appeared to be present in certain circles, but mostly in combination with change if not dilution. I observed a potential for such continuity even in secular families where a lively and self-assured Judaism was being practiced that also proved to be transmissible. But the question is for how long? In light of ongoing mixed marriages, this is probably not sustainable for a considerable length of time. The real question is: are we merely observing ongoing decline and dilution or also a transformation of Judaism/Jewishness in specific subgroups that will prove to be viable in the long run? What are the chances of a revitalization of Judaism in the Netherlands? Even though there are currently no clear signs that point in that direction, it cannot be precluded. Could perhaps an ongoing presence of many Israelis in the Netherlands contribute to it? For the time being, these questions have to remain largely unanswered. It is too early to arrive at a balanced conclusion.

Finally, all this weighing up of the pros and cons and "maybes" with regard to Jewish continuity touches upon more fundamental questions that should be answered first. Questions about content and about boundaries, such as: what *is* Judaism about after all? What really should be considered as "Jewish continuity?" Who is to be regarded as a Jew? And: According to whom? But these are issues to be dealt with at another occasion and within another context than a merely scientific one.

Index

Enlightenment
  of Dutch Jewry
    in general   198, 250–255
    as Orthodox *Haskalah*   254–255
  emancipatory universalism of   195
  of German Jewry   197–199, 250, 256–258
  influence on Sephardi communities   xiii
  literature   191–193, 200–202
  in Netherlands   198, 199–200
  outposts of   193
  role of
    in abolitionism   204–205
    philosophy in   191
    in Surinam/of Surinam Jewry   184–187,
      193–194, 195–196, 197, 202–203, 206
  see also assimilation; emancipation
Erens, Frans   288–289
Esnoga (Sephardim synagogue Amsterdam)
  admiration for   xi
  architecture of   xii
  inauguration of   27–29, 46–51
  as Temple in Jerusalem   29–30, 49
  women's funding of   89
Essen, Sophia Betje van   245
Esther   50–51
Ets Haim (yeshiva)   86, 87, 110–111, 145
European Jewry. *see* Western European Jewry
exile   19–21

Faesch, Isaac   171–172
Felix Meritis Society   200, 206
Ferdinand II, of Aragon   36
Fernandes, Abraham   65 n36
Fernandes, Sara   65 n36
Fernandes Homem, Antonio   67
Fez, Juan de   16–17
Fichte, Johann Gottlieb   199
Fisher, Benjamin   70 n63
Fonseca, Aron de   195
food preparation, kosher   73, 79–82, 275,
  335
France   69, 225
Franco de Medeiros, Isaac   82
Franco, Isaac (Francisco Mendes
  Medeiros)   3
Franka, Gracia   95
Fränkel, Jacob   235
Frankfort, Eduard   271, 273–275, **274**

Frankfurt, Benjamin   106
Frankfurt, Moshe   105, 106–107, 111, 119–121,
  131 n24
Frankfurt, Shimon   105–106, 109–110,
  117–119
Franklin, Benjamin   190, 204
freedom of thought   196, 199
French Revolution   206
Fréret, Nicolas   191
Friedländer, David   212
Frisian language   144
Fuks, Lajb   145

Gabai Enriques, Ribca   85 n154
Gabay Isidro, Abraham   57, 177
Galibi language   189
Gans, Evelien   311
Gauguin, Paul   275, 285
Gelder, M.E. van   291–292
genealogy, of the Dutch   25–26, 52
German Jewry
  and confirmation ceremonies   229, 230,
  231–232
  emancipation of   198–199
  Enlightenment of   197–199, 250, 256–258
  fleeing to
    Dutch Republic   xi
    Netherlands   xvi
  integration of   223, 250
Gobits, Philip   301
Godefroi, M.H.   237
Goethe, Johann Wolfgang von   262
Gogh, Theo van   284–285
Gogh, Vincent van   271, 282–285, **283**
Gomes d'Avero, Luis   67 n46
Gomes, Maria   92
Gompers, Joseph   293
Gonçalves Annes Bandarra, António   40–41
Gossler, Christoph   199
Gottlieb, Maurycy   279 n18
Goudeket, Maurits   **226**
Goudsmit, J.E.   317, 322
Graetz, Heinrich   268, 322
Granada, Ribca de   88 n165
Gris, Ze'ev   105
Groenhuis, G.   38
Groningen   287
  Guyot Institute in   228, 231, 240, 245

The index was prepared by I.S. Pierke
    Bosschieter